Novels
for Students

National Advisory Board

Novels
for Students

Presenting Analysis, Context, and Criticism on Commonly Studied Novels

Volume 21

Ira Mark Milne and Timothy Sisler, Project Editors

Foreword by Anne Devereaux Jordan

THOMSON

GALE

Detroit • New York • San Francisco • San Diego • New Haven, Conn. • Waterville, Maine • London • Munich

THOMSON
™
GALE

Novels for Students, Volume 21

Project Editors
Ira Mark Milne and Timothy Sisler

Editorial
Anne Marie Hacht

Rights Acquisition and Management
Margaret Abendroth, Margaret Chamberlain-Gaston, Edna Hedblad

Manufacturing
Drew Kalasky

Imaging
Leitha Etheridge-Sims, Lezlie Light, Mike Logusz

Product Design
Pamela A. E. Galbreath

Product Manager
Meggin Condino

ISBN 0-7876-6944-X
ISSN 1094-3552

Printed in the United States of America
10 9 8 7 6 5 4 3 2 1

Table of Contents

The Informed Dialogue: Interacting with Literature

When we pick up a book, we usually do so with the anticipation of pleasure. We hope that by entering the time and place of the novel and sharing the thoughts and actions of the characters, we will find enjoyment. Unfortunately, this is often not the case; we are disappointed. But we should ask, has the author failed us, or have we failed the author?

We establish a dialogue with the author, the book, and with ourselves when we read. Consciously and unconsciously, we ask questions: "Why did the author write this book?" "Why did the author choose that time, place, or character?" "How did the author achieve that effect?" "Why did the character act that way?" "Would I act in the same way?" The answers we receive depend upon how much information about literature in general and about that book specifically we ourselves bring to our reading.

Young children have limited life and literary experiences. Being young, children frequently do not know how to go about exploring a book, nor sometimes, even know the questions to ask of a book. The books they read help them answer questions, the author often coming right out and *telling* young readers the things they are learning or are expected to learn. The perennial classic, *The Little Engine That Could, tells* its readers that, among other things, it is good to help others and brings happiness:

"Hurray, hurray," cried the funny little clown and all the dolls and toys. "The good little boys and girls in the city will be happy because you helped us, kind, Little Blue Engine."

In picture books, messages are often blatant and simple, the dialogue between the author and reader one-sided. Young children are concerned with the end result of a book—the enjoyment gained, the lesson learned—rather than with how that result was obtained. As we grow older and read further, however, we question more. We come to expect that the world within the book will closely mirror the concerns of our world, and that the author will *show* these through the events, descriptions, and conversations within the story, rather than *telling* of them. We are now expected to do the interpreting, carry on our share of the dialogue with the book and author, and glean not only the author's message, but comprehend how that message and the overall affect of the book were achieved. Sometimes, however, we need help to do these things. *Novels for Students* provides that help.

A novel is made up of many parts interacting to create a coherent whole. In reading a novel, the more obvious features can be easily spotted—theme, characters, plot—but we may overlook the more subtle elements that greatly influence how the novel is perceived by the reader: viewpoint, mood and tone, symbolism, or the use of humor. By focusing on both the obvious and more subtle literary elements within a novel, *Novels for Students* aids readers in both analyzing for message and in determining how and why that message is communicated. In the discussion on Harper Lee's *To*

Kill a Mockingbird (Vol. 2), for example, the mockingbird as a symbol of innocence is dealt with, among other things, as is the importance of Lee's use of humor which "enlivens a serious plot, adds depth to the characterization, and creates a sense of familiarity and universality." The reader comes to understand the internal elements of each novel discussed—as well as the external influences that help shape it.

"The desire to write greatly," Harold Bloom of Yale University says, "is the desire to be elsewhere, in a time and place of one's own, in an originality that must compound with inheritance, with an anxiety of influence." A writer seeks to create a unique world within a story, but although it is unique, it is not disconnected from our own world. It speaks to us *because* of what the writer brings to the writing from our world: how he or she was raised and educated; his or her likes and dislikes; the events occurring in the real world at the time of the writing, and while the author was growing up. When we know what an author has brought to his or her work, we gain a greater insight into both the "originality" (the world of the book), and the things that "compound" it. This insight enables us to question that created world and find answers more readily. By informing ourselves, we are able to establish a more effective dialogue with both book and author.

Novels for Students, in addition to providing a plot summary and descriptive list of characters—to remind readers of what they have read—also explores the external influences that shaped each book. Each entry includes a discussion of the author's background, and the historical context in which the novel was written. It is vital to know, for instance, that when Ray Bradbury was writing *Fahrenheit 451* (Vol. 1), the threat of Nazi domination had recently ended in Europe, and the McCarthy hearings were taking place in Washington, D.C. This information goes far in answering the question, "Why did he write a story of oppressive government control and book burning?" Similarly, it is important to know that Harper Lee, author of *To Kill a Mockingbird,* was born and raised in Monroeville, Alabama, and that her father was a lawyer.

Readers can now see why she chose the south as a setting for her novel—it is the place with which she was most familiar—and start to comprehend her characters and their actions.

Novels for Students helps readers find the answers they seek when they establish a dialogue with a particular novel. It also aids in the posing of questions by providing the opinions and interpretations of various critics and reviewers, broadening that dialogue. Some reviewers of *To Kill A Mockingbird,* for example, "faulted the novel's climax as melodramatic." This statement leads readers to ask, "Is it, indeed, melodramatic?" "If not, why did some reviewers see it as such?" "If it is, why did Lee choose to make it melodramatic?" "Is melodrama ever justified?" By being spurred to ask these questions, readers not only learn more about the book and its writer, but about the nature of writing itself.

The literature included for discussion in *Novels for Students* has been chosen because it has something vital to say to us. *Of Mice and Men, Catch-22, The Joy Luck Club, My Antonia, A Separate Peace* and the other novels here speak of life and modern sensibility. In addition to their individual, specific messages of prejudice, power, love or hate, living and dying, however, they and all great literature also share a common intent. They force us to *think*—about life, literature, and about others, not just about ourselves. They pry us from the narrow confines of our minds and thrust us outward to confront the world of books and the larger, real world we all share. *Novels for Students* helps us in this confrontation by providing the means of enriching our conversation with literature and the world, by creating an *informed* dialogue, one that brings true pleasure to the personal act of reading.

Sources

Harold Bloom, *The Western Canon, The Books and School of the Ages,* Riverhead Books, 1994.

Watty Piper, *The Little Engine That Could,* Platt & Munk, 1930.

Anne Devereaux Jordan
Senior Editor, TALL
(Teaching and Learning Literature)

Introduction

Purpose of the Book

The purpose of *Novels for Students (NfS)* is to provide readers with a guide to understanding, enjoying, and studying novels by giving them easy access to information about the work. Part of Gale's "For Students" Literature line, *NfS* is specifically designed to meet the curricular needs of high school and undergraduate college students and their teachers, as well as the interests of general readers and researchers considering specific novels. While each volume contains entries on "classic" novels frequently studied in classrooms, there are also entries containing hard-to-find information on contemporary novels, including works by multicultural, international, and women novelists.

The information covered in each entry includes an introduction to the novel and the novel's author; a plot summary, to help readers unravel and understand the events in a novel; descriptions of important characters, including explanation of a given character's role in the novel as well as discussion about that character's relationship to other characters in the novel; analysis of important themes in the novel; and an explanation of important literary techniques and movements as they are demonstrated in the novel.

In addition to this material, which helps the readers analyze the novel itself, students are also provided with important information on the literary and historical background informing each work. This includes a historical context essay, a box comparing the time or place the novel was written to modern Western culture, a critical essay, and excerpts from critical essays on the novel. A unique feature of *NfS* is a specially commissioned critical essay on each novel, targeted toward the student reader.

To further aid the student in studying and enjoying each novel, information on media adaptations is provided, as well as reading suggestions for works of fiction and nonfiction on similar themes and topics. Classroom aids include ideas for research papers and lists of critical sources that provide additional material on the novel.

Selection Criteria

The titles for each volume of *NfS* were selected by surveying numerous sources on teaching literature and analyzing course curricula for various school districts. Some of the sources surveyed included: literature anthologies; *Reading Lists for College-Bound Students: The Books Most Recommended by America's Top Colleges;* textbooks on teaching the novel; a College Board survey of novels commonly studied in high schools; a National Council of Teachers of English (NCTE) survey of novels commonly studied in high schools; the NCTE's *Teaching Literature in High School: The Novel;* and the Young Adult Library Services Association (YALSA) list of best books for young adults of the past twenty-five years.

Input was also solicited from our advisory board, as well as from educators from various areas.

From these discussions, it was determined that each volume should have a mix of "classic" novels (those works commonly taught in literature classes) and contemporary novels for which information is often hard to find. Because of the interest in expanding the canon of literature, an emphasis was also placed on including works by international, multicultural, and women authors. Our advisory board members—educational professionals—helped pare down the list for each volume. If a work was not selected for the present volume, it was often noted as a possibility for a future volume. As always, the editor welcomes suggestions for titles to be included in future volumes.

How Each Entry Is Organized

Each entry, or chapter, in *NfS* focuses on one novel. Each entry heading lists the full name of the novel, the author's name, and the date of the novel's publication. The following elements are contained in each entry:

- **Introduction:** a brief overview of the novel which provides information about its first appearance, its literary standing, any controversies surrounding the work, and major conflicts or themes within the work.

- **Author Biography:** this section includes basic facts about the author's life, and focuses on events and times in the author's life that inspired the novel in question.

- **Plot Summary:** a factual description of the major events in the novel. Lengthy summaries are broken down with subheads.

- **Characters:** an alphabetical listing of major characters in the novel. Each character name is followed by a brief to an extensive description of the character's role in the novel, as well as discussion of the character's actions, relationships, and possible motivation.

  Characters are listed alphabetically by last name. If a character is unnamed—for instance, the narrator in *Invisible Man*—the character is listed as "The Narrator" and alphabetized as "Narrator." If a character's first name is the only one given, the name will appear alphabetically by that name.

  Variant names are also included for each character. Thus, the full name "Jean Louise Finch" would head the listing for the narrator of *To Kill a Mockingbird,* but listed in a separate cross-reference would be the nickname "Scout Finch."

- **Themes:** a thorough overview of how the major topics, themes, and issues are addressed within the novel. Each theme discussed appears in a separate subhead and is easily accessed through the boldface entries in the Subject/Theme Index.

- **Style:** this section addresses important style elements of the novel, such as setting, point of view, and narration; important literary devices used, such as imagery, foreshadowing, symbolism; and, if applicable, genres to which the work might have belonged, such as Gothicism or Romanticism. Literary terms are explained within the entry but can also be found in the Glossary.

- **Historical Context:** This section outlines the social, political, and cultural climate *in which the author lived and the novel was created.* This section may include descriptions of related historical events, pertinent aspects of daily life in the culture, and the artistic and literary sensibilities of the time in which the work was written. If the novel is a historical work, information regarding the time in which the novel is set is also included. Each section is broken down with helpful subheads.

- **Critical Overview:** this section provides background on the critical reputation of the novel, including bannings or any other public controversies surrounding the work. For older works, this section includes a history of how the novel was first received and how perceptions of it may have changed over the years; for more recent novels, direct quotes from early reviews may also be included.

- **Criticism:** an essay commissioned by *NfS* which specifically deals with the novel and is written specifically for the student audience, as well as excerpts from previously published criticism on the work (if available).

- **Sources:** an alphabetical list of critical material used in compiling the entry, with full bibliographical information.

- **Further Reading:** an alphabetical list of other critical sources which may prove useful for the student. It includes full bibliographical information and a brief annotation.

In addition, each entry contains the following highlighted sections, set apart from the main text as sidebars:

- **Media Adaptations:** a list of important film and television adaptations of the novel, including source information. The list also includes stage adaptations, audio recordings, musical adaptations, etc.

- **Topics for Further Study:** a list of potential study questions or research topics dealing with the novel. This section includes questions related to other disciplines the student may be studying, such as American history, world history, science, math, government, business, geography, economics, psychology, etc.

- **Compare and Contrast Box:** an "at-a-glance" comparison of the cultural and historical differences between the author's time and culture and late twentieth century/early twenty-first century Western culture. This box includes pertinent parallels between the major scientific, political, and cultural movements of the time or place the novel was written, the time or place the novel was set (if a historical work), and modern Western culture. Works written after 1990 may not have this box.

- **What Do I Read Next?:** a list of works that might complement the featured novel or serve as a contrast to it. This includes works by the same author and others, works of fiction and nonfiction, and works from various genres, cultures, and eras.

Other Features

NfS includes "The Informed Dialogue: Interacting with Literature," a foreword by Anne Devereaux Jordan, Senior Editor for *Teaching and Learning Literature (TALL)*, and a founder of the Children's Literature Association. This essay provides an enlightening look at how readers interact with literature and how *Novels for Students* can help teachers show students how to enrich their own reading experiences.

A Cumulative Author/Title Index lists the authors and titles covered in each volume of the *NfS* series.

A Cumulative Nationality/Ethnicity Index breaks down the authors and titles covered in each volume of the *NfS* series by nationality and ethnicity.

A Subject/Theme Index, specific to each volume, provides easy reference for users who may be studying a particular subject or theme rather than a single work. Significant subjects from events to broad themes are included, and the entries pointing to the specific theme discussions in each entry are indicated in **boldface.**

Each entry may have several illustrations, including photos of the author, stills from film adaptations, maps, and/or photos of key historical events, if available.

Citing *Novels for Students*

When writing papers, students who quote directly from any volume of *Novels for Students* may use the following general forms. These examples are based on MLA style; teachers may request that students adhere to a different style, so the following examples may be adapted as needed.

When citing text from *NfS* that is not attributed to a particular author (i.e., the Themes, Style, Historical Context sections, etc.), the following format should be used in the bibliography section:

> *"Night." Novels for Students.* Ed. Marie Rose Napierkowski. Vol. 4. Detroit: Gale, 1998. 234–35.

When quoting the specially commissioned essay from *NfS* (usually the first piece under the "Criticism" subhead), the following format should be used:

> Miller, Tyrus. Critical Essay on *Winesburg, Ohio. Novels for Students.* Ed. Marie Rose Napierkowski. Vol. 4. Detroit: Gale, 1998. 335–39.

When quoting a journal or newspaper essay that is reprinted in a volume of *NfS,* the following form may be used:

> Malak, Amin. "Margaret Atwood's *The Handmaid's Tale* and the Dystopian Tradition," *Canadian Literature* No. 112 (Spring, 1987), 9–16; excerpted and reprinted in *Novels for Students,* Vol. 4, ed. Marie Rose Napierkowski (Detroit: Gale, 1998), pp. 133–36.

When quoting material reprinted from a book that appears in a volume of *NfS,* the following form may be used:

> Adams, Timothy Dow. "Richard Wright: Wearing the Mask," in *Telling Lies in Modern American Autobiography* (University of North Carolina Press, 1990), 69–83; excerpted and reprinted in *Novels for Students,* Vol. 1, ed. Diane Telgen (Detroit: Gale, 1997), pp. 59–61.

We Welcome Your Suggestions

The editor of *Novels for Students* welcomes your comments and ideas. Readers who wish to suggest novels to appear in future volumes, or who have other suggestions, are cordially invited to contact the editor. You may contact the editor via e-mail at: **ForStudentsEditors@thomson.com.** Or write to the editor at:

Editor, *Novels for Students*
Thomson Gale
27500 Drake Road
Farmington Hills, MI 48331–3535

Literary Chronology

1775: Jane Austen is born on December 16. She grows up in the country village of Steventon, in Hampshire, England.

1815: Jane Austen's *Emma* is published.

1817: Jane Austen dies of Addison's Disease on July 18. She is forty-one years old. She is buried in Winchester Cathedral.

1865: Rudyard Kipling is born on December 30 in Bombay, India.

1869: André Gide (André Paul Guillaume Gide) is born on November 22 in Paris, France.

1894: Dashiell Hammett (Samuel Dashiell Hammett) is born in Saint Mary's County, Maryland.

1895: Robert Graves (Robert von Ranke Graves) is born on July 24 in Wimbeldon, England.

1901: Rudyard Kipling's *Kim* is published.

1902: Langston Hughes (James Langston Hughes) is born on February 1 in Joplin, Missouri. His unusual middle name had been the birth name of his mother.

1902: André Gide's *The Immoralist* is published.

1905: Jean-Paul Sartre is born on June 21 in Paris, France.

1907: Rudyard Kipling receives the Nobel Prize in Literature "in consideration of the power of observation, originality of imagination, virility of ideas and remarkable talent for narration" which characterize his creations.

1914: Ralph Ellison (Ralph Waldo Ellison) is born on March 1 in Oklahoma City, Oklahoma.

1925: Flannery O'Connor (Mary Flannery O'Connor) is born in Savannah, Georgia.

1926: John Fowles is born on March 31 in a suburb of London.

1930: Dashiell Hammett's *The Maltese Falcon* is published.

1934: Robert Graves's *I, Claudius* is published.

1936: Rudyard Kipling dies on January 18 and is buried in Poet's Corner in Westminster Abbey.

1938: Jean-Paul Sartre's *Nausea* is published.

1940: J. M. Coetzee (John Maxwell Coetzee) is born on February 9 in Cape Town, South Africa.

1947: Octavia Butler (Octavia Estelle Butler) is born on June 22 in Pasadena, California.

1947: André Gide receives the Nobel Prize in Literature "for his comprehensive and artistically significant writings, in which human problems and conditions have been presented with a fearless love of truth and keen psychological insight."

1951: André Gide dies on February 19 in Paris at the age of eighty-one.

1958: Langston Hughes's *Tambourines to Glory* is published.

1960: Flannery O'Connor's *The Violent Bear It Away* is published.

1961: Dashiell Hammett dies of lung cancer.

1964: Jean-Paul Sartre receives the Nobel Prize in Literature "for his work which, rich in ideas and filled with the spirit of freedom and the quest for truth, has exerted a farreaching influence on our age." Sartre declines the prize.

1964: Flannery O'Connor dies of lupus on August 3 at her mother's home in Milledgeville, Georgia.

1967: Langston Hughes dies of congestive heart failure on May 22 in New York City.

1969: John Fowles's *The French Lieutenant's Woman* is published.

1974: J. M. Coetzee's *Dusklands* is published.

1980: Jean-Paul Sartre dies of a lung tumor on April 15. The extent of his international reputation may be gauged by the attendance of twenty-five thousand people at his funeral.

1985: Robert Graves dies at the age of ninety.

1993: Octavia Butler's *Parable of the Sower* is published.

1994: Ralph Ellison dies on April 16 at the age of eighty in Harlem, New York.

1999: Ralph Ellison's *Juneteenth* is published.

2003: J. M. Coetzee receives the Nobel Prize in Literature for portraying "in innumerable guises" "the surprising involvement of the outsider."

Acknowledgments

The editors wish to thank the copyright holders of the excerpted criticism included in this volume and the permissions managers of many book and magazine publishing companies for assisting us in securing reproduction rights. We are also grateful to the staffs of the Detroit Public Library, the Library of Congress, the University of Detroit Mercy Library, Wayne State University Purdy/Kresge Library Complex, and the University of Michigan Libraries for making their resources available to us. Following is a list of the copyright holders who have granted us permission to reproduce material in this volume of *Novels for Students (NfS)*. Every effort has been made to trace copyright, but if omissions have been made, please let us know.

COPYRIGHTED MATERIALS IN *NfS*, VOLUME 21, WERE REPRODUCED FROM THE FOLLOWING PERIODICALS:

American Literary History, v. 13, summer, 2001 for "Ralph Ellison and the American Canon," by Alan Nadel. Copyright © 2001 by Oxford University Press. All rights reserved. Reproduced by permission of the publisher and the author.—*CLA Journal*, v. 46, 2003. Copyright © 2003 by the College Language Association. All rights reserved. Used by permission of The College Language Association.—*Eighteenth-Century Fiction*, v. 14, October, 2001. Copyright 2001 by McMaster University. Reproduced by permission.—*The Journal of Narrative Technique*, v. 13, winter, 1983. Copyright © 1983 by *The Journal of Narrative Tech-*

nique. Reproduced by permission.—*Proteus*, v. 6, 1989. Copyright © 1989 by Shippensburg University. Reproduced by permission.—*The Sewanee Review*, v. 76, April–June, 1968 for "The Symbolic Vision of Flannery O'Connor: Patterns of Imagery in *The Violent Bear It Away*," by Clinton W. Trowbridge. Copyright © 1968 by the University of the South. All rights reserved. Reproduced by permission of the Editor.—*Studies in American Fiction*, v. 27, spring, 1999. Copyright © 1999 by Northeastern University. Reproduced by permission.—*Studies in the Novel*, v. 29, summer, 1997. Copyright © 1997 by North Texas State University. Reproduced by permission.—*Twentieth-Century Literature*, v. 48, spring, 2002. Copyright © 2002, Hofstra University Press. Reproduced by permission.

COPYRIGHTED MATERIALS IN *NfS*, VOLUME 21, WERE REPRODUCED FROM THE FOLLOWING BOOKS:

Butler, Robert. From *Contemporary African American Fiction: The Open Journey.* Fairleigh Dickinson University Press, 1998. Copyright © 1998 by Associated University Presses, Inc. All rights reserved. Reproduced by permission.—Cordle, Thomas. From *André Gide.* Updated Edition. Twayne Publishers, 1993. Copyright © 1993 by Twayne Publishers. All rights reserved. Reproduced by permission of the Gale Group.—Foster, Thomas. From *Understanding John Fowles.* University of South Carolina Press, 1994. Copyright © 1994 by the University of South Carolina Press.

Reproduced by permission.—Gallagher, Susan VanZanten. From *A Story of South Africa: J. M. Coetzee's Fiction in Context.* Harvard University Press, 1991. Copyright © 1991 by the President and Fellows of Harvard College. Reprinted by permission of the publisher.—Gant-Britton, Lisbeth. From "Octavia Butler's *Parable of the Sower*: One Alternative to a Futureless Future," in *Women of Other Worlds.* Edited by Helen Merrick and Tess Williams. University of Western Australia Press, 1999. Copyright © 1999 by Lisbeth Gant-Britton. Reproduced by permission of the author.—Huffaker, Robert. From *John Fowles.* Twayne Publishers, 1980. Copyright © 1980 by G. K. Hall & Co. All rights reserved. Reproduced by permission of the Gale Group.—Jablon, Madelyn. From "Metafiction as Genre," in *Black Metafiction: Self-Consciousness in African American Literature.* University of Iowa Press, 1997. Copyright © 1997 by the University of Iowa Press. All rights reserved. Reproduced by permission.—Marling, William. From *Dashiell Hammett.* Twayne Publishers, 1983. Copyright © 1983 by G. K. Hall & Co. All rights reserved. Reproduced by permission of the Gale Group.—Nolan, William F. From *Dashiell Hammett: A Casebook.* McNally & Loftin, 1969. Reproduced by permission of the author.—Page, Norman. From *A Kipling Companion.* Macmillan Press, 1984. Copyright © 1984 by Norman Page. All rights reserved. Reproduced with permission of Palgrave Macmillan.—Parker, John W. From "Another Revealing Facet of the Harlem Scene," in *Langston Hughes: The Contemporary Reviews.* Edited by Tish Dace. Cambridge University Press, 1997. Copyright © 1997 by Cambridge University Press. Reprinted with the permission of Cambridge University Press.—Symons, Julian. From *Dashiell Hammett.* Harcourt, Brace, Jovanovich, 1985. Reproduced by permission of Curtis Brown Group Ltd.—Tarbox, Katherine. From *The Art of John Fowles.* University of Georgia Press, 1988. Copyright © 1988 by the University of Georgia Press. All rights reserved. Reproduced by permission.

PHOTOGRAPHS AND ILLUSTRATIONS APPEARING IN *NfS*, VOLUME 21, WERE RECEIVED FROM THE FOLLOWING SOURCES:

Algiers, overlooking the harbor, with buildings following from the left and circling the harbor, photograph. © Hulton-Deutsch Collection/Corbis. Reproduced by permission.—Austen, Jane, engraving.—Bogart, Humphrey, Peter Lorre, Mary Astor, and Sidney Greenstreet in the film *The Maltese Falcon,* photograph. Corbis-Bettmann. Reproduced by permission.—British police officers look on as another officer inspects the corpse of a Mau Mau soldier in Kenya, photograph. © Hulton-Deutsch Collection/Corbis. Reproduced by permission.—Butler, Octavia, photograph by Miriam Berkley. © Miriam Berkley. Reproduced by permission.—Cobb breakwater in Lyme Regis, England, photograph. © Alain Le Garsmeur/Corbis. Reproduced by permission.—Coetzee, J. M., walking outside in Lisbon, photograph. © Andanson James/Corbis. Reproduced by permission.—Congregation gathers inside a "storefront" Baptist Church in Chicago, Illinois, photograph. © Corbis. Reproduced by permission.—Ellison, Ralph, photograph. Getty Images. Reproduced by permission.—Emperor Claudius, sculpture. The Library of Congress.—Ezekiel's vision of God, illustration from details in Ezekiel Chapters 1 and 2, photograph. © Historical Picture Archive/Corbis. Reproduced by permission.—Fowles, John, photograph. The Library of Congress.—Gide, André, photograph. © Bettmann/Corbis. Reproduced by permission.—The Golden Temple, Sikhs, India, photograph. Bennett Dean; Eye Ubiquitous/Corbis. Reproduced by permission.—Graves, Robert Ranke, December 27, 1941, photograph. Getty Images. Reproduced by permission.—Hammett, Samuel D., photograph. The Library of Congress.—Hammond, Chris, illustrator. From an illustration in *Emma*, by Jane Austen. 1898. Copyright © by Mary Evans Picture Library. Reproduced by permission.—Hughes, Langston, photograph. AP/Wide World Photos. Reproduced by permission.—"Jesus Walking on Water," from *The Bible*, engraving by Gustave Dore, 1866, photograph. © Chris Hellier/Corbis. Reproduced by permission.—"Kim and the Letter Writer," terracotta plaque, photograph by John Lockwood Kipling. The Granger Collection, New York. Reproduced by permission.—Kipling, Rudyard, circa 1905, photograph. Getty Images. Reproduced by permission.—Livia, illustration on coin. The Library of Congress.—Man holds an umbrella, leaning on a sign for Dexter Avenue Baptist Church in Montgomery, Alabama, while others exit the church in the background, photograph. © Flip Schulke/Corbis. Reproduced by permission.—Man standing under "Colored Waiting Room" sign, photograph. The Library of Congress.—Men among the ruins of Dresden, 1946, Germany, photograph. UPI/Corbis-Bettmann. Reproduced by permission.—Paltrow, Gwyneth, with Jeremy Northam in a scene from the 1996 film version of *Emma*, by Jane Austen. Matchmaker/Miramax/The

Kobal Collection. Reproduced by permission.—Pedestrians walking along Lenox Avenue in Harlem, New York, photograph. © Bettmann/Corbis. Reproduced by permission.—Roman Forum, photograph. © John Madere/Corbis. Reproduced by permission.—Sartre, Jean-Paul, photograph. AP/Wide World Photos. Reproduced by permission.—South Vietnamese family outside their home, with a young boy standing beneath government propaganda during the Vietnam War, photograph. © Bettmann/Corbis. Reproduced by permission.—Streep, Meryl, with Jeremy Irons and director Karel Reisz on the set of the film *The French Lieutenant's Woman*, photograph. United Artists/The Kobal Collection. Reproduced by permission.—Street view outside of the Moulin Rouge in Montmartre in Paris, France, photograph. © Underwood and Underwood/Corbis. Reproduced by permission.—Tibetan Buddhists prostrate at the stupa near the Bodhi tree where Buddha was enlightened, Bodghaya, India, photograph. © Alison Wright/Corbis. Reproduced by permission.—Two young women and two young boys stand in the doorway of a "storefront" Baptist Church in Chicago, Illinois, photograph. © Corbis. Reproduced by permission.—U.S. helicopters coming over open field to land near Bong Son in South Vietnam during Operation Eagles Claw, photograph. © Bettmann/Corbis. Reproduced by permission.—Walled city, sitting atop a hill, Monteriggioni, Italy, photograph. © Nik Wheeler/Corbis. Reproduced by permission.—Wilde, Oscar, photograph. The Library of Congress.—Young, Whitney M., Roy Wilkins, A. Philip Randolph, Walter P. Reuther, and Arnold Aronson, photograph. Still Picture Branch (NWDNS), National Archives at College Park.

Contributors

Bryan Aubrey: Aubrey holds a Ph.D. in English and has published many articles on twentieth-century literature. Entry on *Parable of the Sower*. Original essay on *Parable of the Sower*.

Cynthia Bily: Bily teaches English at Adrian College in Adrian, Michigan. Entry on *Tambourines to Glory*. Original essay on *Tambourines to Glory*.

Liz Brent: Brent holds a Ph.D. in American Culture from the University of Michigan. She works as a freelance writer and editor. Entries on *The Immoralist* and *Nausea*. Original essays on *The Immoralist* and *Nausea*.

Douglas Dupler: Dupler is a writer and has taught college English courses. Original essay on *The Immoralist*.

Tamara Fernando: Fernando is an editor and writer based in Seattle, Washington. Entry on *Kim*. Original essay on *Kim*.

Joyce Hart: Hart is a freelance writer and author of several books. Entry on *Dusklands*. Original essays on *Dusklands*, *Tambourines to Glory*, and *The Violent Bear It Away*.

Catherine Dybiec Holm: Holm is a freelance writer, as well as a genre novel and short story author. Original essays on *Emma* and *The Violent Bear It Away*.

David Kelly: Kelly is an instructor of literature and creative writing at two colleges in Illinois. Entry on *The Maltese Falcon*. Original essay on *The Maltese Falcon*.

Lois Kerschen: Kerschen is a freelance writer and adjunct college English instructor. Original essay on *I, Claudius*.

Uma Kukathas: Kukathas is a freelance editor and writer. Entry on *The Violent Bear It Away*. Original essay on *The Violent Bear It Away*.

Anthony Martinelli: Martinelli is a Seattle-based freelance writer and editor. Entry on *Juneteenth*. Original essay on *Juneteenth*.

Wendy Perkins: Perkins is a professor of American and English literature and film. Entry on *The French Lieutenant's Woman*. Original essay on *The French Lieutenant's Woman*.

David Remy: Remy is a freelance writer in Pensacola, Florida. Original essay on *The Immoralist*.

Kathy Smith: Smith has a Ph.D. in English literature and is a freelance writer, tutor, and nonprofit administrator. Entry on *Emma*. Original essay on *Emma*.

Mark White: White is publisher of the Seattle-based Scala House Press. Entry on *I, Claudius*. Original essay on *I, Claudius*.

Dusklands

J. M. Coetzee
1974

J. M. Coetzee's *Dusklands*, published in 1974 in South Africa, is actually not a novel but rather two short novellas that share a common theme. That theme is an exploration of power, or the lack of it, depending on whose side you are on. It is about the power to rule that is fought for in war, or the power that is exerted in prejudice against a group of people who are considered less than human. It is about the power of the mind to conceptualize how to demean a nation of people; how to propagandize one's beliefs; or how to rationalize one's horrible and disgraceful actions. And it is about the power of survival. But power is not the only theme. *Dusklands* is not only about the power of extensive military machines or the dominance exhibited by white supremacy or the exploitation of colonization. It is also about the sometimes deadly consequences of culture clash, the disintegration of the human spirit, and the complete destruction of a way of life.

Dusklands is Coetzee's first published work. He went on to write many more novels that reached ever-widening, international audiences. He has won numerous prizes for his skill, including two Booker Prizes, the only writer to accomplish this feat. *Dusklands* is not the most extraordinary nor the most popular of his books, but it contains the seed from which his other novels have blossomed. The undercurrent of bigotry, narrow-mindedness, and insensitivity that create the absurdities of Coetzee's novels are all there, as is the suffering of those who are the victims stranded in the futile realities of Coetzee's fictional worlds.

J. M. Coetzee

Author Biography

Booker Prize–winning author J. M. Coetzee, descendant of seventeenth-century Dutch settlers, was born in Cape Town, South Africa, on February 9, 1940. His well-educated parents promoted an interest in learning in the young Coetzee, who loved to read books. When it came time to enter university, Coetzee studied both mathematics and English. Upon graduating with honors from the University of Cape Town, Coetzee moved to England where he found work as a computer programmer. His love of literature had not diminished, however, and two years after marrying Phillipa Jubber, in 1963, he was accepted as a graduate student at the University of Texas at Austin. In 1969, he received his doctorate in English, linguistics, and Germanic languages.

Coetzee would go on to teach literature at the State University of New York at Buffalo (SUNY) for the next three years. He had wanted to stay in the United States but was refused permanent residency, so he returned to South Africa in 1972. In that same year, Coetzee accepted a position as professor at the University of Cape Town, his alma mater, where he taught until his retirement in 2000. Coetzee would return to the United States from time to time, working as guest lecturer at several universities and colleges, including Johns Hopkins, Harvard, Stanford, and the University of Chicago.

Coetzee took up his interest in writing after receiving his doctorate. His first published book was *Dusklands* (1974). His second book, *In the Heart of the Country* (1977) won South Africa's prestigious literary award, the CNA Prize. But it was with his fourth book, Booker Prize–winning *Life and Times of Michael K* (1983) that Coetzee would be fully acknowledged internationally as a gifted author. And his reputation would be solidly grounded with his eighth publication *Disgrace* (1999), which won Coetzee his second Booker Prize. He remains the only author to win this prestigious award more than once.

Coetzee has also written what he calls two fictionalized memoirs: *Boyhood* (1997) and *Youth* (2002). He also has published several collections of essays on topics such as South African literature and culture, and a study of literary censorship. In 2003, for his life's work, Coetzee was awarded the Nobel Prize in literature.

Coetzee is a somewhat reclusive author who seldom grants interviews. But some details about his life other than his publications have been gleaned from news stories. For example, he has suffered personal tragedy in the loss of one of his two children as well as in the loss of his wife, who died from cancer. Coetzee lives with his partner Dorothy Driver in Adelaide, Australia, where he holds an honorary position at the University of Adelaide. Besides his writing accomplishments, Coetzee is well known as a translator of books for South African authors.

Plot Summary

The Vietnam Project

Coetzee's novel *Dusklands* begins with the section (some people refer to it as a novella) called "The Vietnam Project." The protagonist is Eugene Dawn, who is the author of a special report on propaganda in reference to the Vietnam War. The story opens as Eugene considers the merits of his report, which he feels he must defend since his supervisor, named Coetzee, is not quite pleased with it. Coetzee praises Eugene's ability to write but suggests some changes. Eugene, in the meantime, despite his constant reminders to himself to be confident, feels insecure. "He is going to reject me," Eugene says while recounting the day's events in his supervisor's office.

Coetzee tries to explain to Eugene that the report he has written is for the military, which is made up of people who are "slow-thinking, suspicious, and conservative." So Coetzee suggests that Eugene rewrite his report in words of one syllable and more fully clarify Eugene's abstract concepts. Eugene leaves the office depressed.

Eugene tries to rewrite his report in the basement of the Harry S. Truman Library, where he researches topics related to the culture of Vietnam, "mythography," and propaganda. It is while he is surrounded by books that Eugene feels the closest to happiness, an "intellectual happiness," Eugene informs the reader, which in his mind is the highest form. He mentions Harry, the library clerk, who dislikes it when people take down the books from the shelves. Eugene, in turn, appreciates order and hopes that Harry appreciates Eugene's neatness. Eugene also exposes how rigid his habits are. He faces a certain specific direction when he writes. He can write creatively only in the early hours of the morning, before so-called walls appear in his brain, blocking out his inspiration.

Eugene then describes his wife and his relationship with her, which is very dismal. He blames his wife for there not being any feelings between them. And when he refers to their son, he calls him "her child," and mentions that Marilyn's and the boy's conversations disturb his peace. He does not trust his wife. She is a conformist, he says, whereas he is willing to forge new trails, although this nonconformist side of him is slow to emerge. Thus he has given Marilyn the false image that he is a conformist like her. He also believes that she thinks he leans toward violence because of his involvement with the Vietnam project. Marilyn goes to a therapist for her depression once a week. And it is during this time that Eugene misses her. He leaves work early so he can be there and greet her when she opens the front door. While he hugs her, he sniffs at her, trying to catch the scent of another man. Eugene is addicted to marriage, he states, which is a "surer bond than love."

Eugene carries with him a handful of photographs taken in Vietnam. One is of a U.S. soldier having sex with a Vietnamese woman, maybe a child. Another shows soldiers holding two severed heads of Vietnamese men. Another is of a U.S. soldier walking past a Vietnamese man locked in a cage. The man has been tortured, and Eugene discusses the affects of torture.

The second part of the story contains excerpts from Eugene's report. In it, he discusses the aims and

Media Adaptations

- The Nobel Prize committee maintains a Coetzee web page at http://www.nobel.se/literature/laureates/2003/coetzee-bibl.html (accessed November 24, 2004) with links to a brief biography as well as Coetzee's Nobel Prize acceptance speech.

achievements of propaganda and the difference between its affect on people from Western cultures and those from Asian cultures. One theory that Eugene pays special attention to is that of the "father-voice" and how it works to control the common citizen as well as how it fails as a device of propaganda. Intermixed with the narrative of the report are Eugene's interior monologues. His comments tend to exaggerate his position, such as when he refers to himself as a "hero of resistance."

In part three, Eugene reflects on his childhood and how much time he spent with books. Then he quickly returns to the discussion about Coetzee and how much he wants to please him and be more like him. He then discusses how he feels abandoned by Coetzee, how his boss ignores him. Eugene is bored at work. Sometimes he passes the time by calling his wife. After she did not respond to one of his calls, he left work to spy on her.

Eugene marvels at himself, in part four, because he has "done a deed." He has kidnapped his son and is hiding in a motel room, where he hopes to write. He wants to find the peace and order that his mind requires. And by being away from his wife, he thinks he will find it. His son is happy at first, but he soon becomes bored with the inaction of the daily routine. Eugene believes his son fares better when away from his mother who coddles him. After a few days, Eugene's interior dialogue begins to disintegrate as evidenced when he begins to talk about a child who lives inside of him. This is a child who robs him of nourishment and consumes his inner organs. Shortly afterward, Marilyn arrives with the police. Eugene is taken away but not before it is obvious that Eugene has experienced a mental breakdown. He pierces his son's skin with a knife.

Locked away in a hospital, Eugene feels comfortable. Life is simpler. In his thoughts, he is on an equal basis with the doctors, not with the other patients. He talks about wanting to get out eventually, but not yet. He still has much to figure out. Eugene's story ends with the lines: "In my cell in the heart of America, with my private toilet in the corner, I ponder and ponder. I have high hopes of finding whose fault I am."

The Narrative of Jacobus Coetzee

Coetzee's "The Narrative of Jacobus Coetzee" completes the novel *Dusklands*. He begins with a "Translator's Preface," giving the novella the feel of a historic piece. Immediately after this, the so-called journal of Jacobus Coetzee begins. The narrative starts with a brief exposition about the changes that have occurred in relationship to the Boers, the white settlers (of which Jacobus is one) and the native, black African tribes. This theme is discussed throughout the narrative, as Jacobus relates circumstances of his life while living in the northern lands of South Africa.

Although the Hottentots and Boers share similar circumstances and therefore also share a particular way of life, Jacobus states that the main difference between the two groups is Christianity—the Boers are Christian and the Hottentots are not. Even if the Hottentots are converted, their "Christianity is an empty word." The Hottentots, Jacobus believes, use Christianity in order to gain favors from the whites. Jacobus proves, through the tone of his writing, that his understanding of the Hottentots and the Bushmen is stereotypical. This is because he considers himself a master and the black Africans as slaves to help further Jacobus's own cause.

Jacobus goes on to describe the Bushmen, the other major tribe that he encounters. Jacobus describes how the white people set traps for the Bushmen, much like they set for animals. He offers instructions on how to kill them and thus clear the countryside of them. "A bullet is too good for a Bushman," he writes. Then he tells of seeing a Bushman tied "over a fire and roasted."

After these descriptions, Jacobus records the incidents of a journey to the "Great River." He takes some of his men with him on an elephant hunt to gather ivory. He hires one extra man, Barend Dikkop, a good shooter but a troublemaker. Jacobus eventually tells Dikkop to leave the troupe, but before Dikkop takes off, he steals a horse and some supplies. Jacobus beats him when he finds him and leaves him in the desert. As the remaining troupe continues on their travels, the harsh land exhausts them. Although his men do most of the work, Jacobus states that they would have all perished if he had not told them what to do. "They saw me as their father," he writes.

After a few days on the trail, Jacobus and his men encounter members of the Great Namaquas, who are tantalized by the supplies that Jacobus carries in his wagon. They taunt Jacobus, who manages to save his supplies, then promises to visit their village. These people invite Jacobus to join in a meal with them, but he is wary of their motives, suspecting that they will ransack his supplies. When Jacobus finds the villagers doing just that, he cracks his whip into their midst. And then he leaves the village.

Jacobus becomes ill, which he describes in very graphic detail. As his fever takes over, he descends into dreams of his childhood. He awakens for brief moments and hears his men talking. Jacobus suspects they are planning to betray him. Jacobus is taken back to the village, where he is placed in a special isolated hut.

While in the depths of his fever, Jacobus envisions his role in the wild. He ponders death and the boundlessness of the wild land. When Klawer comes to visit him, Jacobus asks why his other men did not also come. Klawer tries to conceal the truth from Jacobus, but Jacobus becomes even more suspicious of the remaining men. Jacobus is fed and cared for but he continues to demean the people who help him back to health. He criticizes their way of life, their food, their lack of spirituality. He sees no sense to their lives.

When he is strong enough to walk, Jacobus leaves the hut and searches for his men. He finds them sleeping off a wild night of drinking and sex. He tries to rouse them but only Klawer pays any attention to him. When Jacobus attempts to awaken Plaatje, the young boy threatens Jacobus with a knife. Plaatje then tries to convince Jacobus that he should leave all the men alone, let them continue to sleep. Jacobus leaves to take a bath in the river. When he is in the water, children come and steal his clothes. Jacobus chases them. When they jump him and punch him, Jacobus bites off one of the children's ears. Men come and insist that Jacobus leave without a horse, supplies, or weapons. Klawer is the only one who leaves with him.

As they travel across the desert, Klawer becomes sick. Jacobus promises to come back for him, but there is no further mention of Klawer.

While Jacobus travels alone, he wishes he could stay in the limitless existence of the wild. He almost fears finding his farm and returning to the domesticity and boredom of routine.

Jacobus finally arrives home and soon after returns to the Great Namaqua village to claim his vengeance. He returns with an army of men, who burn the huts. Jacobus singles out the men who betrayed him and focuses his attention on Plaatje. He tells them he is there to execute them. Jacobus personally kills Plaatje and seems to relish in the act.

There is an "Afterword," supposedly by the author, following Jacobus's account. The afterword, much like the "Translator's Preface," adds authenticity to this fictionalized history.

Characters

Adonis

Adonis (from the second novella) is one of the Hottentots who desert Jacobus at the Namaqua village. Jacobus later executes him.

Coetzee

Coetzee appears in "The Vietnam Project" as Eugene's supervisor and the manager of the assignment called the New Life Project, related in some way to the war in Vietnam. Eugene admires Coetzee but admits that he is afraid of him. Readers see Coetzee only through Eugene, who describes Coetzee as a "powerful, genial, ordinary man, so utterly without vision." Eugene suggests that Coetzee was once a creative person who lost his inspiration and now tries to live vicariously through other creative people, like himself.

Jacobus Coetzee

It is in the second novella, "The Narrative of Jacobus Coetzee," that the protagonist Jacobus Coetzee appears. He is an arrogant white man of Dutch descent who looks down on all black Africans, believing them to be less intelligent, less spiritual, even less human than himself. He relates his experiences of living in the wilds of South Africa and having to deal with the black tribes that live there. It is through his so-called journals that readers learn of Jacobus's beliefs as well as the events of one particular elephant hunt that he undertakes. While searching for the elephants, Jacobus is taken ill and brought back to health by tribal people. Although he appears to go through some changes during his fever, Jacobus does not really change except that,

in the end, he turns out to be even crueler than he was before the illness. He viciously seeks revenge on some of his "slaves" whom he believes betrayed him. Everything in the novella takes place through Jacobus, and therefore the entire narrative is colored by his prejudice and misunderstanding.

Eugene Dawn

The protagonist of the novella "The Vietnam Project" is Eugene Dawn. He describes himself as a person who "cannot stand unhappiness" and needs "peace and love and order." He is a nervous man who believes he is creative. He also believes he envisions things more clearly than his superiors. Although he cannot stand unhappiness, he is anything but happy. He is not in love with his wife. He is not secure in his job. He is not, in general, comfortable with his life. He admits symptoms of depression but claims he is not depressed. However, he feels rejected, throughout most of this story. But he lives in a fog of confusion most of the time. Although he feels rejected by his boss, he also rationalizes that Coetzee is acting out of jealousy when he critiques Eugene's work.

Marilyn Dawn

Marilyn appears in the novella "The Vietnam Project" as Eugene's wife. She has never, states Eugene, "succeeded in freeing me from my rigors." Eugene blames Marilyn for the couple's lack of deep attachment to one another. He does his "duty," Eugene states, but he believes that his wife is "disengaged." He also believes his wife is jealous of his work. In Eugene's eyes, Marilyn leans toward the hysterical. She is empty and expects him to fill her. She gives Eugene, according to him, no privacy, and he must carry his paperwork around with him at all times in order to keep her from going through them. Although he does not love Marilyn, Eugene feels addicted to their marriage. He misses her most when she goes to her therapist because he suspects that Marilyn is having an affair with the doctor.

Martin Dawn

In the novella "The Vietnam Project," Martin is Eugene's and Marilyn's son. Eugene mentions him first as Marilyn's child and speaks about him more as a nuisance than as a child he loves. He claims that the poor child suffers from his mother's frustrations, which she takes out on Martin. When Eugene kidnaps his son and takes him to a motel, Eugene believes that the boy fares better. He believes that Martin is poorly influenced under Marilyn's care. Eugene hopes to bring color and spirit to the boy. But Martin grows bored with the motel room and complains. When the police show up, Eugene pierces Martin's skin with a knife. But the young boy is not seriously wounded.

Barend Dikkop

Barend Dikkop, a Hottentot who appears in the second novella, is a good hunter. For this reason, Jacobus takes him with him when they search for elephants. He had not previously worked for Jacobus and causes trouble during the hunt. Dikkop had been a soldier at one time and believes he is superior to all the other workers, including Klawer, the supervisor of Jacobus's African men. Eventually, Jacobus tells him to leave. Dikkop steals a horse and supplies but Jacobus finds him and beats him, then leaves him in the desert.

Harry

Harry is a clerk in the library where Eugene (from "The Vietnam Project") spends most of his time doing research and revising his report. Harry appears only briefly. Eugene appears to be one of the few people that he in some small way approves of. Harry likes order. He dislikes it when people take books off the shelves because that disrupts order. Eugene tries to gain Harry's approval by neatly stacking the books he uses, demonstrating to Harry that he, too, loves order. Eugene disapproves of a young girl flirting with Harry, but he does not condone the fact that Harry masturbates in a dark corner of the library. This might suggest Eugene's own discomfort in relationship with his wife.

Jan Klawer

Klawer appears in the second novella and is a faithful servant to Jacobus Coetzee. Klawer is a Hottentot on whom Jacobus often depends on for survival. He is the foreman on Jacobus's farm and throughout most of the novel, he supervises the other workers when they accompany Jacobus on the elephant hunt. Of all the men on the elephant hunt, only Klawer remains at Jacobus's side when Jacobus becomes ill. Klawer, alone, leaves with Jacobus once Jacobus is well. The other men all desert them. Klawer becomes sick, himself, however, on the trek back to the farm, and Jacobus leaves him in the desert, promising to return; but there is no mention of his rescuing Klawer.

Jan Plaatje

Jan Plaatje is one of the men that Jacobus (in the second novella) takes with him on the elephant hunt. He is one of the youngest of the Hottentots, and at first Jacobus fully trusts him. When Jacobus first encounters the tribe, the Great Namaquas, Plaatje faithfully protects Jacobus's wagon and supplies. However, after Jacobus becomes ill and is taken to the Namaquas village, Plaatje is one of the men who refuse to return to Jacobus's farm. Later, Jacobus returns to the Namaquas and kills Plaatje.

Themes

Power

Whether it is real or perceived supremacy, whether it is inherent or artificial authority, the theme of power dominates both the novellas in Coetzee book *Dusklands*. In the first novella, there is the authority of Eugene Dawn's supervisor (Coetzee) who has the power to either accept or reject the report that Eugene is working on. Coetzee, because of his rank in the office, has the authority as well as the obligation to make sure that his employees' work matches the criteria of the position or fulfills the needs of the department. In this case, Coetzee, although he praises Eugene's work, suggests that he re-write the study in a less abstract and more comprehensive style. Eugene, however, gives Coetzee even more power than the supervisor requests. Through his own lack of confidence, Eugene imagines Coetzee to be a far greater figure than Coetzee really is. In the process, Eugene sacrifices some of his own power, leading him down a spiraling path that takes him well beyond the definitions of reality into a place where he becomes confused and disoriented.

To make up for his perceived lack of power, Eugene belittles his wife and diminishes his need for her. He also devalues the existence of his son, turning him into an object rather than loving him. And on the other side of the equation, in order to make up for his continual disintegration, Eugene often imagines himself to be more powerful than he really is. For example, despite the fact that he has been committed to an institution or to some psychiatric ward of a hospital, Eugene aligns himself with the doctors who work there, thinking of himself as their equal rather than realizing that he is more the equal of the other patients who live and are cared for there. He belies this notion of power, however, when he states that he wants to stay in the hospital long enough to discover whose "fault" he is.

Power in the second novella is perceived through the protagonist Jacobus, who imagines that

Topics For Further Study

- Research the Zulu chief Shaka. What were his feats? What were his tactics? How did he deal with the Boers? With the British? With his own people? Do the accounts you researched consider him a hero? Why? If not, explain.

- Trace the history of the Boers, then prepare a short report that includes a timeline and a map of their great trek across South Africa.

- Choose another author who has won a Nobel Prize for his or her life's work. Compare the acceptance speeches of this other author with Coetzee's speech. What was the focus of each speech? Which one was more emotional? And why? Which one did you relate to more and why? Then pretend you have been awarded a Nobel Prize for the novels you have produced and write your own acceptance speech. What types of things would you like to say about the art of the novel, or art in general? Who would you count as your influences? Who would you thank?

- Research the political history of the U.S. involvement in Vietnam. Some people have suggested that the U.S. war in Iraq is similar to the war in Vietnam. Research the reasons for the U.S. involvement in both wars. How are they the same? How do they differ? Is either war justified in your opinion? Why or why not?

- The Zulu are a very musical people. Their songs were used during the demonstrations against apartheid in South Africa. Watch the video *Amandla! A Revolution in Four Part Harmony* about the role of the Zulu protest songs and write a review of this movie and present it to your class along with samples of the music that was used. Explain how the music helped the movement.

---

he is the epitome of intelligence and therefore rules over the native Africans. He cracks his whip, and the people obey him. He carries a gun, and they fear him. But without these weapons, he is as frail as they are in the wild, maybe even more so. Once he becomes ill, he must turn to them to be healed. They provide the potion and the food that cure him. He does not accept this notion, however. He always takes credit for his survival. Even when he must take a group of men with him in order to hunt elephants, he states that if he were not in their presence, his men would not survive. He believes that his workers believe this notion too. He says that they think of him as their father. In other words, he is the leader, the ruler, and the final word. And yet his men betray him, choosing to leave his presence when given another choice. It does not take much to defy him. But Jacobus does have the final word, at least according to his journal. For he goes back and kills those who defied him. He goes, however, with an army of men, equipped with modern weapons. The power, therefore, is not in the individual man but in the gun.

Delusion

The protagonists in both novellas are delusional. The author allows them to speak in their own voices, no matter how far from reality their minds, and thus their words, may stray. In the first novella, Eugene becomes so stressed out in his need to prove his intelligence and to therefore impress his supervisor that his mind snaps. In the beginning of the story, Eugene perceives his supervisor as an all-powerful being, someone Eugene would like to emulate, but he lacks the confidence to do so. He flip-flops through varying impressions that he is at one time better than his supervisor and then that he is subordinate to him. He also goes back and forth in his assessment of his marriage and his wife. At one time he says he is bored with her and yet he continually calls her from work to check up on her. And the moment that she turns her attention from him, he cannot stand it. When he thinks that she is having an affair, he craves her the most. Eugene also cannot fully comprehend his relationship with his son. At times he calls him only "her son" referring to his wife's relationship with the boy. And he mentions how distracting the boy's conversations are. But then when he runs away, he takes his son with him. He wants to make his son stronger, and he believes he can only do this away from his wife. He is the one who needs to be made stronger, but he imposes this condition on his son. And from that point, the delusions just get worse. He is not aware that he has done anything wrong in kidnapping the boy. And when the police arrive, Eugene is not fully cognizant of the harm he is causing when he sticks a knife into his son. Coetzee presents Eugene's type of delusional mind as the source of those who create various rationales for going to war with a country that is non-threatening.

Jacobus, the protagonist in the second novella, is likewise delusional but not quite as noticeably. His view of reality is distorted not by a mind disturbed by stress so much as a mind that is unaware of its own prejudice. Jacobus's thoughts are unrealistically inflated. He is so blinded by his prejudice that he belittles everyone around him. He does not see his own weaknesses but rather imposes those weaknesses on the native Africans who serve him. So in conclusion, he believes that he is the only one with intelligence, the only one who has developed a spirituality, the only one who can survive the harsh conditions of the desert. If it were not for him, his men would die, he believes, and yet he does not give credit to tribespeople who have survived in the desert for thousands of years. He does not understand their customs and traditions, so he dismisses them. Their way of life is beneath him, but it is their medicine that saves him. He accuses them of stealing and yet he has stolen their land and hunts their animals, not just for survival but also for profit. By dismissing them as a people not on equal standing with himself, he can justify their murders. He can rid the land of them as some people kill insects that are threatening to eat their crops. He can leave Klawer in the desert and not return to him as he promised, even though if it had not been for Klawer, Jacobus might have been left to rot when he fell sick. Coetzee presents Jacobus's delusional mind as an example of the source of a cruel system such as apartheid.

Style

Journal Writing

The novella "The Narrative of Jacobus Coetzee" is written as if Jacobus himself were taking notes and reflecting on events that have happened to him in the recent past. It is as if he were keeping a journal, recording his thoughts as the actions unfold. This gives the story a strong presence as if the reader had come across a private journal of a settler and was reading the thoughts of a man who had no intention of anyone else ever seeing what he had written. This adds authenticity to the piece, as if Jacobus's story comes unfiltered by any self-conscious feelings or inhibitions. Although his reflections on his actions and those of the people around him are, on the one hand, very haughty, and extremely prejudiced on the other, Jacobus never holds back on sharing them with his journal. He not only exposes his most inner thoughts, he also shares the gruesome details of everything from murder to the movement of his bowels. This type of writing can be somewhat nauseating at times but because the reader feels as if this is a journal, it is excusable.

Interior Monologue

Closely related to the style of journal writing, the novella "The Vietnam Project" is written as if the protagonist were talking to himself, or as if the reader could hear the inner thoughts of the protagonist. The result is similar to the style of the second novella but because it appears to be coming directly from the inside of the protagonist's mind, the reader feels even more closely involved with the protagonist of the first novel than with the protagonist of the second. The inner monologue of a person is even more unfiltered than that of a person who takes the time to write down his thoughts. In the process of writing, one can change or edit an original thought. However, when a story is told as if one were hearing the thoughts of another person, the reader feels as if no editing were done at all. This is demonstrated more clearly when the protagonist Eugene Dawn begins his decline into a mental breakdown. He is confused and his thoughts begin to have very little connection with reality. The reader senses that something is wrong because Eugene is not thinking about what he is doing, or he is misinterpreting what he is doing. In the journal-writing style, used in the story about Jacobus, although the reader might not agree with what Jacobus is doing, Jacobus records his actions accurately.

Fictionalized History

In both of these novellas, Coetzee fictionalizes actual historic events. In the first, he only uses history to construct a story in which a fictionalized character creates a fictionalized method of propaganda for the Vietnam War—a real event. But in the second novella, Coetzee uses real events and writes his story, including a "Translator's Preface" and an "Afterword," as well as footnotes to make the whole piece appear as if it were an actual translation of a real journal of an authentic South African settler. Whether these events really took place is unknown. They may be based on truth, but since Coetzee publishes the account as fiction, one can assume that the history that is presented has basically materialized out of Coetzee's imagination.

Historical Context

Colonization of Vietnam

From about 12,000 B.C. until 200 B.C., the indigenous people of what would later be called Vietnam thrived as farmers and fishermen. Then the first of many invasions from other cultures began. The first outsiders to try to seize control of Vietnam were the Chinese. They would continue to try to push their way into Vietnam for many centuries to follow. The Vietnamese won most of the battles with the Chinese. But this did not stop China from wanting to gain control in Vietnam, which they would try again and again through the eighteenth century.

Things did not improve very much for Vietnam's fight for independence during the nineteenth century. It was during this time that French missionary Pierre Pigneau de Behaine, who had come to Vietnam to introduce Christianity, convinced France to provide money and mercenary soldiers to help reunify Vietnam after a peasant rebellion threatened to tear Vietnam apart. Behaine asked for French support, hoping to gain favors for the French government in Vietnam. However, the Vietnamese soon became suspicious of the French and began persecuting French missionaries. Then in 1845, another country, this time the United States, became involved in the politics of Vietnam when they sent a military ship to Vietnam to rescue some French priests the Vietnamese were threatening to kill. This event would mark the first U.S. military involvement in Vietnam, and it would not be the last.

Two years later, the French returned to Vietnam in force. They were determined to avenge the murders of their citizens. They bombed Da Nang (a major city in central Vietnam that was called Tourane under French occupation) in an attempt to punish the Vietnamese. The French continued fighting the Vietnamese in the following decades, and in 1861, they defeated the Vietnamese army in the south. As the French tried to expand their hold to include northern Vietnam, the Chinese became involved, and a war between the French and the Chinese ensued. In 1885, the French defeated the Chinese and claimed all of Vietnam as French territory. The French colonization lasted until 1945, when Japanese troops defeated the French and occupied Vietnam. The Japanese were in Vietnam for only a short period of time as they were soon defeated in World War II. This left Vietnam temporarily in a political vacuum.

During the Potsdam Conference in 1945, in which the Allied Forces determined how to relegate power after the war, Vietnam was officially divided in two: South Vietnam and North Vietnam. France was given the right to rule the southern portion. Ho Chi Minh, a Vietnamese military leader in the north wanted to unify Vietnam, and so he fought the French in an attempt to rid his country of European rule. China, which was then under Mao Tse Tung's Communist regime, supported the North Vietnamese. To counter the Chinese collaboration in North Vietnam, President Truman, in 1950, authorized millions of dollars to aid the French effort in South Vietnam. In the following years, the U.S. government sent billions of dollars worth of war weaponry to South Vietnam. The term "domino effect" was used by each newly elected U.S. president after Truman to justify U.S. involvement in Vietnam. Like a stack of dominoes falls one by one, each fall affecting the next one, U.S. officials claimed that if Vietnam was allowed to come under communist rule, so would all the other Asian countries. But despite the U.S. financial aid, the French surrendered in 1954, after a horrific war in which more than 400,000 people perished.

Ho Chi Minh then declared war against South Vietnam as he tried to reunite the country. In 1961, President Kennedy sent a small contingency of marines to South Vietnam to train soldiers and to build fortified camps in the jungles to stop the infiltration of North Vietnamese troops into South Vietnam. U.S. involvement quickly escalated from that point. At the height of the war, in 1968, more than one thousand U.S. soldiers died in battle each month. After fifteen years of battle, the last U.S. soldiers finally left Vietnam in defeat. It was the first war that the United States had ever lost. More than two million American people served in Vietnam. Almost sixty thousand of them died.

On April 30, 1975, North Vietnamese soldiers took control of Saigon, the major city in the south.

Compare
&
Contrast

- **1800s:** Napoleon III orders French troops into Vietnam to begin occupation of that country.

  1900s: The French leave Vietnam defeated by the communist Viet Minh after more than 400,000 soldiers, both French and Vietnamese, have lost their lives in continual battles.

  2000s: France and Vietnam enter a period of economic cooperation as exemplified by a code-sharing plan between Air France and Vietnam Airlines, a plan to increase tourism in both countries.

- **1800s:** Chief Shaka of the Zulu people in South Africa rules over the largest tribe of black Africans in South Africa and defeats the British in the Anglo-Zulu War of 1879.

  1900s: Chief Bambatha of the Zulu people fights one of the last battles against the imperial conquest of South Africa. Bambatha becomes an icon in the fight for civil rights against apartheid in South Africa.

  2000s: Zulu music, which is said to raise the spirit through tight harmonic phrasings and was therefore once outlawed by apartheid, is now popularized internationally by the group Lady-smith Black Mambazo.

- **1800s:** Dutch is the prominent language among whites in Africa. When French Huguenots arrive, they are encouraged to forsake their native language in favor of Dutch, which causes both languages to merge and evolve into a language specific to South Africa, now known as Afrikaans.

  1900s: The British government in South Africa at first recognizes only English and Dutch as the official languages. In the 1900s, Dutch is finally replaced with Afrikaans as the official language.

  2000s: There are eleven official languages of South Africa. These include not only English and Afrikaans but also Zulu, Xhosa, and several Bantu languages.

Vietnam was once again unified, this time under communist rule. Today Vietnam has reestablished diplomatic relationships with the United States, France, and China.

Colonization of South Africa

South Africa, for more than 100,000 years, was the land of several different tribes. These included the Xhosa people, the San and Khoekhoe (referred to as the Bushmen and the Hottentots and collectively as the Khoisans), and the people of the Zulu confederation. As maritime trade developed in Europe, it became important for the European nations to establish supply points along the Cape of Good Hope. In 1652, the Dutch East India Company, led by Jan van Riebeeck, established the first European settlement in South Africa. Many of the Dutch who came to South Africa were farmers. They competed with the African tribespeople for land, with such actions often resulting in wars. Over the next century,

the Dutch settlements spread east, away from the coast and deeper into the traditional lands of the tribes. To do this, according to some accounts, the Dutch nearly exterminated the San people. To help them work the land, many of the Dutch settlers imported slaves from Indonesia and India. Descendents intermarried with the Dutch, creating what would later be called the "colored" people of South Africa, as opposed to the darker skinned native Africans.

Another group of white Europeans, the Huguenots (Protestants from France) migrated to South Africa in order to escape religious persecution. They too were good farmers and easily intermingled with the Dutch, gradually adapting themselves to the Dutch language and joining the Dutch in their expansion away from the coast. Together they (the Dutch and the French Huguenots) came to be referred to as the Boers.

In 1795, the British took control of the Cape of Good Hope and tried to impose their lifestyles and laws on the Boers. Unwilling to bear British rule, many of the Boers decided to leave their farms and head even farther into the eastern wilderness. However, as the Boers settled the new land, the British were never far behind, claiming the land for the British crown. The British actions accelerated when gold and diamonds were discovered in Boer land. In 1880 and again in 1899, this led to the so-called Boer Wars, fought between formal British troops and the more renegade Boers. The Boers were able to prohibit the British advances in the first war. But additional forces from Britain were sent to supplement the British soldiers, who were then successful in subduing the Boers in the second war. Many Boers, as well as Africans who worked for them, were placed in concentration camps. (Coetzee's Booker Prize–winning novel *Life and Times of Michael K* is a fictionalized account of this second war.) Outbreaks of fighting continued between the Boers and the British until 1902 when the Boers signed a peace treaty with Britain.

In 1910, the Union of South Africa was created with the most influential political power in the hands of the white minority, both of British and Dutch descent. In 1948, the National Party came into power and the system referred to as apartheid was put in place. Blacks were denied the power to vote; interracial marriages were banned; and Africans were deprived of equal education. Black Africans could only attend agricultural or trade schools. Apartheid would continue for more than forty years. After the release of the political prisoner Nelson Mandela, the first, multiracial democratic elections were held. In 1994, Mandela became the country's first black African president.

Critical Overview

Coetzee's first novel *Dusklands* did not receive a lot of international critical attention. This may have been due more to the fact that he published in South Africa than to the content of his work. Since that time, however, and especially since he won the Booker Prize for his third novel *Life and Times of Michael K*, Coetzee has become an often critiqued author. For instance, in a summary of Coetzee's body of work, Kristjana Gunnars for *World Literature Today* describes Coetzee's style and impact in this way, "J. M. Coetzee's fiction strips bare the veneer that protects us, and it ventures unflinchingly into territory of mind and experience most of us are afraid to face." Gunnars further comments

on a descriptive word that is frequently used to depict Coetzee's style of writing. That word is *sparse*. However, Gunnars explains that since Coetzee's subject matter usually involves human suffering, there is no other way to write. Gunnars states, "The central issue in much of what he [Coetzee] writes is what is often regarded as the fundamental problem of twentieth—and now twenty-first-century literature in general: how do we witness another's pain?" Gunnars concludes that Coetzee's sparse style of writing accomplishes this feat successfully. And in the process, Coetzee "has produced literature of great consistency and accomplishment."

A fellow South African, Tony Morphet, writing for *World Literature Today*, remembers the first time he read Coetzee's *Dusklands* and that he was somewhat baffled by it. "I read the book in one sitting," Morphet states, "exhilarated but confounded. The narratives were intense and compelling, yet, as I progressed, I felt the pattern of meaning eluding me." Morphet continues by stating that although he could not grasp the meaning, he was "convinced" that *Dusklands* "was a herald. A new form of narration, a new way of imagining—a new prose had entered South African literature." Morphet, a teacher of English literature, promoted the book among his fellow teachers and persuaded the department to include the new novel in the curriculum. The book caused a slight uproar. And as Morphet relates, some of the teachers were concerned that "the book would be a danger to students" because of the "disturbing point of view and the vocabulary." Despite this concern, which Morphet states continues today in South Africa, "few question the judgment that Coetzee is the finest writer of his generation—of many generations."

In the article "The Voice of Africa" written for London's *The Observer*, Robert McCrum refers to Coetzee as "the essential novelist of the new South Africa." McCrum explains that having grown up within the apartheid system, Coetzee "absorbed its crimes into his consciousness and published his first book *Dusklands*, paralleling America's role in Vietnam with the early Dutch settlers in South Africa.... He has always wrestled with the peculiar predicament of Africa's white tribe." McCrum continues by stating that Coetzee's "pared-down prose" is particularly "suited to his subject." And McCrum believes that at the time of apartheid, Coetzee "seemed to be the most gifted of a group of South African writers."

And finally, in a *New York Times* article called "A Tale of Heroic Anonymity," which was a

U.S. involvement in the Vietnam War, seen here as U.S. military helicopters fly over a field in South Vietnam, is the subject of the first part of Dusklands

review of Coetzee's award-winning novel *Life and Times of Michael K*, Cynthia Ozick concludes, "Coetzee is a writer of clarifying inventiveness and translucent conviction." She continues, "The grain of his sentences is flat and austere, but also so purifying to the sense that one comes away feeling that one's eye has been sharpened, one's hearing vivified, not only for the bright proliferations of nature, but for human unexpectedness."

Criticism

Joyce Hart

Hart is a freelance writer and author of several books. In this essay, Hart compares the two novellas contained in Coetzee's Dusklands *in search of the not so obvious similarities that link the two stories together.*

None other of J. M. Coetzee's works except for his first novel, *Dusklands*, consist of two separate works combined to create a whole. One might argue that this was done haphazardly or with only a weak link connecting the pieces. The works, after all, take place in two separate countries, at two

separate times. The protagonists live in very disparate circumstances and come to terms with their personal challenges in very dissimilar fashions. But the connections between the two separate parts of this book do take form. Similarities between the protagonists' personalities and their situations are evident. Themes that appear in one story are reflected in the other. And the actions and motives of both protagonists can be defined in relatively parallel details. After exploring these traits of what at first appear to be two unrelated tales, it is difficult to see this novel as anything but a cohesive project.

The protagonist of the first novella, Eugene Dawn, is a rather meek person, living in a quiet environment. He spends most of his life in the library or in a lonely corner of his drab office. His work entails the intellect but little physical exertion and no travel. Immediate danger to his body is nonexistent. In opposition is the protagonist of the second novella, Jacobus Coetzee, the tamer of the wilds; the elephant hunter; the macho slave master—a man who lives in danger of physical harm almost every day of his life. The former lives in the twentieth century in a quiet, modern town, where he ponders war but has little to do with it. In contrast, Jacobus lives two hundred years earlier in a time of colonial expansion, which demands that in order to survive, one must live by one's wits and superior physical conditioning. So how do these two men relate to one another? Where and how do their personalities connect? What could they possibly have in common?

One of the first and possibly most evident characteristics these protagonists share is their isolation. Eugene, although married and a father, demonstrates very slim, if any, emotional involvement with his family. He admits that he is addicted to his marriage, but he also states that he is not in love with his wife. She is an annoyance to him. The only time he is slightly attracted to her is when Eugene believes she is having an affair with her doctor. It excites him to think that another man might be enamored of his wife, or at least physically lustful of her. And Eugene's relationship to his son is even more flimsy. The boy belongs to his wife, as far as Eugene is concerned. Although he kidnaps Martin, he spends very little time actually communicating with him and more often complains that the boy is a young child who craves attention. Away from home, Eugene has very little contact with the people around him. And when he does meet with fellow employees, it is more often in silence. He listens to his supervisor but has little to say to him, even though the dialogue in his head is enormous. Of all the people around him, it is the quiet, mouse-like figure of Harry, the clerk in the library that Eugene relates to the most. And this relationship is fleeting, at best. Eugene is so busy, and therefore so distracted, in analyzing everyone around him, trying to figure out how he either fits into the equation or second-guessing how others perceive him that he devotes little time to actually sharing anything with the people around him. He is isolated by his fear and his lack of confidence. He lives inside his head in a tiny room that becomes more and more distorted.

Although Jacobus, unlike Eugene, appears to have little fear and enough self-confidence to believe that no matter what life-threatening circumstances he might find himself in, he can turn it into a game of possibilities and become excited by the challenges, he too lives in a very isolated world. Not only does he live in a place that he refers to as having limitless boundaries, a place where one can walk for days and never see another human being, he also, like Eugene, lives inside of his head. The room he lives in is also very narrow and distorted. Because of the life-threatening challenges that Jacobus faces every day, he has come to believe that he is superior to those around him. He faces death on a continual basis and eludes it. He has survived because of his outstanding intellect, he concludes. Others

> " Their thoughts, through which these men make themselves feel superior to their fellow beings, keep them locked in a world that has no space for camaraderie. They walk their paths as if they are the only truly human people on earth."

perish in front of him, because of their stupidity or lack of perception. Like Eugene, Jacobus has no friends. The people around him are merely tools that he uses to get what he wants or needs. He has no one to talk to. The one time he attempts to talk to Klawer, one of his workers, Jacobus dismisses the man's responses as trivial. No one understands him, or so Jacobus believes. If given a choice (which he is given, actually, but which he refuses to fully act on), Jacobus would like to live wild in the desert, naked except for his shoes, and very much alone. He refers to his life as a farmer as one of boredom, a life of practiced and repetitive routine. Jacobus's counterpart, Eugene, also mentions how bored he is with his office job. And yet both men remain in their positions, alone and isolated by their thoughts. Their thoughts, through which these men make themselves feel superior to their fellow beings, keep them locked in a world that has no space for camaraderie. They walk their paths as if they are the only truly human people on earth.

The stories that surround these two men also contain similarities. There is the concept of propaganda that unites them, for example. Eugene works on a theory of propaganda, which he hopes the government will use in the war in Vietnam. This work is the focal point of the story, around which Eugene at once excels, flounders, and finally deteriorates. The propaganda is presented as a way of finding victory in Vietnam; a way of suppressing the desires of the Vietnamese people to fight for their land and their way of life. In a comparable way, Jacobus also deals in propaganda. He does so when he deals with the African men who work for him as well as when he must face strangers, such as the Namaqua people. With his own workers, Jacobus continually

What Do I Read Next?

- *The Complete Short Prose, 1929–1989* (1997) is a collection of short stories by Pulitzer Prize–winning author Samuel Beckett. Coetzee wrote his doctorate dissertation on Beckett and is sure to have been influenced by Beckett's work.

- Coetzee's writing is often compared to Franz Kafka, the great Czech author who wrote during the turn of the twentieth century. Kafka's *The Trial* (1925) is considered by many to be his scariest book, as protagonist Joseph K. becomes entangled in a treacherous legal system.

- While working in England as a computer programmer, Coetzee stayed in touch with literature through his studies of British author Ford Maddox Ford. *The Good Soldier* (1915) is one of Ford's best and saddest works. It tackles the subject of infidelity in two marriages, a topic that was more rare in its time than it is today.

- Coetzee won the Booker Prize for two of his novels. The first was *Life and Times of Michael K.* (1983), a story about a young but poor gardener who tries to escape the war that is raging around him; and the second was for *Disgrace* (1999), about a professor who falls from grace because of a brief but rather cruel affair with a student.

- Edward Said's *Orientalism* (1978) is an important work of postcolonial criticism. Said explains how Western people mystified the Orient—through literary, historical, and ethnographic texts—misappropriating the people of that region. The act of understanding other cultures, and writing narratives that depict those cultures, is viewed as a highly political act of power, ultimately marginalizing those who are being depicted by excluding their own voices.

---

reinforces the concept that he is the master and they are the slaves. He does this in words and in actions. These men could easily overthrow him at any time and yet they do not because they believe his propaganda. When Jacobus is in danger of being toppled by the Namaqua people, he praises them for their goodness and charity, claims that he does not fully believe. He tells them these things only to pacify them, to win their temporary willingness to share their hunting fields and to leave Jacobus's supplies in tact. This is a more personal propaganda that Jacobus uses, but its purpose is the same as the propaganda that Eugene creates. Both men's aims are to further exploit another group of people, to win them over, and change their ways. Both stories, in some ways, revolve around the concept of using propaganda to colonize a foreign country.

There is also a lot of blood and guts, rather graphically detailed, in the two separate stories. Eugene, for instance, carries with him, at all times, photographs of severed heads and other atrocities of war. He carries them, he says, so his wife will not meddle in his business. But he also takes the pictures out from time to time to study them. He is somewhat fascinated by them. It is because of these photographs, his wife tells him, that he is changing. The effects of the war in Vietnam have made him a different person, one she knows less well. Later, when Eugene suffers a mental breakdown, he takes a knife and stabs his son. The details of this stabbing are blurred because of Eugene's state of mind, but nonetheless, the reader can imagine the blood and suffering of Eugene's son.

Jacobus's story is more specifically graphic. Killing abounds throughout the telling of his adventures. Animals are killed for food and for profit. People are murdered and tortured. Even in Jacobus's illness, the putrid details of infection, nausea, and diarrhea are reported. He tells of having seen a man roasted. And later, in a struggle with a group of children, (somewhat akin to Eugene stabbing his son), Jacobus bites off a child's ear. After his men betray him, Jacobus returns to the Namaqua village and takes pleasure in slowly killing his former slave, the young boy Plaatje. These bloody deeds are visible signatures in both

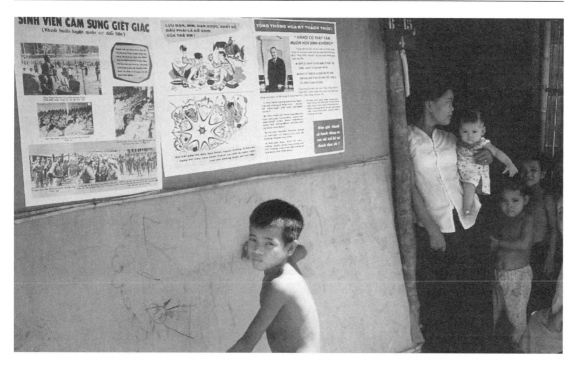

A South Vietnamese family stands amid government propaganda during the Vietnam War, perhaps like the propaganda devised by Eugene Dawn in Dusklands

pieces. They are written in the same tone—objectively and simply. Little emotion is expressed in any of these scenes, whether it is a father wounding his son or a master massacring his slave. The sordid details are presented much as a doctor might record the fine points of a surgical operation. In other words, there is a detachment between the perpetrator and the person he attacks.

And finally, there is the motif of dominance. Even meek Eugene sees himself as one who dominates. He admits, on one hand, that he is insecure, but at the same time (or shortly afterward), he claims his superiority. Eugene is smarter than his supervisor, he says, even though he quakes in his presence. His boss does not understand him or his work. Eugene is the only one who sees the truth, who envisions the true path. He is also better than his wife, who is lost in her depression. His only relationship with his son is that of master. He takes his son to the motel with him and does not in any way attempt to create a child's world for his son's benefit. Rather, the son must adjust to his father's life. And to further prove his dominance, when the police come to reclaim the child, Eugene punctures the young boy in an attempt to further deflate him. The police, like everyone else in Eugene's world, do not understand. "The people in front of me are growing smaller and therefore less and less dangerous," Eugene says, just before the police club him over the head.

Jacobus's goal is also to dominate. He plans on wiping out everyone who stands in his way. He and his fellow farmers clear the land of the Bushmen so they can claim the land for themselves. This is the way the Boers conquer. But the Boers are not the only dominant culture. They have been driven into the interior by the British, whose aim is to conquer the Boers. Dominance, whether played out by men versus animals or man against man, is pressed forward in both of these stories through war, propaganda, slaughter, weaponry, religion, and, in some cases, just an excuse for adventure. One man tries to dominate a whole culture while another attempts to dominate his wife and child. The outcomes vary—one man successfully seeks his vengeance, while the other succeeds only in a total mental collapse. But the desires, motives, and practices of these protagonists, as well as the undertone of these two stories, link the novellas tightly together and present two sides of a compelling narrative.

Source: Joyce Hart, Critical Essay on *Dusklands*, in *Novels for Students*, Thomson Gale, 2005.

Susan VanZanten Gallagher

In the following essay excerpt, Gallagher analyzes the two parts of Dusklands—*"The Vietnam Project" and "The Narrative of Jacobus Coetzee"—within the context of myth-making and colonialism.*

The first dark land we enter is America in the throes of the Vietnam War. *"The Vietnam Project"* is divided into five sections, four of which appear to be diary entries recounting events in the life of Eugene Dawn. In the opening section, Dawn recounts all of his paranoia: his supervisor—one J. M. Coetzee—does not like his writing style; he suspects his wife, Marilyn, is having an affair; he loathes and feels trapped in his body. The second section, written in bureaucratic jargon with subheadings and references, contains Dawn's report for the New Life Project, a propaganda plan that his think tank is preparing for the Department of Defense. An expert in mythography, Dawn argues that the United States should concentrate on forming a counter-myth to the current Vietnamese myth of the sons (Vietnam) banding together to rebel against the father (the United States). After turning this report in, Dawn is convinced that J. M. Coetzee is avoiding him, and he is troubled with bad dreams. Attempting to grasp reality, he runs away with his son, Martin, to a motel in the mountains. When Marilyn and the police come to reclaim the child, Dawn—in a remarkable passage written in the present tense and describing his sense of dissociation—stabs Martin. In the final section of the novella, Dawn writes from a psychiatric hospital, in which the doctors are analyzing his childhood and attempting to discover what made him perform such an atrocious act.

Like Dawn's account, *"The Narrative of Jacobus Coetzee"* has five sections, four of personal recollection and one official document. Dawn's story has numerical divisions; Jacobus gives his sections different narrative titles. In addition, the second half of *Dusklands* is accompanied by a framing device, a preface by a presumed translator (J. M. Coetzee) and an afterword by a South African academic historian (S. J. Coetzee). This framing device directs our attention to the ongoing propagation of the Afrikaner master myth of history.

Jacobus Coetzee, an eighteenth-century Dutch explorer and hunter, opens his narrative with a discourse on the Bushmen and then describes his "Journey beyond the Great River," accompanied by his six Hottentot servants. His "Sojourn in the land of the Great Namaqua" occurs when he becomes ill, and, delirious with a fever, finds himself being taken to a Nama village and nursed in a menstruation hut. While recovering, he is bathing in the river when a group of small boys steal his clothes and begin to mock him. Furious, he falls upon them, and in the ensuing fray, bites the ear off a boy. The Nama physically punish him and then expel him from the village for this savage act of mutilating a child. Accompanied by his faithful servant Klawer, who dies during the journey, Jacobus makes his way back to civilization, only to return with a small armed force to avenge himself on the people who had humiliated him. The final section of his personal narrative, "Second journey to the land of the Great Namaqua," unrelentingly details this cruel punishment. A final account of the first journey appears in the Appendix, which contains the deposition of Jacobus Coetzee, taken down in 1760 at the Castle of Good Hope to serve as the official governmental report. This deposition tells an entirely different story from the personal account, detailing the days of travel, the various natural resources found in the country, and several peaceful encounters with the Nama.

The juxtaposition of these two narratives immediately invites comparison. Both Eugene Dawn and Jacobus Coetzee are explorers. "I have an exploring temperament," Dawn explains. "Had I lived two hundred years ago I would have had a continent to explore, to map, to open to colonization." In the twentieth century, however, what remains to be explored is the human psyche, and instead of mapping rivers and mountains, Dawn sets down body language, dreams, and myths. In their respective roles as government servants, Dawn explores the psychological interior of the Vietnamese rendered in their mythology, and Jacobus journeys into the physical interior of Africa. As explorers, both are driven to know the unknown, to encompass that unknown both mentally and physically. Touching the surface of a photograph of an imprisoned Vietcong, Dawn notes that it "is bland and opaque under my fingers, yielding no passage into the interior of this obscure but indubitable man. I keep exploring. Under the persistent pressure of my imagination, acute and morbid in the night, it may yet yield." Similarly, Jacobus states, "I am an explorer. My essence is to open what is closed, to bring light to what is dark." His "explorer's hammerblow" attempts to crack the bleak desert exterior to reach the "innocent interior."

As Jacobus's imagery suggests, the explorer does not shrink from violence. During the course of their narratives, both Dawn and Jacobus physically

harm a child, which indicates their disturbed estimation of human life. Similarly, they not only are
unmoved by the physical atrocities performed by
their respective colonial powers, but also contribute
to or urge this kind of violence themselves. Dawn
repeatedly examines three photographs that are part
of his material for the Vietnam report: a Vietnamese
prisoner in a tiger cage, a onetime Texas linebacker
copulating with a tiny Vietnamese woman, two Special Forces sergeants holding the severed heads of
Vietnamese "taken from corpses or near-corpses."
The "delicious shame" stimulated by these pictures
provides his imagination with the "slight electric
impulse" needed to stimulate his mythographical
exploration. Dawn's final solution to the problem
of Vietnam is to destroy the land physically by intense bombing and chemical warfare, to "show the
enemy that he stands naked in a dying landscape."
In mythological terms, he advises rape: "assault
upon the mothering earth herself."

With the exception of his attack on Martin,
Dawn's violence is confined to discourse; Jacobus
actually practices violent destruction. Returning to
the Nama village, he coldly watches as his troops
kill, rape, and burn. He personally supervises the
punishment of the four servants who had abandoned him, and recounts the cruelty of these deaths
in horrible detail: "I pushed the muzzle against his
lips. 'Take it,' I said. He would not take it. I
stamped. His lips seeped blood, his jaw relaxed. I
pushed the muzzle in till he began to gag. I held
his head steady between my ankles. Behind me his
sphincter gave way and a rich stench filled the air.
'Watch your manners, hotnot,' I said. I regretted
this vulgarity. The shot sounded as minor as a shot
fired into the sand. Whatever happened in the pap
inside his head left his eyes crossed." The phallic
suggestiveness of this scene typifies the sexual
terms in which the violent assault on interiors is
described throughout both novellas. The rhetoric
suggests the integral connection between political,
economic, racial, and sexual oppression, a connection that Coetzee explores further in his later works.

Dusklands shows how the obsessive drive to
explore and the inevitable acceptance of violence
of both the propagandist and the elephant hunter
are common elements of the master myth of colonialism. But rather than accepting a purely material basis for this behavior, Coetzee points to a
metaphysical origin. In this respect his work differs sharply from the Marxist analysis of the roots
of colonialism. *Dusklands* actually takes several
oblique potshots at the materialistic focus of
Marxism. Jacobus's animal references suggest the

> *Dusklands* shows how the
> obsessive drive to explore and
> the inevitable acceptance of
> violence of both the propagandist
> and the elephant hunter are
> common elements of the master
> myth of colonialism."

inhumanity of pure materialism. His dogs eat the
flesh of the hare, but he obtains "metaphysical
meat" from the death of the hare. Even more sar-
castically, he wonders if when he dies, his organs
will be thrown to "the economic pigs." Dawn also
notes the inadequacy of understanding all human
behavior in Marxist terms, complaining about his
supervisor, "His career has been built on the self
and its interests. He thinks of me, even me, as
merely a self with interests. He cannot understand
a man who experiences his self as an envelope
holding his body-parts together while inside it he
burns and burns." Beyond economics and self-
interest, which Coetzee never completely discounts, are other human drives.

Both Dawn and Coetzee suffer from an onto-
logical problem: they are uncertain about the nature
of their own existence in relationship to the external world. Michael Vaughan observes: "They are
identical, not in character or experience, but in the
mode of consciousness by which they perceive their
world, and their relation to this world." As they
struggle to understand the relationship of their own
subjectivity to the objectivity of the world around
them, both turn to exploration as a means of breaking through their philosophical impasse. Each
moves between total objectivity and total subjectivity, the extremes of annihilation and solipsism.
This desperate search for one's true position in the
universe results both in their use of others as a
means of asserting an identity and in the acceptance
of violence as a copula, a means of establishing and
bridging the gap between self and other. "The gun
and its metaphors," Dawn states, are "the only cop-
ulas we knew of between ourselves and our object."
Similarly, Jacobus claims, "The gun stands for the
hope that there exists that which is other than oneself. The gun is our last defence against isolation

within the travelling sphere." Violence overcomes solipsism: "The gun saves us from the fear that all life is within us. It does so by laying at our feet all the evidence we need of a dying and therefore a living world." The colonizing impetus, then, comes from this divided consciousness, which Stephen Watson identifies as originating with Descartes: "the colonizing project of the West was set in motion when this same man embarked upon his Cartesian project of separating subject from object, self from world in a dualism which privileged the first of the two terms and thereby assured his domination of nature and any other obstacle he might confront ... Just as Western people conquer nature in an effort to conquer their own self-division, so they cannot desist from enslaving other human beings who necessarily confront them as that Other, alien and forever threatening."

The absence that looms for both protagonists is the failure of transcendence, the missing superstructure that controls the relationship of objects and subjects. Their search essentially is religious, as the rhetoric of each narrative reveals. Dawn says about the American presence in Vietnam, "Our nightmare was that since whatever we reached for slipped like smoke through our fingers, we did not exist; that since whatever we embraced wilted, we were all that existed. We landed on the shores of Vietnam clutching our arms and pleading for someone to stand up without flinching to these probes of reality." He realizes that his desire for someone to stand up to reality, to draw a clear line of demarcation between the controlling subjectivity and the controlled object, is actually a "tragic reach for transcendence." The subtext of his meditation is the loss of God:

> We bathed them in seas of fire, praying for the miracle. In the heart of the flame their bodies glowed with heavenly light; in our ears their voices rang; but when the fire died they were only ash. We lined them up in ditches. If they had walked toward us singing through the bullets we would have knelt and worshipped; but the bullets knocked them over and they died as we had feared. We cut their flesh open, we reached into their dying bodies, tearing out their livers, hoping to be washed in their blood; but they screamed and gushed like our most negligible phantoms. We forced ourselves deeper than we had ever gone before into their women; but when we came back we were still alone, and the women like stones.

The same religious reverberations appear in Dawn's search for a father. His advice that the United States employ "the father voice," the voice of authority, in its propaganda broadcasts to the Vietnamese reveals his own longing for transcendent authority. "The

excluded orphan," he dreams of home, "the true home before whose barred gate I have spent this last orphan year." In his orphan state, he is unable to touch the faces from his photographs of Vietnam that populate his dreams; without a home or father, he cannot love others. Instead, as he forces himself deeper and deeper into others in an attempt to reach their subjectivity, he turns them into objects. When guns, drugs, torture, or rape rip open the interior, the subject becomes a mere ghost or absence of self: "where they had once been is now only a black hole through which they have been sucked." Without transcendence, Dawn is unable to escape a solipsistic world.

Jacobus, also, considers the possibility of "a universe of which I the Dreamer was sole inhabitant." In a passage reminiscent of the desire of Melville's Ahab to "strike through the mask," Jacobus wants to discover the reality at the heart of the world. And like Ahab, he fears that perhaps nothing lies behind the material world:

> Behind this familiar red or grey exterior, spoke the stone from its stone heart to mine, this exterior jutting into every dimension inhabited by man, lies in ambush a black interior quite, quite strange to the world. Yet under the explorer's hammerblow this innocent interior transforms itself in a flash into a replete, confident, worldly image of that red or grey exterior. How then, asked the stone, can the hammerwielder who seeks to penetrate the heart of the universe be sure that there exist any interiors? Are they not perhaps fictions, these lures of interiors for rape which the universe uses to draw out its explorers?

The imagery of Jacobus's meditation echoes Dawn's frustration at "the women like stones." The intractable stoniness of the southwestern African terrain—in which Coetzee was raised and Jacobus Coetzee made his discoveries—no doubt contributes to this rhetoric. However, its wildness also helps to form the solipsism of the explorer: "In the wild I lose my sense of boundaries. This is a consequence of space and solitude. The operation of space is thus: the five senses stretch out from the body they inhabit, but four stretch into a vacuum. The ear cannot hear, the nose cannot smell, the tongue cannot taste, the skin cannot feel." Only the eyes are free, and Jacobus becomes an Emersonian "spherical reflecting eye moving through the wilderness and ingesting it." Everything that he sees is included "in his traveling sphere. What is there that is not me? I am a transparent sac with a black core full of images and a gun." The search for the interior is a metaphysical hunt, provoked by the human need to understand the self in relationship to the world.

A British police officer inspects the body of a Mau Mau soldier in Kenya, Africa, which involves the issue of European colonialism, seen in the second part of Dusklands

The fatal loss of transcendence, the obsessive drive to explore, and the recourse to violence are common elements in the colonialism of both the propagandist and the elephant hunter. Jonathan Crewe notes that "we are looking at *recto* and *verso* of the same coin—the Western consciousness in its exploded and imploded condition," and Vaughan implies that Dawn and Jacobus represent two different colonial eras: "the contemporary intellectual . . . of latter-day imperialism" and "the early explorer-coloniser . . . in the epoch of the youthful vigour of Western imperialism." However, *Dusklands* also demonstrates how the practice of colonialism takes

different forms in different times and places. While Coetzee's narrative rejects a pure materialism, he nonetheless acknowledges the contributions of material circumstances to the embodiment of metaphysical questions. Different cultural conditions cause the loss of transcendence to manifest itself in different ways, as well as provide different social and discursive structures within which that loss may be understood. In this respect, the differences in the depiction of Dawn and Jacobus are as significant as the similarities. Their contrasting reactions to the loss of transcendence are particularly noteworthy. Jacobus takes on himself the role of the missing God, exalting in his strength and solipsistic power, but Dawn physically and psychologically disintegrates with the loss of the father. To a certain extent, each is a metonymy of his era and country—Jacobus typifying the physical dominance and religious arrogance of the Afrikaner settlers; Dawn typifying the rhetorical dominance and psychic disturbance of contemporary American society. In an early review of the novel published in South Africa, Lionel Abrahams points out how one part of *Dusklands* is "a story about our origins" while the other is "a story about our possible destination." In the self-aware twentieth century, the myth of masters results not in physical control but in self-doubt and alienation.

Source: Susan VanZanten Gallagher, "The Master Myth of History: *Dusklands*," in *A Story of South Africa: J. M. Coetzee's Fiction in Context*, Harvard University Press, 1991, pp. 57–64.

Sources

Coetzee, J. M., *Dusklands*, Penguin Books, 1985.

Gunnars, Kristjana, "A Writer's Writer: Two Perspectives," in *World Literature Today*, Vol. 78, No. 1, January–April 2004, pp. 11–13.

McCrum, Robert, "The Voice of Africa," in the *Observer*, October 5, 2003.

Morphet, Tony, "Reading Coetzee in South Africa," in *World Literature Today*, Vol. 78, No. 1, January–April 2004, pp. 14–16.

Ozick, Cynthia, "A Tale of Heroic Anonymity," in *New York Times*, December 11, 1983, Sec. 7, p. 1.

Further Reading

Attridge, Derek, and Rosemary Jolly, eds., *Writing South Africa*, Cambridge University Press, 1998.

In the last years of apartheid the world paid a lot of attention to the great literature being produced in South Africa. This book captures some of the breadth and depth of that writing, and there are several references to Coetzee.

Attwell, David, *J. M. Coetzee*, University of California Press, 1993.

Attwell is a professor at a college in South Africa. He offers a critical look into Coetzee's major works, demonstrating how Coetzee's works are complex analyses of the politics in South Africa.

Huggan, Graham, and Stephen Watson, *Critical Perspectives on J. M. Coetzee*, with a preface by Nadine Gordimer, Palgrave Macmillan, 1996.

In this collection of critical essays, Coetzee's works are analyzed with respect to how he deals with colonialism, national violence, and the manipulation of language to promote the ideals of state.

Karnow, Stanley, *Vietnam*, Penguin Books, 1997.

In well-written prose that tries to remain objective, Karnow tries to recapture the events of the Vietnam War as they unfolded in Asia and in the United States. He interviews people on both sides of the war in his attempt to shed light on this topic.

Pratkanis, Anthony, and Elliot Aronson, *Propaganda*, Owl Books, 2001.

Psychologists Pratkanis and Aronson take a look at the subject of propaganda, not just as it has appeared in history but also as it affects everyone today. Propaganda invades the American culture through mass media, whether it is trying to sell merchandise or politics.

Emma

Jane Austen

1815

Of the 2,000 copes of *Emma* printed in 1815, only 563 sold over the next four years. Austen died in 1817 having earned less than £40 for the book during her lifetime. In the early 2000s, the novel was considered a classic of romance comedies and perhaps Austen's best novel of manners and morals. Written at the end of Austen's young life, and hence in her maturity, *Emma* fully demonstrates Austen's narrative power to render witty dialogue, romantic intrigue, memorable descriptions of scenes and situations, and the ironic and satirical treatment of the virtues, vices, and drawing room behavior of the British upper classes at the end of the eighteenth century. To combine both rationality and compassion in one's actions is the mark of true gentility, Austen seems to be saying. Yet, lest readers take this central lesson too much to heart, Austen gives plenty to laugh at and puzzle over as her flawed but redeemable heroine fumbles her way toward womanhood.

Author Biography

Jane Austen was the second daughter and the seventh of eight children born to the Reverend George Austen and Cassandra Leigh. Born on December 16, 1775, she grew up in the country village of Steventon, in Hampshire, England.

Her family was not wealthy, but they were certainly comfortable, for Jane Austen's father earned

Jane Austen

at age nine. In her time, it was not usual for a woman of the "genteel" classes to attend school; rather, she would be expected to attain certain "accomplishments" (singing, sewing, drawing, a speaking knowledge of French, letter writing) to prepare her for an advantageous marriage. Respectable careers (except for those of governess or school teacher) were not open to women, and being married was much preferable to working outside the home. Austen, like most women of her class, was educated at home and read from the books in her father's library. Evident in all her novels is a pointed satire leveled at women who define themselves chiefly by their ability to attract the opposite sex while ignoring the improvement of their minds.

Although Austen was at work on her last novel, *Persuasion*, in 1815, it was published posthumously (along with *Northanger Abbey* which she had written earlier in 1797); *Emma* was the last book to see publication before her death. Austen died July 18, 1817, of Addison's Disease. She was forty-one years old. She is buried in Winchester Cathedral.

£600 a year as the local clergyman. This was a respectable salary but not one that could provide either Jane or Cassandra, her older sister and confidante, a large dowry. Austen lived at the Steventon rectory for 25 years. She never married, although she had more than a passing interest in romance and the society of her peers. Indeed, her keen observation of the society around her is mirrored in her novels, which reflect the manners and morals of her time, the conventions of courtship and marriage, and the psychology of human relationships.

Between 1795 and 1798, Austen wrote the original versions of three novels: *Northanger Abbey*, *Sense and Sensibility*, and *Pride and Prejudice*. However, none of these books was published until well after her father's death (1805) after which Mrs. Austen and her daughters moved from Bath (where the family had lived from 1801 until Mr. Austen's death) to Southampton briefly and then to Chawton, where they lived in a house provided by Jane's wealthy brother, Edward. *Sense and Sensibility* appeared anonymously in 1811, and two years later, *Pride and Prejudice*, the novel that made her reputation. In 1814, Austen published *Mansfield Park*.

Jane Austen received a minimal formal education at the Abbey School in Reading, which she left

Plot Summary

Volume 1

Austen introduces most of the major characters in Volume 1, with the exceptions of Jane Fairfax, Frank Churchill, and Mrs. Elton. Since Jane and Frank are the nucleus around which the central mystery revolves, and yet, since neither character is meant to outshine the hero and heroine (Emma Woodhouse and Mr. George Knightley), it makes good literary sense to save them for Volume 2 and the middle section in which the mystery unfolds and deepens. The book opens with the focus on Emma Woodhouse, whom we find has everything to recommend her as an eighteenth century heroine: She is "handsome, clever, and rich, with a comfortable home and happy disposition." However, Austen makes it clear at the outset that Emma, and indeed all the characters, will take shape not as they appear in and of themselves, but in how they relate to others. Their mannerisms and habits, their allegiance to propriety, their wit and intelligence, and their compassion will mark them as either elegant or common.

Emma is motherless and has been educated by Miss Taylor, her governess of 16 years. "Poor Miss Taylor," as Emma's father calls her (projecting his own loss onto her) has just married Mr. Weston, their close neighbor and friend, and while they will continue to see her everyday, Emma is conscious of her approaching "intellectual solitude." Emma's "evil" character flaw, "a disposition to think a little too well of herself," has ample room for exercise when she meets Harriet Smith. Harriet has neither merit nor birth to urge a friendship between herself and Emma (she is a boarder at Mrs. Goddard's school for girls and her parents are unknown), and yet Emma decides to practice on her, to make for her the perfect romantic match and along the way improve her mind. Mr. Knightley, the novel's paragon of virtue and reason, is skeptical of the friendship. Prophetically, he sees that both must lose by the friendship. No one listens, least of all Emma, for once her imagination has been let loose on a subject, she must follow it to the bitter end. And bitter it does turn out to be.

Emma's designs to "improve" Harriet by association with a "superior" mind and to match her to the eligible bachelor, Mr. Elton, spring from a mix of hubris, boredom, a real intention to do good for both, a romantic detachment from the facts, and an overweening belief in the power of her own ideas. When she learns that Harriet is falling in love with Robert Martin, a simple but honorable tenant farmer (and a man wholly suited to Harriet), she immediately sets about discouraging Harriet by comparing his "clownish" ways to the ways of the "such very real" gentlemen she sees at Hartfield. Of course, Mr. Martin is dimmed by the comparison, at least outwardly. It becomes the cause of a serious disagreement between Emma and Mr. Knightley, who very much wants the union to succeed. Through the critical eyes of Mr. Knightley, and by virtue of her own supercilious airs, readers see how far Emma is from cultivating true grace.

The game of charades that Emma is teaching Harriet to play becomes a metaphor for the dual interpretations of words and motives that Austen cleverly weaves into the scenes assigned to Mr. Elton, Harriet, and Emma. Emma, so blinded by her own intrigues, cannot see that Mr. Elton's true intentions are to win *her* heart. Ever so belatedly, Emma becomes more and more aggravated by Mr. Elton's behavior. At the Weston's Christmas Eve party, his attentions to her are unbecoming, and she wonders why he is not more solicitous for the health of her friend, Harriet, who is home in bed with a sore throat. In the carriage ride home, the suspense is broken when Mr. Elton proposes to Emma, who, in her shock, rudely rejects him. She learns her first lesson here, when she now must comfort Harriet for the illusions that Emma herself has helped put her under. That Harriet does not

Media Adaptations

- *Emma* was adapted for television as a BBC miniseries in 1972. It was directed by John Glenister, and the cast includes Doran Godwin as Emma and John Carson as Mr. Knightley. Since it is four and a half hours long, the series has time to develop fully the themes, characters, and story lines.

- *Emma* was adapted as a full-length movie in 1996. It starred Gwyneth Paltrow and was nominated for two Oscars. The film was released by Miramax and directed by Doug McGrath. It is available on home video.

- *Emma* was also adapted as a full-length British made movie in 1997, starring Kate Beckinsale and produced by Sue Birtwistle. It is available on home video.

judge Emma harshly, if at all, speaks to Harriet's gentleness and sweet nature but also to her inability to be discerning. That Emma truly is mortified by her mistake and compassionate toward Harriet compels us to consider Emma's true depths.

Volume 1 closes with a discussion between Emma and Mr. Knightley on the merits or demerits of Frank Churchill, who is expected to pay a filial visit to his father, Mr. Weston, and his new wife, but who continually makes excuses why he cannot come. The debate grows rather heated since Emma, full of curiosity, imagines Mr. Churchill as someone she might like a great deal, while Mr. Knightley sees in him, although he never admits it, a potential rival to his affections for Emma. In singing his praises (although she has only heard of him by rumor) she claims: "he is very likely to have a more yielding, complying, mild disposition than would suit your notions of man's perfection." Here she hits Mr. Knightley where it hurts, for while he is the perfect specimen of reason and uprightness, the reader cannot help but feel him somewhat rigid and dogmatic in his pronouncements, somewhat bereft of the light-hearted playfulness that would make him truly appealing. For his part, Mr. Knightley, again prophetically, calls Frank's amiability superficial. "He may . . . have very good manners, and be very agreeable; but he can have no . . . delicacy towards the feelings of other people." Although the judgment is not aimed particularly at her, it should have made her blush, for in the department of delicacy she still has much to learn. The exchange shows us the gap between Emma's and Mr. Knightley's sensibilities as well as their carefully guarded feelings toward one another; it also keeps us in suspense about Frank Churchill.

Volume 2

When Jane Fairfax comes to Highbury to live with her aunt (Miss Bates) and grandmother (Mrs. Bates), she serves as a lodestone, attracting the attention of Emma, Mr. Knightley, Mrs. Elton (the former Augusta Hawkins, who has also just come to town with her new husband, the spurned Mr. Elton), the Westons, the Coles, and, surreptitiously, Frank Churchill. It is against Jane's elegance that we must compare all other women and find them wanting, even Emma. Emma, aware of Jane's talents, is determined to like and befriend her; however, her good intentions are shattered when she finds Jane cold and reserved. Jane has come back to Highbury on the occasion of the Campbells going off to Ireland in the wake of their daughter's marriage to a Mr. Dixon. Learning that the former Miss Campbell is not pretty or perhaps as talented as Jane, and, moreover, that Mr. Dixon once saved Jane's life on a sailing expedition, Emma is inspired with "an ingenious and animating suspicion . . . with regard to Jane Fairfax, this charming Mr. Dixon, and the not going to Ireland." She pumps the chattering Miss Bates for more information and, finding nothing to deter her from her suspicions, settles it in her mind that Jane is suffering from an attachment to her friend's husband.

Frank Churchill's arrival corresponds almost exactly with Jane's, although no one regards the timing as anything more than coincidence. His attentions are such that the Westons and Emma herself believe he has fallen in love with her. Here, again, Austen deftly weaves a web of double meanings and possibilities, so that a word, token, or gesture can convey several interpretations. She lets the mystery grow, and readers are none the wiser. Like Emma readers can believe that Frank Churchill is infatuated; however, they are also invited to mistrust his character, as more and more, he enters into the charade of baiting Jane Fairfax over her supposed love affair with Mr. Dixon. In the light of Frank Churchill's attentions, Emma is forced to admit that, although she has vowed never to marry, she might be falling in love with Frank. However, upon reflection, she realizes her attachment is not deep. She becomes increasingly more concerned with how gently to reject him when he does propose to her.

Frank goes off 16 miles to London to have his hair cut (he says), an indulgence that some judge excessive. A few days after he returns, the Coles have a dinner party, during which it is discovered that a pianoforte had arrived mysteriously at the Bates's for Jane. Emma guesses immediately that it is from Mr. Dixon, and those gathered speculate that it must come from the Campbells, since they know how extremely well Jane plays and how much she must miss an instrument at her aunt's home. In the meantime, Mr. Knightley is charitable toward Jane Fairfax and the Mrs. and Miss Bates, and it is not long before Mrs. Weston takes it into her head that he must be in love with Jane. Emma's explosive rejection of such an idea hints at her feelings of propriety regarding Mr. Knightley and her well-hidden jealousy of Jane.

Frank Churchill's youthful energy is contagious. He wants to have a ball, and every plan is made for its going forward, until he suddenly is called away by his ailing Aunt Churchill. His going away is an occasion for sadness, and an opportunity for Austen to introduce the recently returned Mr. Elton with his new wife. All the duties that must be shown to newly-weds—the visits, the teas, the small social indulgences—are given with due regard to their place as a respected couple in Highbury. But Emma soon sees that the new Mrs. Elton is "self-important, presuming, familiar, ignorant, and ill-bred." Harriet, though she lacks birthright or fortune, shines by comparison, an irony that Austen clearly intends for readers to feel. Mrs. Elton takes Jane under her wing, more by persistence and force than by any attraction on Jane's side. Emma is puzzled as to why someone of Jane's gentility would stoop to "chuse the mortification of Mrs. Elton's notice and the penury of her conversation." It is Mr. Knightley, once again, who reminds Emma of her own fault in that she herself deigned it unnecessary to take any further notice of Jane. The volume closes with a dinner party at Hartfield for the Eltons, at which we see Mrs. Elton presumptuously planning to find employment for Jane and Jane politely declining.

Volume 3

At the end of Volume 2, nothing has been resolved: Harriet still has not quite recovered from the loss of *two* potential husbands; Jane Fairfax remains mysteriously reserved; Frank Churchill is returning but no one knows when; Emma is still unclear about her feelings for Frank Churchill; and Mr. Knightley's denial of his matrimonial intentions toward Jane Fairfax does not satisfy the discerning Mrs. Weston. The stage, then, is set for the action's climax. Three scenes in particular are noteworthy for providing encounters among the whole cast of characters, for further developing individual vices and virtues, and for teasing readers with the possibilities of the mystery's solution. The first is the ball at the Crown, a greatly anticipated event that has been delayed until the return of Frank Churchill. Here at the dance Emma is happily engaged for each set, but Harriet is not. At one juncture she is mortified by the snub of Mr. Elton who refuses to dance with her when she is the only woman unengaged. Both Mr. and Mrs. Elton, who are seen to be smugly enjoying the discomfort they have caused, are shown in the worst possible light. Mr. Knightley comes to the rescue and saves Harriet the embarrassment of the moment, an act for which Emma can hardly praise him enough. Frank Churchill continues to flirt with Emma, but his attentions to Jane Fairfax seem pointed. To further complicate matters of romance, some days later, when gypsies accost Harriet, Frank Churchill gallantly comes to the rescue.

The second scene, the "exploration" to Mr. Knightley's estate of Donwell Abbey, once again brings the characters together (all except Frank Churchill, who arrives late after having been called away to attend Mrs. Churchill). At Donwell, Emma notes that Mr. Knightley seems often in conversation with Harriet and wonders what they can be talking about. Much of the scene is taken up with descriptions of the estate, which represent for Austen and for Emma all that is good and right with England. The narrator comments: "It was a sweet view—sweet to the eye and the mind. English verdure, English culture, English comfort, seen under a sun bright, without being oppressive." For her part, Emma "felt all the honest pride and complacency which her alliance with the present and future proprietor could fairly warrant. . . . Emma felt an increasing respect for it, as the residence of a family of such true gentility, untainted in blood and understanding." Clearly, Emma is at home here. Strangely, though, Jane Fairfax bursts into her reverie with the news that she is leaving and, furthermore, walking home alone. Emma is shocked but agrees to let Jane leave. She is clearly upset; earlier, Emma has remarked her conversation with Mrs. Elton, who is still persisting in finding "a suit-

able situation" for her. Finally, Frank Churchill arrives "out of humour," an occasion for Emma to remark to herself that Harriet's "sweet easy temper" will not mind his ill one. Ever since the gypsy rescue, Emma has been considering a match between them not at all to be opposed.

The third important group scene involves a picnic to Box Hill, during which Emma and Frank not only flirt openly, but make the rest of the group uncomfortable by their indelicate gamesmanship and barely disguised taunts. Emma's deliberate insult to Miss Bates makes Mr. Knightley so angry that Emma later feels deep shame and regret. Even Mrs. Elton seems more in the right than Emma, and the party breaks up, leaving Harriet, Mr. Weston, Frank, and Emma to themselves. Jane Fairfax's health becomes a matter of concern after Box Hill, and the next bit of news is that she has decided, on Mrs. Elton's recommendation, to go as governess to a Mrs. Smallridge. At about the same time, Mr. Knightley decides, on a moment's notice, to go to London for several days for no apparent reason. But all news is relegated to the background when it is discovered that Mrs. Churchill has died.

The denouement comes quickly. On the immediate heels of Mrs. Churchill's demise, Emma learns through Mrs. Weston that Frank Churchill and Jane Fairfax have been secretly engaged all along. The Westons are loath to tell Emma for fear she is in love with him. However, Emma is more worried for Harriet, for comically enough, she has really begun to think of Frank and Harriet as a match. Now that Mrs. Churchill is out of the way, Frank and Jane can openly declare their love. Harriet, in the meantime, confesses to Emma that she has fallen in love with Mr. Knightley and believes that he might share her feelings. Emma is astounded. She had thought Harriet in love with Frank after the gypsy episode, but all along it had been Mr. Knightley's saving her at the ball that had overcome Harriet with gratitude. At the moment of Harriet's confession, Emma wakes up: "It darted through her, with the speed of an arrow, that Mr. Knightley must marry no one but herself!"

Romances must have a happy ending, or at least must end in weddings, and this one does in spades. All the eligible young people are married off most appropriately. The ill-bred Eltons have each other; the mysterious but charming and elegant Jane Fairfax and Frank Churchill, free of obstacles, are united. When Mr. Knightley returns from London, it is with the intention of comforting Emma for her loss of Frank. Emma believes his diffident behavior while walking in the garden can only mean he is hesitant to speak of his love for Harriet. Since both are operating under the most mistaken of convictions, it is only by luck (but we feel it is destiny) that Mr. Knightley finds the nerve to propose. As for Harriet, all's well that ends well. Her plain dealing farmer, Mr. Martin, is still in love. With the help of Mr. Knightley (whose attentions to Harriet have been precisely meant to assess her suitability to Mr. Martin) and the approval of Emma, they, too, are married in the little country church. There can be no doubt that Emma has come to value what is most ideal and elegant in herself by her union with Mr. Knightley—the joy that stems from a life ruled by reason and compassion.

Characters

Miss Bates

"[A] great talker upon little matters," Miss Bates is a comic but sympathetic character whose loquacious, hopelessly indiscrete ramblings are the source of much unspoken amusement and, for Emma in particular, some disgust. Taken together, her uncomplaining acceptance of her lot and her well-meant, kind attentions to her neighbors give her poverty some "elegance" and authority. Miss Bates lives with and cares for her aging mother, the two of them surviving by the charitable good graces of their neighbors in Highbury. She also is the loving and solicitous aunt to Jane Fairfax, another major female character in the novel. Miss Bates is important for several reasons. Along with Mrs. Perry, Mrs. Goddard, and Mrs. Cole, she belongs to the country village's mature female circle. Since, on the one hand, her constant chatter is repugnant, but, on the other hand, her morals and her cheerful, good temper are beyond reproach, she is a challenging personality for Emma. It is only when Emma can feel ashamed of her treatment of Miss Bates and learn real patience and charity toward her that Emma herself can take credit for the elegance and breeding she so admires. Miss Bates's position in Highbury society is instrumental to the plot since she provides a source of charity, empathy, and social decorum against which other characters are measured. Moreover, as an "old maid" without means she shares the predicament of certain genteel women in Austen's time (Austen herself had brothers who provided for her) who did not worked and had neither husband nor inheritance on which to rely.

Mrs. Bates

Mrs. Bates is the old and much-respected widow of a former vicar of Highbury and mother of Miss Bates. She rarely leaves her room but to have tea with Emma's father, Mr. Woodhouse, or with Mrs. Perry and Mrs. Goddard. Her principal importance to the novel is as a convenient companion to Mr. Woodhouse and as an example of elderly propriety within the community.

Colonel Campbell

The Campbells are mentioned only in relation to being the benefactors of Jane Fairfax, who is the orphaned niece of Miss Bates. Jane has grown up in the Campbell family and been treated on an equal footing to their own daughter. Their daughter's marriage to Mr. Dixon and the family's temporary removal to Ireland compels Jane to return to Highbury; it also signals the dreaded time of independence, when Jane must seek her living as a governess. So, at least, the good people of Highbury have been led to believe.

Frank Churchill

The mysterious young gallant of marrying age has not yet made his appearance in Highbury, but he is expected every day, for his biological father (Mr. Weston) has just married the elegant Miss Taylor, former governess to Emma. His own mother having died before his was three, Frank Churchill was adopted by his uncle, who was in a position to bestow upon him all of the privileges of rank and wealth that his father could not. Mr. and Mrs. Weston have received "handsome" letters announcing his intent to come and his excuses why he cannot. When he finally arrives, he is liked by all except Mr. Knightley, who finds him less forthright or perfect in his duties and intentions than he ought to be. As it turns out, Mr. Knightley has good reason for his suspicions. Frank is playing a game of deception with the good people of Highbury, and at least two women, Jane Fairfax and Emma Woodhouse, are in danger of falling prey to his manipulative charms. By artifice, Frank Churchill becomes one of Emma's three suitors. In that role readers are meant to judge his character alongside that of Mr. Elton and Mr. Knightley. As importantly, though, he becomes the means by which Emma once again makes critical mistakes in both her assessment of character and in her own powers of reason and observation.

As with most of Austen's characters, Frank Churchill is more complicated than he appears. With Emma, readers learn that charm, good looks, and breeding may serve as a front for sly manipulations and selfish goals. Emma must see in Frank's actions a reflection of her own failings, and she must learn that appearances are not what they seem. With Mr. Knightley, readers must acknowledge that circumstances can sometimes deter good intentions and that although Frank Churchill's actions were not to be condoned, he can easily be forgiven for acting out of love.

Mr. Churchill

While he is never introduced in person, Mr. Churchill is one of the privileged, condescending members of society living outside Highbury whose influence on the story is felt mainly in his role as adopted father to Frank Churchill. Whether and when Frank Churchill will finally come to Highbury to visit his biological father, Mr. Weston, and his new wife, the former Miss Taylor, governess to Emma, is a matter of grave speculation among the neighbors. In fact, one of the key disputes between Mr. Knightley and Emma centers on whether Frank Churchill is being unduly ruled by his feelings of duty toward his adoptive parents and not enough by his filial duty to Mr. Weston. Mr. Churchill also is mentioned early on in the novel as disapproving of his sister's earlier marriage to Mr. Weston on the grounds that it was an unequal match. When that sister dies three years later, their child, Frank, becomes a means of reconciliation. The Churchills adopt him.

Mrs. Churchill

Mrs. Churchill is the sickly wife of Mr. Churchill and adopted mother to Frank. She is regarded by Emma and by the narrator as the chief obstacle to Frank's marrying Jane Fairfax. While, like her husband, Mrs. Churchill is never introduced except as a name associated with Frank's fate, she serves to illustrate the lure and the drawbacks of money and privilege. While Frank expects and needs his inheritance, he is unwilling to act on his own behalf in choosing a wife. Mrs. Campbell is not quite a stereotype. While she indeed appears to be the rich, domineering, condescending society snob that Emma takes her for, toward the end of the novel she actually does die of her illness—poetic justice perhaps, but certainly a very handy plot device, for otherwise Frank and Jane would still be dissembling about their secret engagement.

The Coles

Mr. and Mrs. Cole do not figure largely in the novel except as representatives of a merchant class who have some pretensions to mix with the gentry.

Emma grapples with whether she should attend a dinner party given at the Coles, first thinking it inappropriately beneath her, and later not wanting to be left "in solitary grandeur," she decides to accept the invitation. Austen's irony aims partially at a fixed society so blind in its class-consciousness that it cannot account for good character and breeding unless it is attained by lineage. More importantly, the Coles, like the Martins, serve as lessons in humility to Emma. Austen makes the point through the Coles that when the accepted hierarchies break down and judgments about class and character must be determined, Emma, more often then not, acts out of a desire to be treated as the first person of consequence.

Mr. Dixon

Mr. and Mrs. Dixon do not figure in the action except, as with the Campbells, through their acquainted with Jane Fairfax. However, Mr. Dixon, who has married Miss Campbell (a virtual sister to Jane), is important to the comedy and mystery of the novel. Emma reasons that Jane's sadness and eventual illness can be imputed to an unrequited or ill-fated love for Mr. Dixon. The romance that she imagines is all the more fixed in her mind when the pianoforte arrives for Jane from an anonymous source. She deduces that Jane's decision not to go to Ireland has everything to do with the love she cannot show for the former Miss Campbell's new husband.

Mrs. Augusta Elton

The former Miss Hawkins is coarse, arrogant, and interfering. She is embarrassingly familiar and at the same time unaware of social gaffes. Though orphaned and of dubious breeding, Mrs. Elton takes pride in her sister's having married extremely well, to a Mr. Suckling. Augusta makes odious comparisons between Mr. Suckling's "seat" at Maple Grove and Emma's estate at Hartfield, and her fondest wish is to explore the country in the her sister's barouche-landau, a fancy carriage. Mrs. Elton conspires with Mr. Elton to deliberately humiliate Harriet Smith at the Crown Ball, a social crime for which she is not to be forgiven. She also takes an immediate and therefore controlling interest in Jane Fairfax and her fate. It is Mrs. Elton's persistent haranguing of Jane to take a position as governess that nearly ends in disaster for Jane and Frank. Austen constantly forces Jane into Mrs. Elton's overbearing company to show how elegant Jane Fairfax is by contrast and, as importantly, how superior Harriet Smith appears despite her lack of breeding. Ironically, it might be the anti-heroic Mrs. Elton, so easy to criticize for her hauteur and disdain, who can be fairly compared to Emma at her worst.

Mr. Elton

Having been so successful (at least in her own mind) of having matched Miss Taylor to Mr. Weston, Emma determines to marry off Mr. Elton to her friend Harriet Smith. Mr. Elton, who is the new vicar of Highbury, is single and unhappily so. Readers know little about him except what Emma believes him to be: "most suitable, quite the gentleman himself, and without low connections." Readers have already been privy, though, to Emma's supercilious attitudes toward the Martins, her pride of place, and her vanity in manipulating marriages for her amusement. When it turns out that Emma mistakenly takes his courtship of herself for an attraction to Harriet, Mr. Elton is forever diminished in her eyes. Mr. Elton, to be sure, has her dowry in mind, and when his hopes are dashed, he acts the churl, all pretense of gentle behavior shed like a skin. He soon disappears and only returns to Highbury when he has found a new conquest in the person of Augusta Hawkins. After his marriage to Miss Hawkins, Mr. Elton is relegated to the role of husband and co-conspirator in the couple's haughty treatment of Emma and Harriet Smith.

Jane Fairfax

Jane Fairfax, orphaned at an early age, is raised in privileged circumstances by the Campbells. Of Emma's age and of fine sensibilities, she is beautiful, discrete, and refined. She is Emma's superior in her talent for music, and she is admired for her elegance. She comes to Highbury when the Campbells leave for Ireland and her friend and "sister," Miss Campbell, marries Mr. Dixon. It is expected that she will take a place as governess to a good family in order to support herself now that she is of age. At Highbury she is compelled to live with her chattering Aunt Bates and receive the attentions of the odious Mrs. Elton. While Emma could befriend her and has good intentions of doing so, she finds Jane's reserve and coolness anathema. For her peculiar reserve, indeed, "Emma could not forgive her."

Jane Fairfax can be considered the main female character around which romance and mystery revolve. Although Emma is mistaken in thinking her in love with Mr. Dixon, she is certainly in love. Jane's secret engagement to Frank Churchill, a man with whom Emma initially thought herself in love, is the cause for Jane's reserve and also her shame.

While Jane Fairfax's virtue and intelligence are highly praised, the intrigue she is involved in, as David Lodge points out in his "Introduction" to *Emma*, leaves her "passive and enigmatic." Or as Mr. Knightley describes her, "She has not the open temper which a man would wish for in a wife."

Finally, however, she is redeemed by the same impulse the narrator feels for Frank Churchill. She could be forgiven because she was motivated by love and by a helpless sense of her own inability to choose her fate. She is infinitely finer than Frank Churchill, for in her dissembling, she hurt no one but herself, drew no one into the charade, took no enjoyment in others' ignorance of their secret but only wished for resolution and peace. Except that she lacks a spirit of animation and is not as fortunate in her circumstances of birth, she is Emma's equal or superior in every way. It is indeed necessary for her to leave Highbury soon after her plans to marry Frank are secure, for Highbury is only big enough for one heroine.

Mrs. Goddard

Mrs. Goddard runs a boarding school of high repute at which Harriet Smith is enrolled. She is an honest "plain, motherly kind of woman," a hard worker who is no longer young. She is one of the ladies whom Emma calls on to play cards with her father in the absence of Miss Taylor. She also is the one career woman in town who, by dint of her wholesome, old-fashioned establishment, and her great influence on generations of girls, Emma can accept as proper company for her father. She is one more example of the fluidity possible within a fixed society.

Isabella Knightley

Isabella Knightley is Emma's elder sister, the wife of John Knightley, Mr. George Knightley's brother. Isabella is the quintessential good mother and wife, deferring to her husband in all things, keeping an orderly household, and artlessly adoring her sister and father. Clearly Isabella provides a contrast to Emma, whose intelligence, wit, imagination, and lively projections of her own ego make it extremely unlikely that she will come to regard herself as a passive Victorian housewife.

John Knightley

Mr. John Knightley has, like his brother, a confident sense of self, an Enlightenment zeal for reason and logic, and a temper that does not easily suffer foolishness or inconvenience. His discernment is made evident when he warns Emma that Mr. Elton has designs on her. Austen uses John

Knightley's visits to Hartfield to provide one more model of gentlemanly behavior against which to contrast Mr. George Knightley. In John's inability to be tactful in the face of Emma's father's eccentricities, he is found wanting. His sarcasm, as opposed to his brother's forbearance, adds to Emma's distress over her father's comforts. He also provides a comic, down-to-earth corrective to Mr. Woodhouse's peccadilloes and hobby horses.

However, there is room for education; if Emma must learn reason and gentility from him, he also must study to be more open and less decided in his opinions. He stubbornly clings to his assessments of Harriet and Frank Churchill before he has had a chance to really know them. His jealousy of the latter makes him immune to any of his charms, and his suspicions that the former cannot be improved by Emma's attentions makes him distant and cool to the friendship.

Of all the male characters, Mr. Knightley is the only man whom Emma can marry without fear of discovering a lack of intelligence, compassion, or virtue. He combines all three as well as a promise that things will remain much as they are with the surprising but wonderful addition of marital love and security. Mr. Knightley's absolute steadiness and brotherly affection make it possible for Emma to come face to face with her own desire and sexuality, which until now she has only managed to express in the form of affection for her father, family, and friends.

Mr. Knightley

Mr. George Knightley surpasses all other gentlemen of Highbury for his discernment, reason, kindness, and virtue. He is the owner of Donwell, a large estate comparable only to Hartfield for its size and grandeur, which, if he does not marry, will be inherited by the eldest son of his brother John. While Emma busies herself naïvely making matches, carelessly starting rumors, and meddling in affairs that bring confusion to her friends, Mr. Knightley quietly helps his neighbors, not for his own amusement but out of a sense of responsibility for their well being. It is with his help that Harriet and Robert Martin are finally united, with his care that Mrs. and Miss Bates's needs are often met. With brotherly advice and a firm sense of justice and duty he guides Emma toward more mature behavior. He befriends Jane Fairfax and chides Emma into better intentions on her behalf. He is suspicious of Mr. Elton and Frank Churchill when everyone else is charmed by them, and he turns out to be right most of the time.

Robert Martin

Robert Martin is a tenant farmer of good character and intelligence who has a comfortable and increasingly promising living on Mr. Knightley's estate, Donwell. Harriet is introduced to him and to his sister Elizabeth and the Martin family during a summer recess from Mrs. Goddard's School. Mr. Martin later writes Harriet an eloquent and quite correct letter proposing marriage, which Harriet is inclined to accept until Emma talks her out of it. He is the source of great irritation between Emma and Mr. Knightley, for Emma does not yet know how to value anyone below her own class. She finds a "young farmer . . . the very last sort of person to raise my curiosity. . . . precisely the order of people with whom I feel I can have nothing to do." While Robert Martin plays only a very minor role in the action of the novel, he is important to Emma's education. She finally learns how to value him, despite his station. And through the good offices of Mr. Knightley, Robert Martin finally marries Harriet to the delight of both.

Harriet Smith

Harriet Smith is a boarder at Mrs. Goddard's school, "daughter to someone" but no one knows who. Since Emma needs someone to amuse her after Miss Taylor moves to Randalls, she chooses Harriet, as someone whose sweet and guileless nature could be easily guided and to whom Emma "could be useful."

Harriet takes all her cues from Emma, flattered to be admitted to Emma's inner circle and presented as her special friend. In almost every respect, Harriet has more common sense than Emma, whose imagination leads her to believe that Harriet is of noble birth and therefore should be matched with a gentleman bachelor, the most eligible being Mr. Elton. Emma's misguided interference in Harriet's love affairs threatens to cost her the true happiness of Mr. Martin and loses for her the vague promise of Mr. Elton, who never liked her in the first place except as a friend of Emma's. Emma's "training" of Harriet, which consists of persuading her she is "superior" to anyone but a gentleman, ironically leads Harriet to think of Mr. Knightley as an appropriate and desirable match. It is only when Harriet begins to focus on Mr. Knightley that Emma herself realizes she is in love with him and that she truly has done Harriet great harm.

Harriet's simplicity and naïveté are transformed through Emma's agency to a confidence, maturity, and fuller sense of her own worth without the conceits and arrogance that might accompany such a change. It is to Harriet's credit that she does not judge Emma more harshly for her intrigues, even though they end up costing Harriet much heartache and disillusionment. In the end, it is her own good sense, and not Emma's wisdom, that leads Harriet to the altar and to an appropriate and fulfilling future.

Mr. Weston

Mr. Weston's importance has to do with his early alliance with the Churchills and his son, Frank. His rise in "gentility and property" makes him another example of upward mobility within the early nineteenth-century British class structure. He also presents another "type" of gentleman in Highbury society, who, though very amiable and cheerful of temperament, lacks the judgment and discipline that marks Mr. Knightley as the more reasonable and gentile.

Mrs. Weston

Mrs. Weston, formerly Miss Taylor, marries Mr. Weston at the beginning of the novel and leaves Hartfield where she has been Emma's governess for 16 years. It is her departure for Randalls, only a half-mile away, which occasions the miserable Emma to take on Harriet Smith as a respite to her loneliness. Mrs. Weston is Emma's best friend and confidante. As her governess, and indeed her surrogate mother, she has had a large share in Emma's education; she has also indulged and spoiled her and given her a great sense of her own importance. However, Mrs. Weston is an excellent creature— young, attractive, intelligent and always thinking of others' happiness before her own. Mrs. Weston is the second wife of Mr. Weston. Their marriage sets the stage for the appearance of Mr. Weston's son, Frank Churchill, who owes filial duty to his father and new mother to pay his respects.

Mrs. Weston's story ends almost before it begins with her happy marriage. However, her continuing friendship and devotion to Emma is one of the elevating themes of the novel. Her mistaken interpretations of events and scenes in the novel also endear her to readers. She keeps guessing with her own misguided detective work when she suggests to Emma that Mr. Knightley is really in love with Jane Fairfax, and she adds to the suspense in guessing that Frank Churchill means to propose to Emma. Like readers, Mrs. Weston is beguiled by double meanings and innuendo.

Emma Woodhouse

Emma is an unlikely heroine. She is haughty, immature, rash, overly imaginative, supercilious, and sometimes mean. She finds herself "superior" to almost everyone in her midst, and she is possessed of an undisciplined mind "delighted with its own ideas." Her pride and vanity seem to know no bounds, and her intrigues and manipulations harm or embarrass a number of her friends. But despite her questionable personal charm she is surprisingly able to remake and redeem herself. Where first there is blindness and conceit, later readers see self-awareness and humility. When one moment readers recoil at her arrogance, they are next cheered by her patience and forbearance. Readers almost dismiss her for her rude indiscretions but then are entertained by her candid, honest charm. Just when she is suspected of being ruthless, she is found to be capable of deep compassion and love. Indeed, Emma's very imperfections bind readers to her.

Austen infuses her heroine with such high spirit and determination that her youthful follies can be overlooked. She is motherless, after all, embarked on a project of self-education that begins only when her governess leaves. She is likeable because she refuses to be typical. She refuses to do what is expected of her. She determines never to marry, to continue to improve herself by her own means, and to reject the received wisdom of her times that a woman is nothing without a man. That she does marry in the end does not make her a hypocrite. On the contrary, it is only when she learns that she need not lose herself in a marriage, that her best moral guide and friend has all along been eager for her to make her own mistakes and to wonder in an unselfish way "what will become of her" that she relents.

Mr. Woodhouse

Austen clearly means to equate gentility with the amounts and types of foods one eats, and in his preference for the most abstemious amounts and the least volatile types, Mr. Woodhouse cannot be rivaled. Mr. Woodhouse is old and has a delicate constitution; he is constantly referring to the good advice of his esteemed apothecary, Mr. Perry. It is a source of comic relief when Mr. Woodhouse and his daughter, Isabella, converse about harmful weather conditions, the benefits of one seaside town over another, or the type of gruel that should be preferred on all occasions to avoid an unhealthy constitution. As a quintessential gentleman and undisputed member of the English gentry, Mr. Woodhouse is esteemed as the first citizen of Highbury. His neighbors are solicitous for his health, and he is always careful that people should do their duties toward one another, uphold customs and traditions, and by no means ever give in to excesses or haste. He deplores change and invariably refers to Mrs. Weston as "poor Miss Taylor" and to his own daughter as "poor Isabella," thereby projecting onto their happiness his own dread of their absence from his household.

Austen seems to measure her characters in relation to how they treat the eccentricities and hardships of the most difficult characters. Mr. Woodhouse is one of the characters whose trying personality must be suffered because of his position in society and because he has often been a benefactor to his neighbors. Emma's diligent and dedicated care of her father is perhaps one of her greatest strengths, and Mr. Knightley's unselfish decision to move to Hartfield and give up Donwell to marry Emma is a mark of his true superiority as a man.

Themes

Age of Reason or Age of Enlightenment

Jane Austen was well acquainted with eighteenth-century Enlightenment thinkers such as Dr. Samuel Johnson, whose classical ideals of common sense and moderation were revived during the so-called Age of Reason or Age of Enlightenment. Respect for scientific principles, including human nature, were applied to all aspects of life. While emotion, sentiment, and individual imagination were not absent from Enlightenment thinking, reason and rational thought were highly prized. Characters in Austen's works suffer from her lightly ironic and satirical pen when their wit is unconnected with their powers of reason. (Miss Bates, for example, is kind but "ridiculous"; Mr. Woodhouse is loveable but neurotic about health issues and eating habits; the Eltons' powers of reason are dwarfed by their meanness and pretensions.) But Austen's most heroic characters (Mr. Knightley; the Emma at the end of the novel) have found a balanced way to blend reason and compassion, intellect and virtue.

Manners and Morals

Self-control, decorum, and polite conduct are hallmarks of civilized society, and to be thought well of in society was a mark of good breeding in Jane Austen's privileged world. Although Austen has too keen a sense of humor and too deep a desire for good to triumph to be considered a slave to convention, she imposes limitations on her characters to act with gentility at all occasions. Much can be forgiven in the fictional world of *Emma* if one's

manners are proper and if one acts out of a sense of propriety and decency. Hence Frank Churchill is chastised for having deceived the neighbors but escapes condemnation on account of his good manners, gentility, and well-intentioned heart.

Neoclassicism and Wit

Late eighteenth-century England saw a resurgence of classical forms in art (a period often referred to as Neoclassical)—the comic, the tragic, the epic, and heroic genres in literature reflected the universal truths of human nature. Jane Austen was writing during the Regency period, toward the end of the eighteenth century, when writers of the Romantic Movement were reacting with more lyrical and emotional content to the constraints and limits imposed by neoclassicists. Although Austen was not much influenced by romanticism, her witty dialogue and satire focuses on human foibles within a specific social context that fuels emotion, deep feeling, and sentiment. Austen's wit shows most boldly in her comedy of manners and situations when rules of conduct are broken (Mrs. Elton referring to Mr. Knightley with contemptible familiarity as "Knightley"); when one person's play on words hits on a truth that is unsuspected (Frank Churchill's declaring to Emma that the gift of the pianoforte was certainly "an offer of love"); or when human folly is at fault for uncomfortable social situations ("how peculiarly unlucky poor Mr. Elton was in being in the same room at once with the woman he had just married, the woman he had wanted to marry, and the woman whom he had been expected to marry").

The Novel and Realism

The novel, as a recognized genre, was born in the eighteenth century and in its earliest forms is associated with the writings of Henry Fielding, Samuel Richardson, and Daniel Defoe. However, the novel was as much a female creation springing from the works of Mary Wollstonecraft, Fanny Burney, Ann Radcliffe, and, of course, Jane Austen. The novel was indeed original in that it took for its subject the experiences of ordinary people (rather than mythological, historical, or legendary figures) and based its story on individual expressions of truth common to current times and culture. Jane Austen took the novel to new heights in dramatizing the domestic concerns of her characters. She encompassed the full spectrum of human behavior through situational detail common to her characters and language particular to each character's psychology. The rise of realism and the novel had much to do with the

Topics For Further Study

- How is individual worth determined in a class-conscious society? Was there a clear hierarchical social structure in Emma's world? Did it reflect the reality of Jane Austen's time? What lessons did Emma learn about class and character?

- Under what conditions could women own property in the eighteenth century? Why was it so important for women to marry? What qualities and behavior does Austen believe lead to a happy marriage?

- List the kinds of female accomplishments that would have been considered praiseworthy in Jane Austen's time. Compare them to what women accomplish in the early 2000s. What does the comparison tell you about gender roles then and now?

- Research the British Enclosure Acts of the eighteenth century. What impact did they have on urban and rural culture?

- Austen's novel is full of references to diet and health as well as concern for illness and exposure to bad weather. Much of the concern is treated satirically as the obsession of an aging Mr. Woodhouse. But Harriet Smith's sore throat seems more serious. Describe the living conditions in London during the end of the eighteenth century. Was there any real reason for concern?

- Do some research on the topic of feminism and how it is variously defined. Based on your findings, do you think the character of Emma could be an early proponent of feminism? If yes, what are her qualities that express this? Cite some specific scenes from the novel that you feel express feminist expressions or ideals.

---

rise of literacy and the middle class as well as the examination and scrutiny by women of their roles in both public and domestic spheres.

Style

Bildungsroman

A German term, bildungs, and a French one, roman, combine to form a term that describes the novel of development or formation. This is a story about Emma's formation as a gentile woman. The author intends to show us how a youthful life matures, is educated, and, finally, transformed. In *Emma*, the heroine's development coincides with her attachment to those people in the novel (in particular Mr. Knightley) whose sterling qualities she also must adopt and make her own.

Comedy of Manners

A comedy begins in difficulty and ends happily. At the outset of Austen's novel, Emma is distressed by the thought of her own loneliness that must follow in the wake of Miss Taylor's marriage. The novel ends in the most suitable of companionship and marriage to Mr. Knightley. The major character is often set a task that needs completion or a lesson that needs to be learned. Emma must learn the true nature of discernment of mind and nobility of character. The term, comedy, comes from the Greek (meaning to make merry), and while it is usually lighthearted, a comedy can be serious in intent, as *Emma* certainly is. Austen's novel is not merely a light-hearted romp; its message of compassion and transformation is carefully illustrated. The comedy is not crude; on the contrary, it is subtly ironic and satirical. It revolves around the conventions and manners of an artificial, sophisticated society and depends on small, domestic intrigues and character foibles to generate amusement. Universal truths, however, can be gleaned from the small and particular.

Fatal Flaw

While Emma's personality flaws are not fatal as are those, for example, that mark major characters in Shakespeare's tragedies, hers prevent her from full participation in the life she aspires to—that of a gentile lady. Emma's flaws are treatable; they stem from an excess of imagination, a tendency to think too well of herself, and an inbred bias based on class superiority. At bottom she is well intended and compassionate, animated, intelligent, cheerful and patient. Readers are meant to like her, despite her flaws, but they are also meant to delight in her reinvention of self and the smoothing over of her rough edges.

Gender Issues

Jane Austen is not usually considered a feminist, at least not an active proponent of women's rights such as Mary Wollstonecraft (a contemporary of Austen's who wrote *A Vindication of the Rights of Woman*). But she did believe that women were intelligent, creative equals to men, just as capable of accomplishment and just as liable to shortcomings and, therefore, that they should be judged according to their intelligence and character, just as men were. Emma vows never to marry. It is not because she dislikes men, but because she judges that her life will be just as fulfilling if she remains single. She is well aware of her personal resources, does not behave coquettishly in order to attract men, and prefers to make her own decisions about her welfare, behavior, and attitudes. She is open to instruction from Mr. Knightley, but it is also clear that she will continue to be a forceful, enlightened partner in their marriage.

Mystery

Austen keeps us in suspense as to the nature of the romantic intentions and motives of several of her characters, especially in regard to the central mystery of Jane Fairfax and Frank Churchill. She employs the usual strategies of mystery writing to do so: planting clues, creating dialogue and actions that may have multiple meanings; introducing red herrings to throw us off the trail; and supplying motives that offer possible keys to solving the mystery. Much of the enjoyment in reading is due to Austen's mastery of these techniques, which compels readers to join Emma in playing detective.

Point of View

In *Emma*, there are two perspectives from which to understand the story and the psychology of its characters: that of the author/narrator and that of the heroine, Emma. This limited omniscience provides insights into characters; motives and personalities, but (with the exception of Emma) it does not allow readers to know what characters are thinking. The strategy makes sense in this story since the plot revolves around Emma's process of maturation. Emma's insights are not to be trusted, and so the reliable narrator provides the full truth of the matter.

Satire

A literary strategy for revealing the follies and shortcomings of humankind, satire blends humor and wit with critical attitudes toward human nature and social institutions. Irony, which reveals an often-comic dual reality between what is true and what is illusion, is one of Austen's favorite techniques. She uses it freely to create intrigue and situational comedy. For example, it is ironic when Emma attributes the gift of the pianoforte to Mr. Dixon and Frank Churchill (knowing it is of course from himself) pretends to agree with her suspicions by saying, "I can see it in no other light than as an offering of love." Emma is none the wiser, but the reader sees the double meaning. The Eltons come in for their fair share of satire since they are the perfect pretenders to gentility, being themselves coarse, pretentious, and uneducated.

Social Setting

The novel is set in late eighteenth century England (during the Regency period), in a small countryside village, structured with a conventional hierarchical social ladder. At the top are the landowners (Mr. Knightley, Mr. Woodhouse, and their families); next come the respectable male professionals—the career military officers (Captain Weston, Colonel Campbell), doctors (Mr. Perry), solicitors, and vicars (Mr. Elton). The tradesmen have become more mobile (Mr. Cole), moving up in class as they gain wealth during the Industrial Revolution. Women also can earn respectable wages as teachers and governesses. The tenant farmers (Robert Martin) are near the bottom, followed by the hired servants, and the truly poor (the gypsies). The hierarchy is important to the story since Emma must learn not to be deceived by class when judging a person's character.

Subplot

A secondary plot that develops alongside the main action involving the heroine and which usually influences the major character and the action as a whole is called the subplot. In this case, Jane Fairfax and Frank Churchill are the major characters involved in the intrigue of a secret engagement that leads to mistaken motives and suspicions among the neighbors of Highbury. The mystery of the subplot allows the other characters to reveal their true natures as they interact with the two newcomers.

Historical Context

Jane Austen's *Emma* belongs to a period in English history known as the Regency (1811–1820), during which King George III was considered incompetent to rule and the Prince of Wales acted as Regent. But as a literary figure writing at the beginning of the nineteenth century, Austen can be considered a descendant of the Age of Enlightenment (alternately referred to as the Age of Reason, the neoclassical period, or the Augustan Age). It was a time of economic upheaval, political unrest, and great cultural industry and change.

During much of Austen's life, Europe and England were caught up in the Napoleonic Wars. While the novel itself makes no reference to war, nor is the plot in any way connected to it, military men do play a role as characters. Indeed, it is interesting to note that domestic country life could go on much as usual, despite the political turmoil. The Enlightenment philosophy that sustained the French Revolution and spurred the search for natural laws that would explain human behavior and social institutions did not alter Britain's tradition of monarchy. But it did inspire writers such as Mary Wollstonecraft, Thomas Paine, and William Godwin to pen classic essays on the rights of man, the defense of a just revolution, and the pernicious effects of unjust rule.

The Industrial Revolution grew out of Enlightenment thinking that placed faith in the rational individual and in human progress and science. New inventions such as James Watt's steam engine, Crompton's "mule" (for making yarn), and Jethro Tull's seed planting drill, led to a great increase in agricultural and manufacturing production. When combined with the Enclosure Acts, which radically reduced the number of tenant farmers and drove landless people to cities for jobs, this revolution also led to the spread of contagious disease, an increase in infant mortality, and terrible overcrowding and dangerous working conditions in cities. Social status became more mobile with the growth of the middle class, and confusion about rank and custom prevailed. The wealth and stature of the Coles, for example, comes from trade, and while they belong to a class of people with whom Emma initially does not think she should mix, she

eventually accepts their importance to the community. In Mr. Woodhouse's obsession over food and health, we might read an eccentric but practical wish to stay removed from the evils spawned by urban life. (One of the wonderful discoveries of the time was the smallpox vaccine.) And, through Emma, Austen pokes fun at Mr. Knightley's recurring discussions of agricultural improvements and his need to be in constant communication with his estate's steward.

During Jane Austen's time, satire was a popular literary tool used to critique social institutions and human evils. Ironically, writers associated with the Age of Reason and characterized by Cartesian logic (the thinking of Descartes, as in "I think; therefore, I am.") were not hesitant to parody logical thinking when it came to addressing social ills. Jonathan Swift's great satire, *A Modest Proposal*, for example, uses rational arguments to suggest that the Irish could solve their famine by eating their children. Jane Austen's targets are moral, domestic ones. She satirizes the over-indulgent, supercilious, proud, and coarse whose actions and behaviors lead to crimes of the heart.

It makes sense that the rise of the novel should accompany the rise of the middle class during the eighteenth century. Henry Fielding, Daniel Defoe, Anne Radcliffe, Fanny Burney, and Samuel Richardson were experimenting with realism, and Jane Austen was their literary heir. The Romantic poets (Wordsworth, Coleridge, Keats, Byron, and Shelley among the most prominent) were also emerging, reacting against the cold and impersonal intellectuality of Cartesian logic with lyricism and exotica. Austen was more inclined to observe a unity of form—her novels have a well-conceived beginning, middle, and end, and all parts are related in an organic whole. For example, the action of the novel takes place in the tidy confines of one calendar year.

An influential philosopher of a slightly earlier time was John Locke. His seminal idea that human understanding evolves solely from the experience of the senses had a remarkable influence on the thinking of the next two centuries. The novel, with its focus on social and public discourse, evolved from Locke's stunning postulation that there was a normal shared truth in the collective memory of man and that new ideas did not emerge from private inspiration but from new combinations of old material. If external experience was the measure of knowledge, then essentially, truth was transparent and available to all. The nature of man was knowable and uniform. From this position, it is easy to

Compare & Contrast

- **1815:** Acting as sovereign in place of the ill king, George III, the licentious Prince of Wales (to whom Jane Austen, at his urging, dedicated *Emma*) runs the Regency, which becomes a symbol of British decadence. This era is known for the clash between hedonistic, vulgar behavior and classical standards of elegance.

  Today: Government leaders are held to high standards of behavior and decorum, but, although outwardly public officials maintain a public image of decency, intrigues and scandals are no less common in the early 2000s than they were in Jane Austen's time.

- **1815:** Women have very few legal or personal rights. They are not allowed to vote or to hold wage-earning jobs aside from teaching or factory work. Women cannot attend college. All property and children within marriage belong to the husband, and the eldest male child inherits the family wealth.

  Today: It is unconstitutional to discriminate on the basis of sex. Women have equal access to jobs, exercise complete control over their own property, share control over their children, can achieve a college or university education, and are free to decide their own destiny.

- **1815:** Leisure activities for ladies of the period include walking, drawing, playing a musical instrument, singing, embroidery, and cards. Any strenuous or intellectual activity is placed strictly outside of the woman's role in society. Accordingly, women's fashions are very restrictive.

  Today: Women from all walks of life participate in extreme sports, hard physical work, and challenging intellectual enterprises as well as enjoying more sedentary pursuits. Women's clothing allows complete freedom of movement.

- **1815:** Social relations between well-bred young people follow strict codes of behavior that preclude premarital sex, coarse language or rude behavior, and unchaparoned meetings. Since a woman depends almost entirely on her husband or father to make her way in life, she protects her reputation as a lady.

  Today: People live in a much more permissive society, and the conduct of individuals is not strictly enforced by social codes. Young adults date unsupervised, and cars provide a form of privacy and means of escape. Freed from dependence on husbands, women are likely to worry about education, careers and vocations, politics, among a great many other things once relegated to the masculine social sphere.

- **1815:** Few people move far from the conditions into which they were born. The economic classes do not mix socially, and the higher classes enjoy more privileges and rights than do the lower classes. The barriers that keep the farmer, tradesmen, landed gentry, and ruling elite within their separate spheres begin to break down with the rise of the middle class.

  Today: People pride themselves on living in a time when social barriers can be overcome by merit and education. Education and democratic institutions have created a society more open to mobility and change. However, wealth and status are still associated with privilege and well-being, and those who are economically secure do not usually mix socially with those who are not.

- **1815:** Disease is rampant in large cities such as London. The streets and waterways are dumping grounds for all kinds of animal and human waste; plumbing and refrigeration are primitive; and bathing is not a frequent activity. One of the most dreaded diseases is smallpox, but people also die from seemingly mild afflictions such as colds. Edward Jenner develops a vaccine for smallpox in 1796, and later in the twentieth century, smallpox is virtually eliminated.

  Today: Although knowledge of nutrition and hygiene has increased dramatically, environmental hazards and pollution problems have not been eradicated. People still suffer from plagues such as cancer and AIDS that threaten a growing number of the population. In the early 2000s, treatments for both diseases have been discovered, but there is no known cure.

see why satire and social documentary, science and empirical research prevailed. The influence of Lockian psychology on Jane Austen is suggested in her fondness for characters who show an appropriate public face and her penchant for discovering the true patterns of human nature through interactions in social settings. Other influential social thinkers include John Wesley, who founded the Methodist Church during the eighteenth century; Jean Jacques Rousseau, a radical philosophical voice of the time who distrusted science and valued emotion and intuition; and Adam Smith, called the father of modern economics.

Critical Overview

A collection of responses to Austen's novel (that includes, in fact, all the writers quoted below) is available on the Jane Austen Web site hosted by Brooklyn CUNY. Perhaps the most influential critique of *Emma* written during Jane Austen's lifetime was Sir Walter Scott's in the March 1816 edition of *Quarterly Review,* which that Web site contains. Scott described her as writing "a class of fictions which has arisen almost in our own times, and which draws the characters and incidents . . . more immediately from the current of ordinary life than was permitted by the former rules of the novel." For Scott, Austen's brand of realism was striking and unique, setting it apart from the false sentiment of typical romances or the lurid phantasms of Gothic tales. He praised Austen for "copying from nature as she really exists in the common walks of life, and presenting to the reader, instead of the splendid scenes of an imaginary world, a correct and striking representation of that which is daily taking place around him."

Despite Scott's praise, however, Austen's novels were not a commercial success during her lifetime. Indeed, she was no self-promoter; she published her works anonymously. Because her novels came to be canonized as classics of English literature and because she was so venerated throughout the twentieth and into the twenty-first century, it is difficult to imagine that Jane Austen's art garnered so little notice in her own time. Part of her obscurity as an artist might lie in the fact that most of her books were only actually published at the end of her life. *Sense and Sensibility* was her first book to see publication in 1811. She died in 1817. In the early 2000s, she was probably best known as the author of *Pride and Prejudice* (1813) because of that novel's popularity.

The central argument over her accomplishments tends to revolve around two notions: her narratives' lack of passion and their narrow focus. Some accused her of being blinded by conservative, upper-class views and Enlightenment philosophy. Others wondered how she could ignore the great events of her time. Two critics might serve to represent the critical divide. In the mid-nineteenth century, George Henry Lewes, English philosopher and companion of author George Eliot, heralded Austen as "the greatest artist that has ever written." Where Charlotte Brontë found reason for scorn—"Anything like warmth or enthusiasm, anything energetic, poignant, heartfelt, is utterly out of place in commending these works. . . . The passions are perfectly unknown to her: she rejects even a speaking acquaintance with that stormy sisterhood"—Lewes found plenty of room for praise. He wrote, "There are heights and depths in human nature Miss Austen has never scaled nor fathomed, there are worlds of passionate existence into which she has never set foot; but although this is obvious to every reader, it is equally obvious that she has risked no failures by attempting to delineate that which she has not seen. Her circle may be restricted, but it is complete. Her world is a perfect orb, and vital. Life, as it presents itself to an English gentlewoman peacefully yet actively engaged in her quiet village, is mirrored in her works with a purity and fidelity that must endow them with interest for all time."

Austen's reputation began to grow in the nineteenth century. Professor of English Lilia Melani notes how Victorian scholar and essayist Thomas B. Macaulay praised "the marvellous and subtle distinctive traits" of Austen's characters, and that novelist E. M. Forster preferred to read Austen's work with "the mouth open and the mind closed." Melani also reports, "In the twentieth century, Virginia Woolf rescued [Austen] from the vilification of feminists when she wrote that [Austen] was 'mistress of much deeper emotion than appears on the surface. She stimulates us to supply what is not there.'"

Indeed, devotion to Jane Austen became so commonplace that readers were even satirized for their sentimental devotion to her. The "Janeites" were so called after the title of a short story by Rudyard Kipling (1924), which tells of soldiers forming a secret society based on their admiration and understanding of Jane Austen's novels, a source of solace during the horrors of World War I. The Cult of Janeites originated with the 1870 *Memoir* written by her nephew, James Edward Austen-Leigh. Wanting to portray her as conforming to strict Victorian

Gwyneth Paltrow as Emma Woodhouse and Jeremy Northam as Mr. Knightley in the 1996 film adaptation of Jane Austen's Emma

values, he softened her image, painting her as a kindly old spinster aunt. Anthony Trollope enhanced the image by writing that her novels were "full of excellent teaching, and free from an idea or word that can pollute."

As of the early 2000s, Austen's work was the subject of countless essays, commentaries, dissertations, and media remakes. She is considered one of the greatest novelists in the history of English literature. An American Society of Jane Austen scholars features essays, biographies, book reviews, and web links; scholars continue to discuss and scrutinize her life and work for what it can tell them about her literary style and genius as well as the history, culture, and domestic sensibilities of small-town England in the early 1800s.

Criticism

Kathy Smith

Smith has a Ph.D. in English literature and is a freelance writer, tutor, and non-profit administrator. In this essay, Smith discusses how the comedy of manners and the bildungsroman meet in the education of Emma.

Austen's genius for combining elements of the comedy of manners with the "coming of age" story, or *bildungsroman*, helped legitimize the novel as a literary genre. When *Emma* was published in 1816, the novel was still young. In the early eighteenth century, Daniel Defoe, Samuel Richardson, and Henry Fielding, often referred to as originators of the modern form, wrote what were to become the first canonized novels in British literature. Gothic horror, sentimental romance, satire in the service of reform, and epistolary moralizing characterized the bulk of popular narratives between the 1720s and the 1740s. By the turn of the next century, Austen had teased the novel into maturity by filtering out the sentimental, the fantastic, and the puritanical. In their place, she substituted ordinary domestic conflict, natural dialogue, a plot that progresses causally in real time and in familiar settings. Moreover, she complicated her stories with recognizable human motives, liberally leavened with wit, a dose of light irony, and sprinkled for the most part with sympathetic humor.

In keeping with the conventions of classical drama, Austen provides both enjoyment and instruction as she carefully constructs the events and circumstances under which Emma's education is to take place. We are introduced to the heroine in the

> **We soon find that the first problem to be solved in Emma's social education curriculum is how to cope with boredom. The problem is both serious (her loneliness and isolation are real) and trivial (inasmuch as she seeks mere amusement and diversion)."**

first paragraph by a narrator who is both in and above the action, freely commenting on the story and its individual characters, much like a reporter, while closely identifying with them, in particular with Emma. In "'The Tittle-Tattle of Highbury': Gossip and Free Indirect Style in *Emma*," Casey Finch and Peter Bowen suggest that the effect of this "free indirect style" works on us the way gossip might. Each character's thoughts are "at once perfectly private and absolutely open to public scrutiny." We are "taken in" almost helplessly by our desire both to know what happens to the principles and to belong to the community around which the story unfolds. The narrative voice is comforting. It acts as a corrective to the characters' whims and opinions and also serves to exculpate them (or most of them) from the guilt of their social gaffes. As Frances Ferguson points out in "Jane Austen, *Emma*, and the Impact of Form," Emma (and by extension, the reader) is allowed to make mistakes and to learn "by trial and error" since "sociological knowledge . . . can be learned only experimentally."

Austen drops a clue as to what Emma's trials might involve in the very first sentence: "Emma Woodhouse, handsome, clever, and rich, with a comfortable home and happy disposition, seemed to unite some of the best blessings of existence; and had lived nearly twenty-one years in the world with very little to distress or vex her." Something, Austen implies, is about to change. Our sheltered, privileged but intellectually alive heroine is about to experience some vexation that calls into question the early formation of her character under seemingly fortunate circumstances. We soon find that the first

problem to be solved in Emma's social education curriculum is how to cope with boredom. The problem is both serious (her loneliness and isolation are real) and trivial (inasmuch as she seeks mere amusement and diversion). Emma's fixation on Harriet as the object of *her* tutelage is the ostensible solution to her problem and the first great irony of the novel since it is really Emma who needs improvement. The classical pattern of comedy slowly emerges whereby the protagonist is confronted with a difficulty, undertakes to remedy the situation by self-prescribed methods, and by a naïve series of missteps and adjustments, achieves a reformation of character that is ultimately rewarded, in this case by a new experiential self-awareness and a marriage that seals her achievement of elegance.

The action of *Emma* turns on the domestic scene, on the manners and morals of a country village society designed to represent all that is artificial and sophisticated, ridiculous and honorable, condescending and humble; in short, all the vices and virtues that plague and bless the human condition. It is crucial that we identify with Emma by seeing and judging through her eyes, for as a heroine, she is central to the human portrait, embodying those human qualities and frailties so often at war.

Emma is a meddler. She is presumptuous, haughty, and proud. In the wake of Miss Taylor's loss, she feels compelled to interfere in Harriet Smith's life in a way that brings trouble and shame not only on them both but on their neighbors as well. Moreover, Emma seems happily unaware of her own rectitude; her condescending attitude toward Harriet's beau, Robert Martin, is based on the "rightness" of traditional class structure ("The yeomanry," says Emma, "are precisely the order of people with whom I feel I can have nothing to do."), and seems completely just and rational to her. Upon first meeting Harriet, Emma thinks, "Those soft blue eyes and all those natural graces should not be wasted on the inferior society of Highbury and its connections. The acquaintance she had already formed were unworthy of her." Emma herself would take Harriet's improvement in hand. "[S]he would form her opinions and her manners. It would be an interesting, and certainly a very kind undertaking; highly becoming her own situation in life, her leisure, and powers."

In the abstract, it is difficult to imagine a more smug protagonist. And yet, by chapter three, when Emma reflects with self-satisfaction on the good she can do Harriet, we have already decided to like her, despite, or perhaps because of, her psychological

What Do I Read Next?

- *Pride and Prejudice* (1813) has been the most popular of Austen's six novels. Like *Emma*, it is a comedy of manners, full of satire and irony, wit and sophisticated drawing room exchanges. Blending humor with stunning insight into the domestic scene, human nature, courtship, and the limits and attraction of authority, Austen paints a vivid portrayal of life in the English countryside at the end of the eighteenth century. Like Emma, the protagonists Mr. Darcy and Elizabeth Bennett undergo a moral education, teaching one another through mishap and intention that charm, intelligence, independent-thinking, and vibrancy must ultimately be leavened with humility.

- Mary Wollstonecraft's *A Vindication of the Rights of Woman* (1792) is the first notable feminist essay on gender equality. It takes as its premise that reason, virtue, and knowledge separate humans from beasts. Women, Wollstonecraft argues, should therefore "endeavour to acquire strength, both of mind and body." Men who try "to secure the good conduct of women by attempting to keep them always in

a state of childhood" are "unphilosophical" at best.

- It is hardly possible to understand the Age of Reason without having read John Locke's *Essay concerning Human Understanding* (1690). It changed the nature of inquiry into human consciousness by establishing a cognitive model for analyzing human thought. Locke's notion was that all knowledge was gained by direct experience through the senses and by reflection on those experiences. Hence, individual expression, social interaction, and religious thought could be systematized and explained rationally.

- *The Mysteries of Udolpho* (1794), by Ann Radcliffe—a contemporary of Jane Austen, is considered one of the preeminent Gothic romances of the time, following in the style of the Horace Walpole prototype, *The Castle of Otranto* (1764). The Gothic novel, with its attendant hauntings, sudden storms, sliding tapestries, and generational madness was a very popular genre in the eighteenth century. Jane Austen parodied Radcliffe's work in her posthumously published novel, *Northanger Abbey*.

---

warts. Of course, Emma's animated spirit and intelligence attract our attention. She also has the advantages of wealth and beauty, but what really intrigues us is the pleasure we derive from eavesdropping on her. Austen invites us to critique her and commiserate with her. We feel superior when she expresses ugly sentiments; we are relieved and glad for her when she gets it right. The more we identify with Emma and her predicaments, the more minutely we are obliged to examine our own moral codes. Like Mr. Knightley, we are curious to know "what will become of her!" precisely because she is, like ourselves, a work in progress.

Artlessly, Emma draws us into intrigues that are partly a manifestation of her own active imagination. We don't mind because, like Mrs. Weston, we want to believe that, "[w]here Emma errs once,

she is in the right a hundred times," and if Emma is manipulative, "she will never lead any one really wrong." Austen's narrator confirms Mrs. Weston's good opinion of Emma. If Emma possesses "a mind delighted with its own ideas" she is also full of "real good-will." If she is spoiled by always having been "first" with her father, she is also extraordinarily patient with his tiresome eccentricity. And if she is an intriguer, she is capable of self-criticism and compassion, qualities illustrated in self-reflection when her hopes for Harriet and Mr. Elton are dashed. By the time Emma has "taught" Harriet to be smitten with Mr. Elton, we have been given clues enough that Emma is the real object of Mr. Elton's desire. Of course we relish the situational irony of Emma's self-congratulatory pronouncement that her efforts for Harriet have paid off: "There does seem to be a something in the air of Hartfield which gives love exactly the right direction, and sends it into the very channel where it ought to flow." But by the same token, when the full horror of Mr. Elton's real intentions are revealed as he attempts to "make love" to Emma in the coach scene, her misery and admission of culpability redeem her in our eyes: "Every part of it brought pain and humiliation . . . but, compared with the evil to Harriet, all was light; and she would gladly have submitted to feel yet more mistaken . . . more disgraced by mis-judgment . . . could the effects of her blunders have been confined to herself."

Lest Emma's journey toward true gentility become too didactic or moralistic, Austen introduces a romantic and mysterious subplot involving Frank Churchill and Jane Fairfax, which offers the theme of Emma's education more opportunities for wit and satire. Austen's humor expresses delight with the spectacle of imperfection; however, the tone is far from mocking, for we, like Emma, are still in the dark as to the nature of the mystery, and it is only by a succession of ambiguous hints that we ourselves discover the truth. Although we find little to admire in Emma's jealousy of Jane Fairfax, we do not like Jane's cool reserve any more than Emma does. (By now we are addicted to the gossip.) Moreover, Frank Churchill's deceptions are so clever, that we are able to forgive Emma her favorite new intuition that Miss Fairfax is secretly in love with Mr. Dixon. Despite her foolish mistake with Harriet, Emma has not yet learned the virtue of discretion, but in sharing her gossipy supposition with Frank she is led on deliberately. In fact, the entire community (both the village folk and the literary folk who read the book for the first time) is involved in guessing who has sent Jane the gift of the pianoforte. It is with an almost voyeuristic curiosity, then, that we watch the mystery unfold as the characters gather for a dinner party at the Coles' place.

Frank Churchill's cleverness and acute perception as contrasted with Emma's naïve conjectures set the scene for a comic display of wit during this episode when the major characters come together as a community. The dialogue concerning Jane and the pianoforte is a case in point. "I may not have convinced you perhaps," says Emma to Frank, "but I am perfectly convinced myself that Mr. Dixon is a principal in the business." She is looking for validation of her secret romance idea. Frank Churchill is only too willing to provide it. "Indeed you injure me if you suppose me unconvinced. Your reasonings carry my judgment along with them entirely. . . .

And now I can see it in no other light than as an offering of love." The passage is at once ironic and witty because it is Emma's very lack of considered "reasonings" that allows Frank Churchill to deceive her, and because the pianoforte is indeed an offering of love, but from Frank himself. But wit is a double-edged sword. It can easily injure another (Emma "unwitting" use of wit at Box Hill hurts Miss Bates by implying that the spinster will not be able to limit herself to saying three dull things) as it forces the truth out into the open. Throughout the novel, Austen reveals when wit is appropriate precisely by gauging its effects on members of the community.

The comedy of manners "works" as an educational device only when we have wit enough to see that all in the community are subject to the petty foibles and peccadilloes to which flesh is heir. Even Mr. Elton, whom we hold in disdain both for his cruel treatment of Harriet at the Crown Inn ball and his irredeemable, supercilious behavior after his marriage to the equally ill bred Augusta Hawkins, requires a small measure of sympathy: "how peculiarly unlucky poor Mr. Elton was in being in the same room at once with the woman he had just married, the woman he had wanted to marry, and the woman whom he had been expected to marry."

Austen tends to forgive the improprieties of those who see their own shortcomings but finds little toleration for those who cannot. Frank Churchill is berated for his intrigues and deceptions, especially as they are perceived to compromise the health and future of Jane Fairfax, but his honest apologies, his true regard for Jane, and his loyalty to her friends overcome most objections to his frailties. Mrs. Elton, on the other hand, has no such loyalties and makes no such apologies. The fact that her character, especially, remains "unreclaimed" is important. In "Self-Deception and Superiority Complex: Derangement of Hierarchy in Jane Austen's *Emma*," Shinobu Minma points out what other critics have also noted: the character of Mrs. Elton is meant to "expose" Emma's own pretensions of superiority and her "self-righteous patronage." She is Emma's exaggerated and not so subtle alter ego. Shinobu argues that Austen's intent is to show how the arrival of the nouveau riche (here he includes the Woodhouses who, while well established, "are not a landowning family") tended to upset the traditional hierarchical structure with their need for acceptance into the upper echelons of society. I would argue that Mrs. Elton, unlike Emma, never fits, not merely because of her parvenu pertness, but because she is only superficially self-aware and lacks the talent to belong to any community. Emma's capacity to belong, ultimately, is the true measure of her gentility.

That belonging is finally crucial to Emma's happiness, for like most others in the village, "Not one of them had the power of removal, or of effecting any material change of society. They must encounter each other, and make the best of it." Mrs. Elton considers herself preeminent in Highbury society by connection to and by the trappings of wealth and position. While Emma also feels herself superior and wants to remain so, her social position as "first" is challenged on moral grounds. She submits to the tests of character and admits her vulnerability and failures. Her wedding (the simplicity of which Mrs. Elton finds "extremely shabby") promises, in fact, to make her "first" in social stature, for Mr. Knightley is a member of the true landed gentry. However, that union comes only after Emma realizes the poverty of her own class-based prejudice and rectifies her social behavior. She finds her place and her humility when she can be civil to Miss Bates, accepting of Robert Martin, sociable with the Coles, and intimate with Jane Fairfax. We are left to imagine that because her education has been successful, she will find her happiness among that "small band of true friends" who have vouchsafed her membership among them.

Source: Kathy Smith, Critical Essay on *Emma*, in *Novels for Students*, Thomson Gale, 2005.

Catherine Dybiec Holm

Holm is a freelance writer, as well as a genre novel and short story author. In this essay, Holm discusses how the writing style of this novel differs from a modern fiction novel.

Jane Austen's *Emma* was first published in 1815. Today's readers will note that conventions in written storytelling have changed dramatically since the early 1800s. But Austen's style of storytelling effectively captures the societal nuances that are such a big part of this story. While it may be difficult for modern readers to absorb an older style of writing, it is possible that the older style of writing reflects how people generally communicated during that period in history. In this way, writing is a reflection of the consciousness of society and the trends in communication in general, whether in the 1800s or the twenty-first century. The difference between writing in the 1800s and writing today does not mean that one type of writing is superior to the other, but it does lead to interesting observations about how communication changes over time and what these changes might imply.

> Emma's astute skills of human observation and her attempts at matchmaking have backfired. In a modern novel, a problem like this, or at least some real emotion with something at stake, would have presented itself earlier in the story."

A present-day reader will notice that Austen's book reads differently than a contemporary fiction novel, beginning with the first sentence. Modern fiction is required to "hook" readers right away. Within the first several pages of contemporary fiction (or even the first several paragraphs), there must be the sense of danger, urgency, or a problem (perhaps the central story problem) that the protagonist must deal with. Modern readers have come to expect this. This expectation may be influenced by today's fast-paced life, competing distractions, entertainment media that are short and to the point, or an evolution over time of storytelling methods which have come to be more popular than others.

For a modern-day reader, it may be difficult to discern *Emma*'s central conflict, or the premise of the story, given the first several pages. By contemporary standards, the book starts out quite gently with the following statement: "Emma Woodhouse, handsome, clever, and rich, with a comfortable home and happy disposition seemed to invite some of the best blessings of existence; and had very little to distress or vex her."

Compare this to the beginning of the 2002 bestseller *The Lovely Bones*, by Alice Sebold, which plunges the reader right into the first-person experience of a horrible murder, and one can see how much the conventions of fiction writing have changed in two centuries. Little seems urgent during much of the beginning of *Emma*, which was perhaps typical of 1800s stories but not typical today. One of the first senses of real urgency in *Emma*, which involves the protagonist, does not come until more than a quarter of the way into the book (at least one hundred pages from the beginning) when Elton and Emma are alone in a carriage and Elton reveals his passionate feelings for Emma.

This is one of the first times in the story that emotions from any of the characters truly flare, and there is suddenly a sense of the larger problem at hand. Emma's astute skills of human observation and her attempts at matchmaking have backfired. In a modern novel, a problem like this, or at least some real emotion with something at stake, would have presented itself earlier in the story.

A contemporary reader might assume, after the first few pages of *Emma*, that the governess named Miss Taylor is to be an important character in the story, since much narrative is devoted to Emma's consternation when Miss Taylor moves away. Yet this does not turn out to be the case. Emma does start the novel, as she is mentioned in the first sentence, and the reader might correctly assume (based on contemporary storytelling conventions) that she will be important, even though the urgency to the story is very slow in coming, by modern-day standards. A number of other minor characters make an immediate appearance. Six characters are introduced or mentioned in the first three pages: Emma, Mr. Woodhouse, Miss Taylor, Mr. Weston, Isabella, and Isabella's husband. This convention marks another difference from today's toned down, streamlined fiction. It is impossible to know whether this implies that readers in the 1800s were more patient or could tolerate more narrative complexity, or whether readers today need communications to be as streamlined and concise as possible.

Prose style in a novel such as *Emma* differs from a contemporary fiction novel. Sentences are often much longer than what today's readers are accustomed to. Dialogue is presented in huge chunks, compared to today's standards. Again, the urgent scene between Emma and Elton in the carriage illustrates both the use of sentences and dialogue in this novel. The way the scene is presented is also quite different than it might be written in contemporary fiction. The beginning of this explosive moment is almost lost in the prose.

> To restrain him as much as might be . . . she was immediately preparing to speak . . . but scarcely had she begun, scarcely had they passed the sweep-gate and joined the other carriage, than she found her subject cut up—her hand seized—her attention demanded, and Mr. Elton actually making violent love to her.

It is a very roundabout way of getting to the main point, which reveals itself at the end of this somewhat long sentence. Mr. Elton is "making violent love" to Emma. By contemporary standards,

this scene might be written quite differently, possibly using more dialogue, shorter sentences, and immediately presenting the urgency of the problem at hand: Mr. Elton completely surprises Emma when he passionately displays his feelings for her.

By contemporary story-writing standards, the dialogue in *Emma* often has a character speaking for a long time, longer than may sound natural to contemporary readers. A good example of this, toward the beginning of the book, features Emma and her father discussing their servant James. Mr. Woodhouse goes on for longer than may be comfortable to the modern reader.

> I am very glad I did think of her. It was very lucky. . . . I am sure she would be a very good servant; she is a civil, pretty-spoken girl; I have a great opinion of her. Whenever I see her, she always curtseys and asks me how I do, in a very pretty manner. . . . I am sure she will be an excellent servant; and it will be a great comfort to poor Miss Taylor. . . . Whenever James goes over to his daughter, you know, she will be hearing of us. He will be able to tell her how we all are.

This large chunk of dialogue (with words omitted) is devoted to a servant and his daughter who have little importance in the novel's entirety, or its plot. Contemporary novels often emphasize a pragmatic approach, and very little shows up in the prose that does not advance the plot or serve as an important cue for the reader in some way.

Contemporary literature teachers often advise aspiring writers to "show, don't tell." This phrase is a common denominator of the resources available to writers who want to improve their craft. The narrative style in *Emma* seems to favor the "telling" side of the spectrum, in many cases. This implies no judgment on the quality of the writing, but is another good example of how immensely storytelling craft has changed since the early 1800s. A good example of narrative that tells more than it shows occurs shortly after Emma and her father discuss their servant.

> Emma spared no exertions to maintain this happier flow of ideas, and hoped, by the help of backgammon, to get her father tolerably through the evening, and be attacked by no regrets but her own. The backgammon-table was placed; but a visitor immediately afterwards walked in and made it unnecessary.

The narrative then goes on to describe the visitor at great length, including his age, location of his home, and his "cheerful manner."

Contemporary storytelling would likely handle this series of events quiet differently. Mr. Knightley's (the above mentioned guest) appearance might be worded to stand out more effectively and the reader might not feel like such an observer but instead feel closer to the action. The wording "a visitor immediately afterwards walked in," which is almost lost and hidden at the end of a paragraph, "tells" the reader what is going on but might distance a contemporary reader. A more active way to "show" this action would be to set apart Knightley's arrival with a paragraph break. Then, instead of telling the reader that "a visitor walked in," the contemporary author might say something like, "Emma turned at a rustling behind her, and saw Mr. Knightly coming through the doorway." The contemporary author might immediately follow with dialogue and nuances that would gradually reveal (and "show" the reader) Knightley's character, age, and other details about this new character.

There are moments in *Emma* where the prose stands out with insight and conciseness. During one of these moments, readers gain deep insight into Emma because her honest and blunt (but unspoken) thoughts contrast so effectively with what she has to say. The irony of the contrast highlights the excruciating importance that people (and these characters) placed on social conventions during this time in history.

> 'Yes, good man!' thought Emma, 'but what has all that to do with taking likenesses? You know nothing of drawing. Don't pretend to be in raptures about mine. Keep your raptures for Harriet's face.'

These thoughts are in direct contrast to Emma's polite, socially mannered response, which follows immediately: "Well, if you give me such kind encouragement, Mr. Elton, I believe I shall try what I can do."

Obviously, social conventions and consideration of social standing were extremely important in England's early 1800s. Austin's style of writing, purposefully or not, reflects these societal considerations. In *Emma*, characters spend a lot of time discussing proper behavior, as well as the importance of class and social standing. Emma goes to great lengths to steer Harriet from a romance with a lowly farmer. Emma distresses internally at some length over Churchill's decision to go to London for a haircut. Clearly, these characters pay attention to details, and the modern reader might find them obsessed with such details. There is a self-consciousness that runs throughout most of the book, particularly as characters worry about how to behave in social situations.

> Some change of countenance was necessary for each gentleman as they walked into Mrs. Weston's drawing-room. Mr. Elton must compose his joyous looks, and Mr. John Knightley disperse his ill-humour.

Nineteenth-century illustration by Chris Hammond depicting a scene from Emma

> Mr. Elton must smile less, and Mr. John Knightley more, to fit them for the place.

But, this is a part of the fascination with *Emma*; it is not only a story but an in-depth experience of life in nineteenth-century England. The writing style reflects the social concerns and nuances of the time and might well be difficult to recreate using modern storytelling methods. Critic Frances Ferguson of *Modern Language Quarterly* describes this predicament another way: for the characters in this novel, "desire is always triangulated" because individual choice is always being aligned with larger societal choices, or "what 'everyone' thinks." In the same article by Ferguson, D. H. Lawrence is quoted as saying that Austen "creates a world of 'personality' that identifies characters in terms of their interests and evaluations." In this way, societal trends are reflected in *Emma* and in the way that it reads. Perhaps this can be said of all writing.

Source: Catherine Dybiec Holm, Critical Essay on *Emma*, in *Novels for Students*, Thomson Gale, 2005.

Shinobu Minma

In the following essay excerpt, Minma describes the "old society" in which Emma *takes place and Emma's disruptive effect on its hierarchical system.*

> One's status in society signifies much in *Emma*, and of course it is Emma herself who is most particular about that."

"The neighborhood that did not exist in *Mansfield Park* is everywhere in *Emma*," as Claudia Johnson aptly observes, and this presence of "neighbourhood" has an important meaning. The novel gives a vivid and realistic picture of life in a rural community, and Emma, who attempts to tamper with the destinies of its inhabitants, is a disturber of the order of that community. Moreover, her meddling and mismanagement, though most noticeable in her match-making manoeuvre, are by no means restricted to that; in fact, with all her sensitivity to "rank" or "position," Emma's behaviour threatens to disrupt the system of hierarchy established in the community, and for a full appreciation of the matter we should carefully examine how far her mismanagement extends, and how her rationalizing is interrelated with it.

There is a certain pattern in Emma's disruptive behaviour, and in order to discern this pattern it is important to understand the structural features of "the old society." One's status in society signifies much in *Emma,* and of course it is Emma herself who is most particular about that. For other people, however, "equality" or "inequality" is a matter of no trivial importance; indeed, proper recognition of status is indispensable to daily intercourse among the inhabitants of Highbury. At the same time, it is in fact by no means simple or easy to recognize a person's status properly. In England in Jane Austen's day a small community such as a country village was the basic unit of society, and within each community "a finely graded hierarchy of great subtlety and discrimination" was formed from a wealthy landowner down to the labouring poor. Such differentiation of status was generally accepted as a "part of the given, unquestioned environment into which men were born"; but, owing to its "great subtlety and discrimination," a precise order of precedence in the hierarchy was hardly determinable. People "were acutely aware of their exact relation to those immediately above and below them"; with regard to the whole

social structure, however, they had no more than vague concepts, such as the "upper orders," the "middling ranks," and "labouring men." Moreover, this complicated structure was rendered all the more complicated by remarkable social fluidity. The rise of rich merchants into the gentry was a familiar phenomenon in eighteenth-century England, while younger sons of the nobility and the gentry, who were obliged to enter professions and trades, constantly moved down into the middle ranks. Indeed, large-scale social mobility was a distinct characteristic of English society, where, at least until Waterloo (the year when *Emma* was completed), there were no palpable classes in the sense of mutually exclusive layers and so no strife between them; on the other hand, it certainly increased the complexity of the problem of status identification.

Highbury was meant, no doubt, to be an average country community of the day, and in the portrait of life in this village those features of the old society are quite accurately reflected. Highbury society is a graded status hierarchy, with a squire at the top and a destitute family living in a cottage at the bottom. The story chiefly concerns the upper levels (people in lower grades are only touched on now and then), but regardless of level the inhabitants seem content to live in the traditional framework of society—no rebellious feelings, no smouldering discontent detectable anywhere. If the system of hierarchy itself is not questioned, however, the order of precedence within it is always a problem of great delicacy, which at times arouses controversy. Factors that determine social status are manifold, as indicated in Emma's resentful interior monologue after the scene of Mr Elton's proposal:

> he must know that in fortune and consequence she was greatly his superior. He must know that the Woodhouses had been settled for several generations at Hartfield, the younger branch of a very ancient family—and that the Eltons were nobody. The landed property of Hartfield certainly was inconsiderable, being but a sort of notch in the Donwell Abbey estate, to which all the rest of Highbury belonged; but their fortune, from other sources, was such as to make them scarcely secondary to Donwell Abbey itself, in every other kind of consequence; and the Woodhouses had long held a high place in the consideration of the neighbourhood which Mr Elton had first entered not two years ago, to make his way as he could, without any alliances but in trade, or any thing to recommend him to notice but his situation and his civility.

Here emerges a variety of elements on which the status of a family depends: descent and connections, the length of its residence, wealth and its source, occupation, and so on. To complicate matters further, some of those factors—such as income and official position—are subject to change. The intricacy which attends the process of status discrimination renders it practically impossible to determine an exact and permanent hierarchical order. Oliver MacDonagh sums up the case thus:

> Highbury classified itself internally in a precise though very complex fashion according to income, source of income, prescription, length of residence and function. On the other hand, this ideal arrangement is never matched exactly by the actual social order; or, more correctly, a fixed social order exists only as an abstract notion, or model, to be employed as a point of reference perhaps, but never realized.

Indeed, the absence of a fixed social order is a circumstance which makes it convenient for Emma to rationalize her arbitrary behaviour.

Rank and position are a sort of obsession with Emma, and because of this preoccupation, as well as for the haughty and supercilious attitude she frequently shows, she has been often called a snob. Emma certainly has the appearance of a snob, and, in a sense, she may be one. But, strictly speaking, it is not snobbery that makes her obsessed with social discrimination. To ascertain the spring of her obsession it is necessary to observe carefully how she makes her judgments about the social position of the people around her. As the famous opening of the book points out, Emma enjoys many advantages, in natural attributes as well as in environment; she is endowed with acute mental powers, possesses a large fortune, and occupies a high place in the community she lives in. In addition, she has "a disposition to think a little too well of herself" and takes inordinate pride in her superiority. Also inordinate is her demand for others to acknowledge it; "never loth to be first," she is disposed not only to think a little too well of herself but also to expect others to think a little too well of her. In fact, it is her constant wish to stand "always first and always right" in the eyes of those around her, and the avid desire for the recognition by others of her pre-eminence plays a key role in her personal relations; as Jane Nardin observes, "virtually all of Emma's personal antipathies and preferences can be accounted for by the effects the person in question has upon Emma's self-esteem." Emma's choice of Harriet as a friend is determined by Harriet's "very engaging" manner in "shewing so proper and becoming a deference" to her. Jane Fairfax, on the other hand, inspires enmity in Emma, for her "real" accomplishments and the high favour she wins among the inhabitants pose a threat to Emma's prominent position. Moreover, Jane is reserved and shows no flattering attitude towards Emma, which confirms the latter in her detestation.

It is important to note here that this highly subjective criterion is also applied to her judgment of social status; Emma's assessment of the position of others depends to a great degree on how they satisfy her sense of superiority. Harriet evinces blind adoration for Emma—"a flatterer in all her ways"—and for this reason and with no other legitimate grounds she is pronounced "a gentleman's daughter." The notable difference in Emma's estimation of the social standing of the Westons and the Coles affords another illustration of this arbitrariness. Mr Weston and Mr Cole have both made their fortune in trade, and both have purchased estates in Highbury and settled there. Their careers are analogous, and so is their status in society; or, if there is any difference, it is that the Coles are wealthier, since they are now, "in fortune and style of living, second only to the family at Hartfield." The Coles have hitherto stayed at a respectful distance from Hartfield; but the reserve of this rising family, like that of the "really accomplished" Jane Fairfax, appears to Emma's jealous eyes to be a token of rivalry. Consequently, they are held in contempt for their "low origin" and regarded as "only moderately genteel"; whereas the Westons, the avowed admirers of Emma, are counted among the "regular and best families" in Highbury and so considered on an equal footing with the Knightleys and the Woodhouses. In the case of Elton, Emma's estimate drastically changes. At first Elton is also included, together with Mr Knightley and the Westons, among "the chosen and the best"; indeed, during the period when he earns Emma's favour by his obsequious attentions, he is described as "quite the gentleman himself . . . without low connections." After showing "presumption" by his courtship of Emma herself, however, he is relegated to being a "nobody," with his relatives disparagingly mentioned as "in trade." Emma's severity towards the Coles somewhat softens after the dinner party at their house, where she is "received with a cordial respect which could not but please, and given all the consequence she could wish for"; they are then acknowledged as "worthy people." But Mr Elton, once dismissed, never recovers his former high position.

One notes that "trade," sometimes conveniently overlooked or disregarded, is at other times given great significance as a sign of "low" standing; it serves as a handy tool which Emma uses to validate her arbitrary judgments. But "trade" is not the only device available for her self-justification; Emma often converts her subjective judgments into objective facts, which she then employs as a means of justifying her own egocentric actions. As we have just seen, Harriet's status as a gentleman's daughter, determined according to Emma's peculiar criterion, is pure invention. But once the determining process is obliterated from her mind, the invention gains objectivity as a "fact," in which Emma obviously finds psychological support for her intimacy with a mere parlour-boarder of a common school. Furthermore, in her quarrel with Mr Knightley Emma makes use of this "fact" to vindicate herself. Against Mr Knightley, who reproaches her for inducing Harriet to refuse Robert Martin's proposal, she pleads that Robert Martin is not "Harriet's equal" but "undoubtedly her inferior as to rank in society." The reason she adduces for Harriet's superiority is that "her father is a gentleman." Mr Knightley is incensed at this argument and warmly advocates the farmer's claims. But who is superior is in fact a matter of secondary consideration; what matters is Emma's cunning appeal to the notion of the gentleman. The art of defence she displays with "rank" as a weapon is the highlight of this scene.

In a similar way Emma dexterously handles status to justify her slighting of the Bateses. Miss Bates is a favourite of everybody in Highbury except Emma, who, typically, interlinks her perverse feelings with the question of social position. Among Mr Woodhouse's acquaintants who are on visiting terms with him, Mrs and Miss Bates are classified in "a second set," as following "the chosen and the best." It is of course Emma's view that they belong to a "second" group, but there is something dubious about this classification. Mrs Bates, impoverished as she is now, is "the widow of a former vicar of Highbury," and there was a time, as Mr Knightley says, when Miss Bates's "notice" was "an honour" to Emma; but the Bateses are pushed into a lower class, while the incumbent vicar is placed, as we have seen, among "the chosen and the best." Emma's contemptuous treatment of them is not confined to this instance, and her ill feelings—especially towards Miss Bates—are closely related to her jealous rivalry with Jane Fairfax. As Nardin points out, "it is always clear to Emma that Jane Fairfax, whom she regards as a threatening rival, holds the first place in Miss Bates's affection and esteem," and Emma cannot bear this; she is irritated to see Jane Fairfax "so idolized and so cried up . . . by her aunt and grandmother." This is indeed a circumstance which highly offends Emma's sense of superiority; whence come her ill feelings towards these "idolizers" and her reducing of them to a "second" grade. Emma of course cannot admit this trick of reduction to herself; on the contrary, she ascribes her coldness towards them to their inferiority in

social position. Emma's reluctance to go near the Bateses' house is attributed, among other things, to "the horror of being in danger of falling in with the second rate and third rate of Highbury, who were calling on them for ever." The Bateses, obviously, who enjoy the company of those callers of the "second" and "third rate," are ranked as their fellow creatures (indeed, they and their callers are precisely the constituents of what Emma terms "the inferior society of Highbury,"), and under this "horror" of associating with "inferior" people is concealed her real horror—of associating with Jane Fairfax's idolizers. The Bateses' allegedly low position, together with the allegedly low company they keep, affords a pretext for Emma to justify her own "low" passions.

Thus Emma's enthusiasm for social discrimination is inspired not so much by a snobbish instinct as by an instinct of self-justification. Indeed, when she broaches the subject of rank or position, it is a sign that she has some motives or reasons—usually not laudable ones—to cover up and disguise. She lays exaggerated emphasis on Robert Martin's humble station, not because she actually has a low opinion of farmers, but because she wants to get rid of *this* farmer who stands in the way of her cherished match-making project; it is a stratagem to shuffle off responsibility onto his position. When Frank Churchill proposes the revival of balls at the Crown Inn, Emma at first makes difficulties, pleading the inconvenience of "a confusion of rank"; but it is an ostensible reason to conceal her real sentiment—her unwillingness to mix with those she dislikes. For Emma the social position of other people is an implement with which to camouflage her egotism—a red herring to misdirect herself as well as others. Moreover, this misleading implement is in itself hollow and unsubstantial, as we see in her way of dealing with Harriet and the Bateses. The status she uses as a plea is in many cases arbitrarily determined by herself. In this respect the hierarchical system of her society meets her convenience; its intricacy, plasticity, and fluidity provide a soil very favourable to her machinations. As MacDonagh remarks, a fixed social order exists only as an abstract notion; it is no exaggeration, therefore, to say that everyone has his or her own version of a fixed order. Consequently, no one—even Mr Knightley—can conclusively and convincingly refute Emma's allegations. Indeed, Emma makes dexterous, if unfair, use of the features of her society.

But, if the social order in the old society was unfixed and fluid, the leadership of the gentry in their communities was on the whole firm and indisputable, although their exalted position imposed heavy responsibilities. It was a commonly accepted idea that the gentry's privileges—such as wealth, leisure, and education—were given to them to serve the public. The English gentry, generally speaking, had a strong sense of responsibility and fulfilled "their role as keepers of the peace, unpaid civil administrators, promoters of the public good and benefactors of the poor and unfortunate." This idea of *noblesse oblige* is also prevalent in the world of *Emma*. The way in which those who are in a privileged position should behave towards their inferiors is a recurrent topic in the book. Frank Churchill neglects to make a courtesy visit to his father on his marriage, for which Mr Knightley blames him, putting particular emphasis on his lack of consideration for Mrs Weston: "It is on her account that attention to Randalls is doubly due, and she must doubly feel the omission. Had she been a person of consequence herself, he would have come I dare say; and it would not have signified whether he did or no." A similar view is expressed when Mr Weston advises Frank not to defer his visit to Jane Fairfax: "any want of attention to her *here* should be carefully avoided. You saw her with the Campbells when she was the equal of every body she mixed with, but here she is with a poor old grandmother, who has barely enough to live on. If you do not call early it will be a slight." The lower a person's position or the more adverse a person's circumstances, the more attention is due—this is the principle the two gentlemen formulate, and it is a key principle in a hierarchical society. How, then, is Emma's behaviour to be understood in terms of this principle? And how is her sense of superiority interrelated with her sense of duty?

As a member—or, a "mistress"—of a family who are "first in consequence" in Highbury, Emma is aware that she is expected to offer gracious attentions to the underprivileged, and she believes that she understands her duty well. It is frequently the case, however, that her sense and performance of duty are distorted by the pursuit of her own pleasure. In the midst of the match-making intrigue Emma calls on a poor sick family with Harriet to give them "relief." As Nardin points out, however, Emma performs this charitable act primarily to indulge in the pleasure of feeling her own superiority. Whether the visit is really of benefit to the family is open to question. Emma's "charity" is in fact a pleasure enjoyed in the name of duty, and so is her attempt at match-making for Harriet. When she decides to "notice" her, she regards it not only as "a very kind undertaking" but also as "highly

becoming her own situation in life, her leisure, and powers." Her officious patronage of Harriet allows her to indulge in the pleasure of feeling superior; she defines it as a duty, but it is an invented duty that is superfluous and even pernicious. In her "real" duties, on the other hand, she is often negligent, as is implied in the dissatisfaction Mr Knightley expresses every now and then in regard to her lack of consideration for Jane Fairfax and the Bateses. The cause of her negligence is that she derives no pleasure in discharging such duties.

Yet Emma is by no means always negligent or wrong-headedly assiduous; she can be rational and considerate sometimes, and especially within her own family circle she conscientiously discharges her duties even at the sacrifice of her personal pleasure. The thoughtful attention she shows to Mr Woodhouse is a good example; she is unremittingly careful of his comfort, spares no pains to humour his gentle selfishness, and is always ready to comply with the requests of a fastidious and valetudinarian father. She is an exemplary dutiful daughter. In the scenes of family gatherings she plays the role of a vigilant peace watcher. Mr John Knightley, somewhat intolerant and short-tempered, occasionally provokes Emma or agitates her father by his sarcasm or acerbity. Emma, however, taking it upon herself to "keep the peace if possible," never lets her feelings run away with her on such occasions and, when in a fit of ill humour he darkens the atmosphere, tries sedulously to restore the harmony. Within her own family circle Emma's sense of duty is sound, and her personal pleasure is always subordinated to the performance of her duties. It is when she steps into the outside world that this order of priority is completely reversed; there pleasure obtrudes itself as the primary motivation of Emma's actions, and her sense of duty is either muffled into silence or warped. In *Amelia* Henry Fielding observes through the voice of Dr Harrison that "whoever discharges his Duty well" to blood relations "gives us a well-grounded Hope, that he will behave as properly in all the rest." But Fielding's proposition, sound as it may be as a generalization, does not apply in Emma's case.

Why, then, does Emma's behaviour inside and outside the family circle differ so radically? One may find an explanation in the difference in stability of Emma's own position. Within her family circle, Emma's status as the "first" person is firmly established. With her father she is always first—first in affection and esteem—and she herself confidently says: "I believe few married women are half as much mistress of their husband's house, as

I am of Hartfield." There is actually no one in the family circle—including the sober and unflattering Knightley brothers—who dares to call her position into question or attempt to supplant her. She is of the first importance in her family. In the outside world, however, her premiership is by no means so firm or unchallenged. There appear rivals one after another who, intentionally or unintentionally, present a threat to her foremost position: Jane Fairfax surpasses Emma in accomplishments; the Coles aggrandize themselves at an alarming rate; and Mrs. Elton contests with her for leadership in the village. Emma of course cannot bring herself to accept a subordinate position. She is deeply disconcerted when Mrs Weston suggests the possibility of Mr Knightley's being in love with Jane Fairfax, because, apart from her subconscious affection for Mr Knightley, she cannot bear the idea of Jane Fairfax's becoming "a Mrs Knightley for them all to give way to." But in reality she is more than once obliged to "give way." At the ball in the Crown Inn "Emma must submit to stand second to Mrs. Elton," and, as the narrator ironically adds, "It was almost enough to make her think of marrying." In the outside world where her position is often threatened, she is impelled to do what is unnecessary in the family circle—flaunt her superiority. When she first proposes the theory that Harriet is a gentleman's daughter, she advises Harriet: "you must support your claim to that station by every thing within your own power, or there will be plenty of people who would take pleasure in degrading you." It is not Harriet, however, but Emma herself who faithfully follows this advice; to support her claim to the first position she takes every pain to show off her superiority, "or there will be plenty of people who would take pleasure in degrading" her. And to show off and feel her own superiority is a pleasure to her.

In pursuit of this pleasure she sometimes fabricates superfluous duties, and sometimes neglects to perform her real ones. In both cases she resorts to her characteristic far-fetched rationalization, and in both cases her conduct threatens to deflect or disrupt the village life. To show off her superiority she meddlesomely patronizes Harriet. She thinks she is doing her duty, but thanks to this extra "duty" Harriet loses her way, severed from an environment congenial to her. In her dereliction of duty Emma poses an even more serious threat, and her rationalization there is more glaringly contradictory. In the small society of Highbury she avoids contact as much as possible with those whose company does not gratify her sense of superiority, and so she

seldom goes near the Bateses' house. As we have seen, to excuse her negligence she pleads their low social position. But this method of self-justification carries an obvious paradox. Emma, who takes pride in her high social position, also takes pride in fulfilling those duties which appertain to her high position, and she knows that the first duty of her position is to be a kind friend to the underprivileged. And yet, where the fulfilment of this duty does not minister to her sense of superiority, she evades it by alleging the social inferiority of those to whom she ought to be kind, an inferiority of her own invention. It is natural that such a self-contradictory pattern of behaviour should give itself away. This happens during the excursion to Box Hill, when Emma is unable to avoid contact with Miss Bates, and holds her up to public ridicule. This act—a grave transgression of the principle of patronage in a hierarchy—is not an inadvertent act committed on the spur of the moment; fundamental flaws lurking in her daily conduct manifest themselves in the nasty form of cruel derision. Indeed, this incident exposes the gross paradox involved in Emma's cunning exploitation of the flexibility of her society, and her flagrant offence signals how her frantic superiority-hunting menaces the delicate equilibrium maintained in that flexible social system.

Let us finally consider the peculiar idiosyncrasies of the heroine of the novel in the historical context and the author's intention in delineating them. Emma's superiority complex, as we may call it, has a close relationship to the fact that the Woodhouses are not a landowning family. They derive their income not from land but from "other sources"—presumably from investment. From the statement that they are "the younger branch of a very ancient family," we may assume that the progenitor of the Hartfield Woodhouses was a younger brother in a landed family, who entered trade, made his fortune, purchased the Hartfield estate (from the Knightleys, no doubt), and settled in Highbury (or, the purchase may have been effected by the next generation, as with the Bingleys in *Pride and Prejudice*). It is clear, therefore—as it was no doubt clear to the contemporary reader—that, although they have settled in Highbury "for several generations" and are now admitted to be "first in consequence" there, the Woodhouses in fact stand in almost the same position as the Westons, the Coles, and the Sucklings of Maple Grove. These are all nonlanded rentier families, and the marked increase of such *nouveaux riches* was a distinct characteristic of the society of Jane Austen's days. Claire

Tomalin's biography reveals that the society in which the Austen family moved in Hampshire was by no means an unchanging, orderly rural world, as one would expect, but was a restless fluid world, filled with those who "were what has been called in this century pseudo-gentry, families who aspired to live by the values of the gentry without owning land or inherited wealth of any significance." David Spring, one of the earliest to apply the term "pseudo-gentry" to this group, remarks of the behaviour of those aspirants and the influence they had on their society:

> they had a sharp eye for the social escalator, were skilled in getting on them, and (what was more important) no less skilled in staying on them. They were adept at acquiring what the economist Fred Hirsch has aptly called "positional goods"—those scarce services, jobs, and goods which announce social success. In this they helped to inaugurate a "positional competition" inevitably more widespread than that indulged in by landowners.

As a member of a parvenu family of comparative seniority, Emma struggles to stay on the social escalators, but she goes a little too far; intent upon outdoing her rivals, she becomes obsessed with monopolizing the "positional goods." Indeed, Emma's morbid desire for superiority is an unhealthy symptom of the "positional competition" which was spurred on by the rapid rise of a new social Force.

Was it, then, Jane Austen's intention to criticize the newly emerging gentry? The Woodhouses' nonlanded status is emphasized by several critics as the main cause of Emma's inadequate understanding of her duties. Nardin observes that, in contrast to Mr. Knightley, the landed squire of Highbury, the Woodhouses, though they reside there, "lack the sort of natural, historic ties to the place and its people which land ownership provides for Mr. Knightley," and this lack of real ties, according to Nardin, prevents Emma from cultivating a proper sense of what is due to the inhabitants. Beth Fowkes Tobin develops this argument further and propounds the view that by "idealizing the landlord and criticizing the monied status of the new gentry" Jane Austen attempted to fend off attacks being delivered from several quarters against the landowning classes and thus to advocate the traditional paternalistic system based on land ownership; Emma's moral inadequacies are highlighted in order to lay the blame on the nonlanded new gentry. The "idealized landlord" is of course Mr. Knightley, and there certainly is no objection to seeing him as an exemplary landowner. It is also undeniable that Emma's deficiencies are in many ways linked to her "monied status." But did Jane

Austen really attempt such defence? Given the elaborate and highly systematized description of those deficiencies, one can hardly suppose that Jane Austen's purpose was simply to vindicate one group or class or to blame another; her penetration into the depths of Emma's consciousness even suggests a scientific attitude of mind free from any political bias. What, then, was she doing in this novel?

Fully aware of the rapid growth of the new type of gentry in this period. Jane Austen was also aware that, with their proliferation, a certain ethos—a sort of competitive atmosphere—had become prevalent in society. That she took a keen interest in the matter is obvious, not only from her portrayal in this novel of a heroine obsessed with superiority, but also from her introduction of a caricature of the heroine—Mrs. Elton. Mrs. Elton is herself a daughter of a Bristol merchant of "moderate" dignity, but she has a more prosperous brother-in-law, Mr. Suckling, whose family has been successful enough to purchase an estate, Maple Grove. With this typical parvenu of a brother-in-law and his "seat" as her tower of strength, Mrs. Elton enters Highbury, meaning "to shine and be very superior." Indeed, "extremely well satisfied with herself and thinking much of her importance," Mrs. Elton reiterates many of Emma's own conceited words and deeds. Emma's superiority complex, as manifested in her overweening social pretensions, self-righteous patronage, or petty rivalries, is in an exaggerated way reproduced in this character. Concerning the role of Mrs. Elton, Alistair Duckworth observes that "Jane Austen's intention is clearly to repeat certain of Emma's characteristics in a manifestly inferior personality, and thus to expose them." But what are exposed are more than Emma's personal defects; if "certain of Emma's characteristics" reflect a particular tendency of this period, then the author's intention in parodying them in another character is evidently to "expose" and accentuate the tendency. It is a clever device to indicate that Emma's superiority complex is not just the problem of one individual alone.

But this does not necessarily point to a hostile or aggressive intent of the author against the parvenu gentry; nor was her object in the book merely to lay bare the obnoxiousness of the *arriviste* qualities they possessed. She underlined the cult of arrivism because it was closely related to an alarming phenomenon in her society—the derangement of the hierarchical system. As a keen observer of society; she perceived that the traditional framework of society, its way of life, was being seriously dislocated with the rapid growth of the new social force; with their powerful ambition and vigorous spirit of emulation, those climbers of the social ladder distorted the order and principle of that ladder, the hierarchy. Her main concern in the novel was to carry out a close inspection of this phenomenon. In view of her acute psychological insight into the matter, however, unclouded by emotional involvement but marked by a spirit of detachment, denunciation of the newly risen class or advocacy of the particular social system of the age seems to have formed little part of her plan. Mark Parker remarks that recent Austen criticism, in exploring the political dimension of her novels, "has grappled with the problem of how to attach a context (drawn from a pool of possible contexts) to Austen's novels in the absence of some of the more direct signs of political affiliation and tendency." Yet this "absence" of the "direct signs of political affiliation and tendency" could be regarded as the very sign of Jane Austen's unwillingness to commit herself to a particular political position.

What, then, did she aim at in her inquiry into the phenomenon? Perhaps one could put it this way: well aware of the inevitability of hierarchy in human society, Jane Austen directed her attention to its immutable and enduring, rather than topical and transitory, aspects, and her ultimate object in her inspection of the matter was to elucidate the way hierarchy would function—or, more correctly, the way it would malfunction. To put it another way, the complication of the hierarchical system afforded her an excellent opportunity for studying this problem, and among the factors of the complication what engaged her interest most was the behaviour of the disturbers. The superiority complex which an upstart was prone to, and the self-deception previously examined in several characters, which she knew could easily be united with a superiority complex—these she regarded as essential ingredients of a malfunctioning social hierarchy. Perhaps, while engaged in *Mansfield Park,* she already cherished a design to handle the theme of self-deception on a yet larger scale in future. If so, this design, when she actually put her hand to a new work, entered into happy combination with the task she assigned to herself in it—to illustrate the psychological mechanism of abnormal functioning incident to a system of hierarchy. And, given the masterly delineation of Emma's subtle ways of abusing rank and position, we can say that Jane Austen superbly accomplished her purpose.

Source: Shinobu Minma, "Self-Deception and Superiority Complex: Derangement of Hierarchy in Jane Austen's *Emma,*" in *Eighteenth-Century Fiction,* Vol. 14, No. 1, October 2001, pp. 49–65.

Susan M. Korba

In the following essay, Korba identifies Emma's behavior as similar to that of a dominating male and examines her relationships with submissive females in Emma.

> She always declares she will never marry, which, of course, means just nothing at all. But I have no idea that she has yet ever seen a man she cared for. It would not be a bad thing for her to be very much in love with a proper object.
>
> Intimacy between Miss Fairfax and me is quite out of the question.
>
> —Jane Austen
> *Emma*

Austen critic LeRoy W. Smith asserts that, "contrary to the traditional view, Austen does not avoid the subject of sex in her fiction," that, in fact, "she is well aware of sexuality's powerful role in human behaviour." Similarly, in *Sex and Sensibility,* Jean H. Hagstrum warns readers of Jane Austen against allowing the author's "considerable modesty" to obscure "the real passion that seethes beneath the controlled and witty surfaces" of her novels. He points out that "anyone so seemingly cool and rational has of course invited speculation about what is being kept out of sight" (p. 269). The critical debate over Austen's novel *Emma* may be seen as a case in point. For years, critics of *Emma* have been circling around the apparently disconcerting issue of the protagonist's sexuality. Claudia Johnson finds that "[d]etermining the common denominator in much *Emma* criticism requires no particular cleverness. Emma offends the sexual sensibilities of many of her critics. Transparently misogynist, sometimes even homophobic, subtexts often bob to the surface of the criticism about her." Johnson cites Edmund Wilson's ominous allusions and Marvin Mudrick's dark hints (p. 123) about Emma's infatuations with and preference for other women as examples of the unease aroused by this particular Austen heroine. In examining these critical responses, she concludes that much of the discomfort generated by the novel results from the fact that Emma "is not sexually submissive to and contingent upon men" (p. 123), and that she "assumes her own entitlement to independence and power-power not only over her own destiny, but, what is harder to tolerate, power over the destinies of others—and in so doing she poaches on what is felt to be male turf" (p. 125).

Certainly Emma's adoption of the masculine role and the implications of her usurpation of social power are contentious issues. But it is the doggedly recurrent (yet inevitably dismissed) suggestion of Emma's possible lesbianism that seems to arouse the most critical discomfort. It becomes clear upon examining Smith's and Hagstrum's readings of Austen that the passions "seething" beneath her "controlled and witty surfaces" are seen to be exclusively heterosexual passions. Hagstrum finds no evidence in Austen's works of the "perverse" lesbian sensuality that he briefly examines in other eighteenth-century novels, and which he refers to as "morbidities" or "irregularities." Smith states that Austen "controls her use [of sex] to fit her settings, avoid offence and keep attention where she feels it belongs." One wonders if it is not Austen's critics who are determined to keep attention where they feel it belongs. Although several recent analyses have posited a more sexually radical Austen, Eve Kosofsky Sedgwick's characterization of the bulk of Austen scholarship as critically timid seems largely justified. For the most part, approaches to Austen conform with "the vast preponderance of scholarship and teaching ... even among liberal academics [which] does simply neither ask nor know. At the most expansive, there is a series of dismissals of such questions." Accordingly, while Christine St. Peter challenges readers of Austen to "discover previously unremarked aspects in her treatment of women's relations," her response to the suggestion that Emma's sexual orientation is homosexual rather than heterosexual is emphatically and contemptuously dismissive:

In my rejection of a narrowly defined marital love I do not intend to introduce here a parallel error of discovering in Austen the crypto-lesbian. I know well that in our post-Freudian critical world any mention of intimacy between women conjures up an image of sexual bonding. Austen was aware of this possibility, too, and quite severely rejects it. (p. 475)

Claudia Johnson herself sees the suggestion of Emma's possible homosexual proclivities as nothing more than the misogynistic projections of critics who are "at a loss to account for how Emma could like Harriet more than she likes Mr. Elton." While Johnson's point is well taken, it illustrates the limitations of a feminist perspective that remains resolutely heterocentric. Critics consistently resist what Sedgwick refers to as "the rich, conflictual erotic complication of a homoerotic matrix" present in Austen, refusing to take seriously the possibility of an alternative to the prescriptive heterosexual paradigm. The fact that Emma possesses a measure of social and sexual power, and that she is a woman who, in a number of significant ways, "plays man" throughout the novel, implies as much about Emma's place in the novel's

> In *Emma*, power and sexuality are inextricably linked, and it is Emma's desire for and limited exertion of erotic mastery that provide the framework for Austen's narrative."

sexual configurations as it does about her appropriation of masculine social prerogatives. Her relationships with Miss Taylor (later Mrs. Weston) and Harriet Smith exemplify her attraction to and infatuation with docile and malleable members of her own sex, women over whom she exerts control and influence, and in whose sexual destinies she evinces a passionate and active involvement; and her relationships with the male characters in the novel—Mr. Knightley, Frank Churchill, and even Mr. Elton-serve to demonstrate Emma's marked sexual indifference to men, and, more importantly, her strong sexual identification with them.

Feminist scholar Carole S. Vance suggests that

The external system of sexual hierarchy is replicated within each of us, and herein lies its power. Internalized cultural norms enforce the status quo. As each of us hesitates to admit deviations from the system of sexual hierarchy, nonconformity remains hidden, invisible, and apparently rare. The prevailing system retains hegemony and power, appearing to be descriptive as well as prescriptive, a statement of what is as well as what should be.

Thus, according to Vance "feminism must be a movement that speaks to sexuality ... We cannot be cowardly, pretending that feminism is not sexually radical. Being a sex radical at this time, as at most, is less a matter of what you do, and more a matter of what you are willing to think, entertain, and question" (p. 23, [emphasis mine]). Accordingly, I propose an investigation of the controversial issue of *Emma*'s erotic sub-text that poses the following questions: How do Emma's relationships with the various male and female characters in the novel reveal the nature of her sexual orientation? What are the underlying dynamics that animate her sexual identity? And finally, and perhaps most importantly, why must analyses of this particular heroine ultimately reinscribe a normative heterosexual identity? Why shouldn't Emma be a lesbian?

Susan Morgan, in "Emma Woodhouse and the Charms of Imagination," offers some insights into the psychology informing Emma's relationships. She suggests that Emma is a novel about "the fact that people have an internal life of their own, and that the recognition of this personal existence, this self in someone else, is the necessary requisite for morality and for love." She observes that "within her small world [Emma] knows no boundaries, recognizes no limits. And because there is no point for Emma where her sphere of influence ends there is no room for anyone else's to begin" (p. 37); as a result, Emma constantly "violate[s] the inner lives of the people she tries to control" (p. 46). The unconsummated friendship between Emma and Jane Fairfax is central to her argument: "Emma's inability to go outside herself and grant the value of others must cost her something. And Jane Fairfax is the measure of what Emma loses" (p. 42). Ultimately, Morgan concludes that *Emma* is about the unfolding of an "educational process" in which the heroine learns "to accept her limits and the inviolability of others" (p. 46). Her analysis, despite its avoidance of the sexual/erotic forces afoot within the text, provides a convenient point of departure from which to attempt an investigation of the complexity of Emma's sexual identity: Morgan has identified, albeit unwittingly, both the erotic dynamic at work in *Emma,* which I believe to be a subliminal form of "erotic domination" as delineated by psychoanalytic critic Jessica Benjamin, and the principal erotic relationship within the novel, which, I will argue, is the one that exists between Emma Woodhouse and Jane Fairfax, our heroine's real object of desire. In the discussion which follows, I will examine this concept of "erotic domination" as I see it operating covertly within *Emma,* focusing on several issues that I believe are central to an attempt to understand the complex construction of Emma's sexuality: her relationships with Miss Taylor, Harriet, and Mr. Knightley; her identification with the "male" sexual role, particularly in terms of sexual object choice and the wielding of power; and her involvement with Jane Fairfax, the erotic relationship around which all the others may be seen to revolve. It is this relationship that, for various reasons, is unavailable to Emma throughout most of the novel, and that reveals, finally, the insurmountability of the sexual and social limitations that circumscribe her. It is Jane's ultimate (and, I would argue, necessary) inaccessibility that leads Emma back to Mr. Knightley. Alice Chandler has noted that "marriage

is . . . a sexual act in [Austen's] novels—usually a reconciliation between a man and a woman whose inner feelings and conscious knowledge have been at odds throughout the story"; ultimately, Emma does retreat from "playing man" and marries Mr. Knightley. Nevertheless, I would suggest that the real "reconciliation" in this novel is not between Emma and Mr. Knightley at all, but rather between Emma and Jane—and that, despite this reconciliation, they must then part. Each ends up with her respective husband, and the heterosexual social order is maintained.

However, an examination of the various sexual relationships in *Emma* reveals that this heterosexual social order—"the normal" order, as opposed to "the perverse"—is governed by the same underlying principle that animates Emma's amatory relationships. It has been noted that, in Austen's novels, "love and power cannot be separated as ruling independently in the private and political orders." Accordingly, Sandra Lee Bartky points out that since "the subordination of women by men is pervasive . . . it orders the relationship of the sexes in every area of life . . . a sexual politics of domination is as much in evidence in the private spheres of the family, ordinary social life, and sexuality as in the traditionally public spheres of government and the economy." It would then follow that the dynamic of erotic domination, a concept that "mingles love with issues of control and submission . . . flows beneath the surface of 'normal' adult love" and runs "throughout all relationships of arousal"; in *Emma,* it permeates all sexual relationships, both heterosexual and homoerotic. Indeed, Benjamin contends that domination [is] not a nasty additive to nice eroticism but its essence, for, in patriarchies, domination and submission constitute erotic excitement." Thus, the structure of Emma's intercourse with other women, epitomized in the paradigmatic relationship with Harriet Smith, is mirrored in each of the novel's heterosexual attachments, including those of Mr. Weston and Miss Taylor, Frank Churchill and Jane Fairfax, John Knightley and Isabella, as well as that of Emma and Mr. Knightley. The way in which the desire to dominate is expressed varies in each of the relationships: with Mr. Knightley, it is through overt control and the assertion of superiority; with Frank, it manifests in cruel games and the tormenting of his partner; with Emma, it is through manipulation. The submissive partner in each relationship is usually female, a "sweet, docile, grateful" young woman like Harriet—or a "worshipping" wife like Isabella. Nancy Chodorow points out that "[w]omen find it difficult to integrate agency and love and often accept whatever love they can get in exchange for identification with and love from a man"—for women, this often involves "submission, overvaluation, masochism, and the borrowing of subjectivity from the lover." Mr. Knightley, who is wont to express his views of relationships in language permeated with such terms as "submitting" and "subjection," affirms this view of the woman's role in a discussion with Mrs. Weston, in which he characterizes her as the ideal wife, one trained in "'the very material matrimonial point of submitting your own will, and doing as you were bid'"; he assures her that, as a consequence, had he been asked by Mr. Weston "'to recommend him a wife, I should certainly have named Miss Taylor.'" Ironically, Mr. Knightley credits her relationship with Emma for having turned her into such "an excellent wife"—as Emma's intimate companion, she has been well-trained in the role of the submissive partner.

Typically it is the male partner who occupies the dominant position in the erotic relationship. Susan Contratto observes that "Power has a gender: charismatic power with its excitement, visibility, and privilege is male." Thus, Mr. John Knightley is said to be "no doubt . . . in the habit of receiving" his wife's "pleased assent" to his dicta, despite his tendency to "act an ungracious, or say a severe thing"; Mr. Weston's marriage to Miss Taylor gives him "the pleasantest proof of its being a great deal better to chuse than to be chosen, to excite gratitude than to feel it": Frank Churchill, who behaves with "shameful, insolent neglect" of his betrothed, and, worse, with "such, apparent devotion" to Emma, "as it would have been impossible for any woman of sense to endure" exits the novel with the woman of his choice, having been unable to "weary her by negligent treatment"; and Mr. Knightley, with his "downright, decided, commanding sort of manner" and his fondness for "bending little minds," acknowledges having "'blamed . . . and lectured'" Emma throughout their relationship, conceding that she has "'borne it as no other woman in England would have borne it.'" Emma, however, is able to "bear" Mr. Knightley's attempts to dominate her because she does not recognize his right to dictate to her, and when he refuses to forgive her for contravening his wishes, she is "sorry, but could not repent." Her will—her sense of the legitimacy of her own power—matches his at almost every turn.

Emma occupies a rather unique and peculiar position in the novel's relationship paradigm.

LeRoy Smith finds that, in Austen's fiction, "some women, instead of acceding to dependency, sustain their self-esteem by a compensatory striving for power that takes the form of imitation of the dominant male." Indeed, Austen's creation of Emma at times seems to directly address the kinds of questions that Jessica Benjamin poses in her examination of sexual power: "Why does femininity appear to be linked to passivity? And why do men appear to have exclusive rights to sexual agency, so that women seek their desire in men, hoping to have it recognised through the agency of an other?" As Smith points out

> The hard truth about Austen's world is the fact of male domination. Women, characteristically, are devalued . . . Their social status is narrowly and rigidly defined: passivity is their expected state. Any attempt by them to acquire or exercise power is viewed by men as "manipulative, disruptive, illegitimate, or unimportant." But the female's craving for power is as deeply rooted as the male's [emphasis mine].

Emma firmly rejects the notion of passivity as her "expected state." She is laughingly dismissive of Harriet's wonder that, with all of her charming qualities, she "'should not be married, or going to be married!'," explaining that "'My being charming, Harriet, is not quite enough to induce me to marry: I must find other people charming—one other person at least. And I am not only, not going to be married, at present, but have very little intention of every marrying at all.'" It is clear that Emma recognizes and relishes the power and autonomy of her somewhat anomalous position when she asserts that she has "none of the usual inducements of women to marry'"—that she would, in fact. "'be a fool to change such a situation as mine.'" Austen has placed Emma Woodhouse in the position of sexual dominance usually associated with men. What is more, she possesses a considerable degree of power, which is almost exclusively associated with "male mastery": "'Fortune I do not want; employment I do not want; consequence I do not want; I believe few married women are half as much mistress of their husband's house, as I am of Hartfield'"; Mr. Knightley remarks disapprovingly that "'ever since she was twelve, Emma has been mistress of the house and of you all.'" Arguably, Emma wields a degree of power equivalent to that of any of the male characters within the novel; more, in some cases, as demonstrated by her rejection of Mr. Elton, and her proven ability to deprive Robert Martin of his choice of a wife. This power is one that comes with social prestige, financial security, and a character allowed to develop without the restraints usually imposed upon women; in short, power that usually comes with the label of the male gender. However, Emma is free to exercise her need to control as long she violates only the selfhood of the women with whom she conducts relationships, and not the social boundaries that circumscribe them. Ultimately, Emma will discover that the power she possesses will not allow her to avoid the fate that she attempts to arrange for everyone but herself; her claim to having "very little intention of ever marrying at all" is one she will have to retreat from, once she realizes that if "all took place that might take place among the circle of her friends, Hartfield must be comparatively deserted; and she left to cheer her father with the spirits only of ruined happiness." Once everyone is settled in the security of heterosexual coupledom, Emma will have no outlet for her desire, no object upon which to exert erotic control-her power will no longer mean anything.

In *Emma*, power and sexuality are inextricably linked, and it is Emma's desire for and limited exertion of erotic mastery that provide the framework for Austen's narrative. Susan Morgan identifies Emma's "problem" as a failure to "see the boundaries of oneself and the separate life of others." Similarly, Jessica Benjamin explains "erotic domination" as the failure to recognize the Other "as like, although separate, from oneself'; at the most basic level, it is an impulse imbued with the individual's desire for mutual recognition, for selfhood, and for transcendence. Erotic domination has its psychological origins in an individual's earliest experience, in the failure to achieve "true differentiation." This is a somewhat paradoxical process in which the individual acquires a sense of identity through the development of the ability to see herself and others as independent and distinct beings and learns that her acts and intentions can have an impact on others, and theirs on her; at the same time, the individual is dependent upon the recognition provided by her earliest care-giver, usually the mother, in order to reaffirm this autonomous identity. Benjamin explains that the problem of erotic domination begins with the denial of this dependency—this need for recognition from the maternal Other:

> To escape from this conflict it is all too tempting to imagine that one can become independent without recognizing the other person as an equally autonomous agent in her . . . own right. One need only imagine that the other person is not separate-she belongs to me. I control and possess her.

The resulting relationship is one in which the dominant partner must subjugate the submissive partner as a means of establishing her own autonomy

through the negation of the other person's. In *Emma*, this dynamic is not manifested physically between Emma and anyone else; rather, Emma's need to dominate the women who serve as her objects of desire, to repudiate dependency "while attempting to avoid the consequent feeling of aloneness," is sublimated in her attempts to direct and control their sexual proclivities and to determine the final configurations of their heterosexual unions. In this way, she is able to take an erotic sort of pleasure in exercising mastery, without transgressing the sexual norms of her society or acknowledging the possibility of such desire.

In Emma Woodhouse's case, the failure to differentiate may be seen to have its roots in her early childhood: "Her mother had died too long ago for her to have more than an indistinct remembrance of her caresses: and her place had been supplied by an excellent woman as governess, who had fallen little short of a mother in affection." Miss Taylor, although occupying the maternal space in Emma's life during her formative years, is a problematic figure. In effect, she plays the role of the "permissive parent," as does Mr. Woodhouse, "a most affectionate, indulgent father." We learn that "[e]ven before Miss Taylor had ceased to hold the nominal office of governess, the mildness of her temper had hardly allowed her to impose any restraint"; Emma becomes accustomed to "doing just what she liked; highly esteeming Miss Taylor's judgment, but directed chiefly by her own." Benjamin explains that if

> the first other we encounter is our mother . . . then it is through our . . . impact on her that we experience ourselves as existing and our intentions as meaningful and potent. If our acts have no impact on her, we feel powerless. But if we overpower her, there is no one to recognize us. When we affect her it is necessary that she does not simply dissolve under the impact of our actions . . . If, for example, the mother sets no limits for the child, if she obliterates herself and her own interests . . . she ceases to perform the role of other person . . . If the mother does not at some point remove herself from the child's control she becomes simply an object, which no longer exists outside the self. [(p. 284)]

It is clear that Emma has come to objectify the maternal figure of Miss Taylor, a woman who "had devoted all her powers to attach and amuse her" for sixteen years. Emma considers her an essential appendage to herself, "a friend and companion such as few possessed"; and it is apparent in the first conversation we witness between Emma, Mr. Woodhouse, and Mr. Knightley, that Miss Taylor has long been considered a "possession" of the Woodhouse household. Her function has been "to please" both Emma and her father, a function that she is now expected to perform for her new husband. It is significant that Emma claims to have orchestrated the union between Miss Taylor and Mr. Weston: " 'if I had not promoted Mr. Weston's visits here, and given many little encouragements, and smoothed many little matters, it might not have come to anything after all.' " Emma's view of Miss Taylor's marriage is one that privileges her own role and degree of control rather than that of the actual participants, illustrated by her claim that " 'I made up my mind on the subject' "; she sees the marriage primarily in terms of how it involves and affects herself, much as she sees the objectified person of Miss Taylor. In effect, she is unable to maintain "the essential tension of the contradictory impulses to assert the self . . . without effacing the other." It is this "dialectic of control" upon which the achievement of true differentiation depends: "[I]f I completely control the other, then the other ceases to exist, and if the other completely controls me, then I cease to exist." Benjamin draws upon Freud and Hegel to explain how the breakdown of this tension leads to the desire for domination:

> According to Freud the earliest self wants to be omnipotent, or rather it has the fantasy that it is so. Subsequent omnipotence fantasies are seen as regressions to this necessary first stage. Hegel says that self-consciousness wants to be absolute . . . to be recognized by the other in order to place itself in the world and make itself the world. The I wants to prove this at the expense of the other; it wants to think itself the only one; it abjures dependency.

> For Hegel and Freud, then, the self gives up omnipotence only when it realizes its dependency . . . The subject discovers that if it completely devours or controls the other, it can no longer get what it originally wanted [recognition]. So the subject learns better. But although the subject may relinquish the wish to control or devour the other completely, it does so unwillingly, with a persistent if unconscious wish to fulfill the old omnipotence fantasy. This is a far cry from a real appreciation of the other's existence as a person. The truth in this view of the self seems to be that acknowledging dependency is painful, and that denying recognition to others because of this pain leads to domination . . . predicated on the denial of the other person's independent subjectivity and autonomy . . . It makes the other person an object but retains possession of her. (Pp. 284–85)

Morgan observes that Emma "really sees herself as a director and the other people around her as extensions of her will"; her relationships with the other women in the novel—Miss Taylor, Harriet Smith, and Jane Fairfax—are all shaped by the underlying desire for control and domination. When combined with her passionate and obsessive responses to and interest in each of the women, particularly in their individual sexual relationships, a picture of Emma Woodhouse's own sexual identity begins to form.

Emma's erotic predilection for members of her own sex can be traced throughout the novel and in each of the relationships she has with other women, and it is in these relationships that the underlying dynamics of erotic domination are most in evidence. Emma clearly has identified with the dominant role in the "self-other relationship," a role that Benjamin suggests is usually occupied by the male, while both Miss Taylor and Harriet Smith can be seen to occupy the corresponding submissive role, the "traditionally female side of selfhood" with its characteristics of "dependency, connectedness, [and] yielding" (p. 294). Emma's experience of the failure of differentiation, "the core experience underlying erotic domination," while different from "the male experience of differentiation," has in common with it several important factors. During the formation of male gender identity, the male child repudiates the mother once it is discovered that he "cannot be, or become, her":

> The repudiation of the mother . . . has meant that she is not recognized by the child in the normal course of differentiation. She is not seen as an independent person, another subject, but as something other . . . as an instrument or object, as less-than-human. An objectifying attitude comes to replace the earlier interactions of infancy.

It is the male experience of differentiation that Benjamin links to the tendency to assert control, to make "the other an object and instrument of one's own will" (p. 293)—to subject her to erotic domination. Yet Emma Woodhouse's early childhood experience of the Other, the self-obliterating maternal figure, is one that has placed her in a peculiarly similar position: she also desires the submission of the other, and the mastery that comes with erotic domination. Benjamin points out that the submissive position is generally associated with the female and the dominant with the male and that the basis for this division is found in the mother's "lack of subjectivity for her children." However, the fact that "actual men and women often play the opposite role does not contradict this association. It affirms rather that erotic transgression is an opportunity to express what is ordinarily denied" (p. 294). And, as LeRoy Smith notes, Emma's development appears to be further complicated by her

> identification with the position or role of a model that represents a fantasised projection into the situation and behaviour of the model. The model attracts emulation

because of his or her role or status ... Emma's most influential model is a male figure, Knightley, whose position and role she comes to wish for herself.

Throughout the novel, there are many references to Emma's being identified in a distinctly "male" position, often by other characters. During a discussion about Mrs. Weston's marriage, John Knightley suggests that "'You and I, Emma, will venture to take the part of the poor husband ... the claims of the man may very likely strike us with equal force,'" At times, Emma herself seems to speak from a "male" point-of-view, as when she asserts "'I know that such a girl as Harriet is exactly what every man delights in—what at once bewitches his senses and satisfies his judgment'" (p. 64); she later passionately defends the absent Frank Churchill to Mr. Knightley, saying "I wish you would try to understand what an amiable young man may be likely to feel in directly opposing those, whom as child and boy he has been looking up to all his life'" (p. 148), a statement that reflects her own position in her adversarial relationship with Mr. Knightley. But it is in her dealings with Harriet where Emma's behavior seems most "male." Emma considers Harriet "a valuable addition to her privileges," and is "quite convinced of Harriet Smith's being ... exactly the something which her home required" (p. 26), sentiments reminiscent of a traditionally proprietorial male attitude and more appropriate to a successful young man deciding the time is right to acquire a wife. Emma, in fact, manages to "win" Harriet away from a male rival. When she comes to realize that Robert Martin poses a serious threat to her relationship with Harriet, her amused tolerance of Harriet's connection to the Martin family changes, and "other feelings arose" (p. 27). Emma coolly manipulates the girl into re-evaluating Martin's desirability, and although she encourages her to compare the "very clownish" (p. 32) manners of the young farmer to those of Mr. Knightley, Mr. Weston, and Mr. Elton, it is obvious that it is Emma, and not any of Harriet's more lofty male acquaintances, whom Martin is being matched against. Later, when Martin has proposed, Emma successfully brings about Harriet's refusal of him:

> "You must be the best judge of your own happiness. If you prefer Mr. Martin to every other person; if you think him the most agreeable man you have ever been in company with, why should you hesitate? You blush, Harriet.—Does any body else occur to you at this moment under such a definition? Harriet, Harriet, do not deceive yourself ... At this moment whom are you thinking of?"

> The symptoms were favourable.—Instead of answering, Harriet turned away confused, and stood

thoughtfully by the fire ... Emma waited the result with impatience, but not without strong hopes. (p. 53)

Emma makes it very clear to Harriet in the ensuing conversation that her acceptance of Martin would have precluded further intimacy: "'I must have given you up.'" The choice Harriet makes is between intimacy with herself, or marriage to Martin-and, in this instance, Emma, not Robert Martin, "gets the girl."

Moreover, Emma seems to be impervious to the idea of being attractive/attracted to members of the opposite sex. She is at first amused at the idea of Mr. Elton as a possible suitor: "'Me!' she replied with a smile of astonishment, 'are you imagining me to be Mr. Elton's object? ... What an idea!'" While it is true that Emma's incredulity is based as much on her specious desire for Elton to love Harriet, and her belief that his social inferiority precludes his aiming as high as herself, it is odd that someone of her physical beauty and accomplishments should never even consider herself a potential object of male sexual attraction. In projecting her own feelings about Harriet onto the various men of their acquaintance, she instead repeatedly imagines Harriet as such an object, despite the fact that, except for Robert Martin and Emma herself, no one in the novel evinces any sexual interest in a girl described as merely "'pretty, and ... good tempered, and that is all.'"

Other characters in the novel notice Emma's curious sexual inaccessibility: Frank Churchill, despite the flirtation he indulges in with Emma, admits that "'Amiable and delightful as Miss Woodhouse is, she never gave me the idea of a young woman likely to be attached.'" Her relationship with Frank is one which elicits nothing but the most superficial response from Emma, and begins, in her head, before she has even met him. It is the idea of Frank, rather than the flesh-and-blood reality, which appeals to her. Significantly, she is said to have "frequently thought-especially since his father's marriage with Miss Taylor—that if she were to marry, he was the very person to suit her." She convinces herself that she "'must be in love; I should be the oddest creature in the world if I were not—for a few weeks at least'"; but she is content "'not [to] persuade myself to feel more than I do. I am quite enough in love. I should be sorry to be more.'" Her ultimate desire regarding Frank and "the progress and close of their attachment" is that "she refused him. Their affection was always to subside into friendship ... they were to part." When she later confesses to Mr. Knightley that there was really nothing to the relationship with

Frank, she says that, "'in short, I was somehow or other safe from him,'" the implication being that it is her unrecognized love for Mr. Knightley that has rendered her "safe" from Frank's charms. However, there is little evidence in the novel to suggest that Emma feels any genuine sexual interest in anyone of the opposite sex. In speaking to Harriet of the possibility of falling in love with a man, she states that it will have to be "'somebody very superior to any one I have seen yet, to be tempted . . . I would rather not be tempted. I cannot really change for the better.'" Yet she has "seen" Mr. Knightley all of her life, and she is only "tempted" when her other options have been exhausted.

Emma exercises these other options through her involvements with members of her own sex, in her attempts to establish a form of erotic mastery. In a relationship of erotic domination, "[o]ne person maintains . . . her boundary, and one allows her . . . boundary to be broken"—this seems an accurate description of the sort of dynamic that Emma strives to establish in her relationships with other women. For the most part, she achieves mastery through manipulation, as when she subtly maneuvers the gullible Harriet into spurning Robert Martin's offer of marriage. However, at times she resorts to more overt methods, as when she joins with Frank in humiliating Jane at Hartfield, in an attempt to punish her for her reserve. From the outset of the novel, it is clear that there is a pattern to Emma's choice of female company: she is attracted to women who, like Miss Taylor, possess a "mildness of . . . temper," who defer to Emma's will, and who are "peculiarly interested in herself, in every pleasure, every scheme of hers." These qualities are even more exaggerated in Harriet Smith, described as a "humble, grateful, little girl" whom Emma can mold:

> She would notice her; she would improve her: she would detach her from her bad acquaintance, and introduce her into good society; she would form her opinions and her manners. It would be an interesting, and certainly a very kind undertaking; highly becoming her own situation in life, her leisure, and powers.

One is reminded of Mr. Weston's satisfaction in "its being a great deal better to chuse than to be chosen, to excite gratitude than to feel it" in his own choice of a sexual partner. Miss Taylor's friendship with Emma has consisted of "submitting [her] own will, and doing as [she was] bid"; Harriet comes to "understand the force of influence" as wielded by Emma, whose resolution of "driving . . . out of Harriet's head" any desire or attachment Harriet might feel towards anyone Emma deems

unsuitable seems to her perfectly within her rights. Patricia Meyer Spacks, in "Female Changelessness; Or What Do Women Want?," states: "What do women want? Ideal women want whatever men want them to want." In considering Emma's relationship with Harriet, we could ask: "What does a woman chosen by Emma Woodhouse want? Whatever Emma wants her to want." Accordingly, Emma seems most to love Harriet when she is most effusively humble and compliant:

> "You, who have been the best friend I ever had in my life!—Want gratitude to you!—Nobody is equal to you!—I care for nobody as I do for you!—Oh! Miss Woodhouse, how ungrateful I have been!"

> Such expressions, assisted as they were by every thing that look and manner could do, made Emma feel that she had never loved Harriet so well, nor valued her affection so highly before.

It is significant that Harriet seems to value her relationship with Emma far more than she values a romantic union with Robert Martin. When Emma reveals to her that such a union would have destroyed the possibility of any further intercourse between them, Harriet is "aghast"; she "had not surmised her own danger, but the idea of it struck her forcibly . . . 'What an escape! Dear Miss Woodhouse, I would not give up the pleasure and honour of being intimate with you for anything in the world . . . It would have killed me.'" Interestingly, in keeping with the underlying sexual dynamic that pervades the novel, Harriet's willingness to defer to Emma in all things, to place her in the position of prominence usually occupied by the male suitor or husband, ends when Harriet believes herself beloved by someone whom she perceives as more powerful than Emma—Mr. Knightley.

Emma's attachments to her particular female friends are passionate and somewhat obsessive. Miss Taylor's absence "would be felt every hour of every day," and Emma wonders how she will be able "to bear the change?—It was true that her friend was going only half a mile from them; but Emma was aware that great must be the difference between a Mrs. Weston only half a mile from them, and a Miss Taylor in the house." Certainly Miss Taylor's marriage, despite Emma's self-congratulatory claim of having made the match herself, is an impediment to Emma's desire for dominance, since, as Mrs. Weston, she is no longer subject to Emma's control. Emma must needs find a replacement for Miss Taylor—this will prove to be a pattern in her erotic fixations. As the focus shifts from her feelings of loss at Miss Taylor's marriage to Mr. Weston, to her growing interest in Harriet Smith, the language

Austen employs seems to become increasingly sexual. The relationship that Emma had shared with Miss Taylor is described as that of "friend and friend very mutually attached." It is replaced with something that is described much more overtly in terms that traditionally evoke the romantic heterosexual relationship. Emma's initial interest in Harriet is a very physical one: "Miss Smith was a girl of seventeen whom Emma ... had long felt an interest in, on account of her beauty"; "She was a very pretty girl, and her beauty happened to be of a sort which Emma particularly admired"; on several occasions, we not only find Emma "busy in admiring those soft blue eyes" of her favorite's, but assuring Harriet that her "'soft eyes shall chuse their own time for beaming'" if Harriet will but "'Trust to me.'" A particularly charged scene between the two women occurs after Emma has "decoded" Mr. Elton's riddle:

> "Dear Miss Woodhouse"—and "Dear Miss Woodhouse," was all that Harriet, with many tender embraces could articulate at first; but when they did arrive at something more like conversation, it was sufficiently clear to her friend that she saw, felt, anticipated, and remembered just as she ought.

Significantly, Austen's language here anticipates that used in the romantic declaration scene between Emma and Mr. Knightley, where it is Emma who ultimately finds herself saying and doing "[j]ust what she ought." After all, a lady—a heterosexual lady, that is—always does.

Emma's feelings about Harriet become increasingly possessive; her remarks concerning Harriet are indicative of the way in which she views the younger woman in relation to herself: "The business was finished, and Harriet safe"; "'Now I am secure of you for ever'"; "'We will not be parted. A woman is not to marry a man merely because she is asked.'" Consequently, Emma's desire for Harriet to attach herself to Mr. Elton, although an alliance that would "'confirm our intimacy forever,'" is somewhat questionable. On the one hand, since Emma cannot actually "have" Harriet herself, the power to decide who does in some measure satisfies her unexpressed sexual desire. As well, Harriet's connection to someone whom Emma will be able to interact with socially will ensure Harriet's continued accessibility. (We must wonder, however, how Harriet, as Mrs. Elton, and therefore mistress of her own household, would be any more accessible to Emma in the way she seems to need her to be than Mrs. Weston.) On the other hand, her manipulation of Harriet's sexual focus takes her away from the one man who really does want her, and encourages her to fantasize about belonging to men who do not, and who, in reality, present no threat to Emma's proprietorship. Once Emma has successfully manipulated Harriet into refusing Mr. Martin's proposal of marriage, we learn that Harriet "slept at Hartfield that night," something that occurs with increasing frequency as Emma's influence over her grows.

Not surprisingly, it is Jane Fairfax's lack of Harriet-like humility, her "coldness and reserve," her "indifference whether she pleased or not," which frustrates Emma and creates in her what seems to be a strong repulsion to Jane that lasts until almost the end of the novel. Emma, in her enthusiasm over Harriet's "tenderness of heart" and evaluation of her desirability as a wife, is driven to make unflattering comparisons to Jane: "'Dear Harriet!—I would not change you for the clearest-headed, longest-sighted, best-judging female breathing. Oh! the coldness of a Jane Fairfax!—Harriet is worth a hundred such.—And for a wife—.'" Austen continually emphasizes Emma's resentment over Jane's determination "to hazard nothing," and her feeling that she "was disgustingly, was suspiciously reserved." It is this reserve for which "Emma could not forgive her," a sentence that ends Volume 2, Chapter 2, and that is insistently reiterated at the beginning of Volume 2, Chapter 3. Susan Morgan observes that "Jane, to Emma's outrage, thinks for herself and feels for herself and so controls herself. She does not hand her character over to Emma"; more tellingly, Elizabeth Jean Sabiston states that "Jane Fairfax ... resists all of Emma's efforts to probe her." Jane will not allow Emma to violate her boundaries, and so prevents her from establishing the dominant/submissive dynamic upon which her other relationships are built: "A distinctive quality about Jane is that she is not part of Emma's domain ... primarily because Jane has an independent sense of self which Emma cannot absorb." As a result, her resentment leads Emma to some very adamant disclaimers about any attraction to Jane Fairfax: "'I must be more in want of a friend, or an agreeable companion, than I have yet been, to take the trouble of conquering anybody's reserve to procure one. Intimacy between Miss Fairfax and me is quite out of the question.'" Yet Emma seems to be more than aware of Jane's attractiveness and desirability. Whereas Emma initially thinks of Harriet as "a girl who wanted only a little more knowledge and elegance to be quite perfect," her first impression of Jane after her two year absence is that she is "very elegant, remarkably elegant; and she had herself the highest value for elegance"—she has, in fact, the sort of "elegance, which, whether of person or of mind, she saw so little in Highbury." She recognizes in Jane both "distinction, and merit"; in short, Jane possesses in abundance the qualities that Emma feels would make Harriet "quite perfect." And, despite Emma's declared antipathy towards Jane, she finds her "'the sort of elegant creature that one cannot keep one's eyes from'" and is "'always watching her to admire.'"

Jane's apparent inviolability leads Emma to try and punish her, to force her into the subordinate role she so desperately needs her to occupy in order for Emma to maintain her sense of erotic mastery. She does this through Frank Churchill. Ironically, although Emma cannot know that Frank is Jane's lover, she singles him out as a sort of ally in her attempt to denigrate Jane. Frank and Emma are thus joined in a somewhat bizarre dyad as Jane's persecutors: simultaneously, each occupies the position of rival inamoratos, unbeknown to the other, and, in Emma's case, to herself. It is through their social unity that they manage to inflict the most torment upon Jane, exemplified in their behavior during the word game, when Frank teases Jane with the word "Dixon." Emma reacts with "eager laughing warmth"; Jane "blushed more deeply than [Mr. Knightley] had ever perceived her" the scene is highly charged—with erotic tension? Clearly the prospect of Jane's discomfort and pain affords Emma an exquisite thrill. Emma is complacent in her belief that Frank "perfectly agreed" with her evaluation of Jane and is confident that their feelings are "much alike." The "alikeness" of their feelings lies deeper than Emma is willing to acknowledge. At their second encounter, "Emma felt herself so well acquainted with him, that she could hardly believe it to be only their second meeting"— yet the bond she feels they are developing seems for the most part based on their various conversations concerning Jane Fairfax. In fact, all of their subsequent intercourse revolves around Jane, much of it initiated by Emma, who constantly pumps Frank for details about Jane's behaviour at Weymouth. Despite the fact that outward appearances lead others to suspect that Emma and Frank are interested in each other, for each of them the focus is most decisively Jane Fairfax-her situation, her supposed feelings for Mr. Dixon, her reserve, her musical skills, her complexion—as their common passion, she is endlessly fascinating to them both.

In fact, it is Jane whom Emma most desires, whose recognition she most craves. It is through Jane Fairfax that the possibility of a reciprocal relationship based on an equal and mutual giving of self is presented. Benjamin suggests that the underlying motivation of the dynamic of erotic domination may be the individual's hope of replaying "the original thwarted impulse to discover the other person as an intact being who could respond and set limits at the same time," but that "the original need for a relationship of differentiation with another person is not really solved in erotic domination . . . The aliveness and spontaneity that come from an unscripted relationship is missing." However, Emma continues to resist the sort of intimacy she might find through a relationship with someone like Jane Fairfax, someone who is her equal; Morgan notes that "Emma . . . does not want friendship with a real and independent person. She prefers the indulgence of manipulating Harriet." Yet Emma's passionate attachment to Harriet begins to wane, and she eventually grows tired of her "delightful inferiority"; Harriet begins to figure less and less in Emma's musings, Jane Fairfax more and more. Benjamin explains that the "exhaustion of satisfaction that occurs when all resistance is vanquished, all tension is lost, means that the relationship has come full circle, returned to the emptiness from which it was an effort to escape." As we observe Harriet kiss Emma's hand "in silent and submissive gratitude" for her latest attempt to direct Harriet's sexual interest and "save her from the danger of degradation," it has already become apparent that the focus has shifted quite decisively to Jane Fairfax and to Emma's complex relationship with her.

Susan Morgan suggests that Emma eventually "learns to recognize the presumptuousness of her games, to accept her limits and the inviolability of others" (p. 46), largely as a result of her relations with Jane Fairfax. I would argue that, on the contrary, Emma continues to resist the idea of a relationship based on mutuality until the end of the novel. Her feelings for Jane Fairfax, long denied and twisted into repugnance, are allowed to surface only when she perceives Jane in a powerless and vulnerable state—the desire for mastery informs all of her dealings with Jane. During their first visit, Emma is filled with "complacency" and a "sense of pleasure" over her resolve to be kind:

> When she took in her history, indeed, her situation, as well as her beauty; when she considered what all this elegance was destined to, what she was going to sink from, how she was going to live . . . Emma left her with such softened, charitable feelings, as made her . . . lament that Highbury afforded no young man worthy of giving her independence; nobody that she could wish to scheme about for her.

Emma is reassured by Jane's powerlessness; indeed, she seems to dwell with some lingering pleasure on the idea of Jane's coming degradation. Once again,

Emma's desire to exercise erotic power is manifested in her deliberation over another's sexual fate—and the possibility that she herself might somehow direct it. Emma has previously devoted a great deal of time and thought to Jane's possible sexual relationship with Mr. Dixon; her fixation on this imaginary situation has, in fact, caused her to behave in ways of which she is later ashamed. It is also interesting that Emma should be unable to come up with a "worthy" heterosexual prospect for Jane, considering that she seems to have no trouble when exerting herself on behalf of anyone else. In fact, she expends a great deal of energy in denying the possibility of any such connection for Jane, save for the non-existent romance she creates around Mr. Dixon and the pianoforte. Her reaction to Mrs. Weston's suggestion that there may be something between Jane and Mr. Knightley is one of horror and repudiation: "'Jane Fairfax . . . of all women! . . . Jane Fairfax mistress of the Abbey!—Oh! no, no;—every feeling revolts.'" Similarly, her response to Mr. Knightley's suggestion that she does not "'perfectly understand the degree of acquaintance'" between Jane and Frank Churchill is to protest in hyperbolic, almost manic terms: "'Never, never! . . . Never for the twentieth part of a moment, did such an idea occur to me . . . There is no admiration between them, I do assure you . . . they are as far from any attachment or admiration for one another, as any two beings in the world can be." Since we know that Emma has no real feelings for Frank, her response would be distinctly out of proportion, unless we assume that it is the thought of Jane's attachment that so upsets her. It is obvious that Emma's attraction to Jane becomes more overt as Jane's situation seems to deteriorate. Emma decides, after Jane leaves Donwell in great agitation, that she does, in fact, pity her and her prospects, and that "'the more sensibility you betray of their just horrors, the more I shall like you.'"

Emma's feelings for Jane have been undergoing a change throughout the latter part of the novel; as Jane's autonomy becomes increasingly threatened, Emma's desire for her increases. Once it becomes clear that Jane can no longer avoid the grim necessity of the "governess-trade," and that her departure from Highbury is immanent, her state of pitiable vulnerability is reassuringly confirmed for Emma. It is at this point that Emma desires to "win" her: "the person, whom she had been so many months neglecting, was now the very one on whom she would have lavished every distinction of regard or sympathy." Her interest in Harriet having abated, Emma's behavior to Jane becomes almost obsessive—however, her attempts to visit with and show favor towards the other woman are consistently rebuffed: "It was a more pressing concern to show attention to Jane Fairfax, whose prospects were closing, while Harriet's opened . . . with Emma it was grown into a first wish . . . She wanted to be of use to her; wanted to show a value for her society, and testify respect and consideration." Susan Morgan characterizes Jane as "the measure of what Emma loses" (p. 42); and Emma herself comes to realize what she has missed:

> She bitterly regretted not having sought a closer acquaintance with her . . . had she endeavoured to find a friend there instead of in Harriet Smith; she must, in all probability, have been spared from every pain which pressed on her now.—Birth, abilities and education, had been equally marking one as an associate for her, to be received with gratitude; and the other—what was she?

Unfortunately, Emma's inability to answer this question—to comprehend the inviolability of the other's selfhood (whether that of Harriet or Jane) constitutes her real loss.

Significantly, Emma's realization that "Mr. Knightley must marry no one but herself" directly follows the scene in which she is informed of Jane's elopement with Frank, and Emma feels "most sorrowfully indignant: ashamed of every sensation but the one revealed to her—her affection for Mr. Knightley.—Every other part of her mind was disgusting." D. A. Miller, in his article "Emma: Good Riddance," discusses the way in which Emma is able to block out any previous erotic attachment (his example being that of Frank Churchill) by simply deciding that she "has always loved Mr. Knightley, but simply never knew it; she has never loved Frank Churchill, but only imagined she did." Miller sees this as a "self-revision":

> It would seem as though the psychology of being "really" in love required such retraction to help sustain itself. "This time, it's the real thing": but the reality of the real thing is in part produced by treating previous erotic interest as unreal: inauthentic, delusional, even (as here) non-existent.

> In the proposal scene, this closure of desire becomes institutionalised. Desire has recognised its "proper object" and made itself capable of fixing on it; this recognition can now be incarnated socially, in marriage. (p. 73)

Indeed, Emma has undergone a "self-revision": but the "previous erotic interest" she repudiates is the one she feels for Jane Fairfax. Jane has proven to be an "object" who refuses to engage in the dynamics of erotic domination, and who is leaving her sphere of influence completely, through heterosexual union with Frank Churchill and her removal from Highbury. Emma, who has evinced no previous sexual interest in Knightley, is able to convince herself that he has always been her object of sexual desire, and, what is more, that all erotic interest previous to this is a cause for sorrowful indignation, shame, and disgust. Miller states that "the assumptions under which erotic desire is locked into place . . . [are] in holy matrimony and wholly in matrimony" (p. 73).

Once Jane and Frank have run away together, Emma is forced to deal with what remains to her in the world of Highbury. Harriet's revelation that she is in love with Mr. Knightley and has hopes of reciprocation on his part brings home to Emma the realization that the very fabric of this world, with her at its center, is unraveling:

> Till now that she was threatened with its loss, Emma had never known how much of her happiness depended on being first with Mr. Knightley, first in interest and affection—Satisfied that it was so, and feeling it her due, she had enjoyed it without reflection; and only in the dread of being supplanted, found how inexpressibly important it had been.

This passage is reminiscent of Emma's sentiments about her place in her father's affections: "'never, never could I expect to be so truly beloved and important; so always first and always right in any man's eyes as I am in my father's'" and she feels that "Could she be secure of . . . [Mr. Knightley's] never marrying at all, she believed she should be perfectly satisfied." Thus, Emma cannot bear for Mr. Knightley "to be lost to them for Harriet's sake . . . to be thought of hereafter, as finding in Harriet's society all that he wanted" or for Harriet "to be the chosen, the first, the dearest, the friend, the wife to whom he looked for all the best blessings of existence." When Mr. Knightley does declare his feelings for her, her first thought is "that Harriet was nothing; that she was every thing herself" (emphasis mine); later, when the new alliance between them is established, she congratulates herself on her good fortune in obtaining. "Such a companion for herself in the periods of anxiety and cheerlessness before her!—Such a partner in all those duties and cares to which time must be giving increase of melancholy!" Her "love" for Mr. Knightley seems based on a combination of her desire for ascendancy over Harriet or anyone else in his affections, and her fear of Hartfield's being "comparatively deserted; and she left to cheer her father with the spirits only of ruined happiness." Claudia Johnson observes that the

> "resources"—beauty, wit, employment, money— which Emma thinks can preserve her from sharing Miss Bates's ignominious destiny as a poor old maid finally amount to very little. It is single womanhood

itself, the lack of a circle of people to be "first" with, that turns out to be the evil.

Ironically, the "reconciliation scene" between Mr. Knightley and Emma is yet another manifestation of the dynamic of erotic domination permeating the relations among the characters. Mr. Knightley and Emma have been engaged in a power struggle throughout most of the novel, yet Emma's attitude towards him is generally marked by complacency (save for those instances when she feels deservedly rebuked by him for meanness or bad manners). Having no sexual investment in her relationship with Mr. Knightley, she is able to dismiss his attempts to subjugate her quite easily. While she does "not always feel so absolutely satisfied with herself, so entirely convinced that her opinions were right and her adversary's wrong," she is not so affected by their clashes "that a little time and the return of Harriet were very adequate restoratives." But here, in the reconciliation scene, Emma is finally subdued, "overpowered," in fact, by Mr. Knightley. For the first time, she responds from a position of diminished power—in short, from the "female" position: "What did she say?—Just what she ought, of course. A lady always does." Suffering from "wretchedness," from "loneliness, and . . . melancholy," with a "prospect before her . . . threatening to a degree that could not be entirely dispelled—that might not be even partially brightened," Emma is frightened, vulnerable, and humbled, and she is vanquished by a force more powerful than her own will—Mr. Knightley's declaration of desire, and the comfort and safety to be found in heterosexual union. However, Austen reserves the truly charged and sexually ambiguous moments for the reconciliation between Emma and Jane Fairfax. Emma visits Jane upon her return; she is "longing to see her," and finds that she "had never seen her look so well, so lovely, so engaging." They are unable to exchange confidences in the presence of Mrs. Elton, and Emma, in the few moments they have alone together, tells her that "'Had you not been surrounded by other friends, I might have been tempted to introduce a subject, to ask questions, to speak more openly than might have been strictly correct. I feel that I should certainly have been impertinent.'" Ostensibly she is referring, of course, to Frank Churchill. The two share an emotional exchange: Jane, "with a blush and an hesitation which Emma thought infinitely more becoming to her than all the elegance of all her usual composure," expresses her gratitude to Emma for her interest and forbearance. She chastises herself for her former behavior: "'I know what my manners were to you.—So cold and artificial!—I had always a part to act.—It was a life of deceit! I know that I must have disgusted you.'" Strong words. The encounter ends with Emma's realization that "'we are to lose you—just as I begin to know you.'"

As the novel ends, all of the principals have been matched up with someone of the opposite sex and married off. Heterosexual order is reaffirmed, and everyone is happy. Yet are they? I have attempted to demonstrate that Emma's sexual interest lies, not in Mr. Knightley, or in any of the other men in the novel, but rather in other women. The novel's ending, then, presents a denial of her sexuality. Furthermore, Emma's sexual identity has been formed in a world where the "the question of power affects who and how you eroticize your sexual need"—that is, a patriarchal world. Consequently, as I have suggested, "the question of power . . . is absolutely on the bottom of all sexual inquiry." And, in fact, Emma's sexuality seems to be all about power, expressed through her desire for mastery, for domination, for manipulation. Thus, Emma is subject to a "double whammy," as it were: her erotic predilection for women cannot be openly expressed, and her identification with the "male" role in her most intimate connections with the women she desires renders what is expressed unequal, unhealthy, and ultimately unsatisfying. The only alternative model available to her, which she is forced to embrace at the end of the novel, is no better: Emma must learn to play woman and wife, to submit in her turn.

Source: Susan M. Korba, "'Improper and Dangerous Distinctions': Female Relationships and Erotic Domination in *Emma*," in *Studies in the Novel*, Vol. 29, No. 2, Summer 1997, pp. 139–63.

Sources

Austen, Jane, *Emma*, edited by James Kinsley and David Lodge, Oxford University Press, 1971.

Austen-Leigh, James Edward, *A Memoir of Jane Austen and Other Family Recollections*, edited by Kathryn Sutherland, Oxford University Press, 2002.

Ferguson, Frances, "Jane Austen, *Emma*, and the Impact of Form," in *Modern Language Quarterly*, Vol. 61, No. 1, March 2000, pp. 157–80.

Finch, Casey, and Peter Bowen, "'The Tittle-Tattle of Highbury': Gossip and Free Indirect Style in *Emma*," in *Representations*, Vol. 31, Summer 1990; quoted in Ferguson, Frances, "Jane Austen, *Emma*, and the Impact of Form," in *Modern Language Quarterly*, Vol. 61, No. 1, March 2000, pp. 161–62.

Lynch, Deidre, ed., *Janeites: Austen's Disciples and Devotees*, Princeton University Press, 2000, pp. 25–44, 87–114.

Melani, Lilia, "Discussion of *Emma*," Jane Austen Web page, http://academic.brooklyn.cuny.edu/english/melani/novel_19c/austen/ (accessed December 3, 2004).

Minma, Shinobu, "Self-Deception and Superiority Complex: Derangement of Hierarchy in Jane Austen's *Emma*," in *Eighteenth-Century Fiction*, Vol. 14, No. 1, October 2001, pp. 49–65.

Scott, Sir Walter, Review of *Emma*, in "Reader Response to Austen's Novels," Jane Austen Web page, http://academic.brooklyn.cuny.edu/english/melani/novel_19c/austen/ (accessed December 3, 2004); originally published in *Quarterly Review*, March 1816.

Shaw, Harry, *Concise Dictionary of Literary Terms*, McGraw-Hill, 1972.

Tillotson, Geoffrey, Paul Fussell Jr., and Marshall Waingrow, eds., *Eighteenth-Century English Literature*, Harcourt Brace Jovanovich, 1969, pp. 1–10.

Wollstonecraft, Mary, *A Vindication of the Rights of Woman: An Authoritative Text; Backgrounds; The Wollstonecraft Debate; Criticism*, 2d ed., edited by Carol Poston, Norton, 1988, pp. 1–20.

Further Reading

Austen-Leigh, James Edward, *A Memoir of Jane Austen and Other Family Recollections*, edited by Kathryn Sutherland, Oxford University Press, 2002.

> The memoir written by Austen's nephew James Edward was first published in 1870 and offers the one existing source of family memories about Jane Austen, mostly the recollections, biographical notes, and vivid personal accounts of devoted nieces and nephews.

Copeland, Edward, and Juliet McMaster, eds., *The Cambridge Companion to Jane Austen*, Cambridge University Press, 1997.

> This book is a comprehensive guide to Jane Austen and her work in the context of the times in which she lived. The book includes a discussion of her works and chapters on economics, politics, religion, social class, and literary traditions.

Lynch, Deidre, ed., *Janeites: Austen's Disciples and Devotees*, Princeton University Press, 2000.

> This collection of essays produced since Austen's lifetime demonstrates how wide is the range of interpretations and reader response to her works. It also explores adaptations, reviews, and general reasons for her popularity.

Tomalin, Claire, *Jane Austen: A Life*, Vintage Books, 1997.

> This is a lively and accessible account of the flesh and blood Jane Austen as told mainly from the perspective of family and friends and the many fascinating people she knew.

The French Lieutenant's Woman

John Fowles
1969

One morning, in 1966, at his home on the outskirts of Lyme Regis, John Fowles awoke with a vision of an enigmatic, solitary woman, standing on the Cobb, staring off into the distant sea, a woman who clearly belonged to the past. In an article for *Harper's Magazine*, he writes, "The woman obstinately refused to stare out of the window of an airport lounge; it had to be this ancient quay." The image of the woman haunted him. He notes that she had "no face, no particular degree of sexuality. But she was Victorian." In his vision, she always had her back turned, which to him, represented "a reproach on the Victorian Age. An outcast." He claims, "I didn't know her crime, but I wished to protect her. That is, I began to fall in love with her. Or with her stance. I didn't know which." This mysterious woman would become the inspiration for Fowles's third novel, *The French Lieutenant's Woman* (Boston, Toronto, 1969), an international popular and critical success and the most highly acclaimed work from this prolific author.

The story traces the relationship between a woman, caught between the Victorian and modern ages, and a man drawn to her independent spirit. Charles Smithson, a young English gentleman, becomes fascinated with Sarah Woodruff, a social outcast in the coastal town of Lyme Regis, who is known as "Tragedy," or in a more pejorative sense as "the French lieutenant's woman." Rumors suggest that she gazes continually at the sea, waiting for the sailor who seduced her to return. Charles eventually risks his own social ostracism when he

John Fowles

breaks off his engagement to a perfectly respectable young woman to pursue Sarah. Readers are never given a definite conclusion to the story as they are left to choose among three possible endings.

Fowles's innovative narrative technique, which allows readers to become an active part in the creation of his novel, provides the framework for a fascinating story of passion, the constraints of class, and the struggle for freedom.

Author Biography

John Fowles was born on March 31, 1926, in a suburb of London. Ellen Pifer notes that Fowles characterized his hometown as "dominated by conformism—the pursuit of respectability." His early opposition to conformity would grow into a strong sense of individuality, a subject that emerges in many of his works. He attended Bedford School in London where he admits, he became adept at wearing masks. Pifer writes that Fowles insists the English "very rarely say what they actually think. That could derive from Puritanism—hiding emotions and wearing a public mask." Fowles concludes, "I suffer from it like everyone of my type and background. I've played the game all my life." Pifer argues that

this theme emerges in his fiction as his characters "share their author's facility with masks, and their success at masking their real feelings often proves a hindrance to their internal development."

World War II was raging while Fowles was attending Bedford. He took time off to follow his family to the Devon countryside during the blitz, where he developed a love of nature. Upon graduation, he served as a lieutenant in the Royal Marines. When the war ended, he began studies at Oxford, where he was heavily influenced by the existentialist authors Albert Camus and Jean-Paul Sartre, a subject that would also emerge in his works.

After Oxford, Fowles taught English in Europe and began to write. A few years later, he returned to England where he continued to teach and to work on a draft of *The Magnus*. His first published novel, however, was the popular and critically acclaimed *The Collector* (1963), which enabled him to retire from teaching and devote himself to writing.

After he and his wife moved to Lyme Regis in 1968, he enjoyed continued success as a novelist, especially after the publication of his third novel, *The French Lieutenant's Woman* in 1969. His writing career ended in 1988 after he suffered a stroke. *The French Lieutenant's Woman* earned Fowles the Silver Pen Award, presented by the International Association of Poets, Playwrights, Editors, Essayists, and Novelists, and the W. H. Smith and Son Literary Award in 1970. In September 1981, a celebrated film version of the novel was produced.

Plot Summary

Chapters 1–33

The narrator opens the *The French Lieutenant's Woman* with background information on Lyme Regis, where the story is initially set. He then introduces Charles Smithson, a thirty-two-year-old gentleman and his young fiancee, Ernestina Freeman, who are taking a walk along the Cobb, made famous by Jane Austen in her novel *Persuasion*. The action begins in 1867, but the narrator often breaks into the narrative, noting that the story is being related in the twentieth century. He does this initially by comparing the Cobb to a contemporary Henry Moore sculpture.

Charles and Tina's walk is interrupted by the presence of a woman in a dark cape, standing alone at the end of the Cobb, staring out to sea. Tina explains to a curious Charles what she has heard about the woman, known as "Tragedy" and "the French lieutenant's woman," and her status as a social outcast. Rumors suggest that Sarah Woodruff was seduced and abandoned by a French naval officer who was shipwrecked off the coast. As she nursed him back to health, he reportedly made promises to her that he did not fulfil. Destitute and rejected by most of the Lyme Regis society, Sarah is taken in by the pious Mrs. Poulteney, who plans to "save" the young woman in order to assure her own status as a worthy Christian.

The next day, Charles, whose hobby is paleontology, walks through the Undercliff searching for fossils while Tina visits her Aunt Tranter. The narrator introduces Sam, Charles's servant, who has his eye on Mary, Aunt Tranter's maid. During his walk, Charles comes across Sarah sleeping in a clearing. She awakens with a start, and, after apologizing for disturbing her, Charles departs.

The narrator notes Charles's growing obsession with the mysterious Sarah. After stopping at a farmhouse to refresh himself, Charles again sees Sarah on the path. She rejects his offer to escort her home and implores him to tell no one that she has been walking there, an activity that Mrs. Poulteney has forbidden her. The next day, during a visit to Mrs. Poulteney's, Sarah silently observes Charles and Aunt Tranter's support of the relationship between Sam and Mary. Charles assumes that he has made a connection with Sarah, but the next time their paths cross on the Undercliff, she rebuffs his efforts to help her escape Mrs. Poulteney's control. When she insists that she cannot leave the area, Charles assumes that her feelings for the French lieutenant are the cause. After she admits that the lieutenant has married, her mystery deepens for Charles.

Charles's curiosity concerning Sarah causes him to think about the comparatively one-dimensional Tina and his own needs and desires. During another walk, Sarah finds him, presents him with two fossils, and begs him to hear her story. After determining that listening to Sarah would be a kind act and a useful study of human nature, Charles agrees to meet with her. Sarah admits that Lieutenant Varguennes proposed marriage and seduced her, even though she knew he was not an honorable man. The shame that she has embraced as a result has enabled her to separate herself from a society that would not accept her, due to her common birth. Her education had awakened her to the inequities of social class and gender, and thus her status as an outcast prevents her from having to conform to conventional roles.

Media Adaptations

- The film version of the novel was produced in 1981 by Juniper Films, directed by Karel Reisz, with a screenplay by Harold Pinter. Meryl Streep starred as Sarah, with Jeremy Irons as Charles.

During their conversation, Sam and Mary appear, and Sarah and Charles hide themselves. As she watches Sam and Mary embrace, Sarah turns to Charles and smiles. Charles, noticeably disconcerted at Sarah's open expression of her interest in him, abruptly leaves.

That evening Charles discovers that he is in danger of losing his inheritance and title, which causes tensions with Tina. He later asks his old friend Dr. Grogan to advise him about his relationship with Sarah, who has just been thrown out of Mrs. Poulteney's home for disobeying her orders. Grogan rightly guesses that Sarah engineered this dismissal so that Charles would come to her rescue. Charles, however, chooses not to follow Grogan's advice to stay away from her and meets her the next day on the Undercliff. Charles breaks off an embrace and rushes off, but not before he stumbles upon Sam and Mary who have seen them together. The two servants promise not to tell anyone of the meeting.

Chapters 34–54

Sarah moves to Exeter, aided by money Charles has given her. Charles tries to direct his thoughts to his engagement with Tina, but feels as if he is being trapped by her father who wants him to become his business partner. He is tempted to go to Sarah in Exeter but instead returns to Tina. The narrator provides the first of three endings here—Charles and Tina marry, along with Sam and Mary, and both couples prosper in a contrived Victorian conclusion. Immediately, however, the narrator insists that this ending is only what has taken place in Charles's imagination.

Charles does in fact go to Exeter to see Sarah, who seduces him. Charles discovers that she had not been intimate with the French lieutenant. After returning to his hotel, he writes to Sarah of his plans to marry her, but Sam intercepts the letter. After breaking off his engagement with Tina the next day, Charles returns to Exeter but finds that Sarah has disappeared.

Chapters 55–end

Charles hires private investigators to find Sarah and departs for America. Sam, who has married Mary, spots Sarah in London and notifies Charles. Sarah greets Charles at Gabriel Rosetti's home and explains that she has she has been working as the painter's model and secretary. Charles is shocked at how easily Sarah has fit into the scandalous Pre-Raphaelite group. After Sarah insists that she will never marry, Charles prepares to leave. When Sarah introduces him to their daughter, Lalage, however, the three embrace, suggesting that they will become a true family.

The narrator then reappears, sets his watch back fifteen minutes, and provides the last conclusion to the story. Sarah reasserts her decision not to marry but suggests the two might remain friends and lovers. Charles rejects her offer and leaves, devastated and alone.

Characters

Ernestina Freeman

The narrator introduces Tina, Charles' pretty fiancee, as a typical Victorian woman—obedient and demure, with an intense fear of sexuality. Yet she also displays an uncommonly strong will and a sense of self-irony, along with a sense of humor, without which "she would have been a horrid spoiled child." She reveals her shallowness in her petty response to the news that Charles may lose his inheritance and title.

Dr. Grogan

Dr. Grogan is Charles' old bachelor friend and confidant. He encourages Charles to view Sarah as a fascinating study in human behavior but tries to dissuade him from entering into a relationship with her.

Mrs. Poulteney

Mrs. Poulteney takes in Sarah to prove her own pious, charitable nature. She is "the epitome of all the most crassly arrogant traits of the ascendant British Empire," with her unwavering assurance that she is always right. She refuses any limits to her authority over those with whom she comes into contact.

Sam

Sam, Charles's servant, enjoys a friendly, trusting relationship with his master. Sam, however, betrays that trust when he discovers Charles' relationship with Sarah and determines to blackmail him. His better nature emerges when his guilt prompts him to help Charles find her.

Charles Smithson

Charles is a young, English gentleman whose distinguishing trait is laziness. The narrator describes him as an "intelligent idler" who sets his sights high, "in order to justify [his] idleness to [his] intelligence." His laziness allows him to become engaged to Tina, who does not demand anything but loyalty from him. Yet, his intelligence will not permit him to ignore her shallowness especially as contrasted with Sarah's depth. He also recognizes that "what drove the new Britain was increasingly a desire to seem respectable, in place of the desire to do good for good's sake."

While he wrestles with his position in the world, he turns his attention to science, specifically to a study of fossils. He eventually allows Sarah to pull him away from the confines of his Victorian world, but not without a struggle. He shows his conservative nature in his shock at her behavior— her open expression of her sexuality and her nonconformity. Yet he cannot resist the freedom of the world she reveals to him.

The three endings trace the development of his character during the course of the story. He ultimately discards his more conservative nature, which would lead to the first ending and its happily ever after resolution with Tina. In the second ending, he shows his independence by turning his back on his social class but follows his romantic nature when he reunites with Sarah and their child. In the third ending, he becomes an existentialist hero when he refuses to give himself totally to Sarah and her world and instead chooses a lonely but more authentic life.

Aunt Tranter

Aunt Tranter is a fitting contrast to Mrs. Poulteney. In her role as confident and advisor for both Charles and Tina, she brings out the best in their natures.

Sarah Woodruff

Sarah acts as a counter to Tina, the model of Victorian womanhood. She mystifies everyone, including the narrator in his conventional guise, by her behavior. The modern narrator and reader, however, understand that her actions are governed by her refusal to follow tradition and by her quest for freedom. She rejects the subservient role her society tries to force on her, determined to get what she wants and express her desires freely.

She has been a misfit all of her life, born into the working class but educated like a lady, caught between both worlds, neither of which can offer her the independence she craves. When she determines that she wants Charles, she continually manipulates situations to her advantage. She allows herself to be caught in the Undercliff, which has been forbidden by Mrs. Poulteney, knowing that her actions will cause the old woman to throw her out and thus be able to turn to Charles for help. She feigns a sprained ankle when Charles arrives in Exeter, requiring him to come up to her room to see her. In an effort to help spark Charles' curiosity and desire for her, she remains enigmatic about her relationship with the lieutenant.

In the last two endings, Sarah's need for freedom conflicts with her love for Charles. The first ending suggests that Sarah will be able to remain outside the confines of Victorian society while still being able to establish a family with Charles. Yet, her final emotional state, which causes her breast to shake with "a mute vehemence" when Charles asks her whether he will ever understand her, indicates that marriage will exact its own conventions which will be difficult to escape. The final conclusion focuses on her total freedom but also her estrangement from the man she loves. Fowles never resolves the conflict through his presentation of these two viable conclusions. Yet Sarah has enabled Charles to experience transformation, giving him the strength to break from convention and helping him to discover an authentic selfhood.

Themes

Social Constraints

Each character in the novel is constrained in some way by Victorian society. Tina has never been encouraged to explore her sexuality and so she is afraid of any intimacy with Charles. As a result, Charles gravitates to Sarah, who exhibits a more sensual nature.

Charles is caught up by his comfortable position as an English gentleman, which affords him the opportunity to leisurely dabble in his scientific pursuits and to be in control of his romantic relationships. Yet, he risks banishment from his class if he loses his wealth or behaves in a socially unacceptable way.

Topics for Further Study

- Research the treatment of women in England in the 1860s. How does Fowles depictions of Ernestina and Sarah reflect and challenge Victorian notions of the proper behavior of women?

- Read Fowles *The Collector* (1963) and compare its focus on male/female dynamics to that of *The French Lieutenant's Woman.*

- View the film version of the novel and discuss the changes in Pinter's screenplay as compared to the novel. Explain whether or not you think the film stays true to the thematic import of the novel.

- Investigate British class structure of the period in which the novel is set. What changes were taking place? What rules were maintained? How are these changes and rules reflected in the novel?

He sees evidence of the former in Tina's response when his inheritance is threatened and experiences the latter as a result of his relationship with Sarah. His social ostracism begins when he breaks his engagement to Tina, and is cemented when he aligns himself with the bohemian Sarah.

Sarah has faced social constraints throughout her life. Born into the working class but educated as a lady, she fits into neither world. She becomes a social pariah, however, when rumors surface that she has been seduced by a French lieutenant and are reinforced by her daily position on the Cobb, gazing longingly out to sea.

Freedom

Fowles writes in *The Aristos* that if we strive to be free, the "terms of existence encourage us to change, to evolve." This dominant theme in his work becomes most apparent in *The French Lieutenant's Woman.* Tina never experiences freedom since she does not allow this evolution. Her nature is not strong enough to stand up to the conventions of her world and take a more active part in the determination of her future. She is ultimately controlled by Charles' actions—his proposal of marriage and later his breaking of their engagement.

Charles eventually recognizes the confines of his world and finds the strength to rebel against them, stirred by his interest in Sarah. During a talk with Tina's father, who insists that Charles come into business with him after the wedding, he gains a glimpse of the suffocating life he would have to endure if he married Tina. Attracted by Sarah's open expression of sensuality, Charles breaks his ties with Tina and pursues Sarah, which pushes him to the margins of his society. The last two endings reveal the change that has occurred in Charles's character. In the first, he accepts Sarah's bohemian lifestyle with the Pre-Raphaelites and determines to stay with his family. In the final ending, he gains absolute freedom from social and marital constraints as he refuses to follow the standards of his class or to be possessed by Sarah.

From the beginning of the novel, Sarah resists the restrictions of her age. She allows others to believe that she has been seduced by her French lieutenant, which pushes her outside the boundaries of respectable society. Her search for independence leads her to the bohemian Pre-Raphaelites in London. She refuses to let others dictate her future, deciding when and if she wants to enter into a relationship with Charles.

Style

Narrative

The novel's narrative is postmodern in that it focuses on the self-conscious act of the author telling a story. Fowles discards the traditional, omniscient, Victorian narrator who knows everything about the characters and shares this information with the readers. The narrator in *The French Lieutenant's Woman*, who identifies himself as the author, breaks into the story continuously, providing background information, but also confounding readers' expectations about narrative continuity and clarity. He often moves back and forth in time. For example, he interrupts his description of Lyme Regis by mentioning Jane Austen's use of the Cobb in her novel *Persuasion*, which was written approximately fifty years before *The French Lieutenant's Woman*'s setting date, and by mentioning a twentieth-century Henry Moore sculpture.

He also refuses to give us a clear portrait of Sarah, who remains enigmatic throughout the novel. This more modern narrative sensibility suggests that no one can ever know anyone completely, that some mystery always remains, and that knowledge of others is based on individual perceptions, not universal truths.

As he continually breaks into the narrative, identifying himself in the role of storyteller, the narrator interrupts the reader's suspension of disbelief by continually calling attention to the fictional nature of the tale. This interruption is heightened by the three endings he provides.

Structure

The first ending is a traditional Victorian conclusion. Charles marries the sweetly conservative Tina, deciding that she would provide him with more stability and thus he would retain a secure position in society. He would have risked social ostracism if he had pursued Sarah. The narrator, however, refuses to end in such a conventional way, and so has Charles only imagine this ending.

The narrator reappears after he discards the first ending just as Charles begins his search for Sarah. He sits with a dozing Charles on the train, considering his character's fate and eventually constructing two possible conclusions.

The second ending offers a more modern, albeit still romantic, conclusion, as Charles and Sarah reunite. Refusing to end there, the narrator reappears, this time as an impresario, sets his watch back fifteen minutes, and constructs the final ending, in which Charles is alone. The presentation of these alternate endings forces the reader to recognize the fictional nature of the work and also ultimately to participate in its construction.

Historical Context

Existentialism

Existentialism is a school of philosophical and artistic attitudes that investigates the nature of being. Its basic tenet is that existence and experience rather than essence should be emphasized. The beginnings of existentialism can be traced to the nineteenth-century Danish philosopher Sören Kierkegaard and early twentieth-century German philosopher Martin Heidegger.

After World War II, existentialism reflected on an absurd world devoid of a benevolent creator/protector, where humans must create meaning through their actions and take sole responsibility for their fates. This freedom and responsibility can, however, cause an overwhelming sense of dread. Existentialism has been expressed as a dominant theme

Compare & Contrast

- **Late Nineteenth Century:** A new term, the "New Woman" is used to describe the population of women who challenge traditional notions of a woman's place in society, especially the role of wife and mother. These challenges are seen by much of the current society as a threat to the fabric of the family.

  1970s: Those who fight for gender equality are called feminists, and feminism gains respectability and ground as an area of intellectual and academic study.

  Today: The label "feminist" has fallen out of favor, for feminism is spread over a spectrum of conservative and liberal proponents. Women now do have the opportunity to work inside or outside of the home or both. However, those who choose to have children and a career can face difficult times balancing the often conflicting needs of family and workplace, in part due to inflexible work and promotion schedules.

- **Late Nineteenth Century:** In 1882, the Married Woman's Property Act passes in England, granting women several important rights. In 1888, the International Council of Women is founded to mobilize support for the woman's suffrage movement.

  1970s: In 1972, the Equal Rights Amendment Bill, which proposes that gender equality be

protected by the Constitution, is passed by the U.S. Senate and the House of Representatives, but is not ratified by the required thirty-eight states, so it does not become law.

Today: Women have made major gains in their fight for equality. Discrimination against women is now against the law. However, the Equal Rights Amendment is still not ratified, although it has been presented to each session of Congress since 1982.

- **Late Nineteenth Century:** Feminist Victoria Woodhull embarks on a lecture tour in 1871 espousing a free love philosophy, which reflects the women's movement's growing willingness to discuss sexual issues.

  1970s: The phrase "free love" becomes one of the cultural buzz words—meaning extramarital, noncommittal affairs—as women take birth control pills in order to gain sexual freedom.

  Today: Women engage in premarital sex and have children out of wedlock without experiencing the social stigmas imposed in the previous century. The issue of single parenting causes a furor in the early 1990s when Vice President Dan Quayle criticizes the television character Murphy Brown for deciding not to marry her baby's father. Today, however, single parenting has become more widely accepted.

---

in the literary works of Franz Kafka, Dostoevsky, Camus, Jean-Paul Sartre, and Samuel Beckett.

The New Woman

In the last half of the nineteenth century, cracks began to appear in the Victorians' seemingly stable universe. In 1859, Charles Darwin's *Origin of Species* sparked debates on religious ideology and the development of the human. In 1867, Karl Marx published the first volume of *Das Kapital*, which would challenge notions of class structures and their economic underpinnings. Robert Huffaker writes,

"These eminent Victorians, steadily and without any violent action, helped to shatter the age in which they lived—its faith, morality, confidence." During this period, feminist thinkers contributed to the shattering of traditional social mores as they began to engage in a rigorous investigation of female identity as it related to all aspects of a woman's life. Any woman who questioned traditional female roles was tagged a "New Woman," a term attributed to novelist Sarah Grand, whose 1894 article in the *North American Review* identified an emergent group of women, influenced by J. S. Mill and other

Director Karel Reisz works on the set of the 1981 film version of The French Lieutenant's Woman *with Meryl Streep, who plays Sarah and Anna, and Jeremy Irons, who plays Charles and Mike*

champions of individualism, who supported and campaigned for women's rights. A dialogue resulted among these women that incorporated radical as well as conservative points of view.

The most radical thinkers in this group declared the institution of marriage to be a form of slavery and thus recommended its abolition. They rejected the notion that motherhood should be the ultimate goal of all women. The more conservative feminists of this age considered marriage and motherhood acceptable roles only if guidelines were set in order to prevent a woman from assuming an inferior position to her husband in any area of their life together. This group felt that a woman granted equality in marriage would serve as an exemplary role model for her children by encouraging the development of an independent spirit. Chopin's works enter into this dialogue, exploring a woman's place in traditional and nontraditional marital unions.

Critical Overview

Soon after its publication in 1969, John Fowles's *The French Lieutenant's Woman* became a critically acclaimed best seller in England, America,

and France. Critics enthusiastically praised its rich storytelling along with its innovative style.

Literary scholar Ian Watt, in his review of the novel for *The New York Times Book Review*, declared it to be "immensely interesting, attractive and human" and expressed "awe, at such harmonious a mingling of the old and new in manner and matter." He found the themes "both richly English and convincingly existential." A reviewer for *Life* enjoyed Fowles mixture of existentialism with the previous century's sensualism, which results in "a novel of such riches that it meets the oldest, simplest, and least fashionable test of excellence. You never want it to end." The *New York Times* review insisted it "signals the sudden but predictable arrival of a remarkable novelist."

The novel continues to receive critical attention and high praise. Ellen Pifer writes, "Fowles's success in the marketplace derives from his great skill as a storyteller. His fiction is rich in narrative suspense, romantic conflict, and erotic drama." She praises Fowles's ability, so evident in *The French Lieutenant's Woman*, "to sustain such effects at the same time that, as an experimental writer testing conventional assumptions about reality, he examines and parodies the traditional devices of storytelling."

Criticism

Wendy Perkins

Perkins is a professor of American and English literature and film. In this essay, Perkins examines the dual endings and the role of the reader in the novel.

Several scholars, including Barry Olshen and Elizabeth Rankin, have commented on the problem of the dual endings in John Fowles' *The French Lieutenant's Woman*. Even though the novel's narrator insists that each ending can be perceived as a plausible conclusion to the story, critics have argued that thematic and stylistic textual elements undercut the first ending and support the second. A close examination of the text will prove, however, that such clear determinacy is not possible; the novel's textual elements, in fact, suggest the plausibility of both endings: the possibility of both the union and separation of Charles and Sarah. As Wayne Booth has noted in *A Rhetoric of Irony*, readers will attempt to find meaning in a work that suggests alternate planes of reality by determining a hierarchy of perceptions. Thus, in an analysis of *The French Lieutenant's Woman*, readers will ultimately choose one ending over another in their attempt to establish meaning. In this way, they can actively participate in the creation of the novel's vision.

The second, more contemporary ending, focuses on Charles and Sarah's final separation. When both choose their independence over the confines of marriage, they become models of existential freedom, an important theme that runs through the novel. The narrator notes in the final paragraph that Charles "has at last found an atom of faith in himself, a true uniqueness, on which to build," and Sarah retains her individuality. In order to accept this ending as a satisfying resolution to the novel, certain elements in the first more conventional ending must be plausibly neglected.

The first element that must fade into the background is Charles's love for Sarah, which has become quite evident by his actions in the novel and by the narrator's statement in the first ending, "Behind all his rage stood the knowledge that he loved her still." When, however, in the contemporary ending, Charles recognizes the reality of the arrangement Sarah offers him, he chooses his freedom and dignity over his love for her, recognizing that if he stayed, "he would become the secret butt of this corrupt house, the starched soupirant, the pet donkey." As a result, he feels "his own true superiority to her which was . . . an ability to give that

> And does the union of Sarah and Charles suggest the overtly romantic notion that love conquers all?"

was also an inability to compromise. She could give only to possess; and to possess him." Although his decision to leave tosses him metaphorically "out upon the unplumb'd, salt, estranging sea," his experience has enabled him to discover a firm trust in his own character and abilities.

Sarah's love for Charles, another element of the first ending, is not quite as evident in the text. Sarah admits, in her own words, that she is "not to be understood," a valid statement since neither Charles nor the reader is privy to her thoughts. Yet while the motivations for her behavior remain enigmatic, she ultimately cannot deny her feelings. When Charles entreats her to admit that she never had loved him, she replies, "I could not say that."

The reality of Sarah's love for Charles can be plausibly neglected in the second ending when Sarah realizes her wish that she had earlier expressed to Charles. She explains, "I do not want to share my life. I wish to be what I am, not what a husband, however kind, however indulgent, must expect me to become in marriage." Thus Sarah gains her freedom, but her final reaction to this condition is unclear; from the narrator's ironic vantage point, Sarah is too far away for him to see whether or not there are tears in her eyes.

While critics have overwhelmingly accepted the validity of the second ending, they just as resolutely have denied the validity of the first on thematic and stylistic grounds. The major argument critics have supported is that the first ending is anti-existentialist because it denies to both Charles and Sarah the power of choice, and thus it is a false "Victorian" resolution to the book. One such critic, Ellen Pifer, in her article on Fowles in *Dictionary of Literary Biography*, argues that "the second ending proves more convincing because the artistry is more complete," and it has "a greater impact." She suggests that in the first ending, Fowles is "giving us a taste of old-fashioned assurances . . . in order to brace us for the harsh and lonely realities of the second." Robert Huffaker, in his article on Fowles

What Do I Read Next?

- *The Awakening* (1899) is Kate Chopin's masterful novel of a young woman who struggles to find self-knowledge and inevitably suffers the consequences of trying to establish herself as an independent spirit.

- Kate Millet's *Sexual Politics* (1969) studies the history and dynamics of feminism.

- In *Anna Karenina* (1877), Leo Tolstoy chronicles the passion and tragic fate of his married heroine as she enters into an affair with a dashing officer.

- In the play *A Doll's House* (1879), Henrik Ibsen examines a woman's restricted role in the nineteenth century and the disastrous effects those limitations have on her marriage.

- *The Collector* (1963) is John Fowles's debut novel. Using a butterfly collector as his narrator, Fowles demonstrates an already mature style as he explores issues of class conflict.

---

for *Twayne's English Authors Series Online*, insists that the "final ending is the one supported by the vast thematic network which has woven into the novel the concepts of man's isolation and his survival through the centuries by *evolving*."

While it is apparent that an anti-existentialist ending would be thematically false, it must be noted that Fowles has already provided and discarded one such ending. Charles would have been guilty of acting in bad faith, something no true existentialist would do, if he had conformed to the pressures of his Victorian society and married Ernestina. Recognizing that fact, Fowles has the narrator reveal that Charles had only been imagining this ending, which can be considered the true Victorian conclusion.

If we acknowledge Jean-Paul Sartre's description of an existentialist as one who may choose anything if it is on the grounds of free involvement, we must also acknowledge that Charles and Sarah are given the power of choice in the conventional ending as long as their decision is not made in bad faith.

In this ending, Charles takes personal responsibility for his child, an action that would be commended rather than condemned by existentialists. Also, it is not Lalage's presence that ultimately determines Charles's decision to stay with Sarah. For immediately after Charles's discovery of his daughter, he still cannot resolve his feelings toward Sarah, as the narrator notes, "Still Charles stared at [Sarah], his masts crashing, the cries of the drowning in his mind's ears. He would never forgive her."

A more troublesome element in this scene is Charles's insistence that his reunion with Sarah "had been in God's hands, in His forgiveness of their sins," an image he had previously rejected during his visit to the church. This scene raises three important questions: Is the intervention of God an anti-existentialist turn? Does this ending mean that Charles will not experience the concept of "terrible freedom," a necessary requirement of an existential hero? And does the union of Sarah and Charles suggest the overtly romantic notion that love conquers all? These must be satisfactorily answered in order to accept both endings as plausible.

In the first ending, immediately before Charles's declaration that God has forgiven their sins, he reveals that the stumbling block to his union with Sarah is his own inability to grant this forgiveness. By shifting the responsibility of forgiveness from himself to God, Charles rationalizes in an inauthentic way; however, he ultimately gains what he truly wants. Thus, although his means are existentially inauthentic, the end result is that he has made an authentic choice. Evidence that it is Charles who finally decides to reconcile his feelings for Sarah can be found in his immediate reaction to his declaration that God has forgiven their sins. When Charles asks Sarah, "and all those cruel words you spoke ... forced me to speak in answer?," Sarah replies, "Had to be spoken." It is apparent from

Charles's question that he and not God will have the final responsibility in deciding whether or not to accept Sarah.

The question dealing with the necessary experience of "terrible freedom," defined by the narrator as "the realization that one is free and the realization that being free is a situation of terror," can be answered by examining Charles's reactions while traveling through Europe. Even though during those twenty months he has not been free of his obsession with finding Sarah, he has experienced a certain terrible freedom from the social ties that had previously bound him. As a result, Charles begins to realize his selfhood. He decides that there is "something in his isolation that he could cling to"—his label as an outcast—"the result of a decision few could have taken, no matter whether it was ultimately foolish or wise." Thus, he concludes, "however bitter his destiny, it was nobler than that one he had rejected." It can also be argued that since Charles and Sarah would experience a certain social exile from the community of England, especially if they remained in the notorious Rossetti household, their union would embody the same "pure essence of cruel but necessary . . . freedom" Charles would have experienced with Sarah "on his arm in the Uffizi."

The final element—love conquering all—has been considered by Pifer and others to be one of the major weaknesses of the first ending. However, while there can be no disagreement that the last line of the first ending ("a thousand violins cloy very rapidly without percussion") does suggest an excess of melodramatic, romantic sensibility, we must remember that the violins play in Charles's mind—an imaginative creation that is an immediate reaction to his obtaining something he truly wanted. Here Charles is taking romantic pleasure in the moment, not necessarily in the future.

While this scene does end on a romantic note, it is not quite as closed an ending as critics determine it to be. Charles's final words to Sarah in this scene—"Shall I ever understand your parables?"—suggest that they will face future obstacles. Sarah's silence and her vehemently shaking breast provide evidence that she ultimately will remain inscrutable to Charles and that she will retain some measure of independence.

The action of the novel traces Charles's difficulties in becoming the perfect exemplar of existential freedom. While the placement of the model of existential realization at the end of the novel could be considered the most effective arrangement, we must question the possibility of anyone's achieving this goal. In an interview quoted by Pifer, Fowles has noted the difficulties in obtaining such perfect or absolute freedom with the questions "is there really free will? Can we choose freely? Can we act freely? Can we choose? How do we do it?" Pifer notes that Fowles has admitted that his presentation of the existential man in *The Aristos*, which introduces the major theses of his fiction, is "the ideal model, not a real person. He is a goal, a potential toward which anyone may strive and which in some cases he may realize."

Acknowledging the difficulties in achieving this model or norm, we could argue that the second ending should be considered a wish fulfillment on Fowles' part. Ultimately, however, Fowles is not suggesting that one ending should be chosen over the other; instead he is suggesting the possibility of both. As Pifer notes, Fowles in his role as narrator, "overtly tells the reader that he does not exercise absolute authority over his characters." In essence, he rejects "the notion of a universal creator" and announces in the novel "his abdication from the throne of literary omniscience." Thus the final existentialist exemplar is the reader who recognizes the ambiguity of the text and, as a result, refuses to be manipulated by the author, the narrator, or the critics.

Source: Wendy Perkins, Critical Essay on *The French Lieutenant's Woman*, in *Novels for Students*, Thomson Gale, 2005.

Richard P. Lynch

In the following essay excerpt, Lynch examines social and narrative freedom and their complicated renderings in The French Lieutenant's Woman.

John Fowles has always been concerned with the general issue of human freedom, by which he usually means the freedom of individuals from the constraints of society and its institutions. In the 1960s, he defined this freedom in the context of existentialism, but even after his interest in the broader philosophy of existentialism declined in the 1970s, he maintained a concern with the achievement of "authenticity," the result of the individual's successful struggle with society. *The French Lieutenant's Woman* is probably the best of Fowles's works to examine closely on this subject, but it presents some difficulties, situated as it is on the edge of his change in thinking, perhaps about existentialism and certainly about the novel itself. Fowles experimented with narrative form to some extent in *The Collector* and *The Magus,* but his third novel is his first openly metafictional work—particularly in its double ending and in its use of a twentieth-century

> Sarah, then, has found an alternative symbolic universe, a social frame of reference within which she is able to choose an identity, but Charles has not."

narrator for a novel set in the Victorian period. In itself, the latter would not necessarily constitute an innovation, for as Kerry McSweeney points out, George Eliot's *Middlemarch,* set in the early 1830s, is narrated from the perspective of 1867—not a 100-year gap but an enormous distance in terms of social and historical concerns. In *The French Lieutenant's Woman,* however, we have a narrator who also claims to be the creator of the novel's characters and who makes cameo appearances in the narrative.

The novel is further complicated by the presence of different varieties of freedom, the effect of which, for a reader, can be equivocation on a large scale. Fowles is dealing in particular here with three different kinds of freedom: social, existential, and narrative, though in his statements outside the novel, he does not appear to distinguish between the first two. In *The Aristos,* for instance, he declares, "All states and societies are incipiently fascist. They strive to be unipolar, to make others conform. The true antidote to fascism is therefore existentialism; not socialism." In Fowles's thinking, existentialism is primarily a response to social and political pressures on the individual to conform. His novel can be more clearly understood, however, if the two kinds of freedom are distinguished. Social freedom, a concept that will be elaborated on below, is the opportunity to choose between alternative social "realities" or support groups, which confirm and strengthen one's identity. It is a way, therefore, of choosing an identity. There is some overlap between social and existential freedom in the sense that both give the individual the opportunity to *choose,* but existentialism necessitates a choice independent of any sustaining community. Sartre says that in choosing our own essence we are choosing, in a way, for all humankind, but he also states that "every man, without any support or help whatever, is condemned at every instant to invent man." There is a certain

eventual reassurance, even comfort, that comes with social freedom; the emotions associated with Sartre's existential freedom, in contrast, are anguish over our responsibility in choosing and despair because we know we may rely only on "that which is within our wills."

Narrative freedom, the "freedom" of fictional characters (or the illusion of it) from their authors, is a metaphor for freedom from God, a precondition for existential freedom in Fowles and Sartre. It is the freedom the narrator speaks of when he asserts that a "genuinely created world must be independent of its creator . . . It is only when our characters and events begin to disobey us that they begin to live." Such freedom is always difficult to claim, for although Fowles may not have a God who limits his freedom by determining his "essence" before his "existence," his characters do. Sarah Woodruff does achieve a kind of social freedom in this novel, and she is the primary example of narrative freedom, to the extent that such a thing can be attained. But existential freedom within the possible world of a novel set in the Victorian period is more problematic for its characters, in spite of Fowles's statement in "Notes on an Unfinished Novel" that the Victorian age was "highly existentialist in many of its personal dilemmas." If Charles Smithson, often seen as a potential existential hero by critics, finds a road to freedom in this novel, he does so by learning his own narrative strategies.

Sarah and Charles can be judged, first of all, in terms of their reactions to the social conventions of the late Victorian period. Critics have generally agreed that Charles is a somewhat "conventional" rebel for much of the novel. John Neary, for instance, argues that, rather than achieving or even attempting freedom, Charles has merely replaced Christianity with "Duty, Culture, and Science," which become substitute determiners of his character and actions. And Katherine Tarbox concludes that Charles never does, within the confines of the narrative, shake off the limitations imposed on him by his language and his Victorian assumptions about gender roles and conduct, although she holds out hope for the future Charles. Sarah, on the other hand, is generally perceived as a more genuine rebel against social constraints. Thomas Foster, in fact, calls her a "female Heathcliff," someone who ignores social convention. In spite of this apparent superiority, however, something funny happens to Sarah on the way to the endings: she becomes a catalyst in Charles's development, a secondary character. Both Neary and Foster ultimately see her this way, and McSweeney, in an interesting comment on the narrative that will be discussed later, calls Sarah the "narrator's surrogate," deceiving Charles for his own good. Almost all who have written about the novel see Sarah as a "mystery," but few have any trouble identifying what they see as her function in the novel.

Sarah may not be mere catalyst, though. She may represent a kind of social freedom that has been largely ignored or discounted by critics, perhaps because of Fowles's emphasis on existential freedom. In *The Social Construction of Reality,* Peter Berger and Thomas Luckmann describe the possibilities for attaining what they term "individualism," which they explain as a combination of awareness of choices among discrepant "realities" and identities, and the ability to construct a self out of the choices available (171). (Again, "constructing a self" may appear to be identical with the existential "choosing" of a self, but, as will be explained below, both process and product are substantially different.) Such individualism is made possible by unsuccessful socialization, a situation that may result from any number of causes.

According to Berger and Luckmann, all humans are born into "symbolic universes" (96), social structures a society has institutionalized as "reality." Socialization is the process by which the new individual internalizes that society, making it his or her reality, too. This socialization is accomplished primarily through the mediation of significant others (the parents in childhood; friends, coworkers, and others later on), with whose roles and attitudes, and ultimately with whose world, the individual identifies. In identifying with the significant others and their world, the individual acquires a coherent identity.

Sarah's socialization has been very imperfect, although she is in some respects a type often found in Victorian fiction: the educated woman of limited means who finds respectable employment as a governess. She is different from the type, however, in that she is educated beyond her class at the insistence of her father, a tenant farmer as obsessed with his ancestry as Mrs. Pocket is in *Great Expectations.* Sarah's education is, the narrator tells us, the second curse of her life, the first being an ability to see into others and understand their true worth. She has nothing in common with the other students at the boarding school and, far from internalizing their society and accepting it as "reality," internalizes instead the fictional worlds of Walter Scott and Jane Austen, judging others as fictional characters. Nor does the role of governess

suit her. In her happiest employment, as governess for the Talbot children, she does not understand why she cannot be Mrs. Talbot. She sees no equivalent social position for herself, only the position of outsider, forbidden to enjoy the paradise she sees around her. In a sense, Sarah identifies with Mrs. Talbot—they are the same age—but she cannot enter her world or form an identity for herself based on it. She feels condemned to solitude, "As if it has been ordained that I shall never form a friendship with an equal, never inhabit my own home, never see the world except as the generality to which I must be the exception."

Simply living in the Victorian age is enough to render socialization an unsteady process. Successful socialization requires a close parallel between objective reality (the prevailing version of reality established by the society) and subjective reality (the individual's perceptions and identity). As Berger and Luckmann put it, "Identity, then is highly profiled in the sense of representing fully the objective reality within which it is located. Put simply, everyone pretty much *is* what he is supposed to be" (164). This is very much the sort of society Thomas Carlyle constructs in *Past and Present* around the figure of Gurth, the swineherd from Scott's *Ivanhoe.* Gurth was happy, asserts Carlyle, because he had a definite place in society and a clear relationship to others—in other words, Gurth had no problem with identity: Carlyle laments the absence of such certainty in his own time, and if it was a problem in 1843 (the date of *Past and Present*), it was far more so in 1867, the date not only of John Stuart Mill's attempt to persuade Parliament to grant voting rights to women (calling into question assumptions about gender) and the publication by Marx of the first volume of *Das Kapital* (calling into question assumptions about social class) but also of the Second Reform Bill, which gave the vote to workers in the towns and virtually doubled the total number of voters. Carlyle compared the Reform Bill to "shooting Niagara," and there were fears that Victorian society itself might become radicalized to the point of losing its social and political identity. Sarah, from a social perspective, is one of Carlyle's victims. She is not what she is "supposed to be," either as the daughter of a tenant farmer or, in her own mind, as a governess. She asks Charles, "Where am I not ill placed?"

Conditions sufficient to undermine Sarah's socialization existed, then, both in the world of reference that provides the background to the novel and in her personal life in the narrative, but until the end of the novel, there is no alternative social "reality" available to her, no counterworld within which she could have a counteridentity. There is only the option of pretending to be what she is not (the French lieutenant's woman) as a means of rejecting socialization in a social reality she cannot accept as a verification of her identity. Her role as the "fallen woman" is no threat to society (or to Charles), any more than the roles of other socially stigmatized types, such as those with physical deformities or those born out of wedlock. We can see this in the ease with which Sarah is written off by authority figures: as a social reclamation project (and an opportunity to demonstrate her charity) by Mrs. Poulteney, as a textbook case of the unbalanced woman by Dr. Grogan, and as the sexually exciting "mystery woman" by Charles. She may be more than that to him, but that she assuredly is.

In a society as complex as Victorian England, however, there is bound to be a more complex distribution of knowledge than in, say, the imagined society of Gurth, allowing for the possibility of "different significant others mediating different objective realities to the individual" (Berger and Luckmann 167). The Pre-Raphaelite Brotherhood provides just such an alternative set of significant others for Sarah. Two years earlier, she had made a desperate attempt to discover whether, in other circumstances, she might have had a "gentleman" like Charles—desperate because in fact, as she tells Charles, she never believed there was any chance he would marry her. Indeed, her experiment, if that is a reasonable word for it, had only the effect of expanding the universe within which she was a "nothing." When Charles discovers her two years later, she is manifestly not the Sarah he thought he was seeking. She is, as the young woman who greets him initially says, "no longer a governess." This piece of information is given in response to a question from Charles that is more assumption than question. What else could she be, in her circumstances? But the woman who shows him in reacts to his question with "amused surprise." In social terms, Charles has entered an alternative universe, one in which there are genuine options for intelligent women. Sarah need no longer suffer Victorian stereotypes because she has found that universe and the significant others she needed: "The persons I have met here have let me see a community of honorable endeavor, of noble purpose, I had not till now known existed in this world . . . I am at last arrived . . . where I belong." Sarah is "anchored," as she puts it; she has a secure identity, and it does not appear to be existential in nature, as a number of critics have claimed, but a quite conventional

social identity—although no less hard won in the circumstances.

Tony E. Jackson, in an essay on evolutionary theory in *The French Lieutenant's Woman,* makes an interesting case for Sarah as a "suddenly occurring new kind of self" that "secures its survival" by reproducing itself as a type. Sarah does this, Jackson argues, by causing Charles to reenact her own story and become a social outcast like herself. There could be parallels between such an evolutionary reading of Sarah and the social process described above, but in that process conditions must exist to cause the discontent or "unsuccessful socialization," and Sarah cannot have been from the start "naturally isolated and alienated," as Jackson insists. In Berger and Luckmann's scheme, such alienation can only exist initially as a result of an accident of birth that renders the individual a social outcast, or by the mediation of a significant person other than the parents—a nurse, for instance, who may represent a different social class with a different world view. Neither of these situations applies to Sarah. Her alienation occurs for the very concrete social reasons given earlier, and not "naturally" (a term that begs too many questions). Further, Jackson views Sarah in the final, "existentialist," ending as "the type who is at home with contingency, uncertainty, and anxiety." I would maintain that she is simply "at home." The contentment she expresses with her present situation in the passage quoted above exists in both endings, since the final ending does not begin to displace the one before it until well after that passage. She betrays there neither uncertainty nor anxiety.

Sarah's description of her new community, one "of honorable endeavor, of noble purpose, I had not till now known existed in this world," raises questions about Charles's own options. Should he not have been a member of just such a community, pursuing its own "noble purpose" in the area of science, as the Pre-Raphaelites were in art? Charles likes to see himself as different, "not like the majority of his peers and contemporaries," and he revels in the idea that he and a select few others—Dr. Grogan, for instance—are advanced thinkers. But he wears his Darwinism as comfortably as Ernestina wears the latest fashions, and later in the novel, when Mr. Freeman uses the Darwinian principle of adaptation to changes in the environment to support the idea that "gentlemen" might find it necessary to go into trade, evolution becomes something Charles can do without. The terms *intellectual* or *Darwinist* have about the same reality when applied to Charles as *governess* does when applied to Sarah: they are convenient constructs for those who do not quite fit into mainstream Victorian categories but who are also not regarded as threats to it—as subversive "realities."

This is not to say that Darwinism was not regarded generally as a threat to conventional thinking but that Charles's version of Darwinism is the naïve variety Jackson describes as all too similar to Linnaeus's "ladder of nature"—a comforting reaffirmation of the rightness of one's position at the top of the evolutionary scale. When he goes to visit his uncle at Winsyatt, the estate and its attributes "evoked in Charles that ineffable feeling of fortunate destiny and right order which his stay in Lyme had vaguely troubled." For Charles, unlike Sarah, existence is just, and the order of things seemingly permanent. His satisfaction with Winsyatt as his inheritance "seemed to him to explain all his previous idling through life, his dallying with religion, with science, with travel; he had been waiting for this moment . . . his call to the throne, so to speak." His "real wife," Charles thinks, is "Duty"—the preservation of this order. The scene, like others in *The French Lieutenant's Woman,* contains the intertextual ghost of *Great Expectations*—in this case the scene in which Pip returns to the forge at the end of the novel with the idea precisely that it represents a peace and order he had not recognized earlier, and with the intention of proposing to Biddy (another previously unrecognized destiny). Like Pip, Charles is greeted by empty rooms and changes he did not expect to see—in particular a marriage (his uncle's) that forestalls any return to the past.

In terms of social freedom, Charles is a work in progress at the end of the novel. During his dialogue with himself in the church, where he goes to sort out his thoughts after having become Sarah's first lover, he identifies the age as his enemy, with its

> iron certainties and rigid conventions, its repressed emotion and facetious humor, its cautious science and incautious religion . . . That was what had deceived him; and it was totally without love or freedom . . . but also without thought, without intention, without malice, because the deception was in its very nature; and it was not human, but a machine.

Charles reads a social phenomenon as "nature," something nonhuman that has no choice but to act the way it does. As Berger and Luckmann explain, there is nothing natural or "logical" about such realities; social reality is a purely human, construct. Once it exists, however, reification of the social reality—perceiving it as if it were a "thing" existing independent of humans—is likely. In addition,

Charles, as an amateur scientist, is in the habit of objectifying social realities (making them "things") through scientific metaphors. So the idea that women were brought into creation for the purpose of being wives and mothers is a "natural law," and the continuing descent of a "fallen woman" is determined by "gravity." Perhaps if the oppressions of the age could be read as "nature," as nonhuman, Charles might be seen as a budding existentialist, but even at this stage he has yet to shake off the Victorian conventions he has helped to perpetuate.

Sarah, then, has found an alternative symbolic universe, a social frame of reference within which she is able to choose an identity, but Charles has not. He has been forced to resign his identity as a Victorian "gentleman," but what he will replace it with is not at all clear at the end of the novel. In fact, although Charles is an adult in years (32 at the beginning of the narrative, 34 at the end), the novel has many of the elements of the bildungsroman, or parodies of those elements, and given the many false steps he has made in his development, it is appropriate to see Charles as "starting over." So, in the second ending, the narrator tells us, "It was as if he found himself reborn, though with all his adult faculties and memories . . . all to be recommenced, all to be learnt again!" Fowles claims in his foreword to the revised edition of *The Magus* to have been surprised when a student at Reading University found similarities between *The French Lieutenant's Woman* and his favorite Dickens novel, *Great Expectations,* a classic bildungsroman, but one wonders how much of a surprise it really was. I mentioned above the parallel between Pip's imagined return to the forge and Charles's imagined return to Winsyatt; Fowles's novel is filled with reminders of the Dickens work, even if one discounts the most obvious one: the existence of two endings. The scene at the end of chapter 17, in which Mary holds Sam's hand to keep it from "trying to feel its way round her waist" is taken directly from Dickens's description of the same interplay between Wemmick and Miss Skiffins. Connections with *Great Expectations* in particular may be less important, however, than the bildungsroman category it falls into: a type of narrative that, especially in its emphasis on escape from the effects of primary socialization (the influence of parents and other conservative institutions), deals heavily with the protagonist's attempt to gain social freedom.

The characteristics of this kind of novel are conveniently identified by Jerome Buckley. The four basic elements are the loss of the father (by being either orphaned or alienated), the flight from provinciality (small town to city—usually London), the making of a gentleman (a moral test, since it involves deciding what a "gentleman" is), and trial by love (another test, revolving two love affairs: one dangerous and debasing, the other rewarding). All of these elements can be seen easily in *The French Lieutenant's Woman*. The breakaway from the "father," or an equivalent representative of tradition or conservative values, is parodied in Charles's pseudo-Darwinism, which allows him to see himself as an advanced thinker, in opposition to the narrow-minded views of his time. His actual father, we are told, died of "pleasure" in 1856, and Charles shares no values with the remaining father figure—the fox-hunting turned claret-swilling uncle from whom he stands to inherit wealth. The alienation between father and son in this subgenre is frequently a result of a hostile attitude on the part of the father toward the young hero's new ideas, which are often acquired through reading. One of Charles's faults, we are told, was a "sinister fondness for spending the afternoons at Winsyatt in the library, a room his uncle seldom if ever used." The "immortal bustard," the rare bird Charles mistakenly shot one day on the estate, is a kind of objective correlative for their relationship, evoking different emotions from each: Charles is angry with himself for having helped to nudge the species closer to extinction; his uncle is delighted and has the bird stuffed and placed in a glass case in his drawing room.

The journey from the country, where the protagonist feels stifled intellectually and socially, to the city, where, according to Buckley, the hero is both liberated and corrupted, is also parodied. No doubt Charles feels limited (or just bored) by the provinciality of Lyme, but his "liberation" at the club and the brothel in London is ironic to say the least, and the corruption goes without saying. Buckley notes that the city almost never lives up to the hero's expectations of it, and that is certainly true of Charles's visit to London. He abandons the brothel to go looking for Sarah and ends up with a prostitute (ironically named Sarah) who, on closer inspection, looks disappointingly unlike the original. The third element—the making of a gentleman—is parodied as the unmaking of a gentleman. Charles in fact is forced by Ernestina's father to sign a document stating that he has "forfeited the right to be considered a gentleman."

The two love affairs are with Ernestina and Sarah. The relationship with Ernestina could very well be described as "dangerous and debasing," if our concern is with Charles's social freedom, or

establishment of a self-chosen identity. His marriage to her would be the most conventional of arrangements, suggested in his "dreamed" ending to the novel. As the narrative explains,

> It was simple: one lived by irony and sentiment, one observed convention. What might have been was one more subject for detached and ironic observation, as was what might be. One surrendered, in other words; one learned to be what one was.

The Ernestina connection could also be "debasing" in a comic sense (though not comic from Charles's point of view) if he had to accept Mr. Freeman's offer and go to work in "trade." To the extent that Sarah saves Charles from that surrender and puts him on the road to potential freedom, she represents a "rewarding" relationship, though she is not a reward in herself.

At the end of the bildungsroman, the protagonist is almost always on the road to some undefined destination, with an old identity left behind and a new one still in the process of forming, and that is certainly an accurate description of Charles. There are other parallels with the form—notably the several mock "epiphanies" Charles experiences—and Fowles was quite familiar with most of the novels Buckley discusses. In fact, as he notes in the foreword to the revised *Magus,* he was teaching *Great Expectations* at the time he was writing *The French Lieutenant's Woman.*

Most of these parallels are in the form of parody, and so they appear to bode ill for Charles's development, but as parody they are of a piece with the game-playing antics of the narrator who claims to be author. In the larger context of the narrative and its model author, there is still hope for Charles, whose own socialization has become unsettled, and it is a measure of Sarah's power to affect him that she has been the primary agent of that unsettling. He does not know what she is, but he knows that she is not what she is "supposed to be"—the governess, the fallen woman, or whatever other convenient categories society has assigned her to. And to adapt a phrase from Berger and Luckmann, if fallen women "can refuse to be what they are supposed to be, so can others; perhaps, so can oneself." Unsuccessful socialization begins with such questionings and opens up the essential question, "Who am I?" Once that question has been raised, individualism, as defined above, becomes a possibility. Charles is not there yet when he has his dialogue with himself in the church, but he has taken the first steps.

The conditions necessary for Sarah's social freedom are not available earlier in the novel, so she must rely on a kind of narrative freedom until they

From a vision of a woman standing on the Cobb breakwater at Lyme Regis, England (pictured here), John Fowles first conceived of the character of Sarah from The French Lieutenant's Woman

are, although the latter freedom remains vital to her even at the end of the narrative. It is much easier for an author to give existence to characters than to give them their narrative freedom. In a 1974 interview with James Campbell, Fowles states that he does try to give his characters freedom, "but only as a game, because pretending your characters are free can only be a game." It is an important game in his third novel, however, which straddles two ages with different attitudes toward the novel, and in which Fowles, or at least the narrator, is concerned with Robbe-Grillet's argument that the true modern novelist does not attempt to pass traditional characters off on the reader, and that authors who do so give us mere "puppets in which they themselves have ceased to believe." The only way to avoid the charge of being a puppeteer (a designation Thackeray so cheerfully adopted) is somehow to free the characters in this novel set in a time period conspicuous for the absence of narrative freedom.

Source: Richard P. Lynch, "Freedoms in *The French Lieutenant's Woman*," in *Twentieth Century Literature*, Vol. 48, No. 1, Spring 2002, pp. 50–61.

Thomas C. Foster

In the following essay excerpt, Foster contrasts the characters of Charles and Sarah, exploring

Fowles use of Victorian and post-Victorian elements as part of character development.

Modern readers may be particularly attracted to Sarah because of her existentialist suffering. Although she cannot recognize them (being born a century too early), she exhibits the symptoms of existentialism as delineated by Sartre and Camus. She is alienated from herself, from God, and from society. She has her moments of absurdist recognition and suicidal despair. Her life is without essential meaning, and ultimately she must take charge of her life and invest it with meaning, must create her being as she goes. Like Sisyphus, she has been condemned to a certain life, in her case not rolling a rock up a hill but, instead, living singly in a society that values only wedlock for women, and, after wallowing in misery through the first half of the novel (to the point of contemplating suicide), she chooses the heroic option of embracing that condition and making something positive of it. Unlike Nicholas Urfe, who revels in the poses of existentialism, Sarah is genuinely trapped in an existentialist situation without the knowledge or skills that would provide a guide out of that trap. Her struggle to find her own way out, along with Charles's fascinated observation, forms a large part of the novel's plot.

> One of the attractions of the Victorian society as subject matter for Fowles is its strong impulse toward unipolarism, toward unthinking conformity."

Charles's own grappling with existentialist realities serves as the other major focus. Charles moves from a comfortably conformist role in society, despite his protestations of being his own man, to being an outsider who must confront his own lack of authenticity. While he believes himself to be a Byronic loner and skeptic in the beginning of the novel—and his tweaking of the middle class by following Darwin is his chief supporting evidence—Charles is very much a product of his time and class. He lives on a private income, with expectations of further inheritance of money and title when his uncle dies. He is a nonproductive member of society, and even his fashionable scientific interests are dilettantish, pursued without system or rigor. When he breaks his engagement with Ernestina he is forced outside society, both by Mr. Freeman's threats of exposure and by his own growing sense of alienation, largely brought on by his inability to find Sarah. In "Notes on an Unfinished Novel" Fowles asserts that the Victorian age was profoundly, if unwittingly, existentialist. Certainly, in its fiction, Dickens, Eliot, and Hardy in particular, the age embraced the same concerns as Sartre and Camus and company. Pip's struggle to become a "gentleman" in *Great Expectations* shares many elements with existentialism—that meaning and value must come from within, for instance. Both Hardy's Tess and Jude are tormented by alienation from God and man. The chief difference between their situations and Charles's is that his creator possesses an adequate terminology to discuss his plight.

That plight is central to the novel, for, despite the title and the occasional authorial references to Sarah as "the protagonist," Charles stands as the main figure in the novel. Feminists have rightly noted that Fowles typically concerns himself with male protagonists and male dilemmas, that female characters play secondary roles, and this novel is no exception. This twist, of course, reflects the age;

it may be termed the Victorian era, but it is dominated primarily by such men as Lyell and Darwin, Tennyson and Browning, Marx and Mill, Disraeli and Gladstone, Dickens and Thackeray and Hardy. Even the Pre-Raphaelites, who figure in the novel tangentially, with their fetish of sacred and mythic womanhood, were totally dominated by men— William Morris, Dante Gabriel Rossetti, Edward Burne-Jones. Women were figures of great interest and mystery for the Pre-Raphaelites—in fact, almost the only fit subject for painting—but chiefly because of their Otherness, their foreignness, rather than because of any great understanding on the part of the artists. So, too, with *The French Lieutenant's Woman:* Charles is brought to consciousness through the agency of a woman he admires but does not understand. That woman appears to be miles ahead of him in her own coming into being, yet her presentation in the novel is sufficiently limited that such an appearance may be illusory.

As the novel opens, Charles is the typical wealthy Victorian bachelor on the verge of marriage. Considerably older than his fiancée, he treats her condescendingly, while she behaves like a coquettish and sometimes petulant schoolgirl to his suave Oxford man. He drifts along in what the narrative calls "tranquil boredom," playing his role as young aristocrat. He playfully teases his valet, Sam Farrow, who responds with cockney indignation, both of them conforming carefully to preset roles. His relation with Ernestina is chaste and slightly distant; neither of them ever says anything meaningful or revealing, and even their proposal scene is sealed with a ludicrously asexual kiss. He has followed Ernestina from London to Lyme Regis in an age-old courting ritual of hide-and-seek: if he will follow, then he must be serious. It is, naturally, a game only the wealthy can afford to play.

It is as happily betrothed strollers that they come upon Sarah Woodruff standing at the end of the Cobb, where she rebuffs and attracts Charles with her gaze. He subsequently encounters her on one of his fossil-finding expeditions to the Undercliff, the steep, eroded cliff beyond Ware Commons. When he discovers Sarah sleeping his first impulse is to turn away and not disturb her. But then, prompted partly by the memory of a sleeping prostitute in a Paris hotel, he continues to watch, another of Fowles's voyeurs. Like his counterparts Nicholas Urfe in *The Magus* and David Williams in "The Ebony Tower," he is paralyzed at the brink of action, torn between sexual desire and fear at the risks desire carries with it. And, like them, his voyeurism represents the larger struggle between the impulses of engagement and isolation, of active involvement in life and passive observation of it. She wakes, however, and catches him watching her, and again their gazes lock, with a kind of inevitability: "Charles did not know it, but in those brief poised seconds above the waiting sea, in that luminous evening silence broken only by the waves' quiet wash, the whole Victorian Age was lost. And I do not mean he had taken the wrong path." Readers will instantly recognize the rhetoric of sexual seduction in this passage, with its breathless pause, its lapping of waves—long the cinematic cliché for sexual climax—and in the overstatement of an age being lost. Charles has most certainly started down a different kind of wrong path.

Yet on another level Fowles means exactly what he says about the Victorian age being lost. What is at stake in the novel is nothing less than a way of life. The existing power structure of Victorian society is present throughout the novel, from the odious Mrs. Poulteney and her henchwoman, the misnamed Mrs. Fairley, to the self-made success Mr. Freeman, to Dr. Grogan and his adherence to the best medical opinions of the day, to the Methodist dairyman, to the pert yet orthodox Ernestina. Charles is in danger, as the novel progresses, of becoming merely another pillar of the Victorian establishment. He occasionally displays the humorlessness that passes for moral rectitude, or he wears the mask of "Alarmed Propriety" in dealing with Sarah, or he takes his class privilege too much for granted. The peril is both personal and cultural, since falling into the habits of one's society leads to an ossification of both the individual and the society.

The dichotomy Fowles sets up is between the structures of society, which he feels are inherently fascistic in their efforts to inflict conformity, and the self, which is inherently revolutionary in its insistence on its individuality, in its refusal to conform:

> All states and societies are incipiently fascist. They strive to be unipolar, to make others conform. The true antidote to fascism is therefore existentialism; not socialism.

> Existentialism is the revolt of the individual against all those systems of thought, theories of psychology, and social and political pressures that attempt to rob him of his individuality. (*Aristos*, 122)

One of the attractions of the Victorian society as subject matter for Fowles is its strong impulse toward unipolarism, toward unthinking conformity. The presence of Sarah, then, as one who refuses to conform is not a mere affront to that society but an active threat, since assertion of the Self thwarts

totalitarian impulses. The novelist, however, is interested less in this historical insight than in its modern parallel. The history of the twentieth century has been one of constant assaults on individuals by a host of totalitarian schemes, among which Hitler is the representative figure. Fowles makes this point clear in his repeated analogies and references in the book to the Nazis and those who fought against them. Yet Fowles writes *The French Lieutenant's Woman* in the midst of a decade that stands as one of the premier assertions of selfhood in the history of any century, and he knows that the battle between Self and society is eternal and constant and not yet lost. When Charles loses his way as he gazes into Sarah's eyes, he begins to lose his conformity, begins to see the possibilities of the radical Self.

Those possibilities reside, apparently, in her eyes, for each time they meet Charles is aware of her eyes. When next they meet he notices her eyes are "abnormally large, as if able to see more and suffer more." On this occasion she begs him to tell no one that he has seen her on the Undercliff, thereby implicating his own eyes in her secret. She is forbidden by Mrs. Poulteney, who has what Fowles calls a Puritan fear of nature, from visiting Ware Commons and the Undercliff. During an audience at Mrs. Poulteney's, to which Charles has been dragged by Mrs. Tranter and Ernestina, Sarah and Charles exchange a secret look unnoticed by the others, who have averted their eyes. Sarah's eyes are far-seeing, unlike those of the myopic Ernestina, as she gazes out to sea. She often seems to look through Charles, or past him. Her stare is almost otherworldly; that world, of course, is the twentieth century. If the shortsighted Ernestina represents the present as weighted down by the received ideas of the past (she unpleasantly echoes Mrs. Poulteney during the interview), then Sarah's fixed stare represents the pull of the future.

These two women, then, represent as well as produce the dilemma Charles must struggle with: Will he remain a creature of his own time or move into the future? Ernestina, with her love of bright colors, her adherence to the latest fashions, and her rejection of some of the more outmoded Victorian strictures, stands as a thoroughly "modern" young woman, vintage 1867. Yet her modernity is very much of her time; that is to say, she is as up-to-date as a girl could manage to be while remaining firmly in her own era. Her activities, her speech, her clothing, her taste, are all firmly informed by the culture that contains her. In no measure does she challenge or reject the basic demands and assumptions of Victorian society. Marriage to her would mean ossification for Charles: his tendencies toward stiffness, toward propriety, toward conventionality, would overcome his countervailing impulses toward flexibility, independent thought, and individual action.

Sarah, on the other hand, embodies values more closely associated with the twentieth century, and her influence, her ability to mesmerize Charles, has a great deal to do with the strangeness of that future time. Curiously, Sarah's plight is entirely Victorian in nature: the marital impasse she faces, the ostracism because of her scarlet past, her occupation as governess, and the lack of career paths available to her are all nineteenth-century impositions on her liberty and autonomy. Yet she maintains that autonomy, insists on that liberty, in the face of overwhelming social forces. Even her appearance suggests modernity. Fowles describes her as lacking anything like conventional prettiness yet having a beauty that the High Victorian era could not recognize—full lips, dark eyebrows, dense and wavy hair, and, of course, those astonishingly frank eyes. Modern readers can recognize the features as those of Elizabeth Siddal, Jane Morris, and Alexa Wilding, the favorite models of the Pre-Raphaelites, and the directness as that of our own century. Her look is frequently described as naked, as the narrator emphasizes the eroticism connected with her and also the freedom from conventionally "clothed" responses. This tendency also manifests itself with literal clothing. Repeatedly, Charles encounters Sarah in various degrees of shedding garments: her bonnet, her cloak, and, in the fateful scene in Endicott's Family Hotel in Exeter, her day clothes entirely. He finds her seated in her room in her nightgown, all of the ordinary restraining garments removed. Significantly, when he meets her after their separation she is dressed in a simple shirt and skirt, not at all in the trussed and layered manner of Victorian fashion. The simplicity of her ensemble approximates that of the century to come, in which female modes of dress would become simpler and, ultimately, more masculine.

Sarah's final garments underscore her tendency to usurp what her society views as masculine prerogatives. She often contradicts Charles or else speaks out of turn or too frankly for his comfort. Indeed, she scarcely takes his feelings into account except to manipulate them (or so it seems to him), never to defer to them. She acts toward him, in other words, very much as a woman might act toward a man in the 1960s, not in the 1860s. When the narrator describes her mix of "emotion and understanding," he does so in terms of the past, saying those qualities would have made her "a saint or an emperor's mistress" in an earlier day, yet he cannot say what she might have been in our own day. Nevertheless, readers will recognize in her the beginnings of the liberated modern woman: she thinks her own thoughts, shapes her own identity (the French lieutenant's whore is, after all, her creation), and ultimately pursues her own destiny. Her one sop to her own time is her deferential posture, which she assumes when commanded or corrected, yet even that she typically undercuts with a look or a statement that suggest a less than total submissiveness.

Charles, naturally, sees the choice not between centuries but, rather, between women. His decision is not any easier for that, since he knows so very little of women; indeed, Charles's mystification throughout the novel is largely a product of the Otherness of women. Like many of Fowles's heroes, he has grown up and lived in an all-male environment. His parents are deceased, and his one elder influence is his lifelong bachelor uncle, Sir Robert. The public school and Oxford experience, of course, would have been entirely male in Charles's youth, and among his confederates at his club the only contact with women is with prostitutes and entertainers, two types shaped by men's fantasies of women, rather than by the genuine articles. His chief contact with females has been on the basis of superior power. His class, his masculinity, his educational status, all confer on him the upper hand in contact with women. With such women he is glib and self-assured. Even Ernestina, his intended, is a marked inferior on the basis of age, gender, and class (her father is nouveau riche, a commoner to Charles's aristocrat). Their conversations are shallow, if sometimes sincere; Charles routinely assumes superiority, while Ernestina, who can be quite petulant, consistently defers to him in important matters. When she does contradict him, during their meeting with the abominable Mrs. Poulteney, it is on the subject of the unreliability of domestic servants, an area of supposed female expertise. Even then she realizes her transgression and apologizes immediately when they are alone. What Charles lacks, then, is any knowledge of a woman as a complete person, someone with views, feelings, and a history that are hers alone, rather than a concoction brewed up to please the dominant male power structure.

Because of his lack of information, Sarah poses a significant problem of interpretation for Charles. He becomes the readers' representative within the novel, trying to decode and understand Sarah, just as the readers on the "outside" of the text must try to interpret each character. Some critics, like Mahmoud Salami, have seen her as a creator of texts, of stories and parables that teach. It is perhaps more accurate, however, to understand Sarah herself as a text to be read. Not only her narratives but her sheer presence require active reading by Charles, as well as by others in the novel. Such a view of the novel can be quite fruitful, since it gives readers a means of understanding the different Sarahs presented to different audiences. The general public of Lyme Regis is presented with a very simple text: Sarah as fallen woman, ruined by a wicked foreign seaman, sensual and unrepentant. To Dr. Grogan she is another text, a case study of an unbalanced woman. In fact, he turns her literally into a text by presenting Charles with the medical documents pertaining to a similar case revolving around another young French officer, a Lieutenant La Roncière, falsely charged with raping the young daughter of his commanding officer. Grogan attempts to explain Sarah's behavior in terms of Marie, the girl in the case study.

To Charles, however, Sarah presents another, very different, text: constantly shifting, sometimes contradictory, unpredictable, unfinished. Each time they meet she produces some new bit of information, some new slant on her personality. She is occasionally the wanton, more commonly the damsel in distress (a role made more plausible by living in the house of Mrs. Poulteney, a reasonable facsimile of a wicked stepmother), borderline madwoman, solitary, villain, victim, lover, betrayer. She places herself in his path by going repeatedly to Ware Commons and the Undercliff, where she knows he goes to pursue his fossil collecting, then asks to be left alone. Making sure he sees her, she asks him to tell no one that he has seen her, thereby implicating him in her secret. She seeks out his help but does so clandestinely, appealing both to his gallantry and his ego (he is special, he alone can help her). She reveals progressively more of her story, yet it is not always consistent, and the main point, as he discovers, is untrue. When Charles finally goes to Endicott's Family Hotel and they make love, he finds to his shock that she is a virgin. She has never made love to the French lieutenant. His reading of her moves from victim of romantic impulses to victim of a narrow-minded society to manipulative, selfish marriage wrecker. That last image settles in more firmly when, having broken his engagement and returned to Exeter, he discovers that she has vanished.

Yet even then he is not satisfied with his interpretation, like a reader who finds a novel missing its last, most critical chapter. He waits for two years while his agents search for her, partly out of love and partly out of an anxiety of uncertainty: he wants to know why she has done what she has done. Unlike ordinary readers, Charles gets his chance to question this extraordinary author. If the text of Sarah is radically unstable, it is sufficiently provoking to spur him to action. The search for her authentic text is complicated by Charles's construction of a fantasy text, onto which he projects his desires. That alternative text, as Salami notes, is a "masculine narrative" in which Sarah is "a mystery, a dangerous Eve, and a contradictory subject." Charles can never understand, or "read," Sarah until he learns to accept her feminine narrative without bending it to the will of his masculine desires and prejudices.

Throughout Charles's search for the "real" Sarah, readers are confronted with an analogous search for the real novel. *The French Lieutenant's Woman* has become famous for its twin endings, yet they stand as merely the final instance of narrative gamesmanship in a long catalog of slippery practices. The most obvious example is the use of the nineteenth-century novel form itself, for, while Fowles makes faithful use of the elements of that form, he never pretends to be writing a Victorian novel. Carefully assembling the elements of such a work—the story of Charles and Sarah could easily be by Eliot or Hardy—he repeatedly violates the illusion of reality by intrusive comments and stratagems. From the outset he insists on the differences between the nineteenth century and the twentieth, and he compares characters and situations to literary examples from the major Victorian novels. He compares the valet Sam Farrow, for instance, to Dickens's Sam Weller and, at another point, asks if he is a Uriah Heep. No Victorian, and certainly not one of the great realists, would risk damaging the presentation of their illusion with such an artful reference. Elsewhere he compares gentlemen of Charles's day with those of our own, again reminding readers of the artifice of his creation. His crowning moment, though, is chapter 13. Having asked, in closing the previous chapter, who Sarah is and what drives her, he opens this new installment by saying frankly: "I do not know. This story I am telling is all imagination. These characters I create never existed outside my own mind." He goes on to discuss the conventions of Victorian storytelling, including the omniscient, godlike narrator. He says, however, that that mode can never be his own, since he lives in the age of Alain Robbe-Grillet, the driving force behind the New Novel, and Roland Barthes, the French structuralist and narrative theorist.

His assertions put him firmly and consciously in the postmodernist camp, exploring its concerns, especially those of self-conscious narrative, distrust of realism, exploitation of previous forms, and narrative indeterminacy or unreliability. The effect of these concerns is to thwart the readers' desire for *story,* even while fulfilling it. If a writer believes that realism is essentially false, that it is an effect produced by a series of devices designed to trick the reader, among them the pretense that the writer is not making it all up, then his response may be, like Fowles's, to call attention to the artifice of his enterprise. The self-consciousness he displays in chapter 13 is characteristic: he reminds the reader that none of this is literally true or that it is true only in imaginative terms. In fact, Fowles chooses chapter 13 very carefully, on the basis of two well-known antecedents. One is Samuel Taylor Coleridge's *Biographia Literaria,* the first thoroughgoing treatment of literary theory in English. In his chapter 13 Coleridge discusses, in what is probably the most famous passage in the work, the distinction between fancy and imagination. George Eliot's *Adam Bede* includes, in chapter 17, "In Which the Story Pauses a Little," a discussion of her theory of novel writing and her views on imitating reality in her works. Fowles, then, conflates these two preoccupations into his profession of artifice, reminding readers that they should not confuse the action of the novel with real life and inviting their complicity in pursuing this view of the novel. What he finally argues for is the aesthetic consistency of fiction: it need not imitate any external reality so long as it provides an aesthetically satisfying whole.

And if the novel's wholeness is internal—that is, the narrative is true only to its own principles, not to any outside "standard"—then the readers' perceptions of those principles, and that truth, is as important as anything imposed on the narrative by the author. What he begins to argue for in chapter 13 is the aesthetic autonomy—the self-containedness—of the novel as well as the primacy of imagination in its creation. Aesthetic autonomy, however, is a function not only of the writer's creation but also of the readers' perception: How do readers view and understand the wholeness, the integrity, of the novel? The novel is a transaction between the two parties, then: the creator and the audience. For instance, the narrator is unable to fill in all the details of Sarah's motivations and internal life, so readers must surmise for themselves what drives her. The rightness of their interpretation is determined not by the narrator stepping in with a "final" version of Sarah but, rather, by how completely each reader's interpretation fits the facts of the narrative and explains her actions to that reader's satisfaction. There are numerous possible Sarahs in the novel, and different readers will undoubtedly reach different conclusions about her, many of them equally valid in the context of the novel.

Source: Thomas C. Foster, "*The French Lieutenant's Woman*: Postmodern Victorian," in *Understanding John Fowles,* University of South Carolina Press, 1994, pp. 72–85.

Katherine Tarbox

In the following essay excerpt, Tarbox examines the often "deceptive appearances" of the characters and the narrator, and the resulting effect on perceptions and actions in The French Lieutenant's Woman.

While it might appear that Charles distorts Sarah in a neurotic way, his case simply demonstrates how extremely difficult it is to know anything objective about another human being. If the narrator (whose brainchild she is) cannot grasp her troth, how could Charles? In fact, the narrator, by his own problematic and intrusive presence, forces us to examine the very word "I," to recognize what a shifty and complex thing it is. Fowles poses the old problem of identity in a new way. The narrator brings up the problem himself as he has Charles on the train thinking about Sarah: "I say 'her,' but the pronoun is one of the most terrifying masks man has invented; what came to Charles was not a pronoun, but eyes, looks . . . a nimble step, a sleeping face." Language contributes, then, to the difficulty of knowing the truth about one's neighbors; it allows one to limit, classify, and collect; it puts all things in parity. The narrator reproduces the entire text of "To Marguerite" to suggest these distances between enisled individuals.

The sustained theme of "hearsay" is an illustration of these same distances. Much of what the reader knows of the people in this book emerges from stories, usually several times removed. The first information of Sarah comes from a story the Vicar (who heard it from another vicar, who heard it from Mrs. Talbot) is telling to Mrs. Poulteney. She processes the reformation and categorizes Sarah based on criteria mentioned in the story (which, the narrator confides, the Vicar is amending slightly as he speaks). Sarah earned the appellation Tragedy through similar apocryphal stories that flew through Lyme. Through the novel many different versions of the Varguennes story are told (most notably the double version from Sarah herself), demonstrating the spurious or tentative nature of what the individual tellers assume to be truth. In the opening scene the voyeuristic narrator establishes the specious nature of appearances by giving first a long then a close shot of Charles and Ernestina: "The local spy . . . might have deduced that these two were strangers . . . On the other hand he might, focusing his telescope more closely, have suspected that a mutual solitude interested them." The contradictory nature of the sightings (both of which are untrue) shows the deceptiveness of visual information. Similarly, Sam first introduces Mary by a story in which she falsely appears to be a prostitute. Mr. Freeman seeks to know Charles before he allows him into the family. Charles gets top honors because the dossier of appearances that he has constructed around himself defines him, ironically, as a fine Victorian gentleman. When people see Sarah standing on the Cobb and staring out to sea, "There it was supposed, she felt herself nearest to France." As we later learn, Sarah cares not a whit for Varguennes, but the natives interpret her solitariness according to the conventions of romance. In truth, any walk in Lyme commands a view of the sea, and the Cobb and Cliffs are the only places to get away from the local eavesdroppers.

The narrator enjoys playing a game of appearances. One of his favorite tricks is to set the reader up to feel one way about a thing; then he makes a quick reversal and twits the reader for feeling as he does. For example, he labors the fact of Charles's extreme and foolish overdressing as he goes out to find fossils. He prompts a feeling of superior judgment in the reader, then derides him for his condescension: "We laugh . . . We make, I think, a grave—or rather frivolous mistake about our ancestors . . . Their folly in that direction was no more than a symptom of their seriousness in a much more important one. They sensed that current accounts of the world were inadequate; that they had allowed their windows on reality to become smeared by convention, religion, social stagnation." If the laughter is unjust it is because all human beings are handicapped by having to see life through a haze of complex and virtually unavoidable prejudices. The reader's laughter says much about the dirtiness of his own windows, and points to his arrogance in thinking he has the right angle on things, an attitude for which the narrator soundly condemns Mrs. Poulteney. The reader may feel compassion for Sarah that all condemn her on the strength of appearances; but the narrator often makes him feel guilty of the same crime.

Characters in the novel frequently sit in judgment on each other, and the bases for their

> "The narrator enjoys playing a game of appearances. One of his favorite tricks is to set the reader up to feel one way about a thing; then he makes a quick reversal and twits the reader for feeling as he does."

decisions are always these deceptive appearances. The draconian Mrs. Poulteney presides, for example, over a great number of questions involving hirings, firings, matters of taste, and morality. She fires Millie for some minor domestic crime until Sarah, characteristically, uncovers the truth behind the crime and finds that the girl is ill. Sarah forces Charles to judge her by choosing him as her confessor. Grogan, at the end of the novel, finds himself having to pass judgment on Charles. The narrator spends much of his intellectual energy on judging an entire age. The narrator even judges himself at the end when he appears in fancy dress. All the judgmental situations meet in the breach-of-promise writ that Mr. Freeman hands down against Charles. The crude and only vaguely accurate language of that document conveys how ill founded most judgments are and how shortsighted we are when we seek to judge. The errors that mark and defile Sarah and Charles are the same errors that send LaRoncière to prison.

The story of LaRoncière, the other French lieutenant, is the most extreme case of maladroit judgment in the book. Like Sarah, he is a victim of the universal human penchant for collecting and categorizing. In the same way that the accumulation of apparent evidence sends LaRoncière to jail, various sorts of circumstantial evidence nearly send Sarah to the lunatic asylum. Grogan examines Sarah and accepts a good deal of slanted evidence about her behavior, and promptly diagnoses her as melancholic and hysterical (and he would have Charles do the same; Grogan is another who is convinced he has the right angle on things). Ironically, given all the extenuating and existing information, his diagnosis seems perfectly plausible. She does indeed suffer purposefully, as do all the other hysterics in Grogan's grisly catalogue. But to put Sarah in the same category as Charcot's famous patients is a gross parody of science similar to the diagnosis of Nygaard in *The Magus*. The only thing certain about Sarah is that she can be neither classified nor explained; she has motives that cannot be comprehended by Grogan's philosophy. It is not Sarah but Ernestina who commits hysterical acts in the novel, as when she "faints" as Charles leaves her. Charles smells that rat, as well as Grogan's.

Grogan himself best plays out the sense of crippling schizophrenia, the war between facile appearances and contradictory intuitions. When Charles refuses to admit that he loves Sarah, Grogan counters, "Do you think in my forty years as a doctor I have not learned to tell when a man is in distress? And because he is hiding the truth from himself? Know thyself, Smithson, know thyself." Ironically, Grogan should be giving this advice to himself. He is a "dry little kestrel of a man" who has never known real commitment to another human being. He showed Charles the telescope with which he enjoys Lyme's bathing beauties, and as he did, "his tongue flickered wildly out and he winked." In this rather disgusting image Grogan-the-voyeur reveals himself as one who looks but does not leap. In many ways Grogan is a retarded adolescent who plays with ideas rather than living them, as he demonstrates in his childish playing with Charles at a secret society of Darwinism, in his histrionic swearing on Darwin rather than the Bible. Both are embarrassingly juvenile acts committed by one who constantly conjures his forty years' wisdom. But there is much in Grogan that is likable, that is even wise; he speaks perhaps the most meaningful words in the book when he sends Charles off for the last time, warning him about the wages of freedom. The narrator also suggests that Grogan is a bit taken in by Sarah. But he is pathetically torn; as is Charles, who eventually goes way beyond his mentor in existential awareness.

Fowles creates in this novel an intricate web of errors in fact, judgment, awareness, intuition, and perception. Sarah elects Charles in order to save him. Her godgame involves training Charles away from contradictions, appearances, superficies, and conventions. Why Sarah chooses to work her game on Charles is a moot consideration. It seems easy enough to accept on simple faith her simple explanation: she loves him. With her uncanny perspicacity—"She saw through people in subtle ways . . . She saw them as they were and not as they tried to seem"—she sees the real Charles in hiding. She sees that he has the potential to become existentially aware (as she is). His trial is a test of his fitness, of his worthiness to be naturally selected. She does not see the same potential in Grogan, whom she knows to be firmly attached to the status quo, and she refuses to tell her story to him. She sees that Charles, caught in an evolutionary incident and metaphorically buried in a landslide, is becoming fossilized. She simply tries to show him the way out; or, as Ronald Binns suggests, her game is designed to make Charles aware that he has a destiny over which he has control.

Her methods—like those of the god of the universe and the author-god—are strange. It is probable that she has her plan fairly well defined from the start. Before she and Charles have gotten very far he says to her, rather avuncularly, "If he does not return, he was not worthy of you. If he returns, I cannot believe that he will be easily put off, should he not find you in Lyme Regis, as not to discover where you are and follow you there." What he says is an excellent description of his own future conduct toward Sarah. Her reply is, characteristically, a look: "Her expression was strange, almost calm, as if what he had said had confirmed some deep knowledge in her heart." The test becomes a question: Will you follow me out of the landslide?

Sarah teaches, as Conchis teaches, by parable, by telling stories. Both involve their listeners in fictitious situations that seem to be real. Sarah's method is to tell a plausible story about herself and Varguennes and then to maneuver Charles into the plot in her former role, so that he always has a mysterious sense of deja vu. The Varguennes story is, for Sarah, a metaphor (like Conchis's masque) for how she achieved here own sense of freedom. She explains to Charles why she gave herself to Varguennes: "I did it so that I should never be the same again. I did it so that people *should* point at me, *should* say, there walks the French Lieutenant's Whore . . . I threw myself off a precipice . . . What has kept me alive is my shame, my knowing that I am truly not like other women." What she means to do (to mirror what was ostensibly done to her) is involve Charles in a relationship far outside the bounds of propriety, to make it impossible for him to return to his former life. Then, like her, he will have to suffer the burden as well as the exhilaration of his freedom. In effect, she makes him walk in her shoes.

After Charles becomes enchanted by Sarah he walks as furtively on the Ware Cliffs as she does; he even learns all the paths only she knows, to keep away from the eyes, the spies. Sarah begins slowly to cut him away from Ernestina and respectability.

When she relates how she and Varguennes deceived Mrs. Talbot, Charles becomes opprobrious until he realizes that he has been deceiving Ernestina about his meetings with Sarah. At the end of her confession Charles is extremely aroused by her, and he thinks, "He would be to blame, of course, if he did not now remove himself, and for good, from the fire." Sarah offers him the same position she was in with Varguennes: the knowledge that he has a choice and that his choice entails responsibilities either way. He is at the point where, no matter what he chooses, he will never be the same again. Sarah takes him farther away from safety after she gets herself dismissed from her position. She sends him a note at his hotel (knowing that word will get around, which it does) where she again offers him the existential choice that, according to her story, Varguennes offered to her. She writes in French (allowing her to be more maudlin than she could be in English), reinforcing the equivalence that is being built up between her and Varguennes: "Une femme à genoux vous supplie de l'aider dans son désespoir. Je passerai la nuit en prières pour votre venue." Even Charles gets the connection: "The French! Varguennes!"

Charles's demise becomes inevitable when he succumbs to her clever machinations. When he decides to go to Sarah on the Undercliff despite (and in opposition to) Grogan's diagnosis, he has already begun to walk in her shoes. After he spends a frantic night in self-questioning, he walks off into the dawn to this clandestine meeting. But instead of showing the meeting, the narrator interrupts with an entire chapter describing Charles's walk. The chapter is a lovely, lyrical pastoral, a hiatus in the despair and confusion. We see how gorgeous the morning is; we see Charles looking up rather than down, thinking of the living things rather than the dead. He stops to listen to the wren's song and feels that "the heart of all life pulsed there in the wren's triumphant throat." He realizes that he now feels more outside the drawing-room world than inside: "Charles felt in all ways excommunicated . . . He was like Sarah."

Charles's undoing happens in many steps and runs parallel to other events in his life that prove helpful to Sarah's endeavors. He is, after all, stripped of his estate, title, and fortune. And then he is, to his horror, invited to go into trade. These circumstances help to create the air of fatedness that hangs over his relationship with Sarah. But his fulcrum moment arrives in Exeter. When he goes to Sarah's hotel he is literally in the same position she was in with Varguennes at Weymouth. The edict of both Sarah and her metaphorical French Lieutenant is: you must come to me of your own will; you must choose to cut yourself off with your own will. Sarah feigns a sprained ankle for this reason: so that Charles should have to come up to her room knowing fully what he is doing. As he climbed the stairs "he remembered Varguennes; sin was to meet in privacy." She makes certain that she is helpless, that she can take no active part in the sexual encounter, because it must be all his doing. He must take command completely, become existential action personified. He appreciates the real spirit of the moment: "He felt borne on wings of fire, hurtling." And he does indeed become action: he strides around the room, knocks over chairs, rips clothes, half kills Sarah with violent kisses, throws her across the bed. Sarah fulfills the requirements of the rest of her story by disappearing, as Varguennes did. Charles's education is not complete until he proves that he can bear the burden of freedom. In his exile he moves closer and closer to Sarah until the two virtually merge in an image: "One calm evening while still at Charleston, he chanced to find himself on a promontory facing towards Europe." Immediately after that he is told, "She is found."

Source: Katherine Tarbox, *"The French Lieutenant's Woman,"* in *The Art of John Fowles*, University of Georgia Press, 1988, pp. 67–73.

Robert Huffaker

In the following essay excerpt, Huffaker examines the historical aspect of The French Lieutenant's Woman *and the novel's narrative technique, including narrative intrusion.*

III The Novel's Historical Quality

At its elementary level, *The French Lieutenant's Woman* is a magnificent historical novel. It is the story of a Dorset farm girl whose strange revolt against Victorian convention frees her for a womanhood among the Pre-Raphaelites in London, while toppling an intelligent young gentleman from the upper class into exile. It is also the story of a city valet and a provincial housemaid who succeed in marriage and mercantilism, of a scholarly old bachelor physician, of a kind old spinster aunt, of a frivolous London girl whose wealth has barely failed to spoil her, and of a bigoted old widow who thinks Heaven operates on the points system. The novel's panorama of Victorian England bears close-ups of such specialized activities as London whoring and legal negotiating. The book documents discussions of Victorian science, politics,

> One reason *The French Lieutenant's Woman* succeeds is Fowles's using the old omniscient and intrusive point of view with such grand style."

economics, and social custom, and it describes both urban and pastoral England. Such illumination is expected of a historical novel, and this one provides it. But *The French Lieutenant's Woman* is far more than a historical novel. Fowles denies interest in that genre and does not consider this book part of it. He compares it to other artists' using earlier form and technique: "Stravinsky's eighteenth-century rehandlings, Picasso's and Francis Bacon's use of Velasquez. But in this context words are not nearly so tractable as musical notes or brushstrokes." Prokofieff's *Classical Symphony* ran through his mind as he wrote the novel, and he must feel his technique's kinship to Prokofieff's early twentieth-century renovation of mid-eighteenth-century classical style. Both Fowles and Prokofieff handled forms of previous centuries with loving irony. Fowles describes the central painting in "The Ebony Tower" as growing out of "a homage and a kind of thumbed nose to a very old tradition," a phrase he might also have applied to his own earlier book. Such artistic use of outmoded form is not purely parody or pastiche, terms implying some disrespect for the model; nor is such reworking simply imitation or emulation, words suggesting parasitic cribbing. *The French Lieutenant's Woman*, like the *Classical Symphony*, is an original modern expansion upon older traditional forms. Written both admiringly and ironically, both works pay tribute to past techniques while gently spoofing them.

Because some of Fowles's effects blend epochs a century apart, there is temptation to call them anachronisms. His technique occasionally resembles Bernard Shaw's sicking ancient Egypt's Ra upon his British audience or Mark Twain's transporting his Connecticut Yankee back to Camelot. Fowles's narrator, in many ways a character as well, is part Fowles himself and part device. Since this author-persona is a modern novelist who slips into his own created past, his time-linking effects appear deceptively anachronistic. But his appearances in

the novel are more synchronistic than anachronistic, since he remains obviously the twentieth-century novelist, merely disguised as Victorian for trips into the book—complete with contemporary transportation and timepiece. Such synchronic elements establish the perpetuity of existence and carry the theme of evolution: "Mary's great-great-granddaughter, who is twenty-two years old this month I write in, much resembles her ancestor; and her face is known over the entire world, for she is one of the more celebrated younger English film actresses." The narrator carries out this sense of sempiternality by including such specifics as Ernestina's birth in 1846 and her death on the day the Nazis invaded Poland (1 September 1939). Such references link fictional characters to known reality in recent history, and the device is neither anachronistic nor hard to believe, since people often live ninety-three years. The author's toby jug which once belonged to Sarah, the Undercliff from the air, Mrs. Poulteney as inhabitant of the "Victorian Valley of the Dolls," today's public urinal replacing yesterday's Assembly Rooms—all such details destroy the separateness of the two ages and support Fowles's attitude toward existence as a horizontal concept without beginning or end. Such linking elements not only demonstrate his concept of time but also intensify the authenticity, the reality of his story.

IV The Intrusive Author

Fowles fuses the old ingressive and omniscient point of view with his modernity as another way of showing the continuum of time. He also uses that traditional narrative technique to accomplish feats unavailable to contemporary novelists who refuse the old omniscience. In the process, he makes considerable fun of the tradition which has in recent decades come to insist that the author himself be ousted from his own fiction. Fowles ironically protests that the modern novelist (in the age of Robbe-Grillet and Barthes, leaders in the form-obsessed *nouveau roman* school) must give his characters freedom; then he rides smugly into his own fiction as novelist-god to parody the notion of an intervening deity. He is intervening in the name of nonintervention.

The question of the novelist's role is inseparable from the idea of God's, and this book's central concern with narrative point of view is as theological as it is literary. His ironic treatment notwithstanding, Fowles is quite serious about the godlike function performed by creators of fiction. Whatever narrative technique an author uses, it is ultimately impossible for him to avoid being omniscient and omnipotent in his own fiction; he knows his own creation and may share it as he likes. But because twentieth-century man no longer sees himself as manipulated by an intervening god, the modern novelist who hopes to create a believable world must avoid the appearance that he as creator can know and control that world. Since an omnipotent god no longer pulls the strings, today's novelist considers himself presumptuous if he seems to do so. Such was not the case in the Victorian novel, as Thackeray's conclusion to *Vanity Fair* illustrates: "Let us shut up the box and the puppets, for our play is played out." Fowles directly contradicts Thackeray's metaphor:

> Perhaps you suppose that a novelist has only to pull the right strings and his puppets will behave in a life-like manner; and produce on request a thorough analysis of their motives and intentions . . . The novelist is still a god, since he creates (and not even the most aleatory avant-garde modern novel has managed to extirpate its author completely); what has changed is that we are no longer the gods of the Victorian image, omniscient and decreeing; but in the new theological image, with freedom our first principle, not authority.

Although Fowles mentions the leaders of the *nouveau roman,* his antipathy to their style-consciousness is well known. And his return to Victorian narrative is partly a mockery of their transmitting novels almost entirely through sensory perceptions of their characters. As if to emphasize that the modern novelist *does* exist in his fiction, Fowles returns unreservedly to the previous century's intrusiveness—editorializing, footnoting, quoting prose and poetry at will, taking every license of omnisience, even surpassing Trollope by writing himself into the plot, complete with physical description.

Nonetheless, in his jarring thirteenth chapter, Fowles also preserves his own theological image of god-novelist by rejecting omnipotence and refusing to trespass upon Sarah's inner mind: "There is only one good definition of God: the freedom that allows other freedoms to exist. And I must conform to that definition." Fowles could have chosen *not* to conform to that image; his refusing to do so betrays the seriousness behind his irony. In *The Aristos,* he presents the same theology: that "god" is a situation rather than a power, being, or influence—and that man's freedom proves the situation's sympathy despite its general indifference to the individual: "Freedom of will is the highest human good; and it is impossible to have both that freedom and an intervening divinity."

One reason *The French Lieutenant's Woman* succeeds is Fowles's using the old omniscient and intrusive point of view with such grand style. Having established theoretical freedom of his characters, Fowles proceeds to assume the older technique with boldness which uses its best qualities. The result is so pleasant as to cast doubt upon some of today's avant-garde techniques. The current aversion to authorial involvement, especially as seen in the *nouveau roman,* has so limited narrative technique that such critics as Wayne C. Booth and Norman Friedman question its validity and defend advantages of omniscient narrative. Today's proponents of authorial detachment defend their principles in the name of artistic illusion, as if the reader is supposed to forget he is holding a book, which someone must have written. Fowles, using the intrusive method unavailable to them, anticipates their criticism of his old-fashioned approach; his narrator discusses his own technique.

In chapter 13, Fowles drops his own fictional pretense: "This story I am telling is all imagination. These characters I create never existed outside my own mind. If I have pretended until now to know my characters' minds and innermost thoughts, it is because I am writing in (just as I have assumed some of the vocabulary and 'voice' of) a convention universally accepted at the time of my story: that the novelist stands next to God. He may not know all, yet he tries to pretend that he does." By exposing his own mechanism, Fowles defies both Victorian preoccupation with the illusion of omniscience and contemporary fixation upon the illusion of detachment.

Bradford Booth defends the Victorian intrusive author on the basis of nineteenth-century reality: "It is charged that he does not maintain a consistent point of view. What matter, if his characters live? It is charged that he sees human nature only from the outside. What matter, if his view be not distorted?" Fowles defends his simultaneous breach of Victorian omniscience and twentieth-century detachment with contemporary philosophy nearer, for example, Joyce's:

> I have disgracefully broken the illusion? No. My characters still exist, and in a reality no less, or no more, real than the one I have just broken. Fiction is woven into all, as a Greek observed some two and a half thousand years ago. I find this new reality (or unreality) more valid; and I would have you share my own sense that I do not fully control these creatures of my mind, any more than you control—however hard you try . . . your children, colleagues, friends, or even yourself.

In essence, Fowles presents a reality akin to such as that of Joyce and Durrell, whose artist characters create their own existence. He says of himself and his fellow novelists, *"We wish to create worlds as real as, but other than the world that is. Or was."* With modern aesthetic reality entirely different from the Victorian kind, Fowles can flout both the nineteenth-century author's pretense to all knowledge and the contemporary one's obsession with impersonal narration.

Fowles is not the first novelist to dispel his own illusion. There are two particularly notable Victorian precedents. A near parallel to his fiction-shattering chapter 13 is Trollope's conclusion to the fifteenth chapter of *Barchester Towers:* "But let the gentle-hearted reader be under no apprehension whatsoever. It is not destined that Eleanor shall marry Mr. Slope or Bertie Stanhope. And here, perhaps, it may be allowed to the novelist to explain his views on a very important point in the art of telling tales . . . [T]he author and the reader should move along together in full confidence with each other. Let the personages of the drama undergo ever so complete a comedy of errors among themselves." Perhaps the classic breach of illusion in the Victorian novel is the one George Eliot commits in her seventeenth chapter to *Adam Bede*, entitled "In Which the Story Pauses a Little":

> "This Rector of Broxton is little better than a pagan!" I hear one of my readers exclaim. "How much more edifying it would have been if you had made him give Arthur some truly spiritual advice. You might have put into his mouth the most beautiful things— quite as good as reading a sermon." Certainly I could, if I held it the highest vocation of the novelist to represent things as they never have been and never will be. Then, of course, I might refashion life and character entirely after my own liking.

Eliot, like Fowles, devotes her entire chapter to this extended aside. And also like Fowles, she pleads for truth in portraying characters. That argument for reality is one reason Fowles insists that his characters are *free*. In addition to establishing a metaphor for his theology, he is explaining that he cannot violate today's informed ideas of human behavior. But the characters of Trollope, who *has*, perhaps, "disgracefully broken the illusion," are not free in the same sense of realistic probability. In contrast to Fowles, Trollope gains the reader's confidence at the expense of his characters. By conferring metaphorical freedom upon his characters, Fowles gives the opposite impression—seeming to protect his characters from the reader. Earlier parallels to Fowles's declaration of character independence are not unheard of; Fielding, two centuries earlier, protests in *Tom Jones* that he is obliged to divulge certain information himself

because he cannot prevail upon any of his characters to speak. To Fielding, the characters are "actors," and unmistakably *his;* their taciturnity is only the author's whimsical humor.

Fowles's often playful intrusions are sometimes as near to devices of Fielding and Sterne as to techniques used by their Victorian successors, but his personal appearance in the novel is more extreme than most inventions of either century. In older traditions, the author sometimes steps into the presence of his *reader,* but Fowles keeps the reader at some distance and actually joins his *characters.* Fielding climbs into a coach with the reader of *Tom Jones,* and Dickens yanks the reader of *The Old Curiosity Shop* away by the hand on a cross-country trip, but neither ever barges into a character's railway compartment.

However much Fowles's showmanship may resemble his capriciously introducing the film of *The Magus* or Hitchcock's popping up in his own cinema, a seriousness underlies this novel's wit and humor. Fowles uses his unconventional techniques purposefully as well as effectively: both his intrusions and his self-limited omniscience are essential to his themes and plot.

By establishing himself candidly as a twentieth-century novelist writing of the preceding century, Fowles assumes the unique vantage point to command the necessary historical view. The narrator needs such perspective to understand Charles's confronting evolution's particular segment which made the twentieth century what it is. Omniscience enables Fowles's narrator to step into pre-1867 past as well as into twentieth-century present and to summarize extensive plot material with economy. And the reader must consider the narrator qualified to make the judgments he proposes and to depict reliably the events, people, and places he describes. The omniscient viewpoint further enables Fowles to expose various characters' thoughts without elaborate technical ruses. Omniscience would not have been the only way to do so, but it effectively gives the reader insight to such internal feelings as Charles's misgivings about involvement with Sarah, Ernestina's longings and sexual inhibitions, Sam's class-conscious resentments and schemes, and Mrs. Poulteney's rivalry for a first-class seat in Paradise. Such mental processes could have been revealed through an objective omniscience which exposed without comment. But Fowles's editorial interpretations make possible his Victorian irony, an important part of the book's humor. This point of view is also the simplest way to accomplish the job of narration—just as the easiest way to solve problems and know reality is to believe in the Victorian God, another irony in Fowles's technique.

Interpolating essay material serves the same kind of double purpose, making the plot believable while widening the reader's perspective. Sometimes the essay comprises an entire chapter, in the manner of Fielding and George Eliot. Chapter 35, an essay on lower-class sexual freedom and the problem of incest in Thomas Hardy's life, informs the reader and removes all doubt about why Sam and Mary appear together at the hay barn. The history of the gentleman, interpolated within the thirty-seventh chapter, also informs the reader historically, while explaining Charles's antipathy to Mr. Freeman's offer of a mercantile career.

Fowles exults in all available Victorian devices to link the epochs and show history's horizontality: brief authorial comments, footnotes, essay materials, and epigraphs foreshadowing the chapters they precede. By using these conventions as a Victorian novelist might have, he forcefully connects past and present. To heighten suspense, he abruptly shifts scene, once leaving Charles peering over a barn partition for an entire chapter. Except in Sarah's case, he reveals character through direct narration. He sprinkles his text with documents, stories-within-stories, and personal letters: the Freeman attorneys' legal paper, Grogan's case histories, Ernestina's sentimental novel, the eighteenth-century account of a London brothel, and written correspondence between Charles and other characters—to mention several. The narrator's intrusions often control the reader's sympathy for characters: the term "catatonia of convention" increases one's distance from the jilted Tina; and the comment on Charles's first poem, "to get the taste of that from your mouth," moves the focus away from his character's aching heart. Fowles's sometimes clinically probing his characters' minds is another way of keeping the reader's sympathy at proper distance.

But Sarah is the novel's one thoroughly modern character, and Fowles strengthens her contemporary quality, along with her mystery, by making her the only one whose mind he will not enter. In the Darwinian sense, she is the cultural "missing link" between the centuries—more modern than Victorian. By voluntarily limiting his Victorian omniscience in her case alone, Fowles adds another dimension to the evolution theme. His other restriction of Victorian narrative technique—his

demurral over authorial omnipotence—further links by showing the evolution of the novelist's role, especially as it applies to man's evolving concept of a god. The narrator's appearing as character and the reader's choosing between multiple endings emphasize concepts of literary, theological, and social evolution.

V The Novelist as Character

The novelist enters his book in three appearances—first like an owl who becomes human beneath Sarah's window. And he gives the novel three endings—the first of which damns Charles to a lifetime of reading that maddening verse Ernestina has stitched on his watch pocket, then more justly, plummets Mrs. Poulteney into Tartarus. But that tongue-in-cheek denouement is only how Charles dreams things *might* have turned out, with each winding of his watch reminding him indeed of love: the love he had missed. The last two endings—one Victorian, the other contemporary—are the ones which determine the book's final impact, just as do the narrator's diverse personae on his two more blatant trips into the novel.

When the narrator first intrudes upon Charles's railway compartment, he is incognito as the archetypal Victorian novelist. Like Thackeray, he is "prophet-bearded," the bullying "tabernacle" preacher, his top hat squared, "aggressively secure," with the look of an omnipotent god—"if there were such an absurd thing"—who wonders of his character, "Now could I use you? Now what could I do with you?" But his habit and demeanor are only a disguise; he is still the contemporary novelist, who is really wondering what the devil he is to do with Charles in a novel whose Victorian conventions forbid an open, inconclusive, ending and whose contemporary views preclude "fixing the fight." Having vowed to take neither Charles's nor Sarah's side, he decides upon two endings to their story and is caught tossing a florin to determine which will be the last, and therefore the more powerful.

When the narrator at last reappears to effect that final ending, his new disguise clarifies why the toss has gone to the contemporary, open, ending. No longer done up as the preaching, Victorian, omnipotent-god novelist, he is now the successful novelist-impresario (notorious "fixers" of their dramatic enterprises, despite their respectable pose). He, "as he would put it, has got himself in *as he really is*. I shall not labor the implication that he was previously got in as he really wasn't." Now he has "an almost proprietary air," dandified clothes, a "foppish and Frenchified" beard, the look of a "tycoon." Contrary to protests of *nouveau roman* stylists, the modern novelist is no less in control of his own fiction than the Victorian who acknowledged his omniscience: "In this he has not changed: he very evidently regards the world as his to possess and use as he likes." As the contemporary novelist carried grandly into his unique, part-Victorian novel, the dandified narrator is making his point about the evolution of both theology and literary technique: the Victorian novelist, in the context of Victorian reality, could assume the omniscience which his age attributed to God; but the contemporary novelist, in the context of twentieth-century reality, must maintain the illusion of non-intervention, in this age which no longer believes in a controlling deity. But both Victorian and modern authors have always controlled their own fiction, as Fowles's contemporary impresario-novelist demonstrates. Although he refuses the role of intervening god, he accepts the role of novelist with all of its dramatic manipulations. The Victorian novelist might have tossed a coin, but the contemporary writer can control his novel's *time.* And this one does—thus giving the existential perspective on events which themselves cannot be controlled, i.e., changed. It is *his* florin (a two-headed one, perhaps) which has determined the final ending; now it is *his* watch (a Breguet, the finest) which effaces the previous quarter hour to make way for that final and contemporary ending.

VI *The Endings: Victorian and Modern*

From its ancient beginnings in magic, then religious, ritual and drama, fiction was characterized by closed endings: victories, sacred marriages, births, and deaths. If the hero lost, his defeat grew out of some tragic flaw—some misunderstanding with the gods which alienated their affections. If he won, his victory came from the gods as a reward for his virtue. For centuries, fiction's closed endings assured the accomplishment of divine justice—however miraculous and improbable the *deus ex machina* necessary to bring it about. Even well into the Victorian Age, the novel's closed ending remained a function of divine intervention—although often, at this stage, a sort of secularized version in which the hero was rewarded with the girl and the wealth. However materialistically, the novelist-god gave the protagonist justice—at least until Dickens dropped Stephen Blackpool down a mineshaft and Hardy's heroes began to suffer from their author's deterministic views.

Except for such writers as Hardy and the later Dickens, the novelist in the epoch of the decreeing

Victorian god had no qualms about intervening in his story to effect the closed ending of his choice. And to make his ending happen, the novelist frequently relied upon the most improbable of coincidences. Infants abandoned in railway stations miraculously reappeared years later to claim inheritances; long-lost relatives were reunited across continents and oceans; and heroes were catapulted from poverty to wealth by convergences of the most unlikely circumstances. Although today's novel usually shuns even the barely coincidental, the Victorian novel's closed endings often defied all natural law and mathematical probability. And Lalage, the child whose birth to Charles and Sarah provides the denouement for the first, the closed, ending, is one of those improbable Victorian devices. Lalage is the conventional *deus ex machina*—or more accurately *dea ex uno coito*—whose birth is believable enough in a Victorian context. But the modern reader who knows his physiology would, however willing, require a block-and-tackle to suspend disbelief. Although it is certainly *possible* that Sarah might have conceived from a single union, the odds against that eventuality are better than five-to-one, even under the best of conditions. The conditions, however, are not optimum. The brief consummation of Charles and Sarah may be literature's definitive premature climax: its ninety seconds include not only Charles's feverish undressing but also his travel time—for two-and-a-half round trips between sitting room and bedroom. Charles attributes the happy ending to "God's hands." And rightly so, since biological probability weighs against Lalage's birth, which might have been prevented by variations in ovulation, spermatogenesis, sperm motility, and other factors—not the least of which is genetic mutation, the evolutionary process mentioned in the final chapter's first epigram: "Evolution is simply the process by which chance ['hazard,' in British usage] (the random mutations in the nucleic acid helix caused by natural radiation [gamma-ray particles]) cooperates with natural law to create living forms better and better adapted to survive."

Fowles instructs the reader, "But what you must not think is that this is a less plausible ending to their story. For I have returned, albeit deviously, to my original principle: that there is no intervening god beyond whatever can be seen, in that way, in the first epigraph to this chapter; thus only life as we have, within our hazard-given abilities, made it ourselves, life as Marx defined it—*the actions of men* (and of women) *in pursuit of their ends.*"

Not only is this final ending not less plausible, it is by far the more probable—biologically, as well as psychologically. For, in protesting that his impresario-novelist is "as minimal, in fact, as a gamma-ray particle," Fowles links him to the Gardner epigraph and shows him to intervene as *chance, hazard*—natural radiation, the evolutionary agent which might have inhibited Lalage's birth.

The final ending is thus true to Fowles's biological view. But it is also true to his sense of mystery, for even biology cannot explain it completely. Even in this final ending, there is an unidentified child. Lalage, perhaps? We shall never know.

But this thoroughly contemporary final ending is the one supported by the vast thematic network which has woven into the novel the concepts of man's isolation and his survival through the centuries by *evolving*. Finally, even the reader himself must choose whether to evolve: if he takes the final ending, he has chosen evolution. But if the accepts the happy ending, he must accept along with it its Victorian intervening God, its biological and psychological improbability, its heavy-handed rendering, and its wretched musical accompaniment—the "untalented lady" attempting a Chopin mazurka.

Source: Robert Huffaker, *"The French Lieutenant's Woman,"* in *John Fowles*, Twayne Publishers, 1980, pp. 98–108.

Sources

Fowles, John, *The Aristos: A Self-Portrait in Ideas*, Little Brown, 1964.

————, *The French Lieutenant's Woman*, Signet, 1970.

Huffaker, Robert, "Chapter 4: *The French Lieutenant's Woman*," in *John Fowles*, Twayne's English Authors Series Online, G. K. Hall, 1999; originally published as Twayne's English Author Series, No. 292, Twayne Publishers, 1980.

Pifer, Ellen, "John Fowles," in *Dictionary of Literary Biography*, Vol. 14, *British Novelists Since 1960*, edited by Jay L. Halio, Gale Research, 1983, pp. 309–36.

Review of *The French Lieutenant's Woman*, in *Life*, May 29, 1970, p. 55.

Review of *The French Lieutenant's Woman*, in *New York Times*, November 10, 1969.

Watt, Ian, Review of *The French Lieutenant's Woman*, in the *New York Times Book Review*, November 9, 1969, pp. 1–2.

Further Reading

Brantlinger, Patrick, Ian Adams, and Sheldon Rothblatt, "*The French Lieutenant's Woman*: A Discussion," in *Victorian Studies*, Vol. 15, March 1972, pp. 339–56.
In their discussion of the novel, the authors conclude that all the endings suggest Charles is "left between Victorian repression and modern freedom, having lost Ernestina but not clearly having gained Sarah."

Olshen, Barry N., *John Fowles*, Frederick Ungar, 1978.
In his section on the narrative structure of the novel, Olshen rejects the first ending as "traditional, romantic wish fulfillment."

Palmer, William, *The Fiction of John Fowles: Tradition, Art, and the Loneliness of Selfhood*, University of Missouri Press, 1974.
In an examination of the novel's endings, Palmer suggests that the introduction of the child is "an anti-existentialist resolution that runs against the grain of Fowles's intentions as expressed in his own voice within this very novel."

Rankin, Elizabeth D., "Cryptic Coloration in *The French Lieutenant's Woman*," in *Journal of Narrative Technique*, Vol. 3, September 1974, pp. 193–207.
Rankin argues that the first ending should be seen as an "imperfect stage in the evolution of an existentialist," and so the second ending should be considered the novel's true conclusion.

I, Claudius

Robert Graves

1934

The initial reason Robert Graves set out to write *I, Claudius* (1934) was for money. Living on the Spanish island of Mallorca with the poet Laura Riding, Graves fell into some financial difficulties, which he hoped to resolve through the writing of the historical epic. The book, the first of two fictionalized accounts of Claudius, the Roman emperor from 41 to 54 A.D., was a great success. Within a couple months it had gone into four printings both in the United States and in Great Britain. In 1937, one of Hollywood's biggest directors, Josef von Sternberg, made a failed attempt at filming Graves's epic, a failure that only enhanced the book's growing prestige.

Told from the point of view of the stuttering, physically deformed Tiberius Claudius Drusus Nero Germanicus (most commonly referred to as "Claudius,"), *I, Claudius* covers the reigns of Augustus, Tiberius and Caligula, and ends at the point of Claudius himself reluctantly assuming the position of emperor shortly following Caligula's assassination.

Laden heavily with political intrigue, sexual depravity, incest, conspiracies, family strife, war and pagan rituals, *I, Claudius* was seen by contemporary readers as an allegory of the current times and was awarded both the James Tait Black and the Hawthornden Prizes in 1935.

While the book takes poetic and historical license in several key areas, it has been widely hailed as a masterful portrayal of the Roman Empire and

Robert Graves

the families that ruled it. In Graves's version of events, Claudius was seen by most around him as a bumbling, deformed, and mentally handicapped, but generally harmless, individual who, because of those traits, was able to survive the capriciousness of Tiberius and the madness of Caligula. While those around him plotted endlessly for political power and revenge, Claudius kept to himself, quietly recording his history of Rome and of the Etruscans, but all the while keeping a keen eye on the Empire's goings-on—observations of which formed the basis of Graves's novel.

Author Biography

Robert von Ranke Graves was a noted English poet, classical scholar, translator and novelist. Born July 24, 1895, in Wimbeldon, England, Graves was one of five children born to Alfred Perceval Graves, a poet and Gaelic scholar, and Amalie von Ranke Graves. (Graves's father also had five children from a previous marriage.)

After attending Charterhouse, a private English preparatory school, Graves in 1913 received a scholarship to St. John's College at Oxford. But with the outbreak of World War I, he enlisted and was seriously injured in 1916. This was clearly a crucial event in his life. During the Somme offensive, he had been abandoned as dead and only much later rescued from a pile of corpses. He was eventually nursed back to health and sent back to the front, but the event would scar Graves for years. While recovering from the wounds, he published his first collection of poetry, *Over the Brazier*, and over the next two years, while still enlisted, he would publish two more collections of poetry.

Although Graves would eventually become most famous for his historical novels and his studies on mythology, he considered himself first and foremost to be a poet, producing over 50 volumes of verse in his career. But his first commercial success as a writer came with the publication in 1929 of *Goodbye to All That*, his controversial autobiography in which he recounts his difficulties in school as well as the horrors of war. The book would quickly lead to a falling out with one of Graves's good friends, the English poet, Siegfried Sassoon.

In 1918, Graves married the painter and feminist activist Nancy Nicholson with whom he would have four children. Shortly following the war he took up a teaching position at St. John's College. He soon became known as one of the country's finest "war poets."

A turning point in both Graves's personal and poetic life occurred in 1926 when he met the poet Laura Riding. Together, they founded a press and collaborated on several publishing projects. After a series of infidelities with Riding, Graves permanently separated from his wife in 1927. In 1929 Graves and Riding moved to the Spanish island of Mallorca, but with the outbreak of the Spanish Civil War in 1936, they were forced to move to America. Riding would soon fall in love with Schuyler B. Jackson, whom she would marry in 1941. Graves would meet and fall in love with Beryl Hodge, the wife of a good friend. In 1946 Hodge and Graves moved back to Mallorca, and they married in 1950.

The books that gave Graves his international reputation and greatest commercial successes were *I, Claudius* in 1934, and its 1943 sequel, *Claudius the God*. In 1948 he turned to mythology with his classic, but highly controversial, study *The White Goddess*. His attention turned would soon to Christianity, with the publication in 1946 of *King Jesus*, and by the 1950s, the publication of several more significant works had cemented his international reputation as a novelist, poet, translator and scholar.

In 1962, W. H. Auden called Graves England's "greatest living poet," and in 1968 he was the recipient of the Queen's Gold Medal for Poetry. From 1961 to 1966, Graves was Professor of Poetry at the University of Oxford, and by the time of his death in 1985, at the age of ninety, he had published more than 140 books.

Plot Summary

Chapters 1–6

The Robert Graves novel *I, Claudius* begins with a depiction of the title character as a child. Claudius suffers from many ailments that cause him to stutter and give him a permanent limp. Although reviled by most of his relatives, he is prophesized by a sibyl to one day rule Rome, and as a young child a tiny wolf cub, which eagles had been fighting over, falls into his arms, a sign that he will become the protector of Rome.

Considered by most to be an idiot, Claudius is given the love of history through his tutor Athenodorus, and he eventually grows to write several historical studies, of which *I, Claudius* is one.

Claudius's grandmother Livia is the most important figure in these early chapters. "Augustus ruled the world, but Livia ruled Augustus," Claudius writes, and he describes how his grandmother turns Augustus into an instrument for her ambition to take control of Rome through her son Tiberius.

For starters, Livia uses her position to create discord between Marcellus, Augustus's son-in-law and leading candidate to succeed Augustus, and Agrippa, Augustus's oldest friend and most successful general. The end result of Livia's complex ruse is that Marcellus eventually dies of mysterious ailments (this is the first of many hints that implicitly tie Livia to the rash of food poisonings that infect Rome for generations) and Agrippa is left free to marry Augustus's daughter Julia. Nine years later, in 12 B.C., after Agrippa dies while alone in the country, Julia is free to marry Tiberius, a man Claudius describes as "morose, reserved, and cruel."

Claudius's father Drusus, on the other hand, is a virtuous man. A successful general widely known for his Republican values, he suffers a riding accident on the Rhine. Tiberius rushes to his side, but it is too late. Drusus is dying of gangrene, and his final words, whispered to Tiberius and in reference to Livia, are, "Rome has a severe mother."

With Drusus dead, Livia's plan to rule Rome through Tiberius moves forward. But now Gaius and Lucius, the sons of Julia and direct descendants to Augustus, are in her way. Gaius has become the favorite to follow Augustus as emperor. Livia, in another cunning set of moves, succeeds in getting Tiberius relocated outside of Rome, leaving his wife Julia behind. All along Livia had been feeding Julia an elixir she claims will make her irresistible to Tiberius, but it is actually an aphrodisiac that only increases Julia's sexual appetite. With Tiberius away, Julia goes wild, and her nightly orgies become legendary. When Augustus learns of Julia's activities, he banishes her for life. Meanwhile Gaius, who is sent away to Asia Minor, is given the wrong treatment for a battle wound and is forced for health reasons to retire, and Lucius, in transit to Spain, dies mysteriously. Thus, with no one else remaining to take over as emperor, Augustus has to accept Tiberius back to Rome and adopt him and Postumus jointly as his sons and primary candidates to succeed him.

Chapters 7–14

After his first love is poisoned, and after Livia's plans to have Claudius married to a girl named Aemilia are thwarted when Aemilia's parents are accused of a conspiracy against August, Claudius is forced to marry the six-foot-two inch Urgulanilla. A week after his marriage, Claudius comes across Pollio and Livy, two of Rome's most famous historians. In the course of discussions, Pollio tells Claudius how Claudius's father and grandfather were poisoned. Henceforth Claudius would be on the look-out for further clues to support Pollio's contention.

Meanwhile, Livia and Augustus's views of Postumus begin to change for the worse, and Livia conspires with Livilla, Castor's wife, against Postumus by inviting him to her room and seducing him. As soon as he embraces her, she cries out and Livia immediately breaks through the door and has Postumus arrested. Postumus is banished for life and disinherited, but not before he can tell Claudius the entire story of Livia's conspiracy against him. With Postumus gone, the lone heir to Augustus is now Tiberius.

Soon after returning to Rome to help the aging Augustus, Germanicus learns from Castor of Livia's plot to banish Postumus, and in turn he tells Augustus. On the pretence of taking another trip to one of the colonies, Augustus visits Postumus on his island to help him escape. Livia catches wind of Augustus's plan, and assuming he would bring Postumus back to Rome and restore him to favor, she has to act quickly. She knows that with Postumus restored, her own life will be in danger. Coincidentally, Augustus falls sick, and though he eats only from the common table and of the figs he

Media Adaptations

- The most comprehensive Web site on Robert Graves can be found at http://www .robertgraves.org/ (accessed November 24, 2004) with links to many data bases and material related to Graves's scholarship, including *Gravesiana: the Journal of the Robert Graves Society* and archived audio recordings of the writer.

- Academy of American Poets houses a Robert Graves page at http://www.poets.org/poets/ poets.cfm?prmID=197 (accessed November 24, 2004) with audio recordings and links to other sites.

- Blackstone Audiobooks released an unabridged audio recording of *I, Claudius* in 1994 that is available both through bookstores and online as a digital download.

- One of the most critically acclaimed television series of all time, Masterpiece Theater's *I, Claudius*, starring Derek Jacobi as Claudius, and also staring John Hurt and Patrick Stewart, is available both in DVD and VHS format. Included in the DVD format is the 1965 television production, *The Epic That Never Was*, a documentary of director Josef von Sternberg's failed 1937 filming of Graves's book.

himself has picked, out of fear of being poisoned by Livia, he dies.

Prior to his death, Augustus expresses to Claudius his deep apologies for how he has been treated throughout his life, and says that he has taken care of a certain "document" and that Claudius will one day be compensated. Claudius assumes Augustus is referring to his will, and surmises that the emperor has come to learn of Livia's conspiracies. But Augustus did not safeguard his changes well enough, and the previous version of the will, which names Tiberius as successor, is read to the Senate. Livia finally gets her wish, and when Postumus is reported killed by a captain of the guard, her final problem, it seems, is solved.

Chapters 15–34

Soon rumors that Postumus is still alive begin circulating through Rome. The rumor proves true, but Tiberius is able to catch him and have him tortured and killed.

Roman troops in the Rhine mutiny upon Augustus's death, angry over the few shares they are given. Germanicus, remaining faithful to Tiberius, borrows money from Claudius and pays the men under the pretence that the money has come directly from Tiberius. In Rome, Sejanus, Tiberius's Commander of the Guards, begins poisoning the

emperor's mind against Germanicus with several lies. Sejanus had also forms a group of professional informers whose job it is to infiltrate the populous for the purpose of weeding out Tiberius's potential opponents. When Germanicus is sent with his family, including his son Caligula, to the East, Sejanus revives Tiberius's fears by reporting a statement that Germanicus allegedly says in front of one of Sejanus's secret agents. Livia and Tiberius then send a man named Gnaeus Piso to work with Germanicus. Piso also reports back statements construed to make Germanicus appear unfaithful to the emperor. Soon Germanicus finds that his orders to his regiments or cities are not being followed; they are all being overridden by contradictory ones from Piso.

Germanicus soon falls ill and starts smelling "death" in his house. A superstitious man, he sleeps with a talisman, or good luck charm, under his pillow. A slave soon reports finding the body of a dead baby beneath the house, and soon similar discoveries are made throughout the house. After several strange and near-hallucinatory experiences, Germanicus becomes certain that Piso is trying to murder him through black magic. Germanicus dies, and for years the murder remains a mystery. Aggripina returns with her children to Rome, where the public grieves for the popular Germanicus for days.

Sejanus continues to consolidate his power and even tries to become related to the imperial family by marrying his four-year-old daughter to Claudius's son Drusillus. But a few days later Drusillus is found dead with a pear stuck in his throat. Soon Sejanus, Livia and Livilla, Castor's wife, conspire against Castor, who has just been named Protector of the People by Tiberius, a sign that Tiberius is aware of Sejanus's ambitions and intends to check them. The conspiracy works, and Castor quickly falls out of favor with Tiberius. Soon thereafter he falls ill with symptoms of consumption and dies.

Treason trials soon proliferate throughout Rome, and Sejanus once again plots to gain entrance into the imperial family by arranging Claudius's divorce and marrying his adopted sister Aelia to Claudius.

Tiberius, getting old and weak, retires to Capri, thus leaving control of Rome in the hands of Sejanus. He remains there eleven more years until his death, practicing acts too obscene for Claudius to recount.

Livia calls on Claudius and confesses all of her murders, including those of Claudius's father and son, as well as Agrippa, Lucius, Marcellus and Gaius. She also tells him of the prophecies that Germanicus's son, Caligula, will be emperor, and that Claudius will avenge Caligula's death. Livia also makes Claudius promise to deify her when he becomes emperor. In 29 A.D., Livia finally dies.

Under Sejanus's rule, Rome suffers from endless capricious arrests and executions. Claudius's mother happens to find drafts of letters between Livilla and Sejanus, implying a conspiracy to kill Tiberius. She sends Tiberius the letters, and Tiberius has Sejanus arrested for treason. After Sejanus's gruesome execution, a whole crop of equally grim executions follow.

In his final years, Tiberius indicates Caligula as his successor. After Tiberius's death, the Senate confirms Caligula's accession, and in the first days of his rule, Caligula generously pays off Tiberius's debts, observes the terms of Tiberius's and Livia's will, doubles the pay to the army, and sends millions of gold pieces from the treasury into general circulation. General amnesty is declared, and when Caligula falls ill with what is called a "brain fever," the popular consternation is so great that thousands of people stand in vigil day and night outside of the palace.

When Caligula "recovers," however, one of his first acts is to call Claudius into his room where he reveals to his uncle his "metamorphosis" into a divine being and also reveals, with pride, how as a young boy he had murdered his father Germanicus by frightening him to death and stealing his talisman.

Quickly thereafter, Caligula indiscriminately begins killing friends and family members, marries other men's wives at a whim, and puts men to death for such crimes as selling hot water. When the treasury is nearly depleted, Caligula empties the prisons by executing the prisoners and feeding their bodies to wild beasts in the amphitheaters. Claudius's own mother, rather than living under the reign of this madness, kills herself.

Caligula's "divinity" continues; he argues daily with Neptune and with the river gods. No one feels safe around Caligula, and when Claudius is summoned to the palace one night, he assumes his end is at hand. But instead he is awarded with a play in which Caligula plays the "rosy-fingered Goddess," after which Claudius is given the beautiful young Messalina in marriage.

Caligula grows madder by the day, until finally Cassius, one of his soldiers, kills him during a festival. In the melee that follows, soldiers tear through the palace, intent on plunder, and notice two feet sticking out from behind a curtain. Claudius has tried to hide out of fear for his life, but one of the soldiers recognizes him, and the group proclaims him emperor. After a brief protest, he gives in and is soon being carried around the court, fulfilling the sibyl's prophecy and the omen of the wolf cub.

Characters

Agrippa

The most important man in Rome after Augustus, Agrippa is Augustus's oldest friend. Livia favors Augustus's stepson, Marcellus, over Agrippa for the purposes of making Agrippa jealous. When a strange sickness overcomes Augustus, he is forced to name an heir. He chooses Marcellus at Livia's behest, forcing Agrippa to request a relocation out of Rome.

Agrippina

The daughter of Julia and widow of Germanicus, Agrippina becomes the de facto leader of Rome's anti-Tiberius faction following Germanicus's death.

Athenodorus

Athenodorus is Claudius's second tutor. Described by Claudius as "a stately old man with dark gentle eyes," Claudius credits the tutor with instilling in him self-confidence and a love of history.

Augustus Caesar

Augustus, or "Octavian" as he was known before he became Emperor in 27 B.C., claims to be Caesar's heir. Claudius portrays him as essentially a just, though generally weak leader, who defers to his wife Livia and is blind to her numerous conspiracies. "Augustus ruled the world, but Livia ruled Augustus," Claudius tells his readers early on. Every attempt he made at placing one of his direct descendants in line for succession, his second wife Livia succeeded in either killing them off or having them exiled. For most of his marriage to Livia, Augustus was unaware of his wife's conspiracies. It was not until Germanicus returns from his military excursions and informs Augustus of Livia's evil-doings does he catch on. But by then it is too late; Livia poisons the figs directly on the tree, and Augustus becomes one of her many victims.

Briseis

Briseis, one of Claudius's slaves, offers faithful friendship and support to her master, and is most remembered in the narration by a dream she relates to Claudius that foretells the way in which he will assume the position of Emperor.

Caligula

After Tiberius dies in 37 A.D., Caligula, takes over. His first acts as Emperor are to make amends for the unjust reign of Tiberius, and in the first months of his own reign, the Roman public comes to love him. However, after a "brain fever" nearly kills him, Caligula comes to believe he has metamorphosed into a god. Thereafter his reign as Emperor is marked by madness and capricious acts of sadism, sexual depravity, and cruelty. Friends and family members are killed for no reasons, the private fortunes of citizens are plundered, and the women of Rome are considered the emperor's personal property. Caligula is eventually killed at the hands of Cassius, one of his soldiers, and succeeded by Claudius.

Calpurnia

As Claudius's longtime mistress, the prostitute Calpurnia provides Claudius with advice and friendship and is the only woman who ever truly loves him. Her true feelings for Claudius are revealed by her visible hurt when Claudius announces his marriage to the beautiful Messalina.

Cassius

First known for surviving the massacre in the German forests, Cassius becomes more famously recognized as the solder who assassinates Caligula.

Castor

Castor is Tiberius and Vispania's son and the husband of Livilla. He is as cruel as his father. When he was named Protector of the People by Tiberius, a clear sign that he would be heir to the emperor, a conspiracy against him unfolds. He dies of consumptive-like symptoms, thus leaving Sejanus with even greater power.

Claudius

Officially known as Tiberius Claudius Drusus Nero Germanicus, and referred to variously as "Claudius the Idiot," "Claudius the Stammerer," and "Clau-Clau-Claudius," he is the narrator of the story and emperor of Rome during his narration. The son of Drusus and grandson of Livia, Claudius is considered by most Romans to be little more than a harmless, if bumbling, idiot, allowed to remain in the company of the imperial family only because of his birthright. But Claudius, over time, proves to be a keen observer of the political and familial intrigue that Rome had become famous for. While taking no sides in any of the familial struggles, he is able to survive the poisoning of Livia, the tyranny of Tiberius, and the madness of Caligula. His deformities make him a figure of scorn, but they also help to keep him under the radars of the legion of conspirators stalking Rome's streets. Upon Caligula's assassination in 41 A.D., Claudius is forced against his will to accept the position of emperor, a title he maintains for 13 years.

Drusilla

Drusilla, one of Caligula's sisters, is known for having sexual relations with him from a very early age. She is referred to as a "she-beast" by Claudius's mother.

Drusus

Drusus is Claudius's father. He is highly respected by his son and wildly popular with Romans for his belief in the liberties of the Republic. As a general in the army on the Rhine he is wounded slightly. In a letter to his brother Tiberius, he exhorts Augustus not to continue his rule, for the sake of Republican values. The letter is accidentally read aloud to Augustus and Livia. Augustus replies immediately, asking Drusus to return to Rome, but by the time Augustus's letter arrives, Drusus has fallen from a horse and is severely injured. It is revealed later that Livia poisoned him. At his deathbed he whispers to Tiberius, in reference to Livia, "Rome has a severe mother." His death feeds into Livia's plan to rule Rome through her son, Tiberius.

Gaius

Gaius is Julia's oldest son by Marcus Agrippa and a favorite of Augustus. Shortly after being made Governor of Asia Minor, he falls sick and dies, another of Livia's poison victims.

Gemellus

Gemellus is the young son of Livilla and Castor. Caligula kills him for no apparent reason.

Germanicus

Germanicus is the older brother of Claudius and a hugely popular general in the Roman army. Devoutly faithful to Tiberius, Germanicus borrows money to pay mutinous troops and forges a document indicating that the gift came directly from the emperor. As Tiberius's military successes grow, he becomes more and more unpopular among the populace. Tiberius sends him and his family to Antioch, where a series of foreboding and mysterious events unfold, culminating in his death. It is eventually revealed that his son Caligula had killed him, but the belief at the time is that Piso and his wife Plancina, had done the deed.

Julia

Julia is Augustus's daughter by his previous marriage. She is married to Marcellus until he dies, then to Agrippa until he dies, and then to Tiberius. Tiberius never loves her, and after he leaves Rome, she engages in nightly orgies throughout the city and is eventually banished for life by Augustus. It is eventually revealed the Livia has been feeding her an aphrodisiac under false pretences. Julia dies of starvation during Tiberius's reign.

Livia

Livia, the second wife to Augustus and mother of Tiberius and Drusus, is undoubtedly the most powerful individual in the Roman Empire. Her name, Claudius tells us, relates to the Latin word meaning "malignity," an apt description of her relationship to Rome. "Augustus ruled the world, but Livia ruled Augustus," Claudius writes. Livia has fooled her husband into divorcing her so she can marry Augustus, whom she has convinced, falsely, that his wife, Scribonia, is having an adulterous affair. Livia's marriage to Augustus is never consummated; Augustus is a mere instrument in her boundless ambitions. She even provides Augustus with beautiful women with whom he can satisfy his sexual needs. Just before dying, she admits to Claudius that she poisoned several political opponents, including Claudius's father and son. Livia's

monomaniacal desire is to bring her son Tiberius into the line of succession to the emperor, and she uses every ounce of cunning to see that desire through.

Livilla

Livilla is Claudius's sister, Castor's widow, and Sejanus's mistress. She helps conspire against Postumous by seducing him and having him arrested for attempted rape.

Lucius

Julia's second son by Marcus Agrippa and adopted son and heir to Augustus, Lucius is an obstacle in Livia's plan to control Rome. On a trip to Spain, Lucius mysteriously dies, leaving Tiberius as Augustus's obvious heir.

Macro

Commander of the Praetorian Guard under Tiberius following Sejanus's execution, Macro serves briefly under Caligula until he is executed by Caligula.

Marcellus

Octavia's son and Julia's husband, and adopted son of Augustus, Marcellus is considered a leading candidate to be Augustus's heir. After being named Augustus's heir, thus taking Agrippa out of the picture, he is elected to a city magistracy. However, he quickly dies from the same sickness as Augustus, thus leaving Agrippa as the only possible successor. Like so many others, Marcellus falls victim of Livia's touches of poison.

Medullina

A beautiful girl of thirteen who befriends Claudius and whom Claudius loves and sets out to marry, Medullina is poisoned on her way to the wedding and dies before the marriage can take place.

Messalina

Claudius's third wife, Messalina, is given to him by Caligula. She is the first woman Claudius loves since his youth. Although *I, Claudius* ends before Messalina's true colors are revealed, she comes to be known as one of the most famous harlots in history.

Aelia Paetina

Claudius's second wife and Sejanus's adopted sister, Aelia is used by Sejanus to help him become a member, by marriage, of the imperial family.

Piso

Appointed the Roman governor of Syria and Tiberius's agent, Piso conspires against Germanicus by spying on him and sending false reports back to the Roman Senate. When Germanicus becomes ill, he suspects Piso of black magic. Following Germanicus's mysterious death, Piso is accused of the murder and forced to stand trial. Because he holds documents that indict the emperor and his wife, before a the trial can be completed, Livia arranges for his wife Plancina to kill him and make the death appear to be a suicide.

Plancina

Out of fear of losing everything she owns, Plancina, Piso's wife, with Livia's help, kills her husband Piso and makes the death appear to be a suicide. She herself is then tried, and acquitted, of Germanicus's murder.

Postumus

One of Claudius's best friends and grandson to Augustus, and therefore a possible successor to Augustus, Postumus is daring and adventuresome. At the age of fourteen, he protects Claudius from a beating by Cato, Claudius's tutor. He loves Livilla, which proves to be his downfall. Livilla seduces Postumus and then cries rape, causing Postumus to be banished from Rome. He was eventually freed secretly by Augustus, who had finally come to learn of Livia's treachery, but it was too late for him to become Emperor. Livia's further treachery kept him out of Augustus's will, and when his whereabouts were eventually discovered, he was tortured and killed by Tiberius.

Sejanus

Born of humble origins, Sejanus becomes Commander of the Praetorian Guard under Tiberius and effectively ruled Rome with an iron fist when Tiberius retired to Capri. His thirst for power became too much, however; his excesses, which cause the indiscriminate arrests and deaths of many officials and everyday citizens, lead to his own hideous execution at the hands of Tiberius.

Sibyl at Cumae

Claudius relates his visit to the Sibyl at Cumae, who foresees his ascension to emperor and further tells him that 1900 years hence, despite his "stammer, cluck and trip," he "shall speak clear," a reference to the history he writes.

Tiberius

When Augustus dies in 14 B.C., Tiberius, his adopted son and the natural son of Augustus's wife Livia, becomes emperor. His lasts for twenty-two years, most of them in self-imposed exile on the island of Capri. Claudius portrays Tiberius as being a cruel and degenerate ruler who comes to power primarily as the result of his mother Livia's murderous plots. Claudius also tells us of Tiberius's depravity, hinting at acts of bestiality and other depraved sexual practices. Tiberius is on his deathbed, but not quite dead, when he is suffocated by Caligula's commander Macro.

Urgulanilla

A huge, six-foot two-inch woman whom Livia forces Claudius to marry, Urgulanilla has little to do with Claudius.

Themes

Fatalism

The Romans believed that the Fates had already determined their futures, which could not be altered. Claudius describes a visit to the Sybil of Cumae, who foretells of his becoming emperor. He also describes how the Roman Senate would order consultations with the books of prophecies whenever strange portents or disasters occur. Tiberius consults Thrasyllus and acts in response to the soothsayer's prophecies. Livia, near her own death, calls Claudius to tell him of the omens that point to him both becoming emperor and eventually avenging Caligula's death. As described by Claudius, these omens and prophecies were far more than mere superstitions; they effectively guided the Romans in their decision-making and actions. Both Livia and Caligula, for instance, had ample opportunities to kill Claudius, and given all that Claudius knew about their goings-on, it would have made sense to do so. But the fact that Claudius is prophesied to become Emperor and one day avenge Caligula's death helped explain his ability to stay alive.

The Recording of History

Claudius is, first and foremost, a historian. His explicit aim with these chronicles is to offer "readers of a hundred generations hence" this "confidential history" of his life. In what seems at first a digression, Claudius, shortly after his first marriage, meets the historians Pollio and Livy in the

Topics For Further Study

- In Chapter IX of *I, Claudius*, the reader is introduced to two historians of the day, Pollio and Livy. They proceed to argue over their respective views of historical writing. Livy maintains one can spruce history up by providing its figures with "poetical feelings" and "oratorical ability." Pollio asserts that "Poetry is Poetry . . . and History is History, and you can't mix them." Explain in fuller detail the basic arguments that each historian is presenting here. Which side do you think Graves would side with? Which side do you agree with, and why?

- Caligula is presented by Graves as a perverted, capricious, and certifiably mad emperor. However, not all historians agree with this account. Research Caligula's life and explain how your findings either support or reject Graves's portrayal.

- Research the meaning of the term "femme fatale." Are there any "femme fatales" in *I,*

Claudius? If so, who are they and what function do they play in Claudius's narration?

- Sibyls play a major role in Roman society during Claudius's lifetime. Research the history of sibyls in Ancient Rome. What literary function do they serve in *I, Claudius*? Similarly, astrologers are also important in the story. How do astrologers and sibyls differ? How are they similar?

- In Chapter 17 of *I, Claudius*, Claudius goes on record as saying that he and "never at any time of [his] life practices homosexuality" and goes on to explain his position. Although sexuality plays a major role in the book, this is one of the few occasions where homosexuality is mentioned. Whey does Claudius feel compelled to make this assertion? Research the life of Robert Graves and describe his views on homosexuality. How do they fit with these remarks by Claudius?

library. While there, they have a discourse on the uses and abuses of history. "Yes, Poetry is Poetry, and Oratory is Oratory, and History is History, and you can't mix them," Pollio chides his fellow historian. Ironically, Claudius, the narrator of *I, Claudius*, claims to be following Pollio's dictum, but Graves, in his creation of Claudius and his imaginative turns of events, certainly mixes "poetry," or imaginative liberties, with "history." While Graves rightly argues that the characters and events of *I, Claudius* are all historically based, he nevertheless took great liberties in enhancing the characters' traits and filling in the historical detail. Perhaps Graves's most liberal use of "poetry" occurs in his depiction of Caligula. While there is general agreement as to the vicious and capricious nature of Caligula's reign, there is no consensus as to Caligula's psychological state. History certainly suggests that Caligula may have been certifiably mad, but Graves offers an extreme view of that madness that few others have previously, or since, depicted.

Nepotism

Much of the political power in the novel is relegated according to the nepotistic desires of the characters, or the characters' desire to secure the emperor's seat for their own blood relatives, resulting in conniving and murderous competition. With the demise of the Republic, political power in Rome has become concentrated in the hands of the emperor. It is through the emperor's will that a successor is chosen, and it is clear in Augustus's case, at least, that he wants at all costs to choose one of his direct descendants. Unbeknownst to him, however, Livia is constantly scheming to place her own son, Tiberius, in the line of succession. Throughout most of the narrative, it is unclear exactly how Livia is doing this, but near her deathbed, she admits to several poisonings and plots that effectively kept Augustus's children and grandchildren from being able to take over as Emperor. In fact, one could argue that the primary tension that fuels the early action of *I, Claudius* is the continual battle between the wills of Livia and Augustus in this regard. Livia is able to manipulate Augustus through her strategic use of poisoning and plotting, and she wins supremacy for her bloodline.

Paganism

Rome, during these years, is still a pantheistic pagan society, with multiple gods. Christianity, as such, has not yet been established. The Senate, for instance, allows Augustus to be deified in Asia Minor; Livia asks that Claudius promise to deify her upon her death; Caligula believes himself to be a god and, in fact, goes to war, like a god, against Neptune. Sibyls and oracles are consulted, and the emperors retain astrologers to advise them on political matters.

Political Tyranny

Under the Republic, a considerable amount of power was conferred upon the elected officials of the Senate. When August was made emperor, the senate conferred all power to him. As a result, Rome suffers under years of endless plots and conspiracies as Augustus's potential successors and their followers vie with one another for advantage. The winners of these stratagems tend to be those who are most merciless in their acts, such as Livia, Sejanus and Macro, and otherwise innocent politicians, officials and citizens are denied their basic rights and summarily exiled or executed. Although Augustus was generally viewed as a just leader, the reigns of Tiberius and Caligula are noted for their brutal and tyrannical characteristics.

Sexual Activity

Although Claudius is, on most accounts, remarkable for the objectivity of his narration, he does not hesitate in passing judgment in regards to issues of certain types of sexuality. In one noted digression, he states emphatically that he has never engaged in homosexual practices, a sexual lifestyle he considered degenerate. This digression is all the more odd considering that at no time in the narration does he explicitly describe observing any homosexual practices. Also, on several occasions he remarks that the depravity of Tiberius was too revolting to describe, without actually stating what that depravity is, though he does allude to the emperor's practice of bestiality, and he describes one of the Roman wives killing herself as a result of being forced to endure unspeakable acts by Tiberius. Julia is described for her excessive wantonness, and Caligula comes off as being the most depraved of them all, with his inclination to sleep with his sisters and couple with whomever he desired. The sexuality that Claudius describes is effectively used to enhance the atmosphere of "depravity" in Rome; since Claudius makes little, if any, mention of his own sexual activity, this effectively lends a greater air of objectivity to his narrative. (Though it is interesting to note that Claudius is more judgmental of Roman sexual practices than he is of his family's proclivity for grisly murders.) As is the case in virtually all aspects of his life, Claudius is a passive observer of Rome's sexuality; he only acts when acted upon.

War and Xenophobia

Part of the popularity of *I, Claudius* when it was first published may have had to do with the historical and political context in which Graves was writing. The year before the book's publication, Hitler had just come to power in Germany, and although it was still early, there was growing sentiment that Germany would one day soon be on the march to war. *I, Claudius* depicts one of the most aggressive imperial forces in world history. The Roman Empire was able to expand throughout the world as a result of its continual military incursions and victories. Augustus was one of the most successful emperors in this regard, helping Rome to solidify its holdings in the Balkans and Germany. Roman citizens were generally excited at the news of new military victories, for it usually meant that they would soon profit from new supplies of food and an infusion of new wealth into the Roman economy. War also provided military leaders, such as Germanicus, with a way to advance themselves in the eyes of the Roman Senate and emperor. And as in the case with most imperial forces, Rome played on its citizens' fear of the foreign "barbarians." Such a fear of foreigners is known as xenophobia. Without vigilance, these barbarians could one day be knocking down Rome's gates. In Rome's particular case, just as it already was for Graves to a large degree, the Germans were considered particularly barbaric, and Augustus and Tiberius expend serious resources on their German military incursions. Claudius describes massacres of Roman regiments at the hands of the German barbarians, and he describes the fear of the citizens when news of Rome's losses spreads.

Style

Foreshadowing

I, Claudius is narrated by Claudius during the final years of his life. Throughout his narration, Claudius hints at events that are yet to come, oftentimes with the help of sibyls, oracles or other methods of divination. His visit to the Sybil of Cumae, for instance, foretells of his becoming emperor, and a dream that his slave Briseis has describes how his succession would take place.

Historical Novel

As a novel relating a particular period in the history of the Roman Empire, *I, Claudius* relies on certain, verifiable historical facts. The characters he describes all existed in the chronology and relationships that he lays out. Graves seldom fudges dates or the details of significant events, such as the deaths of major Roman figures. However, much of *I, Claudius* is based purely on the author's power of speculation and imagination, and as such should be considered for what it is: a fictional account of the reign of three Roman emperors. However, the purpose of historical fiction is not to portray the "facts" of a particular historical time or event as would a scholarly study; rather, its purpose is to portray the general "truth" of the times in the hopes of providing insights in the readers' contemporary times. A good historical novel reveals universal truths about other people and cultures, and transports us to another historical time through good storytelling, but not through ponderous academic research.

Narrative Objectivity

While Claudius, by the nature of his own existence as a member of the imperial family, cannot but help to be involved in many of the plots and subplots unfolding around him, he nevertheless consciously strives to provide his reader with an objective view of events. His early speculation of Livia's involvement in various deaths is eventually proven true, establishing his credibility as a narrator, and rarely do his other speculative thoughts fail on the grounds of his own biases and subjectivity. Claudius is an historian. As such, he should not lift one historical character above another in the eyes of his eventual readers, but rather reveal the truth as he sees it. This narrative technique is one of the most remarkable characteristics of *I, Claudius*, and Claudius himself, as depicted through his narration, is one of Graves's most ingenious inventions and certainly one of literature's most memorable. Claudius—introduced to his readers as "'Claudius the Idiot,' or 'That Claudius,' or 'Claudius the Stammerer'"—comes across as a remarkably self-deprecating individual. A stuttering, limping, bumbling fool, he is seemingly out of favor with Rome's power structure. But the course of his narration proves him to be an insightful and brilliant figure with a sharp intellect and flawless memory, and as a result, he is able to survive the caprices of Augustus, Tiberius, and Caligula before being named emperor himself.

Historical Context

I, Claudius was written from the Spanish island of Mallorca in 1934. Within two years, the Spanish Civil War would force Graves and his partner, the poet Laura Riding, to flee for America. Meanwhile, the Italian fascist dictator, Benito Mussolini, Spain's right-wing General Francisco Franco, and the German National Socialists, under the leadership of Adolph Hitler, were gaining power in their respective countries and threatening greater Europe.

To understand how the convergence of these historical and political events affected the reception of *I, Claudius*, it is necessary to understand the historical background of the book's story. Although a work of fiction that relies on the author's imagination to fill in some historical voids, the book itself is generally accepted by critics as a historically accurate reflection of the Roman Empire.

In 23 B.C., the Roman Senate granted Gaius Julius Caesar Augustus Octavianus, the grandnephew of Julius Caesar and more commonly known simply as Augustus, the titles and powers of *Imperium proconsulare maius* and *tribunicia potestas* for life, effectively ending the Roman Republic and turning over to him the complete control of the Roman state.

Although Augustus's reign is generally viewed as a just one, with the growing stability of the empire listed as one of his greatest achievements, the seeds of what would evolve into decades of capricious, corrupt and vengeful rulers were planted with the demise of the Republic. In 14 A.D, Augustus died and Tiberius Claudius Nero, commonly referred to as Tiberius, came to power. For twenty-three years, until his death in 37 A.D, Roman citizens and political leaders were on the receiving end of Tiberius's reign that was marked by seemingly capricious assassinations, poisonings, and banishments. In 26 A.D, Tiberius retired to the island of Capri, where he is said to have lived a life of complete depravity and debauchery, effectively leaving Rome in the hands of the praetorian prefect Sejanus, a man whose sole vision was to become emperor at all costs. But the brutality and corruption of Sejanus was even too much for Tiberius to ignore, and in 31 A.D he was arrested and executed.

Compare & Contrast

- **1934:** After years of unprecedented economic growth in the 1920s, the United States suffers from the stock market crash of 1929, leading to the Great Depression.

  Today: After years of economic growth and prosperity in the 1990s, stemming from the unprecedented growth of the hi-tech industry, the United States enters into their greatest recession since the Great Depression.

- **1934:** Europe faces the rise of anti-democratic movements in Germany, Italy and Spain. Fascism and National Socialism are threatening the stability of Europe and, by extension, of the world.

  Today: Although Europe has experienced the spread of democracy since the fall of communism in the 1980s and 1990s, the region faces increased threats of terrorism from Islamic extremists and Russian secessionists.

- **1934:** Labor unions are still struggling to make inroads into the private sector. As a result, workers do not have basic benefits such as guaranteed wages, overtime pay, or health insurance.

  Today: Although labor unions made huge advances following World War II and helped union and non-union workers achieve basic rights, since the 1980s unions have lost political ground, and the wages and rights of many United States workers are being threatened.

- **1934:** Germany is in the early stages of trying to extend its influence across Europe and around the world. Hitler makes no pretence in his desire to spread the ideology of National Socialism around the world.

  Today: While generally speaking there are no military powers that are explicitly trying to take over the world, in the eyes of many the world over, particularly in the eyes of many observers in the Middle East, the United States, with its invasion of Iraq, is trying to extend its influence and ideology across the globe.

- **1934:** Classical education, especially among the upper classes, is very much in vogue in colleges and universities, both in the United States and in Great Britain. Most students in private schools must learn Latin and Greek, and most students are well versed in the Greek and Roman classics and history.

  Today: With some notable exceptions, most students are not required by colleges or universities to study foreign languages or the classics. Classical studies, including the study of Greek and Latin, has been relegated to small academic departments, and the vast majority of students graduate with very little knowledge of the classics or classical languages.

With Tiberius's death, rumored to have come from the hands of his praetorian prefect Macro, his nephew Caligula took over, and thus began a reign marked by what many believe was the apex of Roman madness. Shortly after becoming emperor, Caligula suffered what doctors at the time referred to as a "brain fever." He survived, but his mental acuity suffered irreparable damage. For the remainder of his reign he believed himself to be immortal, was known widely to be having incestuous relationships with his sisters (often with his wife in attendance). His acts of cruelty to opponents, common citizens and criminals were unprecedented in Roman history. After only five years in his reign, an officer of the praetorians, or imperial guard, with the help of several colleagues, assassinated him. In the melee that followed, Claudius was found, literally hiding behind some curtains. The praetorians guards dragged the fifty-year-old, stuttering and physically deformed uncle of Caligula to their camp, where they named him emperor.

I, Claudius covers the period of the Roman Empire that saw the end of the Republic and an increased concentration of power in the hands of the emperor, thus leading to an endless number of conspiracies and political intrigues among the Roman elite. Each successive emperor seemed to outdo the previous in capriciousness and terror, with the innocent bystanders and citizens suffering the most. It also covers a period in which Rome was intent on consolidating, and increasing, its hold on outlying territories, particularly Germany. Claudius's descriptions of the Germans in particular paint an unflattering picture of barbarity.

Graves wrote *I, Claudius* shortly after the tremendous and hedonistic excesses of the 1920s had imploded with the Great Depression and left the Western industrialized world in economic collapse. By 1934, there was also a growing anxiety with respect to Germany's intentions and Italy's growing fascist threat. Europe seemed to be precariously balanced between hyper-anxiety that fueled the 1920s and the hyper-aggression that would erupt with World War II. Europeans watched helplessly as the influence of fascists and Nazis grew. The severe prejudice against the German race as a result of World War I was also fueled by Hitler's rise to power. The rest of the Western world felt helpless as Europe seemed fated to repeat the debacle of World War I. As a result Western society seemed to be suffering from a severe moral angst that led to several unanswered questions: How can an individual survive in such a seemingly unresponsive and amoral world? What can the average person do to positively contribute to such chaos? Is it possible for a society to move forward without repeating its destructive past? These questions were questions of life and death for millions of Europeans in 1934, and by addressing these issues through the eyes of a seemingly powerless, and even inept, individual, and by using an ancient time and world as the backdrop, Graves was able to throw light on the dark questions that the readers of 1934 in Great Britain and the United States may have been asking themselves.

Graves was not alone in using the Roman Empire as a backdrop for epic stories at this time. In 1934, the novelist Jack Lindsay published *Rome for Sale* and *Caesar is Dead*, and within a couple years several more would appear, including Phyllis Bentley's *Freedom Farewell* in 1936, Leslie Mitchell's *Spartacus* in 1937, and Naomi Mitchison's *The Blood of the Martyrs* in 1939. Rome, with its fascist-like praetorian guards and regalia, proved to be a good backdrop to explore issues of the political tyranny and excesses that were spreading across Europe. Even more important, *I, Claudius* covers the period of Roman history that followed

A likeness of Roman Empress Livia, wife to the Emperor Augustus, on a coin

the demise of the more democratic principles of the Republic. Democracy across Europe was on the defensive in 1934; Tiberius and, possibly, Caligula-like rulers were threatening Western civilization.

Critical Overview

I, Claudius was the most widely read and commercially successful book Robert Graves had written to that point. Although his autobiography *Good-Bye to All That* and his growing reputation as a war poet had placed him on the literary map, it was not until *I, Claudius* that he was able to make a reasonable living from his writing.

Within a few months of its publication, the book had been reprinted four times in Great Britain and the United States. Although Graves considered the book to be a potboiler that he wrote only for the money, it went on to win the James Tait Black and Hawthornden Prizes of 1935. Writing in *The Nation & Atheneum*, the novelist Mary McCarthy wrote that the book was "amazingly full of color and imagination." In 1935, Alexander Korda purchased the film rights to *I, Claudius* with the intention of making a movie starring Charles

Laughton. The movie, eventually to be directed by one of Hollywood's finest directors, Josef von Sternberg, was never completed.

Posterity was very kind to Graves. In 1976, the British Broadcasting System produced a television series based on *I, Claudius* and its successor, *Claudius the God*, starring Derek Jacobi, Patrick Stewart and John Hurt. The series was one of the most successful mini-series ever produced, and following its broadcast in the United States, the book, which has been selling a couple thousand copies a year, was reprinted by Vintage for its Vintage Classics series and became an international bestseller. The book's crowning achievement came in 1998 when the Modern Library listed it as the fourteenth best novel of the twentieth century.

Criticism

Mark White

White is publisher of the Seattle-based Scala House Press. In this essay, White argues that while Graves's novel is well-researched and well-written, it does not deserve the critical acclaim it has received.

In 1933, Robert Graves and the poet Laura Riding Jackson were living on the Spanish island of Mallorca and in desperate need of money. Graves' brilliantly received 1929 autobiographical book *Good-Bye to All That* was a commercial success, but its royalties only helped Graves to get out of debt and set himself up for a writing life with Riding on Mallorca. So when pleas to friends, including the British poet Siegfried Sassoon, failed to rescue them, Graves turned to a project he had been working on for some time.

Written primarily for the money and referred to variously by Graves as a "potboiler" and as a "bestseller," *I, Claudius* was a huge success, selling out of three printings within its first year of publications in both Great Britain and the United States. By the end of 1934, Graves was not only temporarily out of financial difficulties, but he had also become an international literary sensation.

Over the years, *I, Claudius* would continue to do reasonably well, selling on average some 2,000 copies a year. But in 1976, when the British Broadcasting Company produced a mini-series based on *I, Claudius* and its successor, *Claudius the God*, and a few years later when the series ran on American television, sales of Graves's fifty-year old

" A good historical novel, in addition to offering the reader a compelling story to follow, should also provide an insight into the times in which it was written."

novels skyrocketed, and the eighty-year old writer suddenly found himself on the bestseller lists again on both sides of the Atlantic. In 1998 the book would receive another unexpected boost when the Modern Library named it as number fourteen on its list of the best 100 novels of the twentieth century. So not only did this unlikely story of a stuttering and limping Roman Emperor dig Graves and his lover out of financial ruin, it also helped to secure him a place in literary posterity.

There is certainly no question that Graves would have deserved to have his name etched into the annals of literary posterity regardless of the fate *I, Claudius*. The author of more than 140 books, including over 50 volumes of poetry, several studies of mythology, and scores of critical studies, Graves was, by any standard of measure, deserving of a respectful place in English literary history.

But does he deserve to remembered critically for *I, Claudius*? Certainly the success of the television productions alone have guaranteed him many more years of popularity, but has it been a popularity that the book deserves in its own right? Does it belong alongside the likes of James Joyce's *Ulysses*, William Faulkner's *The Sound and the Fury*, and Vladimir Nabokov's *Lolita*, as the Modern Library list suggests? In other words, should one take Graves at his word when he called the novel a potboiler, or is there something lurking behind the words of the stuttering emperor that give this novel a greatness beyond its obvious commercial attributes?

As is usually the case with such queries, the answers to most of these questions are yes, and no. Yes, *I, Claudius* is far better than a mere "potboiler." Graves knew how to write, he knew how to tell a story, and he knew the point at which history should stop and fiction should begin. But no, the book does not deserve the critical immortality that it seems to be on the verge of acquiring. *I,*

What Do I Read Next?

- Paul Fussell's *The Great War and Modern Memory* (1975) received the National Book Award, the National Book Critics Circle Award, and was named by the Modern Library as one of the twentieth century's 100 Best Non-Fiction Books. It analyzes the effects of World War I on several major writers, including Graves, Siegfried Sassoon, and Wilfred Owen.

- Known as one of the bitterest autobiographies ever written, Graves's *Good-Bye to All That* (1929) is a scathing critique of World War I and the military and political leaders who led Great Britain during the war.

- *Wild Olives: Life in Majorca with Robert Graves* (1995), by William Graves, and *A Woman*

Unknown: Voices from a Spanish Life (2000), by Lucia Graves, offer glimpses into the writer's life from the perspectives of two of his children.

- In 1937, shortly following her husband's success with *I, Claudius*, Laura Riding published *A Trojan Ending*, her attempt at classical historical fiction. Graves supplied Riding with the necessary historical material that formed the basis of the book.

- *In Broken Images: Selected Letters of Robert Graves, 1914–1946* (1982) and *Between Moon and Moon: Selected Letters of Robert Graves 1946–1972* (1984), both edited by Paul O'Prey, are the first collections of Grave's abundant correspondence to have been published.

Claudius was written to make money, and it succeeded brilliantly because its author was a brilliant enough scholar and writer to make all the right literary moves. With *I, Claudius*, Graves fed on Great Britain's and America's bottomless appetite for sexual depravity, political intrigue, femme fatales, and even good, old fashioned German bashing. Add to the mix his ingenious use of age-old fairy-tale themes that one finds in such stories as "Cinderella" and "The Ugly Duckling" and in such venues as elementary school playgrounds where bullies are forever beating up on the lame and innocent, along with an atmosphere beginning to smell ripe with the familiar stench of war, and the result was well-timed, well-written and imaginatively inspired historical soap opera that hit the hearts and charts of the English-reading populace.

Graves was, by any account, a serious scholar and a man of high literary talent. With *I, Claudius*, Graves spent several years of assiduous research into Roman history and customs. While *I, Claudius* relies on Graves's boundless imagination for its storytelling, the major events depicted in the novel have a historical basis, and the dates within the story coincide with what we know of Rome's history. But a historical novel must do more than simply

provide an accurate recording of history. A good historical novel, in addition to offering the reader a compelling story to follow, should also provide an insight into the times in which it was written. By any measurement, did *I, Claudius* provide its readers of 1934 insights into their own worlds?

An obvious place to look for an answer to this question is in the way the book portrays Rome's relationship with its outlying areas, particularly the Germans. Doing so would show how Graves presented his reader, if he did so at all, with insight into the "German question," a growing and pressing concern for him and his fellow Europeans in 1934.

In 1933, Adolph Hitler had come to power in Germany. While it would be a few more years before Germany would invade its neighbors, the psychological and political war had already begun. Europe could already hear the figurative echoes of the marching black boots of the National Socialists.

A large part of Graves' novel is devoted to the German campaigns of Claudius's brother Germanicus. The Germans that Germanicus' and Claudius's father Drusus had conquered, Claudius tells us, had quickly adapted to "Roman ways, learning the use of coinage, holding regular markets and even meeting in assemblies that did not end, as their former assemblies had always ended, in armed battles." In other words, Roman occupation had relieved the Germans of "their old barbarous ways," but when Varus, a political appointee of Augustus, entered the picture, he began abusing the Germans who, in turn, secretly planned a mass rebellion. Varus, believing the Germans to be a "stupid race" of men who respected you only when you hit them, ignored warnings of a rebellion from his own staff, and a horrible massacre ensued, in which only Cassius, the officer who would one day assassinate the Emperor Caligula, survived. News of Rome's previously unimaginable defeat spread panic throughout Rome, and Romans believed that the German hordes were ready to knock on the city gates. News and rumors of German barbarity spread. As Claudius/Graves note:

> Meanwhile, the Germans hunted down all the fugitives from Varus's army and sacrificed scores of them to their forest-gods, burning them alive in wicker cages ... The Germans also enjoyed a long succession of tremendous drinking-bouts on the captured wine, and quarreled bloodily over the glory and the plunder."

When Germanicus later returned to the front to avenge the massacre, he wrote to Claudius:

> The Germans are the most insolent boastful nation in the world when things go well with them, but once they are defeated they are the most cowardly and abject. Never trust a German out of your sight, but never be afraid of him when you have him face to face.

Can an argument be made that Graves is merely using the facts of Roman history to lift a mirror to the situation of 1934 Europe? If that is the case, then what "insight" does Claudius's account afford the reader?

Any possible argument that Graves is building a case for Great Britain to defend itself against Germany here falls short when one considers the story of *I, Claudius* as a whole. Rome, under Augustus, and then less successfully under Caligula, was an imperial country with imperialistic aims. Its vision was to rule the world, from horizon to horizon; any useful analogy in this context would bring the reader to view Germany, not Great Britain, as the modern day Rome. If that is the case, then who would the Germans be? Certainly not the Brits, and certainly not the Americans—both races of people who considered themselves among the most civilized in the world and far from the barbaric natures that Claudius depicts.

The problems Rome was having with its colonies were problems all imperial forces have always had, and will always have, with their colonies: whenever the colonizer has tried to impose its own will on its subjects, the subjects have rebelled forcefully and usually violently.

No, the only purposes these passages effectively served, aside from the obvious ones of relating the history of Rome as it actually was, were to feed into the existing and growing fear of the German threat. After World War I, European leaders could not trust Germany's intentions, and their imposition of the humiliating Versailles Treaty only fanned the flames of German anger. That anger, in turn, fanned the flames of hatred against and fear of the German race. Whether conscious or not, Graves had pulled from ancient history the same themes of fear of the "outsider" and "other" that Europeans were still experiencing nearly 2000 years later. Graves is offering nothing insightful here; he is merely fanning the flames of anti-German sentiment, a sentiment that would help in the sales of his book.

So what of the possible argument that Graves is using ancient Rome to depict Germany or, better yet, the fascist states of Italy or Spain? On a superficial level, one could make this argument, as there are several characteristics that both the fascists and the national socialists shared with Rome of Augustus, Tiberius and Caligula. For starters, as already mentioned, the Roman Empire, like Nazi Germany, had visions of world domination. The consolidation of political power in the hands of a single individual—Franco in Spain, Mussolini in Italy and Hitler in Germany—also mirrored that of Rome, and like Rome, once power was consolidated by the respective parties, no method was considered too cruel to help the parties retain that power. Rome's praetorian guard also found distant relatives in the fascist and nazi states, as did Roman regalia and the classical attributes and themes on which the Roman Empire was built. But beyond that, one would be hard pressed to see any useful parallels. For instance, one of the most striking features of Germany and Italy were their regimentation; while the elites certainly had opportunities for the same illicit and licentious behavior as the Roman elite, and while they certainly did not hesitate to indulge in them, the ultimate ideology of the parties was always of paramount importance. Although the Holocaust was certainly as "depraved" as anything that Claudius described, Germany's execution in exterminating Jews and other "undesirables" was far more planned and systematic than any of the cruelties enacted by Rome.

What *I, Claudius* does offer contemporary readers, however, is the opportunity to rubber-neck

View of the Roman Forum, which was extensively built up by Augustus, the first emperor of the Roman Empire

at the figurative train wrecks that littered the Roman empire. Powerful men and women, immortalized by their lineage and their positions of power and prestige, were done in by their own lasciviousness, greed, sexual depravity, and conspiracies. *I, Claudius* was provided with all the makings of a high-brow soap opera decades before *General Hospital*, *As the World Turns*, or *West Wing* would rivet generations of Americans and Brits to their couches. And comparing *I, Claudius* to television series is by no means anachronistic or mixing metaphors, for it was the British Broadcasting Company and America's Public Broadcasting System, with the help of a brilliant performance by the British actor Derek Jacobi playing Claudius, that one could argue ultimately raised the book from its place as a solid, if forgettable, novel, to that of one the greatest novels ever written, at least in the eyes of Modern Library's panel of judges.

Of course, one could argue with equal vigor that regardless of the success of the television series, the book would not survive if it was not good. There are countless examples, after all, of stellar movies that are based on all-but-forgotten books. This is true, and this brings us back to the original argument that Robert Graves knew what he was doing. By creating an archetypal character in Claudius

(a composite "ugly duckling," "Cinderella," and bullied school boy), surrounding him with some of the richest and most memorable characters in history, and describing their respective demises in agonizing detail, Graves found for himself a winning recipe for a money-maker. But to be considered great, Claudius's account of his life through 41 A.D. would have to have offered us insights into the 1934 world of its readers. If the insight that Graves is offering his readers is how train wrecks rivet us, then, yes, his novel is a great one, but otherwise *I, Claudius* the book offers little more than *I, Claudius* the television series and takes much longer to get through.

Source: Mark White, Critical Essay on *I, Claudius*, in *Novels for Students*, Thomson Gale, 2005.

Lois Kerschen

Kerschen is a freelance writer and adjunct college English instructor. In this essay, Kerschen shows how Graves used the structure of the historical novel, as well as imaginative speculation, to create a new portrait of the Emperor Claudius.

The historical novel is a type of novel that generally distinguishes itself by being set in a time period previous to the one in which the author lives.

Most storylines can be set in the past, usually for the simple purpose of establishing a backdrop to a story that is peopled by fictional characters. Even when the social situation of the time period is essential to the plot, it is the characters that dominate the story. For some plots, the historical time period is an interesting enhancement but is otherwise irrelevant; for example, the plot and characters of *Cold Mountain* could have been set in any war time, just as *Romeo and Juliet* has been adapted to a variety of time periods and worked very well in the twentieth-century New York City adaptation we all know as *West Side Story*. Certainly, the author and editor take pains to assure the accuracy of the historical setting, being careful not to use inappropriate fashion or language, or mention any event that had not yet happened or any device that had not yet been invented. With some historical novels, such as the currently popular Patrick O'Brian naval series set in the Napoleonic era, it is the remarkable extent of the detail about life in those times that has fascinated readers and gained the most acclaim. Then there is the type of historical novel as written by Robert Graves in *I, Claudius*.

From among the genre's options, Graves chose to write a fictional story using real characters in a real setting; that is, his story was based on historical figures as well as a historical time period. The difference between a history book and a historical novel about real people is that the history book should be based solely on known facts, while the historical novel contains elements that may not be verifiable. In fact, some of the story may be a total invention of the author. Richard Cavendish, a reviewer for *History Today*, commented that "When the authors know their stuff, historical novels can make as enticing and informative a path to history as proper history books, which are not after all invariably free of fiction." In the case of *I, Claudius*, the story is based on careful and extensive research on the part of Graves, but then he filled in the areas that historians would ordinarily leave blank or mark as questionable, unknown. Graves connects the known history with plausible assumptions and unique interpretations about the unknown motivations and behind-the-scene intrigues of the figures involved.

Graves took theories and suggestions from historians and wrote a story that plays out the possibilities. Daniel Aaron in an article for *American Heritage*, suggests that when a novelist, such as Gore Vidal writing *Lincoln* as a novel and not as a biography, "mixes disagreed-upon facts and agreed-upon facts, he is creating an extra but not

> " ... Graves may have assigned guilt or credit to different parties than the ordinary history book would because he felt that he had discerned the truth that was kept out of the public record."

necessarily nonhistorical compound." In other words, when Graves addressed the "what if" of history through fiction, he might have actually guessed the truth. After all, those who were recording events at the time they were occurring might have done so with bias or malicious intent. Is a record of history always a fact just because it is written down, or might there be more to the story? Might some important link have been left out for purposes of discretion or just lack of space? If so, might not a writer be able to reconnect the links through both research and imagination?

Graves was actually a poet who brought his literary sensitivities to his historical research as well as a gift for psychological analysis. With these attributes, he was able to discern relationships and an unfolding of events that an academic historian would not have reported. Graves was also aware of the social and political biases of Roman historians such as Suetonius and Tacitus that caused them to disregard any evidence of intelligence and savvy in Claudius. In an interview about *I, Claudius*, Graves explained that he felt that Roman historians:

> ... had obviously got Claudius wrong ... I didn't think I was writing a novel. I was trying to find out the truth of Claudius. And there was some strange confluent feeling between Claudius and myself. ... It's a question of reconstructing a personality.

Graves studied a number of documents that Claudius wrote in an effort to get to know the one-time emperor of Rome. Adding this knowledge to the realization that Claudius had cerebral palsy led Graves to conclude that "The whole scene is so solid, really, that you feel you knew him personally, if you're sympathetic with him. The poor man."

Thomas Fleming, himself a historical novelist, notes that "Sometimes it is a special insight into a historical character that triggers an imaginative explosion." Indeed, when Graves dared to venture into the mind of Claudius, he discovered that Claudius was perhaps not the deformed idiot that his family thought him to be, but a wily intellectual with enough survival instincts to play up his infirmities and thus put himself at a safe distance from the imperial intrigues. Then Graves was ingenious enough to construct the novel as if it were the autobiography of Claudius. What better proof of Claudius' abilities and insights? Who better to explain his deception and serve as a bird's-eye observer to important historical events than Claudius himself?

Fleming also advises that "fact can and should be woven into fiction so seamlessly [that] readers never stop to ask what is true in the literal sense and what is imaginative." Graves certainly accomplishes that feat, even though he uses language that is very British, which sometimes jars the reader out of the illusion that the novel is the autobiography of Claudius. When Tiberius calls for an omelet and a couple of beef-cutlets, one has to wonder if these items were ever really on the menu in ancient Rome. "It has been difficult at times to find suitable renderings for military, legal and other technical terms," Graves tells the reader in the "Author's Note." Nonetheless, his care in using correct terms in technical areas may or may not have carried over to other areas as well. In addition, the plan to hide the autobiography "in a lead casket and bury it deep in the ground," trusting the Sibyl's prophecy that it will be found in nineteen hundred years, is a contrivance of the author, as is the "confidential history" explanation. Therefore, the reader starts out knowing what game the author is playing with imagination and historical events. Nonetheless, as the novel progresses, everything seems so perfectly plausible that readers eventually forget the device of the novel. As Fleming adds, "All that should matter is the conviction that they are being taken inside events in a new revelatory, personal way." There is nothing more personal than an autobiography, and revelations abound as Claudius confides in the audience.

Graves also saw the members of the Roman imperial family during the life of Claudius in a different light from historians. Using the character of Claudius as an observer and astute, skeptical reporter, Graves is able to turn rumors—that historians are obligated to ignore—into the juiciest parts of the novel. Consequently, there are some differences between his characters, drawn from history, and the generally accepted description of these people found in the annals of history. In other words, Graves may have assigned guilt or credit to different parties than the ordinary history book would because he felt that he had discerned the truth that was kept out of the public record.

Although some critics feel that historical fiction is most successful when it precisely and consistently reproduces the attitudes and lifestyles of its time period, it seems to be the nature of historical novels that they include a note of satire on contemporary times. Graves indicated an interest in using his novels to convey a modern message, and there are some telltale signs of this practice in *I, Claudius*, written in 1934. Graves was one of the first in Britain to warn of the potential trouble with the growth of fascism in Europe, particularly Germany. His description of Germans in *I, Claudius* are quite revealing of an attitude:

> If Germans ever become civilized it will then be time to judge whether they are cowards or not. They seem, however, to be an exceptionally nervous and quarrelsome people, and I cannot make up my mind whether there is any immediate chance of their becoming really civilized.

Some readers feel that *I, Claudius* was written to parallel the fall of the British empire, although the fall of the Roman empire came long after the life of Claudius. Since the novel concentrates on relationships within the ruling family, other readers might suspect that *I, Claudius* is a parody of the Mafia since there are coincidentally so many striking similarities in the operation of this "family business." For example, the remorseless Livia said that she "never contrived a murder" for her own benefit but only to remove those people who might stand in the way of the succession of her own sons and grandsons. This mentality is classic Mafia: knock off the competition to increase your own power and territory, but do not feel guilty because it is only business.

The historical novel can be a valuable educational tool because it teaches history in a format that readers find palatable and enjoyable. Readers start out reading a story and end up with new knowledge about a certain time period. Also, just as when movie-goers see "based on a true story" in the credits and dash home to look up the facts or check to see if there is a book on the subject, the historical novel has the potential to revive popular interest in the time period of the story (e.g., the renewed interest in the actual events connected to the Titanic after the blockbuster movie named after the ill-fated ship). Even more, Aaron, writing about what we can learn from a historical novel, speculated that "in reshaping popular conceptions of the past [historical fiction] might even revolutionize the study of history." An ethical historical

A bust of the Roman Emperor Claudius

novelist will not purport that his/her version of history is closer to the truth than what has been previously established, but will stimulate scholars into considering the "what ifs" and perhaps re-examining the records in a new light. Such is the accomplishment of Graves and *I, Claudius* in that his extensive research, combined with psychological analysis and compassionate sensitivity, results in previously unconsidered possibilities for the motivations, credit, and blame for some of Roman history's most famous people, and perhaps raises the reputation of "poor Claudius."

Source: Lois Kerschen, Critical Essay on *I, Claudius*, in *Novels for Students*, Thomson Gale, 2005.

Sources

Aaron, Daniel, "What Can You Learn from a Historical Novel?" in *American Heritage*, Vol. 43, No. 6, October 1992, pp. 55–56.

Blowen, Michael, "How the Movie Sells the Book," in *Boston Globe*, January 12, 1986, Sec. B, p. 1.

Buckman, Peter, and William Fifield, "The Art of Poetry XI: Robert Graves," in *Conversations with Robert Graves*, edited by Frank. L. Kersnowski, University of Mississippi Press, 1989, p. 100.

Burton, Philip, "The Values of a Classical Education: Satirical Elements in Robert Graves's *Claudius* Novels," in *Review of English Studies*, Vol. 46, No. 182, May 1995, pp. 191–218.

Cavendish, Richard, "Historical Novels," in *History Today*, Vol. 53, No. 5, May 2003, p. 88.

Fleming, Thomas, "How Real History Fits into the Historical Novel," in the *Writer*, Vol. 111, No. 3, March 1998, pp. 7, 11.

Graves, Richard Percival, "Book Four: Robert Graves and Laura Riding in Majorca, 1929–1936," in *Robert Graves: The Years with Laura, 1926–1940*, Viking, 1990, pp. 125–244.

Hopkins, Chris, "Robert Graves and the Historical Novel in the 1930s," in *New Perspectives on Robert Graves*, edited by Patrick J. Quinn, Susquehanna University Press, 1999, pp. 128–35.

McCarthy, Mary, Review of *I, Claudius*, in *The Nation & Atheneum*, June 13, 1934, quoted in Snipes, Katherine, "Historical Novels: On Claudius" in *Robert Graves*, Ungar Publishing Company, 1979, p. 180.

Snipes, Katherine, "Historical Novels: On Claudius," in *Robert Graves*, Ungar Publishing Company, 1979, pp. 173–88.

Further Reading

Gibbon, Edward, and David Womersley, *The History of the Decline and Fall of the Roman Empire*, abridged ed., Penguin, 2001.

    First completed in 1788, Gibbon's classic study of the Roman empire continues to be considered one of the major works on the subject. Womersley's abridgement keeps the major themes and style of the original.

Graves, Richard Percival, *Robert Graves: The Years with Laura, 1926–1940*, Viking, 1990.

    The second of a three-volume biography of Graves by his nephew, *The Years with Laura* covers the period in which *I, Claudius* was written.

Graves, Robert, *Claudius the God: And His Wife Messalina*, 1940, reprint, Vintage, 1989.

    Picking up where *I, Claudius* left off, *Claudius the God: And His Wife Messalina* covers the 13-year reign of Claudius as emperor of Rome.

Seymour, Miranda, *Robert Graves: Life on the Edge*, Doubleday, 1995.

    One of the most insightful biographies of Graves available, Seymour's work profited from the unprecedented cooperation she received from Graves's widow and son.

Seymour-Smith, Martin, *Robert Graves: His Life and Work*, rev. ed., Bloomsbury, 1995.

    This 1995 edition, updated from its original 1983 edition on the occasion of the centennial of Grave's birth, is considered among the finest of Grave's biographies, even if it is also considered one of the most opinionated.

The Immoralist

André Gide

1902

André Gide's controversial short novel *L'Immoraliste* (1902; *The Immoralist*) describes a journey of self-discovery by which a young man becomes increasingly aware of his homosexual inclinations. *The Immoralist* is based on Gide's personal experience of discovering his homosexuality while traveling as a young man in North Africa.

The Immoralist is narrated by Michel, a young man who describes his marriage to Marceline, a woman he hardly knew, and lays bare the developments of his inner life during the first few years of their marriage. While on an extended honeymoon in North Africa, Michel finds himself attracted to young Arab boys. This experience inspires him to embark on a journey of self-discovery through which he eventually finds himself leading a double life: he presents a false facade to his wife, while going out on his own to follow his natural inclinations and experience his true inner being. Back home in France, Marceline announces that she is pregnant. Meanwhile, Michel finds himself increasingly drawn to healthy and attractive young men. Becoming ill from tuberculosis, Marceline suffers a miscarriage. Michel, motivated by a strong desire to return to North Africa, pushes her to travel with him, despite her deteriorating health. After she dies, Michel is left to grapple with the meaning of his own life, and to come to terms with his homosexual tendencies.

The central theme of *The Immoralist* is repressed homosexuality. Gide's narrative further explores themes of life versus death, mind versus body, and the process of self-discovery.

André Gide

Author Biography

André Gide was one of the most important French writers of the twentieth century. He was born André Paul Guillaume Gide, 22 November 1869, in Paris, France, the only child of Paul Gide, a professor of Roman law, and Juliette Rondeaux Gide, a Norman heiress. When Gide was eleven, his father died of tuberculosis. Soon after, Gide developed a predilection for faking illness, and was often kept home from school, receiving an uneven education from private tutors. Upon passing his baccalaureate examination at the age of twenty, he determined to devote his life to writing. His first book, *Les Cahiers d'André Walter* (1891; *The Notebooks of André Walter*), is an autobiographical novel based on his youthful experiences.

In 1893, Gide made his first trip to North Africa, where he had his first homosexual experience. That year, he suffered from tuberculosis, though he soon recovered. Two years later, he returned to North Africa, where he met with the well-known homosexual Irish writer Oscar Wilde. In important conversations with Wilde, Gide was encouraged to admit his homosexual tendencies to himself and his friends. Gide's trips to North Africa became the basis of *The Immoralist*, in which Michel, the central character, travels twice to

Algeria. The character of Menalque in *The Immoralist* is based on Wilde, and Michel's late-night conversation with Menalque in which his friend hints at his homosexual tendencies is based on Gide's discussions with Wilde. Gide's mother died in 1895. Soon after, he married his cousin, Madeleine Rondeaux. At the age of twenty-seven, Gide was elected mayor of La Roque, making him the youngest mayor in France.

The Immoralist, one of Gide's most important works, was first published in 1902. Like Michel in *The Immoralist*, Gide struggled in his marriage with feelings of genuine love for his wife that conflicted with his homosexual inclinations and his strong need for individual freedom. These tensions resulted in many years of estrangement between husband and wife. When she learned of Gide's love affair with a young man in 1918, she retaliated by burning all of his letters to her. In 1923, Gide's daughter, Catherine, was born to Elisabeth van Rysselberghe, a married woman with whom Gide had an extramarital affair. However, Gide's paternity of the child was kept secret from Madeleine. After a lengthy illness, Madeleine died in 1938. Gide's lifelong concern with individual freedom lead him to advocate for the social, economic, and political liberty of oppressed peoples throughout the world, and he is remembered as a great humanitarian. During World War I, he worked for the Red Cross, then in a convalescent home for wounded soldiers, and later offered shelter to war refugees. During the 1920s, he became an advocate for the oppressed peoples of colonized regions, as well as for women's rights and the humane treatment of criminals. In 1947 he was awarded the Nobel Prize for Literature. Gide died in Paris on 19 February 1951, at the age of eighty-one.

Plot Summary

Part 1

Michel, the protagonist of *The Immoralist*, has spent his early adulthood as a scholar of ancient Greek and Roman cultures. He describes his marriage at the age of twenty-five to Marceline, a twenty-year-old woman whom he hardly knows. Shortly after their engagement, Michel's father dies. The newlyweds travel on their honeymoon to North Africa, a region that at the time was colonized by the French. During their travels, Michel becomes ill from tuberculosis. By the time they arrive in the city of Biskra, Algeria, he is gravely ill and close to death.

Media Adaptations

- *The Immoralist* was adapted as a play written by Ruth Goetz and Augustus Goetz, first staged on Broadway in 1954. This production starred James Dean as an Arab teenager, Louis Jordan as Michel, and Geraldine Page as Michel's wife Marceline.

Throughout his illness, Michel and Marceline stay at a hotel in Biskra, where Marceline nurses him. Michel is so ill that he does not even leave their hotel room for a long time. As he begins to recover, Marceline brings Bachir, a local Arab boy, to play in Michel's room and cheer him up. Eventually, Michel recovers enough from his illness to go out for a walk with Marceline in a park near their hotel. When they meet a group of local Arab boys in the park, Michel feels that he would prefer to go there without his wife. He realizes that, as a scholar, he has been living the life of the mind, while neglecting his physical being. Finding a renewed sense of life and a new awareness of his physical senses, Michel determines to devote himself to improving his health.

As Michel's health continues to improve, he begins to take walks alone among the orchards of a nearby oasis, where he meets and befriends more Arab boys. He and Marceline begin to invite the Arab boys to their hotel lodgings to play and eat sweets. One day, Michel sees one of the boys, Moktir, steal a pair of his wife's sewing scissors. Instead of reprimanding Moktir, or taking the scissors away from him, Michel lies to his wife about why the scissors are missing. After this incident, Michel finds that Moktir is his favorite of the children.

After staying in Biskra for several months, Michel and Marceline decide to leave. They continue to travel in North Africa, Italy, and the Mediterranean region, passing through Tunis, Malta, and Syracuse. With his newfound health and excitement about life, Michel finds himself losing interest in his scholarly research. While staying in Salerno, Michel spends many days off on his own exploring the area, leaving his wife behind at their hotel. He becomes very focused on his body and his physical health. He soon finds himself leading a double life. Away from his wife, he continues to focus on his newly emerging sense of self and renewed excitement about life. In his wife's presence, however, he presents a false persona as a loving and attentive husband.

One day, Michel gets into a fight with a drunken coach driver, who had been driving recklessly while Marceline was a passenger in the coach. That night, two months after their wedding, Michel and Marceline make love for the first time.

Part 2

In the spring, the newlyweds return home to France. They spend the summer at Michel's childhood home in Normandy, in northern France, where he has inherited a large estate called La Morinière. Michel becomes acquainted with Bocage, his estate manager. When Charles, Bocage's seventeen-year-old son, arrives at La Morinière, Michel is immediately drawn to the young man, and the two of them go horseback riding together every day. Michel becomes increasingly involved in the management of his estate. Marceline informs him that she is pregnant.

In the fall, Michel and Marceline move back to Paris, where he begins his teaching post at the College de France. In Paris, Michel is bored by the demands of their social life. One day, he meets Menalque, a former acquaintance, with whom he strikes up a friendship. Menalque explains that he has traveled to Biskra and met many of the Arab boys whom Michel had befriended while on his honeymoon. One night, Menalque hands Michel the pair of scissors that Moktir had stolen from Marceline. Michel arrives home that night to find that Marceline has had a miscarriage and is gravely ill from tuberculosis.

When the academic year ends, Michel and Marceline return to La Morinière for the summer. Marceline becomes more and more ill. Michel, meanwhile, spends more and more time with the peasants on his estate. He even joins Alcide, the youngest son of Bocage, in secretly poaching game on his own grounds. He finds himself intrigued by the lives of the peasants, particularly those whose behavior is morally questionable. Although Marceline continues to be very ill, the couple decides to leave La Morinière and travel.

Part 3

Michel and Marceline travel throughout Switzerland, Italy, and North Africa. Marceline becomes more and more ill, while Michel finds himself increasingly full of health and vigor. They return again to Biskra. Michel cares for Marceline during the day, but after she goes to sleep, he goes out prowling the streets at night. He meets many of the children they had befriended two years earlier. However, the boys have become young men, and have gone on with their lives. Some of them have married and found work, while others have become criminals and spent time in jail. Moktir, the boy who once stole the pair of scissors, has recently been released from prison. Michel is disappointed that these boys have lost the health and freshness that had first drawn him to them.

One night Moktir takes Michel to a prostitute. Michel returns home from this encounter to find that Marceline is dying. After Marceline dies, Michel remains in Algeria for three months. During this time, he befriends an Arab boy named Ali. Ali eventually introduces Michel to his sister, who is a prostitute. Michel sleeps with Ali's sister on several occasions. However, Michel soon becomes bored of her, and feels that Ali seems to be jealous, so he tells the girl he no longer wants to see her. Ali continues to spend time with Michel, and to do various errands for him, "in exchange for the odd caress." Afterward, when Ali's sister encounters Michel on the street, she teases him that he is more interested in her brother than in her, and that Ali is the reason he stays in Algeria. Michel's response, which is the closing line of the novel, is "Perhaps she is not altogether wrong . . ."

Characters

Alcide

Alcide is the youngest son of Bocage, the caretaker of Michel's estate at La Morinière. When Michel learns that Bocage has been poaching on the estate, he decides to join the young man in secretly poaching on his own land.

Ali

Ali is a little Arab boy whom Michel befriends during his second visit to Biskra. Ali introduces Michel to his sister, who is a prostitute. After Marceline dies, Michel sleeps with Ali's sister several times, but soon notices that Ali seems to get jealous of his sister. Michel thus decides to stop sleeping with the girl in order to maintain his relations with Ali. When Ali's sister teases Michel that he is more interested in Ali than in her, Michel reflects, "Perhaps she is not altogether wrong . . ."

Ali's Sister

Ali's sister is an Arab girl who works as a prostitute. On his second visit to Biskra, Michel befriends Ali, who introduces him to her. Michel sleeps with Ali's sister several times after his wife's death. However, Michel decides not to sleep with her anymore, in part because he is bored by her, and in part because he feels that Ali gets jealous of his attentions to the sister. After this, Ali's sister teases Michel that he prefers the little boy to her, and that Ali is the reason Michel continues to stay in Biskra. Michel confirms that she may be right about this.

Bachir

Bachir is a little Arab boy whom Michel and Marceline befriend during their first visit to Biskra. Bachir is the first of the boys whom Marceline brings home to Michel to cheer him up while he is recovering from tuberculosis. On their second visit to Biskra, Michel learns that Bachir has gotten a job as a dishwasher.

Bocage

Bocage is the caretaker of Michel's estate in Normandy. Michel finds Bocage irritating because of his incessant demands on Michel's attention in reporting to him about the managing of the estate. Michel eventually realizes that Bocage is not altogether honest in his running of the estate.

Charles

Charles is the seventeen-year-old son of Bocage, the caretaker of Michel's estate at La Morinière. Michel takes an immediate liking to Charles, and the two of them spend their days together riding horseback around the estate. When Michel and Marceline return to La Morinière a year later, Michel finds that Charles has changed, and he is no longer attracted to the young man.

Daniel

Daniel is one of the three friends Michel summons to visit him in North Africa after Marceline dies, so that he may confide in them by telling his story.

Denis

Denis is one of the three friends Michel summons to visit him in North Africa, so that he may confide in them by telling his story.

Marceline

Marceline is Michel's wife. She is twenty years old when she marries Michel. Although their families had been friends when they were growing up, Michel and Marceline do not really know each other. While they are traveling in North Africa on their honeymoon, Michel becomes gravely ill with tuberculosis, and Marceline is very attentive and caring in nursing him back to health. When he starts to feel better, she brings Bachir, a little Arab boy, back to their hotel to play, as a means of cheering Michel up during his recovery. While the couple eventually befriend a number of Arab boys, Marceline prefers the sickly and weaker children, while Michel prefers the strong and healthy ones.

After they return to France from their honeymoon, Marceline becomes ill with tuberculosis, which she contracted while nursing Michel. While they are staying at La Morinière, Marceline announces that she is pregnant. When they move to Paris, she becomes increasingly ill, soon losing the baby in a miscarriage. While she is still very sick, she and Michel take off again to travel in Switzerland, Italy, and North Africa. Michel insists that they are traveling to areas where the climate will help to improve her health, but Marceline grows increasingly ill as they travel. After they arrive in Biskra for the second time, Marceline dies.

Menalque

Menalque is an acquaintance of Michel who shows up at one of his university lectures in Paris. He and Michel immediately strike up a friendship. Gide based the character of Menalque on his friend Oscar Wilde, a well-known Irish playwright of the time. In *The Immoralist*, Michel mentions that there had recently been a public scandal and lawsuit regarding Menalque; this refers to a widely publicized trial in which Oscar Wilde was accused of homosexual relations with the son of a wealthy Englishman. In *The Immoralist*, Michel asserts that the lawsuit and scandal against Menalque were absurd and unfair. When he greets Menalque after his lecture, Michel makes a point of hugging him in front of everyone, demonstrating that he is not ashamed to be associated with him.

While in Paris, Michel and Menalque have several late-night conversations. Menalque tells Michel that he had traveled in North Africa, following the path that Michel and Marceline had taken on their honeymoon. Menalque explains that he had questioned many of the Arab boys they befriended in Biskra, and that he became intrigued by Michel's behavior there. One day, Menalque hands Michel the pair of scissors that had been stolen by the boy Moktir. Menalque tells Michel that he believes in following one's natural impulses, regardless of the judgments of society.

Michel

Michel is the narrator and central protagonist of *The Immoralist*. Michel's mother died when he was fifteen. His father, a scholar of ancient Greek and Roman culture, raised Michel to follow in his footsteps in devoting his life to scholarship. When Michel is 25, his father becomes gravely ill, and Michel marries Marceline, a young woman whom he hardly knows, in order to please his dying father. Michel and Marceline spend many months traveling in Italy and North Africa on their honeymoon. However, they sleep in separate bedrooms and their marriage is not consummated until two months after their wedding. During the course of their travels, Michel becomes gravely ill with tuberculosis, but recovers under the loving care of his wife.

As his health improves, Michel finds himself focusing on his physical body and sensual experiences for the first time in his life. He experiences this profound change in himself as a sort of rebirth, an emergence of his true, natural self that had previously been concealed from him. At the same time, Michel finds himself attracted to healthy young men and boys in North Africa as well as at home in France. Although Marceline has a miscarriage and becomes increasingly ill with tuberculosis, Michel convinces her to travel with him through Europe and back to North Africa. Soon after they return to Biskra, Algeria, where they had spent much of their honeymoon, Marceline dies. Finally freed from all obligations to others, Michel remains in Biskra for several months. He sleeps several times with a girl prostitute, but soon discovers that he prefers the company of her little brother, Ali. Torn between his natural homosexual inclinations and the traditional societal values with which he was raised, Michel finds himself in a state of personal crisis. He contacts his three closest friends from childhood, begging them to come to his home in North Africa. When the three friends arrive, Michel proceeds to recount to them the story of his experiences of personal transformation, and to express his feelings of distress about how to proceed with his life.

Moktir

Moktir is a little Arab boy whom Michel befriends during his first visit to Biskra. One day, Michel spies on Moktir as he steals a pair of sewing scissors belonging to Marceline. Michel is fascinated by this incident, and decides not to reprimand the boy or take the scissors back. Instead, he lies to his wife about how the scissors were lost. After this incident, Michel finds that Moktir is his favorite of the boys. Later, when Michel is back in

Paris, his friend Menalque hands him this pair of scissors, which had been recovered from Moktir. When Michel and Marceline travel to Biskra the second time, Michel learns that Moktir has become a criminal and has recently been released from prison. One night, Moktir takes Michel to a prostitute; when Michel returns home from this encounter, he finds that his wife is dying.

Monsieur D. R.

Monsieur D. R. is the addressee of the letter written by an unnamed friend of Michel to his brother. This letter opens the novel and serves as the frame narrative of the central story.

Unnamed Friend

The Immoralist begins with a letter, addressed to a Monsieur D. R., written by one of the three friends whom Michel had summoned to North Africa in order to tell them his story. The unnamed author of the letter, addressing the recipient of the letter as "my dear brother," explains that he has written Michel's story down on paper, as it was narrated to the three friends, and included his transcription with the letter.

Themes

Homosexuality

The central theme of *The Immoralist* is the growing self-awareness of a repressed homosexual whose natural inclinations are at odds with societal conventions. Gide's narrative is based partly on his own experiences as a young man whose sexless marriage came into conflict with his homosexual tendencies. Written nearly a century ago, *The Immoralist* describes Michel's process of self-realization in subtle, veiled terms. There is no direct reference in the novel to homosexuality, but only indirect hints regarding Michel's physical attraction to adolescent boys and his general lack of interest in maintaining a sexual relationship with his wife. However, the closing lines of the novel are the most direct indication of Michel's homosexuality: Michel loses interest in a female prostitute, and indicates that he prefers the "odd caress" of the girl's brother Ali.

Self-Discovery

Michel's narrative describes a journey of self-discovery. Until his marriage, Michel had lead a very limited and sheltered life as a young scholar

living under the wing of his father, who was also a scholar. Michel's honeymoon travels with his wife to North Africa, however, open up new vistas to him, and he becomes increasingly aware of his own body and of physical, sensual experiences. As time passes, Michel discovers the emergence of his true inner self, which had previously been repressed. With his increasing awareness of his true nature, Michel finds that he must present a false outer appearance to his wife. Michel's late-night discussion with Menalque encourages his conviction that it is more important to live according to one's natural desires than to stifle the true inner self in accordance with societal conventions. By the end of the novel, however, Michel finds that his journey of self-discovery has left him feeling confused and uncertain about his life. As he tells his friends, "Knowing how to free oneself is nothing; the difficult thing is knowing how to live with that freedom."

Mind versus Body

As a studious scholar, Michel before his marriage had lived a life of the mind. In North Africa, as he is recovering from tuberculosis, however, Michel becomes increasingly focused on the life of the body. His interest in his physical being begins when he sees the fresh and healthful bodies of the young Arab boys. This inspires him to devote himself to improving his own physical health through diet and exercise. As he recovers from his illness, Michel becomes increasingly aware of physical and sensual experiences. One day he goes off by himself in the wilderness and sunbathes nude, then dives into a mountain stream, thus acting upon his desire to engage in physical experiences and to celebrate his physical being. As an expression of his newfound sense of self, he decides to shave his beard and let his hair grow long, thus outwardly demonstrating the profound change that has come over him. Michel's interest in physical health is also indicated by the fact that he finds himself drawn to the most healthy and attractive looking Arab boys, while his wife tends to prefer the sickly and homely looking children.

Life versus Death

Life and death are also central themes of *The Immoralist*. During the course of the novel, Michel and then his wife are brought to the brink of death. While on their honeymoon, Michel becomes gravely ill from tuberculosis. Although he eventually recovers his health, Marceline later becomes ill from tuberculosis, which she had contracted

Topics For Further Study

- The region of North Africa includes the modern nations of Algeria, Tunisia, Morocco, and Liberia. Research and report on the political, social, cultural, and economic conditions of one of these nations.

- Although tuberculosis was more widespread during the 19th century than it is today, it continues to be a deadly disease in areas throughout the world. Find out more about the disease of tuberculosis as it impacts today's world. How prevalent is tuberculosis in your own nation? In what regions is it most prevalent and most deadly? What efforts are being made to prevent and cure tuberculosis today?

- *The Immoralist* is the story of a repressed homosexual man in the late 19th century, struggling to make sense of his natural sexual tendencies. Societal attitudes toward and treatment of homosexuals has changed in the century since Gide's novel was first written. Write an essay describing the societal attitudes and legal status of homosexuals in your own society. What is your own opinion of the status of homosexuals in today's society?

- *The Immoralist* is a short novel in which the narrator describes a process of discovering aspects of himself that he was not previously aware of. Thus, it is a story of self-discovery. Write your own short story, narrated in the first person, in which the protagonist describes a process of discovering some aspect of her or his personality that he or she was not previously aware of. Describe in what ways this process of self-discovery affects the narrator's approach to life and relationships with others.

while nursing him through his illness. Marceline's illness causes her to have a miscarriage, and she herself soon dies. Michel, in recovering from sickness, discovers a new sense of physical health and passion for life. Michel is a scholar of ancient civilizations, and so has spent most of his life studying dead peoples and dead cultures. With his new love of life, Michel loses interest in studying a dead past. As his story progresses, he finds himself desiring more and more to experience life to its fullest extent. He describes his new appreciation for life as a process or rebirth. Ironically, though his baby dies before it is born, Michel experiences a feeling of rebirth in his own life. As his wife is dying, Michel finds himself embracing and celebrating life.

Style

Preface

The Immoralist was first published in 1902 without a preface. However, in later editions of the novel, Gide included a brief "Preface" in response to the reactions of readers and critics to certain aspects of his story. In this preface, Gide explains that many people have misunderstood *The Immoralist* and criticized it unfairly. He states that he has been blamed for not ending his story with a clear moral condemnation of Michel's behavior. However, Gide insists that it was not his intent to provide moral conclusions to his tale, but to pose a problem. He asserts that the problem represented in *The Immoralist* is one commonly experienced by many men of his day. He states, "I don't pretend to have invented this 'problem'—it existed before my book came along," and that, regardless of the fate of the character in the novel, "the 'problem' continues to exist." Finally, Gide notes, "I am not trying to prove anything, merely to paint my picture well and set it in a good light."

Frame Narrative and Point of View

The narrative structure and point of view of *The Immoralist* is somewhat complex. The novel begins with what is called a *frame narrative*, meaning a brief explanation of the context of the central narrative. Thus, the first two pages of *The Immoralist* are written in the form of a letter from an unnamed man to his brother, a Monsieur D. R., explaining that Michel summoned his three longtime friends—Denis, Daniel, and "I"—to travel to his hotel in Sidi, North Africa, on an urgent matter. The letter states that Michel told his story to these three friends one night while lounging on his terrace. The letter writer indicates that he has written down Michel's story as it was told to these friends, and that this transcript of the story is enclosed in the letter.

Within this *frame narrative*, the main body of *The Immoralist* is a first-person narrative from the point of view of Michel. Michel thus opens his story by addressing his three listeners as "My dear friends," informing them that he is at a point of crisis, and that he is going to tell them the story of his life. Michel explains that he no longer understands anything about life, and that he needs this opportunity to talk with loyal friends about what he has experienced. Thus, the remainder of the novel is narrated in the first-person "I" form; except at several points Michel again addresses his three listeners in the second-person "you" form, in commenting on his own story.

Psychological and Confessional Literature

The Immoralist is considered one of the greatest early psychological novels. A psychological novel is focused primarily on the internal life and development of the individual, stressing thoughts, emotions, and character over plot and external events. *The Immoralist* is also regarded as one of the great novels in the *confessional* mode. A confessional novel is a first-person narrative in which an individual character, whether fictional or autobiographical, describes personal experiences expressive of some internal moral or psychological conflict or dilemma. Michel in *The Immoralist* "confesses" to a group of three close friends the intimate details of his psychological development as a young man, and the conflicts he experiences between the expectations of his marriage and his yearning for personal freedom.

The Récit

Gide referred to the novel form of *The Immoralist* as "récit," meaning a "narrative" or "account." A récit is a brief novel with an essentially simple narrative focus in which a first-person narrator explores deep psychological and social dilemmas through a personal reminiscence. Gide's short novel *La Porte etroite* (1909; *Straight is the Gate*) is also regarded as a récit, as is the novel *La Chute* (1956; *The Fall*), by the French existentialist writer Albert Camus.

Historical Context

France: The Third Republic

The Immoralist takes place in France, Europe, and North Africa during the 1890s. Michel's family estate is located in Normandy, a province in northern France. While teaching as a professor, he lives with his wife in Paris. The French government at this time was in the era of the Third Republic, which began in 1871, adopting the Constitution of the Third Republic in 1875. France's colonial holdings increased during the era of the Third Republic, and by 1900 France was the second greatest colonial power in the world, after Great Britain. The Third Republic was dissolved with the invasion of France by Germany during World War II, and French colonial holdings were greatly reduced during the post–World War II era.

North Africa

Many of the important events in *The Immoralist* take place during Michel and Marceline's travels in the region of North Africa. North Africa encompasses the modern nations of Algeria, Tunisia, Morocco, and Libya. This region is also sometimes referred to as the Maghrib, which in Arabic means "West." The Atlas Mountains in the north, the Sahara desert in the South, and coastal regions along the Mediterranean Sea characterize the terrain of North Africa. The inhabitants of North Africa are primarily Arabic Muslims, who were subjugated and dominated by French and other European colonial powers beginning in the 19th century. During the nineteenth and early twentieth centuries, France invaded, conquered, and colonized much of North Africa. France conquered Algeria in 1830. Tunisia came under French control between 1881 and 1883. France did not conquer Morocco until 1912. Libya, which had been within the domain of the Ottoman Turks since 1835, was invaded and occupied by Italy in 1931. Thus, the events of *The Immoralist* are set in the French controlled areas of Algeria and Tunisia. Biskra, the city in which Michel befriends a number of Arab boys and makes important discoveries about his own nature, is located in northeastern Algeria.

The political and national conditions of North Africa have changed greatly since the 1890s. In the post–World War II era, French colonial control gave way to national sovereignty. Libya, which had come under Italian and then British control, was granted national independence in 1951. Tunisia and Morocco were granted sovereignty by the French

Compare & Contrast

- **1890s:** The French government is in the era of the Third Republic, under the Constitution of 1875. France is a parliamentary democracy with a president and prime minister. Voting privileges are extended to all adult men.

  Today: The French government is in the era of the Fifth Republic, under the Constitution of 1956. France remains a parliamentary democracy with a president and prime minister. Voting privileges are extended to all adult men and women.

- **1890s:** The region of North Africa includes colonial territories of several European nations. Algiers and Tunisia are French colonies, while Libya and Morocco are colonial holdings of the Ottoman Turkish empire.

  Today: The former colonies of the North African region include the four sovereign nations of The Democratic and Popular Republic of Algeria (Algeria), the Republic of Tunisia (Tunisia), the Socialist People's Libyan Arab Jamahiriya (Libya), and the Kingdom of Morocco (Morocco). All of these nations are members of the League of Arab States, a multi-nation alliance of Middle Eastern countries sharing economic, political, and cultural interests.

- **1890s:** France is a major colonial power, second in size only to Britain.

  Today: In the post-colonial era, most former French colonial holdings have been granted national sovereignty. France is a member of the European Union, a multination alliance sharing many social, economic, and political interests.

---

government in 1956. France at this point hoped to maintain control of Algeria. However, Algerians wishing to attain the same national independence granted to their neighbors had begun a rebellion against French rule in 1954. Finally, in 1962, after eight years of civil war, France admitted defeat and granted national sovereignty to Algiers.

Tuberculosis

During the course of *The Immoralist*, both Michel and his wife Marceline suffer from tuberculosis. While Michel recovers from the disease, Marceline, who becomes infected while nursing him, eventually dies from it. Tuberculosis is an infectious disease that reached epidemic proportions during the nineteenth century. Tuberculosis affects the lungs, making breathing difficult. One of the most dramatic symptoms of tuberculosis is the coughing up of blood, which Michel in *The Immoralist* describes in graphic detail. During the nineteenth century, there was no known cure for tuberculosis, and lengthy bed-rest or staying in temperate climates was often recommended. The bacteria which causes tuberculosis, *bacillus*

Mycobacterium tuberculosis, was identified in 1882 by the German physician Robert Koch. Beginning in the 1940s, antibacterial drugs that can effectively treat and cure tuberculosis first came into use. However, tuberculosis continues to be a widespread disease today, killing some three million people per year, many of them in developing or third world countries where sanitation and medical care are inadequate.

Critical Overview

The first printing of *The Immoralist* in 1902 consisted of 300 copies, of which the majority were circulated among Gide's friends and his intellectual circle. While it caused a small scandal among this limited readership, subsequent editions of the novel brought Gide increasing controversy. Many critics regarded Michel's narrative as a celebration of behavior which society in general deemed immoral. These early reviewers regarded Michel's behavior in terms of selfish "individualism," thus avoiding all reference to homosexuality.

André Gide's encounter with poet and playwright Oscar Wilde in North Africa influenced the storyline of The Immoralist

Nonetheless, Gide was widely criticized for endorsing Michel's behavior, rather than condemning it. Gide, however, defended his narrative in a "Preface" to later editions of the novel, asserting that, as an artist, his intent was not to judge his character, but to represent a set of experiences common to many men. In the latter half of the twentieth century, as homosexuality became a more acceptable subject of public discussion, critics came to view *The Immoralist* as the tale of a repressed homosexual struggling to come to terms with his sexual orientation in a societal context of late-Victorian values. Albert J. Guerard, in *André Gide* (1951), asserted that *The Immoralist* "is one of the first modern novels to deal at all seriously with homosexuality." Alan Sheridan, in an "Introduction" to a translation of *The Immoralist*, published in 2000, observed that Gide's novel:

> . . . examines the case of a man with wife and child, means and career, a man caught up therefore in a complicated network of overlapping relations and responsibilities, who comes to see his whole life as a hypocritical sham and, in pursuit of his true, authentic, homosexual self, abandons everything.

Thomas Cordle, in *André Gide* (1993), similarly remarked, "The central strategy of *L'Immoraliste*

is . . . the dissolution of the heterosexual relationship and its replacement by a homosexual one." Cordle added, "The essential action of the story is this protracted conversion from the normal, socially sponsored sexual relationship that is inimical to Michel's nature to the forbidden relationship that satisfied his native desires."

However, Cordle pointed out, "Michel never fully recognizes that he is a homosexual." In the late-twentieth-century, *The Immoralist* became identified with a larger body of gay and lesbian literature. In 1999, the *Advocate*, a national gay and lesbian news magazine, listed *The Immoralist* as fifth on a list of the "100 Best Lesbian and Gay Novels," while in 2000, the *Lambda Book Report* named *The Immoralist* among the "100 Best Lesbian and Gay Books of the 20th Century." Following a different line of literary criticism, postcolonial critics in the late twentieth century criticized *The Immoralist* as an expression of European colonial attitudes toward the cultures of the Middle East. These critics argued that Michel's sexual attraction to young Arab boys in colonial North Africa must be seen in a broader cultural, political, and historical context of European subjugation of Arabic peoples. Regardless of judgments of the cultural, social, and political implications of *The Immoralist*, most reviewers agreed that Gide's prose style in this narrative is admirably spare and elegant. *The Immoralist* is further regarded as an important work in the development of the psychological novel. Gide's skillful use of first-person "confessional" narration has been widely praised for its subtlety and complexity.

Criticism

Liz Brent

Brent holds a Ph.D. in American Culture from the University of Michigan. She works as a freelance writer and editor. In the following essay, Brent discusses scents, odors, and smells in Gide's novel.

Michel's experience of personal rebirth in *The Immoralist* is characterized by an increased awareness of his physical being. His sense of touch, taste, and smell become heightened, and each new sensation represents a celebration of life. The more alive he feels, the more he seeks out sensual experiences. As he explains, "The only way I could pay attention to anything was through my five senses." Throughout *The Immoralist*, Gide uses sensual

> " While traveling from Ravello to Sorrento, Michel again experiences his sense of smell as a celebration of his excitement about life."

descriptions, particularly the sense of smell, as an important indication of Michel's growing self-awareness and lust for life.

Michel first experiences his sense of smell as a celebration of life while traveling in North Africa and Italy on his honeymoon. The first instance in which he mentions the sense of smell is while he and Marceline are in Biskra, Algeria. As Michel recovers from tuberculosis, he finds himself more and more focused on his physical health. When he becomes well enough to take walks in the park near their hotel, Michel experiences a new sense of life welling up within him. During one of these walks, he enters the park "with a sense of rapture."

> The air was luminous. The cassias, which flower long before they come into leaf, gave off a sweet scent— or perhaps it emanated from everywhere, the light, unfamiliar smell which seemed to enter into me by all my senses and filled me with a feeling of exaltation.

This first powerful sensual experience of his heightened sense of smell represents for Michel a sign of the new life emerging within him. "Was this finally the morning when I was to be reborn?" he asks.

With Michel greatly recovered from his illness, he and Marceline leave North Africa to travel through Italy. In each new location, Michel experiences new fragrances that further awaken his growing lust for life. He frequently describes his experience of the smells around him as intoxicating and rapturous. In Salerno, he walks among a grove of lemon trees in a state of dreamy intoxication. His experience of the lemons is described in lush detail, exulting in their look, taste, and smell.

> The fragrant lemons hang like thick drops of wax; in the shade they look greenish-white; they are within reach, and taste sweet, sharp, refreshing.

In Ravello, Michel becomes bolder and more adventurous in his new celebration of life through physical and sensual experience. He wanders in the woods by himself, enjoying his new physical strength, focusing on the aesthetic qualities of his own body. He finds a remote clearing in the woods where he sunbathes nude, experiencing the forces of life through the physical sensations of his skin. With the heat of the sun's rays, he states, "my whole being surged up into my skin." One day, he dives naked into a clear mountain stream and comes back to shore to bath in the sun. To enhance this rejuvenating physical experience, Michel adds the smell of fresh mint.

"There was some wild mint growing there," he relates. "I picked some, crushed the sweet-smelling leaves between my fingers and rubbed them over my damp but burning body."

While traveling from Ravello to Sorrento, Michel again experiences his sense of smell as a celebration of his excitement about life. As he describes their journey:

> "The roughness of the sun-warmed rocks, the rich, limpid air, the smells made me feel so alive. . . . 'Oh joy of the body!' I exclaimed to myself."

Upon returning home, Michel and his wife stay for the summer at La Morinière, their estate in northern France. While there, Michel spends most of his time out roaming in the fields and woods, where he experiences a whole new range of smells that further inspire him to pursue his natural desires. He describes with exaltation the smell of the sea air, the odor of wet leaves, and the fragrance emitting from the crops as well as the earth itself. During the apple harvest, he describes the rich fragrances filling the air: "A sickly sweet scent rose from the meadow and mingled with the smell of the ploughed earth."

Interestingly, while Michel and Marceline spend the winter in Paris, Michel makes no mention whatsoever of any smells, odors, or fragrances, whether good or bad. This represents Michel's feeling of sensory deprivation while in the city, where he finds the social atmosphere stifles his quest for natural, physical experiences. When they return to La Morinière the following spring, Michel once again celebrates his strong impressions of the smells of country life. During the hay harvesting season, he observes:

> The air was full of pollen, of scents, and it went to my head like strong drink. It was as if I hadn't breathed for a year, or else had been breathing nothing but dust, so smoothly did the honey-sweet fill my lungs.

As he spends more and more time with young peasant men on the estate, Michel begins to associate his sense of smell with his attraction to these vigorous youths. He becomes fascinated with the

What Do I Read Next?

- Gide's short novel *La Porte étroite* (1909, *Strait is the Gate*) is written in the mode of the *récit*, which Gide identified as a narrative form conducive to expressing some of his central literary themes. The first part of *Strait is the Gate* is narrated by Jerome, who recounts his love for his cousin Alissa, her refusal to marry him, and her early death. The second part of this story consists of Alissa's diary, which Jerome discovers after her death, and which explains their complex relationship from her perspective.

- *Si le grain ne mert* (1926, *If It Die . . .*), considered one of the great works of confessional literature, is Gide's autobiographical account of his life from birth to marriage.

- Gide's novel *Les faux-monnayeurs* (1926, *The Counterfeiters*) is one of his best-known works. It concerns a group of boys prone to getting in trouble, and depicts the responses of their teachers and parents to their misbehavior.

- *La Chute* (1956, *The Fall*), by French existentialist author Albert Camus, is regarded as a *récit* in the manner of Gide's *The Immoralist*. *The Fall* is a first-person narrative in which Jean Baptiste Clamence, a former lawyer, confesses his feelings of personal guilt to various sailors at a bar in Holland.

- *The Ballad of Reading Gaol* (1898) is a long poem by Gide's friend Oscar Wilde, written while Wilde was imprisoned on charges of homosexuality. Wilde criticizes the inhumane conditions of the British prison system.

- In the biography *André Gide: A Life in the Present* (1999), Alan Sheridan argues that Gide's works addresses many themes and social issues, still relevant today, including responsibility, freedom, morality, sensuality, spirituality, and homosexuality.

- *André Gide*, (1993, updated ed.), by Thomas Cordle, provides a critical introduction to Gide's life and work. Cordle examines the influence of the literary movements of symbolism, romanticism, and socialist realism on Gide's writings.

---

earthy existence of the peasants, and intrigued by their secret lives. The young man who fills him in on local gossip tells Michel stories that "gave off vapours of the abyss; I inhaled them uneasily, feeling my head spin." Alcide, the young man whom he helps to poach on his land, sleeps in the barn, and Michel even enjoys the odor of Alcide's clothes, which "still bore the warm smell of poultry."

During Michel and Marceline's second trip through Europe and North Africa, Michel continues to associate his sense of smell with his love of life. He hates being in Switzerland, because he finds the people lacking in vitality. However, as they leave Switzerland to enter Italy, he becomes aware of the vigorous sense of life associated with Mediterranean culture. He comments that traveling from Switzerland to Italy, "was like exchanging abstraction for life, and even though it was still winter, I thought I could smell scents everywhere."

As they continue their travels through Italy, Michel continues to delight in the rich scents of the land and people. In Naples, he is drawn by the scent of the orange blossoms to go out prowling the streets at night, for "the slightest breath of wind carried their scent." In Taormina, Michel is so charmed by a Sicilian coach driver, whom he describes as "resplendent, fragrant and delicious as a piece of fruit," that he spontaneously kisses the man. In the ports of Syracuse, Michel finds that he is enchanted even by the unpleasant odors of life on the docks, "The smell of sour wine, muddy backstreets, the stinking market frequented by dockers, tramps and drunken sailors."

While Michel associates a strong sense of smell with the love of life, he likewise associates those who are repulsed by smells with death and morbidity. During their stay in Florence, Marceline becomes increasingly ill while Michel finds

Moulin Rouge (French for "red mill"), a cabaret built in 1889 and situated in the red-light district near Montmartre, Paris, France, may symbolize the hedonist culture that attracts Michel in The Immoralist

himself more and more invigorated. One day, enchanted by their fragrance, he buys a huge bundle of almond blossoms to bring home to his wife. He excitedly arranges the flowers throughout their hotel room. But when Marceline returns and steps in the door, she is nauseated and upset by the odor of the flowers, "a faint, very faint, discreet smell of honey." It is as if even this subtle fragrance of life is overwhelming to the dying woman.

The Immoralist has been widely praised for its elegant and affecting prose. Gide's vivid descrip-

tions of Michel's sensation of smells, odors, and fragrances are brilliantly expressive of his celebration of life through sensual experiences.

Source: Liz Brent, Critical Essay on *The Immoralist*, in *Novels for Students*, Thomson Gale, 2005.

Douglas Dupler

Dupler is a writer and has taught college English courses. In this essay, Dupler discusses the moral quandaries in a novel that contains a quest for freedom.

The title of André Gide's novel, *The Immoralist*, refers to a protagonist who consciously experiments with his moral boundaries. In the beginning of the novel, this protagonist, named Michel, is prompted by a serious illness to find a new way of living. His strained efforts to get well lead him to loosen or discard the moral fabric which once enveloped him. By the end of the novel, Michel has so adopted a philosophy of personal freedom, and challenged his belief system, that he seems adrift in a sea of uncertainty and experiences an intense solitude that he calls an "empty liberty." During the story, Michel gains firsthand experience of sickness and health, love and marriage, and life and death. During these deep experiences, the protagonist struggles both for his own truths and to affirm his life amidst his solitude and his increasing amount of freedom.

From the beginning of the story, the conflict between individual and culture is hinted at; the question arises, "In what way might Michel be useful to the state?" As Michel begins telling the story of his life, in retrospect, he shows the point of uncertainty to which he has arrived when he states, "I no longer understand anything." The story Michel begins to tell is his personal quest for freedom, which includes freedom from accepted moral laws, and that quest has left him in a place where he acknowledges, "the difficult thing is knowing how to live with that freedom."

When describing himself at the beginning of the story, before changes have occurred to him, Michel portrays his life as normal to the point of being almost unnoticeable. He has been a man of placid emotions and calm passions. He marries Marceline because his father is dying, and he believes that the marriage will please his father during his last days. Michel states that he did not love his wife at the beginning, and instead of passion he felt "a tenderness, a sort of pity" for her. He is very aware of the intricacies of social convention when he notes that his wife was Catholic and that he is Protestant. Michel is a successful academic, although his work has been published under his father's name. When speaking of himself, he notes how "the early moral lessons of childhood . . . exert an influence," and mentions an "austerity" that he inherited from his "mother's indoctrination" and his "puritanical childhood." Michel points out that he has friends, but that he "loved friendship more than the friends themselves," revealing the mental abstraction that permeates his bookish life. Michel notes his "thrifty habits" and the "detached" quality of his life. In short, Michel describes himself as

> The illness is representative of how restricted and contracted his life has become, and his efforts to overcome the sickness become efforts also to find a new and more vital way of living."

influenced by the cultural rules in which he is immersed, so much so that he remarks that, "It never occurred to me that I could lead a different life."

Michel's illness produces deep inner questioning in him. The illness takes him to the edge of life and death, where he has to affirm his desire to live. In the throes of sickness, he realizes a "wild, desperate drive towards existence." The illness is representative of how restricted and contracted his life has become, and his efforts to overcome the sickness become efforts also to find a new and more vital way of living. Michel becomes so debilitated that he has to learn to do basic tasks again, and he feels a "thrill of discovering life afresh" as he makes slow steps toward recovery. During his recovery, Michel organizes his life in order to "concentrate solely" on his cure, and he "would identify as *good* only those things that were salutary," a new change in his moral system. Michel decides that survival is simply a "question of willpower," and he begins living his life in a way that enables him to exert his will over his situation. Michel is exiled from his homeland by illness and by choice. Leaving his culture behind during his convalescence frees him from cultural constraints, and he realizes that he must seize this freedom. In his new situation, he states that his "salvation depended on myself," while the new life he envisions will be "an exaltation of the senses and the flesh," quite different from his previous life.

Michel's illness forces him out of his dualism between mind and body; he claims he does not have the "strength to lead a dual life," and that he would "think about the life of the mind later," when he is better. He abandons intellectual activity and begins a willful and organized program to strengthen his body and overcome his illness. As his body heals, he experiences a transformation. Michel discovers a "newfound awareness" of his senses; he delights in the feeling of sunshine on his body and of taking cold plunges in water. The countryside of North Africa becomes beautiful to him, which he describes with poetic and graceful language. He cuts off his beard and allows his hair to grow longer to reveal his "new self," and his body becomes muscular and tanned. He becomes "no longer the pale, scholarly creature," but a person who is determined to allow a "voluptuous enjoyment" of himself and "of everything that seemed . . . divine." Michel also changes how he views his body, seeing it "no longer with shame" that he perhaps inherited from his culture, "but with joy." By the second part of the novel, Michel's belief system has changed in the way that he views his mind and body; before, the life of the mind had precedence, but his transformative illness forces him to prioritize the health of his physical body.

Michel, throughout the story, strongly attests to the transformation that the illness brings about. He emphasizes the change in himself when he states that, "Everything that was painful to me then is now a delight." When he returns to France, he is "constantly reminded" of the change that has occurred to him, and he states that he "had only just been born." He further abandons his old life when he declares he would prefer to adopt a "provisional mode" of living, and he begins to experience life as "nothing more" than the "passing moment." Michel becomes a more advanced immoralist when he begins to rebel intellectually against his old way of thinking. He claims, "I started to despise the learning," and he made efforts to "shake off these layers" that he had acquired from his culture. He comes to believe that underneath a "secondary" layer of himself, put there by culture, there is an "authentic being" that is primal and vital, and that by getting back to that more essential part of himself he can make his life more "harmonious, sensuous, [and] almost beautiful." His personal philosophy becomes one of both striving for perfection and ridding himself of cultural programming, and he states, "How could I be interested in myself other than as a perfectible being?"

The transformation affects other areas of Michel's belief system. In one instance, Marceline prays for Michel during Mass, to which Michel responds, "There is no need to pray for me." He rejects an appeal to God because he claims he does not want any obligations, while Marceline refuses to believe that he can heal without divine help. In another scene, further delineating the change in Michel's moral system, he observes one of the children, with whom he has made a friendship, steal a pair of scissors from his room. Assuming the boy has no idea that he has been observed, Michel allows the incident to pass without comment or reproach. Instead, this boy, named Moktir, now becomes Michel's "favourite," and this incident becomes "a strange moment of self-revelation." The scissors also have an interesting symbolism; this incident, of tolerating and even admiring the act of stealing, represents a break, or a cutting away, of some of Michel's morals.

Michel also questions his love for his wife. He analyzes his love for her, and he tries to will himself to love her more. Love becomes an act of self-creation for Michel, when he makes a promise to force his love to "grow with my health." He shields his inner reality from his wife, stating, "it was important that she didn't interfere with my new self-awareness." He mentions how he has to lie to Marceline about his feelings for her, and that he began to "enjoy this dissimulation" at the same time their love "deepened," a strange contradiction but one that tests his "new, unknown faculties" of pushing his moral edge. At one point, Michel declares that his "veneration" for his wife grew in "inverse proportion to my self-respect."

Michel also tests his morals when he goes to his family farm and interacts with the farm workers. Michel finds out that one of them is poaching from him, and rather than stop the illegal act, he becomes interested in it, condones and assists it, and eventually even pays one of the perpetrators unknowingly. By transgressing long-held agreements and codes of conduct, Michel gets taken advantage of and the workers become exasperated with him. In the end, the farm becomes uninteresting to Michel, he becomes alienated from the people who had been close to him, and he flees as "everything was unraveling" around him.

In the end, Michel meets suffering and illness again as his wife's health deteriorates. He seems to play a disturbing part in her decline, pushing them to repeat the exhausting journey that Michel had made to overcome his own sickness. In his quest to find what "man is still capable of," he becomes driven by an "irresistible demon." His narrative contains contradictions that reinforce his sense of confusion toward the end. He asks, "how many . . . conflicting thoughts can coexist within a man?" and decries his "insufferable logic." Of his wealth, he "grew to hate this luxury and yet enjoy it." Of people, he states that "the worst instincts . . . seemed

The harbor of Algiers, Algeria, the city where André Gide almost died from a serious illness, much like the character Michel in The Immoralist

to me the most sincere." He keeps his distance from other people, claiming that "the very things that separated me . . . were what mattered." His loneliness is palpable when Marceline dies; he states, "I no longer know the dark god I revere." Michel acknowledges his predicament and confusion in the end, when he states that consistency in thinking is "what makes a real man." Instead of seeing the potential of the future, which he once proclaimed, he ends his story by remarking on the "intolerably long, dreary days" that lie ahead of him, as he has freed himself from both constraints and safety nets.

Source: Douglas Dupler, Critical Essay on *The Immoralist*, in *Novels for Students*, Thomson Gale, 2005.

David Remy

Remy is a freelance writer in Pensacola, Florida. In the following essay, Remy examines Gide's use of natural imagery to mirror his protagonist's psychic state.

André Gide's *The Immoralist* is a novel of exploration and discovery, albeit within a psychic realm. Michel, an accomplished archaeologist and scholar, embarks upon a journey of self-exploration that is guided by his subconscious as much as it is by any willful decision to abandon the social mores

that have imposed themselves upon him. As the novel progresses, Michel's spirit remains rebellious, unbridled, and this spirit gathers in intensity with each layer of his former self that he casts aside. Throughout *The Immoralist* Gide incorporates natural images that mirror Michel's psychic state, especially the process of psychic renewal that results from stripping away the patina of education, family relationships, and respectability that have provided Michel with a foundation and direction for his life.

For Michel, a man whose mentality is tied to his physical surroundings (a fact attested to by his incessant wandering), environment plays a key role in shaping his attitude toward life, and for this reason much of the imagery Gide uses to represent Michel's psychic state is associated with nature. Early in the novel, after a brief stay in Paris, Michel and Marceline journey to Michel's farm, La Morinière, near Lisieux, which is, according to Michel, "the shadiest, wettest countryside" he knows. The farm, which had formerly been the domain of Michel's father, who is now deceased, offers Michel an opportunity to put his imprimatur upon the family's history.

With the aid of Charles, the caretaker's son, Michel tours the farm, inspecting its pastures and orchards and formulating a plan for the future.

> " Michel understands that, in order for him to uncover his true self, the one that lies beneath the 'text' his life has composed thus far, he must remove each outer layer of his being until he reaches the core."

From this orderly abundance, from this happy subservience, from this smiling cultivation, a harmony was being wrought, no longer fortuitous but imposed, a rhythm, a beauty at once human and natural, in which one could no longer tell what was most admirable, so intimately united into a perfect understanding were the fecund explosion of free nature and man's skillful effort to order it.

This plan is nothing less than grand in design, but Michel, his "old turmoil" having been displaced by a feeling of serenity, must assess the amount of energy he will bring to the task of reshaping the farm. He must plumb the depths of his psyche and determine his ability to combat the forces of nature, much less the sense of family history associated with the farm, if he wishes to demonstrate a "disciplined intelligence" over the land and all it produces.

With a characteristic transition that fosters a strong connection in the novel between actions and the ideas that motivate them, Gide employs imagery that places his protagonist's psychic state in bold relief. For example, when Michel finds Bocage, the caretaker who has known him since he was a child, beside a pond that must be drained and cemented to repair a leak, Gide describes the scene with images that are laden with symbolic meaning. According to Michel, the pond had not been drained in "fifteen years," thus indicating a certain neglect that has resulted from the inexorable progress of time as well as human indifference. The pond is full of "very large" carp and tench (another bottom feeder) that had "never left the deepest parts" of the containment. The fish, like Michel's memories of La Morinière, are firmly established and will not give way easily. "Occasionally a great shudder ran over the surface, and the brown backs of the disturbed fish appeared," says Michel as memories, like the denizens that have surfaced, rise from deep within his subconscious. Moreover, the

fish represent Michel's desire to master the "powerful savagery" that exists within nature and within himself, for he wishes to control the land with that "disciplined intelligence."

By wading in and joining the farmhands and their children in an impromptu "fishing party," Michel physically immerses himself in the land he claims as his own. Water, long a symbol for the unconscious because of its translucent qualities and interminable depths, becomes a medium for exploration as Michel and Charles, with mud-splattered faces, wade into deep holes and attempt to catch a large, slippery eel, itself a symbol for Michel's nascent freedom once the eel emerges from the pond's murky depths into the light of day. Gide's choice of imagery and symbolism may lack subtlety, but they nevertheless bind the novel's ideas with actions that the reader can easily interpret.

Later in the novel, once Michel has returned to La Morinière after a series of journeys abroad with Marceline, who now lies gravely ill, Gide employs nature's stark contrasts to underscore Michel's growing frustration and impatience at the responsibilities he must uphold. Once again, Michel, lord of the manor, inspects his property in an effort to distract himself from what he calls his "disheveled life," only to find that the farm now exhibits laxity instead of the organization he had witnessed there before. Burdened by the constant demands that have been placed upon him, Michel seeks the ordered harmony a farm embodies as an ideal, a harmony arrested from the surrounding wilderness, as well as the organic hierarchy that exists within nature itself.

Instead of finding woodlands that have had their timber cut according to a long-standing agreement, one that leaves no doubt as to how the wood should be cut, divided, and sold, Michel discovers that Heurtevant, the contractor, has allowed trees felled in winter to occupy the lot well after spring, the traditional time for harvesting, so that the forest's new growth must overcome these obstructions if the forest is to revive and replenish itself.

Similarly, Michel feels trapped by the responsibilities he must bear, especially those that result from other people's negligence. Though Michel breaks with the past, he cannot assert his independence completely because obstacles remain in his path. The new Michel cannot emerge because the old Michel, the one who was encumbered by family obligations, stands in the way.

Gide's use of these natural images attains greater symbolic importance when one considers that Michel, in search of "the old Adam" within him—an entity who cannot be suppressed by family, education, nor by Michel himself—has decided to abandon the past. In removing the "encrustations" that have, in his view, prevented him from becoming an "authentic being," Michel compares himself to a palimpsest, a piece of writing that, upon close examination, reveals previous drafts or texts underneath. Each layer builds upon the other to form a composite text, a complete entity. Michel understands that, in order for him to uncover his true self, the one that lies beneath the "text" his life has composed thus far, he must remove each outer layer of his being until he reaches the core. "In order to read it," he muses, extending this metaphor, "would I not have to erase, first, the more recent ones?"

When considered in light of Michel's self-image, Gide's use of imagery from nature mirrors the idea of a palimpsest, for layers of soil, water, and timber are removed to reveal a landscape that represents a new beginning; layers are uncovered so that others may push through. The pond is drained so that it may be repaired and replenished; like the formal education that Michel rejects, the dark, murky waters of the pond are drained away to reveal what is at the core: a primal, pristine state represented by the large fish that swim along the bottom. Similarly, the felled trees in the woods around La Morinière represent a thinning, or removing, of old growth so that new growth may emerge. Combining ideas with actions that resonate throughout the novel, Gide presents the reader with images that create visually Michel's process of psychic renovation.

More than one hundred years after its initial publication, *The Immoralist* remains a novel of startling ideas and confessions. Gide's use of strong visual imagery, particularly that found in nature, serves as a metaphor for Michel's transformation from aesthete to debauched and broken hedonist. Thus, by mirroring his protagonist's psychic state with images from the natural world around him, Gide marks Michel's existential journey indelibly for the reader with each page turned and each layer of being uncovered.

Source: David Remy, Critical Essay on *The Immoralist*, in *Novels for Students*, Thomson Gale, 2005.

Thomas Cordle

In the following essay excerpt, Cordle shows how Gide's The Immoralist *precipitates "the dissolution of a heterosexual relationship and its replacement by a homosexual one."*

L'Immoraliste (*The Immoralist*) (1902) is the first representative of that most remarkable

> What the psychological novel offered Gide was a means of dramatizing his inner turbulence in terms appropriate to it. The *action* of these books is in the conflict between desire and inspiration on the one hand and the restrictive force of pain and obligation on the other hand."

category of Gide's work, the psychological novel. Gide did not invent the genre, but he did revive it in a period when prose fiction was more or less divided between the pseudosociological chronicles of the Naturalists and the delicately perverse romances of the Decadents. Gide's models, we may reasonably presume, were *La Princesse de Clèves, Manon Lescaut, René, Adolphe,* and *Dominique.* But there was something in this type of fiction that was more important for him than any model, and that was the kind of action that the narrative represented. In "Un Esprit non prévenu" (An unbiased mind) Gide made a distinction between two sorts of novels, "or at least two ways of depicting life":

> The one, exterior and commonly called "objective," which visualizes first of all the other person's gesture, the event, then explains and interprets it.

> The other, which seizes first of all emotions and thoughts, then creates the events and characters most fitted to bring these out and runs the risk of being powerless to depict anything that the author has not first felt himself. His inner riches, his complexity, the antagonism of his too diverse possibilities, will allow the greatest diversity in his creations. But everything comes out of him. He is the only guarantee of the truth he reveals, the only judge. The hell and the heaven of his characters is in him. It is not himself that he depicts, but what he depicts he could have become if he had not become precisely himself.

What the psychological novel offered Gide was a means of dramatizing his inner turbulence in terms appropriate to it. The *action* of these books is in the conflict between desire and inspiration on the one hand and the restrictive force of pain and obligation on the other hand. Physical encounters and displacements are to be interpreted as symbolic inventions employed to reflect and enrich the psychological action. This does not make them any less important: indeed, one of the outstanding qualities of Gide's psychological novels is to be found in the suggestive power of these secondary effects of scene and situation. (Such effects, we must remember, were the *primary* value of his symbolist tales.)

The central strategy of *L'Immoraliste* is one that we have already seen in Gide's work: the dissolution of a heterosexual relationship and its replacement by a homosexual one. The difference here is that the strategy is neither concealed nor abbreviated; it is the subject of the story from beginning to end, and the course of its development is punctuated with peripeties and discoveries. Gide found the way to involve all the motives and countermotives of his personality in this one plot. The result is a story that is at once direct and clear in its depiction of the growth of a desire and complex and ambiguous in its thought about the demands of that desire.

The attack upon heterosexuality (which for Gide was always an attempt to be rid of the frustration oedipal relationship) begins on the first page of Michel's story when he says of his bride Marceline: "I had married her without love, mainly to please my father, who, dying, was worried at leaving me alone" (*Romans, Récits et Soties, Oeuvres lyriques*, hereafter cited as *RRS*). The illness that strikes him on their wedding journey to North Africa is not an accident but rather a defense against the undesired relationship.

Michel begins his recovery by refusing Marceline's attentions. He avoids her and seeks health in the company of a band of Arab boys. When he sees one of these steal Marceline's sewing scissors he is delighted to be a silent accomplice in the theft. He does not understand his joy, but its reason is not to our eyes impenetrable: the scissors are an emblem of feminine power, an instrument of castration. When the child takes them he disarms Marceline and displaces her as an object of erotic interest. Michel not only recovers from his illness, he becomes a new man whose strength and vitality are based upon his acknowledgment of the claims of his fundamental being—what he calls, in biblical language, "the old man." As a sign of rebirth he shaves his beard. (So did Saül, and so did Gide.) At this point there occurs a reversal in the process of homoeroticism. In southern Italy, on the way home, he finally accomplishes his conjugal duty to Marceline—but it is of the utmost importance to note that this act takes place after he has wrestled with and thrashed a drunken coachman.

At home on his Norman farm Michel puts his new strength to work practicing in all things what he calls "a science of the perfect utilization of self through an intelligent restraint" (*RRS*). He is relieved of his marital obligations by Marceline's pregnancy, and he enters into a warm virile relationship with the 17-year-old son of his farm manager. Together they plan to carry out certain projects in agricultural economy. Michel's latent homosexuality finds a sort of symbolic expression and a partial satisfaction when, one day, he paddles around barefoot in a pond helping Charles catch the eels that have been exposed by draining the pond.

The next major episode of the novel is the turning point in Michel's history. He meets Ménalque, a godlike figure who manifests and professes a doctrine of risk, expenditure, and egoism. Ménalque is a notorious homosexual. (His name, of course, recalls *Les Nourritures terrestres*, and still more pertinently Virgil's *Bucolics*.) In token of his authority over Michel he brings the scissors that Moktir stole from Marceline. In a single conversation he undermines the prudent plan of Michel's life and teaches him to despise his possessions and his expectations. On the night of their meeting Marceline suffers a miscarriage and becomes very ill. The accident marks the end of her ascendancy in Michel's life. Ménalque plays no other role in the story than this one of being the means through which Michel discovers a little more of his hidden and repressed nature. He is a kind of demonic intercessor who could better be called a force, or an idea, than a character.

When Michel and Marceline return to the farm, Michel no longer has any thought for productive economy. He poaches game on his own lands with the disreputable young son of his farm manager. This relationship has the same homoerotic character as the one with Charles, but the setting of Michel's encounters with Alcide endows them with an illicit and clandestine value. Finally, restlessness overcomes him and, abandoning the farm, Michel drags the ailing Marceline away on a journey that leads them step by step back to Africa.

Michel's conduct this time is the reverse of what it was coming north out of Africa. He is no longer prudently building his health and strength but recklessly expending and risking both by drinking with the riffraff of Naples and Sicily, and sleeping in their company on tavern floors. On one occasion he frankly embraces and kisses his carriage driver. Back in Africa, he seeks out his former companions and, freeing them from want and subservience, he indulges their appetite for pleasure, as well as his own. Marceline, weakened by his demonic pursuit of satisfaction, dies; Michel consoles himself with the little boy Ali. It is in this manner that the heterosexual marriage is definitively destroyed and the homosexual encounter put in its place.

The essential action of the story is this protracted conversion from the normal, socially sponsored sexual relationship that is inimical to Michel's nature to the forbidden relationship that satisfies his native desires. The knowledge of who and what he is, and of what he must do to become who he is, comes in the form of impulses rather than decisions. The powers of clear vision and determination are stifled in him by his moral and intellectual culture, which has proscribed the solution that he is unconsciously striving to find.

It is in the conflict between the hero and his culture that Gide develops his accompaniment to the main action. This secondary conflict seems at times to override the major one because its terms are clearer and franker. Being more verbal than imagistic, and conscious rather than unconscious, it tends to seize tonal control of the narrative.

At the very beginning of the novel Michel is referred to as "the very learned Puritan," and as he begins to tell his story he mentions "the grave Huguenot teaching" given him by his mother. This is his moral capital: a stock of austere, inflexible precepts. To his father he owes a similarly dogmatic training in classical philology, which has taught him to regard Athens and Rome as the two foci of human history.

Michel's bondage to his culture is symbolized by his marriage to Marceline, who represents the Christian ideal at its most excellent. Her virtues of devotion, abnegation, restraint, and pity are all expressions of the triumph of human weakness. To complete the image of submission Gide makes her a Catholic.

In going to North Africa, Michel crosses the frontier of his culture, and when he loses its protection and guidance he fails ill. His recovery is owed entirely to the assertion of a primitive power within him that is independent of traditional and collective values. This "authentic being" is discovered only when the veneer of acquired knowledge peels off. "There was more here than a convalescence; there was an augmentation, a recrudescence of life, the inflow of a richer, warmer blood which was to touch my thoughts, touch them one by one, penetrate everything, stir, color the most remote, delicate, and secret fibers of my being" (*RRS*).

Michel's first task is to create physical strength, but concurrently he must reshape his moral and intellectual being to conform to that strength. The first stage in his moral revolution culminates in that "perfect utilization of self through an intelligent restraint" that he formulates in the midst of work on the farm and the preparation of the course that he will give at the Collège de France. This course entails a complete revision of his historical studies. He is no longer interested in the "abstract and neutral knowledge of the past." Philology is now a means of approaching the human personality of an earlier time. He is drawn more and more to the rough, uncultured Goths and especially to the rebellious and debauched young King Athalaric (A.D. 516–534). The thesis that he subsequently proposes is that culture, born of life, ends by stifling life and preventing the contact of mind with nature.

Michel's critical thought has in fact preceded and opened the way to a new conduct. His prudent, economical way of living is in conflict with this new conception of man. When he meets Ménalque after his first lecture his thought is: "The life, the least gesture of Ménalque, was it not a thousand times more eloquent than my course?" (*RRS*). This new man enunciates a doctrine of radical individualism, sensualism, and consumption that makes the ground give way under Michel's feet, as he puts it. From that moment forward, his thought and conduct are directed toward a new end: to discover what man is yet capable of. "And each day there grew in me the obscure feeling of untouched riches, covered over, hidden, smothered by cultures, decencies, moralities" (*RRS*).

When Marceline says to him: "I understand your doctrine—for it is a doctrine now. It is fine, perhaps ... but it suppresses the weak," Michel replies: "That is what is needed" (*RRS*).

Up to this point, Michel's "immoralism"—his rejection of conventional Christian, middle-class morality and his effort to found a vital and authentic ethic on the acknowledgment and pursuit of desire and possibility—bears a close resemblance to the Nietzschean "revaluation of all values." Gide was familiar with Nietzsche's work and had written about it in 1898 in his "Letters à Angèle." In later years he attempted to minimize the influence of Nietzche on the book, and in a sense he may have been justified in doing so. Ménalque could be called a genuine Nietzschean hero: his life is a risky pursuit of his own unrealized possibilities; he refuses the restraint of principles and retrospective judgments; and still he sublimates his more aggressive instincts, finding in ascetic self-denial a pleasure superior to that of indulgence and satisfaction. Michel is another matter. He is very unsure about the grounds of his revolt. With Marceline very near death, he reflects: "Ah, perhaps there would still be time . . . Shall I not stop?—I have sought, I have found what makes my value: a sort of stubborn commitment to the worst" (*RRS*). And to the friends who have answered his call for aid after his wife's death he says: "It seems to me sometimes that my real life has not yet begun. Drag me away from here now and give me reasons for existing. I no longer know how to find them. I have freed myself, possibly, but what difference does it make? I am suffering from this unutilized freedom. Believe me, it is not that I am overcome by my crime, if you choose to call it that—but I must prove to myself, that I have not overstepped my rights" (*RRS*).

This speech, and indeed the whole development of the moral countercurrent in the novel, imply that Michel's erotic impulse has not been able to conquer altogether his moral resistance. The erotic has achieved its end but at the cost of painful division within the hero's soul. He feels that he was right to follow his own desire and Ménalque's teaching, but the puritan in him is still alive, and he has not been proven wrong. It is on this ambiguous note that Gide ends his story. The erotic conflict provides the basic energy of the novel. That is the problem that has to be solved. Unlike Gide, Michel is unable to create and play two lovers' roles. One has to be sacrificed to the other. But there is ambiguity in this, for Michel never fully recognizes that he is a homosexual, and that his conduct is inspired by *distaste* for the heterosexual relationship he has passively accepted and by *desire* for love with a boy. Instead of seeing his problem for what it is, he does something extravagant: he poses it in terms of the entire moral and intellectual order of his world. He effects a transference that makes his personal dilemma appear, in the first place, to be directly related to the revolution in Western moral thought that is represented principally by Friedrich Nietzsche, and in the second place he assimilates it to the revolution in historical thinking that established philosophical anthropology as a rival to antiquarian historiography (another development in which Nietzsche played a primary role).

It is this elevation and expansion of his personal anomaly that makes Michel a hero. He attacks the very heart of the ideology of his society, and he offers himself as an example of the new thought that he is advancing. But his heroic rebellion, by its very vigor and honesty, turns Michel into a satanic figure, for it leads him to destroy a gentle and unprotesting victim who is sacrificed as a representative of her culture. The immolation of Marceline casts a deep shadow over Michel's entire venture, obscuring its value and making it profoundly questionable.

The result is, as we have seen, a downcast hero, one who has asserted his notion of the truth and had it strike back at him in its consequences. However, there is no inscrutable fate working against him, nor any vengeful god. His difficulty is located entirely in the human condition, and more specifically in the fact of human freedom. The problem is one of conflicting rights among persons, and Michel's action in attempting to resolve it becomes an episode in a continuing drama within Western civilization. He illustrates with great force and clarity the manner in which the conflict may appear to a particular man in a set of particular historical circumstances.

Gide's artistry is abundantly displayed in *L'Immoraliste*, and nowhere more impressively than in the narrative style. The story that he invents is a romantic one in all essential respects—in its glorification of self, of desire, and of will; in the excesses of action and thought that it depicts; and in the ironies that it sustains from start to finish, the irony of Michel and the irony of freedom. But the narrative is the work of a symbolist who foregoes all rhetorical effects in order to make his language a purely descriptive instrument. The voice that recounts is that of Michel, not that of Gide. The haughty tone, so often stiff and artificial, is precisely that of a scholarly puritan who is trying to set forth his turbulent inner experience without knowing quite what it is all about. This austere, insensitive voice is Gide's primary means in making the character of Michel. It is an unceasing evidence of what he is, a man whose action and thought are governed by impulses that he either fails to comprehend or misrepresents to himself.

The symbolical representation of ideas in the story is extraordinarily rich, and so too are the symbols that reveal the constant presence of the erotic motive. The composition of the narrative mirrors both the Gidean personality division and the antithetical character and action of Michel. Half the story is allotted to the productive, or angelic, phase of Michel's reform and half to the consumptive, or demonic, phase. The encounter with the mythical, archangelic Ménalque stands at the midpoint. The effect of this perfect division can hardly be overestimated. It gives the book an air of equilibrium and resolution that is at odds with the ambiguous sense of the story. Perhaps it is to this aspect of his work that Gide was alluding when, after declaring in his preface that he had intended to pose a problem and not to judge it or solve it, he added: "I use the word 'problem' here with reluctance. To tell the truth, in art there are no problems—of which the work of art is not a sufficient solution" (*RRS*).

However important a work *L'Immoraliste* may appear to be today, at its publication it found few readers, and among those few some greeted it with hostile indignation. Gide felt that this reaction was wholly unjustified since he had not sought to make Michel's excesses seem anything but ignoble. The indignation, however, was probably provoked by something deeper than Michel's *conduct*. What he *does* is easy enough to judge and condemn. What he *is* would have been harder for Gide's indignant readers to get at. Michel's arrogance, anarchism, and insensitivity are essentially class attributes, and the readers of the novel were mostly of Michel's class. Their outcry was provoked really by Gide's association of their guilty being, which they had felt was adequately hidden, with guilty deeds that could not be concealed.

Source: Thomas Cordle, "Romantic Resurgence," in *André Gide*, updated ed., Twayne Publishers, 1993, pp. 48–98.

Sources

Cordle, Thomas, *André Gide*, Updated Edition, Twayne, 1993, pp. 67, 69, 71–72.

Gide, André, *The Immoralist*, translated by David Watson, Penguin Books, 2000, pp. 15, 34, 45, 47, 50, 69, 89, 95, 97, 98, 111, 114, 115.

———, *The Immoralist*, translated by Richard Howard, Alfred A. Knopf, 1970.

Guerard, Albert J., *André Gide*, Harvard University Press, 1951, p. 106.

Sheridan, Alan, "Introduction," in *The Immoralist*, by André Gide, translated by David Watson, Penguin Books, 2000, p. x.

Further Reading

Ahmida, Ali Abdulolatif, ed., *Beyond Colonialism and Nationalism in the Maghrib: History, Culture, and Politics*, Palgrave, 2000.
> Ahmida provides a collection of critical essays by various authors on the history, culture, and politics of North Africa and Egypt in the nineteenth century.

Barnes, David S., *The Making of a Social Disease: Tuberculosis in Nineteenth-Century France*, University of California Press, 1995.
> Barnes offers a cultural, medical, and socioeconomic history of tuberculosis in France during the nineteenth century.

Benjamin, Roger, *Orientalist Aesthetics: Art, Colonialism and French North Africa, 1880–1930*, University of California Press, 2003.
> Benjamin discusses the influence of North African culture on French art during the period of the French colonial occupation.

Fryer, Jonathan, *André & Oscar: Gide, Wilde, and the Gay Art of Living*, Constable, 1997.
> Fryer examines the friendship between André Gide and Oscar Wilde in terms of homosexual identity and lifestyles during the late-nineteenth and early-twentieth centuries.

Hayes, Jarrod, *Queer Nations: Marginal Sexualities in the Maghreb*, University of Chicago Press, 2000.
> Hayes examines representations of homosexuality in North African literature.

Merrick, Jeffrey, and Bryant T. Ragan, Jr., eds., *Homosexuality in Modern France*, Oxford University Press, 1996.
> Merrick and Ragan provide a collection of essays on the history of homosexuality in nineteenth- and twentieth-century France.

Walker, David, *André Gide*, Macmillan, 1990.
> Walker provides a critical analysis of narrative techniques in Gide's novels.

Juneteenth

Ralph Ellison

1999

Juneteenth (New York, 1999) is Ralph Ellison's posthumous publication composed of nearly four decades and thousands of pages of work. The book was started in 1955. Pieces of *Juneteenth* were published during his four decades of work. In 1960 the literary magazine *The Noble Savage* published a portion entitled "And Hickman Arrives." Seven years later, a fire razed the Ellison's summer home, destroying a significant portion of *Juneteenth*. Given this setback, Ellison's forthcoming second novel continued to be delayed and was left unfinished even after his death in 1994. However, in 1999, after countless hours of work, John F. Callahan, Ellison's literary executor, pieced together cohesive selections from the mammoth, unfinished manuscript creating a cogent work of vast literary merit.

The title comes from an event that occurred on June 19, 1865. On this date in history, General Gordon Granger landed in Galveston, Texas to deliver the news that the Civil War had ended and that Abraham Lincoln had freed the slaves. What is most notable about this event was that Lincoln's Emancipation Proclamation was given on January 1, 1863, nearly two and half years before Granger reached Texas. Hence the vague term "Juneteenth" holds the innuendo of a vague date in history.

Similar to Ellison's other works, most notably his first novel *Invisible Man*, *Juneteenth* questions the cultural fabric of the United States. It digs into the underbelly of America, uncovering the foul history of racism and segregation in America. However, in classic Ellison style, the work does not

Ralph Ellison

fester in the negative. *Juneteenth* is an affirming narrative in that the black characters are strong, educated and cognizant. They do not cling to their oppression. Instead they yearn for something better and strive to find a way to achieve a better America—not a better *black* America—but a better *overall* America where the segregated races coexist and prosper, where racism is not forgotten, but absolved. Unfortunately, Ellison's dream as it existed in his mind and the minds of his protagonists has yet to be achieved. Nonetheless, his works, like *Juneteenth*, can only help to enable Americans with the knowledge necessary to move the nation closer to Ellison's aspiration.

Author Biography

Ralph Waldo Ellison, a twentieth-century African American writer and scholar, is one of America's most powerful and notable voices in the history of black America. A productive writer of essays and criticism, Ellison only wrote two novels during his lifetime, *Invisible Man* and the posthumously published *Juneteenth*. Although not prolific in the world of fiction, Ellison's writing changed the way Americans thought about race, politics, religion and culture through his essays and teachings.

Ellison was born into segregation on March 1, 1914 in Oklahoma City, Oklahoma. His father died only three years later, leaving his mother alone to raise their poverty stricken family. In 1933, Ellison attended Tuskegee Institute with the intentions to pursue a career in music. However, studying modern literature piqued his interested in writing. After leaving Tuskegee Institute in 1936, Ellison moved to New York City, where he met the author Richard Wright. From this friendship, Ellison was inspired to write and became associated with the Federal Writers' Project and published his first short stories and articles.

In 1945, Ellison began work on his most famous work, *Invisible Man*. Ellison's friendship with Wright helped to develop his most notable character, the nameless black protagonist in *Invisible Man*. Unlike Wright's angry, uneducated and inarticulate character in his powerful novel *Native Son*, Ellison's character was educated, well spoken and self-aware. Although both characters sprung from the consequences of oppression, Ellison focused his attentions on affirming what blacks have achieved as opposed to Wright's protest literature focused on the brutality of racism. In 1946, Ellison married Fanny McConnell who helped support them during the writing of *Invisible Man*. Finally, seven years after he began, Ellison achieved international fame with the publication of *Invisible Man*. In 1953, Ellison became the first black American to win the National Book Award when *Invisible Man* was awarded the coveted prize.

Although his first novel took seven years to complete, it would be a short duration in comparison with his second novel. Ellison began work on his second novel in 1955 while in Rome as a fellow of the American Academy of Arts and Letters. In 1958, Ellison accepted a position at Bard College as an instructor in Russian and American literature. In 1962, Ellison took a creative writing position at Rutgers University. Ellison continued to work on his second novel. Sadly, in 1967, a substantial portion of the manuscript was destroyed in a fire that burned the Ellison's summer home in the Berkshires. Although the fire was a setback, Ellison continued to garner praise and was appointed Albert Schweitzer Professor of Humanities at New York University in 1970. He served in this position until 1980.

Over the four decades following the publication of *Invisible Man*, Ellison published countless reviews, interviews, essays and critiques of literature, folklore, jazz and other aspects of race and culture. A collection of his work was published in 1964, *Shadow and Act*, and another in 1986, *Going to the Territory*. Yet, during his lifetime he never published a second novel. At the age of eighty, on April 16, 1994, Ellison died in Harlem, New York. Some five years after the author's death, through keen selections from thousands of pages of Ellison's unfinished magnum opus, John F. Callahan, Ellison's literary executor, helped finally publish Ellison's second novel, *Juneteenth*.

Plot Summary

Chapters 1–3

The novel opens with Reverend Hickman and the members of his parish attempting to see the racist Senator Adam Sunraider. They are denied entry to the senator's office and, eventually, they are thrown out of the lobby by Sunraider's security. The parish moves on to Senate's Visitors' Gallery to watch Sunraider in action. He is giving a riveting speech about black Americans. It is a racist monologue, even containing the demeaning phrase "Coon Cage Eight"— a Cadillac full of "eight or more of our darker brethren crowded together enjoying its beauty, its neo-pagan comfort, while weaving reckless through the streets." While giving his speech the senator is having hallucinatory visions of the emblematic eagle from Great Seal. Alas, as Hickman and his parish watch on from the Visitors' Gallery, an unnamed black man rises up and shoots Sunraider several times. Fleeing the pursuit of security, the assassin falls to his death from the Visitors' Gallery down to the Senate floor. Hickman is distraught. His only son, the adopted white Sunraider, has somehow transformed himself into racist and, now, he has been mortally wounded right before his eyes.

Chapter 4

The unnamed assassin found his mark, but Sunraider is holding on to the last strings of life in a hospital bed. After falling from the assassin's bullets, Sunraider began calling for his adoptive father, Reverend Hickman. From his deathbed, Sunraider, with the help of Hickman, begins a lengthy series of flashbacks and recollections to his past. Before becoming a racist senator, Sunraider was a young, white preacher named Bliss Hickman, raised by a parish of kind, religious black Americans. Bliss is a young boy with a remarkable skill for preaching. Sometimes his skill made him the envy of others. On one such occasion, a young black boy was taunting Bliss about being a preacher. The boy teased

Bliss and eventually Bliss hit the boy with a rock. Bliss is an important aspect to Reverend Hickman's revivals. He lies in a coffin and eventually rises up representing the resurrection and the life. Bliss moves the parishioners. He is a great preacher, even at his tender young age.

Chapters 5–7

In the hospital Sunraider again flashes back to his early years, remembering his first love and his years as an unsuccessful filmmaker. A young woman named Laly is accompanying Bliss on a picnic under a tree out in a field. Bliss calls Laly a "Teasing Brown" and she calls him "Mr. Movie-Man." The two enjoy an enormous picnic of sandwiches, fried chicken, Texas hots, boiled eggs, cake and tea with lemon and mint. The two are in love and eventually have sex underneath the tree.

Bliss also recollects his unsuccessful attempts at filmmaking with his partners Lester Donelson and Karp. They have a run-in with unfriendly townspeople, who beat them and pour whiskey on their heads, and forgetful Donelson ruins a remarkable scene when he forgets to load film in the camera.

Senator Sunraider wakes up in the hospital and is pleasantly surprised that Reverend Hickman is still by his side. The unlikely father and son team discuss the past and, eventually, Hickman convinces Sunraider to preach to him. Hickman continues their discussion, redirecting it through his recollections about their teamwork at the revivals. Hickman is using his time by the senator's side to re-educate his son about the struggles of black Americans. The Reverend talks about the history of Juneteenth and how it was not the first, nor the last, step of the black American on his road towards freedom.

Chapters 8–10

Hickman and Sunraider recount a crucial revival in which a deranged white woman, Miss Lorelli, storms through the meeting, claiming that Bliss is her son. She grabs the young white preacher and tries to kidnap him. The women of the parish attack her and try to wrestle Bliss from the crazed woman. The church is in an uproar. Eventually, Sister Bearmasher grabs Miss Lorelli by her hair and drags her out to her carriage. Hickman and Bearmasher take Lorelli to jail, where, subsequently, they are incarcerated for being black.

Knowing that Hickman may meet opposition at the jail, Sister Georgia takes Bliss back to her home for the night. The two share a melon and conversation. Bliss is attracted to Georgia in a way he cannot understand because of his youth. Following a nightmare, Georgia allows Bliss to sleep in her bed, where he sneaks a peak under her nightgown. He catches a glimpse of her womanhood and is ashamed of his immorality. He admits his indiscretion to Georgia, and she condemns his act, calling him a "jackleg" and throwing him crying out of her bed.

After being beaten by the police and released from jail, Hickman returns to Bliss. Bliss asks if Lorelli is his mother. Hickman tells the boy that she is just a crazy woman who comes from lots of money. She has a history of kidnapping children and claiming they are her babies.

Later, Bliss is laying under the porch in the shade when he decides to eavesdrop on Mrs. Proctor and Body's Mother. The two women discuss the episode with crazy Miss Lorelli and some of her other more bizarre habits. However, although both women cannot believe the woman could be Bliss' mother, they both admit that they do not know for sure.

Chapters 11–14

Hickman takes Bliss to his first movie. The Reverend explains that the film must be Bliss's first and last movie because films are of bad shadow worlds that are too sinful to make a common practice in a preacher's life. They attend the film and Bliss is terrified because he believes that the woman in the picture is his mother, the deranged woman from the revival, Miss Lorelli.

From the revival forward, Bliss begins to pull away from Hickman and the parish. Soon he runs away and goes to the all-white movie houses to escape from the searching parishioners. As Hickman recounts these memories, the senator begins experiencing frantic, fragmented recollections of his life—who he was, what he has become—and how his past and his emotions have shaped and morphed him into his present being. Soon both men, Hickman and Sunraider, sleep in the hospital room. Hickman dreams and contemplates freedom, violence, *blackness* in America and his role in it all. It is insightful, but vague.

Chapters 15–16

Hickman recollects how Bliss came to him. Bliss's mother, an unnamed woman, accuses Hickman's brother, Robert, of rape. Although innocent, Robert is murdered by a lynch mob. The woman is shunned from the community for engaging in sex with a black man. Pregnant and needing to give birth, the woman turns to the most unlikely of places, Alonzo Hickman's home. Hickman takes

Media Adaptations

- Segments of an interview conducted by Elizabeth Farnsworth with Ralph Ellison in the 1960s, followed by an interview in 2000 with John Callahan, the editor of *Juneteenth* and Ralph Ellison's literary executor, is available at http://www.pbs.org/newshour/bb/entertainment/jan-june99/ellison_6-21.html (accessed November 24, 2004) and maintained by The Public Broadcasting Service Web site.

- An interview from 1977 is available at http://www.nytimes.com/books/99/06/20/specials/ellison-conversation.html and is conducted at Ellison's home by Ishmael Reed, a novelist and poet.

her in and plans to kill her, the child and himself after she gives birth. However, after the child is born, Hickman feels pity for the pathetic woman and begins to love the young boy. He cannot carry out his original plan. The woman abandons the child and leaves Hickman's home. Hickman names the child Bliss "because they say that's what ignorance is." With the birth of Bliss, Hickman experiences his own rebirth, finding God and changing his ways from a partying jazz musician to a powerful preacher. Hickman raised Bliss to the best of his abilities, but the boy grew up, went out on his own, and became a multimillionaire, a racist and senator.

After this final recollection, Sunraider appears to be reaching the last moments of his life. Laying in his deathbed, the senator begins a hallucinatory journey through a landscape composed of people shooting pigeons, foxes that bring men to tears, and a rude boy from a Goya painting. It ends with a massive, ominous black car full of black men. It is no ordinary car—it hovers, screeches and appears to be an amalgamation of random parts. The occupants of the car dislike Sunraider because they know he is a racist. Yet instead of running him over, they load the senator into the car taking him away on his final ride.

Characters

Sister Arter

Sister Arter is one of the members of Reverend Hickman's parish that accompanies him to Washington, D.C. with the hopes of making contact with Senator Sunraider.

Sister Bearmasher

Sister Bearmasher is a member of Reverend Hickman's parish who wrestles Miss Lorelli away from Bliss during a revival. During the revival, an unfamiliar, wild, red-haired white woman rushes through the procession, grabbing the young preacher, Bliss, and rips him from his little coffin. The woman appears insane and is screaming that the boy is her son. Many women from the parish attempt to pull Bliss from Miss Lorelli. However, the woman's craziness makes her incredibly powerful. Finally, Bearmasher pushes her way through the crowd to Miss Lorelli where she winds handfuls of the woman's hair around her arms and pulls the woman free of Bliss. Reverend Hickman loads Miss Lorelli, whose hair is still wound up in Bearmasher's fists and arms, and Bearmasher into Miss Lorelli's buggy. The three speed off through the night to delivery the crazy woman to the police.

Bliss's Mother

Bliss's Mother is an unnamed woman who accused Robert Hickman, Alonzo's brother, of rape. Her false accusation leads to Robert's murder at the hands of a lynch mob and her banishment from the white community. Pregnant and with nowhere to turn, Bliss's mother goes to Alonzo's home to give birth to her son. She admits that the boy could not have been Robert's and Alonzo decides to murder the woman, her child and himself after the child is born. Alonzo finds it impossible to commit the crimes because he begins to pity Bliss's mother and love the young, white boy as his own. Bliss's mother flees his home, leaving her son, never to be heard from again.

Body

Body is a black boy who is one of Bliss's best friends. Bliss often calls Body his "right hand." The two spend all of their time together, except in church where Bliss is too busy preaching. Body often questions Bliss about scripture and preaching, but Bliss does not want to talk of things when he is spending time with Body because preaching is his work. Bliss enjoys playing and being a kid with Body. During one such time, Body and Bliss are

on the porch and Body tries to explain Sammy Leaderman's movie projector to Bliss. Unfortunately, since neither child has the vocabulary or understanding to simply talk of a movie projector, they banter back and forth as Body tries to explain the box that has the people in it. Eventually, Bliss ends up frustrated, believing that such a thing cannot exist. Regardless of the outcome of this conversation, Body and Bliss's friendship represent one of the few opportunities for Bliss to behave like a little boy, thus, Bliss cherishes the moments he is allowed to spend with Body.

Body's Mother

Body's Mother, as the name implies, is the mother of Bliss's friend, Body. Bliss is envious of the love between Body and his mom because Bliss is an orphan. In addition to being an orphan, he has been forced to grow up fast because of Reverend Hickman's efforts to cultivate Bliss's natural preaching talent. Body's Mother was also at the revival when Miss Lorelli came storming in like a mad woman. At one point, Body's Mother and Mrs. Proctor are having a discussion on Body's Mother's front porch. Unbeknownst to the ladies, Bliss is laying silently underneath the porch in the shade. The two discuss Miss Lorelli, her craziness and whether or not she could truly be Bliss's mother. Both agree it is unlikely, but they admit that they cannot say for sure. Eager for any type of maternal love, this overheard conversation confuses Bliss and leaves him wondering whether or not Miss Lorelli is his mother.

Bowlegs

Bowlegs is a black boy who comes to Bliss's defense during an encounter with some young boys. A group of boys are hanging around an empty lot pushing a truck around in the dirt, when Bliss walks through. A young, unnamed boy begins to taunt Bliss, teasing him about being a preacher. Bowlegs steps to Bliss's defense, stating that the young white boy is a real preacher who is capable of delivering salvation. He criticizes the unnamed boy for his rudeness and blasphemy.

The Boy at Waycross

The Boy at Waycross is the nameless black boy who taunts Bliss during an encounter in an empty lot. The unnamed boy mocks Bliss's preaching and insults him. Eventually, Bliss turns the table on the unnamed boy, trapping the boy in an idiom that makes him look foolish. All the taunting angers Bliss, but he tries his best to hold his composure. Yet, in the end, Bliss's verbal jabs back at the boy incite the nameless youth to charge the young preacher. Bliss smashes an egg-sized rock against the boy's forehead and runs from the crowd of young boys.

Lester Donelson

Lester Donelson is Bliss's cinematographer partner during his years as an unsuccessful film-maker wandering through rural, Midwestern towns. Donelson is a lazy, volatile man who frequently forgets to do important tasks, like load the film into the camera.

Sister Georgia

Sister Georgia is a member of Reverend Hickman's parish who takes Bliss to her home after the meeting when Miss Lorelli attempted to kidnap him. After Sister Bearmasher ripped Miss Lorelli from Bliss, the congregation fussed over what to do with Bliss since Reverend Hickman left to deliver the crazed woman to the police. Eventually, the women decide it was best for Sister Georgia to take him home because she is younger, has no children and lived close by. Sister Georgia scoops up the scared, little preacher and runs through the woods with him to her home. During the run through the woods, Bliss feels a response to her womanly aspects and scents. He feels ashamed. Once home, the two share a melon and talk on the porch. Soon, Sister Georgia puts Bliss to bed on the couch. He wakes Sister Georgia because he is tossing and turning with a nightmare. She decides it is best for Bliss to sleep with her that night. Bliss agrees, but succumbs to his temptations and his earlier feelings about Sister Georgia, sneaking a peak at her womanhood underneath her sleeping gown while she sleeps. Ashamed and writhing with sin, Bliss admits his dishonorable act and cringes under his own immorality. However, Bliss also recognizes that the impure glimpse could have been less disreputable if Sister Georgia would have been a little girl of Bliss's own age, again showing that he has been forced into adulthood at too early of an age.

Reverend Alonzo Hickman

Reverend Alonzo Hickman is the man responsible for adopting and raising Bliss. He is the leader of the parish and an accomplished trombone player. Hickman, also called A. Z. and Daddy Hickman, slowly moves towards a life devoted to God after his brother is unjustly lynched for raping a white woman. The woman, pregnant and shunned by her community, goes to Hickman's house as a last resort to give birth. Hickman plans to kill the woman, her child and himself, but cannot complete the task.

He begins to feel pity for the woman and love for the child. The woman leaves Hickman with the child, and he names the boy Bliss.

Hickman had wild younger years playing trombone with bands, drinking, dancing and fornicating. However, such behavior becomes too difficult with a young boy and soon his musical talent leads him to play tamer venues, such as churches. Finding God, Hickman begins to not only play music in churches, but also preach the Word. As Bliss gets older, Hickman sees and cultivates a natural talent for preaching in the young, white boy. Soon, Bliss becomes an important part in Hickman's meetings and revivals. Hickman tries his best to teach the young boy about race, religion, politics and sermonizing because he sees that the young boy could be a bridge or a "tie that binds" between the two segregated cultures of America. However, Hickman's eager prodding eventually pushes his white son away and, although Hickman loved the boy, he allows Bliss to become his own person. Watching from a distance, Hickman is saddened by what has become of his son. Eventually, with a letter from Janey Mason outlining the racist Bliss has become, Hickman forces himself to go to Washington, D.C. to confront and question his confused, beguiling son. Unfortunately, he is too late, and he witnesses Bliss being shot on the Senate floor.

Bliss Hickman

Bliss Hickman is a young, white orphan left in the hands of a black jazz musician, Alonzo Hickman, by his mother. Alonzo raises Bliss the best way he can, trying to make enough money playing trombone in jazz clubs. However, the lifestyle is hardly an acceptable way to raise a child. Soon Alonzo begins playing trombone at churches and eventually finds his own voice as a preacher. At a very early age, Bliss also shows great promise as a preacher. He is incredibly skilled in the understanding and memorization of scripture. Bliss has a voice and delivery enviable of any full-grown preacher. Alonzo sees this gift as an opportunity that could benefit all of America. A young, intelligent, religious white boy raised to love and understand black culture, with the capacity to speak with eloquence beyond his years, could be a bridge that spans the gap between the two segregated American cultures. Unfortunately, this burden is too much for young Bliss to bear and he runs away. The boy grows older, explores filmmaking, falls in love and travels with his friends. All the while Alonzo keeps a close eye on him through the help of his far-reaching constituents. Much to Alonzo's dismay, his young hope eventually turns against his upbringing, becoming a vile racist: Senator Adam Sunraider.

Robert Hickman

Robert Hickman is Reverend Alonzo Hickman's brother. He is murdered by a lynch mob after being accused of raping a white woman. Robert Hickman is innocent, yet he is still killed for the crime. The woman who accuses him is Bliss's mother.

Karp

Karp is Bliss's production partner during his years as an unsuccessful filmmaker wandering through rural, Midwestern towns. Karp is a kind man who does not seem as driven as Bliss, but is also much more dedicated and adept than their third partner, Donelson.

Laly

Laly is Bliss's "Teasing Brown" love interest from his filmmaking years. The two share a beautiful afternoon together picnicking and making love under a tree. Laly calls Bliss "Mr. Movie-Man" and the couple talk of love and the future. Their relationship is precious in that Bliss finally feels true love for a woman, but it is also short-lived.

Miss Lorelli

Miss Lorelli is the crazed woman who storms into Reverend Hickman's meeting, crashes through the members of the parish and attempts to kidnap Bliss from his coffin. The woman is eventually wrestled away from Bliss by Sister Bearmasher and delivered to the authorities by Bearmasher and Hickman. According to Hickman, Miss Lorelli has a torrid history of kidnapping children and claiming them as her own. She is not so much wicked as she is deranged. Hickman assures Bliss that Miss Lorelli is certainly not his mother, but the boy is left skeptical, both from his yearning for a mother and an overheard conversation between Body's Mother and Mrs. Proctor.

Sister Lucy

Sister Lucy is one of the members of Reverend Hickman's parish that helped care for Bliss after Miss Lorelli attempted to kidnap the young preacher.

Janey Mason

Jane Mason is one of Hickman's many constituents who is instructed to keep an eye on Bliss after he leaves the parish. Mason sends Hickman a letter stating that Bliss has become a horrible, racist Senator and that there is little hope for his recovery. She also fears that the Senator's life may be in danger. Mason's letter prompts Hickman and members of his parish to leave the south and head for Washington, D.C.

Sister Neal

Sister Neal is one of the members of Reverend Hickman's parish that accompanies him to Washington, D.C. with the hopes of making contact with Senator Sunraider. Sitting in the Senate's Visitors Gallery, Sister Neal is horrified at what has become of the once-shining hope the preacher Bliss had been.

Mrs. Proctor

Mrs. Proctor is a friend of Body's Mother and was present during the meeting in which Miss Lorelli attempted to kidnap Bliss. At one point, Body's Mother and Mrs. Proctor are having a discussion on Body's Mother's front porch. Unbeknownst to the ladies, Bliss is laying underneath the porch in the shade. Mrs. Proctor tells a story about one of her former white employers who always had to complain about some aspect of Mrs. Proctor's work. Eventually, the white woman found herself caught in a lie, accusing Mrs. Proctor of doing something impossible, and Mrs. Proctor called her out, stating she was only looking for something to complain about. The altercation led to Mrs. Proctor losing her job.

Senator Sunraider's Secretary

Senator Sunraider's Secretary refuses to contact the Senator when Hickman and the members of his parish arrive at his office in Washington, D.C. Eventually, the secretary has them thrown out and never mentions anything of their visit to Senator Sunraider.

Senator Adam Sunraider

Senator Adam Sunraider is the racist outcome of young Bliss Hickman. After leaving the parish and stumbling through years as a filmmaker, Bliss eventually finds wealth and a desire for politics. Somehow, whether it be through his indoctrination into his culture as a white American or his revolt against his upbringing as a black American, Bliss is morphed into the vicious Sunraider. Sunraider is outspoken about the evils of black America. He uses the skills he learned behind the pulpit in Reverend Hickman's parish to scrutinize and deprecate the very culture that raised him. Sunraider's speeches eventually lead to his tragic demise at the hands of young, black assassin, but not before he spends several days on his deathbed recollecting

Topics For Further Study

- Ellison's characters express their feelings through speeches and sermons, both political and religious. Describe at least two speeches or sermons, whether they be famous or personal, that have affected your life. Examine the impact and message of these speeches. Are they of a religious or political nature? Both? Neither? Who are the people addressing you and how do you relate to them and their place in time and history? Write a short essay summarizing the speeches and examining these questions.

- Bliss Hickman and Adam Sunraider are effectively the same individual. However, they are polar opposites with regards to their beliefs, understandings and perceptions of race, culture, religion, and politics. This type of juxtaposition is popular in fiction. Try to come up with other characters that share the polarity of Reverend Bliss and Senator Sunraider and compare their differences. What makes the characters change? What are the different personalities of the different characters? To get you started, it may be helpful to think about Dr. Jekyll and Mr. Hyde.

- *Juneteenth* as it is published is only a fragment of the work that Ellison put into developing his second novel. Select two to four aspects from *Juneteenth* that you feel were left underdeveloped and write a short passage that would help to clarify or further explicate the character, scene, setting, or theme that left you unfulfilled and wondering.

- Music is an important factor not only in Ellison's life but also in the characters he develops. Jazz music in particular plays an important role in the development of Ellison's writing. As a young man, Ellison was an accomplished trumpeter and as an older, educated scholar, Ellison made many accomplishments writing about jazz music and musicians. Reverend Hickman is also tied to music, as his life before Bliss was dedicated to the trombone. Spend time listening to some jazz music from the 1950s and 1960s, like Charlie Parker, Miles Davis, and Charles Mingus. How does this music feel in relation to the tone established in *Juneteenth*? Do the characters move in a way that mimics jazz music? Do you believe jazz music could be the soundtrack to *Juneteenth*? Why? Would you select a different type of music or different jazz musicians to compose your soundtrack of *Juneteenth*? If so, what would you pick and why?

and recounting what had occurred to drive him to this, his final place in history.

Deacon Wilhite

Deacon Wilhite is a member of Reverend Hickman's parish that helps lead revivals with Bliss, the young preacher. He is an honest man with a powerful voice and message. Wilhite stands tall and proud as a leading member of Hickman's congregation.

Sister Wilhite

Sister Wilhite is one of the members of Reverend Hickman's parish that helps care for Bliss after Miss Lorelli attempted to kidnap the young preacher.

Themes

Darkness and Light

Darkness and light play an important role in Ellison's *Juneteenth*. The words both represent race, Caucasian and African American, and are personified in the white preacher, Bliss, and his grown-up alter ego, racist senator Sunraider. The term *bliss* means complete happiness or paradise. It is heavenly, full of light and devoid of evil and immorality. On the other hand, the term *Sunraider* carries the implied meaning of an individual that raids the sun, i.e., removes all aspect of light. Sunraider is the personification of darkness, just as Bliss is the personification of light. The importance of light and darkness appears in other places. When Bliss is contained within the coffin at the revivals he is trapped inside the darkness. However, inside the darkness of the box the young, white preacher is dressed in his white satin outfit and upon his cue, he is reborn from the darkness into the light of the parish. His repeated rebirth is a metaphor for the resurrection. The metaphor, in turn, builds Bliss up as an allusion to Jesus. Like the savior, Bliss possesses a remarkable ability to preach salvation. In addition, his rebirth at revivals instills faith in the parishioners. Finally, with Bliss's actual birth, he brought Hickman out of the darkness and into the light of God. If Bliss would not have instilled light in Hickman, the Reverend would have murdered him, his mother and himself in a fit of rage, shrouded in the darkness of his brother's unjust lynching. Ellison uses light and darkness to repeatedly create strong metaphors throughout *Juneteenth*, describing race and religion through a figurative use of language.

Dualism

Dualism is an important theme in Ellison's *Juneteenth*. Bliss is an example of the dualism of flesh and spirit. He is young and, although his body is youthful, his spirit is advanced. Thus, with an advanced spirit, he is expected to deny his flesh as it catches up with his mind. He is forced to ignore his physical yearning for swimming, ice cream, playing with his friends, girls and living a carefree, young life. Bliss is forced into a spiritual recognition that most adults never achieve. His identity is built upon his understanding of scripture and his ability to preach salvation. Hickman saw this ability in his young, adopted son and wanted to cultivate it. However, his pressures eventually drove Bliss away, sending him to chase his lost childhood and seek out his physical nature. Unfortunately, Bliss did not achieve a balance between his dual natures. Instead of falling temporarily into the grips of the flesh to again return and tend to his spirit, Bliss continued away from his spiritual upbringing. He tried his best to deny his other side, to squelch it from existence, by becoming his own antithesis: a rich, racist senator.

Memory and Reminiscence

Memory, or reminiscence, is the most central theme of Ellison's work. The device is used both by Hickman and Sunraider to recount feelings, emotions and actions. In fact, there are often memories within memories that create a collage-like narrative.

It is very effective in creating a relationship between Hickman and Sunraider, especially since their emotions are presented as collage-like, too. Without the tool of memory, or reminiscence, it would be hard to develop the fabric that binds the two very different men together. They, in many ways, grew up together. Bliss was a mature, spiritual young preacher, just like his adoptive father. Although they ended up standing diametrically opposed to one another, they seemed permanently intertwined, as if their shared memories held them together as a unit even though they grew apart as individuals.

Style

Juxtaposition

Through the use of contrasting images, e.g., light and darkness, and emotions, e.g., bliss and fear, Ellison underscores the impact race has on the characters in the South prior to the Civil Rights movement. In one scene, parishioners are engrossed in the power and vitality of salvation and the Word, and then they are suddenly wrought with fear regarding the backlash they will endure from having to wrestle a deranged, white woman out of their revival. Juxtaposing these feelings and images allows Ellison to reveal the heart of race relations in the South. He is able to exemplify the intelligence, integrity and devotion of black Americans in opposition to the oppression and racism imposed on them during this time in history.

Figurative Language

Figurative language is a technique imposed by Ellison in *Juneteenth* to interrupt the order of his storytelling. The novel is composed of the linear story of Bliss, Hickman and Sunraider. However, the literal use of language to explain their history is broken up by dreams and memories that are brought to life through hyperboles, similes and ironic visual constructs. For example, when Sunraider is giving his speech before the Senate, he is hallucinating that the eagle from the Great Seal is attacking him, flapping its wings in front of his face, clutching the olive branch and the arrow. The bird is staring deep into the speaking senator's eyes. All the while, Sunraider is delivering a speech before his fellow senators and those in the Visitors' Gallery. This is one of several examples of a literal description of an event being interrupted by a figurative use of language.

Compare
&
Contrast

- **1930s–1940s:** Benjamin Davis Sr. becomes the first black general in the United States Army in American history.

  Today: African Americans hold important positions in Congress and all divisions of the armed forces. Colin Powell, an African American, held the prestigious position of Secretary of State under the first term of the George W. Bush presidency.

- **1930s–1940s:** Jackie Robinson becomes the first black to play Major League Baseball.

  Today: Players of all ethnicities, races and nationalities play throughout the United States in Major League Baseball, National Basketball Association, National Football League and the National Hockey League.

- **1930s–1940s:** Franklin Roosevelt signs the Social Security Act and the Wealth Tax Act is passed, helping alleviate the unjust concentration of wealth and power.

  Today: The United States is enduring a struggling economy. In the last quarter of 2003 the Bureau of Labor Statistics reports nearly 8.8 million people are unemployed. By October 2004 there are still about 8.2 million people without work.

- **1930s–1940s:** The apartheid program is established in South Africa. Racial discrimination is institutionalized in laws that marginalize black Africans, often defining specific areas where they can live and work. Many black Africans are relocated several times to various locations determined by a prejudiced government.

  Today: South Africans crushed apartheid in 1994 with the all-race elections and, although the nation still suffers, they are making strides to becoming a safer, democratic state.

Historical Context

Pre-Civil Rights Movement America and the Emancipation Proclamation

The title of this novel is pulled from a moment in history known as *Juneteenth*. The term refers to June 19, 1865. Although Abraham Lincoln gave the Emancipation Proclamation on January 1, 1863, it took nearly two and a half years for the news to spread. On June 19, 1865, General Gordon Granger rode into Galveston, Texas with news that the Civil War had ended and, along with it, slavery. The enslaved were elated. Many moved north as it symbolized freedom. Others left for the deeper South to try and find relatives and family members. Still others stayed to see what type of employer-employee relationship would develop out of slavery. Much is unknown as to why there was a two-and-a-half year delay in delivering the news of freedom to the slaves in Texas. One story that is often told is that the messenger delivering news of

freedom was murdered on his way to Texas. Another is that the plantation and slave owners deliberately withheld the news in order to maintain the labor force. Lastly, it is speculated that federal troops waited for one last cotton harvest to financially benefit the slave owners. Of course, none of these speculations has been proven true. Regardless, what is known is that Texas retained the status quo, enslaving blacks for two years beyond what was lawful.

Although Ellison's book does not take place during this historical time, the term *Juneteenth* acts as metaphor for all of the steps black Americans have taken, and continue to take, towards ending slavery, achieving equality and eliminating racism. Reverend Hickman states, "There's been a heap of Juneteenths before this one and I tell you there'll be a heap more before we're truly free!" The novel takes place in the decades prior to the Civil Rights movement. Although this is not explicit, the time and setting implies this period of history.

Racial segregation, racism, and the legacy of racism in the United States are themes addressed in Ralph Ellison's novel Juneteenth

In relation to the fifty years following the Emancipation Proclamation, the two decades before the Civil Rights movement, 1935–1955, were a time of relative prosperity and growth for black Americans. Black Americans were being recognized for their work and achievements. Authors, activists, athletes and educators were voicing opinions, spurring change and stirring people of all races to action. However, there were still many who were opposed to the equality march of the black American. Black Americans were still being quickly convicted of crimes they did not commit. Lynch mobs still roamed the South, murdering unsuspecting and innocent black men. Black women were still exploited and demeaned in the homes of rich whites. Yet, black Americans still strived to overcome the oppression of white Americans. Jesse Owens won four gold medals at the 1936 Summer Olympics in Berlin. In 1941, A. Philip Randolph pressured Franklin D. Roosevelt, who eventually issued an executive order to end discrimination in the defense industries. The United Negro College Fund was founded in 1944. In 1954, the first giant step to overturn segregation was completed with the Supreme Court ending legal segregation in all American schools. These are only a few of the many *Juneteenths* paving the way on the African American journey towards equality, true freedom and a better America.

Critical Overview

Ellison's novel *Juneteenth* was only recently published in 1999, thus there is not a great deal of criticism written about the book. It has received a vast amount of praise, but also some reviews critical of the novel construction. Nonetheless, there has not been enough time for concrete reflection to develop a corpus of lengthier criticism. Richard A. King stated in *Journal of American Studies* that Ellison's *Juneteenth* "can be read as an allegory of the history of America." Though nurtured and cared for by long-suffering blacks, white Americans have spent their lives—and the nation its history—denying that originary link of intimacy." King is touching on what has made Ellison one of America's most important and cherished authors. Ellison is capable of creating a story that is rich with history, entrenched with allegories and metaphors, but not hinged to oppression or evil. Ellison's other works, most notably *Invisible Man*, all explore and shed light on the evils of racism, segregation and hatefulness, but they are rooted in the affirmation of *blackness*, not in the literal exploration of the obviously negative, incredulous evils of racism.

Yet, although this book has received much praise in terms of reviews from magazines and newspapers, the academic journals that have delved into the book note several problems with the book. Again, from Richard A. King in *Journal of American Studies*, "In structural terms, too much of *Juneteenth* is made up of the two men's [Hickman and Sunraider] exchanging set speeches about their shared pasts. Upon reflection, none of this is surprising considering Hickman's religious and [Sunraider's] political vocation." Although the sermonizing and speechmaking of both characters helped to develop their relationship and the collage of their intertwining emotions, it is excessive.

Overall, *Juneteenth* is an incredible work. With Ellisonian wit, humor, assumption and evocation the novel explores the ever-changing climate of race in America. Yet, as forthcoming criticism will analyze, this book is the construct of over two thousand pages of work and, albeit far from perfect, a remarkable novel has sprung forth from that formidable collection of thoughts, ideas, allegories and anecdotes.

Criticism

Anthony Martinelli

Martinelli is a Seattle-based freelance writer and editor. In this essay, Martinelli examines the effects of race—as personified by the opposing characteristics of Bliss Hickman and his adult self, Senator Adam Sunraider—on religion and America during the decades prior to the Civil Rights movement.

In *Juneteenth*, Ralph Ellison tells the story of a young, white orphan, Bliss, who is taken in and adopted by a black musician, Alonzo Hickman. Although completely white in appearance and blood, Bliss developed an incredible understanding of black culture and religion. In fact, he had such a keen knowledge of scripture that it becomes apparent to Hickman that Bliss had a prodigious ability for preaching the Word. Hickman became righteously devoted to cultivating Bliss's abilities because he saw in Bliss the qualities of a savior, not only for individuals but also for America. Unfortunately, Hickman's focus on Bliss's religious development blinded him to a wholly necessary

> No longer Bliss—an individual of enlightenment, happiness and a union of the spirits of the races—the boy preacher was transformed into Sunraider—an individual devoid of light, rooted in wretchedness and the Archfiend of the democratic spirit."

development of his son's being: his physical, flesh side. It was apparent that Bliss had a strong inclination for the spirit and, thus, an ability to be the "the tie that binds" blacks and whites, unifying America through the Word and the light of goodness. However, given such blind one-sidedness, without proper attention given to his duality as a flesh-and-bone human being, it became inevitable that Bliss was doomed to fall victim to himself. Through being denied access to tactile things, e.g., playing with friends, attending movies, flirting with girls, Bliss was forced to revolt against Hickman and his black upbringing in order to pay needed attention to his physical side. He ran from his adoptive father's parish to pursue filmmaking, sleep with women, make millions and eventually turn into an antithesis of his former, younger self: a white, racist Senator named Adam Sunraider. The duality of the protagonist-antagonist character in one single body, i.e., Bliss and Sunraider, is a representation of race and its effect on religion and America.

Bliss came to Hickman through an extraordinary and sad turn of events. Bliss's mother had accused Hickman's brother, Robert, of rape. A lynch mob heard of the accusation, sought out Robert and murdered him. Bliss's mother was, in turn, shunned by the white community. Pregnant with not Robert's but an unnamed white man's child, Bliss's mother turned to the most unlikely of individuals: Alonzo Hickman. Hickman brought the woman into his home and planned to murder the woman, her child and himself once she gave birth. However, upon the child's birth, Hickman, a jazz musician with a lewd and hedonistic past, began to feel pity for the woman and a deep love of the new-born boy. The birth of the small child pulled Hickman from the darkness of his past and his murderous plan, removing him from his past and future sins, showing him goodness. Recalling holding the newborn Hickman thought, *"I'll call him Bliss, because they say that's what ignorance is. Yes, and little did I realize that it was the name of the old heathen life I had already lost."* Bliss's birth is also a rebirth of Hickman in that he has found a new life and a new beginning, refocusing his life and passion on religion and preaching instead of jazz music, drinking and women.

With Hickman on a religious path and Bliss as his catalyst, it is no wonder that it became important to Hickman to introduce his young, white adopted son to religion and the Word. As the boy grew, Hickman realized that at an early age Bliss possessed a natural talent for preaching salvation. Even though Hickman told Bliss, "I still couldn't tell who your daddy was, or even if you have any of our blood in your veins," Hickman believed the boy possessed an ability that transcended his race. Bliss was a *white* boy bringing salvation to the souls of *black* parishioners in a time of deep segregation and racism in America. Bliss had learned and cultivated so much of the black culture that his race was no detraction from his preaching of the Word. However, for Bliss, black culture, even though he was white, became his integrated pattern of knowledge and belief. He personified an American race battleground—a white-skinned, black-spirited boy. Alan Nadel supports this claim in *American Literary History*:

> . . . the problem for Bliss is to remember. He must take himself—and us—to the depths of that American unconscious where the contradictions that undermine democracy can be confronted. Pursuing that search from Bliss's and Hickman's perspectives makes clear that Bliss is not only Christ but also America, both the sacrificial spirit and the historical embodiment of democracy.

Although Nadel takes Bliss to a higher religious standpoint as Christ, his statement supports the concept of Bliss as a personification of the American democratic dream of true equality and understanding, free of racism and violence.

Yet, for all that Bliss was, Hickman's desires pushed Bliss away. In opposition to Nadel's statement, Bliss was not Christ. He was not the Son of God; he was merely man. As to be expected from all youths, Bliss had to revolt against his father to become his own man. He fled from the parish, disappearing into whites-only movie houses to escape the parishioners' attempts to reclaim their prodigy preacher. Films were Bliss's most effective form of rebellion against father, because Hickman told his son that "if they look at those shows too often they'll get all mixed up with so many of those shadows that they'll lose their way. They won't know who they *are* is what I mean." Hickman's lesson proved true. The catalyst for Bliss's transformation into the racist Sunraider was the young preacher's decision to leave the parish, the Word and his culture to wander the Midwest unsuccessfully attempting to make movies.

Upon Bliss's final decision to leave, Hickman decided to no longer attempt to bring the boy back to the parish. Hickman was full of anxiety because he still believed the boy held the key to the future of America. However, he understood that continued pressure would only further drive Bliss from what Hickman believed was his true calling: to bind America and the races together. Unfortunately, Bliss continued to rebel, to the point of complete cessation. No longer Bliss—an individual of enlightenment, happiness and a union of the spirits of the races—the boy preacher was transformed into Sunraider—an individual devoid of light, rooted in wretchedness and the Archfiend of the democratic spirit.

Sunraider is assassinated on the Senate floor. On his deathbed and with Hickman by his side for the first time in decades, Sunraider recounted his youth as Bliss, the white preacher boy who could have been *the tie that bound* America together. He told Hickman, "I couldn't understand my creation. Didn't you realize that you'd trapped me in the dead-center between flesh and spirit, and that at my age they were both ridiculous?" This was Sunraider's first explication of his own rebellion. He articulated an understanding of where he came from and, more importantly, from what he rebelled. Hickman embraced Sunraider's memories. Yet, as Nadel states in *American Literary History*, "Bliss ought to have destroyed the myth of segregation." Hickman saw this power in Bliss and was thus willing to pressure the boy's growth as the grand unifier of America. Also, Hickman was complacent and eventually willing to let the boy rebel and temporarily flee from his calling. However, he was surprised as to the extent that Bliss was willing to wander from the Word, his culture and, most unbelievable, the community that loved him. Hickman told his son, "Bliss, how after knowing such times as those you could take off for where you went is too much for me to truly understand. At least not to go there and *stay*." Hickman believed that when his adopted son left him he would eventually return. He believed he had instilled in his son a true love of the Word and of the *blackness* that was imbedded under his white skin, deep within his spirit, and that these concepts would lead Bliss back to his calling.

Unfortunately for Hickman, Sunraider, and America, the savior-son Bliss left, never to return. His solitary position between black and white, racism and democracy, the spirit and the flesh, all created too much anxiety for such a young man. The powerful, unseen force of Bliss's position is clarified in a scary, lengthy passage from Sunraider's memory of being locked in a coffin at Hickman's revival:

> ... Screaming, mute, the Senator thought, Not me but another. Bliss. Resting on his lids, black inside, yet he knew that it was pink, a soft, silky pink blackness around his face, covering even his nostrils. Always the blackness. Inside everything became blackness, even the white Bible and Teddy, even his white suit. Not me! It was black even around his ears, deadening the sound expect for Reverend Hickman's soaring songs; which now noodling up there high above had taken on the softness of the piece of black velvet cloth from which Grandma Wilhite had made a nice full-dress over coat—only better, because it had a wide cape for a collar. *Ayee*, but blackness.

On his deathbed, Sunraider was ravaged by his tumultuous position between the races of America. The passage is riddled with oppositions and references to black and white, religion and rebirth. Sunraider's memory is still vivid, even on his deathbed. Internally, he is violently pulled in multiple directions by everything that he was supposed to bind together. This responsibility was simply too much and, thus, Sunraider gave in, releasing himself from the daunting task that Hickman had lain out before him.

In the final moments as Sunraider fades into death, the American dream of a true freedom and unification of the races slips away with Bliss's life. Hickman called out, "Bliss! You were our last hope, Bliss; now Lord have mercy on this dying land!" Although Ellison does not hold Hickman's opinion, the death of Sunraider-Bliss does represent Ellison understanding that even up to the author's own death in 1994, the American dream was still unrealized. The death of the Sunraider-Bliss character is not one of doom for America, it simply represents that there still exists a chasm between the races, one that will not disappear until Americans have moved beyond their final Juneteenth, forming a "tie that binds," unifying all Americans under a true democracy.

The black church has a significant role in Juneteenth, *as Reverand Alonzo Hickman narrates parts of the novel, and protagonist Adam Sunraider is raised to be a black minister*

Source: Anthony Martinelli, Critical Essay on *Juneteenth*, in *Novels for Students*, Thomson Gale, 2005.

Robert J. Butler

In the following essay excerpt, Butler examines the narrative structure of Juneteenth, *positing that critics who find the novel too "loosely connected" misinterpret the way the structure is "inspired by musical techniques rather than conventional narrative plotting."*

A close reading of *Juneteenth* reveals that the novel is anything but the "Frankenstein monster" which [Louis] Menand described and much more than the loosely connected fragments which several other reviewers perceived. But the book's principle of organization, like the structure of *Invisible Man* which early reviewers and critics were also unable to see, is not apparent on a first or second reading because it is inspired by musical techniques rather than conventional narrative plotting. The structural "patterns" of *Juneteenth* which are used to give shape and meaning to the "raw experience" which Ellison struggled for over forty years to refine, are, like those of an impressionistic symphony

> And like America, Sunraider is sharply divided—he is both a racist demagogue and someone who takes seriously the America created by 'our visionary fathers.'"

or a jazz composition, based upon free rhythms and loose repetition rather than a mechanical plan or linear plot.

The most important structural device employed in *Juneteenth* is the careful placement of three key scenes, the assassination of Senator Sunraider at the beginning of the novel, the Juneteenth celebration at the center of the book, and Hickman's meditations at the Lincoln Memorial toward the end of the narrative. Each of these scenes takes place in a setting of great national and cultural importance and, as they resonate against each other like the movements of a symphony or the parts of a jazz performance, they not only give the book a loose but discernible overall shape, but they also allow Ellison to develop central themes, define important characters, and provide a comprehensive vision of American experience. For unlike Ellison's earlier fictions, which are centered in quintessentially modern figures who are alienated from a social context, *Juneteenth* is, in the best sense of the word, a "national" narrative which is centered around a large-scale figure of epic proportions who heroically assumes the "socially responsible role" which Invisible Man seeks but has trouble finding at the end of the novel. Father, minister, and citizen, Alonzo Z. Hickman is no underground or marginalized person afflicted with twentieth-century *anomie*; rather, he is a "citizen-individualist" whose story is integrally related to a larger national narrative which provides *Juneteenth* with a power and resonance missing in much modern and postmodern literature.

The first major scene, the assassination of Senator Adam Sunraider on the floor of the United States Senate in the mid-1950s, dramatizes the disastrous cultural conflicts and contradictions of post–World War II American culture. Like the battle royal scene in *Invisible Man*, it is a frightening epiphany of a disintegrating society because it reflects a fundamental conflict between democratic ideals and racist practices. Just as the battle royal is an ironic inversion of the Alger myth, Sunraider's speech is an ironic commentary on the classic pre-Civil War myth of America as a pre-fallen Eden. Carried away by his own "verbal exhilaration," he releases the "full resonance of his voice," giving "expression to ideas the likes of which he had never articulated." The first part of the speech is a powerful evocation of the "transcendent ideas" that go to the heart of the American myth, picturing America as an "edenic landscape" which has broken free of a corrupt European past and promises "a more human future." Sunraider urges his audience to embrace a "democratic passion" and assures them that "we are defeated only if we fail in the task of creating a total way of life which will allow each and every one of us to rise above his origins." He then concludes this unlikely speech, which arises from "some chaotic region deep within him," by citing two African American figures, Booker T. Washington and George Washington Carver, as people who did indeed establish themselves as exemplary American men who rose well above their origins, black men from the "dark side" of America who became prominent at a "dark time" of African American history. They are evidence for Sunraider of the fluidity of American life and the fact that "brightness sometimes hides itself in darkness."

The setting in which this scene is enacted emphasizes the mythic resonance of Sunraider's speech. His audience is seated behind "circular, history-stained desks," and as he delivers this speech, he gazes at another circular object which calls to mind the nation's history and mission, "the Great Seal" containing the "national coat of arms." Gazing at this "mystic motto of national purpose" and especially the "emblematic" eagle at the center of the seal, he is shaken for a time from racist diatribes which he has used to gain power and delivers an uncharacteristically democratic speech arising from a subconscious self "deep within him." Spurred on by his audience's rapt attention as they await "some crucial and long-awaited revelation that would make them whole," Sunraider taps into an ideal vision of America which is diametrically opposed to the racism and demagoguery he has used to vault himself into a position of national prominence and power.

But if the first section of Sunraider's speech expresses that part of his divided personality suggested by his first name, Adam, the second part of his speech comes from his outward political self which divides people by exploiting their baser selves. (This part of the speech could well be suggested by the initials of his two names, B.S.) Shifting from a "lovely dream of progressive idealism," he launches into his stock-in-trade, a Negro-baiting invective eliciting "enthusiastic rebel yells." It is precisely at this point that he is shot by an anonymous assailant whose motives and racial origins are not clear. Is he a black man who objects to the crude racism of the second part of the speech, or is he a white man offended by the democratic idealism of the first part of the speech? The text remains ambiguous on both points.

In his *New York Times Book Review* article, Louis Menand argued that the scene culminating in Sunraider's being shot is not successful because its two parts blatantly contradict each other:

> Callahan's insertion of the excerpt from "Cadillac Flambé"—an anti-black diatribe—into the speech Sunraider is delivering when he gets shot is consistent with the rest of his speech which is in praise of democracy and diversity. Did Ellison want his character to have undergone a political conversion on the eve of his assassination? If he did, it's too late now.

But Menand's criticism misses the point which goes to the heart of the scene's meaning. Sunraider's sometimes raving speech is a surprisingly lucid example of what he calls "our national ambiguities"— America is both a visionary world defined by lofty ideals and a historical entity which has consistently contradicted those ideals. And like America, Sunraider is sharply divided—he is both a racist demagogue and someone who takes seriously the America created by "our visionary fathers." The first part of his speech is rooted in his childhood past when as Hickman's adopted son and revivalist partner he would have indeed embraced the mythic vision of America as a new Eden, a redemptive force transforming human history. But he is also Senator Sunraider, the man who defiled American ideals to secure his own political advantages. Although the scene stresses the ambiguous duality of both America and Sunraider's own nature, it is altogether lucid on this point which Sunraider makes midway through his speech—America's "transcendent ideals" do indeed "interrogate us, judging us." Just as Sunraider is judged and found wanting in this scene and pays the price of his demagoguery with an assassin's bullet, so too is post–World War II America interrogated and judged by Ellison for failing to square its democratic ideals with its history.

Underneath the bitter ironies of Sunraider's speech, therefore, emerge important thematic matters which the novel's other key scenes will attempt

to clarify. Among these important ideas are the three questions which Sunraider raises: "How can the many be one? How can the future deny the past? And how can the light deny the dark?" These "three fatal questions" which "history has put to us" are not answered by Sunraider, but Ellison does make him the frail vessel who poses such questions, which the remainder of the novel will meditate upon seriously.

The Juneteenth celebration, which is located in the two chapters at the exact center of the novel, also takes place in a setting of profound national and cultural importance, a campground which in the past has served as a sacred burial ground for slaves and in the present is the place where Hickman and seven other ministers hold a weeklong celebration of African American freedom promised by the Emancipation Proclamation. Indeed, Hickman regards Juneteenth as a day of enormous cultural importance, a "God-given day" to "celebrate our oneness." It is in fact a day when the "transcendent ideals" described in Sunraider's Senate speech are finally extended to black Americans and, accordingly, Hickman sees this day as "a great occasion. A great occasion." A crucial moment in the historical experience of all African Americans, it is also a pivotal moment in Sunraider's personal life since it is at this point that a white woman claims him as her son and begins a process which eventually culminates in his leaving Hickman and denying his profound ties with black people. And Sunraider's betrayal of his roots reflects a larger betrayal of blacks by American society since the promises of freedom and justice which were made in the original Juneteenth in 1865 were eventually reneged upon by the Compromise of 1877, which laid the groundwork for the re-enslavement of American blacks through a system of racial segregation. As was the case with the assassination scene at the beginning of the novel, Ellison connects personal and cultural narratives to stress the integral connection between individual lives and the life of the nation.

And Hickman's extraordinary sermon, like Sunraider's speech, is heavily infused with myth and rituals which help to define American identity. But unlike Sunraider, who evokes the romantic pre-Civil War myth of America as Eden before the Fall, Hickman conjures up a tragic post-Civil War vision of America as a postlapsarian world in which the "calamity" of slavery betrays "the principles of Almighty God," making America a kind of "hell." But if slavery is linked to "the fall of proud Lucifer from Paradise," Hickman's powerfully Christian imagination offers hope for a redeemed America by drawing skillfully upon the paradox of the Fortunate Fall which is central to Christian theology. Hickman assures his congregation that the "calamity" of slavery was "laced up with a blessing," and this blessing is "the Word." And the Word empowered blacks to transcend the "pain and suffering" of slavery by constructing a spiritually rich African American culture.

The most compelling image Hickman uses to dramatize the concept of the Fortunate Fall is the underground, a rich and complicated symbol of the historical experience of black people in America. Designed by whites as a tomb into which slaves would fall, it becomes transformed in Hickman's mythic imagination as a transcendent symbol of regeneration:

> Ah, but though divided and scattered, ground down and battered into the earth like a spike being pounded by a ten-pound sledge, we were on the ground and in the earth and the earth was red and black like the earth of Africa. And as we moldered underground we were mixed with this land. We liked it. It fitted us fine. It was in us and we were in it. And then—praise God—deep in the ground, deep in the womb of the land, we began to stir!

Seen in this context, the minuses of African American experience become plusses and, to use the metaphor of electricity which Ellison employed so brilliantly in *Invisible Man*, the minuses and plusses together produce energy and power. Converting their dead underground tomb to a live womb, African Americans are "rebirthed dancing" and "crying affirmation." Deprived of their African languages, they create "a new language and a brand-new song" which enables them to found a new culture in America. As Hickman envisions the history of black people in America, therefore, he sees blacks as "a new kind of human," a "well-tested people" who are charged with the sacred task of "transforming God's Word into a "lantern." They are what Albert Murray called "omni-Americans" whose historical mission is to resolve the kinds of contradictions in American history which were dramatized in Sunraider's Senate speech.

Seen in this light, Hickman's Juneteenth sermon provides real answers to each of the "three fatal questions" posed in that speech. While Sunraider can provide only abstract and highly rhetorical responses to these questions which he contradicts in his personal and political life, Hickman's sermon answers these questions in ways which are morally compelling because his responses are rooted in the concrete facts of lived African American experience. The many *are* one

because all Americans share a common history in the New World and are unified by a coherent set of moral and political principles. The "communion" that Hickman finally celebrates transcends racial limits and is not only a "coming together" of black people but all people because the principles epitomized by Juneteenth are broadly American values unifying all races and creeds. Thus, Ellison stressed in a testimonial to John Wright given in the early 1980s, "Fortunately American experience is of a whole and despite the differences of race and religion, class and region, it is still inspirited by the same ideals" (Callahan, "Reflections" 20). Hickman also provides a clear and emphatic answer to the second question posed by Sunraider— the future can deny the past only by destroying itself. Just as Sunraider brought about his own moral disintegration and death by denying his past, America will be destroyed by larger versions of the senseless violence which claims Sunraider's life if it forgets the sacred principles of its founding. For this reason, Hickman exhorts the wounded Sunraider to "Continue! Remember!" as a way of reviving himself in the present by recalling and re-experiencing the richly human life he shared in the past with Hickman. And in a similar way, Ellison is telling late twentieth-century Americans that there is still hope for the country if it can "remember" the founding principles of America and "continue" on with them. Lastly, Hickman's sermon provides a lucid answer to the third question raised in Sunraider's speech, "How can the light deny the dark?" As Bliss's/Sunraider's life vividly demonstrates, the experience of blacks and whites in America are integrally bound up with each other, and terrible personal and political calamities will result from the separating of the two races. By recreating his Juneteenth sermon to Sunraider, he tries to remind him of the central mistake of his life and urges him to rejuvenate himself psychologically and spiritually by reintegrating himself with the black people who provided him with the only family he has ever known.

Sunraider's response to Hickman's redeeming words, however, is a curious mixture. Part of him reacts favorably to Hickman's evocation of a past world centered in communal love and purpose, and he is at times "dragged irresistibly along" by Hickman's "reminiscing voice," which compels him "to make the connections." But throughout Hickman's meditations in Chapters 7 and 8, Sunraider also stubbornly resists the voice which asks him to rejuvenate his life by moving beyond the self. As Hickman encourages him to assume a "discipline" needed to overcome a condition of being "self-blinded," he thinks, *"No . . . no more of it! No!* And at the end of Chapter 7 he reduces Hickman's magnificent sermon to "Words, words" as he "wearily" tries to sink back a state of safe but enervating isolation. In Chapter 8 when he remembers his own participation in the Juneteenth celebration which Hickman so lyrically recreates, he is able to recall only negative memories which serve to alienate him further from the past. Even in the transcendent moment when he rises from the coffin, he can think only in trivialized terms, resenting the fact that Hickman refuses to reward him outwardly for his services by providing him with ice cream:

> *And not even ice cream, nothing to sustain myself in my own terms. Nothing to make it even worthwhile in Bliss's terms.*

In essence, Bliss's life is destroyed because of his very modern insistence on having everything on his "own terms," and this gives him momentary outward satisfactions but locks him into a selfishness which separates him from a nourishing past and a vital community. Like the woman claiming to be his mother and who asserts, "He's mine, MINE!," Bliss is destroyed by the selfishness which compels him first to become "Mr. Movie Man" and later Senator Sunraider, roles which provide him with various forms of "ice cream" (sex, money, power) but destroy him as a person. Appropriately, he is assassinated by a nameless, lone gunman whose identity, like Sunraider's, is indeterminate.

So Hickman's heroic efforts to save Sunraider by reconnecting him to his past and his community probably fail. But Hickman succeeds magnificently on another level, for he provides the novel's modern readers with an eloquent and potent vision of personal and cultural revival. And this is made clear not only in the Juneteenth sermon but also in the novel's third major scene, Hickman's meditation at the Lincoln Memorial at the end of the novel.

Significantly, this scene is recalled through memory as Hickman is nearly overcome in the present by a rare moment of self-doubt and depression as he gazes at the dying Sunraider and thinks "[w]hat an awful time" his visit to Washington has "turned out to be." Not only has his group been insulted by being treated as an "annoyance" precisely at the point when they have "arrived" in Washington to plead their case as American black people seeking delivery on the promises of American democracy set forth by our founding documents such as the Constitution and the Bill of Rights, but Hickman is also terribly disappointed in his at-

tempts to rejuvenate Sunraider. At this stage of the novel, therefore, Hickman is beginning to lose confidence in his ability to succeed on both personal and cultural levels, losing faith in his ability to find some meaning in the tragic events of Bliss's life, his own life, and the life of the nation. Indeed, he wonders if "[t]here are simply too many snares and delusions, too many masks, too many forked tongues. Too much grit in the spiritual greens."

He is saved from such despair as he closes his eyes and remembers an earlier point in the day when he and his group went to the Lincoln Memorial to pray after they had been turned away so rudely from Sunraider's office. Experiencing "a sudden release from the frame of time," he moves away from a troubled present and is refreshed by the "awe and mystery" of the "serene, high-columned space" of the Lincoln Memorial. Indeed, the transcendence he experiences in this scene is comparable to the ecstasy he had felt as a blues musician "improvising on some old traditional riffs" or the rapture he had felt as a minister preaching the Gospel, feeling "the Sacred Word surging rapturously within him."

His physical eyes closed but the eyes of his soul awakened in an "inward-turning vision," Hickman experiences an epiphany which enables him to reaffirm a strong belief in his own life, Bliss's life, and the life of the nation. More importantly, he comes to a powerful understanding of how all three are related. Gazing at the statue of Lincoln, "the great image slumped in the huge stone chair" and then peering into Lincoln's "great, brooding eyes," he is uplifted by the tragic vision of America embodied in Lincoln's story. And he realizes how that story is connected to the experience of African Americans, since Lincoln's own suffering and his emancipation from his culture's hatreds, fears, and divisions convince Hickman that he was one of them:

> *So yes, he's one of us, not only because he freed us to the extent he could, but because he freed himself of that awful inherited pride they deny to us, and in doing so he became a man and he pointed the way for all of us who would be free—yes!*

Hickman finds in Lincoln a heroic man whose life embodied positive answers to each of the "three fatal questions" which Sunraider poses in his Senate speech. For he made it possible for the "many to be one" by preserving the union; he guaranteed the American future by squaring it with sacred principles from its past; and he did his best to ensure that the "light" not deny the "dark" by extending citizenship to black Americans. He truly possessed the "balanced consciousness" necessary to perceive "unity in diversity" which Sunraider rhetorically describes but which Lincoln lived and paid for with his life.

Lincoln, therefore, becomes the true "Father" of the United States in ways that George Washington, a slaveholder, failed to be. For Lincoln was able to link all Americans together by healing "wounds that have festered and run and stunk in this land." Although his vision of America "has been undone" in the "betrayed years" after the Civil War, people such as Hickman can be inspired by Lincoln's example and get their "second wind" and then "do all over again what has been undone." The values which Lincoln embodied are rooted in the country's founding documents and can be used to rejuvenate America in the present.

Thus "possessed by the experience at the Memorial," Hickman surely does get a "second wind" which helps him to recover belief in himself, his nation, and even Bliss/Sunraider. Reminded that "for a hope or ideal to be real it has to be embodied in a man," he has witnessed the purest American ideals embodied not only in Lincoln but in himself as well. Just as he regards Lincoln as the true father of the nation, he envisions himself as "Daddy Hickman," the true father of Bliss and the spiritual father of his congregation. And as Lincoln strove to preserve the Union, Hickman has come to the conclusion that America is one people, "human cloth" which is "woven too fine" to be cut in pieces. His extraordinary vision at the Lincoln Memorial, therefore, rejuvenates him by reminding him that—"the big things can save us." In so doing, he links the novel's three major scenes together in an impressively affirmative way—the doubts which were generated by him as he witnessed the shooting of Senator Sunraider are resolved by his creative acts of memory. Distilling a faith in America and himself from his meditation on Lincoln in the near past, he links this vital moment with an equally vital moment in the distant past, his Juneteenth sermon. In the process, he joins the "light" and the "dark," rather than denying them, and thus avoids the despair that consumes Sunraider.

With this restored belief in himself and his people, Hickman is then able to productively revisit the most troubling episode in his personal past: the lynching of his brother, the death of his mother, and the birth of Bliss. The outlines of these events were vaguely suggested in Chapters 8 and 9 but are fully dramatized in Chapter 15, which directly follows the scene at the Lincoln Memorial. This story of personal anguish and tragedy is a microcosmic version of the story of post-Civil War America, a world betrayed by racism and violence but containing the possibility of redemption through love. In both personal and national narratives, to use a metaphor from Hickman's Juneteenth sermon, "calamity" is mysteriously "laced up with a blessing."

The scene begins with Hickman expecting his death as he awaits the white men who lynched his brother Bob for allegedly impregnating a white woman. Hickman has actually recorded his own death in the family Bible and is fatalistically "dedicated to one last act," retaliating against the whites by killing them as they seek him out. What the reader expects from this scene is a miniature version of the Civil War, but what follows is a masterfully written parable of regeneration through love, a tale of "Eden and Christmas squeezed together."

Intent on racial violence and his own death, Hickman is surprised by the appearance of the white woman who was responsible for Bob's death by naming him as the father of her unborn child. Hickman's first response is to kill both the woman and her child, gaining the satisfaction of a "God-cursing crime" as an act of pure revenge. But when she asks for his assistance in delivering the child and tells Hickman that she is a Christian, he is strangely moved by her pleas and actually delivers the baby and nurses its mother back to health. It is precisely at this moment that Hickman begins his "change," eventually undergoing a conversion from a roustabout who centers his life in "heathen freedom" to a heroic person who will sacrifice the self in order to assume two important social roles—first, a father who names and raises Bliss and, later, a Christian minister dedicated to the "Christ-like" ideal of being a self for others. His story, therefore, dramatizes in a powerful way the Christian concepts of good coming out of evil, growth emerging from suffering, and life growing out of death. In an altogether mysterious way, the terrible violence inflicted upon his brother and the death of his mother has resulted not only in Bliss's birth but also Hickman's rebirth.

Here again, Hickman's story is strongly connected to Lincoln's life, death, and rebirth as a mythic figure who helped create a new America after the Civil War. Like Lincoln, who had to free himself of "that awful inherited pride" in order to become a leader for the whole nation, Hickman must overcome his socially constructed "pride" in order to transcend his desires to murder the white woman who gave birth to Bliss. And like Lincoln, who had a profound belief in the basic unity of American society and gave his life to preserve the "Union,"

A group of African American protestors participate in a Civil Rights march from the Washington Monument to the Lincoln Memorial in Washington, D.C.

Hickman overcomes his early perception of Bliss and his mother as strangers, sensing on a very profound level "some cord of kinship" between them which is "deeper than blood, hate, or heartbreak." Just as Lincoln preserved the unity of the nation, Hickman as father keeps his small family together and as a minister brings his people together in a vibrant, unified community. A person who has successfully harmonized private and public selves, he is one of the "citizen-individualists" whom Sunraider describes in his Senate speech but fails to become.

Throughout his career, Ralph Ellison expressed a strong dissatisfaction with the stylistic limitations and philosophical gloom of the modern American novel, tracing both problems to the twentieth-century writer's recoil from public experience into a world of narcissistic privacy. In his 1953 acceptance speech for the National Book Award, for example, he objected to the "narrow naturalism" and "unrelieved despair" which he felt characterized "so much of our current fiction" (*Shadow and Act*) and observed that "something vital has gone out of American prose after Mark Twain" (*Shadow*). Ellison therefore found his inspiration in the work of nineteenth-century masters such as Twain, Melville, and Emerson, who envisioned America as a democratic society endowed

with an "almost magical fluidity and freedom," a country that provided both "individual self-realization" and "human fraternity" (*Shadow*).

In "Twentieth Century Fiction and the Black Mask of Humanity," written in 1946 but published in 1953, Ellison argued this point more fully, claiming that "the broad conception of democracy which vitalized the work of our greatest writers" (*Shadow*) had disappeared from American fiction, citing Hemingway as a particularly vivid example of a writer who had withdrawn from public reality into an "artistic individualism" (*Shadow*) which produced a narrow "technical perfection" at the expense of "moral insight." He felt that Hemingway paid an unacceptably steep price for rejecting "national myth" and retreating into "personal myth" (*Shadow*) because such a strategy robbed his art of social relevance and moral resonance, trapping Hemingway into a "tradition of intellectual evasion" (*Shadow*).

By the time that Ellison was engaged in the writing of *Invisible Man,* he was deeply committed to the belief that "Art by its nature is social" and that one of the most important responsibilities for the writer was to shape experience into "socially meaningful patterns" (*Shadow*). He therefore devoted himself to recovering "a body of unassailable public beliefs" (*Shadow*) which would enable him to write fiction which would harmonize American individualism with the life of a democratic society. Like Melville, Emerson, and Twain, Ellison was seriously interested in "portraying the moral situation of a nation" (*Shadow*) rather than making his writing "the instrument of a questionable personal freedom of the artist" (*Shadow*).

Juneteenth, much more fully and explicitly than *Invisible Man*, fulfills the exceptionally high standards which Ellison set for himself as a twentieth-century American novelist. *Invisible Man* concludes with the central character rejecting the narcissism that has nearly destroyed him and searching for the "next phase" (*Invisible*) of his life in which he hopes to play a "socially responsible role" (*Invisible*). But *Juneteenth* carries this story much further and is centered in a hero who is a "citizen-individualist," one whose personal life is nourished by a series of important social roles. Father, minister, and leader, Hickman draws from his nation's traditions and performs a series of heroic actions which have great personal and cultural importance. His narrative stands in stark contrast to Bliss's/Sunraider's story, which reads like a cautionary tale warning against what Robert Bellah and others have defined as a major problem in modern American culture, an individualism which has become "cancerous" because it produces a "socially unsituated self," resulting in a sterile narcissism and cultural disintegration.

By artfully structuring *Juneteenth* in terms of scenes which draw heavily from national myth and ritual, Ellison endows Hickman's story with a power and resonance missing from much modern literature. The novel has a special significance for twenty-first century Americans because it is much more than a diagnostic tool which can bring our cultural problems into sharper, clearer focus. Offering imaginatively compelling strategies for creatively handling and perhaps solving such problems by a renewed commitment to public reality, *Juneteenth* is that rare thing in modern fiction, a robust national narrative which is a genuine curative force.

Source: Robert J. Butler, "The Structure of Ralph Ellison's *Juneteenth*," in *CLA Journal*, Vol. 46, No. 3, 2003, pp. 291–311.

Alan Nadel

In the following essay excerpt, Nadel considers Juneteenth *a version of "Ellison's America," in which Ellison tries to reconcile the American psyche with the repressed "sin of American racial pride."*

The point I am making—and I cannot stress it strongly enough—is that for Ellison, the Negro represents the return of the repressed in the American psyche:

> The Founding Fathers committed the sin of American racial pride . . . In failing the test of what was after to be termed the American dilemma, they prepared the way for the evils that Jefferson had hoped to pile upon the royal head of England's king, and loaded them upon the black backs of anonymous American slaves. Worse, these Americans were designated as perfect victims for sacrifice, and were placed beyond any possibility of democratic redemption . . . Indeed they were thrust beneath the threshold of social hierarchy and expected to stay there.

> To further justify this act of pride and failure of nerve, myths of racial superiority and inferiority were evoked, and endless sacrificial rites of moral evasion were set in motion.

Thus the artist has the moral burden of helping America confront its repressed self-contradiction, and the surreal dream worlds of Ellison's novels create the symbolic space in which repressed guilt and unfulfilled desire take visible form. Ellison's craft adapts the techniques of high modernism to the moral imperative of an integrated American consciousness, because that integrated consciousness is mandated by the articulation on which democracy depends. Ellison's work over the last 50 years, as *The Collected Essays* makes clean, is underpinned by this complex mandate he has conceived for the American artist, and particularly the Negro American artist, who has privileged information about America's self-contradictions. One sees why the transitions always gave Ellison trouble. The task he set for himself was to reveal the dissociation of American sensibilities lodged in the sacrifice of a race to the political interests of a nation, so that his surreal vision had to present the segregated world while exposing the myth of segregation by demonstrating an infinite network of connections. To this end, Ellison's transitions, puns, images, and allusions create a ghost network of language and craft that integrate the sundry aspects of the American Nightmare.

In this light, *Juneteenth* is an admirable attempt to accomplish the impossible. Perhaps, given the impossibility of the task, it is apt, even fortunate, that the novel is an unfinished portion of a larger unfinished work, a larger work moreover that admits infinite possible versions. Only Ellison, himself—and perhaps not even he—could know definitively which passages in the material he left behind were alternative versions of the same section, and which were additional sections. While in jazz, alternative versions are always additions, in fiction, we generally rely, albeit imprecisely, on the principle of unity that delimits a work by separating what it is from what it is not. In an irony that Ellison might have appreciated, his unpublished works bring us to an impossible impasse guaranteeing that the limits of Ellison's second novel will be no more clearly defined and finalized than the subject of that novel: America.

In giving us his version of *Juneteenth,* editor Callahan has no doubt deprived us of another version. That is the problem endemic to *versions,* a problem that cannot be solved by Callahan's promise to produce a scholar's edition or to make all the Ellison papers available at the Library of Congress. Of course I regret that the book entering the public consciousness and the American canon as Ellison's last novel does not contain more of the material he wrote over the last 45 years of his life.

By the same token, pursuing this line of regret at the expense of the text we do have in its (artificial) entirety is a great mistake. In *Juneteenth,* Callahan has made available a strong and important piece of literature rich in its exploitation of the themes and techniques Ellison devoted over half a century to refining. The same cannot be said, I'm afraid, of *Flying Home and Other Stories,* the collection of Ellison's early short fiction, also edited by Callahan. Although the work will no doubt be of interest to Ellison scholars because it identifies a body of concerns and images that inform Ellison's entire opus, it reveals little of the rich dynamics that characterize Ellison's mature fiction and criticism. If the *Collected Essays* provide a long-overdue comprehensive introduction to Ellison's novels, then the short stories provide a useful footnote. They are particularly useful, for instance, in highlighting the nostalgic quality of *Juneteenth* in that they contain several child protagonists on whom Ellison seems to be drawing in his creation of the child Bliss whose story *Juneteenth* tells.

Juneteenth's plot is constructed primarily in "flashbacks" that summon Ellison's wealth of memory, in the fullest sense of that term, so that the novel presents characters, styles, scenes, and allusions that comprise a composite of Ellison's America. The setting is a bedside vigil that counterpoints the memories of one character with the dreams/fantasies of another. Reverend Hickman, a Negro minister, had been the adoptive father of Bliss, who was raised in the Negro community as a Negro, despite his fair appearance and indefinite origins. In that community, even as a child he was one of the spiritual leaders: Reverend Bliss. But

> **This battle for the life and soul of Bliss, for the history and promise of America, takes place, moreover, in uniquely Ellisonian terms."**

Bliss, partially in search of his origins and partially in denial of them, left the community, first to become Mister Movie-Man, a director of silent films, and then Adam Sunraider, a white racist senator from a New England state. The community's loss of Bliss, in other words, starts out as an unfulfilled promise and becomes an overt betrayal.

The attempt to understand that betrayal focuses the novel. It motivates Hickman to lead an entourage to Washington (in the mid-1950s) to speak to Sunraider, to redeem him, to return him to Bliss. Critically wounded by an assassin, Sunraider calls Hickman to his hospital bed, motivated by a desire to understand his own history. Thus we enter the hallucinatory dream world of the semiconscious Bliss/Sunraider as he remembers his past. At times he comes to consciousness and speaks with Hickman. And Hickman too remembers. In the composite, we mix memory and desire in an attempt to find the key that will impel the rebirth of the dying Bliss. The influence of *The Waste Land* (1922) is even stronger in *Juneteenth* than in *Invisible Man,* especially since Bliss is identified from the outset as a Christ figure. Lying in his hospital bed, he wonders, *"LORD, LORD, LORD WHY HAST THOU . . ."* And his response to hearing Hickman call his name is "to dream, to remember, recall himself an uneasy dream," in which he returns to a bright day in his childhood when "Daddy Hickman" shows him a coffin out of which he will jump in a revival meeting to reenact resurrection "so the sinners can find life everlasting." In a section replete with evidence of Ellison's skill at making words serve many masters at once, the Easter bunny to which Bliss clings for comfort in the dark of the coffin becomes as well Brer Rabbit, the trickster, and the dark itself becomes the miraculous blank of Bliss's origin. The tension between Bliss's desire for a teddy bear and an Easter bunny returns us to the Brer Bear/Brer Rabbit motif in *Invisible Man,* just as this scene that merges the coffin and the hospital bed evokes the

What Do I Read Next?

- *Invisible Man* (1952) is Ralph Ellison's first novel. It is about a nameless black man traveling through the perils of American racism and cultural blindness.

- *The Collected Essays of Ralph Ellison* (2003) contains some of the greatest essays, criticisms and interviews, both published and formerly unpublished, from one of the most cogent and vital voices in American race commentary and examination, Ralph Ellison.

- *Living with Music: Ralph Ellison's Jazz Writings* was published as a collection in 2002. Before ever becoming a renowned writer and scholar, Ellison was an accomplished trumpeter. This collection is full of great meditations on jazz classics and profiles of famous jazz musicians. It also offers a window into the lives and culture of black Americans.

- *Flying Home and Other Stories* (1998) is a collection of thirteen previously unpublished works of short fiction that depict Ralph Ellison's interesting development as a writer.

- *Beloved*, by Toni Morrison, won the Pulitzer Prize in 1988. The novel traces the life of a slave woman, Sethe, who decides to kill her infant daughter rather than allow her to be enslaved. The novels explores the atrocities of slavery and the deep struggles of a woman entrapped by a lifetime of unbelievable pain.

- *Native Son* (1940), by Richard Wright, is a powerful novel set in the 1930s about the hopelessness and destitution of black Americans in the inner city. The meditation of the book reflects upon the ever-changing question of what it means to be black in the United States.

- *The Fire Next Time* (1963), by James Baldwin, was a plea to "end the racial nightmare." The book has proven timeless, not only as a galvanizing voice of the Civil Rights movement, but also as a personal and provocative work reflecting upon a changing nation through the eyes of a brilliant black American.

---

coffin/bed in the factory hospital, where the invisible man underwent an electric lobotomy to sever him from his origins. "What is your mother's name?" the doctors asked the invisible man in order to determine whether the operation was a success (*Invisible Man.*) Returning us to that primal site of death and resurrection, *Juneteenth* asks the same (unanswerable) question, implicitly associated with the trickster rabbit, in all his incarnations. The nature of the meditation in this case, however, is quite different. Bliss is not a *sign*—as the invisible man was—of the disintegration of American sensibility; rather he *is* disintegrated America. His problem, therefore, lies not in the eyes of his beholder, but in the way that he beholds himself. While the problem for the invisible man was to be seen, the problem for Bliss is to remember. He must take himself—and us—to the depths of that American unconscious where the contradictions that undermine democracy can be confronted. Pursuing that search from Bliss's

and Hickman's perspectives makes clear that Bliss is not only Christ but also America, both the sacrificial spirit and the historical embodiment of democracy. As such, his origins can never be completely ascertained, and his search for his true mother is a folly, for Hickman did not know, he explained to Bliss, "who your daddy was, or even if you have any of our blood in your veins." Too much violence, too many lies, too much faith in the idea of racial purity obscure the origins of Bliss. But the improbable circumstances that brought him to Hickman served to redeem Hickman from the cycles of hatred and violence that circumscribed Hickman's life as a Southern Negro.

In theory, Bliss ought to have destroyed the myth of segregation. Having been born to a white woman and unknown father, left in Negro hands, and then becoming the spiritual leader of a Negro community, he understood from his firsthand experience the connection between Brer Rabbit and the Easter bunny. Thus Hickman, praying over Bliss/Sunraider's unconscious body, is also praying for America: "We asked nothing for ourselves, only that he remember those days and what he had been at that time. Remember the promising babe that he was and the hope placed in him and his obligation to the babes who came after."

What then made Bliss forget? The movies: they were the fatal temptation for this potential savior, the cunning seductress for this representative American. Bliss's transformation into Mister Movie-Man draws its significance from Ellison's carefully orchestrated tension between image and word, which functions in *Juneteenth* in much the way that the tension between sight and blindness, light and dark, do in *Invisible Man*. Throughout the novel, image competes with the other common senses, so that the fascination with image comes to supply Bliss with an identity at the price of forgetting the sound, taste, sight, and feel of his experience. And most significantly, for Bliss the image replaces the word, which means forgetting that, for a democracy, in the beginning was the word.

Armed only with words, Hickman throughout the novel is trying to save Bliss from his obsession with image. This struggle takes myriad forms. Hickman engages folklore and scripture; he wrestles with angels, with demons, and with history. And he wrestles with his own conscience, for in an integrated society no one escapes culpability. This battle for the life and soul of Bliss, for the history and promise of America, takes place, moreover, in uniquely Ellisonian terms. By representing America as the Negro's adoptive child, Ellison has inverted the traditional historical poles. Since the Negro in North America antedates the American nation, it was the Negro who adopted America, and not the other way around. But the America that the Negro adopted was not a nation represented by the white, privileged image of the founding fathers but the promise of their words. Thus the decision to adopt America was an act of faith, and Bliss's rejection of his adoptive father, of his integrated history, of the truth of his senses, is a breach of faith with the Constitution and the Declaration of Independence. To discover his origins, therefore, Bliss must go back to the act of blind faith that allowed Hickman to adopt him, that is, if he does not die first, which remains a strong possibility.

Although this schematic description of *Juneteenth* may help explain how it reflects some of the intricacies of Ellison's thematic concerns, it doesn't do justice, I'm afraid, to the craft with which he develops those concerns. *Juneteenth*, page by page, is a text of rare resonance, full of strains, motifs, harmonies, allusions. Reading the novel, one moves through the dark and darkly enlightening echo chamber of the American canon, a canon that is being adopted in the same way that Coltrane adopted "My Favorite Things."

In its intricate harmonics, *Juneteenth* manifests a perhaps impossible faith in the power of art to reformulate history. Like the protagonist of *Invisible Man*, Ellison may be one of American literature's most sophisticated naïfs, or he may have played the role with unparalleled skill. Only someone naively seduced by the propaganda of the American Dream and an essentialist notion of individualism could articulate some of the positions that Ellison held. But only by assuming that naïve role and rhetoric could Ellison put himself in the position to make so fully visible the contradictions between the imagined (or imaginary) America and its lived practice. Perhaps Ellison knew about the invisible *n* in "can(n)on." Perhaps he knew the can(n)on was not a neutral or natural mechanism but a weapon, loaded and pointed at someone. Perhaps he understood, as well, the labor that went into mining its ore, the crucible that forged its shape, and the source of the shrapnel with which it is loaded. Perhaps he understood how much work was necessary to make that *n* invisible.

Ellison suggested that the reason Duke Ellington failed to receive the nation's highest honors was that "his creations are far too *American*. There is also the fact of Ellington's aura of mockery. Mockery speaks through his work and his bearing . . . [T]o many his stage manners are so suave and gracious that they appear a put-on—which quite often they are. His manner, like his work, serves to remind us of the inadequacies of our myths, legends, conduct, and standards. However, Ellington's is a creative mockery in that it rises above itself to offer something better, more creative and hopeful, than we've attained while seeking other standards" (*Collected Essays*).

Source: Alan Nadel, "Ralph Ellison and the American Canon," in *American Literary History*, Vol. 13, No. 2, Summer 2001, pp. 393–404.

Sources

Ellison, Ralph, *Juneteenth*, Vintage, 2000, pp. 23, 38, 112, 131, 143, 162, 223, 307, 311.

King, Richard A., "The Uncreated Conscience of My Race/The Uncreated Features of His Face: The Strange Career of Ralph Ellison," in *Journal of American Studies*, Vol. 34, Pt. 2, August 2000, pp. 306–07.

Nadel, Alan, "Ralph Ellison and the American Canon," in *American Literary History*, Vol. 13, No. 2, Summer 2001, p. 402.

Further Reading

Burke, Bob, and Denyvetta Davis, *Ralph Ellison: A Biography*, Oklahoma Heritage Association, 2003.
> This biography spans the entirety of Ellison's life, most notably chronicling his experiences with segregation in his hometown of Oklahoma City.

Eichelberger, Julia, *Prophets of Recognition: Ideology and the Individual in Novels by Ralph Ellison, Toni Morrison, Saul Bellow, and Eudora Welty*, Louisiana State University Press, 1999.
> This book explores the treatment of the individual in relation to society through the four of America's greatest literary giants. Questioning more than just race, the novels of Ellison, Toni Morrison, Saul Bellow and Eudora Welty explore ethnicity, gender, class, and religion during the most volatile years of American history.

Ellison, Ralph, Albert Murray, and John F. Callahan, *Trading Twelves: The Selected Letters of Ralph Ellison and Albert Murray*, Vintage Books USA, 2001.
> This collection of letters spans a decade of friendship between the remarkable authors Ralph Ellison and Albert Murray. Beginning in 1950, the letters exchanged over the following ten years offers a glimpse into literary history and race in America.

Jackson, Lawrence, *Ralph Ellison: Emergence of Genius*, Wiley, 2001.
> This biography recreates the first forty years of Ellison's life, taking us through the publication of his greatest masterpiece, *Invisible Man*.

Tyson, Tim, *Blood Done Sign My Name*, Crown, 2004.
> In this incredible personal history, Tyson, a professor of African American studies from University of Wisconsin–Madison, examines with a blunt, precise eye the struggles of black Americans and the Civil Rights movement in the South.

———, *Radio Free Dixie*, University of North Carolina Press, 2001.
> This biography traces the remarkable life of Robert F. Williams, one of the most influential and powerful black activists in American history. Although his name is often overshadowed by Malcolm X and Martin Luther King Jr., Williams played an integral role in the Civil Rights movement pushing blacks towards "armed self-reliance."

Kim

Rudyard Kipling
1901

Rudyard Kipling was one of the most popular writers of his era, and his novel *Kim*, first published in 1901, has become one of his most well-known non-juvenile works.

The novel takes place at a time contemporary to the book's publication; its setting is India under the British Empire. The title character is a boy of Irish descent who is orphaned and grows up independently in the streets of India, taken care of by a "half-caste" woman, a keeper of an opium den. Kim, an energetic and playful character, although full-blooded Irish, grows up as a "native" and acquires the ability to seamlessly blend into the many ethnic and religious groups of the Indian subcontinent. When he meets a wandering Tibetan lama who is in search of a sacred river, Kim becomes his follower and proceeds on a journey covering the whole of India. Kipling's account of Kim's travels throughout the subcontinent gave him opportunity to describe the many peoples and cultures that made up India, and a significant portion of the novel is devoted to such descriptions, which have been both lauded as magical and visionary and derided as stereotypical and imperialistic.

Kim eventually comes upon the army regiment that his father had belonged to and makes the acquaintance of the colonel. Colonel Creighton recognizes Kim's great talent for blending into the many diverse cultures of India and trains him to become a spy and a mapmaker for the British army. The adventures that Kim undergoes as a spy, his endearing relationship with the lama, and the skill

Rudyard Kipling

and craftsmanship of Kipling's writing have all caused this adventurous and descriptive—if controversial—novel to persist as a minor classic of historical English literature.

Author Biography

Poet, novelist, and short story writer Rudyard Kipling, the first English writer to receive the Nobel Prize in literature, was the most popular literary figure of his time. He was born December 30, 1865, in Bombay, India, to John Lockwood Kipling and Alice MacDonald Kipling. John Lockwood Kipling, who was an anthropologist and curator, inspired the character of the Keeper of the Wonderhouse in *Kim*.

Kipling spent his early childhood in India and was cared for by a Hindu nanny; as a young child he spoke Hindi. However, as was the custom of the time, at the age of six Kipling was sent to boarding school in Britain where he unfortunately was subjected to severe strictness and bullying. His poor eyesight kept him from advancing into a military career, so at the age of sixteen Kipling returned to his parents in Lahore, India, and began his career as a journalist, first at the *Civil and Military Gazette*

(1882–1887) and then as a worldwide correspondent for the *Pioneer* (1887–1889). He became quite popular for his work, especially for his satirical and humorous verse. When he returned to England in 1889 at the age of twenty-four, he was already regarded as a national literary hero.

In 1892, Kipling married the American Caroline Balestier and moved to Vermont. Their two daughters, Josephine—who was to die at the age of six of pneumonia—and Elsie, were born here. The Kiplings returned to England in 1896; their only son, John, was born later that year. The Kiplings remained based in England and traveled regularly around the world.

Although Kipling did not live for a long period of time in India after his childhood and his early adult years, his love of India and interest in the subcontinent and his memories of the India of his childhood figured greatly in his writing. Kipling is best known for his works about India, most notably *Kim*, a novel that covers all corners of the continent and in which Kipling lavishly describes the many different cultures and native peoples of the empire. Published in 1901, *Kim* is widely regarded as his most mature and polished work.

Kipling was a prolific writer, and his skill at storytelling, his immensely readable and songlike verse, his refusal to mince words, and the strong sense of British patriotism that characterized his work made him immensely popular with the common readership. However, his receipt of the Nobel Prize in 1907 was met with disapproval from other literary critics and writers, who considered him vulgar and lacking in craftsmanship.

The death of his son, John, during World War I, combined with failing health, affected Kipling's writing deeply. His output decreased dramatically after this period. He died on January 18, 1936, and is buried at Poet's Corner in Westminster Abbey.

Among Kipling's other most well-known works are *Captains Courageous* (1897), *The First and Second Jungle Books*, and the poems "If," "White Man's Burden," and "Recessional."

Plot Summary

Chapter 1

The novel *Kim* by Rudyard Kipling takes place in British India in the 1880s and 1890s. The novel opens with the introduction of the title character: Kim is a thirteen-year-old boy of Irish heritage who has been orphaned in India and raised by an opium den keeper in the city of Lahore, amid the myriad cultures of India. Because of the ability he has developed to blend in seamlessly among many different cultures through language and his broad knowledge of customs, Kim is known to his acquaintances as Friend of All the World.

Kim meets a Tibetan lama—a Buddhist—who has come to India in search of the Holy River that sprang from the arrow of the Buddha and which promises Enlightenment to its believers. The River proves elusive; even the learned museum curator at Lahore knows nothing of its location. Kim learns that the lama is traveling alone, as his *chela*, or follower and servant, died in the previous city. Seeing that the lama is an old man in need of assistance, Kim, dressed in the manner of a Hindu beggar child, agrees to be the lama's new *chela* and accompany the lama on his quest. He informs his friend and sometime guardian, Mahbub Ali, a well-known Afghan horse trader, that he will be leaving Lahore with the lama, and he agrees to carry some vague documents from Ali to an Englishman in Umballa as a favor. However, later that night Kim observes two sinister strangers searching Ali's belongings. Realizing that his favor to Ali smacks of danger, he and the lama, who remains ignorant of Kim's secret dealings, depart early for the road.

Chapter 2

On the train to Umballa, Kim and the lama meet a Hindu farmer and several other characters all representing an array of customs, languages, and religions from all over India, illustrating—as Kipling will often make a point of doing—the diversity of peoples that make up India's native population. Upon arriving in Umballa, Kim secretly seeks out the home of the Englishman—whom he discovers to be a colonel in the army—and delivers Ali's documents. He overhears word of an impending war on the border and realizes that Ali's documents were directly related to this development.

Chapters 3–4

The next day, Kim and the lama proceed to the outskirts of Umballa in search of the River, where they accidentally trespass in a farmer's garden. He curses them until he realizes that the lama is a holy man. Kim is angry at the farmer's abuses, but the lama teaches him not to be judgmental, saying, "There is no pride among such who follow the Middle Way." In the evening they are entertained by the headmaster and priest of a village. Kim, who loves to play jokes and games, pretends he is a

Media Adaptations

- *Kim* was adapted as a film in 1950. Directed by Victor Saville, it starred Errol Flynn as Mahbub Ali and Dean Stockwell as Kim. It was released as a VHS recording in 1996 and on DVD in 2003.

- In 1984, a made-for-television movie adaptation of *Kim* was released in the UK, starring Peter O'Toole as the lama and directed by John Howard Davies. It was released as a VHS recording in 1996.

- An unabridged audio recording of *Kim* is available through Audible.com. It is read by Margaret Hilton and was originally recorded in 1988.

prophet and "forsees" a great war with eight thousand troops heading to the northern border, drawing on what he had heard in Umballa. An old Indian soldier, who had fought on the British side in the Great Mutiny of 1857, calls Kim's claims to question until Kim makes an accurate description of the colonel—which convinces the soldier of his authenticity.

The old soldier, with renewed respect, accompanies Kim and the lama the next morning to the Grand Trunk Road. During their journey, the lama preaches to the soldier the virtues of maintaining detachment from worldly items, emotions, and actions in order to attain Enlightenment; however, when the lama goes out of his way to entertain a small child with a song, the soldier teases him for showing affection. It is the first evidence of the lama's truly human struggle with maintaining distance from his human emotions.

Eventually, the small party comes upon the Grand Trunk Road, a fifteen-hundred-mile-long route constructed by the East India Company that connected east Calcutta, East Bengal, and Agra. A vivid, detailed description of the masses of travelers is given, including descriptions of several different religious sects, including Sansis, Aklai Sihks, Hindus, Muslims, and Jains, as well as the various wedding and funeral processions marching along the road. This section provides yet another instance of Kipling's travelogue-type digressions to paint a vivid picture of India for his British and American readership. Kim is utterly delighted by the masses of people traveling before his eyes. The lama, however, remains deep in meditation and does not acknowledge the spectacle of life surrounding him.

In the late evening, Kim, utilizing his sharp wit and cunning, procures the aid of a rich old widow from Kulu, herself of a sharp and salty tongue, who is traveling in a royal procession from the northern lands to her daughter in the south. She offers food, shelter, and care for the lama in exchange for the holy man's charms and prayers interceding for the birth of many future grandsons for her.

Chapter 5

While resting along the Grand Trunk Road, Kim comes upon an English army regiment, which bears a green flag with a red bull on it. Since he was a young child, Kim had been told by his guardian that his father—a former soldier—had said that a red bull in a green field would be Kim's salvation. With excitement at having found the sign of the bull, he sneaks into the barracks to find out more information, only to be captured by the Protestant chaplain, Mr. Bennett. Together with Father Victor, the Catholic chaplain, he discovers the personal documents that Kim carries with him everywhere, which reveal him to be not a Hindu beggar but an Irish boy—and the son of Kimball O'Hara, who himself had been a member of this same regiment. Seeing that he is white and the son of a soldier, the chaplains do not allow Kim to continue on as a servant to a Buddhist monk. Kim stays reluctantly with the regiment, and the lama takes his leave abruptly, saying only that he must continue on his Search.

Chapters 6–8

Kim is put under watch of a drummer boy, who, having been born and raised in England, holds Kim and everything having to do with India in contempt, and subjects Kim to verbal and physical abuses. Kim, nevertheless, manages to easily outsmart the boy and procure a letter-writer to send word to Mahbub Ali of his whereabouts. Later, Father Victor shows Kim a letter from the lama indicating that he will pay for Kim's education at the Catholic school of St. Xavier's—a school for Sahibs, or white men. Kim is inconsolable at the thought of the lama traveling without him and fending for himself.

Mahbub Ali comes to Kim after receiving his letter. Seeing the good in Kim's future schooling,

he tries to convince Kim that is it for the best, for, as he says to Kim, "Once a Sahib, always a Sahib," indicating that he should not only learn the ways of his own people but take advantage of the privilege that being a Sahib has to offer.

Colonel Creighton, the English colonel whom Kim first secretly encountered in Umballa, shows up. After conversing with Ali about Kim's peculiar history, he shows an interest in Kim's welfare and schooling. He accompanies Kim to Lucknow—the location of St. Xavier's—and gently plies Kim with questions, revealing indirectly that he has a keen interest in ascertaining Kim's suitability for future employment as a spy.

Upon arrival at St. Xavier's, Kim encounters the lama, who says that he is staying at a Jain temple in Benares and that he is helping Kim financially in order to acquire spiritual merit. His voice, however, betrays feelings of tenderness.

Kim's first year at St. Xavier's is skimmed over in the narration. The scene quickly skips to summer vacation, during which Kim has decided, against Creighton's wishes, he will take to the road. He dons the disguise of a Hindu beggar child and eventually meets up with Mahbub Ali, who takes him in as an assistant. Kim reveals to Ali his knowledge that the documents he had delivered to Creighton in Umballa had directly related to the war at the northern border. They reach an unspoken understanding between them that Ali serves as a spy for the British Army in what he calls the Great Game and that Kim is in training to become such a spy. Historically, the Great Game was a colloquial term for the espionage network across British India working to protect the northern border from invasion from Russia.

Later in the horse camp, Kim overhears two strangers looking for and plotting against Mahbub Ali. Kim proceeds to warn the horse trader, saving his life.

Chapters 9–10

Kim is sent, per Creighton's instructions, to the home of the antiques and jewel dealer, Lurgan Sahib, who is another "player" in the Great Game. Lurgan Sahib is a hypnotist and a master of disguise. He, along with his servant, a small Hindu boy, teaches Kim to master many mind games to train his powers of quick observation, in preparation for his future work as a "chain-man" in the spy network. Another key chain-man, the Bengali Hurree Chunder Mookerjee, visits Lurgan Sahib and Kim and approves of Kim's potential and progress in his training. Mookerjee returns Kim to Lucknow and presents him with the gift of a medicine toolkit.

Kim completes his next year at St. Xavier's with great success as a student. He spends his summer holidays working as an assistant to Mahbub Ali and his Christmas holiday continuing his training with Lurgan Sahib.

After Kim returns for his third year of school, Mahbub Ali and Lurgan Sahib convince Creighton that Kim is ready, at the age of sixteen, to be discharged from school and put into chain-man training directly in the field. After he is discharged from school, Kim is taken to Huneefa, a blind prostitute and a sort of sorceress, who puts him in an authentic disguise as a young Buddhist priest and places a charm against devils upon him. Kim is also provided with all of the trade tools of a chain-man, and Mookerjee informs him of the secret code for recognizing another chain-man, or "Son of the Charm." Kim has officially been initiated into the network.

Chapters 11–12

Kim, now completely alone and having been schooled as a Sahib but then thrust into the world in the guise of a Buddhist priest, begins to question what his identity is and where he belongs, asking, "Who is Kim—Kim—Kim?" a question that will remain with him. Kim travels to Benares to meet his holy lama. On the way, he encounters a Punjabi farmer who, seeing Kim in the guise of a priest, begs help for his sick child. Kim cures the child with medicines from his kit. Upon reaching the temple where the lama is lodging, he is ecstatic to be reunited with the lama and to continue upon the quest for the Holy River. The lama shows Kim a piece of artwork that has been occupying his time: the Wheel of Life, an intricate, complex chart he has drawn in great detail, illustrating the cycle of life that traps the soul. The lama, ever intent upon attaining Enlightenment and thus escaping the Wheel of Life, carries the chart with him constantly.

On the train, Kim encounters E23, a chain-man in the disguise of a Mahratta, who, having intercepted enemy documents, is under hot pursuit. Kim puts his training as a master of disguise to use and, in order to protect E23, transforms him into a Saddhu—a member of a sect of ascetic priests. The lama, who knows nothing of Kim's training as a spy, believes that Kim has acquired the ability to cast spells and charms, and he warns Kim against using his powers for prideful reasons. Kim and the lama enter a discussion about the virtues of action versus inaction. While the lama advises Kim to abstain from "Doing"

except to acquire merit towards Enlightenment, Kim responds that "to abstain from action is unbefitting a Sahib." The lama answers, "There is neither black nor white. . . . We be all souls seeking to escape."

The old woman whom Kim and the lama had previously encountered on the Grand Trunk Road hears of the lama's proximity and summons him to her home to request further blessings from the lama for her grandchildren. Here, Kim finds Mookerjee waiting for him in the guise of a hakim, or healer. Mookerjee reveals to Kim the details of the spy mission that has been occupying the Great Game for the past few years: the northern border is being jeopardized by five kings who rule over the independent regions bordering British India and are believed to be allying with the Russians, thus creating a significant security hazard for the British Empire. Mookerjee has been enlisted to intercept two Russian spies in the northern hill country and relieve them of their documents. He asks Kim to help him. Kim, eager to participate in the Great Game, convinces the lama to travel to the northern countries.

Chapters 13–14

Finally having reached the northern lands, Kim finds the cold, wet weather and the dramatically hilly landscape difficult to travel; however, the lama is happy to be back in a region and environment familiar to him. All the while, Mookerjee has been stalking the two enemy spies, who turn out to be a Frenchman and a Russian. He eventually crosses their path and introduces himself to the spies as a welcoming emissary from the Rajah of Rampur, offering them his services and hospitality as a guide through the hill country. His true aim, of course, is to knock the spies off their course and relieve them of their secret documents before they are delivered into enemy hands.

Mookerjee leads the spies as if he is a travel guide and happens upon Kim and the lama, who is expounding on his Wheel of Life. One of the spies demands that the lama sell him his drawing of the Wheel. When the lama refuses, the spy reaches out to grab the paper and rips it, much to the chagrin of the lama, who in anger rises and threatens the spy with his lead pencase—inciting the Russian spy to punch him full in the face. Kim immediately tackles the Russian spy and beats him, while the spies' servants—who are Buddhists and therefore enraged at the attack on a holy man—drive away the French spy and run off with the luggage.

Kim, leaving the spies to the care of Mookerjee, convinces the servants that the luggage, being the possession of two evil men, is cursed. He obtains the package with the secret documents and heads to Shamlegh-under-the-snow for shelter, where they stay with the Woman of Shamlegh.

The lama, meanwhile, is shaken at his inability to resist his passions and at his gross display of attachment to his artwork and to his emotions. The excitement and worry have made him ill. In his illness he spends much time in meditation and, after a few days, informs Kim that he has seen "The Cause of Things": his bodily desire to return to the hills caused him to abandon his search for the River; his act of giving into his desire led him to further give in to his passions and attack the spy— thus moving farther and farther from his quest on the Way to Enlightenment. Having come to this conclusion, the lama demands that he be taken back to the lowlands of India to continue his search for the Holy River.

The woman of Shamlegh, in spite of receiving gentle rebuke from Kim for her attempts to seduce him, provides a litter to carry the lama back through the hills and food for their journey. Kim kisses her on the cheek at his departure and, as a gift to her, reveals that he is not a priest but a Sahib. Kim and the lama, who is now ill, continue on the road, Kim with the intercepted documents hidden in his luggage.

Chapter 15

Kim and the convalescent lama travel for over twelve days and return to the home of the old woman of Kulu, where Kim collapses into a feverish illness. The old woman nurses him out of his illness, for which he is grateful. Having acquired many father figures throughout his journeys, he has now acquired a true mother figure. Mookerjee, hearing that Kim is awake and well, relieves him of the secret documents and proceeds to deliver them to the Colonel.

Coming out of his fever and suddenly relieved of the burden of the secret documents, Kim is overcome by a sense of displacement that has visited him several times throughout his travels. He repeats to himself, "I am Kim. What is Kim?" At this point, he experiences an epiphany of his existence. Having previously seen himself as detached and somewhat alienated from the world, he comes to a feeling of utter belonging among all people.

Meanwhile, during Kim's illness, the lama, having foregone food for two days and nights in the pursuit of meditation, has attained the Enlightenment he has been seeking. He relates to Kim how his soul released itself from his body, how he flew up to the Great Soul to meditate upon The Cause of Things. However, a concern came to him suddenly regarding Kim's well-being, and so, for Kim's sake, his soul returned to his body and landed, headlong, in the Holy River of his seeking. He declares his Search is over and that he has attained Deliverance from sin for both himself and his beloved *chela*.

Characters

Abdullah

The son of the local sweetmeats seller, Abdullah is one of Kim's playmates in Lahore.

Mahbub Ali

Known throughout India as the most famous horse trader, Mahbub Ali, characterized by his red beard and his quick temper, is a devout Muslim from Afghanistan and a close friend to Kim. It is he who bestowed Kim with his moniker "Friend of All the World." While in public Ali is a horse trader, in secret he is a chain-man, or a spy, who works in close collaboration with Colonel Creighton in what he calls the Great Game—the intricate system of espionage the British government used to maintain the security of British India's northernmost borders. At the opening of the novel, Ali entrusts a packet of secret documents to Kim for delivery to Colonel Creighton. It is this action that starts Kim in the direction of becoming a chain-man himself. During Kim's vacations from school, he works as an assistant to Mahbub and apprentices with him in the ways of espionage. Like many of the other male characters, Mahbub Ali is a surrogate father figure to Kim.

The Amritzar Girl

A courtesan whom Kim and the lama encounter on the train to Umballa, she graciously pays for their ticket fare, ensuring them safe passage.

The Arain Farmer

Kim and the lama accidentally trespass on his land as they leave the town of Umballa. His coarse treatment of them, and Kim's subsequent judgment upon him, leads the lama to one of several important sermons on Buddhist practice.

The Babu

See Hurree Chunder Mookerjee

Reverend Arthur Bennett

The Protestant chaplain for the Maverick Irish regiment in India, Mr. Bennett discovers Kim snooping around the barracks and uncovers his identity as the son of a deceased fellow soldier, Kimball O'Hara. Kipling's unsavory portrayal of Mr. Bennett, who is coarse and ignorant of the customs of India, represents his lifelong disapproval of Christian missionary work in India.

Colonel Creighton

Colonel Creighton is a British officer of the army and the supervisor of the "chain men" who work as spies along British India's northern border. Creighton sees that Kim has potential as a spy, and he takes a keen interest in procuring education and training for the boy.

The Curator

The kindly British keeper of the anthropological museum in Lahore, the Curator is also called the "Keeper of the Wonder House." The lama comes to him for guidance in finding the Holy River; he is unable to give guidance but presents the lama with an indispensable pair of reading glasses.

The Drummer Boy

Described as a fat boy of fourteen years with freckles, the drummer boy of the regiment has the job of keeping Kim from running away from the army barracks. He is ignorant of the ways of the native people of India and has a hatred for the country and its people, and he refers to them in derisive language.

E23

Kim encounters E23, a chain-man, on a train being hotly pursued by enemies. Kim uses his spy training to disguise E23 as a Saddhu, thus saving the man's life and acquiring his first taste of life as a spy.

The French Spy

The French spy accompanies the Russian spy on a mission to deliver enemy documents, only to be waylaid by Kim, the lama, and Mookerjee.

The Hindu Farmer

A kindly farmer from Umballa, he offers Kim and the lama lodging and food during their stay in his town.

Hindu Servant

When Kim initially arrives at Lurgan Sahib's home for his apprenticeship, Sahib's young servant boy grows jealous and attempts to harm Kim. Later,

he becomes Kim's tutor in mastering various aspects of the craft of espionage.

Huneefa

A blind prostitute, Huneefa is also an expert in disguise as well as a sort of soothsayer. At Mahbub Ali's behest, she outfits Kim in his first chain-man disguise as a Buddhist monk, and she casts several good luck spells over him.

Kim

Kim is the title character of the novel. Born in Lahore, India, Kim is orphaned as a baby after his Irish mother dies in childbirth and his father, a soldier in an Irish regiment, slowly dies of an opium addiction. He is raised by the keeper of an opium den in the streets of Lahore. Kim is characterized by a sharp tongue, a tireless wit, a powerful sense of observation, and a keen sense of humor, as well as an untiring appetite for playing pranks and games of wit and trickery. Although he is a white child, he grows up as a "native," with the uncanny ability to blend in to any of the many cultural and religious groups that make up the Indian population—an ability that earns him the moniker "The Friend of All the World." This uncanny ability, together with his sharp, conniving nature, makes him a prime candidate for becoming a spy for the British government.

The novel develops along two interconnecting threads of Kim's life from age thirteen to seventeen: his adventures as he traverses India both as the servant of Teshoo Lama, a Tibetan monk, and as a spy-in-training for the British government, and his eventual hand in saving British India from a Russian invasion; and his conflicted identity as both a "Sahib"—a member of the white ruling class in India—and a child born and bred as an Easterner. This sense of displacement and identity loss comes to Kim when he is removed from the company of Indians whom he has known all his life and placed for three years in a Western, Catholic school, where he masters the culture, academic knowledge, and language of the British rulers.

This sense of displacement overcomes Kim several times throughout the novel; however, the novel concludes with Kim's experience of an epiphany: Having previously seen himself as detached and somewhat alienated from the world, he comes to a feeling of belonging among all people.

Chota Lal

Chota Lal is one of Kim's playmates in Lahore, prior to his departure as a servant of the lama.

Teshoo Lama

Teshoo Lama, the second most important character of the novel, is Kim's master, guardian, father figure, and companion throughout most of the novel, who both cares for Kim and is cared for by Kim. A Buddhist abbot from Tibet, he has come to India in search of the Holy River that sprang from the arrow of the Lord Buddha. Kim accompanies him as his servant throughout the whole of India. While Kim is constantly enchanted by the myriad of people they encounter in their travels, the lama remains fixedly detached from any interest in humanity or the machinations of human life. He spends his time in meditation, and he interacts with his fellow travelers only to preach the ways of Buddhism to them: specifically, that all souls are equal, that all souls are trapped in the cycle of life, and that the only way to escape the cycle of life is through detachment from all things worldly. However, although he strives for utter detachment, the lama occasionally slips and reveals his true affection for his servant, Kim, who likewise adores his master.

The lama carries with him an intricately drawn chart mapping of the Wheel of Life—a symbolic representation of the cycle of life that, according to Buddhist teaching, all souls strive to escape from in order to be reunited with the Great Soul. However, the lama struggles throughout his pilgrimage to remain on the path to Enlightenment and to let go of the attachments of the world, specifically his emotions and bodily desires. The climax of the novel is reached when a Russian spy, desiring the lama's Wheel of Life, rips it from his hands and incites the lama to violence. These actions lead the lama to the absolute realization that he is not free of the emotions of pride and desire. Through this realization, he attains the Enlightenment he has been so strenuously seeking.

In a twist of spiritual irony, his love for Kim leads him not to escape to the Great Soul but to selflessly remain with Kim until his well-being is assured.

Lispeth

See The Woman of Shamlegh

Lurgan Sahib

Lurgan Sahib is a "half-caste" and a chain-man in the Great Game. He is a jeweler, an antique dealer, and a master of hypnotism and disguise. Kim is sent to Lurgan Sahib as an apprentice in order to learn the craft of espionage.

Hurree Chunder Mookerjee

Also known as The Babu, Mookerjee is a Bengali and a chain-man in the Great Game. He holds several Western degrees and is an anthropological expert. When he is not explicitly performing spy work, he collects information on various cultural and religious practices across India, for the purpose of anthropological study.

Mookerjee assists in Kim's training as a chain-man throughout the novel and officially initiates him into the brotherhood of the Sons of the Charm. When it is discovered that Russian spies are attempting to organize a breach of the northern border, it is Mookerjee who, with the help of Kim, intercepts their documents and thwarts their mission.

Kimball O'Hara

O'Hara is the deceased father of Kim, previously a soldier in an Irish regiment in India and the victim of a debilitating opium addiction. Upon his death, Kim is orphaned and left to the streets of Lahore.

The Old Soldier

Kim encounters the old soldier outside of Umballa. A retired soldier who commands the respect of the local Sahibs for his service in the Great Mutiny of 1857, he serves as Kim and the lama's guide to the Grand Trunk Road.

The Old Woman of Kulu

Kim and the lama first encounter the old woman on the Grand Trunk Road. She is a wealthy widow from the hill country. A salty-tongued character, she is taken by Kim's ability to match her wit. Kim and the lama are the recipients of her hospitality on numerous occasions. When Kim falls ill, she nurses him back to health, becoming not just a benefactress but a mother figure to the orphaned Kim.

The Opium Den Keeper

After the death of Kimball O'Hara, the woman who kept the opium den where he met his demise was left to care for young Kim from the age of three to thirteen.

The Punjabi Farmer

Kim, disguised as a Buddhist priest, is begged by the Punjabi farmer to heal his sick child. Kim uses his medicine kit to cure the child, thereby earning the gratitude of the farmer. In thanksgiving, he serves as Kim's companion for a brief time.

The Russian Spy

One of two spies who breach the northern border in order to deliver enemy documents, the Russian spy picks a fight with the lama after he refuses to sell him a precious drawing. During the ensuing fight, Kim and Mookerjee manage to procure the enemy documents.

Father Victor

The Catholic chaplain of the Maverick Irish regiment in India, he is instrumental in obtaining an education for Kim at St. Xavier's school.

The Woman of Shamlegh

The Woman of Shamlegh takes Kim and the lama into her home after they are attacked by the Russian spies. She makes a failed attempt to seduce Kim. Like most of the women portrayed in *Kim*, Lispeth presents a dual nature: both caretaker and temptress.

Themes

Equality and Unity

The ideal of the equality and unity of men echoes across several motifs in *Kim*, most notably through the Buddhist teachings of Teshoo Lama. He tells Kim, "To those who follow the Way there is neither black nor white, Hind nor Bhotiyal. We be all souls seeking to escape." This ideal of the equality and unity of men transcends the stringent caste, or class, distinctions of the predominantly Hindu society that Kim has known.

The lama carries with him a diagram called the Wheel of Life, which is a symbolic representation of the Buddhist doctrine that all lives are equally bound in the cycle of life and that all souls seek release from this cycle by attaining Enlightenment. The numerous references to the Wheel of Life throughout the novel serve to reinforce the message of equality and unity. The lama's teachings and his quest for Enlightenment are never the subject of Kipling's criticism, as are other religious beliefs presented in *Kim*; rather, the resolution of the novel includes the lama's triumphant attainment of Enlightenment, which serves to authenticate, rather than disprove, the doctrine of equality and unity echoed throughout.

Kipling also uses the theme of unity to portray an ideal India that is not divided by imperialism but rather is unified under it. This is especially evident in the relationships between the characters who par- ticipate in the Great Game: Mahbub Ali, an Afghan; Lurgan Sahib, a person of "mixed" race; Hurree Chunder Mookerjee, a Bengali; and Colonel Creighton, an Englishman, an officer, and therefore a member of the ruling class. Despite their disparate backgrounds, all these characters are united in a tight brotherhood of espionage that functions specifically to protect the interests of the British Empire in India. It is especially significant that Kipling shows both British and Indian characters alike operating on an equal basis for the good of the empire. This serves to promote an idealized, unrealistic portrayal of a specifically united, inclusive British India.

Imperialism

John A. McClure writes in his essay "Kipling's Richest Dream," "In *Kim* ... brotherhood and despotism keep uneasy company." In other words, the finely crafted portrayal of unity and equality Kipling develops between "native" and "Sahib" conflicts with the unavoidable fact that the British are the governing class, and the Indians are the governed. Kipling, however, presents the imperialist presence in India as unquestionably positive. This is done most effectively through the main plot of the novel—the endeavors of Indian and British spies to protect the northern border of British India from the encroachment of Russia, thus protecting the imperial interests of the British Empire. It is especially significant that Indian spies are shown protecting British interests. In this way, Kipling constructs an India in which the native population supports the British Empire and thus presents Britain's imperialist presence as a positive good.

Orientalism

In recent years, orientalism has come to be defined as the knowledge and beliefs about the peoples of "the Orient"—that is, of the Middle East, South Asia, and East Asia—as constructed and imposed by their Western European colonizers. Many of the observations of Indian life presented in *Kim* as fact are derogatory stereotypes, derived from such orientalists' beliefs.

For example, Edward Said writes in his introduction to *Kim*:

> Sihks are characterized as having a special 'love of money'; Hurree Babu equates being a Bengali with being fearful; when he hides the packet taken from the foreign agents, the Babu 'stowed the entire trove about his body, as only Orientals can.'

These derogatory ethnic stereotypes are sharply contrasted with Kipling's portrayals of the

Topics For Further Study

- Modern readers of *Kim* will find many of the descriptions of the Indian people throughout the novel grossly stereotypical. In Kipling's day, it was deemed factual and common knowledge by Westerners that Asiatic peoples were, on the whole, lazy, superstitious, and conniving, and these myths are repeated and perpetuated throughout *Kim*. Although our modern society is much more sensitive to the inaccuracies and harmfulness of cultural and racial stereotypes, there still persist stereotypical representations of Asians in popular culture. What other examples of racial or cultural stereotyping can you identify in our culture?

- Many scholars argue that *Kim* is a novel motivated by masculinity: All of the main characters are male, and females show up largely as plot devices. How do the male characters in *Kim* regard women? How are women portrayed? What do you think Kipling's portrayal of women in *Kim* reflects about his attitudes towards women?

- India is the location of the origin of many of the Eastern world's major religions. India is also home to numerous religious sects, many of which are mentioned in *Kim*. Choose a sect with which you are unfamiliar, and research the history and primary beliefs of this sect.

- Much of *Kim* is set along the Grand Trunk Road, which was a main highway that crossed the Indian subcontinent. This highway has played a major role in the history of India. Research the history of the Grand Trunk Road. Where did it come from? What importance has it played over the centuries?

British and British culture as more advanced. For example, when Lurgan Sahib attempts to hypnotize Kim, Kim recites the multiplication tables he learned at English school to resist—sharply symbolizing Kipling's belief in the advancement of British law over the superstitious ways of the Asians. Such contrasts throughout *Kim* serve to support and justify the rule of the "more capable" British over the Indian people.

Identity

The character of Kim is placed in a predicament of identity: Kim, an Irish orphan, grows up in the streets of the Indian city of Lahore and adapts to the culture and languages of India—so well, in fact, that he can pass himself off as a member of almost any religious or cultural group of India. He is at once a Sahib and, by virtue of his upbringing, a part of the colonized society.

Kim, who is known as "Friend of All the World" and includes "this great and beautiful land" as all his people, begins to undergo a crisis of identity when he is first made to go to school to become a Sahib.

This question of identity and belonging plagues Kim throughout the novel, leaving him with a feeling of loneliness. Although Kim's conflict of identity is brought about by being suddenly thrust into the British culture, it is significant that Kipling does not make Kim's identity crisis one in which he must choose between living as a Sahib—the member of the governing class—and as a "native—a member of the governed. Through Kim's eventual ability to reconcile both, Kipling symbolizes his larger ideal of a unified British India.

Religion

One of *Kim*'s major plotlines is the quest for Enlightenment undertaken by Teshoo Lama. While the lama faces both external and internal obstacles to fulfilling his quest, the novel culminates with his triumphant attainment of his goal. The novel is threaded throughout with the lama's Buddhist spirituality and teachings; and while many of the characters, including Kim, question and are mystified by his philosophies, the lama's success at attaining Enlightenment at the end of the novel serves to validate the authenticity and truth of his messages.

In marked contrast to the validation of Buddhism in *Kim* is a censure of Christianity, as represented by Father Victor and the Reverend Bennett. Unlike the lama, who inspired Kim's complete adoration, the Christian chaplains are portrayed as ignorant and undignified, therefore inspiring Kim's disgust. Although the chaplains try to convert Kim to Christianity, he remains devoted to his Buddhist master. This symbolic "defeat" of Christianity can be read as evidence of Kipling's lifelong loathing of Christianity and missionary work in India.

Women and Treachery

Kim is a markedly male story, featuring an all-male cast of characters and focusing on traditionally male relationships: that of Master and Student and the initiation of Kim into a brotherhood—the Sons of the Charm. The women characters factor mostly as plot devices. The old woman of Kulu provides a place for Kim and the lama to rest, as does the Woman of Shamlegh.

However, even though women play a very minor role in the novel, the representation of women denotes a regard for women as treacherous obstacles to the goals of men, be they spiritual pursuits or political games. For example, the lama complains that the old woman of Kulu has derailed him from his Search: "Take note, my *chela*, that even those who would follow the Way are thrust aside by idle women!" Kim is likewise warned of the machinations of women by his other father figure, Mahbub Ali, during his training as a spy: "Mahbub was exact to point out how Huneefa [a prostitute] and her likes had destroyed kings."

The absence of women from most of the novel, therefore, not only creates a sense that spiritual quests and adventures in travel are the realm of men but that it is an absolute necessity for the success of the male characters in being successful in their goals.

Style

Epigraph

An epigraph is a piece of writing that is used at the beginning of a work to set the tone of that work or to highlight thematic elements. Each chapter of *Kim* opens with an epigraph. Kipling prefaces each chapter with an excerpt of verse, many of which are taken from his own works. For example, chapter 5 is the chapter in which Kim is reunited with his father's army regiment and therefore with his own people. The chapter is prefaced by an excerpt from the poem "The Prodigal Son":

> Here I come to my own again
> Fed, forgiven and known again
> Claimed by bone of my bone again,
> And sib to flesh of my flesh!
> The fatted calf is dressed for me,
> But the husks have greater zest for me . . .
> I think my pigs will be best for me,
> So I'm off to the styes afresh.

The excerpt tells of a person who is not at home with his own people and thus sets the tone for the chapter in which Kim struggles with the alien British language and culture.

Travelogue

Kim's plot, based on a pilgrimage, a quest, and the adventures of international espionage, by nature encompasses a vast geographic setting; almost the entirety of the Indian subcontinent is covered. Kipling uses Kim's vast travels to provide his readership with detailed descriptions of the widely varied landscape of India, as well as of the native inhabitants. His numerous digressions into travelogue-type accounts reveal a narrative voice aimed at a specific audience: that of the English in Great Britain. India was the largest and most lucrative possession of the British Empire, and the British in England remained fascinated with exotic portrayals of the subcontinent, which Kipling provides with the expert eye of a former resident.

Epiphany

An epiphany is a sudden revelation experienced by a character, often representing resolution of an internal conflict. Kim, plagued throughout the novel by a feeling of displacement and a confusion of identity, has an epiphanic moment at the end of the novel as he is coming out of illness:

> With almost an audible click he felt the wheels of his being lock anew on the world without. Things that rode meaningless on the eyeball an instant before slide into proper proportion. . . . They were all real and true . . . clay of his clay, neither more nor less.

This sudden sense of understanding—his epiphany—helps Kim come to a sense of belonging, thus resolving one conflict presented in the plot.

Another epiphany occurs when a Russian spy rips the lama's Wheel of Life from his hands, which incites the lama to violence. Because of these actions, the lama comes to the absolute realization that he is not free of the emotions of pride and desire. This realization helps him to attain the Enlightenment he has been so strenuously seeking.

Compare & Contrast

- **1890s:** English readers were fascinated by portrayals of "exotic" British colonies like India, written primarily by British writers such as Rudyard Kipling and E. M. Forster, which offered depictions of India from the perspective of the British colonizer.

  Today: Ethnic Indian writers and novelists writing in English, such as Salman Rushdie and Arundhati Roy, offer today's English-language readership award-winning work portraying the life and culture of India from an Indian perspective.

- **1890s:** The practice of British imperialism reflects a racist belief of white, British superiority over the non-white nations of the world, rationalizing their government-sanctioned conquest and rule of other races. A need for knowledge about the peoples that Britain was governing led to the study and classification of the non-Christian, nonwhite races governed under the British Empire. Such studies offer the West a wealth of translations of writings from India and knowledge of religious practices; but it also has the effect of lumping together diverse groups of people into a generalized, homogenous group that was characterized as "needing" governance.

  Today: In 1978, the scholar Edward Said named the definitions, generalities, and stereotypes placed by the imperialistic West on the diverse cultures and peoples of the East—from the Middle East to the Far East—"Orientalism." Said's breakthrough studies on the objectification of Eastern lands and cultures by the imperialistic West are part of the pioneering efforts of sociological scholarship and theory today known as postcolonial studies, which have made lasting inroads into recognizing, and thereby dismantling, harmful, inaccurate generalizations that persist in Western culture about Asiatic peoples.

- **1890s:** England commands the largest worldwide empire, spanning the globe, of which India is one of the largest and most important components. However, despite Britain's attempts to keep control over the vast subcontinent, army mutinies and the growing educated class of Indians create more and more opposition to British rule.

  Today: India, Pakistan, and Bangladesh, formerly the Indian Empire of Great Britain, are each independent, self-governing nations. Strong influences of British rule remain, including forms of government and the adoption of English as an official national language.

Historical Context

British Imperialism in India: Its Intellectual Roots and the Role of Orientalism

When *Kim* was published in 1901, the British Empire was still the most powerful empire in the world. The Indian subcontinent was one of the most important parts of the empire, which thousands of "Anglo-Indians," like Kipling himself, called home.

Imperialism was not just the practice of the British Empire's acts of colonization of other lands and people; imperialism was a philosophy that assumed the superiority of British civilization and therefore the moral responsibility to bring their enlightened ways to the "uncivilized" people of the world. This attitude was taken especially towards nonwhite, non-Christian cultures in India, Asia, Australia, and Africa.

This driving philosophy of moral responsibility served to rationalize the economic exploitations of other peoples and their lands by the British Empire and its subsequent amassing of wealth and power. It was nevertheless, during Kipling's time, largely embraced and unquestioned by the worldwide British population, and Kipling, being no exception, reflected this philosophy of cultural superiority and patriotism in much of his writing.

The acquisition of knowledge of the people that they governed, and the dissemination of this knowledge, was key to the formulation of the ingrained Western notion of superiority and their belief in the inferiority of Eastern peoples. The Western scholars who studied the customs and peoples of the East were called orientalists and their studies orientalism. While many of their works brought valuable translations of Eastern literature to the West—the most famous and influential of which is Edward Fitzgerald's translation of *The Arabian Nights*—orientalism also had the unfortunate effect of creating the ethnic stereotypes that caused the nonwhite, colonized peoples to be generalized as weak, conniving, and immoral—and therefore very much in need of British law, rationale, and morality. Such descriptions that were brought back and perpetuated by orientalist "scholarship" have been ingrained into the Western psyche. The greatest evidence is Kipling's own derogatory descriptions found in *Kim*: Bengalis are cowardly, all Asiatics are superstitious, and Kim himself had the ability to "lie like an Oriental."

The Great Mutiny of 1857

Edward Said calls The Great Mutiny of 1857 "the great symbolic event by which the two sides, Indian and British, achieved their full and conscious opposition to each other," and he states that "to a contemporary reader [of *Kim*] 'The Mutiny' meant the single most important, well-known and violent episode of the nineteenth-century Anglo-Indian relationship." During the Mutiny, Indian soldiers who served the British government under white, British officers captured the city of Delhi. The Mutiny eventually became part of the larger Sepoy Rebellion (1857–1859) against the British government. While their efforts were eventually squelched, it was the first and one of the most violent acts of rebellion of Indians against the forced rule of Great Britain. The Indian National Congress, a party made up of Western-educated Indians whose aim was to acquire independence from Britain, was formed in 1885; so when *Kim* was published only fifteen years later, the political landscape of India was characterized by a tension between the Indians who wanted independence and the British who struggled to remain in control. It is of marked interest to note that Kipling largely ignores this tension between Indian and English in *Kim* and portrays all of his Indian characters as being pro-British—certainly not accurately reflecting the true political landscape of India at the time, which was instead characterized by growing discontent and the desire for Indian independence.

The Great Game

The Great Game referred to in *Kim* was the colloquial term for the British government's Survey of India, which began in 1767 and continued until India's independence in 1947. The players in the Great Game were trained surveyors who worked undercover for the British government. It was especially dangerous in the northern parts of the region, particularly Tibet, which was not under the jurisdiction of the British Empire; and thus surveyors sent out to map such forbidden areas were sent in disguise. It was this type of espionage work for which Colonel Creighton was training Kim.

The espionage work of the Great Game extended beyond mapmaking to collecting counterintelligence against the Russians immediately to the north. In particular, the British aim was to keep the independent regions of modern-day Afghanistan, Tibet, and Nepal from allying with Russia, in order to protect the security of their empire. The climax of *Kim*, in which Kim, the lama, and Babu Mookerjee effectively disarm and rob two Russian spies, is a direct reference to the threat that the British felt from the Russian presence.

Critical Overview

Although Kipling was one of the most popular writers of his time, his work was often met with sharply differing criticisms by the literary establishment. His work previous to *Kim*, which included more verse, political essays, and children's stories than longer works, was often met with contempt and scorn; indeed, his receipt of the Nobel Prize in 1907 was criticized by the literary establishment, who viewed him more as a popular writer than a true artist, a writer of verse rather than a poet, and who disapproved of the often coarse nature of his political writings.

When *Kim* was first published in 1901, however, it was largely met with praise both from the press and the general readership; most critics agreed that it was Kipling's most polished work to date. J. H. Millar wrote in *Blackwood's Magazine*, December 1901, that "Mr. Kipling has decidedly 'acquired merit' by this his latest essay. There is a fascination, almost magic, in every page of the delightful volume, whose attractiveness is enhanced by . . . superlative excellence." William Morton Payne, writing on recent fiction in *The Dial* in November of that same year, called *Kim* "singularly enthralling" and said that "few Europeans understand

Tibbetan Buddhists, similar to the lama whom Kim meets in Kipling's novel, worship beneath the Bodhi tree, where it is recorded that Buddha achieved enlightenment

the working of the Oriental mind as Mr. Kipling understands them, and far fewer have his gift of imparting the understanding to their readers." While *The Bookman* ran a piece calling *Kim* "mediocre and meaningless," it seems that they were equally enthralled by Kipling's riveting and enjoyable descriptions of life in India. The article states, "The author would be applauded for his very minute and exact knowledge of Asiatic life and Oriental superstition." While Kipling's contemporary critics discussed and argued his merit as an artist, it appears that the most praiseworthy item they agreed on in *Kim* was Kipling's vivid descriptions of Indian life and India's native peoples.

Throughout his career, Kipling wrote many works of fiction and nonfiction that gave strong voice to and supported the imperialist efforts of the British Empire, especially its governance over India. While the idea of imperialism was popular and well supported by the intellectual community during the first part of Kipling's life, by the 1920s—after Britain had fought a major world war and was struggling with more difficulty to maintain its enormous empire—the romance of colonization had been replaced by world-weariness,

and Kipling's work suddenly came to be viewed as utterly old-fashioned, if not incorrect and vulgar.

It was not, however, until the school of thought known as postcolonial studies emerged in the 1960s that criticism of *Kim* was taken up again in a whole new light. Postcolonial study concerns itself with the effects and methods of subjugation and colonization on a subordinate people. In other words, postcolonial studies see imperialism from the point of view of the colonized. Most notable in postcolonial criticism of *Kim* is Edward Said, whose groundbreaking work *Orientalism* explores how Western concepts of the colonized peoples of the East created unflattering, generalizing, inaccurate stereotypes—such as the Asian as a liar, the Asian as conniving, and the Asian as superstitious and irrational, which contributed greatly to the rationalization for the imposition of Western rule. Said has edited an annotated edition of *Kim*, in which he writes in the introduction: "*Kim* is a major contribution to [the] orientalized India of the imagination, as it is also to what historians have come to call 'the invention of tradition. . . . Dotting *Kim*'s fabric is a scattering of editorial asides on the immutable nature of the Oriental world . . . for example, 'Kim could lie like an Oriental.'" What Said points out is that the "exact knowledge" of Asiatic life so extolled as by Kipling's contemporaries were not accurate at all, but were myths that Kipling and his Western contemporaries not only bought into, but perpetuated.

Kim has not received only negative criticism in recent years, however. The reintroduction of Kipling's work through the growing popularity of postcolonial studies has brought about a renewed interest in the novel, especially its role in and its use of historical occurrences of British India, from interest in the Great Game of espionage between Russia and Britain to examinations of how Kipling portrayed The Great Mutiny of 1857. Today, *Kim* is still considered a minor classic, more for its historical interest than for its artistry.

Criticism

Tamara Fernando

Fernando is an editor and writer based in Seattle, Washington. In this essay, Fernando argues that Kipling misrepresented the political environment of late-nineteenth-century India in order to promote the validity of British imperialism.

Much of Rudyard Kipling's writing, both fiction and nonfiction, focuses on India. Kipling—himself an Englishman born in Lahore, who lived and wrote during the late nineteenth and early twentieth centuries at the height of the British Empire—was known as one of the most vocal proponents of his time of British rule in India. His writing reflected the largely common belief held by Britain that the Western world had a moral obligation to provide the Eastern, nonwhite world with what they saw as their superior political and intellectual guidance. This complex of superiority was coupled with the largely held and promoted stereotypical portrayals of the Asiatic person as weak, immoral, and incapable of independent advancement. Of course, hand in hand with this sense of moral obligation to impose British government on the "dark races" of the world was the amassing of economic and global power for Britain itself, the largest empire the world had ever seen. Thus, the maintenance of the sense of moral obligation in India was a significant part of the ideology behind the economic welfare of the empire.

Kipling's nonfiction work was bluntly polemical, but a pro-imperialist message pervades his fiction as well. Even though the novel *Kim*, with its vibrant descriptions of the geography and cultures of India, seems to be a celebration of the subcontinent and its native peoples, it nevertheless is structured as a pro-imperialist work. Specifically, Kipling creates a very particular portrayal of the political environment of India that pointedly ignores the growing conflict between the native Indians and their British rulers. His constructed misrepresentation of the Indian political environment serves to maintain the strength and validity of the British presence in India.

One of the most telling scenes in *Kim* is in chapter 3, when Kim and the Tibetan lama come upon an old soldier who had fought on the British side in The Great Mutiny of 1857. The mutiny was the first and one of the most violent uprisings of Indians against their colonizers, in which Hindu and Muslim soldiers, who vastly outnumbered their British superiors, stormed and took over the city of Delhi. It is recognized historically as a starting point for the division between Anglos and Indians and as a starting point for the push for Indian independence (which would come almost one hundred years later, in 1947). Edward Said writes in his introduction to *Kim*: "For the Indians, the Mutiny was a nationalist uprising against British rule, which uncompromisingly re-asserted itself despite abuses, exploitation and seemingly unheeded

> That Kipling characterizes an uprising based on resentment towards imperialist rule and the attempt to resist this rule as merely 'madness' reduces the Indian nationalist cause to irrationality and, therefore, to meaninglessness."

native complaint." The British, on the other hand, saw the mutiny as an act of irrational and unwarranted aggression.

The language that Kipling uses to describe this mutiny is markedly from the British point of view, so it is significant that the account comes not from a British soldier but from an Indian:

> A madness ate into all the Army, and they turned against their officers. That was the first evil, but not past remedy if they had then held their hands. But they chose to kill the Sahibs' wives and children. Then came the Sahibs from over the sea and called them to most strict account.

The Indian soldier describes the cause of the mutiny as "madness" that made the soldiers turn against the officers. That Kipling characterizes an uprising based on resentment towards imperialist rule and the attempt to resist this rule as merely "madness" reduces the Indian nationalist cause to irrationality and, therefore, to meaninglessness. Because there is no rational reason for the uprising, the murder of officers—the most egregious act of disloyalty—is cast as "evil." And while the murder of civilians, especially women and children, is deemed universally unacceptable, that the soldier chooses to focus on this aspect of the mutiny serves to further demonize the actions of the Indians and invalidate their nationalist cause and the reality of their discontent.

Furthermore, the Indian soldier frames the British in a pointedly paternalistic light in describing the British retaliation against the Indian mutineers: The Sahibs "called them to most strict account" for their actions. This particular choice of phrasing casts the governing British in a parental role; the British counterattack and squelching of the

What Do I Read Next?

- *Quest for Kim: In Search of Kipling's Great Game* (1999) is a historical analysis written by Peter Hopkirk. Hopkirk explores the real history of the Great Game, which was Britain's quest to map the entire Indian subcontinent in an effort to control the region as well as to keep it out of the hands of the Russians. His specific focus is on the real people upon whom Kipling based many of his characters, such as Muhbub Ali, Lurgan Sahib, and Colonel Creighton.

- *Midnight's Children*, first published in 1980 and awarded the Booker Prize in 1981, is Salman Rushdie's complex, brilliant novel that uses magical realism to explore the sociological and political issues created in newly independent, postcolonial India. Rushdie, who is a Muslim Indian, is one of the most important writers from India today.

- Joseph Conrad's novel *Heart of Darkness* was published one year after *Kim*, in 1902, and is set in colonial Africa. Conrad's writing style is markedly different from Kipling's, and *Heart of Darkness* remains a classic of English literature. It is a good example of writing on imperialist themes contemporary with *Kim*.

- *A Passage to India*, a novel by English writer E. M. Forster, was first published in 1924 when India was still a part of the British Empire. The novel, although written from a distinctly British colonial point of view, explores the controversies surrounding relationships between the different races. It offers another comparable version of India through colonial eyes.

- *Orientalism*, a work of criticism by the postcolonial theorist Edward Said, first published in 1978, is a seminal criticism of British imperialism and its aftermath. In particular, Said concentrates on the use of literature by Victorian Britain to promote colonization and the exploitation and oppression of other races.

---

insurgency—and all of the brutality likely thereafter—is cast as a just punishment that brings the unruly back to their rightful order. And that rightful order, of course, is to remain the governed, rather than the governing. Through the language he gives the soldier, Kipling frames the mutiny not as a group's legitimate attempt for independence and nationalization, but as an unjustified, irrational, and isolated act of brutality, thus not only ignoring but invalidating the existence of legitimate conflict.

While the mutiny is largely regarded by historians as the turning point in Anglo-Indian relations and the true first attempt by Indians at retaliating against the British colonizers, the future of the independence movement in India was not characterized by violence, but was instead orchestrated politically through the growing British-educated Indian middle class. The regime of Britain in India was not one of intellectual oppression—indeed, the British saw it as part of the white man's moral obligation to educate the Oriental in ways of Western morality and rationality, and so Indians were not denied, but encouraged to obtain, a British education. Nevertheless, many British did not regard the Indian, even a British-educated Indian, to ever be able to govern himself. Blair B. Kling writes in the Norton critical edition of *Kim*: "To the British in India the Bengalis might be English educated, but they were still racially inferior and did not have the moral fiber, manliness, or common sense to warrant more than subordinate administrative appointments." This wide-reaching British sentiment towards the educated Bengali class is specifically reflected in Kipling's characterization of Hurree Chunder Mookerjee.

The character of Mookerjee in *Kim* is one of the educated Bengali class to which Kling refers. Indeed, Kipling does portray Mookerjee as highly educated and extremely competent in his work as a spy in The Great Game, especially in his heroic, skilled, and dangerous success at the climax of the novel, in which Mookerjee, with the help of Kim, tricks the

Russian spies out of their goods and leads them astray. He is extremely competent at his work, even described, when he is in the midst of his anthropological studies, as a "sober, learned son of experience and adversity." However, as learned as Mookerjee may be, Kipling treats him not as an equal to the British whom he emulates, but rather as a caricature. This is especially evident in the way that Kipling has rendered his English speech patterns. Mookerjee's English speech is liberally peppered with highly British expressions, such as in a conversation with Kim: "By Jove . . . why the dooce do you not issue demi-offeecial orders to some brave man to poison them . . . That is all tommy-rott."

No other character in Kipling uses such a highly concentrated smattering of idiomatic expressions. Kipling also renders Mookerjee's English in an unorthodox spelling—such as "dooce" for "deuce"—to highlight the Bengali's non-British accent. This has the effect of portraying Mookerjee's English as not "true" English, but almost as a dialect. The dialect-type spelling, together with the almost laughable, exaggerated use of British figures of speech, has the effect of making Mookerjee's speech a caricature of the English language—the opposite of authentic English language. Said writes of Kipling's cartooning of Mookerjee: "Lovable and admirable though he may be, there remains in Kipling's portrait of him the grimacing stereotype of the ontologically funny native, hopelessly trying to be like 'us.'"

This parodying of Mookerjee devalues him—and, by extension, the educated Indian class to which he belongs—and places him on a field unequal to the British, thus rendering the Indian educated class—and therefore their cause for independence—impotent.

The misrepresentation of the Indian historical and cultural experience in these two specific instances is tantamount to Kipling outright ignoring that a very real conflict of interests existed in the Anglo-Indian relationship. The very absence of conflict between the Anglo and Indian characters in *Kim* is in fact not limited to specific instances, but is intrinsic in the plot of the novel, the centerpiece of which is The Great Game. The Great Game was the complex espionage operation that the British government used to collect information about the northern borders of the Indian Empire and the independent regions bordering on it—such as Afghanistan, Nepal, and Tibet—chiefly to protect their northern border against the threat of the Russians.

The main action of the plot of *Kim* involves the participation of Mahbub Ali, Colonel Creighton, and other key characters—including, of course, Kim himself—in a dangerous game of espionage against what remains a largely vague and unnamed enemy throughout the book. It is not until chapter 12 that the enemy is finally given a concrete identification: They are Russian spies, and the climax of the novel involves Mookerjee and Kim successfully disarming and derailing the spies from their mission. Thus, the main action of the plot of the novel results in nothing less than the preservation of the British Empire.

In addition to the Indian characters working actively as supporters of the British government is the complete absence of any Indian characters who were working in opposition to the imperial presence and for independence. Kipling would have been quite aware of the very real and vocal organizational work of the educated Indian elite to challenge British rule and bring about independence. So it is of great significance that Kipling not only completely leaves out any characters representing the independence movement, but also puts the preservation of the British Empire directly in the hands of Indians. The absence of dissension, coupled with the complete devotion of the Indian characters to the British cause, works towards a representation of India that completely denies any conflict in the Anglo-Indian relationship. Kipling, by extension, therefore denies any validity to the very real independence movement. The fact that Kipling portrays the Russians as the sole threat to British sovereignty also denies that the independence movement posed a real threat to British sovereignty. The act of completely ignoring Indian national movements on Kipling's part symbolically invalidates it and renders it harmless.

Kipling's purposefully constructed misrepresentation of the political environment of India thus leaves the reader, in the end, with an image of an India not divided by conflict, but happily united under the British Empire. Even the spiritually transcendent closing scene of the novel reflects Kipling's aim in portraying an utterly unified India: The book closes with the Tibetan lama attaining Enlightenment after finally finding the Holy River of his pilgrimage—and even in the description of the lama's Enlightenment, Kipling manages to make a final, overreaching impression of an India not divided by strife, but unified in harmony:

> Yea, my soul went free, and, wheeling like an eagle . . . my Soul drew near the Great Soul which is beyond all things. At that point, exalted in contemplation, I saw Hind [India] from Ceylon in the sea to the Hills, and my own Painted Rocks at

"Kim and the Letter Writer," terracotta plaque made by John Lockwood Kipling, the father of Rudyard Kipling, for the first edition of Kim *in 1901*

Such-zen; I saw every camp and village to the least, where we have ever rested. I saw them at one time and in one place, for they were within the Soul.

Source: Tamara Fernando, Critical Essay on *Kim*, in *Novels for Students*, Thomson Gale, 2005.

David H. Stewart

In the following essay, Stewart explores the influences of orality on Kipling and its manifestations in Kim.

Recent studies of the oral or performative element in literature provide novel methods for understanding the work of Rudyard Kipling. In this essay, I shall review Kipling's peculiar approach to the creative process, demonstrates its applications to *Kim,* and note some ways of modifying critical response to Kipling and perhaps other writers.

Everyone concedes Kipling's exploitation of the visual possibilities of print. Many of his poems and pages of prose foreground the typesetter's paraphernalia: dashes, leaders, apostrophes, quotation marks, exclamation marks, and uncommon capitalizations appear constantly. The word "telegraphic" is often used to describe his style. He was

delighted to include his father's illustrations to enhance the visual appeal of his books. Having mastered the journalist's craft at an early age, he sensed the power and romance of highspeed presses and made print-technology serve his ends, so that critics often credit him with helping initiate the enhancement (or subversion) of literature by incorporating journalistic techniques.

But this conventional sense of Kipling's procedure cannot be reconciled with his own statements. Late in life, he described his early efforts as a writer:

> I made my own experiments in the weights, colours, perfumes, and attributes of words in relation to other words, either as read aloud so that they may hold the ear, or, scattered over the page, draw the eye. There is no line in my verse or prose which has not been mouthed till the tongue has made all smooth, and memory, after many recitals, has mechanically skipped the grosser superfluities.

Here the emphasis is clearly on the acoustic element in his work, although he acknowledges the importance of visual and other sensory elements. His is an excellent example of writing that poses problems for readers in our century because, according to Walter Ong, literary criticism ignores auditory, olfactory, gustatory and tactile imagination and imageries. We are "addicted" to the visual—and thereby "impoverished."

The importance of the oral-aural elements in Kipling can be demonstrated in a number of ways. He once admitted that "three generations of Methodist Preachers lie behind me—the pulpit streak will come out!" Probably the moralizing strain was foremost in his mind, but this is inseparable from the oral medium of evangelical, indeed of Christian, tradition. How this tradition affected Kipling can be witnessed in a negative and positive way by noting his childhood experiences, first in the House of Desolation, where fundamentalist piety took venomous forms, and second in the presence of his mother and his sisters, women with an uncommon "command of words" inherited directly from a Methodist environment.

Kipling spoke often of his "Daemon." "My Daemon was with me in the *Jungle Books, Kim,* and both Puck books, and good care I took to walk delicately, lest he should withdraw . . . When your Daemon is in charge, do not try to think consciously. Drift, wait, obey." In some sense, Kipling believed that he "heard" what to write and transmitted the message. To whom was he listening? Psychologists might say, "to his alter ego or subconscious;" but he also conversed about and read his work to his parents. Another hypothesis claims that it is small groups of orally bonded individuals who create all literature. Writers must listen and speak before they write. Until populations became too large, you simply asked an author or his acquaintances what he meant if his poem puzzled you. The coffeehouse or salon provided appropriate settings. Literary works existed within an oral network that obviated explication. When the network broke down, as it did at first between dominant critics and Wordsworth or Kipling or Faulkner, wild allegations began to fly; but the normal fabric of communication ordinarily restored itself and conversation resumed. Isolated writers such as Emily Dickinson or Kafka, who worked somewhat outside the network, remained enigmatic until critics brought them inside. In our century, local networks continue to function (for example, the Inklings at Oxford, the Black Mountain poets, the New York Review of Books coterie), but there is no general network, hence every author requires a biographer and dozens of academic explicators. This situation gives credence to the alternative hypothesis that books are made not from living language but from reading (or *mis*reading) other books, which seems unsatisfactory when applied to Kipling, although he read widely all his life.

That Kipling chose isolation by listening to his Daemon and by using as a sounding board his parents rather than contemporary writers is confirmed in another way when he told Rider Haggard that "we are only telephone wires;" that is, we transmit messages rather than originating them. He amplified this by explaining that neither he nor Haggard actually wrote anything. "*You* didn't write *She* you know; something wrote it through you!"

Given this assumption about the genesis of his fictions, we can understand why he confessed to writing not from notes but from memory. "I took down very few notes except of names, dates, and addresses. If a thing didn't stay in my memory, I argued that it was hardly worth writing out." Moreover, we can imagine why Kipling's reading his tales aloud was such a compelling experience for the auditor. He became a rhapsode, as Plato would have it, disclosing messages to the souls of those who can hear rightly and respond beneficially. At the very end of his life, when he revised his work for the definitive Sussex and Burwash editions, the only significant change he made in the text of *Kim* was italicizing key words, evidently to guide the voice of his reader toward correct rhythms, accents, and intonations.

Perhaps this helps explain the violent reactions of readers to Kipling from the first. Of course, his

> Like Twain and other American vernacular writers, Kipling transcribed English that was under the stress of an alien environment, which wrenched it with new words and accents, as well as novel concepts."

imperial posturing and anti-intellectualism can account for the intelligentsia's repudiation of his work; but the unique vehemence of this repudiation suggests that something in Kipling triggers extraordinary responses. Working by ear as well as by eye, he breaks into our consciousness in ways that prevent our keeping the text at arm's length. Nietzsche called the ear "the organ of fear," and Kipling assaults our ears. The "voices" of *Kim* occupy us, so that we become bridges threatened by the marching feet of a verbal legion, glass strained to the shatter-point by the pitch of words. His books talk in ways that force us to answer, and we try to reduce the stress of invading language by talking back—by humming along or humming against.

How is it that a writer so expert with typographic conventions manages to neutralize them, to elicit continually an aural as well as a visual response? As critics recognized when Kipling's career began, his writing is like speech or music. Already in 1890, Barry Pain wrote a parody of Kipling that included the observation that

> when we speak . . ., we often put a full stop before the relative clauses—add them as an afterthought . . . But when we write we only put a comma. The author of *Plain Tales from the Hills* saw this, and acted on the principle. He punctuated his writing as he did his speaking; and used more full stops than any man before him. Which was genius.

George Moore claimed that Kipling's language is rhetorical, "copious, rich, sonorous . . . None since the Elizabethans has written so copiously." And T. S. Eliot believed that, like Swinburne's, Kipling's work "has the sound-value of oratory, not of music. [His] is the poetry of oratory; it is music just as the words of orator or preacher are music; they persuade, not by reason, but by emphatic sound." That this is equally true of Kipling's prose seems clear from the testimony of Henry James and other critics who sought musical analogs to describe Kipling's style.

Of greater importance than these impressionistic responses is an approach through Kipling's use of colloquialism, which many critics mistook for journalism. Richard Bridgman examined the rise of colloquialism in American literature, tracing the slow and clumsy process by which authors discovered how to convey dialect and direct speech in a convincing way. He concludes that Kipling's contemporaries, Twain and James, were the first writers to succeed and that, except for James' experiments, "nothing very clear or purposeful happened to the vernacular in literature for a quarter of a century following the publication of *Huckleberry Finn.*" Bridgman refrains from noting the parallels between Twain and the so-called "regional" writers all over Europe during this period, from Leskov in Russia to the practitioners of *Heimatkunst* in Germany; nor does he call attention to the similarities between Twain and Kipling as uneducated ex-journalists who expanded the literary lexicon by successfully importing colloquial language. He does not ask the obvious question: Would English and American literature have diverged so significantly in the twentieth century if English writers had capitalized on Kipling's stylistic explorations as American writers did on Twain's?

Approaches to Kipling through dichotomies between journalism and "true art" or between imperialist vulgarity and compassionate humanism can be productively supplemented by examining the tension between oral and literate strategies. To be sure, others have noted what we may call the "gestic" component in Kipling's language. Even in German translation, Berthold Brecht evidently heard "vividness and epigrammatic directness of speech" in Kipling's diction, which can be called gestic. R. G. Collingwood described Kipling as the one who shocked late nineteenth century aesthetes by reviving "magical art," dead since the Middle Ages. It is an art that has strong vocal overtones which he calls "speech-gestures."

Kim invites us to hear how Kipling conveys orality through print. In chapter seven, there are two descriptions that provide entry to the book in a new way. First, Colonel Creighton explains Kim's future in school and as a government servant. "Kim pretended at first to understand perhaps one word in three of this talk. Then the Colonel, seeing his mistake, turned to fluent and picturesque Urdu, and Kim was contented." The second

passage is a description of the language of schoolboys at St. Xavier's:

> And every tale was told in the even, passionless voice of the native-born, mixed with quaint reflections, borrowed unconsciously from native foster-mothers, and turns of speech that showed that they had been that instant translated from the vernacular. Kim watched, listened, and approved. This was not insipid, single-word talk of drummer-boys.

Both passages remind readers that the novel is mainly "oral" (three-fourths is direct discourse) and also that it is a "translation." *Kim* contains four "languages," each with its own distinctive style. First there is Kipling's (or the omniscient narrator's) style, that encyclopedic, confiding, emphatic, and often elliptical language that was his trademark. We hear it, with all its commas, dashes and foreign words, in the first paragraphs of the novel and from time to time thereafter. For some readers, it obtrudes, as Thackeray's voice does. For most readers, however, it is a supple instrument with astonishing versatility that enables him to present superb descriptions, for example of the Grand Trunk Road in chapter four. It also provides him the latitude to adopt the second person singular ("Therefore, you would scarcely be interested in Kim's experiences as a St. Xavier's boy . . .," chapter seven), the first-person plural (". . . almond-curd sweetmeats (*balushai* we call it) a fine-chopped Lucknow tobacco," chapter eight), the imperative mood (the Babu: "Behold him . . . Watch him, all babudom laid aside, smoking at noon . . .," chapter 15), and the ironic voice (the Babu: "Never was so unfortunate a product of English rule in India more unhappily thrust upon aliens," chapter 13). One added trait of this "narrator's language" is the high incidence of compounds, frequently hyphenated: "*fiend-embroidered* draperies," "*brow-puckered* search," "*many-times-told* tale," "*quick-poured* French," "*de-Englishised,*" "*be-ringed,*" "he . . . was *bad-worded* in clumsy Urdu." In addition to these verbs and verbals, compounding can be found in other parts of speech; and it led one critic to speculate that this is an important source of Kipling's epic flavor and fairy-tale quality. Certainly it is Kipling's "deviant language" in *Kim* (whether the narrator's or some character's) that makes his idioms so emphatic and that gives the novel a kind of deep-structure that takes us back to Anglo-Saxon word-formation.

The second language of *Kim* is the voice of the homeland (*Balait,* as Kim calls it). Creighton, the Reverend Bennett and Father Victor, even the drummer boy from Liverpool speak "standard English"—more or less. That is, each speaks his own dialect of English, always signaled by the appearance of contractions: "'em" for them, "an'" for and, "ud" for would, "amazin'" for amazing. Moreover, Kipling distinguished Victor's Irish from Bennett's English.

It is this conglomerate "normative language" that gives special flavor to what might be called "native English," the third language of the novel. This is Kim's "tinny saw-cut English" ("oah yess") before he attends school. It is the English of the bazaar letter-writers, for example "*Sobrao Satai Failed Entrance Allahabad University*" who added *P.M.* (sic) to the lama's letter to Kim: "*Please note boy is apple of eye, and rupees shall be sent per hoondie* [cheque] *three hundred per annum. For God Almighty's sake*" (chapter six). This is also the Babu's English, which Kipling exhibits frequently: "the best of English with the vilest of phrases" (chapter 13). For example, in chapter 12, the Babu describes himself to Kim in English: "By Jove! I was such a fearful man. Never mind that. I go on colloquially ..." Then he switches to Urdu, which Kipling translates into standard English. But the signal for this switch is not buried for most readers. The compulsory examination for British officers in Hindustani was called the "colloquial." Kipling provides an aural sign for the switch between languages.

It is in this third language that Kipling often devises colloquial deformations that accentuate an aural response to words. When the Babu says that something "is creaming joke" or refers to "locks, stocks and barrels," we must "sound out" the right meaning, as we do when Huck Finn describes a subject taught by the Duke as "yellocution." Kipling was especially adept with deviant verbs. Thus a scribe, writing English translated from the lama's dictation in imperfect Urdu, records: "*Then Almighty God blessing your Honour's succeedings to third and fourth generation and . . . confide in your Honour's humble servant for adequate remuneration . . .*" (chapter six). The most dramatic example of Kipling's foregrounding of verbs occurs in chapter three when Kim converses with Father Victor:

"They call me Kim Rishti-ke. That is Kim of the Rishti."

"What is that—'Rishti'?"

"*Eye*-rishti—that was the regiment—my father's."

"Irish, oh I see."

"Yes. That was how my father told me. My father, he has lived."

"Has lived where?"

"Has lived. Of *course* he is dead—gone out."

Incorrect present perfect "has lived" is exactly right in place of a past tense or the verb "died" for conveying the un-Western blur of life with death. It is this "translated" Urdu and Hindi (for example, the boys' talk at St. Xavier's) that comprises perhaps ten percent of the novel.

Finally there is *Kim*'s fourth language in which over half of the book is written. It is "actual" Urdu, often spoken with an accent. Kipling performs an impressive feat here by making English sound (and look) non-English. He does it by leaving remnants of the original vernacular, single vocables, sometimes translated in parentheses but always italicized as if inviting us to sound them aloud, however senseless and alien. He does it by "Germanic" capitalizations, a typographic trick which accentuates nominals. He does it by studding the language with borrowed, sometimes inflected words (usually mispronounced) from English, for example, *terain* (for "train"—"Quick: she comes!"), *Berittish* (for "British"), *tikkut* (for "ticket"), *takkus* (for "taxes"), *Ker-lis-ti-an* (for "Christian"), and a number of corrupted proper names. He does it by punning—in both English and Urdu and once in Pushtu. He does it with archaic and Biblical constructions: "We *be* craftsmen," "the gates of his mouth were loosened," "if so be thou art woman-born," "whoso bathes in it washes away all taint and speckle of sin," "thou wast born to be a breaker of hearts." Finally, he does it with a variety of malformations. In chapter seven, Kim leaps from a cab to greet the lama. The driver exclaims, "What is to pay me for this coming and recoming?" A moment later the lama explains his own sudden appearance: "perceiving myself alone in this great and terrible world, I bethought me of the *te-rain* to Benares." "Recoming" and "bethought" are little surprises in Kipling's rhetorical armory that make his language vitally oral.

In addition to these four distinct languages of *Kim*, there are several other features of the text that enhance its aural appeal. The poetic epigraphs for each chapter serve as a musical paradox. Kipling's habit of radical excision and compression of his manuscripts (*Kim* "as it finally appeared was about one-tenth of what the first lavish specification called for") has the paradoxical effect of accelerating the reader's vocalization by forcing him to fill in the gaps. Kipling's prodigal descriptions seem all the more copious because they are rare. They are show pieces set in a tale that advances almost exclusively by laconic dialog. More importantly, Kipling's visual imagery is usually random and non-cumulative. Except for such obvious links as between Kim and a colt or horse and the recurrent allusions to the Wheel, River and Road as metaphors of life, Kipling's images rise momentarily to the surface and then vanish. By no means does this minimize Kipling's appeal to the eye (or indeed the other senses). His repeated use of horizontal lighting to intensify physical descriptions gives *Kim* its visual brilliance. But Kipling never organizes and unfolds his texts the way Joyce, for example, does. As Hugh Kenner has observed, Joyce depends on "technological space;" that is, on the printed page exclusively, on "the antithesis between the personal matrix of human speech and the unyielding formations of the book as book." *Ulysses* strives for a kind of simultaneity in which incremental repetitions and recurrences call attention to themselves. We must refer constantly to the text to see them. *Kim* inhabits the aural recesses of memory, creates echoes in addition to visions.

Still more important in *Kim* is the constant "translation" from the vernacular, which creates an unusual aural medium. For example, characters "speaking" Urdu at times use an "elevated vocabulary that would be inappropriate in plain English. Kim tells Colonel Creighton, "it is *inexpedient* to write the names of strangers." The Jat farmer says of his sick son, "he *esteemed* the salt lozenges." Later when Kim scolds him for meddling, he says, "I am *rebuked.*" Kim describes the ash in the farmer's pipe as "*auspicious.*" Such diction is incompatible with these characters' vocabularies in English, but here in "translation" it seems normal, therefore doubly suggestive.

A second example: the novel is full of oral formulas ("let the hand of Friendship turn aside the Whip of Calamity;" "I am thy sacrifice") that are unknown in English yet familiar because they conform to the structure of maxims. A speaker of Urdu can actually translate some of them back into the original, so that he may read "I am thy sacrifice" but hear *"Main tum pe qurban jaoon,"* a Moslem oath of fidelity. An English reader hears, instead, echoes from an archaic, perhaps Biblical, past that authenticates such statements. Curses ("Room for the Queen of Delhi and her prime minister the gray monkey climbing up his own sword!"), oaths ("I am thy cow!"), and proverbs ("For the sick cow a crow; for the sick man a Brahmin") abound in *Kim.* The structure is unmistakable although the words are strange, so that meaning comes as emphatically through rhythm and intonation as through diction. The continual appearance of conventionalized and formulaic locutions makes *Kim* rhetorical, dialogic. Its compressed style, confiding narrator, and loquacious characters everywhere reinforce an apothegmatic quality that transforms the book into a sustained enthymeme which, as students of rhetoric know, forces auditors to participate in and contribute to verbal transactions.

A final striking characteristic of *Kim* is the appeal to our ears through frequent use of exclamations and the imperative mood that they create. Hear and obey! Let all listen to the Jâtakas! The search is sure! Hear the most excellent Law! It is found! Be Quiett! These are cries that leap above the "surface noise" of Indian life and Kipling's high volume prose. The mood is so strong that it deflects the narrator's voice from its normal indicative mood. For example, in chapter five, there is a description of the Maverick regiment's setting up camp for the night, pitching tents, unpacking equipment, "and behold the mango-tope turned into an orderly town as they [Kim and the lama] watched!" In chapter 15, after summarizing Hurree Babu's hoodwinking the foreign agents, the narrator's voice suddenly rises: "Behold him, too fine-drawn to sweat, too pressed to vaunt the drugs in his brass-bound box, ascending Shamelegh slope, a just man made perfect." The epigraph of chapter one and the second sentence of the novel ("Who hold Zam Zammah, that 'fire-breathing dragon,' hold the Punjab . . .") are emphatic generalizations that sound like a Commandment.

If it is true that Kipling managed his typographical medium in a way that recreates the illusion of hearing rather than reading, then perhaps we can explain *Kim*'s "magical" appeal to readers and also its peculiar isolation as a modern classic. It speaks to us from an oral-aural world not only of nineteenth century Anglo-India but of childhood. It seems to short-circuit the alphabetical print medium and operate in terms of the seven features of oral cultures that Walter Ong has listed:

> (1) stereotyped or formulaic expression, (2) standardization of themes, (3) epithetic identification for "disbambiguation" of classes or of individuals, (4) generation of "heavy" or ceremonial characters, (5) formulary, ceremonial appropriation of history, (6) cultivation of praise and vituperation, (7) copiousness.

Illustrations from *Kim* for each of these come to mind at once and suggest the profoundly conservative tendency of the novel. Formulaic language, cliches, incantatory and exclamatory expressions withdraw us from the abstract, objective world of print, according to Ong, and reintroduce us to a world of matter, potency, indistinctness and subjectivity. This occurs because voice "signals the present use of power," sound being "more real or existential than other sense objects, despite the fact that it is more evanescent."

Like Twain and other American vernacular writers, Kipling transcribed English that was under the stress of an alien environment, which wrenched it with new words and accents, as well as novel concepts. Anglo-Indian English was as different as American English from the language of the homeland. Kipling's typographical medium captured the sense of adventure and expansiveness that rapid language modification conveys as it assists us in the struggle to assimilate new experience. His lexical and syntactic innovations explain in part why *Kim* is a valuable book for people learning to read.

To the triumph of print technology, Kipling reacted one way, Joyce another. Both of them listened diachronically to language and tried to transmit the word they heard. But Kipling's creed said, "drift, wait, obey," which meant that he affirmed traditional wisdom. Joyce followed a more romantic and modern path, preferring what Ong calls the "irenic" stance and avoiding the "free dialogic struggle with an audience," which was the older, perhaps more venerable, way to speak.

Source: David H. Stewart, "Orality in Kipling's *Kim*," in *Critical Essays on Rudyard Kipling*, edited by Harold Orel, G. K. Hall, 1989, pp. 114–24.

The Golden Temple of the Sikh religion is just one example of the religious and cultural diversity in India, the setting for Kim

Norman Page

In the following essay excerpt, Page outlines Kim *and its place in Kipling's oeuvre, and comments on Kipling's particular gifts as a short-story writer.*

Kim took considerably longer to grow than most of Kipling's books: according to J. I. M. Stewart, 'there was nothing which gave him more trouble.' Its origins belong to the period of residence in Vermont, and it is 'said to have been first conceived during a visit of Lockwood Kipling's to Naulakha' (Hilton Brown). It perhaps grew out of the early abandoned Anglo-Indian novel *Mother Maturin*, and Kim has also something in common with the Mowgli of the *Jungle Books*. But its deeper origins belong to Kipling's childhood and his earliest experiences of the sights, sounds and smells of India. It has been suggested, on the basis of internal evidence, that the dating of the action precedes by a generation or so the date of composition, and that Kim was born in 1865 and joined the Lama in 1878; if so, it may be significant that Kipling, who gave his own initial to his boy-hero, was himself born in 1865. The book is, among other things, an exploration of the writer's earliest memories, and Hilton Brown has called it '*the* nostalgic throwback of his career.'

The book was serialized in *McClure's Magazine* (December 1900 to October 1901) and almost simultaneously in *Cassell's Magazine* (January–November 1901), and appeared in book form in England and America in 1901. The New York edition includes ten illustrations by John Lockwood Kipling. For Kipling's own comments on the book, see *Something of Myself,* Chapter 5.

By general consent *Kim* is the best of Kipling's longer works of prose fiction and by any standards a masterpiece. There is less agreement on what kind of book it is and on what is its central theme. Kipling himself characterized it as 'nakedly picaresque and plotless,' but even a careless reading suggests that it contains something more than a mere string of colourful incidents. J. I. M. Stewart considered that it ought to be seen primarily as 'a book for young people.' Edmund Wilson claimed that the book deals with 'the gradual dawning of [Kim's] consciousness that he is really a Sahib.' Rupert Croft-Cooke took the line that it is really two stories in one, and that one of them is greatly inferior to the other:

> But the Great Game follows them. It is made eventful, even exciting . . . but the secret service story is

no better than John Buchan might have written and
never ceases to be a tiresome distraction from the
'nakedly'—and magnificently—picaresque.

Charles Carrington probed somewhat deeper in
stressing that Kim has to face a decision how to live:

> he must choose between contemplation and
> action . . . Though it is not expressly stated, the reader
> is left with the assurance that Kim, like Mowgli and
> like the Brushwood Boy, will find reality in action,
> not in contemplation.

Edward Shanks stated the theme somewhat differently: 'it must be said that *Kim* is *about* the infinite and joyous variety of India for him who has
the eyes to see it and the heart to rejoice in it.' This
view is endorsed by Arnold Kettle: 'There is in fact
a strong case for describing *Kim* as being essentially about India the subcontinent rather than about
Kim the boy.'

A brief outline of the main action will indicate
some of the book's main features. Kimball O'Hara,
the son of an Irish Colour-Sergeant and a nurse-
maid in a Colonel's family (the mother's race and
nationality are unspecified, but there are grounds
for supposing she might have been a Eurasian), is
an orphan who runs wild in the streets of Lahore.
When we first see him he is seated astride an antique bronze gun in front of the Museum (Kipling's
father was, of course, curator of the latter). He
meets a Tibetan lama who has embarked on a quest
for a river that will wash away sins, and the two
set off on a pilgrimage to the Buddhist holy places
of India. Since the priest is a kind of saintly innocent and the boy is precocious and knowing, the
quasi-paternal and quasi-filial roles are to some extent reversed. The situation is traditionally picaresque in so far as the hero and a companion set
forth on a journey and encounter numerous persons
and adventures along the way.

They travel widely by railway and along
the Grand Trunk Road, but when Kim encounters

the Mavericks, his father's regiment, he falls into
the clutches of the chaplains, who cause him to be
sent to school (with the Lama's agreement and at
his expense) in order to be turned into a sahib. During the school holidays, however, Kim escapes and
returns to his old ways; he is taken up by British
agents and trained for secret service work ('the
Great Game'). In the latter part of the book he travels to the Himalayas with the Lama, who eventually finds the river he is seeking. His goal is
therefore achieved, but Kim's position at the end
of the story remains a little ambiguous.

As this summary shows, *Kim* presents a man's
world and most of the major characters are male.
Women appear fleetingly in minor roles, but at one
point Kim reflects: 'How can a man follow the Way
or the Great Game when he is so-always pestered
by women?' (The narrator informs us that Kim
'thought in the vernacular' on this occasion, and we
are bound to recall the young Rudyard Kipling thinking and talking in the vernacular in his early years.)

'The Way' and 'the Great Game' are the two
antithetical sets of values—the life of contempla-
tion versus the life of action, asceticism versus
materialism—that confront Kim. In a sense both
reach their climax towards the end of the novel, for
not only does the Lama find his river but Kim succeeds in obtaining vital documents and delivering
them to the authorities. When it comes to the
choice, however, Kim does not opt exclusively for
either. As Arnold Kettle says:

> Kim is a man in the world of men, neither more nor
> less. It is a real world, not an illusion (as the Lama's
> philosophy would have it), a world of Doing in which
> action is neither an irrelevance nor an end in itself
> but a necessary element in the relationship between
> men and nature, man and man. This is what Kim has
> come through to. . . . Kim has escaped from the false
> antithesis, the choice between action on the one hand
> and truth on the other, between an amoral material-
> ism and an unworldly idealism. The new materialism
> to which he advances, and of which the emblem is
> his sense of identity with the earth and its processes,
> no longer excludes the human values encompassed
> in his relationships with the Lama. ('What is Kim?,'
> in *The Morality of Art,* ed. D. W. Jefferson [1969]
> pp. 219–20.)

In other words, Kim opts for a synthesis or golden
mean, avoiding both fanaticism and a crass rejection of the spiritual life. His 'sense of identity with
the earth and its processes' is a natural outcome of
the sustained picture of India's teeming landscapes
and townscapes that the novel has presented.

There is a large descriptive element in *Kim* but
Kipling's scenes are only occasionally presented as

set-pieces; more often the touches, while intensely vivid, are highly economical, as a few quotations will suggest:

> [during a railway journey] Golden, rose, saffron, and pink, the morning mists smoked away across the flat green levels. All the rich Punjab lay out in the splendour of the keen sun. The lama flinched a little as the telegraph-posts swung by . . .

> They all unloosed their bundles and made their morning meal. Then the banker, the cultivator, and the soldier prepared their pipes and wrapped the compartment in choking, acrid smoke, spitting and coughing and enjoying themselves. The Sikh and the cultivator's wife chewed *pan;* the lama took snuff and told his beads, while Kim, cross-legged, smiled over the comfort of a full stomach. (Ch. 2)

> The lama squatted under the shade of a mango, whose shadow played checkerwise over his face; the soldier sat stiffly on the pony; and Kim, making sure that there were no snakes, lay down in the crotch of the twisted roots.

> There was a drowsy buzz of small life in hot sunshine, a cooing of doves, and a sleepy drone of well-wheels across the fields . . . (Ch. 3)

> And truly the Grand Trunk Road is a wonderful spectacle. It runs straight, bearing without crowding India's traffic for fifteen hundred miles—such a river of life as nowhere else exists in the world. They looked at the green-arched, shade-flecked length of it, the white breadth speckled with slow-pacing folk; and the two-roomed police-station opposite. (Ch. 3)

For an example of more sustained description, see the account of the Great Trunk Road and its travellers in Chapter 4, beginning: 'They met a troop of long-haired, strong-scented Sansis with baskets of lizards and other unclean food on their backs, their lean dogs sniffing at their heel.'

After all, it is India that binds together the two main strands of the novel, for its restless, endlessly varied life is both the scene of adventure and 'the very Wheel itself, eating, drinking, trading, marrying, and quarrelling—all warmly alive' (Ch. 12) from which the holy man seeks escape. The India of *Kim* is not that of the early short stories—primarily, that is, the India of the sahibs and tourists—but the land of the Indian peoples themselves in all their diversity. As J. I. M. Stewart has said, 'At least to a Western reader, it is the Indian characters in the story who appear most real and, in a deep sense, most beloved.' When Kim is asked in Chapter 8 'And who are thy people, Friend of all the World?' he replies, 'This great and beautiful land.' Kipling, who was never to see India again, enshrined in the book his own love for the land to which his earliest memories belonged.

'Why did the author of the brilliant short stories never develop into an important novelist?' asked Edmund Wilson in 1941. The answer surely has to be the obvious one: that the gifts demanded of a writer of 'brilliant short stories' will not necessarily sustain the same writer through a full-length work of fiction. In his early stories, Kipling is indeed brilliant in contriving situations that present a crisis in one or more human lives: a crisis that may be comic, serious or tragic. But the characters who enact the drama are usually conceived and presented in the sketchiest terms: it is significant that most of Kipling's descriptive writing evokes places rather than people. Rarely do his characters develop, and this not because the form of the short story cannot accommodate development but because the matter holds little interest for him. Much of his work shows the strengths and the limitations of a journalist of genius: he is superb at catching the quality of a moment or an episode, but virtually a non-starter when it comes to tracing the slow evolution of a personality or a relationship. And it is after all the latter—to endow a character (in Henry James's phrase) with 'the high attributes of a Subject,' and to describe (in George Eliot's phrase) 'the stealthy convergence of human lots'— that was seen in Kipling's time as the business of the novelist. The absorbing concern of the modern novel is with inwardness, and its techniques have been largely devoted to the task of conveying a sense of the inner life. But Kipling, fascinated by externals of every kind and every degree of significance, had little time for inwardness. That indifference did not vitiate his work as a writer of short stories (though he is significantly different even in this genre from, say, James Joyce or Katherine Mansfield); but it prevented him from becoming a novelist in the main realistic tradition of English fiction. In fact, with the exception of the strongly autobiographical *The Light that Failed,* he never even attempted to write a novel of this kind.

Some of Kipling's later stories are more ambitious and even constitute fragmentary novels (like 'Mrs Bathurst') or incredibly compressed novels-in-miniature (like 'The Gardener'). In such characters as Helen Turrell and Mary Postgate he succeeded in giving a sense not just of a passage of experience but of the quality of a whole life. But compression was an essential condition of high quality.

Source: Norman Page, "The Novels," in *A Kipling Companion*, Macmillan Press, 1984, pp. 151–56.

Sources

Gilbert, Susan M., and Sandra Gubar, "The War of the Words," in *No Man's Land: The Place of the Woman Writer in the Twentieth-Century*, Vol. 1, Yale University Press, 1989.

Maurice, Arthur Bartlett, "Rudyard Kipling's *Kim*," in *Kim*, by Rudyard Kipling, edited by Zohreh T. Sullivan, W. W. Norton, 2002; originally published in *Bookman*, October 1901.

McClure, John, "Kipling's Richest Dream," in *Kim*, by Rudyard Kipling, edited by Zohreh T. Sullivan, W. W. Norton, 2002; originally published in *Kipling and Conrad: the Colonial Fiction*, Harvard University Press, 1981.

Millar, J. H., "A 'New Kipling,'" in *Kim*, by Rudyard Kipling, edited by Zohreh T. Sullivan, W. W. Norton, 2002; originally published in *Blackwood's Magazine*, December 1901.

Payne, William Morton, "Mr. Kipling's Enthralling New Novel," in *Kim*, by Rudyard Kipling, edited by Zohreh T. Sullivan, W. W. Norton, 2002; originally published in *Dial*, November 16, 1901.

Said, Edward, *Orientalism*, Vintage, 1979.

Further Reading

Cain, Peter, and Tony Hopkins, *British Imperialism, 1688–2000*, 2d ed., Longman, 2001.
    When this comprehensive history of the British Empire was first published, it was received with critical acclaim. It has since been updated to relate imperialism to modern-day international politics.

Gilmour, David, *The Long Recessional: The Imperial Life of Rudyard Kipling*, Farrar, Straus and Giroux, 2003.
    Kipling's legacy has endured a long history of vilification, but this biography offers a fresh, early-twenty-first-century perspective on his life and ideologies.

Mallett, Phillip, *Rudyard Kipling: A Literary Life*, Palgrave Macmillan, 2003.
    Another very recent biography on Rudyard Kipling, this work concentrates especially on Kipling's writing life and family life.

Wilson, Angus, *The Strange Ride of Rudyard Kipling: His Life and Work*, House of Stratus, 2002.
    An older biography of Kipling first published in 1977, Wilson's work on Kipling concentrates on his personal life and its relationship to his work.

The Maltese Falcon

Dashiell Hammett
1930

Readers who have never picked up Dashiell Hammett's 1930 detective novel *The Maltese Falcon* nor viewed the classic 1941 film adaptation, which follows the novel practically word-for-word, might feel a strong sense of familiarity when they first encounter the story. In this book, Hammett invented the hardboiled private eye genre, introducing many of the elements that readers have come to expect from detective stories: the mysterious, alluring woman whose love may be a trap; the search for an exotic icon that people are willing to kill for; the detective who plays on both sides of the law to find the truth, but who ultimately is driven by a strong moral code; and enough gunplay and beatings to make readers share the detective's sense of danger. Throughout the decades, countless writers have copied Hammett's themes and motifs, seldom able to come anywhere near his near-perfect blend of cynicism and excitement.

Hammett is considered one of those rare writers whose critical esteem has exceeded the small genre in which he wrote. A former detective himself, he wrote about the business with a sharp eye for procedural details, but he also showed a knack for engaging dialogue and understanding of the depths of the human soul. In his lifetime Hammett was considered an excellent detective writer, producing five novels, over eighty short stories, and numerous scripts for Hollywood and radio. Today he is respected as one of America's most important and original authors.

Dashiell Hammett

Author Biography

Born in 1894 in Saint Mary's County, Maryland, Samuel Dashiell Hammett grew up in Philadelphia and then Baltimore. He attended the Baltimore Polytechnic Institute, dropping out at age fourteen to help his family financially. That led to a series of positions, including store clerk, newsboy, machine operator, and stevedore. Eventually, he became an operative for the Pinkerton Detective Agency, a nationwide franchise.

Hammett served as an ambulance clerk during World War I. During the war, he contracted influenza, which affected his health for the rest of his life. Returning to civilian life, he settled in San Francisco, the city that has become associated with him through his works. Hammett married Josephine Dolan, a nurse he met while recuperating, in 1921. From 1922 to 1926, most of his living was made writing copy for advertisements. He also worked part-time for the Pinkerton agency, when his health allowed.

His first short story was published in 1923. After that, he published detective stories regularly. His first novel, *Red Harvest*, was published in 1929, followed by *The Dain Curse* that same year, and *The Maltese Falcon* the year after. In all, he wrote only a handful of novels, concentrating his efforts on short stories and screenplays. The residual payments from radio and film spin-offs of *The Maltese Falcon* and his 1934 novel *The Thin Man* supported him financially.

In the mid-1930s, Hammett began an affair with famed playwright Lillian Hellman, who was to be his true love for the rest of his life. He divorced Josephine in 1937. He became active in the Communist party in the 1930s, when many other writers did. During World War II, Hammett, despite failing health and severe alcoholism, served as a sergeant in the Aleutian Islands, editing an army newspaper.

When he returned home after the war, his health was ruined, his writing was infrequent, and he was subject to persecution by the country's growing anti-Communist sentiment. In 1951, Hammett went to prison for five months when he refused to testify in a trial against four Communists charged with conspiracy. He was blacklisted and unable to sell his works; in addition, the Internal Revenue Service attached his income to collect back taxes owed. After his release, he taught in New York at the Jefferson School of Social Science. Hammett died of lung cancer in 1961.

Plot Summary

Chapter 1: Spade & Archer

The Maltese Falcon begins when a beautiful woman, who gives her name as "Miss Wonderly," comes into the Spade & Archer Detective Agency and who wants to have a man named Floyd Thursby followed. Miles Archer, one of the partners in the firm, agrees with a lecherous grin to help Miss Wonderly personally.

Chapter 2: Death in the Fog

Sam Spade is phoned in the middle of the night and told that Miles Archer has been shot dead. He goes to the scene of the crime and then phones his secretary, Effie Perine, and tells her to break the news to Archer's widow, Iva. When he returns to his apartment, he is met by two policemen, who ask if he knows anything about the death of Archer or the subsequent shooting of Thursby.

Chapter 3: Three Women

When Spade arrives at his office the next morning, Iva Archer is there. They are having an affair. Effie later tells him that Iva had been out when Effie arrived at her house in the middle of

Media Adaptations

- The first screen adaptation of *The Maltese Falcon* was the film *Dangerous Female* (1931). It was directed by Roy Del Ruth and stars Ricardo Cortez as Sam Spade and Bebe Daniels as "Ruth Wonderly."

- Another adaptation was made in 1936, as *Satan Met a Lady*. Starring Bette Davis and Warren William, this version gives Dashiell Hammett credit for his novel but alters the characters and situations: In it, detective Ted Shayne is hired by Valerie Purvis to locate a ram's horn covered with precious jewels. It was directed by William Dieterle and is available on videocassette from Warner Home Video.

- The 1941 film of *The Maltese Falcon* is one of the most influential Hollywood movies ever made, defining the detective picture for generations to come. It is noted for its close adherence to Hammett's original dialogue, its near-perfect casting, and for being the first film in legendary director John Houston's long and distinguished career. Starring Humphrey Bogart, Mary Astor, Sidney Greenstreet, Peter Lorre, and Elisha Cook Jr., the film is available on DVD and VHS from Warner.

- The 1974 film *The Black Bird* parodied the *The Maltese Falcon*, presenting the son of Sam Spade, who has inherited his father's detective agency and set out on his own quest for the Maltese falcon. The film stars George Segal, Lee Patrick, and Elisha Cook Jr. (from the 1941 version), and was directed by David Giler. It is available on videocassette from Columbia/Tristar.

- In the 1982 film *Hammett*, directed by Wim Wenders and produced by Francis Ford Copella, the author becomes involved in investigating the disappearance of a cabaret singer. This fictional story is based in fact and recreates the world in which Hammett lived and traveled. Frederick Forrest plays Hammett. It is available on VHS from Warner.

---

the night. Spade goes to Miss Wonderly's hotel, only to find her gone. There is a message from her when he returns to the office, telling him to come to a different hotel, where she is registered under the name "Leblanc."

Chapter 4: The Black Bird

At her hotel, Spade finds out that she is neither Wonderly nor Leblanc, but Brigid O'Shaughnessy. She acts frightened and begs Spade to help her. She admits to having been untruthful and says she met Thursby in Hong Kong and counted on him for protection against enemies who might try to kill her.

After stopping at his attorney's office to ask how far he can go in refusing to answer the police's questions, Spade returns to his office. There he meets Joel Cairo, who offers him five thousand dollars to find a statue of a bird. Before leaving, Cairo draws a gun to make Spade sit still while he searches the office.

Chapter 5: The Levantine

Spade takes the pistol from Cairo, knocks him unconscious, and then searches his pockets. When Cairo comes to, he asserts that he is still willing to pay five thousand dollars for the statue. When Spade returns his belongings, Cairo aims the gun at him again and proceeds to search the office.

Chapter 6: The Undersized Shadow

That night, Spade goes to the Geary Theatre, having noted earlier that Cairo had tickets to the show there. He sees a young man following them. He sees the same youth later, on his way to meet Brigid, and loses him. When he mentions having met Cairo, she says that she must talk to him, but not at her place. They take a cab to Spade's apartment for a meeting. When they arrive, Iva Archer is waiting there for Spade and is upset when he says she cannot come upstairs with him.

Chapter 7: G in the Air

Waiting for Cairo, Spade tells Brigid a story about a man who, after a near-death experience, abandoned his wife and children, only to eventually settle down to the same kind of life with the same kind of family. Cairo arrives, and he and Brigid talk about how the black bird was smuggled out of Hong Kong. At one point she slaps him, and Spade intervenes. While he is standing between them, though, the doorbell rings.

At the door are Dundy and Polhaus, the two policemen who interrogated Spade on the night of Archer's murder. Spade refuses to let them in, until they hear Cairo inside screaming for help.

Chapter 8: Horse Feathers

The two detectives find that Cairo has blood on his head. Brigid accuses him of attacking her, and Cairo accuses her and Spade of holding him prisoner. Just as the policemen are about to take everyone to jail, Spade laughs and says that it has all been a joke. His claim that he did it to trick the policemen angers Dundy, who punches him in the jaw. Enraged, Spade refuses to answer any more questions and insists that they leave. Cairo leaves with them.

Chapter 9: Brigid

Alone with Brigid O'Shaughnessy, Spade lies and says the apartment is still being watched by the boy he saw before. He insists that she tell him the truth about what is going on: She reveals some facts about having been to Marmora and Constantinople, but he still accuses her of lying. She pulls him down against her for a long kiss.

Chapter 10: The Belvedere Divan

In the morning, Spade sneaks out before Brigid wakes up and, with the key he found in her purse, goes to her hotel, where he finds a receipt showing that she rented it the month before. Returning with breakfast, he puts the key back before she knows it was gone. He takes her back to her hotel and then goes to Cairo's hotel. Waiting in the lobby, he sits next to the young man who has been tailing him and talks cheerfully. The young man takes a threatening tone, but Spade tells him to tell G. to call him. He then humiliates the young man by bringing the house detective over and asking him, "What do you let these cheap gunmen hang out in your lobby for, with their tools bulging in their clothes?" After the young man has been forced to leave, Cairo comes in and says that he has been interrogated by the police all night but that he stayed with the same story Spade made up in his apartment.

Spade returns to his office and learns that G. has tried to reach him. Brigid is there, afraid because her apartment has been searched. Spade arranges for her to stay with Effie, his secretary.

Chapter 11: The Fat Man

Mr. Gutman calls Spade and tells him to come to his hotel. Iva Archer comes to Spade and says that she sent the police to his apartment, jealous of the other woman she saw. He tells her that lying to the police might be illegal and sends her to his lawyer, Sid Wise.

Gutman is a cheerful fat man who is very interested in finding the black bird. He is amiable, yet unwilling to tell Spade any details about the value of the bird or why it is interesting to so many people. At the end, the friendly conversation turns hostile. Spade stands up, throws his glass down so that it breaks, and shouts that he will not deal with Gutman unless he is told the truth.

Chapter 12: Merry-Go-Round

Spade's attitude in the elevator while leaving Gutman's suite reveals that his anger was just a bluff. He stops at Sid Wise's office and finds out what Iva said about her whereabouts on the night Archer was killed. At the office, Effie says that Brigid never arrived at her house. Spade hunts down the cabdriver who drove her. The cabdriver says that after picking up a newspaper, she asked to be dropped off at the Ferry Building.

Wilmer, the tough young man, is waiting for Spade at his office building. He leads Spade to Gutman's hotel at gunpoint, but before going into the suite, Spade takes his guns away from him.

Chapter 13: The Emperor's Gift

Gutman tells Spade the history of the Maltese falcon: how it was created as a present for Emperor Charles V in 1530 but disappeared in transit, showing up in various places over the course of centuries. He himself came on the trail seventeen years earlier, following it from one place to another, up to a Russian named Kemidov, in Constantinople. Gutman sent Brigid and Thursby to get it from the Russian, and they never brought it back. Spade says that he can get the bird for Gutman in a few days, but while they are talking, Gutman receives a secret message. He drugs Spade's drink, and as Spade loses consciousness, he feels Wilmer kick him in the face.

Chapter 14: La Paloma

Spade returns to his office where Effie tends to his bruise, and he offers to see her cousin, a history professor, about Gutman's tale about the Maltese falcon. He goes around to the hotels and cannot find Brigid or Gutman. At Cairo's hotel he has the house detective let him into the room, where he finds that the piece of the newspaper regarding ship arrivals is missing. Checking against another newspaper, he notes that the ship *La Paloma* is coming from Hong Kong, the last place the search for the falcon stopped. Effie returns to the office and says that she saw *La Paloma* ablaze in the harbor.

Chapter 15: Every Crackpot

Spade has lunch with Detective-sergeant Tom Polhaus and then meets with District Attorney Bryan, who tries out various theories about the murders, including one that has Thursby killed by rivals of the mobster he used to work for. Spade ends the interview by declaring that he will find the killers and give them to the authorities.

Chapter 16: The Third Murder

Spade meets with a prospective new client, talks to his lawyer about the district attorney, and then goes out to find Brigid. When he returns, he tells Effie that Brigid had been to the *La Paloma*, along with Gutman and Cairo. The ship's captain, Jacobi, met with them all in his cabin and then left the ship with them around midnight. As Spade is telling the story, a man comes into the office, staggers a few steps, and then falls to the floor. It is Jacobi, and he has a parcel in his arms that contains the Maltese falcon. At the same time, a call comes from Brigid O'Shaughnessy, who says that she is in trouble and needs Spade's help. Spade takes the package, tells Effie to phone the police about the dead man, but not to mention the falcon or the phone call.

Chapter 17: Saturday Night

Spade checks the parcel at a locker at a bus terminal, mails the key to his post office box, and then goes to Gutman's suite, where he finds Gutman's daughter, Rhea, drugged. He helps her walk around to stay awake, and she tells him that Brigid has been taken to an address in a faraway suburb. He goes to that address and finds it empty and showing no sign that anyone has been there recently. Returning to Gutman's hotel, he finds that Rhea left before the ambulance that he called for her could arrive. He stops to talk to Effie at her house and then returns home. Brigid meets him out on the street, and when he brings her inside his apartment, Gutman, Cairo, and Wilmer are there—with guns.

Chapter 18: The Fall Guy

Spade expresses pleasure at seeing them so that he can sell them the falcon. Gutman gives him an envelope with ten thousand dollars in it, which is less than they had talked about, but, as he explains, actual money is worth more than talk. As a condition for selling the falcon, Spade insists that they have to provide a fall guy, so that the police can consider the murders solved. At first, his suggestion that they provide Wilmer is met with derision, but after he explains his case, Gutman and Cairo help him knock Wilmer unconscious.

Chapter 19: The Russian's Hand

Spade has Gutman explain the details about how Thursby and Jacobi were killed. Gutman goes through the envelope with ten thousand dollars, which Brigid has been holding, and only finds nine thousand-dollar bills: Spade takes Brigid into the bathroom and makes her take off all of her clothes, eventually coming to the decision that Gutman has palmed the missing bill in order to make him distrust her. In the meantime, Wilmer escapes.

When morning comes, Effie picks up the falcon at the bus station and brings it to Spade's apartment. Gutman is excited, until he scratches away the black enamel coating and finds out that it is not gold but lead. He comes to the conclusion that the Russian in Constantinople must have substituted a fake bird for the real one, and he extends invitations to Cairo, Brigid, and Spade to join him in going after it. Cairo accepts, and they leave.

Chapter 20: If They Hang You

Spade immediately calls the police and tells them all that he knows about the Maltese falcon, the murders, and the suspects who are escaping. Then he talks with Brigid, explaining that he knows that she must be the one who killed Miles Archer. She tells him that if he loved her, it would not matter, and he admits that he actually might but that there are too many reasons on the other side of the equation to make love matter much. When the police arrive, they tell Spade that they caught up with the others just as Wilmer was in the process of killing Gutman. Spade turns Brigid O'Shaughnessy over to them.

The next morning, Spade arrives at the office to find that his faithful secretary, Effie, is angry at him for turning on Brigid. When he enters his private office, Iva is there, and the novel ends with his preparing to face her again.

Characters

Iva Archer

Before the novel began, while Miles Archer was still alive, Sam Spade was having an affair with his wife, Iva. After Miles's death, Spade goes to lengths to avoid her. Iva asks Spade if he killed Miles so that he could marry her, an idea that Spade finds humorous. When she sees him with Brigid O'Shaughnessy, Iva becomes jealous and sends the police to his apartment. Spade convinces her that she could be in trouble for giving the police false information, and he sends her to talk to his lawyer for advice, giving him the chance to find out, through the lawyer, what Iva was doing around the time of Miles's death.

Miles Archer

A partner in the Spade and Archer detective agency, Miles, leering wolfishly at Brigid O'Shaughnessy, offers to handle her case personally and is lured to his death because of his lechery. He dies forgetting his better instincts and behaving inappropriately as a detective, letting a pretty girl, Brigid, lure him up a dark alley, where she shoots him. Spade has no fondness for his dead partner, remembering that he "was a louse. I found that out the first week we were in business together and I meant to kick him out as soon as the year was up."

Phil Archer

Phil is the brother of Miles. Although he does not appear in the novel, Phil Archer is instrumental in the plot: When he finds out that Spade was having an affair with Iva, Phil suspects that Spade might have had a motive for killing Miles, and he tells it to the police.

Joel Cairo

Cairo is frequently referred to as "the Levantine," referring to the eastern Mediterranean area he appears to have come from. He is described as effeminate in the way he dresses and in his behavior. From his tender concern for Wilmer and from references to a "boy" he had in Constantinople, it is inferred that Cairo is probably homosexual. He originally hires Spade to find the Maltese falcon, but only after searching Spade's office at gunpoint. From the way that Gutman describes Cairo, it is clear that, when the situation requires it, he can be deadly. In the end, after losing his temper with Gutman, Cairo decides to join Gutman in continuing to travel the globe looking for the falcon.

Ted Christy

Christy, Effie Perine's cousin, is a professor of history at the University of California at Berkeley. Spade sends Effie to him to confirm whether the facts of the falcon story are plausible.

Wilmer Cook

Formally known as Gutman's "secretary," Wilmer is a young man who tries to be tough and intimidating, a facade that Spade through verbal and physical attacks makes difficult to maintain. When Wilmer is trying to act cool in the lobby of Cairo's hotel, Spade points him out to the hotel detective, who asks him to leave. Before entering Gutman's hotel suite, Spade takes Wilmer's guns away from him, telling him, "This will put you in solid with your boss." After convincing Gutman and Cairo that they should give Wilmer up to the police, Spade punches him and knocks him unconscious. Wilmer's hatred for Spade projects out toward other people. There is some indication, from the way that Cairo talks gently to him, that he and Cairo may once have had a romantic relationship, but Wilmer shouts obscenities at him. In the end, the police report that Wilmer killed Gutman, a father figure to him, with multiple shots.

Lieutenant Dundy

Of the two policemen who repeatedly come to visit Spade to find out what he knows about the events related to Miles Archer's death, Dundy is the unsympathetic one, constantly looking for ways to have Spade's detective's license revoked or even to have him arrested.

Mr. Flitcraft

Spade tells Brigid O'Shaughnessy about a case he worked on as a detective in Seattle: Mr. Flitcraft, nearly killed by a falling beam from a skyscraper, ran away from his family to embrace life. After a few years, when the fear of death no longer haunted him, he remarried a similar woman and began a similar life in another nearby town.

Mr. Freed

Mr. Freed works at a desk in the St. Mark's Hotel, where Brigid is registered as Miss Wonderly at the beginning of the novel. He is an acquaintance who gives Spade information and is discreet enough never to mention it to anyone else.

Casper Gutman

Gutman enters the novel as an almost mythical figure, as Cairo and Brigid refer to him in conversation by drawing the first letter of his name in the air, to keep his identity from Spade. When he does meet Spade, Gutman turns out to be a jolly, affable man, taken to frequent exclamations about one aspect or another of Spade's character that he admires. He takes a paternal stance toward Wilmer, the gun-toting youth who works for him, while his own daughter, Rhea, is never seen anywhere near him.

Gutman is obsessed with finding the Maltese falcon, having pursued it across the globe for seventeen years. He is willing to devote still more years toward his quest. In spite of his cheerful demeanor, he is perfectly willing to kill or betray anyone who stands in the way of his quest.

Rhea Gutman

Gutman's beautiful seventeen-year-old daughter only appears in one scene in the book: After Spade has been called to the Alexandria Hotel to help Brigid O'Shaughnessy, he finds Rhea there, allegedly drugged, scratching her own stomach with a pin to keep awake. He later finds out that, after sending him off to a bogus address, she quickly exited the hotel, not drugged at all.

Captain Jacobi

The captain of the ship *La Paloma*, he carried the falcon from Hong Kong for Brigid O'Shaughnessy. When he delivers the bird to Spade's office, he has already been shot several times, and he dies on the office floor.

Miss Leblanc

See Brigid O'Shaughnessy

Luke

Luke is the house detective at the Hotel Belvedere, where Joel Cairo is staying. He keeps Spade informed of Cairo's activities, and when Spade points out that Wilmer is loitering in the hotel lobby, he chases the gunman out.

Brigid O'Shaughnessy

Brigid O'Shaughnessy originally hires Spade and Archer with a phony story about trying to find a man who ran off with her younger sister. She gives them a phony name, Miss Wonderly. Her objective is to have her accomplice in stealing the falcon, Floyd Thursby, followed. After Thursby and the detective following him, Miles Archer, are shot, she turns to Sam Spade for protection, telling him more and more about the falcon and why it is so valuable, but never fully revealing all that she knows. She is manipulative, telling Spade several times how much she needs him but then disappearing

from his protection when she sees a chance to attain the falcon without his help. In the end, Spade finds out that O'Shaughnessy herself killed Miles Archer and, although he believes that he may in fact be in love with her, turns her over to the police.

Effie Perine

Effie is Sam Spade's secretary, confidante, and, in some ways, surrogate lover. She knows enough about Spade's tastes to convince him to talk to Brigid at the start of the story by pointing out how good-looking the potential client is; later, she champions Brigid, telling Spade that her women's intuition has convinced her that Brigid is a good woman; at the end, when she finds out that he has turned Brigid over to the police, she turns against Spade in a way that she has not throughout the book. Spade's interactions with Effie frequently include the kind of physical contact and terms of endearment that people of contemporary society find inappropriate in a business situation.

Tom Polhaus

Polhaus is Spade's friend on the police force, a detective-sergeant. When he and Dundy interrogate Spade, it is Polhaus who asks Spade to behave reasonably, interceding between the two men when they start fighting.

Sam Spade

Spade is the hero of the novel. He is a veteran detective, telling a story at one point about a case he handled several years earlier when he was with a large agency in Seattle. He is defiant toward the law, but careful about just how defiant he can be without endangering his practice, consulting with his lawyer when necessary to make sure that he is not putting himself in legal jeopardy. And he gives clients and potential clients the impression that he is willing to break the law if he has to in order to attain the results they need. As Spade points out late in the book, he finds it good for his reputation as a detective to project this impression of corruptibility.

Spade is cynical in his relations with women. Before the start of the novel, he has been having an affair with Iva Archer, the wife of his partner. When she finds herself free to marry him after Miles Archer's death, Spade makes it clear that he was just toying with her. He is in fact sick of Iva and angry when she manages to catch him alone. He never fully trusts Brigid O'Shaughnessy, forcing her to submit to a strip search in order to see if she has stolen some of the reward he has received for the Maltese falcon. Still, in spite of taking precautions against her possible betrayal, there are clear indications that he is in love with her.

The force that drives Sam Spade is a moral code that is more important than financial gain, power, or love. He has a sense of what is right and what is wrong, regardless of his personal feelings. He does, however, try to hide the fact that he is acting morally, preferring to explain away his actions as good business moves. Turning in Gutman and his crew, for instance, entails giving up the ten thousand dollars that they gave him, but he says that there is no other way to escape culpability in the crimes that they committed. In the end, though, after examining all of the reasons why it is right to send Brigid to jail, he cannot overcome his love for her without pointing out the bedrock moral rule that a man cannot let the murder of his partner go unpunished, even if it was a partner whom he detested.

Floyd Thursby

Thursby never appears in the novel. He is a hoodlum from St. Louis and Chicago, who met Brigid O'Shaughnessy in Hong Kong and helped her steal the Maltese falcon. In San Francisco, she hired Spade and Archer to follow him, assuming that Thursby would either be killed or scared away. He was killed by Wilmer to scare Brigid into giving up the falcon.

Sid Wise

Spade's lawyer is a member of the firm Wise, Merican, and Wise. Several times, Spade consults with him about whether actions he is considering are legal or could be prosecuted. Spade sends Iva Archer to Wise after she has given the police false information, saying that Wise will protect her legally. Later, Spade has Wise tell him what Iva has said.

Miss Wonderly

See Brigid O'Shaughnessy

Themes

Code of Honor

Throughout most of this novel, the protagonist, Sam Spade, seems to be too cynical to hold any deeply held convictions. His love life is defined early on by his affair with Iva Archer, the wife of his business partner, whom he openly detests. Financially, he seems perfectly willing to sell his services to whoever offers him the most money, at one point taking on both Joel Cairo and Brigid O'Shaughnessy as clients, even though their interests clearly conflict.

His encounters with the police and the district attorney imply that Spade is more interested in making sure that his business is not disturbed by the events surrounding Miles Archer's death than he is in seeing justice prevail.

And so it is a surprise when, at the end of the novel, Spade's behavior turns out to be directed by a code of honor that he understands clearly and respects. He seems frustrated and a little embarrassed when trying to explain to Brigid O'Shaughnessy why he cannot take the corrupt and easy solution, which would entail accepting the money that he has been given by the criminals and going on to live his life with the woman he loves. Most of his reasons for turning away from the easy solution are based in logic—the police would find out about his involvement in the affair anyway, and he would never be able to fully trust Brigid, no matter how much he might or might not love her. In the end, Spade's decision to turn Brigid in to the police comes down to one basic rule that he cannot bring himself to break: "When a man's partner is killed he's supposed to do something about it. It doesn't make any difference what you thought of him. He was your partner and you're supposed to do something about it." Spade's shift in diction, into the "you" perspective, indicates that he believes this to be an absolute law that applies to all cases at all times, regardless of individual circumstances.

Single-Mindedness

Most of the characters in this novel are motivated by the dual interests of greed and self-preservation. Joel Cairo, Brigid O'Shaughnessy, and even Sam Spade himself are intrigued with the untold wealth that is promised to come with the retrieval of the Maltese falcon, so long as the wealth will not come with the price of death or imprisonment. For Casper Gutman, though, the search for the falcon is so personal that it has become his identity. Having devoted the past seventeen years of his life traveling the globe and spending untold money on his quest, Gutman can imagine no other existence. For a moment, on finding that the falcon brought to San Francisco is just a leaden replica, Gutman allows despair to take over his usually cheerful optimism, but almost immediately he gathers his wits about himself and is ready to start off in search of the bird once again.

Although the novel gives little background about Gutman, Hammett makes it clear that his obsession with the falcon is the most important thing in his life by showing how callously he treats his family and surrogate family. He only seems aware of the

Topics For Further Study

- Research the development of detective work from the 1930s through today. How do the methods of a detective like Sam Spade relate to the methods of detectives today? What are the differences and similarities between the way private detectives conduct their work when compared with public detectives? How has modern forensic study changed the nature of detective work and solving crimes?

- Research the history, structure, and work of the Order of the Hospital of St. John of Jerusalem. Why do you think Hammett chose this organization as part of the motivation for the plot of *The Maltese Falcon*? How likely is it that the order might have given a jewel-encrusted falcon to the Emperor Charles V, as is mentioned in Hammett's novel?

- Sam Spade refuses to talk to the District Attorney, saying that he may be forced to testify before a grand jury or even a coroner's jury. Find out the legal status of witnesses before either of these two juries where you live, and prepare a report that outlines what Spade would be in for if either jury were convened in the deaths of Miles Archer and Floyd Thursby.

- After Spade, the second most famous American detective of the twentieth century could be Raymond Chandler's Philip Marlowe. Humphrey Bogart, who played Sam Spade in the acclaimed 1941 film adaptation of *The Maltese Falcon*, also played Marlowe five years later in the adaptation of Chandler's *The Big Sleep*. Watch both movies, and write a comparison/contrast paper about Bogart's acting styles in portraying these two different yet similar characters.

---

existence of his daughter, Rhea, when he is able to use her to distract Spade from getting the falcon before him; he is willing to put Rhea in legal and even physical jeopardy without a second thought. As Gutman explains to Wilmer, after offering to make him the "fall-guy" for the police: "I couldn't be any fonder of you if you were my own son; but—well, by Gad!—if you lose a son it's possible to get another—and there's only one Maltese falcon."

Homosexuality

The Maltese Falcon presents an acknowledgement of homosexuality that is rare in 1920s fiction, especially in mainstream popular fiction. There is no question that Joel Cairo is gay, a fact that is implied frequently throughout the novel, as when Brigid O'Shaughnessy laughingly suggests that the boy outside shadowing them might be "the one you had in Constantinople" or, even more pointedly, when Sam Spade asks Wilmer where Cairo is, referring to him as "the fairy."

Most of the references to Cairo's sexuality are derogatory stereotypes. Hammett describes him as an overly preened dandy, with "slightly plump hips," wearing fawn spats, chamois gloves, and "the fragrance of *chypre*." He gives Cairo dialogue such as "Oh, you big coward" and has him call for help with a "high and thin and shrill" voice. Still, Hammett offsets this offensive caricature by giving Cairo some degree of individual dignity as a criminal: He stands up to an all-night interrogation from the police without cracking, and he decides in the end that his attraction to Wilmer, who must be turned over to the police, is less important than the profit he stands to make from the falcon. Cairo's homosexuality is mocked throughout the novel, but as a man he is taken seriously.

Style

Antihero

While a traditional hero might be counted on to do the right thing for the common good, the protagonist of *The Maltese Falcon*, Sam Spade, responds to every situation by examining what he himself stands to gain from it. Spade is willing to betray his friends, and he has an affair with his business partner's wife. He does not work within the law, but checks in with his lawyer regularly to see how far outside of the law he can go. And he is an untrusting lover, accusing Brigid O'Shaughnessy of duplicity the moment that the falcon is discovered to be fake. Hammett establishes his questionable moral position in the novel's first paragraph, describing him as looking "rather pleasantly like a blond Satan."

In the end, Spade explains to Brigid O'Shaughnessy that his seemingly amoral behavior is just a ruse that he uses to draw criminals to him, which is good for the detective business. He behaves heroically, forsaking the money and the girl who is begging for his support, in favor of a higher ideal. The novel successfully mocks traditional heroic values and at the same time reinforces them.

Metaphor

The Maltese falcon that is at the center of this story is described as being made of gold and jewel encrusted, making it very valuable, with a unique history that makes its value inestimable. Readers never see the real Maltese falcon in the story, but its importance drives the plot ahead. It is a metaphor for Gutman's obsession, Cairo's greed, O'Shaughnessy's duplicity, and Spade's curiosity.

Film director Alfred Hitchcock is said to have coined the phrase "the MacGuffin" to represent the object in a film or novel that all of the characters are seeking. The object can be something of monetary value, like the Maltese falcon, or of strategic value, such as top-secret government documents. Sometimes, novels never even tell readers what is in the briefcase or vial or envelope that is being hunted. The reason that an otherwise irrelevant term like "MacGuffin" is used is that the desired object usually is irrelevant, in and of itself, becoming important only when it is interpreted as a metaphor for the characters' motives and desires.

Historical Context

Prohibition and Gangsters

Sale of alcohol had been illegal in the United States since 1920, when the 18th Amendment was ratified and signed into law. Congress passed the National Prohibition act, also referred to as the Volstead Act, to provide law enforcement agencies with the means to enforce the ban. While the intent of the amendment was to hinder the use and abuse of alcohol, it ended up having the unintended effect of creating a profitable industry for criminals to rise to power.

As federal agents struggled to control the production, sale, and transportation of alcohol, those who were willing to take chances and oppose the law saw great profits. As a result, criminals found it in their best interests to organize their distribution networks to regional chains. Although illegal, liquor became easily available, most notably in "speakeasies," which were underground nightclubs. Profits were high enough to absorb the costs incurred when federal agents raided speakeasies and confiscated or destroyed liquor supplies, and local law enforcement agencies were bribed to make sure that such raids were infrequent.

Each town had its criminal empire. Chicago, for instance, spawned the most famous gangster of the time, Al Capone, who rose to power in 1925. In the next two years, he made 60 million dollars through the sale of liquor alone. Criminal syndicates like Capone's, and dozens of others like it across the land, were manned by low-level foot soldiers and those who patterned themselves after the gangsters. By the late twenties the gangster image was well known in American popular culture. Hammett gives Floyd Thursby, murdered early in *The Maltese Falcon*, the background of a typical gang member of the time. Wilmer Cook, the young henchman for Casper Gutman, clearly patterns his menacing stance after pop culture images of hoodlums of the time, an image that Sam Spade openly mocks.

The Great Depression

The Maltese Falcon was published at a time when America needed escapist literature to deal with the harsh economic realities that had suddenly come crashing down, first on the nation and then on the whole world. During the 1920s, the economy had sailed along at a comfortable rate, with stock prices climbing year by year. In the absence of any major international conflict, the overall mood was one of peace and prosperity. That changed on October 29, 1929, just months before this novel was printed. On that day, known as Black Tuesday, the stock market lost about 12 percent of its value, which, combined with massive losses the day before, started a downward trend that continued for the next three years. By the end of November, investors had lost 100 billion dollars; by mid-1932 the stock market was worth only 11 percent of its value before the crash.

The instability in the market drove America into one of the worst depressions it has ever

Compare & Contrast

- **1930:** It is considered acceptable and even friendly for an employer like Sam Spade to address an employee like Effie Perine with terms of affection such as "angel" and "precious."

  Today: The use of such terms, usually associated with romance, is socially and legally forbidden, as they might be used to pressure an employee into an unwanted relationship.

- **1930:** Steamship passage from Hong Kong to San Francisco can take weeks but is the most common way of travel.

  Today: The trip from Hong Kong to San Francisco can be done by jet plane in a matter of hours.

- **1930:** Hotels have house detectives who keep an eye on the guests to make sure that they are not bringing illegal activities into the hotel. Usually, house detectives are retired policemen.

  Today: Computerized information systems make it easier for ordinary desk clerks to check background information more thoroughly than house detectives were ever able to do.

- **1930:** Americans think of private detectives as being on the border between legal and illegal activities.

  Today: The private eye mythos still appears sometimes on television, but people generally do not believe the job to be as glamorous as it once was presented to be.

---

experienced. Banks and businesses closed, causing ordinary people to lose both their jobs and their savings. Unemployment went from around 6 percent before the crash to nearly 25 percent in the 1930s. The government tried policies meant to stimulate the economy, but real economic growth was stalled until the start of World War II, in 1939, when America provided munitions for the warring countries before being drawn into the conflict itself.

Critical Overview

When *The Maltese Falcon* was first published, Dashiell Hammett was little known outside of the small, specific world of crime fiction. This is the book that changed that and brought his name to the attention of reviewers of literary works. For instance, William Curtis, reviewing the book in *Town & Country*, an upscale leisure publication, admitted, after comparing Hammett to literary figures of the time (including Ernest Hemingway):

> I think Mr. Hammett has something quite as definite to say, quite as decided an impetus to give the course of newness in the development of the American tongue, as any man now writing. Of course, he's gone about it the wrong way to attract respectful attention from the proper sources. . . . He has not been picked up by any of the foghorn columnists. He's only a writer of murder mystery stories.

In his review for the *New York Herald Tribune*, Will Cuppy wrote, "This department announces a new and pretty huge enthusiasm, to wit: Dashiell Hammett. Moreover, it would not surprise us one whit if Mr. Hammett should turn out to be the Great American Mystery Writer." The humor magazine *Judge* pronounced the writing in *The Maltese Falcon* to be "better than Hemingway."

By 1934, the novel was so recognized for its literary merit that it was included in the Modern Library collection. Hammett's subsequent novels—*The Glass Key* and *The Thin Man*—were championed by reviewers, but they also found more flaws in them than they did in *The Maltese Falcon*, which remained the high point of his literary output.

Hammett's reputation remained static throughout the 1930s and 1940s, as he went year after year without producing another novel, though interest in *The Maltese Falcon* surged when the film version

The Maltese Falcon *was adapted in 1941 into an Oscar-nominated film starring Humphrey Bogart as Sam Spade, Mary Astor as Brigid O'Shaughnessy, Peter Lorre as Joel Cairo, and Sydney Greenstreet as Kasper Gutman*

starring Humphrey Bogart was released in 1941. In the 1950s, Hammett was sent to jail for his association with Communists, and the House Un-American Activities Committee actively worked to keep his works banned from libraries. By the 1960s, though, the anti-Communist hysteria was forgotten, and soon after Hammett's death in 1961 the reading public returned to him. In the early 1980s, in particular, there came a slew of biographies and critical studies of him, firmly ensconcing Hammett's name into the halls of American literature. As the great crime novelist Ross MacDonald took time to observe in his 1981 autobiography, *Self-Portrait: Ceaselessly into the Past*, "I think *The Maltese Falcon*, with its astonishingly imaginative energy persisting undiminished after a third of a century, is tragedy of a new kind, deadpan tragedy."

Criticism

David Kelly

Kelly is an instructor of literature and creative writing at two colleges in Illinois. In this essay, Kelly traces the facts that can be deduced about

Sam Spade's true personality from his interactions with characters who are not involved in the Maltese falcon caper.

In *The Maltese Falcon*, Dashiell Hammett has produced a detective novel format that is so compelling that it has been done and redone over and over. It is a pattern that any moviegoer or television watcher is familiar with by now: The detective, Sam Spade, finds himself pulled into a web of intrigue surrounding a mysterious, valuable object that brings three murders to his doorstep. Readers follow the story because they want to know who committed the killings and where the valuable black bird is. Keeping them interested is the work that a mystery story is supposed to do. What elevates this book from being a good read to being literature, though, is the interest that Hammett shows in Sam Spade's personality and the way that he provokes readers to wonder about it. In the end, the mystery of the man turns out to be more compelling than any questions about who did what, with what, and how.

Who is Sam Spade? At the end of *The Maltese Falcon*, readers find out that he is not the person that he has pretended to be all along. He proves to be a man driven by a sense of honor, which he has kept hidden throughout, a man who has known the answer to who killed his partner, Miles Archer, but who has kept on pursuing clues anyway, allowing himself to be seduced by Archer's killer, but not so far taken in by love that he is willing to let the woman he loves escape justice. He is a man with an agenda so deeply buried under his placid demeanor that it is very likely that he himself is not aware of it.

In addition to Spade's probable lack of self-awareness, Hammett makes his personality even more difficult to understand with the way that he tells this story. The third-person narrative voice is distant, never allowing access to what Spade really thinks. Readers never enter into his mind. Although Spade's job is to observe the other characters and surmise from their behaviors what they are thinking, he applies no such scrutiny to his own actions. Without access to his thoughts, readers find themselves, at the end of the book, knowing the least about the character that they thought they knew the best.

Deception is a tool in the detective's arsenal. Without access to his thoughts, readers can be deceived just as much as the characters that Spade is trying to fool. For instance, when Spade walks out of the fat man's suite at the end of chapter 11, shouting and threatening, readers have no way of knowing that he has not actually lost his cool until the next chapter when he sighs in relief that his posturing has gone so well. He shows similar temper with Lieutenant Dundy and District Attorney Bryan, using the pretense of emotion to leverage the situation. Over the course of the novel, he hides from Brigid O'Shaughnessy what might be the most important fact of all: that he knows, and probably has known from the moment he surveyed the crime scene, that she and only she could have killed Miles Archer.

Of course, this detective story would hardly be worth following through to the end if readers knew early on that Spade had identified O'Shaughnessy as the murderer of his partner and that all of her whispery pleas for his devotion and trust were wasted in the air. It is good for the story to have Spade withhold his knowledge. In the context of the story, though, he never adequately answers why it was better to hold this knowledge back than to tell it to the police and thereby wash his hands of the whole affair. He says that it is his duty to turn in the killer of his partner, and that is what Spade eventually does, but Hammett does not make clear whether that is Spade's intention all along or something that he settles on at the last minute. Spade's

> **Spade's ambivalence is understandable—he is, after all, a man in love—but the fact that even he might not know his own intentions combines with Hammett's narrative distance to make Spade the darkest mystery in the book."**

ambivalence is understandable—he is, after all, a man in love—but the fact that even he might not know his own intentions combines with Hammett's narrative distance to make Spade the darkest mystery in the book.

The best way to separate Spade's true self from the various bluffs that he goes through to track down the Maltese falcon is to look at how he is with characters who are not even involved with the affair of the black bird. There are few people in the book who do not relate to the search for the falcon, which makes them exceptional when they do appear.

In order of least importance, the first of these characters would be the theater manager who hires Spade in a quick, one-paragraph scene in chapter 16. Spade is in the thick of his search for the falcon, and, in fact, comes into possession of the object of everyone's murderous interests later in that same chapter. But he takes time to listen to the man and accept a retainer from him. This small touch is seldom noticed. The man is so insignificant to the story that Hammett does not even bother to describe him, beyond referring to him as "swart." Still, his significance to understanding Spade's character is great. In taking the man's retainer, Spade makes it clear that, this deeply into the case, with the police pressuring him with jail and the fat man offering him unimaginable riches, he does not expect his life to change much. It might even be unconscious, but Spade behaves as if he sees neither wealth nor jail in his immediate future. This affirms his behavior at the end, when he tells O'Shaughnessy that he would still have turned her in if the falcon had been real, and he had collected his ten thousand dollars.

A more significant indicator of Spade's true psychological state is the story that he tells

What Do I Read Next?

- Fans of this book will see an entirely different kind of detective in debonair Nick Charles, the hero of Hammett's next and last novel, *The Thin Man* (1934).

- While Sam Spade is a rugged individualist, Hammett's previous detective character, The Continental Op, was a pudgy, nameless operative of the Continental Detective Agency. He is the protagonist of two earlier novels, *Red Harvest* and *The Dain Curse*, both published in 1929.

- Brian Lawson's novel *Chasing Sam Spade* (2002), published by Booklocker Press, presents a man who goes to San Francisco to investigate the murder of his father, only to become wrapped up in a web of intrigue with clues taken from Hammett's novel. The city's atmosphere plays a strong role.

- The writer who is most often associated with Hammett is Raymond Chandler, whose stories of Los Angeles detective Phillip Marlowe have a sense of hardboiled fatalism and a verbal style that approaches Hammett's skill. Of the Marlowe books, *The Big Sleep* (1939) is the most popular, possibly because Humphrey Bogart played Marlowe in the 1946 film.

- Many crime-novel connoisseurs consider James Ellroy to be the modern-day heir to Hammett and Chandler. Of his novels, *L.A. Confidential* (1997) is often singled out for its seamless storytelling and its dark vision. It tells the story of three policemen involved in a scandal-ridden case in Los Angeles in the 1950s.

- Though many literary studies have been made of Hammett's life, a more personal look at him, including family photos, was done by his daughter Jo Hammett in her book *A Daughter Remembers* (2001).

O'Shaughnessy in chapter 7 about the man named Flitcraft, who, having been nearly hit by a falling girder, abandoned his wife and infant child, traveling the world for a few years before settling down to almost the exact same situation that he left. The story is mostly notable because of its irrelevance to what is going on in Spade's life at the time that he chooses to tell it: He is falling in love and on the verge of finding out about the mystery of a lifetime. It takes a strong man to rein himself in and put the events surrounding him into perspective. Literary critics can debate whether the moral of the story is fatalism (that a man is going to be what his destiny dictates, despite moments of awareness) or freedom (that Flitcraft, shaken by the awareness of death, realized that his former life had been just fine). The important thing is that Spade focuses on this story when he feels the falcon intrigue drawing him in. "I don't think he even knew he had settled back naturally into the same groove he had jumped out of in Tacoma," Spade explains to O'Shaughnessy, who is barely listening and certainly not ascribing any importance to this weird little tale. "But that's the part of it I always liked." As with the episode of the swart man, it seems that, beyond wealth or love, what Spade expects of himself is consistency.

And that is why, in the end, he resigns himself to accepting Iva Archer as a part of his life. The wife of his murdered partner, Iva appears to be involved in the falcon case in some way, but she really is not. She is an independent entity, a constant factor that was in Spade's life before the case started and one that will be there when it is over. When Spade finds out that Iva was not home on the night Miles was shot, he has her story checked out in a roundabout way, having her tell her alibi to his lawyer, who in turn, unethically, tells it to Spade. He still does not seem convinced, but expresses satisfaction that the police will believe it. But Spade's own skepticism of Iva's story is suspicious: If he is not convinced that Iva was where she said she was when Miles was killed, then why is he so certain of Brigid O'Shaughnessy's guilt? Or, conversely, if Spade knows that

O'Shaughnessy killed his partner, then why does he show such interest in Iva's whereabouts? Throughout the story, Iva jealously stakes out Spade's apartment and his office, and he tries his best to avoid her. Apparently, though, he is curious about what she does when she is not around to bother him. The man of conviction loses the money and the girl—this is the price of having convictions—but he ends up in the arms of a woman that he claims to detest. This might just be bad luck, but it could also be the fate that Spade, consciously or unconsciously, wants. He might realize that, whatever he does to escape, he, like Flitcraft, will end up with Iva or someone like her.

If Hammett had given more direct access to Spade's thoughts, the story would have been less interesting, and the lead character would certainly have been less compelling. Sam Spade seems to be a complex, interesting man trying to hold onto a simple, uninteresting life, even as he stands in the middle of a hurricane of love and intrigue. Readers do not know what he is thinking; Spade himself might not even know, in any depth, what motivates him. The important thing is that he is so well realized in what he says and does that readers can recognize his fate and accept that it is right for him.

Source: David Kelly, Critical Essay on *The Maltese Falcon*, in *Novels for Students*, Thomson Gale, 2005.

William Marling

In the following essay, Marling uses a then-and-now approach to analyze how Hammett weaved various period and stylistic references into his characters and their actions in The Maltese Falcon.

The Maltese Falcon is our greatest detective novel, but its status as such is the product of a continuing cultural consensus. When published it announced a new style, one adopted widely, which we, viewing it in retrospect, have come to accept as *the* style of the period. In other words, *The Maltese Falcon* is a classic not only because of its literary quality and response to its age, but because when we look back on it we recognize the origins of what we have become. Alternate genealogies are always available, but we do not see ourselves in *The Benson Murder Case* or *Little Caesar* or even in Dashiell Hammett's other work as we do in this novel.

Recently the style of *The Maltese Falcon* has been questioned, a sign that the consensus is no longer solid. James Guetti, in his instructive 1982 essay in *Raritan,* "Aggressive Reading: Detective Fiction and Realistic Narrative," examined the prose of Hammett, Chandler and Macdonald from

> " The emotional and behavioral model that is Sam Spade defines itself most vehemently in opposition to the 'sap.'"

the paired perspectives of information theory and reader response criticism. He found Hammett's style, especially his descriptions of characters, "provoking, even irritating" because they are a "collection of visual fragments."

> We may know from information theory that the information present in any situation is proportional to the "resistance" of that situation. We may feel "informed" while reading Hammett's prose, then, because all these separate items, all these details, compose a resistance to our reading efforts, and our response to that resistance is to increase those efforts. We try harder and harder to smooth the story out, to break it down to something hardier and neater than this list of details, to reduce it in volume by somehow changing its state from a mixture of separate things to a more homogeneous solution.

Guetti does not ask questions about readers of 1929 or their horizon of reading expectations. Given his approach, that is perfectly acceptable. He is not interested in questions of genre or the way in which emerging and declining styles mediate one another. He is a "modern reader," whose critique suggests that we no longer read Hammett in a context that makes his style meaningful. Albeit indirectly, Guetti does the signal service of suggesting a discussion of the function of this style, and whether it has a relation to history.

The passage that most provokes and irritates Guetti is Hammett's introduction of the villain, Casper Gutman:

> The fat man was flabbily fat with bulbous pink cheeks and lips and chins and neck, with a great soft egg of a belly that was all his torso, and pendant cones for arms and legs. As he advanced to meet Spade all his bulbs rose and shook and fell separately with each step, in the manner of clustered soap-bubbles not yet released from the pipe through which they had been blown. His eyes, made small by fat puffs around them, were dark and sleek. Dark ringlets thinly covered his broad scalp. He wore a black cutaway coat, black vest, black satin Ascot tie holding a pinkish pearl, striped grey worsted trousers, and patent leather shoes.

Guetti's critique is out of sympathy: "It repeats itself dissonantly and insistently. . . . Its sentences lose their grammar and become lists . . . Its concern with explanatory clarity becomes overextended and boring. . . . And it is so intent upon its variation of detail that its construction becomes gratingly unvarying." In Guetti's estimate, this stylistic debacle exists to challenge the reader, to provide "resistance" to his aggressive drive to solve the mystery. The "mystery," in this sense, is some withheld feature of plot: who done it.

Surely this is to impute to Hammett, the advertising copywriter, a disinclination to meet his readers on their own terms that would have doomed him to the same obscurity that has claimed S. S. Van Dine. We know that these descriptions were deemed by such literary lighting-rods as Dorothy Parker to be the essence of Hammett's modernity. There is little testimony that Hammett was read by readers who placed their wits in competition with his. Unfortunately the cultural conflict that gave *The Maltese Falcon* its stylistic power has evaporated. A cluster of emerging design values and economic forms found crystallization in this novel, and we forget that it could ever have been otherwise.

From its opening words *The Maltese Falcon* concerns itself with what I will term the clash of the rough and the smooth in the domain of popular style. These design values are best illustrated by Hammett's own change from the rumpled, anonymous, fat Continental Op to an art nouveau detective:

> Sam Spade's jaw was long and bony, his chin a jutting v under the more flexible v of his mouth. His nostrils curved back to make another, smaller, v. His yellow-grey eyes were horizontal. The v motif was picked up again by thickish brows rising outward from twin creases above a hooked nose, and his pale brown hair grew down—from high flat temples—to a point on his forehead. He looked rather pleasantly like a blond satan.

As more than one scholar has noted, this is an impossible face. If you attempt to draw it, you have a design of V's that caricatures a devil. The point of opening the book with this description is that the unusual visual emphases relate the book to socioeconomic change immediately. The whiplash angles of Spade's face echo the most popular curvilinear motif of Art Nouveau, already familiar to the public visually, whether in the typography of Eugene Grasset and Otto Eckmann, the illustrations of Aubrey Bearsley or the industrial designs of Henri van de Velde and Hector Guimard. Charles Chaplin had already used this V-face on a villain in *Easy Street* (1917). It is by now well known that these artists and designers were adapting the organic, nature-based forms of Victorian picturesque design to the demands of modern industrial manufacture, which required functionality. They facilitated the coming triumph of Modernism by providing a brief period in which new products, for new ends, made by new processes, were given a hint of reassuring organic familiarity. Hammett, designing a new hero for new readers in a new era, suggests no less for his readers.

Hammett's opening description tells readers that Sam Spade is not a Victorian detective, not the Continental Op or Philo Vance. Spade is modern, seemingly amoral, but organic and familiar. What will be new is mediated by such conventional descriptions as the "steep-rounded slope of his shoulders [that] made his body seem almost conical—no broader than it was thick—and kept his freshly pressed grey suit from fitting very well." This appearance, along with his cigarette rolling when upset and occasional animal grunts and nervous sweats, gives Spade the organic familiarity of the past.

The function of representing the nakedly modern falls to his opposite number, Miss Wonderly (Brigid O'Shaughnessy), whose multiple names suggest her indefiniteness.

> She was tall and pliantly slender, *without angularity anywhere*. Her body was erect and high-breasted, her legs long, her hands and feet narrow. She wore two shades of blue that had been selected because of her eyes. The hair curling from under her blue hat was darkly red, her full lips more brightly red. White teeth glistened in the crescent her timid smile made. [emphasis added]

"Without angularity anywhere," "long," "narrow," "pliantly slender," and attired in red (hair and lips) and two shades of blue: could Brigid's glistening white teeth complete a pun on the national banner? Miss Wonderly is thoroughly modern: smooth, aerodynamic and painted in primary hues. Just as the newly designed typewriters, automobiles and telephones were *sheathed* by metal skins, her style is the smooth. Her interior processes—emotions, motives—are not visible. The faring of "Miss Wonderly," will soon be stripped away to reveal the less modern sounding Brigid O'Shaughnessy, a rough name whose ethnicity is an implicit critique of corrupt urban politics of the 1920s.

The visual styles of Spade and Wonderly are opposed within the first 300 words of *The Maltese Falcon*. The cultural context of this opposition is next:

> The tappity-tap and the thin bell and the muffled whir of Effie Perine's typewriting came through the closed door. Somewhere in a neighboring office a

power-driven machine vibrated dully. On Spade's desk a limp cigarette smouldered in a brass tray filled with the remains of limp cigarettes. Ragged grey flakes of cigarette-ash dotted the yellow top of the desk and the green blotter and the papers that were there. A buff-curtained window, eight or ten inches open, let in from the court a current of air faintly scented with ammonia. The ashes on the desk twitched and crawled in the current.

The modern workplace is the terrain to be contested. Its portrayal as ammonia-scented and ash-dotted dates to the 1890s and Ash Can School painters; its literary rendering, beginning with Stephen Crane and proceeding through the muck-raking journalists, became such a convention of the period that Scott Fitzgerald could depend on such a scene's implicit meaning (the Valley of Ashes) for *The Great Gatsby* (1925). By 1930 a few details of mechanization and the sensory texture of industrial life were sufficient to evoke the anxiety of technological change in the workplace.

In Spade and Wonderly then, the reader faces two styles of response to this anxiety. Miss Wonderly is completely identified with the stylistic values of the New, the Modern, and therefore to be suspected. Her stammering inarticulateness cues the reader: "Spade smiled and nodded as if he understood her, but pleasantly, as if nothing serious were involved." With his familiarizing look of the past, Spade wants her to begin "as far back as you can." Miss Wonderly anxiously questions her own actions—"I shouldn't have done that, should I?" "That is what he would tell me anyhow, isn't it?" The reader cannot trust her because, while design designates her as the future, she expresses a fear of the future.

On the other hand, Spade's guarded way of speaking and showing emotion, in keeping with his visual persona, manifests a concern for survival that reassures the reader. But this guarded quality is really a kind of ideological sleight-of-hand, an elision by which the modern implies (only) those traditional qualities it requires. Spade may not be the most modern character, but he is more modern than others, a realization that comes only after the reader has taken his side and which finally leads to the novel's endorsement of a new style of behavior.

Spade's sub rosa modernity is developed by the conventions of description—Guetti's "reading resistance"—that Hammett employed to set Spade off from the other male characters. There is no chance that the reader will opt for Spade's partner Miles Archer, for he is a draft horse from the past: "medium height, solidly built, wide in the shoulders, thick in the neck, with a jovial heavy-jawed

red face and some grey in his close-trimmed hair." "His voice was heavy, coarse." Miles is killed early, by that avatar of the modern, Miss Wonderly. Spade's ironic "You've got brains, yes you have" at the moment he is cuckolding Archer makes clear that he is not Modern enough. Sgt. Tom Polhaus and Lt. Dundy not only belong to the Victorian past but to the same ethnic factionalism implied in Brigid O'Shaughnessy's name.

> The Lieutenant was a compactly built man with a round head under short-cut grizzled hair and a square face behind a short-cut grizzled mustache. A five-dollar gold-piece was pinned to his neck-tie and there was a small elaborate diamond-set secret-society emblem on his lapel.

Dundy's description is like that of Archer; along with Polhaus and Shilling, they are variations on a type that Hammett sets up as The Sap, to contrast with Spade. The essence of this older Victorian type is the absence of sheathing. They are rough. These characters have an almost chemical reaction to stimulae in terms of the job; Dundy's eyes fix Spade "in a peculiarly rigid stare, as if their focus were a matter of mechanics, to be changed only by pulling a lever or pressing a button."

On Miss Wonderly's side of the stylistic dialectic, the crooks appear, one by one, as progressively more flawed versions of the smooth.

> Mr. Joel Cairo was a small-boned dark man of medium height. His hair was black and smooth and very glossy. His features were Levantine. A square-cut ruby, its sides paralleled by four baguette diamonds, gleamed against the deep green of his cravat. His black coat, cut tight to narrow shoulders, flared a little over slightly plump hips. His trousers fitted his round legs more snugly than was the current fashion. The uppers of his patent-leather shoes were hidden by fawn spats. He held a black derby hat in a chamois-gloved hand and came towards Spade with short, mincing, bobbing steps. The fragrance of *chypre* came with him.

Like Miss Wonderly, Cairo is fashion-conscious and "glossy," but like Gutman his plumpness and "bobbling" intimates some threat in the smooth. In holding Spade at gunpoint to search his office, Cairo is more overtly duplicitous than Wonderly. But the hidden threat in Cairo and Wonderly is only made stylistically clear by the appearance of Gutman. He is the quintessentially unsmooth smooth character: in his bubbles, ringlets, eggs, pearls and patent leather, he has subdivided his smooth surface until it becomes rough. By reticulating and dispersing smoothness, Hammett found a phenomenal way of making it rough and repulsive, and the sensory impact diffuses to color Cairo and Wonderly.

Pure smoothness is not to be trusted. The conventions of characterization limit the appropriate range of smoothness to Spade's activities.

Of the remaining characters, less description is given. Effie Perine, who helps define the Sap, is a "lanky sunburned girl whose tan dress of thin woolen stuff clung to her with an effect of dampness. Her eyes were brown and playful in a shiny boyish face." Her visual style, like Spade's, suggests the mediation by the Victorian of the modern: exterior not completely smooth, but smooth enough, with a self-preserving guarded emotional smoothness.

These descriptions are not intended, then, as a devilish obstacle to the resolution of the mystery, but as ideological bracketing. What we already sense in such repeated details as the "patent leather" shoes of Cairo and Gutman are markers in the "fashion rhetoric" of larger social forces outside the text. "The Fashion text," as Roland Barthes noted, "represents as it were the authoritative voice of some one who knows all there is behind the jumbled or incomplete appearance of the visible forms." That such signs should be perceived by Guetti as "resistance," rather than a path to the solution of the conflict, simply means that the older conflict, now that we live in its outcome, is ceasing to concern us.

The climax of *The Maltese Falcon* is not the unmasking of the falcon as a fake, but Spade's revelation that he is turning his client and romantic interest, Miss Wonderly (Brigid O'Shaughnessy) over to the police.

> "You didn't—don't—I-love me?"
>
> "I think I do," Spade said. "What of it?" The muscles holding his smile in place stood out like wales. "I'm not Thursby. I'm not Jacoby. I won't play the sap for you."

This response suddenly makes clear a complex of stylistic and emotional elements in the novel, which are crystallized in the commonplace of "sap." Among other things, this invocation subordinates romance to self-discipline, professionalism and class interest. It opens a view of Spade's character, which had been concealed by his familiar exterior, that now may be seen to accommodate feigning both love and hate. It reveals what is modern about him, which is his interior.

Spade's list of reasons for not being a sap strikes many readers today as stammeringly inarticulate, as hypocrisy, though it is valued by scholars for updating the "detective code." In 1930, however, this list was necessary to explain the curious behavior that Spade had exhibited throughout the novel and to illuminate in retrospect his actions—for a good deal of the mystery in this novel is why Spade acts the way he does.

Spade's list begins with an appeal to the traditional, broad social bonds that typified the undifferentiated members of a 19th century community: "When a man's partner is killed he's supposed to do something about it." But neither partnership nor community have a role in Spade's life: he is a loner, without wife or coeval. He is emblematic of the emerging structure of society, which Hammett quickly suggests: "Then it happens we were in the detective *business*. Well when one of *your organization* gets killed, it's *bad business* to let the killer get away. It's bad all around—bad for that one *organization*, bad for *every detective everywhere*." [emphasis added] This second reason reflects a narrower allegiance to a specific profession and the perception by its members of the world in terms of their class interests: Spade as a small businessman.

The third reason tightens this focus to Spade's specific profession: "I'm a detective and expecting me to run criminals down and then let them go free is like asking a dog to catch a rabbit and let it go." But in the 19th century the dog did that frequently, when larger interests dictated. Philo Vance did it. So did the Continental Op. However, the new standards imposed by getting a living in a narrow trade preclude the acknowledgement of traditional community ties and emotional bonds, even his feeling for Brigid.

The fourth and following reasons explain the preclusion of emotion in terms of self-preservation: "No matter what I wanted to do now it would be absolutely impossible for me to let you go without having myself dragged to the gallows," and "I couldn't be sure you wouldn't decide to shoot a hole in *me* some day." If competition and survival are suggested here—residual elements of social Darwinism—it is because the emerging economic ideology seizes useful elements of the preceding system, such as individualism while dropping elements such as cooperation and charity.

In this enumeration Hammett manages to strip from the previous social model its communal and affective aspects while retaining its laissez-faire emphasis on economic freedom and self-interest. The net result is to establish the primacy of self-interest, which Spade then turns on Brigid's championing of affective ties. "All we've got is the fact that maybe you love me and maybe I love you." He accuses her of encouraging his affection in order to reap economic gain, as though he were an unwary consumer: "I won't because all of me wants to—wants to say to hell with the consequences and do it—and because—God damn you—you've counted on that with me the same as you counted on that with the others." These lines perform important ideological work. The commodification of emotion, especially sexuality, was taboo under the old system, because promiscuity undermined the economic unit of the family; but under the new system, its role is not yet clear. The commodification of sexuality seems to threaten the illusion of individual uniqueness necessary to synchronous isolated work. Yet the discovery that sexuality could be managed by serializing its form and denying it an affective content is implicit in Spade's behavior, for he sleeps with Brigid in order to search her apartment.

The emotional and behavioral model that is Sam Spade defines itself most vehemently in opposition to the "sap." A word with roots in England of the early 1800s, sap is a short form of "saphead," which connotes a fool or dupe. Tom Sawyer applied the word to Huck Finn in response to the latter's anti-romantic hardheadedness in 1884. The image of the human head covered by "the circulating fluid of a plant or animal" is worth pondering. On being "sapped," a plant or animal is pierced so that its vital fluid runs out: what should be inside comes outside. A "saphead" or "sap" is someone whose fluid inner essence has leaked in unseemly fashion to the exterior. The implied norm against which the epithet works is a contained inner essence and a hard, smooth exterior. But it is not a model that denies fluid inner emotions—anxiety, depression, love. Instead it emphasizes their management.

That the indulgence of emotion results in becoming a "sap," Hammett leaves no doubt. The first character in the novel identified as a sap is Spade's partner Miles Archer. Both his cuckolding by Spade and his death at Brigid's hands can be traced to insufficient self-discipline. Archer can't see beyond the quick $100 and Miss Wonderly's trim figure—he's for the immediate, visceral reward. Not accidentally he is married and that "partnership" undermined. Archer's petty venality represents the passing economic phase, as Hammett reminds us by describing him with the 19th century conventions of the "jovial heavy-jawed red face" and "solidly built" body. Spade has Archer's name taken off the door almost immediately, for if Spade were Archer he'd be dead, just as Thursby is dead, both of them "saps."

To a lesser degree but in more instructive fashion Lt. Dundy, the Irish cop who is Spade's nemesis, is a sap. Spade defines himself against Dundy by incidents that reflect the latter's inability to see where his real interests lie. Dundy treats Spade like a criminal for most of the narrative, trying to provoke him with heavy-handed interrogation, unfounded accusations and late night telephone calls. He can't see that Spade has a professional value to him, and vice-versa. The conventions of his description—"compactly built," and "square face," but particularly the five dollar gold-piece tie-clasp and "small elaborate diamond-set secret society emblem"—connote an older character model. The last detail identifies him as a lodge member at a time when the Lynds, in their study of *Middletown* in 1925, tell us that such heterogeneous forms of male organization had given way to associations of lawyers, doctors and businessmen, even in Muncie, Indiana. These new associations were highly competitive, professionally oriented class interest groups. They replaced the geographically based lodges such as the Elks and Moose. But Dundy, who always shakes hands "ceremoniously," and whose admonitions—"I've warned you your foot was going to slip one of these days"—echo religious imagery that dates to Jonathan Edwards, still belongs to this world.

When Dundy finds Spade with Brigid and Cairo and threatens to haul them to jail, Spade says, "Don't be a sap, Dundy." Immediately Dundy hits Spade: he understands the charge and responds in the old mode of physical violence. Unlike Polhaus, who perceives his common professional interests with Spade and passes information to him with an easy informality, Dundy subscribes to the grand conspiracy theories of District Attorney Bryan, which preclude effective professional cooperation. Hammett parodies their conception of crime, which links the falcon to "Dixie Monahan" and Chicago gamblers (by which readers are to understand "Al Capone.") This conception of problems is passe, failing to perceive that professional interests are narrow and solution-oriented.

All of Gutman's gang are saps: conventions and commonplaces aided Hammett in detailing them. Wilmer is undersized, homosexual and profane. Cairo is a dandy and homosexual. Gutman is fat and abuses his daughter. Brigid is a serial seductress and gold-digger. Their common pursuit of the falcon, emblem of materiality, defines them as anachronistic adventurers from a previous economic life. They represent a prodigality that once astonished Hammett in the person of Roscoe "Fatty" Arbuckle, so the rotund Gutman is their natural leader. They live well and dress lavishly, without holding jobs, without any explained funding. After they have the falcon, they propose to leave their "legal difficulties" to Spade. Hammett's personal fondness of prodigality glints along Gutman's "cherub" smile when he proposes to seek the falcon in Constantinople, but he enforces thematic closure by having the betrayed Wilmer kill Gutman minutes later. "He ought to have expected that," remarks Spade, who understands that romantic treasure-hunting is a thing of the past.

Spade, with his efficiency apartment, Murphy bed, store bought products, office and secretary, epitomizes the emerging economy. Compared to the Continental Op, Spade's lack of heterogeneous social contact is clear. In *Red Harvest,* the Op had Mickey Linehan and Dick Foley for partners, on the street he met Bill Quint and Dinah Brand, and he achieved camaraderie with Reno Starkey among the crooks. When Sam Spade walks down the street, he is likely to be shadowed. He trusts no one. Yet he knows at least as many people, has more useful professional contacts than his predecessor. Among his acquaintances of instrument value are hotel detectives, cabbies, policemen and lawyers. But there is no geographic or community relation among these economic isolets, no sense of polity. The same technological forces that provide them with Murphy beds and billboards require that their work be narrowly and efficiently organized. Like the urban office-worker of the late '20s, Spade's life has the spheres of self-preservation and work, which for him are synonymous. He has no informal or community ties: no church, no lodge, no hobbies, no affective ties or neighbors.

This lack does not glare because it is depicted as difficult to achieve: it is emotional smoothness. When Effie Perine sees Spade perplexed by Brigid, Iva and Dandy, she cues the reader to its demands: "You always think you know what you're doing, *but you're too slick for your own good. . . .*" This slickness—mental and emotional "smoothness"—and its cost are the center of the novel's ideological innovation. Even the most alluring models of exterior smoothness, such as Brigid, may be simply examples of *sheathing* that disguise the anachronistic values of the old economic model. True smoothness is interior as well as exterior: its manifestations are coolness, skepticism, feigned comprehension, suspension of judgement, self interest, observation, the ability to wait, a sense of humor.

The genuinely smooth is not easy. Hammett's descriptions of Spade's "growl," the "wales" that stand out in his cheeks, his "harsh gutteral voice," and the "dreamy" quality of his face when he is about to hit someone—all these are meant to testify to its difficulty and to offer the reader a model sufficiently complex to be worthy of emulation. One suspects that Dorothy Parker, among others, took Sam Spade to heart because he embodied not only the new behavior of the emergent economy but its cost as well. He can be hurt, but he polices his wound. Spade contains himself without a price: both Iva and Effie ask if he killed Archer, and Spade's flinch reveals his pain at their presumptions.

As Hammett indicated by titling an important chapter "Three Women," Brigid O'Shaughnessy, Effie Perine and Iva Archer serve, in one sense, as the fates. They ask questions, represent mysteries, and possess occult powers: Brigid can solve the mystery of the falcon, Iva can implicate or exonerate Spade in her husband's murder, and Spade depends particularly on Effie's "female intuition." As we shall see, however, Hammett folded into this essentially archetypal presentation of women a number of potent psychological and socioeconomic analogues, the upshot of which will be (especially in Raymond Chandler) to suggest the emergent economic ideology in a female foil to the main female character.

Psychoanalytic analyses of *The Maltese Falcon* have pointed out that the deaths of Archer and Thursby leave Spade in possession of two women formerly attached to other men. They postulate that he is subject to a "fear of Oedipal victory" with regard to Effie Perine, his "desexualized daytime mother." But the imperative of ideology to manage popular energies consumes just such shibboliths and taboos relentlessly. Effie is purposely just like Mom; sublimated Oedipal victories were old news in popular narrative by 1930. All the ideological hints in the novel point to Effie as Spade's appropriate partner. Only her disappointment that he does not believe in Romance—a concession to sentiment—keeps them apart in the final scene.

As potential spouses these three women represent the choices faced by Hammett's male readership. Effie is the girl next door: lanky, sunburned, playful, boyish, earthy and candid—echo of Sinclair Lewis' widely praised Leora Tozer of *Arrowsmith* (1925). Her "de-sexualization" must be understood against the prevailing convention of popular literature in the early '20s that a woman serving a man in the workplace would be sexually exploited. From this vantage Effie appears to be empowered by Hammett. She becomes a kind of office wife—an economic partner who is competent, efficient, honest and a team player. Spade's physical intimacies with her seem as uncharged as a small child's bedtime hug in the kitchen. When the falcon comes into their possession, they are not mesmerized like Gutman but quickly dispose of it. The only male/female unit in the novel, they function ideologically as the Nuclear Family.

The falcon must be exposed as a fake in the presence of Brigid, to show that she lacks potential as a spouse. Her "gold-digger" profligacy and Bad Girl sexual liberality (overt depiction of unmarried sex was still at the edge of the popular reading horizon in 1930) must be exposed as a threat to social stability. Brigid's name, like that of Gabrielle Leggett in Hammett's preceding novel, *The Dain Curse,* suggests a foreignness, and when, early on, she calls herself Miss Le Blanc, she suggests her archetype Blanchfleur, who nearly diverted Sir Galahad from his guest for the grail. "I always lie," Brigid confesses. "Can I buy you with my body?" she asks.

A type since the Middle Ages, the femme fatale evolved from the succubus. Heroes of the early grail romances, such as Percival, were afflicted by succubi. Disguised as sensual, alluring maidens, these hags misled the hero when he was lost or tempted him to sexual intercourse while he slept. At consummation he forfeited his soul to them. The succubi developed distinct physical features that became conventions of several genres. Pointed ears, sharp teeth, angular noses and cheekbones, epilepsy and other seizures have traditionally been the means by which readers recognized the succubus and her threat to the hero. In *Red Harvest,* Hammett confined the succubus to a cameo appearance in Myrtle Jennison. In *The Dain Curse,* the Op cures Gabrielle Dain, the heroine, of her archetype; even her ears and teeth are rounded off. In Brigid's smoothness, sheathing, and green, his personal sign for lust, Hammett definitively articulated the femme fatale that had fascinated him since "The Girl with the Silver Eyes" (1924). In subsequent work, variations on Effie would dominate.

Iva Archer falls between Effie and Brigid, though closer to the latter, with whom she shares some characteristics. Like Myrtle Jennison, Iva has cheated on her husband: both serve as cautionary examples of the wages of sin. As with Myrtle, Spade's inclination is to pull up the covers over Iva and to say "thank you" when he is done. Yet Iva is his lot when the novel ends. She is so shallow emotionally as to be non-human; she makes Spade

shiver, as if having Iva was to become Archer, to cuckhold oneself.

Clearly it would be better to have Effie. Only the rogue male in Spade refuses to face the logic that makes Effie Perine his domestic partner. Only Effie has a mother, a brother, a family of any sort; only Effie can speak to Spade candidly about a woman's "shape" or about his business. She uses his chair when he is absent, she massages his temples in a scene which by its isolation and physical contact is provocative. If she offers Spade no knowledge about himself, none of the allure of death that Brigid represented, that is well lost. Effie is the economic truth about marriage: mundanity and the sacrifice of romance to expediency and money-getting. That Effie should reprimand Spade for his unromantic behavior in the end is not only a brilliant concession to sentiment, but a recognition that women transmit the core beliefs of society. Men adjust, bear new tensions, fit themselves to a changing social grid, but the affective tradition in 1930 is still passed down through mothers.

By far the most influential interpretation of *The Maltese Falcon* in Robert Edenbaum's brilliant perception that "in the last pages of the novel . . . the reader (and Brigid O'Shaughnessy) discovers that he (and she) has been duped all along." Spade, says Edenbaum, has known from the moment he saw Archer's body that Brigid was the murderer. "Spade himself then is the one person who holds the central piece of information. . . . he is the one person who knows everything, for Brigid does not know that he knows. And though Spade is no murderer, Brigid O'Shaughnessy is his victim." Edenbaum concludes that "Brigid . . . is the manipulated, the deceived, the unpredictable, finally, in a very real sense, the victim." In his view, the course of the action is "the demolition of sentiment" through the "all but passionless figure of Spade."

The key to this interpretation is Edenbaum's insight that Spade is a kind of "daemonic agent," that is, a vehicle of allegoric impulse. Those who try to redeem the sentimental level of the action have missed the point, says Edenbaum. They say "You're right, you're right, but couldn't you better have been wrong?" This is the point made via Effie Perine in the novel's last scene. But the point about Spade is that allegorically he could not have been wrong: neither the form of allegory nor his revelation of his knowledge in the climactic scene permit the reassumption of values that have been sloughed.

Edenbaum's feat of reading the novel against the grain of sentiment (and the 1943 film version) also sheds a revealing light on Brigid. Untouched by affection herself, she counts on Spade's automatic response to her pretended helplessness, her sexual attractiveness, her love. She "falls back on a set of conventions that she has discarded in her own life, but which she naively assumes still hold for others," writes Edenbaum. Spade, seen from the retrospect of the finale, reveals how a "modern" self-interest identifies sentiment, encompasses it and reveals it to be an unsophisticated form of emotional manipulation for economic ends.

This retrospective understanding of the novel's action may finally be more important than its allegoric impulse. In allegory, by and large, meaning develops concurrently with the reading experience; nothing is withheld from the reader by the central character. If the reader knows, with Spade in chapter two, who killed Miles Archer, only then is he reading allegory. If he does not, if he is lulled by sentiment, if he fills in Spade's growls and Brigid's stammerings with affective meaning, then the retrospect shows he has been insufficiently suspicious of the motives of others, less than comprehensive in his canvassing of the data. There is no way to press the novel, as Guetti implies, and wrest the "mystery" from its resisting details.

The form of the novel, like the economic ideology it endorses, is an instance of "instrumentality." I mean this word exactly in the sense popularized by John Dewey and his pragmatist fellows in the teens and twenties: that the truth of ideas or forms (in this case persons might be included) is determined by their success in solving actual problems. Retrospectivity has great instrument value for ideological suggestion in narrative. And the ideology of *The Maltese Falcon* completes the circuit by endorsing instrumentalism.

No better example of this reinforcement (and the limits of an allegoric reading) exists than the "Flitcraft parable." Just before he sleeps with Brigid, Spade tells her a long story about a real estate agent who leaves his office for lunch one noon and never returns. He passes a construction site and "a beam or something fell eight or ten stories down and smacked the sidewalk alongside him." Suddenly Flitcraft's eyes opened: "He felt like somebody had taken the lid off life and let him look at the works." Life was not a "clean, orderly same, responsible affair," and he saw rather that "men died at haphazard like that, and lived only while blind chance spared them." According to Spade, "What disturbed him was the discovery that in sensibly ordering his affairs he had got out of step and

not into step, with life. He said he knew before he had gone twenty feet from the fallen beam that he would never know peace again until he had adjusted himself to this new glimpse of life . . . Life could be ended for him at random by a falling beam: he would change his life at random by simply going away."

This naturalistic conception of the universe leads Flitcraft to wander for several years, eventually marrying a woman similar to his first wife and replicating his old circumstances. Spade "always liked" this part of the story: "I don't think he even knew he had settled back naturally into the same groove he had jumped out of in Tacoma . . . He adjusted himself to beams falling, and then no more of them fell and he adjusted himself to them not falling."

In Robert Edenbaum's reading, Spade subscribes to the "Dreiserian" nature of Flitcraft's insight. Beams do not continue to fall in Flitcraft's world, but they do in Spade's. Edenbaum turns to the analogue between Spade recounting her husband's sea-change to the first Mrs. Flitcraft and Spade's recounting the story to Brigid. "If Brigid were acute enough—or less trammelled by conventional sentiment—she would see in the long, apparently pointless story that her appeals to Spade's sense of honor, his nobility, his integrity, and finally, his love, will not and cannot work . . . Brigid—totally unscrupulous, a murderess—should understand rather better than Mrs. Flitcraft, the bourgeois housewife. But she doesn't."

Edenbaum halts here. Since in his view Spade is a daemonic agent, the stories he tells are to be comprehended allegorically in relation to the action. Yet Spade's ironic appreciation of Flitcraft's naturalism is plainly evident. In fact, it has a genealogy. Hammett's first version of Flitcraft was the English character Norman Ashcraft, an Englishman, in the short story "The Golden Horseshoe." Resenting his wife's wealth and desiring to prove his independence, Ashcraft migrates to America, leads a scruffy life and is in a sense reincarnated in the criminal Ed Bohannon, who kills him and assumes his identity. A strong and attractive aspect this story is the fantasy of an enjoyably disreputable life available beyond the marital confines. It is also a variation of the theme of the prodigal son that fascinated Hammett. Ashcraft sheds his wife's stultifying fortune, just as Flitcraft walks out on $200,000, "a new Packard, and the rest of the appurtenances of successful American living." But Ashcraft dies: prodigal sons always fail for Hammett.

The *urban setting* of the Flitcraft parable, given short shrift in a strictly allegoric reading, is also important. Increasingly *safer* than rural life, as well as materially better, it was perceived by recently urbanized readers as straitened by its greater organization. The threat of death by falling beams is a *post hoc* justification of the original departure, from the small town and traditional family, just as Flitcraft's second family in idealized solution. If one can go away and come back to the same family as before, one has both affective ties and complete independence. The Prodigal Son lives! He reads the universe as material, organized by chance, and decides on a course of prodigality. But Hammett knew that prodigals were never welcomed back by stay-at-home brothers.

Hence the instrumental lesson of the Flitcraft parable. The universe may not be rational—random events like the falling beam and prodigal son punctuate life—but rationality is the best instrument with which to go hunting. The chance event drives men away from cover and adaptive or habitual responses for only a short time. Prodigal sons return.

Were Brigid at all perceptive about the Flitcraft parable, as Edenbaum says, she would see that each time she tries to deceive him, Spade becomes more sure of her guilt. But Spade never even reveals his suspicion to the reader, and his certainty is withheld until it can most emphatically endorse the instrument value of narrow self-interest and professional class consciousness by the brothers of prodigal sons, which is how Hammett defines his readers. Retrospect allows them this ironic appreciation, which allegory does not.

It also performs another service that allegory cannot, which is to distinguish "useful" instrumentality from the false and "serial" version that characterizes Brigid. Ideology selects existing features for their appropriateness to the emerging system, in this case the credit economy. Just as Art Nouveau mediated the arrival of modernism in art and design, popular acceptance of the credit economy was smoothed by ideological mediations in popular art. Instrumentalism provides a way of assessing credit, sentiment, smoothness—so as to preclude the kind of misevaluation that leads one to speculate in stocks or to invest in Ponzi pyramids, much less quest after Maltese falcons or trust Brigid O'Shaughnessys. The resistance that James Guetti, and no doubt others, perceive in a text that we had presumed a stylistic forebear, may mean that we are so far along the road of a subsequent socio-economic phase—that of the

service economy—that our genealogy requires redefinition.

Source: William Marling, "The Style and Ideology of *The Maltese Falcon*," in *Proteus*, Vol. 6, No. 1, 1989, pp. 42–50.

Julian Symons

In the following essay excerpt, Symons explores symbolism, including the meaning of the Flitcraft story, in The Maltese Falcon.

The actual writing in *The Maltese Falcon* shows the author's determination to move out of the pulp world into that of the genuine novelist. It is not only the guns pumping lead that have gone. Slang is used less liberally, and attention is paid to the need for continuity and to the development of character. In the lectures on the mystery story that he gave years later in New York, Hammett stressed, as one student remembered, "that tempo is the vital thing in fiction, that you've got to keep things moving, and that character can be drawn *within* the action." It was such drawing of character within the action, including action within the dialogue, that Hammett achieved here and in later novels to a degree approached among his contemporaries only by Hemingway. The good, hard phrases found in the earlier work were not sacrificed. Typical of them are the lawyer Sid Wise's remark, "You don't cash many checks for strangers, do you, Sammy?" and Spade's caustic observation to Gutman after he has disarmed Wilmer and given Wilmer's pistols to the fat man, "A crippled newsie took them away from him, but I made him give them back." It is true that the style has its limitations, or rather, that there are some clichés of the pulp story that Hammett never discarded. Spade does too much "wolfish grinning," and his eyes are "hard and cold," "narrow and sultry," "wary and dull," "angry," "bulging," "brooding"—all within a few pages.

The book's effectiveness rests in part in the realization, fuller and richer than in the short stories, of San Francisco's streets and scenes. Spade waits for Cairo outside the Geary Theater on Suffer Street, sits with Effie Perine in Julius's Castle on Telegraph Hill, has an apartment on Post Street. Joe Gores, author of the novel *Hammett,* has traced many of the places exactly, for instance identifying Brigid's room at "the Coronet on California Street" as the Yerba Buena Apartments on Sutter Street.

There remains the question of symbolism. The falcon itself is often seen by critics as symbolic, because what should be a jeweled bird proves to be no more than black enamel coating lead. It is "a suitable symbol for illusory wealth" in "a novel about the destructive power of greed," Richard Layman

> One can read symbols into anything, but there is no indication that the falcon was chosen for any reason other than to provide a good focal point for a thriller, a focal point which also had a basis in fact."

says, and William F. Nolan thinks that "the falcon is a symbol for the falseness and illusions of life itself." Ross Macdonald suggested that the falcon might symbolize the lost cultures of the Mediterranean past "which have become inaccessible to Spade and his generation," or might even stand for the Holy Ghost itself. The absence of spiritual beliefs in Spade, he wrote, "seem[s] to me to make his story tragedy, if there is such a thing as dead-pan tragedy." This surely goes much too far. Almost any crime story can be said to express the destructive power of something or other, whether it be greed, sex, hatred, or envy. We are all aware of the deadliness of the Seven Deadly Sins. And although it may be that a true awareness of past, or indeed present, culture is absent in a man like Sam Spade, his solution can surely be called tragic only if Spade, even momentarily, suffers tragically. But the detective's emotional struggle is merely between the romantic feeling of his love for Brigid and the practical need to offer the police a murderer, and there is no doubt that the practical approach is going to win. One can read symbols into anything, but there is no indication that the falcon was chosen for any reason other than to provide a good focal point for a thriller, a focal point which also had a basis in fact.

There is more reason for attributing symbolism to the Flitcraft story, told by Spade to Brigid as one of his detective experiences. Flitcraft is a Tacoma real estate executive who has a pleasant house, a new car, and "the rest of the appurtenances of successful American living," including a wife and two sons. He goes out to lunch one day and never comes back. Spade finds Flitcraft five, years later, living in the Northwest with another wife, and a baby son—the same kind of woman and the same kind of life. What had happened to him? On the way out to lunch Flitcraft was almost hit by a beam

falling from an office building in course of construction. The near escape from injury and possible death showed him that the life he was living, "a clean, orderly, sane, responsible affair," was really a foolish one. "Life could be ended for him at random by a falling beam: he would change his life at random by simply going away." So he leaves, but after a couple of years he duplicates his previous existence. "That's the part of it I always liked," Spade says. "He adjusted himself to beams falling, and then no more of them fell, and he adjusted himself to them not falling."

The Flitcraft story is extremely well told. It has nothing to do with the plot, but we, like Brigid, find it absorbingly interesting. The records of any police department will confirm that its basic elements are not unusual. Apparently happy husbands or wives often disappear from their pleasant homes to lead a new life, generally with another woman or man but sometimes for no obvious logical reason. In fiction Georges Simenon has played several variations on the theme, as in *The Man Who Watched the Trains Go By,* in which Kees Popinga suddenly realizes that the pattern of his respectable life is a fraud, abandons his wife and family, becomes a multiple murderer, and ends up in an asylum. There he starts to write an article, "The Truth about the Kees Popinga Case," but fails to complete it because, as he says to his doctor, "Really, there isn't any truth about it, is there?" Undoubtedly Hammett meant something by inserting this enigmatic story into a tale to which it bears no obvious relation, but what?

Most of the interpretations are based on the falling beam and what it made Flitcraft understand about the universe. "The randomness of the universe is Spade's vision throughout," says Robert I. Edenbaum. Layman points out that the nineteenth-century American philosopher Charles Sanders Pierce (Flitcraft changes his name to Charles Pierce) wrote about random occurrence. John Cawelti suggests that Hammett's vision is of an irrational cosmos in which all the rules can be overturned in a moment, and William Ruehlmann that the tale is meant to show that Spade, like Flitcraft, is incapable of emotional involvement and so is truly committed to nobody. All the characters in the book, according to this view, are counterfeits: Brigid a counterfeit innocent, Gutman a counterfeit sage, Wilmer a counterfeit tough guy. "Worst of all is Spade, a counterfeit hero." George J. Thompson, one of the most intelligent critics of Hammett's work, says that "the meaning of the Flitcraft parable is that if we can see clearly enough to understand that external reality is unstable and unpredictable, then one must be ready to react to its ironies. . . . To some extent the Flitcraft parable, like the Maltese falcon, stands for the absurdity of assuming that the external world is necessarily stable."

There are other theories, all based on Hammett's belief in the random nature of life. Without expressing positive disagreement with any of them, it should perhaps be added that with Hammett the most straightforward, least high-flown view of the Flitcraft story is likely to be the one he had in mind. It is possible that he was not contemplating a grand application of the story to all human existence but merely a personal reference to his own career to date. In that case the key sentence is "What disturbed him was the discovery that in sensibly ordering his affairs he had got out of step, and not into step, with life." Up to the time of his departure from San Francisco, Hammett had done his best to order his life sensibly, without much success. For several years afterward, however, he made no attempt to order it at all.

Whether or not this idea has any validity, those prone to fine-spun theories about Flitcraft in particular and Hammett's work in general should remember his response to Lillian Hellman on an occasion when he had killed a snapping turtle, first by rifle shot and then by an ax blow almost severing the head, only to find that the dead turtle had moved down the garden in the night. When Hammett started to cut away one leg from the shell, the other leg moved. Was the turtle alive or dead? Hellman rang the New York Zoological Society and was told that it was scientifically dead but that the society was not equipped to give a theological opinion.

"Then how does one define life?" Hellman asked Hammett. "Lilly, I'm too old for that stuff," he replied.

He would always have been too old for some of the theories put forward about the meaning of Flitcraft.

Source: Julian Symons, *"The Maltese Falcon,"* in *Dashiell Hammett*, Harcourt, Brace, Jovanovich, 1985, pp. 66–72.

William Marling

In the following essay excerpt, Marling examines Spade's philosophical outlook and detective's code as they relate to the moral climate in The Maltese Falcon.

In his 1934 introduction to *The Maltese Falcon* Dashiell Hammett wrote:

If this book had been written with the help of an outline or notes or even a clearly defined plot-idea in

> "Hammett made Spade's code an innovation on the generic standard, a new version that allows him not only deception, but the pleasures of adultery and the rewards of betrayal."

my head I might now be able to say how it came to be written and why it took the shape it did, but all I can remember about its invention is that somewhere I had read of the peculiar rental agreement between Charles V and the Order of the Hospital of Saint John of Jerusalem, that in a short story called "The Whosis Kid" I had failed to make the most of a situation I liked, that in another called "The Gutting of Couffignal" I had been equally fortunate with an equally promising denouement, and that I thought I might have better luck with these two failures if I combined them with the Maltese lease in a longer story.

The hallmark of the best modern American novelists has been an ability to recognize in the themes and plots of early work those conflicts that can sustain even greater elaboration. Call it a sieving or a critical eye, in 1928 Dashiell Hammett had it.

Hammett had written two novels in two years, had rewritten his old stories, and he claimed to have 250,000 words—an amount equal to half of the Bible—available for publication. This work was at once recapitulative and boldly innovative. In 1925, before he wrote "The Big Knockover" and "$106,000 Blood Money" to train up to the length of the novel, he had written two stories that were good but not quite finished. In "The Whosis Kid" most of the action took place in the apartment of Inés Almad, an alluring foreigner who fled with the loot from a robbery. The Op was in her apartment when three former partners showed up. The "situation" that Hammett liked was the "apartment drama," in which the rising action was heightened by the physically confining space and mutual hostility of the characters. The tension built extraordinarily well while it was submerged in the dialogue, but the climax had been an ineffectual spate of bullets.

Hammett had known the advantage of tempting the hero's code with a beautiful woman since

"The Girl with the Silver Eyes." But in "The Gutting of Couffignal" he attempted to increase the tension by making the Op's surrender circumstantially plausible. It failed. The Op seemed so uninvolved with the temptress that he sacrificed little in adhering to his code. In *The Maltese Falcon* Hammett clarified the archetypal traits of this femme fatale—beauty, mutability duplicity—and involved the detective with her romantically from the first to the last chapter.

The Maltese Falcon is also given impetus by Hammett's elaborations on "classical" mystery formulas and by the reality/illusion debate that he explored in *The Dain Curse*. The use of violence to move the plot is much reduced; there are three murders, only one of them onstage. There are, however, ten important deceptions and reversals, and the detective himself is a deceiver, whose code takes shape from a parable about self-deception at the novel's core.

The detective is a new incarnation. In *The Dain Curse* Hammett seemed stumped about his hero's evolution and fell back on pure chivalric code. The hero of *The Maltese Falcon* recurs to the hero of *Red Harvest* in some traits, but in a more important way, as Hammett noted, he is an idealized vision of independence and self-reliance:

> Spade had no original. He is a dream man in the sense that he is what most of the private detectives I worked with would like to have been and what quite a few of them in their cockier moments thought they approached. For your private detective does not—or did not ten years ago when he was my colleague—want to be an erudite solver of riddles in the Sherlock Holmes manner; he wants to be a hard and shifty fellow, able to take care of himself in any situation, able to get the best of anybody he comes in contact with, whether criminal, innocent by-stander or client.

Sam Spade is the hero who looks "rather pleasantly like a blond satan." From jaw to widow's peak, his face repeats a *V* motif. He is slope-shouldered, compact, and muscular, so that mien and physique together suggest an extroverted, physical man. His partner Miles Archer is a similar but less intelligent type. Their office is managed by Effie Perrine, a "lanky, sunburned girl" with a "shiny boyish face," who became Perry Mason's Della Street and every private eye's secretary afterward.

The action begins when Effie escorts into Spade's office a Miss Wonderly, really Brigid O'Shaughnessy: she asks Spade to rescue her sister from a hoodlum named Floyd Thursby, and she advances $200 for the work. Miles Archer walks in, sizes her up, and volunteers to do the job.

A 2 a.m. call from the police informs Spade that Archer has been murdered. He taxis to the scene but declines to examine the body or answer questions. "I'll bury my dead," he says. He asks Effie to call Iva Archer with the news. At home Spade is questioned by policemen Polhaus and Dundy, who have learned that he was cuckolding his partner, which makes him a suspect. They also reveal that Thursby is dead.

Miss Wonderly disappears, and has changed her name to Miss LeBlanc when Spade finds her. She only confesses her real name in the first "apartment scene," a histrionic meld of confessions, tears, and innuendos that does not fool Spade. But he agrees to help her recover a "valuable object" for an additional $500.

At the office the next day Effie ushers in Joel Cairo, who also gives Spade a retainer to help him find the object, which he identifies as the Maltese falcon. He pulls a gun on Spade, is disarmed, but repeats the trick as he leaves—all to no avail. After his contact with Cairo a man begins to shadow Spade, necessitating elaborate dodges. Brigid will not divulge details about the quest for the falcon, but, like Princess Zhukovski, offers to buy Spade's trust with her body. This disturbs Spade, who arranges a meeting between Cairo and Brigid.

Waiting for Cairo, Spade tells Brigid the story of Flitcraft. It seems like idle conversation, but it is a parable explaining, indeed forecasting, Spade's behavior. When Cairo arrives, he trades sexual insults with Brigid (he is a homosexual) until Dundy and Polhaus appear again. The police threaten to jail all three. Only Spade's brilliant improvisation, in which he persuades Cairo to play a part, prevents their arrest. Dundy again accuses Spade of Archer's murder, and punches him on the way out. Drawing on his deepest reserve of discipline, Spade refrains from striking back, but after the police and Cairo leave, he flies into a rage. The scene ends with Spade and Brigid on the way to bed, but readers are warned away from assuming paramount importance for the love interest. Spade wakes before Brigid the next morning, and searches her apartment while she sleeps.

With a clue garnered the previous night, Spade finds the man shadowing him and says he wants to see "G." When he returns to his office, Spade has a call from G., who is Casper Gutman. The shadow, a "gunsel" or kept-boy named Wilmer, escorts Spade to see Gutman. Like Effie, Wilmer has passed into the archetypal library of the detective novel. From Gutman Spade learns more about the "black bird" and those who seek it; he pretends to possess it and gives Gutman a dead-line for his participation in its recovery.

Fearing that Gutman will kill her, Brigid goes into hiding. When Spade applies himself to tracking her down, he can find no clues except a newspaper clipping about a ship due from Hong Kong called *La Paloma*. When Gutman calls and opts in, Spade learns the entire story of the falcon. Hammett embellished the history of the icon's later travels, but the data on the Hospitalers of Saint John is basically correct. They were a religious order in the Middle Ages, located on the Isle of Rhodes, and charged with providing lodging and care for pilgrims on the way to Jerusalem. They built up tremendous wealth between 1300 and the early 1500s, but were displaced by Suleiman the Magnificent and his Turkish armies in 1523. They wandered until 1530, when they gained the patronage of Charles V, who gave them four islands, including Malta (not three, as Gutman says). The actual Hospitalers were displeased by the barren islands and savage inhabitants, but delighted that the only required tribute was "simple presentation of a yearly falcon on All-Saints Day." Initially they gave a live bird, but as their wealth grew they substituted jewel-encrusted statuettes.

At the finish of the history, Spade passes out—Gutman had drugged him. On waking, he finds Gutman, Wilmer, and Cairo gone. When he goes to search Cairo's room, he finds another clue leading to *La Paloma,* but is prevented from pursuing it by appointments with Polhaus and the district attorney. Then as Spade and Effie discuss the day's events at the office, Captain Jacobi of *La Paloma* enters, carrying the wrapped falcon, and falls dead at their feet.

Spade instructs Effie to phone the police while he hides the falcon. He tries to contact Gutman, but the criminals conspire to send him on a wild goose chase. Since Brigid participates in the deception, Spade is suspicious when she appears outside his door that evening. Gutman, Cairo, and Wilmer are waiting upstairs; Spade knows he is trapped. He accepts $10,000 to deliver the falcon, but insists that a "fall-guy" be given to the police for the murders. First he suggests Wilmer, then Cairo. Gutman suggests Brigid and attempts to impeach her by suggesting that she stole one of the ten $1,000 bills that she has been holding for Spade. When this ploy fails, Gutman and Cairo agree to make Wilmer the fall guy.

As dawn approaches, Spade phones Effie to retrieve and deliver the falcon. Unwrapped, it turns out to be a worthless imitation; Gutman asks for his money back, and Spade gives him all but $1,000, which he later turns over to the police. The irrepressible Gutman decides to continue his search, and Cairo joins him. As they leave Spade alerts Polhaus and Dundy, but before the criminals can be arrested Wilmer kills Gutman.

Spade urges Brigid to tell all before the police arrive. She confesses to conspiring to get the falcon, but denies involvement in Archer's murder. However all of the evidence points to her. "Miles hadn't many brains," says Spade, "... but he'd have gone up [the alley] with you, angel, if he was sure nobody else was up there." When Brigid confesses, she attempts to force Spade's loyalty by invoking their love. In the stunning climax, Spade says that "maybe you love me and maybe I love you" but that he "won't play the sap for her." He enumerates seven reasons why, then turns her over to Polhaus and Dundy.

The novel ends on a melancholic note the next morning as Effie Perrine will have nothing to do with Spade because he has betrayed the cause of true love. Iva Archer waits outside, however, and when Effie ushers her in Spade shudders and seems resigned to an emotional wasteland.

The Importance of Flitcraft

The rightness of the ending, as well as an understanding of Spade's earlier actions, rest on the story that he told about Flitcraft. Occurring before he goes to bed with Brigid, the parable's structural position is like that of the dream sequence in *Red Harvest* or the fight with the ghost in *The Dain Curse*. But thematically it is better integrated. Flitcraft is a reinterpretation of the character Norman Ashcraft in "The Golden Horseshoe," and like other aspects of the novel he has become immortal—there are probability statistics in the insurance business known as *Flitcraft Reports*. In Hammett's first treatment, Ashcraft resents his wife's wealth and wants to prove that he can support himself independently. He moves to America, leads a scruffy life, and is in a sense reincarnated in the criminal Ed Bohannon. The fantasy of an enjoyably disreputable life available beyond the marital confines is a strong and attractive aspect of the earlier story.

In Hammett's reworking, Flitcraft is a real estate agent who leaves his office for lunch one noon and never returns. He passes a construction site and "a beam or something fell eight or ten stories down and smacked the sidewalk alongside him." Suddenly Flitcraft's eyes opened: "He felt like somebody had taken the lid off life and let him look at the works."

Life was not a "clean, orderly, sane, responsible affair," he saw rather that "men died at haphazard like that, and lived only while blind chance spared them." According to Spade, "What disturbed him was the discovery that in sensibly ordering his affairs he had got out of step and not into step, with life. He said he knew before he had gone twenty feet from the fallen beam that he would never know peace again until he had adjusted himself to this new glimpse of life . . . Life could be ended for him at random by a falling beam: he would change his life at random by simply going away."

This naturalistic conception of the universe leads Flitcraft to wander for several years, eventually marrying a woman similar to his first wife and replicating his old circumstances. Spade "always liked" this part of the story, which shows the primacy of the adaptive response: "I don't think he even knew he had settled back naturally into the same groove he had jumped out of in Tacoma. . . . He adjusted himself to beams falling, and then no more of them fell and he adjusted himself to them not falling."

The moral, which Brigid misses, lies at the level of Spade's ironic appreciation rather than in Flitcraft's insight into the nature of the universe. The universe may be material and organized by chance, one may die any second; but such an insight, as Flitcraft demonstrates, does not mean that randomness constitutes a way of life. Man is above all adaptive and habitual, traits not only rationally intelligible but rather predictable. Information keeps crystallizing in a chaotic universe. Spade, for example, has found Flitcraft. Herein lies the basic irony that pervades Spade's outlook: the world may not operate rationally, but rationality is the best net with which to go hunting. The chance event—the falling beam—drives men away from cover and adaptive responses for a short time.

In telling Brigid this, Spade is explaining that his code is primary for him. It is the best adaptive response to the world in which he lives, a version of James Wright's advice to Hammett back in 1915. Spade has seen the potency of chance events—and love might be numbered among them—and he understands their relation to the patterns. Were Brigid at all perceptive about this story, she would see that each time she deceives him, Spade becomes more certain of her pattern. His "wild and unpredictable monkey-wrenches" repeatedly unseat her from romantic postures and reveal her fundamental avarice. But the uncomprehending Brigid only says "How perfectly fascinating" at the end of the Flitcraft story.

The Moral Climate *of* The Maltese Falcon

Hammett's most extraordinary fictional feat is the embodiment of this world view in the character of Sam Spade. Spade is a continuation of that interest, which Hammett expressed in *The Dain Curse,* in the deceptions that veil reality. Reality is Spade's psychological fulcrum, and yet he is more perfectly than the Op a knight of the detective code. But readers perceive him as flawed, cruel, and human, rather than as the holder of God-like powers. Hammett masks his character's power primarily by eliminating the first-person narrator, whose intimacy with the reader revealed his minor infidelities to the code and implied that he discussed his cases, a weakness alien to the entirely private personality of Spade. With a third-person point of view, the hero's person becomes more distant and independent. In addition, Hammett made Spade's code an innovation on the generic standard, a new version that allows him not only deception, but the pleasures of adultery and the rewards of betrayal. Such variations are the key mode of creativity in popular literature, allowing readers to enjoy generically or conventionally forbidden desires.

Yet Spade's code is only one of three moral climates. The reader is exposed equally to the worlds of the police and of the criminals, whose ethos Brigid shares. The exact distinctions between these worlds are blurred, and the reality/illusion question makes it clear that both Spade and the reader function, when they judge, on the basis of only some of the facts. More facts may be produced by "heaving a wild and unpredictable monkey-wrench into the works," as Spade says, but he never forgets that his facts, once linked, are still a construction of reality. As he tells his lawyer of Iva Archer's alibi, "I don't believe it or disbelieve it. . . . I don't know a damned thing about it." What counts, he explains, is that it seems "to click with most of the known facts" and "ought to hold." Spade operates on this view of reality for the entire novel; at its end he refuses to tell Brigid whether he would have acted differently had the falcon been real and they shared its wealth.

Hammett had a bit of fun articulating Spade's world view: when Flitcraft assumes his new existence, he changes his name to Charles Pierce, a variation on Charles Sanders Peirce, the nineteenth-century American philosopher who wrote extensively about chance and probability. Peirce also identified a logical process between induction and deduction called "abduction," in which the investigator accepts an event as having happened, then imagines the state of affairs that produced the situation. Its common use in detective fiction, as Hammett saw, reinforced the role of the detective as the author of reality.

The method is apropos, since the characters with whom Spade must deal live according to illusions. Most of them are greedy; they want the falcon. For some, such as Gutman, this greed is overlain with the illusion of personal quest. Others, such as Brigid, believe the world is made up of "saps," who can be manipulated by their sexual desires. All such illusions are, on the allegoric level, symbolic sins. Those of Joel Cairo, the effete criminal, and Wilmer, the homosexual gunman, have become less obvious as their characters became more stereotyped. Rhea Gutman's self-abuse is a continuation of Gabrielle Leggett's morbid self-destruction. Miles Archer, with his sartorial self-confidence, represents a traditional pride, while Effie Perrine, with her romantic conception of love, is a more simply deluded, but nonetheless erring, variation on a generic norm.

Reasoning as he does by abduction, Spade maintains his personal distance on these characters until he abduces (authors) their formative situations. He understands that everyone lives in his illusions, so he believes nothing, trusts no one, and rejects real emotional contact. Critic Bernard Schopen points out that Gutman, Cairo, Wilmer and Brigid are moral primitives, who "create those illusions which assist them in their rapacious pursuits." Most affective are those of Brigid, whose continual lies and deceptions readers excuse as long as she feigns inchoate personal emotions—claiming thus an emotional sanctity. This implication of mystery makes her character far more interesting than those of Jeanne Delano in "The Girl with the Silver Eyes" or the princess in "The Gutting of Couffignal." Yet it is the reader, not Spade, that she seduces with her sentiments. Spade merely speaks the lingua franca of each character's illusion and avoids the fate of "saps" like Archer and Thursby, who are induced to participate.

The abductive method is complicated by those properties of the formal mystery that Hammett appropriated for the structure of *The Maltese Falcon*. He had been experimenting with analytic detection in *The Dain Curse*, and was fond of the trail of false clues that he used in "The Tenth Clew." The ten deceptions in *The Maltese Falcon*, according to George Thompson, begin with Brigid's representation of herself as Miss Wonderly and her portrayal of Thursby as Archer's killer. The third is Dundy's opinion that Spade murdered Archer, a view supported by new information about Spade's affair with Iva and testimony from Archer's brother. If the reader is suspicious of Spade at this point, Hammett has successfully involved him in the skeptical world view that is Spade's *modus operandi,* and the point of the Flitcraft parable. The fourth deception is Brigid's story connecting herself and Thursby to the falcon, for she says that she is the victim of the latter's greed. Later, the implication in her disappearance is that she has become the victim of foul play. The sixth deception occurs when she calls Spade for help, the seventh when the police theorize that Thursby's death is the result of underworld warfare. The wild goose chase to Burlingame is the eighth false clue, and the ninth is the $1,000 bill that Gutman palms in the final showdown. That the falcon itself is a worthless phony is the tenth and paramount deception. It suddenly illuminates the moral and spiritual emptiness of the co-conspirators, and ironically belittles their quest. It also links the nine previous deceptions in one paramount symbol of the three plot elements—the investigation of Archer's death, the mystery of the falcon, and the romance between Spade and Brigid.

The Flitcraft parable itself shines through the ten plot deceptions to illuminate the grail/quest structure in a new light. When the grail is found to be worthless, the implication is that the emotion Brigid generates is a "falling beam," discredited by her greed. But it is also true that while they seek it, the grail holds Spade and Brigid together. It represents the emptiness of sentimental emotion, but its pursuit is, paradoxically, an adaptive response, a confirming, stabilizing influence in Western society. But it no longer provides a "solution." Like so many American writers of the late twenties, Hammett sees continual emotional improvisation as the only answer. The fact that Flitcraft's life is Hammett's personal meditation on what he himself should do next makes the symbol extraordinarily compelling.

Source: William Marling, "The Falcon and the Key," in *Dashiell Hammett*, Twayne Publishers, 1983, pp. 70–78.

William F. Nolan

In the following essay, Nolan provides an overview of the creation of and critical response to The Maltese Falcon, *focusing on dialogue, characterization, and censorship. Nolan is the award-winning author of the science fiction classic* Logan's Run, *adapted to film in 1976, starring Michael York. Nolan has been cited as "the leading Hammett scholar." In addition to his critical study* Dashiell Hammett: A Casebook, *Nolan is also*

> *The Maltese Falcon,*
> when closely studied, is basically
> a series of brilliant dialogues, set
> in motion and bolstered by
> offstage events."

the author of a full biography entitled Hammett: A Life at the Edge *(Congdon & Weed, 1983). He has written extensively on Hammett for magazines and has just completed a third book on the author,* A Life beyond Thursday: Solving the Hammett Mystery, *now in submission by the Trident Media Group in New York.*

Recalling the San Francisco of Hammett, and *The Maltese Falcon,* veteran columnist Herb Caen vividly described the gritty atmosphere of this fog-haunted northern California city: "The Hall of Justice was dirty and reeked of evil. The criminal lawyers were young and hungry and used every shyster trick . . . The City Hall, the D.A. and the cops ran the town as though they owned it, and they did. Hookers worked upstairs, not on the street; there were hundreds, maybe thousands, most of them named Sally. The two biggest abortion mills—one on Market the other on Fillmore—were so well-known they might as well have had neon signs. You could play roulette in the Marina, roll craps on O'Farrell, play poker on Mason, get rolled at 4 A.M. in a bar on Eddy, and wake up at noon in a Turk Street hotel with a girl whose name you never knew or cared to know. . . . San Francisco was a Sam Spade city."

And Sam Spade, the satan-faced private eye, was Dashiell Hammett's man—the cool, untrickable lone sleuth who stood between the law and lawbreakers, despised by both, respected by both, who could deal from the top or bottom of the deck, as occasion demanded, who grinned at loaded guns and told politicians and cops to go to hell, who bluffed, cracked wise, bedded his women, and handled his booze, who called San Francisco "my burg," and knew every hood in it, a man of cynical humor, direct action and a man, above all else, who followed the ritual code of his profession.

"When a man's partner is killed he's supposed to do something about it," he says, after his agency co-partner, Miles Archer, is gunned down in the fog. What he does about it, and to whom, forms the backbone of Hammett's most famous novel, the prototype of a thousand others, the book which in the very act of remaking its field transcends it. Many critics have called it the finest crime novel ever written; certainly it is one of the half-dozen best, a classic which *The New Republic* (in a 1930 review) cited for its "absolute distinction of real art."

Editor Joseph Shaw, reading the 65,000-word manuscript in 1929 as a five-part serial, enthused to his readers: "In all of my experience I have never encountered a story as intense, as gripping or as powerful as this one . . . It is a magnificent piece of writing. With all the earnestness of which I am capable, I tell you not to miss it."

The Maltese Falcon is remarkable in many respects. Aside from a bit of scuffling and a punch or two, all of the violence takes place offstage; the four killings are done "out of range," and we are shown the effects of murder rather than its execution, what its factual existence does to the men and women who share in it. Hammett gives us implied violence; guns are drawn and flourished, never fired; threats are made, tempers flare, accusations and cross-accusations abound—but Hammett keeps the tension taut as a stretched wire without ever resorting to overt violence. This is all the more fascinating in a book which most readers recall as "full of action and death." (Jacobi, the doomed ship's captain staggers into Sam's office and dies there, but he has been shot elsewhere; his ship has burned beyond our vision; we are shown only the end result of what has been done to him.) There is the constant, immediate feeling that, at any given moment, the scene will literally explode into bullets and blood, but Hammett resists the temptation, and suspense is therefore greatly intensified. Even at the climax, when one expects the usual shoot-out we are given only conversation—crackling, menace-laden conversation, laced with double and triple meaning—designed to do the job we have come to expect from overt violence. When the fat man, Gutman, is finally killed by one of his own gang we learn this as it is reported to Spade—just as we learned of the deaths of Archer and Thursby. And Spade, a man of violence, uses only his personality, his shrewdness, to hold the game in check. (Admittedly, in the course of the book, he disarms two of Gutman's hoods, but casually and with no fuss. Unlike the Op, he does not carry a gun, use a gun. Yet, always there is the feeling that he *would* use it—if he had to—as casually as he swats the pistol out of Cairo's grasp.)

The Maltese Falcon, when closely studied, is basically a series of brilliant dialogues, set in motion and bolstered by offstage events. The book could easily be translated into stage drama, with no more than minor cutting needed for the new form. The sets are all there: Spade's office, the girl's apartment, the fat man's hotel room where the last-act climax is played.

The characters in *Falcon* are etched so deeply that once encountered they cannot be forgotten: Casper Gutman, the florid fat man seeking the elusive gold-and-jewel-encrusted statuette, who speaks effusively in a "throaty purr" and whose eyes are "dark gleams in ambush behind pink puffs of flesh," who finds the resourceful Spade a more-than-worthy opponent; red-haired, blue-eyed Brigid O'Shaughnessy, the culmination of Hammett's good-evil women, the lying temptress who changes identity as often as she changes her old lies for new ones; Joel Cairo, the soft-voiced, perfumed homosexual; Wilmer Cook, the sadistic, baby-faced gunman; and Sam Spade himself, with his V-shaped face and sharp predator's teeth ("He looked . . . like a blond satan and grinned . . . showing his jaw teeth").

Effective, too, is Effie Perine, Sam's secretary—and Lieutenant Dundy and detective Polhaus of Homicide, the coppers who dog Spade closely throughout the narrative. ("I've warned you your foot was going to slip one of these days," Dundy tells the detective. Spade remains unruffled. "It's a long while since I burst out crying because policemen didn't like me.")

The author had real people in mind when he created these characters (as he so often did with his detective fiction): "I followed Gutman's original in Washington," stated Hammett, "and I never remember shadowing a man who bored me so much. He was not after a jeweled falcon, of course; but he *was* suspected of being a German spy. Brigid was based, in part, on a woman who came in to Pinkerton's to hire an operative to discharge her housekeeper. [And, although Hammett didn't say so, she was also patterned on the advertising artist he'd shared an office with in San Francisco, Peggy O'Toole.] I worked with Dundy's prototype in a North Carolina railroad yard. The Cairo character I picked up on a forgery charge in 1920. Effie, the good girl, once asked me to go into the narcotic smuggling business with her in San Diego. Wilmer, the gunman was picked up in Stockton, California, a neat small smooth-faced quiet boy of perhaps twenty-one. He was serenely proud of the name the papers gave him—The Midget Bandit. He'd robbed a Stockton filling station the previous week—and had been annoyed by the description the station proprietor had given of him and by the proprietor's statement of what he would do to that little runt if he ever laid eyes on him again. So he'd stolen a car and returned to stick the guy up again and see what he wanted to do about it. That's when we nabbed him."

Hammett's detective, in this novel, bears his own first name, Samuel, but the author denied autobiographical intent, declaring that "Spade had no original," that he was "idealized . . . in the sense that he is what most of the private detectives I've worked with would *like* to have been." The average detective, stated Hammett, cares nothing for the Sherlock Holmes image: "He wants to be a hard and shifty fellow, able to take care of himself in any situation, able to get the best of anybody he comes in contact with."

Hammett used several disguised San Francisco hotels in the course of the novel. Casper Gutman lives at the St. Mark, "a combination of the St. Francis and the Mark Hopkins." Cairo lives at the Belvedere, which was "based on the Bellevue."

Hammett's cross-and-double-cross scene writing reached its apex with the hotel room sequence wherein Sam tells Gutman that they must rig a "fall guy" for the police to pin all the murders on. He suggests the boy, Wilmer, and although Gutman is shocked ("I feel towards Wilmer just exactly as if he were my own son") the fat man considers the idea. Meanwhile, Spade offers to make Cairo the fall guy, and when the little man protests and says, "Suppose we give them . . . Miss O'Shaughnessy," Spade agrees that if "she could be rigged" he's willing to discuss that idea. She is horrified—and the boy is finally chosen. This entire sequence, in which Spade plays off one member of the gang against another, weakening all of them, sowing mistrust and hatred, is Hammett at his most masterful; his control is superb, and the scene could not be improved upon.

At Tony's Bar in New York, a few years after the book was published, Hammett told James Thurber that *Falcon* had been influenced by Henry James' *The Wings of the Dove.* "In both novels," related Thurber, "a fabulous fortune—jewels in *Falcon,* inherited millions in *Dove*—shapes the destinies of the disenchanted central characters, and James' designing woman, Kate Croy, like Hammett's pistol-packing Brigid O'Shaughnessy, loses her lover in a Renunciation Scene."

The late W. Somerset Maugham, who basically admired Hammett's work, found Spade to be

"... a nasty bit of goods ... an unscrupulous rogue and a heartless crook. ... There is little to choose between him and the criminals he is dealing with."

Yet this is precisely the character Spade wants to project to Gutman; it is imperative that the fat man think him capable of anything; he must play villain to defeat a villain. Later he says, to Brigid, "Don't be too sure I'm as crooked as I'm supposed to be. That kind of reputation [makes it] easier to deal with the enemy."

Actually, Spade wears many masks throughout the book—pretending to go along with the girl although he knows she killed Archer; stringing the police; working himself into a false rage for Gutman's benefit—and as each mask is removed a new one appears; total honesty is a luxury Sam cannot afford. The masks must remain in place. ("Everybody has something to conceal," he says.)

It would be a mistake to judge Spade as "unscrupulous" and "heartless." In the climactic sequence in which he finally turns Brigid over to the police he reveals the emotions of a man whose heart is with the woman, but whose code forbids his accepting her. Spade knows that he cannot continue to function if he breaks his personal code and goes off with Brigid—even while he admits that Miles Archer was "a louse" and that the agency is better off without him. Sam can sleep with Iva, the dead man's wife; he can bed down his secretary ("... his hand on her hip ... 'Don't touch me now—not now.'") and he can spend the night with Brigid, but he must never make a permanent alliance with any of them, the good or the evil. He must remain, like the Op, a free lance for hire. He may love Brigid ("I think I do") but he cannot trust love any more than he can trust the girl herself ("I am a liar," she tells him, "I have always been a liar"). Spade refuses to "play the sap" for her, giving her all the code reasons for turning her in, then admits that after she's jailed "I'll have some rotten nights." Finally, emotionally, he tells her he won't let her go free "because all of me wants to—wants to say to hell with the consequences and do it—and because-God damn you—you've counted on that with me the same as you counted on that with the others."

This is not Maugham's heartless crook; this is a shaken man fully aware that emotion can destroy him if he lets it. Spade ultimately rejects Brigid, "sends her over," with the outwardly cruel and cynical line (which may have helped deceive Mr. Maugham): "You're an angel ... [and] if they hang you I'll always remember you." Spade meant it literally.

But if not a villain neither was Sam Spade a hero. In fact, Hammett was presenting a new breed of antihero, a man whose rigid personal code is placed above that of the society he inhabits. He becomes, in effect, the individual lawmaker, a danger to any society. And Spade *is* a dangerous man, capable of using the corruption around him, admitting that "most things in San Francisco can be bought or taken."

In the midst of the case Spade tells Brigid a long, seemingly irrelevant story she does not understand, about a man named Flitcraft who left his wife and family suddenly one day, starting a whole new life—all because, while walking along the street, he had narrowly missed being killed by a falling beam, and "he felt like somebody had taken the lid off life and let him look at the works." Spade is telling the girl, in parable, that life is a series of falling beams and that some of us find out about them and some don't. He is telling Brigid, in effect, not to be surprised when one hits her—as it finally does. Spade lives longer because he knows the beams are falling, and is watching for them.

Ceremony helps hold Sam's world together. He follows a stylized pattern in handling small details (the rolling of a cigarette, the ritual handshake, etc.) so that he may deal creatively with larger ones. Order within disorder. Mysticism mixed with hard practicality. Yet no more mysterious than Hemingway's war veteran (and Spade is a veteran of many wars) ceremoniously fishing on the Big Two-Hearted River. It is pertinent to note that in his magazine-to-book revisions Hammett substituted "They shook hands ceremoniously" for "They shook hands with marked formality." This same calming ceremony is present in the way Spade dresses, ransacks an apartment, disarms a gunman.

Novelist Kenneth Millar sees in the search for the jeweled falcon "a fable of modern man. ... The black bird is hollow, worthless. The reality behind appearances is a treacherous vacuum. ... The bird's lack of value implies Hammett's final comment on the inadequacy and superficiality of Spade's life and ours. If only his bitterly inarticulate struggle for self-realization were itself more fully realized ... Sam Spade could have been a great indigenous tragic figure. ... I think *The Maltese Falcon,* with its astonishing imaginative energy persisting undiminished after more than a third of a century, is tragedy of a new kind, deadpan tragedy."

Critic Allen Eyles termed it "a study of a group of people affected by the weakness of greed, realized with a force and a psychological aptness that gives it a moral purpose."

Hammett's involved blood history of the falcon, as told to Spade by Gutman, was partially—as with the characters themselves—based on fact. The author stated that "somewhere I had read of the peculiar rental agreement between Charles V and the Order of the Hospital of St. John of Jerusalem." He refers to the agreement of 1530 between the Order and Emperor Charles V, under which, as "rent" for the island of Malta (then under Spanish rule), they would pay Charles an annual tribute of a single falcon. One of the birds they gave, according to Hammett's account, was "a glorious golden falcon encrusted from head to foot with the finest jewels in their coffers." It moves from country to country down the years, leaving a trail of death and theft and deceit, until Gutman goes after it some seventeen years before the story opens. It is against this highly romantic background that Hammett plays out what editor Shaw called his "saga of a private detective."

That the bird is a worthless fake when Gutman finally gets it is no real surprise to Spade. He never believed in it anyhow; men who live in seedy apartments and work out of seedy office buildings may dream of fabled riches, but they know such riches will not be seen in their lifetime. Gutman is crushed (by the falling beam), but Spade is safe and free to continue as before, lonely, embittered, but able to function on a realistic level. He still has his job. He's been "through it all before" and expects to go through it again.

In 1929, when Hammett wrote *Falcon,* rather strong editorial censorship existed in the popular magazines. When Hammett's serial arrived Shaw checked it carefully. Sex came first. Brigid's line, "I'm not ashamed to be naked before you," was dropped, as was a line from Cairo directed to her regarding a boy she had failed to sleep with. ("The one you couldn't make.") A damn or a hell was permitted, but outright swearing or foul language was not. (Hammett got around this neatly, losing none of the intended impact. "The boy spoke two words, the first a short guttural verb, the second 'you.'") Hammett's line from Spade, "How long have you been off the gooseberry lay, son?" was changed to "How long have you been off the lay?" since Shaw was certain Hammett had something dark in mind. Actually, "the gooseberry lay" was crook slang for stealing wash from a clothesline!

However, Shaw did not touch the line "Keep that gunsel away from me . . ." because he assumed the word "gunsel" meant gunman. He was wrong. It was a homosexual term, meaning "a kept boy."

Yet, to this day, mystery writers continue to misuse it, following Shaw's line of thought as to its origin.

Homosexuality in general was not censored nearly as much as heterosexuality in those early pulp days. In the book version, when Spade questions a house detective about Joel Cairo, the man answers with a leer, "Oh, that one." The original magazine version was bolder in the detective's reply, "Oh, *her!*"

Another interesting Hammett magazine-to-book change, having nothing to do with censorship but dealing with clarity, consisted of his switching "You'll want to sleep if you've been in the grease all night" to "You'll want to sleep if you've been standing up under a police storm all night." Hammett was always working to improve his writing for hard-cover publication.

The Maltese Falcon became an immediate best-seller (surpassed only by *The Thin Man* in overall sales through the years). In *Falcon*'s first decade and a half the book saw two dozen hard-cover printings in three separate editions. Fifteen of these printings were issued out of Modern Library.

With the successful publication of *Red Harvest, The Dain Curse,* and now with *The Maltese Falcon,* Samuel Dashiell Hammett had achieved a major critical and financial breakthrough.

Source: William F. Nolan, "Hammett's Black Bird," in *Dashiell Hammett: A Casebook,* McNally & Loftin, 1969, pp. 56–65.

Sources

Cuppy, Will, "Mystery and Adventure," in *New York Herald Tribune,* February 23, 1930, p. 17.

Curtis, William, "Some Recent Books," in *Town & Country,* February 15, 1930.

"Judging the Books," in *Judge,* March 1, 1930.
MacDonald, Ross, *Self-Portrait: Ceaselessly into the Past,* Capra Press, 1981, p. 112.

Further Reading

Gregory, Sinda, *Private Investigations: The Novels of Dashiell Hammett,* Southern Illinois University Press, 1985.
   Coming from outside of the small, specific world of detective fiction, Gregory examines Hammett's novels with the same critical eye that one might apply to the works of Dostoyevsky or John Updike.

Layman, Richard, *Dashiell Hammett: A Descriptive Bibliography*, University of Pittsburgh Press, 1979.

This book gives a comprehensive, painstakingly assembled survey of Hammett's many novels and stories, with the detailed publication history of each.

Marling, William, "Dashiell Hammett, Copywriter," in *The American Roman Noir: Hammett, Cain, and Chandler*, University of Georgia Press, 1995, pp. 93–147.

Marling's analysis of Hammett, and of *The Maltese Falcon* in particular, fits into a larger context of detective fiction in books and films.

Wolfe, Peter, *Beams Falling: The Art of Dashiell Hammett*, Bowling Green University Popular Press, 1980.

Wolfe approaches the author's life as a mystery, piecing together clues from his writings to create a convincing portrait of the man.

Nausea

Jean-Paul Sartre
1938

Jean-Paul Sartre's philosophical novel *La Nausée* (1938; *Nausea*) is a seminal text of the existential movement that emerged in France during the 1940s and 1950s. In *Nausea*, Sartre, who became a figurehead of existential philosophy, explores fundamental questions and ideas that he elaborated upon in his later works.

Nausea is written as the diary of Antoine Roquentin, a thirty-year-old man who is grappling with a sense of revulsion at his consciousness of his own existence and of the existence of the people and objects around him. Roquentin, who is profoundly lonely, without friends or family, expresses a sensation of "sweetish sickness" in contemplating the absurdity of life. He refers to this sensation, which is both mental and physical, as the Nausea.

Nausea takes place primarily in the fictional French seaport town of Bouville, where Roquentin has been living for the past three years, while he works on research for a biography he is writing of an eighteenth-century French politician. Roquentin eventually decides to abandon the biography, as he has come to the conclusion that it is a meaningless project. He begins to hope that he and his former girlfriend, Anny, will get back together again and that their love will cure him of his Nausea. However, when he goes to visit Anny, she once again rejects him, and Roquentin is plunged into crisis, for his existence seems all the more repulsive to him. He ultimately resolves his philosophical crisis by deciding to take on the creative project of

Jean-Paul Sartre

writing a novel, which he feels will be an antidote to the Nausea.

Nausea exemplifies a philosophical exploration of the nature of existence and the challenge faced by an individual who becomes keenly conscious of the fundamental absurdity of life. Sartre further explores themes of consciousness, loneliness, transformation, and freedom, in terms of his existential philosophy.

Author Biography

Jean-Paul Sartre was born June 21, 1905, in Paris, France. His father died when he was only one year old, after which he and his mother lived with his maternal grandparents. When he was eleven, his mother remarried, and they moved to La Rochelle. Sartre described his childhood and young adulthood in his Nobel Prize–winning autobiography *Les Mots* (1964; *The Words*). He studied philosophy at the Ecole Normale Superieure, in Paris, from which he graduated at the top of his class in 1929. It was there that he met Simone de Beauvoir, who graduated second in their class and was to become his lifelong companion as well as a major feminist and existentialist writer in her own right. The

relationship between Sartre and de Beauvoir, which has become legendary, lasted over half a century and was characterized by the intense intellectual sharing of two great minds made complicated by Sartre's numerous extended affairs with other women.

Upon graduating from the Ecole Normale, Sartre served for two years in the Meteorological Corps of the French military. During the 1930s, he taught at several different secondary schools throughout France. His first novel, *La Nausée* (*Nausea*), was published in 1938. In 1939, with the outbreak of World War II, he was drafted into the army. He was captured by Germans in 1940 and spent nine months in a prisoner of war camp. In 1941, he was released from the prison camp and returned to Paris, which was by then occupied by German forces. Sartre joined the French Resistance movement and wrote for the underground Resistance newspapers *Combat* and *Les Lettres Francaises*. The publication of his greatest philosophical tract, *L'etre et neant* (*Being and Nothingness*), in 1943, established him as a leading figure at the forefront of existential philosophy. By the end of the war, Sartre's combined working out of existential philosophy and his passionate commitment to political causes had earned him celebrity status. He was awarded the French Legion of Honor in 1945 but refused to accept it.

After the war, Sartre became increasingly committed to active participation in political causes, and his existential philosophy developed along these lines as well. He and de Beauvoir founded the literary, philosophical, and political journal *Les Temps Modernes* in 1945, which became a major forum for debating existential ideas. Among his major works may be included the novel *Nausea*, the philosophical tract *Being and Nothingness*, the play *Huis-clos* (1944; *No Exit*), and the autobiography, *The Words*. In 1964, Sartre was awarded the Nobel Prize in literature for *The Words* but refused to accept the honor.

Starting in 1960, his eyesight began to seriously deteriorate, and he was nearly blind by the time of his death. In the last decade of his life, he essentially stopped writing, although he continued to be involved in political causes through ongoing activism and remained in the public eye by giving widely publicized interviews. Sartre died of a lung tumor on April 15, 1980. The extent of his international reputation may be gauged by the attendance of twenty-five thousand people at his funeral.

Plot Summary

Nausea is written as a diary begun by Antoine Roquentin in January of 1932. Roquentin, a thirty-year-old man, has been living in the small French seacoast town of Bouville for the past three years, during which he has been researching and writing a biography of the Marquis de Rollebon, an eighteenth-century political figure. Roquentin lives alone in a one-room apartment near the train station. Before moving to Bouville, he had spent many years traveling throughout the world.

Roquentin begins writing the diary in order to record a subtle change he has noticed in his perceptions of himself and the world around him. He is disturbed by his own consciousness and by uncertainty about the significance of his life, and he is questioning the meaning of the existence of objects and people in the world. He has recently begun experiencing episodes in which he is overcome with a sense of revulsion, or "sweetish sickness," in grappling with these questions. Roquentin refers to this sensation, which is both mental and physical, as the Nausea:

> Then the Nausea seized me, I dropped to a seat, I no longer knew where I was; I saw the colours spin slowly around me, I wanted to vomit. And since that time, the Nausea has not left me, it holds me.

Roquentin spends his days in the Bouville library working on his book, and he often spends his evenings sitting in local cafés. Sometimes he walks through the streets at night, observing the people. On Sundays, Roquentin strolls through the streets of the town, observing the respectable, middle-class townspeople in their Sunday promenade as they exchange pleasantries with passing acquaintances.

At the library, Roquentin has become acquainted with a man whom he refers to as the Self-Taught Man because he is in the process of reading all of the books in the library in alphabetical order. The Self-Taught Man asks to see Roquentin's picture postcards from his world travels, and the young man reluctantly invites him up to his room to oblige him in this.

One day, Roquentin unexpectedly receives a letter from Anny, an English actress with whom he had a relationship for three years. He and Anny broke up six years ago, and he hasn't seen or heard from her in about four years. Anny tells him that she is going to be passing through Paris in a few days and begs him to come to visit her while she is there.

Roquentin goes to the Bouville art museum and examines the paintings in the portrait gallery, which contains portraits of the city's many founding fathers, local politicians, and influential businessmen. Roquentin ridicules these portraits, which are designed to justify the existence of these men by emphasizing their power and influence over the town.

After three years of working on his history of the Marquis de Rollebon, Roquentin comes to the conclusion that the project is meaningless, and he decides to abandon the writing of the book altogether. As his research and writing of this book has been the focus of his life for several years, Roquentin is thrown into an even greater sense of crisis. He realizes that he has been writing the book in order to avoid facing his own existence.

Roquentin reluctantly agrees to meet the Self-Taught Man for lunch at a local restaurant. The Self-Taught Man explains that he is a communist and a humanist. While he seems to expect that Roquentin will be sympathetic to his political and ideological attitudes, Roquentin is critical and disdainful of both communism and humanism. In the midst of this awkward and unpleasant conversation, Roquentin is overcome with the Nausea and abruptly leaves the restaurant without explaining himself to the Self-Taught Man.

Roquentin takes the train from Bouville to Paris to visit Anny. He realizes that he is still in love with her and is hoping that they may be able to get back together again. When he visits Anny at her hotel in Paris, they have a long conversation in which she explains to him how her attitudes about life have changed, and he tries to explain to her the thoughts he's been having about the Nausea. Roquentin feels that although they have been separated for several years, they have both been thinking about the same things and have changed in similar ways.

Anny, however, does not take much interest in his ideas and makes it clear that she has no interest in becoming involved with him again. She explains that she is living as a "kept" woman, meaning that she is financially supported by a wealthy man to whom she is not married and does not love, but with whom she travels throughout the world. She rather coldly dismisses Roquentin, telling him he does not mean anything to her anymore. Roquentin later sees her at the train station, where she boards a train in the company of the man by whom she is "kept." Although Anny sees Roquentin from the train window, she remains expressionless and does not acknowledge him.

Roquentin returns to Bouville, but he has decided that he is going to move to Paris in a week.

On his last day in town, he stops by the library. There, he witnesses a scene in which the Self-Taught Man makes sexual advances toward a young schoolboy. Roquentin says nothing, but the Corsican who guards the library yells at the Self-Taught Man that he has seen what he did to the boy. The Corsican punches the Self-Taught Man in the nose and tells him never to come back to the library again. As the Self-Taught Man is walking out of the library, blood streaming from his nose, Roquentin attempts to help him. But the Self-Taught Man refuses his help and walks off down the street.

In his final two hours before catching the train to Paris, Roquentin goes to the Railwaymen's Rendezvous café to say goodbye to the waitress, Madeleine, and the café manager, Francoise, and to write in his diary what has just happened with the Self-Taught Man. While he is at the café, Madeleine offers to play a certain jazz record that he likes, which contains the song "Some of These Days." While listening to this song, Roquentin imagines that it has been composed by a Jewish man sitting at a piano in New York City and sung by an African American woman. In contemplating the creative process that resulted in this song, Roquentin realizes that he wants to try writing a novel. The idea of writing a novel seems to him to be a sort of resolution to the Nausea that has been distressing him.

Characters

Anny

Anny is an English actress with whom Roquentin was in a relationship for three years. They broke up about six years before the events of the story take place and have not seen, written, or talked to each other in about four years. One day, Roquentin unexpectedly receives a letter from Anny, stating that she will be passing through Paris in a week and asking him to come visit her while she is there. Roquentin goes to visit Anny in her hotel room in Paris with the hope that she will want to get back together with him. He and Anny have a long conversation in which she explains to him that she had always wanted to experience "perfect moments" in life but that she now realizes there are no perfect moments, and so she no longer expects to have them. Roquentin tries to explain to her his own thoughts about the Nausea, but Anny does not seem interested in what he has to say. She tells him

that she is living as a "kept" woman, meaning that she is being supported as the mistress of a wealthy man whom she does not love and whom she is not going to marry. Anny rather abruptly tells Roquentin to leave, because a young man (presumably a lover) is coming to visit her. She tells Roquentin that she no longer has any use for him. Later, at the train station, Roquentin sees Anny board a train with a tall, Egyptian-looking man who is presumably the man by whom she is being "kept." Although Anny sees Roquentin from her window on the train, her face remains expressionless, and she does not acknowledge him. In visiting Anny, Roquentin had hoped that the answer to his internal struggles would lie in renewing his love relationship with her. However, when he realizes that this is not possible, he is once again left to grapple alone with the significance of his existence.

The Corsican

The Corsican is the man who serves as a security guard for the library in Bouville. Toward the end of the novel, he sees the Self-Taught Man making sexual advances at a young schoolboy. The Corsican immediately walks over to the Self-Taught Man and yells at him and then punches him in the face, causing his nose to bleed profusely. The Corsican then orders the Self-Taught Man to leave the library and never come back.

Francoise

Francoise is the manager of the Railwaymen's Rendezvous café, and also works as a prostitute in an upstairs room of the café. Roquentin maintains a purely sexual relationship with Francoise, although she does not charge him for sex, as she does with her customers. During his last few hours in Bouville, Roquentin sits in the café. He had hoped to be with Francoise one more time before leaving town, but she is entertaining another male customer and does not have time for him.

Madeleine

Madeleine is the waitress at the Railwaymen's Rendezvous café. During Roquentin's last few hours in Bouville, while he is sitting at the café, Madeleine offers to play a record of the jazz song "Some of these Days." Although he has listened to the song many times before, he finds on hearing it this time that it helps him to realize that he wants to write a novel.

Ogier P.

See The Self-Taught Man

Antoine Roquentin

Antoine Roquentin is a thirty-year-old man who begins keeping a diary in January of 1932. Roquentin has spent several years traveling throughout the world. He is supported by a modest family inheritance, so he does not have to work to make a living. For the past three years, he has been living in the small seacoast town of Bouville, France, while doing research and writing a history of the Marquis de Rollebon, an eighteenth-century French political figure. Roquentin begins his diary in order to record the subtle changes he has been experiencing in his perceptions of himself and the world around him. He finds that he has been experiencing a "sweetish sickness," which he calls the Nausea. The Nausea, which is both a physical and a mental sensation, comes over him at moments when he is feeling overwhelmed by a sense of disgust at the absurdity of existence.

Roquentin eventually decides to abandon his book about the Marquis de Rollebon because he feels that the project is meaningless. One day, he receives an unexpected letter from Anny, an English actress with whom he had a relationship for several years. Roquentin and Anny broke up about six years ago, and they haven't seen or heard from one another for several years. Anny's letter states that she will be passing through Paris in a few days and begs him to come visit her while she is in town. Roquentin realizes that he is still in love with Anny, and he hopes that they will get back together again. He imagines that this love will be the answer to his confusion over the nature of his existence and the significance of his life. However, when he goes to visit Anny in her hotel room in Paris, she makes it clear that she has no interest in getting back together with him, and she rather coldly informs him that she no longer has any use for him.

Toward the end of the novel, Roquentin decides that he is going to move to Paris and work on writing a novel. He feels that this creative process will serve as some kind of resolution to his struggles over the meaning of his existence.

The Self-Taught Man

Roquentin meets the Self-Taught Man during his daily visits to the Bouville library. The Self-Taught Man sits at the library reading during his free time, and Roquentin figures out that he is trying to read all of the books in the library in alphabetical order. The Self-Taught Man explains that he began this project about seven years ago and

expects that he will have read them all within another six years. Although they have often exchanged pleasantries while at the library over the past three years, Roquentin and the Self-Taught Man have never socialized together outside of the library.

The Self-Taught Man asks to see Roquentin's picture postcards from his world travels, and Roquentin reluctantly invites the man up to his room to see them. He gives the Self-Taught Man a handful of postcards to take home with him, and the man then offers to take him to lunch sometime, to which Roquentin reluctantly agrees. When Roquentin and the Self-Taught Man meet for lunch, the man tells him that he is a communist and a humanist. Although the Self-Taught Man seems to expect that Roquentin holds these same values as well, Roquentin is disdainful of these views.

On Roquentin's last day in Bouville, while he is at the library, the Self-Taught Man is caught making sexual advances toward a young schoolboy. The Corsican also sees this, and he yells at the Self-Taught Man and punches him in the face, causing his nose to bleed profusely. The Corsican tells him to leave the library immediately and never come back again. The Self-Taught Man takes this punishment passively and quietly leaves. Roquentin offers to help him, but the Self-Taught Man refuses to accept his help and walks off down the street.

Themes

Change, Transformation, Metamorphosis, Rebirth

Roquentin begins writing his diary because he has noticed a subtle change in his perceptions of himself and the world around him. He hopes that by recording his daily perceptions, he will be able to make sense of the nature of this change, which he describes as "an abstract change without object." He realizes that, at various points in his life, he has been "subject to these sudden transformations," in which "a crowd of small metamorphoses accumulate in me without my noticing it, and then one fine day, a veritable revolution takes place." Roquentin expresses that he is terrified of this "new overthrow in my life" because "I'm afraid of what will be born and take possession of me." *Nausea* describes the process of transformation that Roquentin experiences. Images of metamorphosis and rebirth throughout the narrative emphasize the centrality of this theme to the novel as a whole.

Topics For Further Study

- Sartre was one of the philosophers at the forefront of the French existential movement. Learn more about another major existential thinker, such as Søren Kirkegaard, Arthur Schopenhauer, Friedrich Nietzsche, Martin Heidegger, Karl Jaspers, Martin Buber, Albert Camus, or Simone de Beauvoir. What are the major works of the philosopher or writer you choose? What are the central ideas put forth by this philosopher or writer? Explore your opinions in comparison to these ideas. To what extent do you agree or disagree with them, and why?

- Learn more about another important French writer from the twentieth century such as Andre Breton, Louis Aragon, Paul Eluard, Andre Malraux, Louis-Ferdinand Celine, Alain Robbe-Grillet, Samuel Becket, Eugene Ionesco, or Marguerite Duras. What literary movement (or movements) was this writer associated with? What are some of the major works of this writer?

How is this author's writing characterized, in terms of style, theme, and subject matter?

- In *Nausea*, Roquentin's experience of listening to a jazz record helps him to define and make sense of his own purpose in life. Research a major jazz musician from the twentieth century. What were this musician's major works (songs, albums, compositions, etc.)? How has this musician's unique style of playing or composition been described? To what extent did this musician influence other musicians or the development of jazz music in general? If you are able to find and listen to a recording of this musician's work, pick one song, musical number, or composition, and describe the music in your own words. What thoughts, feelings, or mood does this music evoke?

- *Nausea* is a novel written in the form of a fictional diary. Write your own original short story in the form of a fictional diary.

Consciousness and Self-Reflection

The narrative of *Nausea* is motivated by Roquentin's extreme consciousness of his own perceptions of himself and others. His diary is an exercise in self-reflection, an attempt to express and record the details of this extreme self-consciousness. On several occasions, Roquentin examines his face in the mirror for long periods of time. He seems to be trying to evaluate the physical features of his face, but this exercise serves as a metaphor for Roquentin's struggle to make sense of his own humanity. This motif of gazing at his reflection in the mirror symbolizes his process of self-reflection, as recorded in his diary. At a point of crisis in the story, Roquentin is overwhelmed by his consciousness of his own existence, to the extent that he feels plagued by his own thought processes. "If I could keep myself from thinking!" he cries. Roquentin eventually comes to the conclusion that his constant thinking and his consciousness of himself constantly thinking are precisely what define his existence. Because he

exists, he can't help but think. He asserts, "My thought is *me*: that's why I can't stop. I exist because I think . . . and I can't stop myself from thinking." Later, he states:

> I am. I am, I exist, I think, therefore I am; I am because I think, why do I think? I don't want to think any more, I am because I think that I don't want to be, I think that I . . . because . . . ugh!

Loneliness

Roquentin's experience of extreme loneliness, and his perception of the people around him as lonely, is a significant element of *Nausea*. Roquentin lives an extremely lonely life. He has no family, no friends, no girlfriend, and few acquaintances. He explains, "I live alone, entirely alone. I never speak to anyone, never; I receive nothing, I give nothing." Although he has been essentially alone for the past three years, Roquentin realizes, "For the first time I am disturbed at being alone." Because he himself is so alone, he is keenly aware of the loneliness of other people around him.

Roquentin tries to cure his loneliness with the idea that perhaps he and Anny may get back together again. When Anny once again rejects him, Roquentin must return to his previous state of utter loneliness. By the end of the novel, he does not seem to have resolved the problem of his loneliness.

Freedom

Freedom is another important theme of *Nausea*. Roquentin frequently mentions the fact that he is entirely "free." He has no commitments to family or friends, and, because he is financially supported by a small inheritance, he has no commitments to holding a job or earning a living. At one point he states, "All I wanted was to be free." The idea that every individual is free is central to Sartre's existential philosophy. Sartre asserted that every individual is faced with complete freedom to choose how she or he responds to the world. Sartre believed that this fundamental freedom carries an enormous responsibility, for each individual is accountable for his or her own actions. In *Nausea*, Roquentin is keenly aware of his freedom to act in the world, and yet he is unsure of what to do with this freedom.

The Nature of Existence and Experience

The central thematic concern of *Nausea* is with questions of the nature of existence and experience that came to define the philosophy known as existentialism. Throughout the novel, Roquentin grapples with uncertainty about his own existence and the existence of objects and people in the world around him. He finds existence itself to be meaningless and repulsive. However, in a moment of crisis, he realizes that the fact of his own existence constitutes his only reality and that there is nothing more to life than this fundamental existence. He comes to the conclusion: "I am the Thing. Existence, liberated, detached, floods over me. I exist."

Style

The Fictional Diary

Nausea is written in the form of a fictional diary. An "Editors' Note" that opens the novel states that the diary was found among the notebooks of Antoine Roquentin. Since the diary is entirely fictional, as is the character Roquentin, Sartre's inclusion of this "Editors' Note" adds a sense of authenticity to the story. The "diary" also includes several editors' footnotes, which explain certain

inconsistencies in the entries. For example, one footnote explains that a word has been crossed out in the handwritten original of Roquentin's diary, while another clarifies a date that was not specified in the original. Like the "Editors' Note," these footnotes create a sense of authenticity, as if Roquentin had been a real person and his original diary were a real document. These elements in the novel contribute to the story's sense of realism.

First-Person Narrative

As a fictional diary, *Nausea* is written in the first-person singular narrative voice. Roquentin is the narrator of the story, and all of the events are described from his unique perspective. The first-person narrative device is effective as a means of conveying one individual's internal thought processes and his struggles with the nature of his own consciousness. The reader is thus immersed in Roquentin's perceptions of the world around him and his efforts to grapple with the nature and meaning of his own existence.

The Philosophical Novel

Nausea is a philosophical novel, or novel of ideas. Although it is a work of fiction, Sartre utilized the novel form in order to express and explore his philosophical ideas. Many critics have been impressed with Sartre's success in expressing his existential philosophy through the medium of fiction. Through this approach, as compared to a purely philosophical work, Sartre gives his philosophical ideas a sense of immediacy and relevance to the experience of the individual trying to make sense of his existence.

Historical Context

France Between the Wars

Nausea is set in 1932 and was first published in 1938. The 1930s are often referred to as the interwar period, which spanned the years between the ending of World War I and the beginning of World War II. During this time, the French government was known as the Third Republic. In World War I, which began in 1914, the Germans invaded France. World War I ended when the Allied forces defeated Germany in 1918. With the outbreak of World War II in 1939, Germany once again invaded France. In order to avoid further conflict, the French government made an agreement with Germany in 1940. According to this agreement, the

Compare & Contrast

- **1930s:** The French government is a constitutional democracy known as the Third Republic, based on the Constitution of 1815.

  Today: The French government is a constitutional democracy known as the Fifth Republic, based on the Constitution of 1958.

- **1930s:** France is a member of the multination alliance known as the League of Nations, which formed in the wake of World War I and was designed to maintain world peace.

  Today: France is a member of the United Nations, which replaced the League of Nations at the end of World War II. France is also a member of the multination political and economic alliance known as the European Union.

- **1930s:** France is a colonial power with national sovereignty over regions of North Africa and Indochina.

  Today: France is no longer a colonial power, as most former French colonies have established national sovereignty.

- **1930s:** The French unit of currency is the franc.

  Today: The French unit of currency is also that of the European Union, the euro.

Third Republic was dissolved, and France was divided into a German-controlled region, which became known as Vichy France, and a French-controlled region that served in weak acquiescence to German forces. In 1942, Germany invaded this French-controlled region as well. During this period of German occupation, a French resistance movement formed to sabotage German forces and undermine the occupation. Sartre was very active in the French Resistance, as well as writing for underground Resistance newspapers. In 1944, the American allied troops landed in Normandy, which served to turn the tide of the war against German forces. This period of the war is known as the Liberation because it resulted in the freeing of France from the German occupation.

Existentialism

French existential philosophy emerged in the 1940s and 1950s. It developed out of the philosophical school of thought known as phenomenology. Existentialism is a philosophy that questions the nature of human existence. According to existentialism, man is defined by the simple fact that he exists. Sartre put forth that each individual is constituted by a numerous series of choices that she or he makes throughout life and that everyone is fundamentally free to make such choices from a vast array of possibilities. Existentialism further stresses the fundamental absurdity of human life and tends to focus on negative experiences, such as pain, despair, and fear of death. Sartre posited in *Being and Nothingness* (1943) that the opposite of existence is nothingness and that by choosing to live, one chooses existence over nothingness.

French existentialism is rooted in ideas of the nineteenth-century philosophers Søren Kierkegaard, Arthur Schopenhauer, and Friedrich Nietzsche. During the 1920s and 1930s, the German philosophers Martin Heidegger and Karl Jaspers laid the foundation for French existentialism. Sartre was particularly influenced by Heidegger's *Being and Time* (1943), to which he paid homage with his title *Being and Nothingness*, the defining text of the existential movement. Sartre's contemporary, the French Algerian Albert Camus, developed his own existential ideas in the essay "The Myth of Sisyphus" (1942) and his philosophical novels *The Stranger* (1942) and *The Plague* (1947). Simone de Beauvoir, another important French existential thinker, elaborated upon Sartre's ideas in her novels, particularly *She Came to Stay* (1943) and *The Mandarins* (1954). De Beauvoir further introduced a feminist perspective to existential philosophy.

Twentieth-Century French Literature

Nausea is a work of existential fiction and is generally grouped with the existential novels and memoirs of his fellow French authors de Beauvoir and Camus. The existential novel is regarded as a transitional form that bridged the development of post–World War I and post–World War II French literature.

In the immediate post–World War I era, an avant-garde literary and artistic movement called dadaism emerged and flourished for several years. Dadaism developed as a reaction against the horrors of World War I and the bourgeois values of the middle class. The dadaists disdained rationalism and reason in trying to create works of poetry that defied conventional uses of language. Dadaists were more concerned with the response of the reader or viewer to their work than to the intrinsic aesthetic value of the work itself. However, because dadaism was defined more by what it was reacting against than by constructive aesthetic principles, it evolved after several years into the more positive approach of surrealism. Surrealist literature, which took form primarily through poetry, is characterized by an antirationalist sensibility, with an emphasis on unstructured writing that expresses irrational, unconscious states of mind. The surrealists were strongly influenced by the psychoanalytic theories of Sigmund Freud and were concerned with the deep psychological element of human experience. The French writer Andre Breton emerged as the major spokesperson for the surrealist movement, which he delineated in his *Surrealist Manifesto* (1924).

In the post–World War II era of the 1940s and 1950s, a new movement in the French novel emerged and came to be known as the *nouveau roman* ("new novel") or anti-novel (a term coined by Sartre). The writers of the *nouveau roman* were strongly influenced by existentialism, in that they emphasized the absurdity of life and reacted against normalizing bourgeois values. Thus, the *nouveau roman* is characterized by a defiance against conventional expectations of narrative, story structure, and character. One of the leading writers of the *nouveau roman* was Alain Robbe-Grillet, whose novel *Jealousy* (1957) is one of his best-known works. Existentialism was also an important influence on the theater of the absurd, which emerged in France during the 1950s and 1960s. Theater of the absurd draws on the philosophies of existential writers, such as Sartre and Camus, and emphasizes the absurdity of human life. Samuel's Beckett's play *Waiting for Godot* (1953) is regarded as the most representative work of the theater of the absurd.

Devastation such as this from World War II profoundly influenced the philosophy of existentialism, of which Jean-Paul Sartre was a major proponent

Critical Overview

Nausea is considered to be the seminal text of French existential philosophy. The influence of *Nausea*, along with Sartre's other writings, on twentieth-century thought has been profound and pervasive. Roquentin's philosophical dilemma, as expressed in *Nausea*, has been regarded as representative of the experience of modern life in the twentieth century. As Hayden Carruth, in an introduction to an English translation of *Nausea*, remarked, "*Nausea* gives us a few of the clearest and hence most useful images of man in our time that we possess," adding, "The power of Sartre's fiction resides in the truth of our lives as he has written it."

Critics generally agreed that, in *Nausea*, Sartre effectively utilizes the medium of fiction to explore philosophical ideas that he would later develop in *Being and Nothingness*. However, critical opinions have varied on the question of how successful *Nausea* is as a work of fiction in its own right. As Marie McGinn, in an essay in the *British Journal of Aesthetics*, commented:

> [*Nausea*] remains a collection of striking illustrations of philosophical ideas, but never gels into a unified

> " Roquentin comes to feel that adventures are not so much a matter of traveling to exotic places and meeting interesting people, but that an adventure can be something that happens internally, such as a change in one's state of mind."

work of art in which all the parts are motivated by an overriding aesthetic aim.

Critics have debated the philosophical implications of the novel's ending with Roquentin's decision to make his life meaningful through the pursuit of an artistic endeavor—the writing of a novel. Many agree with Sartre's conclusions about the role of the artist—be it a musician, novelist, or painter—in society and the redeeming qualities of artistic endeavor. A. van den Hoven, in an essay in *Sartre Studies International*, remarked:

> Roquentin ultimately favors music and writing because they allow him to entertain the possibility of composing 'an adventure that can't take place;' a story that may redeem his existence retrospectively and shame the readers into recognizing the facticity of their existence.

Whatever the evaluations of *Nausea*, as a work of philosophy or of literature, Sartre is universally recognized as one of the most profoundly influential thinkers of the twentieth century.

Criticism

Liz Brent

Brent holds a Ph.D. in American culture from the University of Michigan. She works as a freelance writer and editor. In the following essay, Brent discusses the theme of storytelling in Sartre's novel.

At the very end of *Nausea*, Roquentin comes to the conclusion that he wants to write a novel and that this process will serve as a solution to the problem of existence that he has been grappling with. During the course of *Nausea*, Roquentin's thinking

about the concepts of adventure, heroes, and storytelling gradually develop to the point at which he comes to conceive of the process of writing a novel as an adventure and the role of novel-writer as that of a hero.

During the many hours Roquentin spends sitting in cafés and overhearing the conversations of the people around him, he is aware of people's tendency to tell one another stories. However, he realizes that because he is always alone and has no one to talk to, his ability to tell stories to others has deteriorated. He says, "When you live alone you no longer know what it is to tell something. . . . [Y]ou plunge into stories without beginning or end."

On the other hand, he feels that being so alone has made him more observant of the stories he sees taking place in the world around him, through his observations of people interacting with one another in cafés and on the streets.

Roquentin has recently gotten the urge to tell someone about the changes he is experiencing, which is why he decides to start writing the diary. In the beginning of the diary, he feels somewhat uncomfortable trying to write down what happens to him. He comments, "I am not in the habit of telling myself what happens to me, so I cannot quite recapture the succession of events. I cannot distinguish what is important."

Meanwhile, as Roquentin has been conducting research and writing his biography of the Marquis de Rollebon, he is in the process of writing the story of the Marquis's life. Yet he feels that the distinction between a factual history and a fictional novel has begun to blur in his own writing:

> I have a feeling of doing a work of pure imagination. And I am certain that the characters in a novel would have a more genuine appearance, or in any case would be more agreeable.

He briefly toys with the idea of writing a novel about the Marquis de Rollebon, instead of a history, but quickly dismisses the notion.

Roquentin begins to think about the concept of adventure and what it means to him. He knows that he has certainly experienced many "adventures" in the conventional sense of the term. He has traveled all over the world, had strange and exciting experiences, and met many different kinds of men and women. "I have had real adventures," he says. But then he wonders where all of these adventures have led him and if he has really learned or gained anything from these exciting experiences. He admits, "I am generally proud of having had so many adventures." But he suddenly begins to think that these

What Do I Read Next?

- *L'Etre et le néant* (1943, *Being and Nothingness*) is Sartre's masterpiece of philosophical writing. In this work he directly expresses his fundamental philosophical ideas, which became the foundation of French existentialist thought.

- *Huis-clos* (1945, *No Exit*) is regarded as Sartre's greatest dramatic play. *No Exit* concerns three characters who have died and who find themselves in an afterlife in which they are stuck together in a room. Through this fantastical premise, Sartre explores some of his fundamental philosophical ideas.

- *Les mots* (1964, *The Words*) is Sartre's Nobel Prize–winning autobiographical account of his childhood and early adulthood.

- *Mémoires d'une jeune fille rangée* (1958, *Memoirs of a Dutiful Daughter*), by Simone de Beauvoir, is an autobiographical memoir, including discussion of de Beauvoir's experiences as Sartre's personal companion.

- *L'étranger* (1942, *The Stranger*), an existential novel by Albert Camus, is on par with Sartre's *Nausea* as a seminal work of existential fiction. *The Stranger* expresses Camus's existential philosophy through the experiences of a young man whose mother has recently died and who finds himself committing a brutal crime.

- *Jean-Paul Sartre* (1992), by Philip Thody, offers a general introduction to the life and works of Sartre.

- *Situating Sartre in Twentieth-Century Thought and Culture* (1997), edited by Jean-Francois Fourny and Charles D. Minahen, offers a collection of essays discussing the works of Sartre in the social, cultural, political, and historical context of the twentieth century.

- *Introducing Sartre* (1998), by Philip Thody and Howard Read, offers a fun and easy-to-digest introduction to the life, work, and thought of Sartre.

---

were not truly adventures at all, and he starts to feel as if "I have never had the slightest adventure in my life, or rather, that I don't even know what the word means any more." He then comes to the conclusion, "No, I haven't had any adventures."

Roquentin makes a connection between the concept of adventure and the act of storytelling. Because he has had so many adventures during his world travels, he knows that he has many stories to tell that others would find quite interesting. However, he begins to question the value of such adventures and of the stories that can be made of them. He thus begins to wonder what the concept of "adventure" truly means to him.

Roquentin comes to feel that adventures are not so much a matter of traveling to exotic places and meeting interesting people, but that an adventure can be something that happens internally, such as a change in one's state of mind. He comes to the conclusion, "This feeling of adventure definitely

does not come from events." Roquentin wants very much to experience this sense of adventure in his life, but he realizes that it is not something he has any control over:

> Perhaps there is nothing in the world I cling to as much as this feeling of adventure; but it comes when it pleases; it is gone so quickly and how empty I am once it has left.

In a moment of revelation, Roquentin realizes that the very fact of his existence is an adventure in itself, that his consciousness of his existence is an adventure, and that he himself is the hero of the adventure of his own existence:

> Nothing has changed and yet everything is different. I can't describe it; it's like the Nausea and yet it's just the opposite: at last an adventure happens to me and when I question myself I see that it happens that I am myself and that I am here; . . . I am as happy as the hero of a novel.

Roquentin comes to realize that adventure is not an experience a person can actually live, but that an adventure is defined by the telling of the story of an experience. He concludes that while a person is living through an experience, it never seems like an adventure; one never feels like a hero. But when a man tells the story of his experience after the experience has ended, the story itself is what makes it an adventure and what makes the teller of the tale the hero of the adventure:

> This is what I thought: for the most banal even[t] to become an adventure, you must (and this is enough) begin to recount it. This is what fools people: a man is always a teller of tales, he lives surrounded by his stories and the stories of others, he sees everything that happens to him through them; and he tries to live his own life as if he were telling a story.

In the ending of *Nausea*, Roquentin puts together his ideas about storytelling, adventures, and heroes in a sudden realization of how he might find a way to justify his existence and perhaps rid himself of the Nausea. He has a sort of revelation while listening to a record of a jazz tune called "Some of These Days." Roquentin finds that, in listening to this tune, his sense of Nausea seems to dissipate, and he even feels a sense of joy. He imagines the process by which the tune was created. He imagines a Jewish man sitting at a piano in an apartment in New York City, composing the music and writing the lyrics. He imagines an African American woman singing the tune in a recording session from which the phonograph record is produced. He feels that the man and woman who created this recording are "a little like the heroes of a novel."

From this thought, Roquentin realizes that he, too, could create something that might have the same effect on himself and others that the jazz tune has on him. Since he is not a musician, he knows that he is incapable of composing a song. However, he knows that he can write well, and so he comes to the conclusion that he wants to try writing a novel. He imagines himself writing "[a] story, for example, something that could never happen, an adventure. It would have to be beautiful and hard as steel and make people ashamed of their existence."

So Roquentin's desire to have adventures of which he is the hero evolves into a desire to write a work of fiction that would be an adventure in itself and of which he, as the author, would be the hero.

Source: Liz Brent, Critical Essay on *Nausea*, in *Novels for Students*, Thomson Gale, 2005.

Sources

Carruth, Hayden, "Introduction," in *Nausea*, by Jean-Paul Sartre, New Directions, 1964, pp. v–xiv.

McGinn, Marie, "The Writer and Society: An Interpretation of *Nausea*," in *British Journal of Aesthetics*, Vol. 37, No. 2, April 1997, pp. 118–28.

Sartre, Jean-Paul, *Nausea*, translated by Lloyd Alexander, New Directions, 1964.

Van den Hoven, A., "Some of These Days," in *Sartre Studies International*, Vol. 6, No. 2, December 2000, pp. vi-xxi.

Further Reading

Fullbrook, Kate, and Edward Fullbrook, *Simone de Beauvoir and Jean-Paul Sartre: The Remaking of a Twentieth-Century Legend*, Harvester Wheatsheaf, 1993.

Fullbrook and Fullbrook provide critical discussion and reevaluation of the legendary relationship between Simone de Beauvoir and Jean-Paul Sartre.

Fulton, Ann, *Apostles of Sartre: Existentialism in America, 1945–1963*, Northwestern University Press, 1999.

Fulton discusses the influence of Sartre's existentialist thought and writings on American intellectuals of the post–World War II era.

Giles, James, ed., *French Existentialism: Consciousness, Ethics, and Relations with Others*, Rodopi, 1999.

Giles provides a collection of essays by various authors discussing the fundamental ideas of French existential philosophy.

Murphy, Julien, ed., *Feminist Interpretations of Jean-Paul Sartre*, Pennsylvania State University Press, 1999.

Murphy offers a collection of critical essays by various authors examining the life and work of Sartre from a feminist perspective.

Sartre, Jean-Paul, and Benny Levy, *Hope Now: The 1980 Interviews*, University of Chicago Press, 1996.

Levy provides interview material from a series of long interviews with Sartre, conducted during the last year of his life.

Scriven, Michael, *Jean-Paul Sartre: Politics and Culture in Postwar France*, St. Martin's Press, 1999.

Scriven provides critical and historical discussion of Sartre's life and work in the cultural and historical context of France during the post–World War II era.

Shack, William A., *Harlem in Montmartre: A Paris Jazz Story between the Great Wars*, University of California Press, 2001.

Shack provides historical discussion of the jazz music scene in Paris during the 1930s. Shack particularly focuses on the presence of African American jazz musicians who came to Paris during this period.

Parable of the Sower

Octavia Butler

1993

Parable of the Sower (New York, 1993) by Octavia Butler is set in California and covers a period of three years, from 2024 to 2027. It is a grim near-future novel that exaggerates trends in American life that were apparent in the late 1980s and early 1990s, such as fear of crime, the rise of gated communities, illiteracy, designer drugs and drug addiction, and a growing gap between rich and poor. Climate changes brought about by global warming are also central to the novel.

The protagonist is Lauren Olamina, an African American girl who is fifteen years old when the novel begins. She lives in Robledo, about twenty miles from Los Angeles, which has become a walled enclave only partially protected from the rampant lawlessness and desperate poverty that exists beyond the walls of the neighborhood. When the enclave is completely destroyed by bands of arsonists and thieves, Lauren is one of the few survivors. She heads north, on foot, with a couple of companions in a perilous search for a better life.

Butler's disturbing dystopia, written in the form of Lauren's diary entries, is at once an adventure story, a coming-of-age story, and a thought-provoking exploration of some negative trends in American society that have become more pronounced in the decade that has elapsed since the novel was written.

Octavia Butler

Author Biography

Octavia Estelle Butler was born in Pasadena, California, on June 22, 1947, the daughter of Laurice and Octavia Margaret (Guy) Butler. Her father died when she was a baby, and her mother supported the family by working as a maid. Butler loved reading science fiction stories as a child, and she soon started writing them herself. At the age of thirteen she was submitting her own stories to magazines.

Butler attended Pasadena City College, and while a student there she was awarded fifth prize in the *Writer's Digest* Short Story Contest. She received an Associate of Arts degree in 1968 and went on to attend California State University, Los Angeles, in 1969, and the University of California, Los Angeles.

In 1969, Butler entered the Open Door Program of the Screen Writers' Guild, where one of her tutors was Harlan Ellison. At Ellison's suggestion she enrolled in the Clarion Science Fiction Writers' Workshop, held in Pennsylvania. As a result of taking the workshop, she sold two short stories. Deciding she wanted to be a writer, she supported herself with low-paying jobs such as dishwashing and cleaning, while continuing to write, often getting up at three o'clock in the morning to do so. When she was laid off from a telephone sales job

in 1974, she decided to use the time to write her first novel, the science fiction tale *Patternmaster*, which she completed in less than a year and sold to Doubleday. *Patternmaster* was published in 1976 and was quickly followed by three more novels in the *Patternmaster* series: *Mind of My Mind* (1977), *Survivor* (1978), and *Wild Seed* (1980). In between, Butler published *Kindred* (1979), a mainstream novel focusing on African American history.

In 1984, St. Martin's published *Clay's Ark*, a fifth volume in the *Patternmaster* series. In that year she also won the Hugo Award, for her short story "Speech Sounds," and in 1985 she won the three most prestigious science fiction awards for her novelette *Bloodchild* (1985): the Hugo Award, the Nebula Award, and the Locus Award. After this, Butler turned her attention to the science fiction trilogy, *Xenogenesis*, which was published by Warner Books. The three novels were *Dawn: Xenogenesis* (1987), *Adulthood Rites* (1988), and *Imago* (1989).

Butler then hit a barren spell. She knew she wanted to write about a woman who wanted to start a new religion, but she could not produce a manuscript that satisfied her. Eventually the ideas flowed smoothly, and the result was *Parable of the Sower* (1993).

Butler received a MacArthur fellowship in 1995. In 1998, her novel *Parable of the Talents*, which she described as a continuation of *Parable of the Sower*, was published by Seven Stories Press and republished by Warner in 2000. The novel won the Nebula Award for best novel, 1999. Also in 2000, the three novels in the *Xenogenesis* were collected under the title of *Lilith's Brood* and published by Warner Books.

Plot Summary

Chapters 1–3

Parable of the Sower begins in July 2024, in Robledo, in southern California. It is Lauren Olamina's fifteenth birthday. California has changed drastically over the past three decades. Water is scarce and expensive, there are few jobs, and climate changes have produced massive rains followed by years of drought. Lauren lives in a neighborhood that is walled off for protection from the homeless people, drug addicts, vandals, arsonists, and thieves who roam the unwalled residential areas. Lauren's father is a Baptist minister, and Lauren goes to church to be baptized, even though she no longer believes in the Christian God. The church is outside the wall, and the family goes armed. Many of the houses are burnt out and have been looted, and homeless families wander the streets. Lauren feels their pain because she suffers from "hyperempathy syndrome," also called "sharing."

Several weeks later, a neighbor named Mrs. Sims shoots herself. She was in despair after her family died in a house fire started deliberately. Meanwhile, Lauren tries to form a new concept of God. She decides that God is change, because the reality of life is that everything changes.

Chapters 4–9

In February 2025, Lauren goes to the hills with a neighborhood group for target practice, where they encounter a pack of feral dogs. They shoot one dog, and as it dies, the hyperempathic Lauren feels its pain. Guns are essential because the family cannot rely on the police to protect them. In Lauren's neighborhood, every household has at least two guns.

In March, after three-year-old Amy Dunn wanders off and is shot dead, Lauren talks with her friend Joanne Garfield about how they need to make plans to survive before their neighborhood is overrun by thieves and killers. She wants to learn how to live off the land, and she plans to create emergency packs of supplies should they have to leave in a hurry. She tries to enlist Joanne's help, but Joanne tells her parents, exaggerating what Lauren said. Lauren's father tells her to stop panicking people, but he does allow her to start teaching the neighborhood kids about her ideas.

When thieves rob the gardens, the community sets up an armed neighborhood watch. But the thieves keep coming, and Lauren is desperate to think of a way out. She develops her God-is-Change belief system further, calling it Earthseed.

Keith, Lauren' thirteen-year-old brother, slips out of the neighborhood, stealing Cory's key. He returns, beaten up. Two weeks later he disappears again for nearly two weeks. When he returns, he is wearing new clothes, but he will not say where he has been. His father beats him severely. Two months later, Keith leaves again, this time returning with money, which he gives to Cory. Then he leaves again.

Chapters 10–13

In June 2026, Keith returns after an eight-month absence. He has been squatting in an abandoned building with friends but will not say how he acquires his money. Later, he admits to robbing and shooting. In August, he is tortured and killed, probably by drug dealers.

There are more robberies, and by October the community is starting to come apart. The Garfields move to Olivar, a coastal suburb of Los Angeles, which has been bought by a company called KSF. Lauren fears that the company will cheat and abuse people. She decides that next year she will go north, maybe as far as Canada.

In November, Lauren's father disappears and is assumed dead. Lauren speaks at a church service for him, and she begins to emerge as a leader in the community. She takes over her mother's teaching responsibilities.

The day before Christmas Eve, the Olamina house is robbed. Another house, where the Payne and Parrish families live, burns down, leaving only one survivor.

Chapters 14–19

In July 2027, the entire neighborhood is overrun by violent intruders. Fires blaze everywhere. Lauren is one of the few to escape. When she returns, the place is littered with corpses, and scavengers are at work. Lauren gathers supplies, and as she leaves she meets Harry Balter and Zahra Moss. Learning that her entire family is dead, Lauren decides to head north, and Harry and Zahra go with her. Lauren cuts her hair so she can be taken for a man. They buy supplies and begin walking on the freeway, heading for the 101 that would take them up the coast toward Oregon. Hundreds of other people are walking the highways. Lauren has a gun and Harry a knife to protect themselves against predators. Lauren insists that they trust no one. At night, they take turns keeping watch. On their first night, they are attacked by two men. Lauren and Harry kill them both.

They replenish their water supplies from a commercial water station. It is a dangerous place, and Lauren and Harry help to scare off two men who attempt to rob a woman and her husband. They reach the ocean, and Lauren improves their survival skills by devising a method to make seawater drinkable. The couple they helped, Travis and Natividad, and their six-month-old baby, Dominic, join up with them, although the newcomers are suspicious at first. As the days go by, Lauren talks to her group about Earthseed. Travis and Zahra are interested, and Lauren regards Travis as her first convert.

There is an earthquake, and fire breaks out in a community as they pass. Scavengers flock to it and there is gunfire. Lauren meets another traveler, Taylor Franklin Bankole, and he stands guard as Lauren and her friends pull two young women, Allison and her sister, Jill Gilchrist, from the rubble of a house. A man attacks Lauren, and she kills him with her knife. Allison, Jill, and Bankole travel on with Lauren's group. They reach Salinas, where they replenish their supplies, using money they have taken from corpses.

Chapters 20–25

They avoid the Bay area because the earthquake has created chaos there. Camping just east of San Juan Bautista, they emerge unscathed after a nearby gunfight at night. Bankole brings in a three-year-old child, Justin Rohr, whose mother has just been killed. Allie soon takes charge of him.

They reach the San Luis Reservoir. A friendship springs up between Lauren and Bankole, and she explains her Earthseed philosophy to him. They become lovers, and he is shocked when he finds out she is only eighteen.

By September, they reach Sacramento. They pass some horrible sights, including a dog with a child's arm in its mouth and a group of kids who are roasting a severed human leg. Bankole tells Lauren that he owns three hundred acres of land in the coastal hills of Humboldt County, where his sister lives with her husband and three children. He wants her to leave the group and go with him. Lauren thinks it might be a good place to begin the first Earthseed Community.

The group is surprised to discover that a ragged woman, Emery Tanaka Solis, and her nine-year-old daughter, Tori, have crept into their camp at night. After some discussion, the group decides to take them along with them. The next day, they are joined by Grayson Mora and his eight-year-old daughter, Doe. Grayson does not trust the group but stays for the sake of his daughter. It later turns out that Grayson, like Lauren, is a "sharer," as are Emery and Tori.

Several days later, a man tries to grab Tori and attacks Emery. Lauren shoots him, and the rest of the group fight off the remainder of the gang, but Jill is shot dead. They continue on their way, narrowly escaping a raging fire before they arrive at Clear Lake. Eventually they reach Bankole's land, but the house has been destroyed and all his family killed. They decide to stay and build Acorn, their Earthseed community.

Characters

Harry Balter

Harry Balter is a young white man from the same neighborhood as Lauren. His girlfriend is his first cousin, Joanne Garfield, but they split up when the Garfield family moves to Olivar. Harry survives the violent attack on the neighborhood and is one of the original members of Lauren's group. His new girlfriend is Zahra Moss. Harry is more trusting than Lauren, and on the road he has to learn to become more ruthless.

Taylor Franklin Bankole

Taylor Franklin Bankole is a fifty-seven-year-old black doctor who joins Lauren's group halfway through their journey. Since he is much older than the others, he is able to give them steady advice and support. Bankole is from San Diego, and he left his community after it was destroyed by arson. Five years earlier, his wife died after being beaten by thieves. Bankole and Lauren are attracted to each other and soon become lovers. He tells Lauren that he is on his way to three hundred acres of land that he owns in the coastal hills of Humboldt County, California. He hopes to meet up with his sister and her family who live there. Lauren and the group make this their destination, but when they arrive, they find that the house has been destroyed and the family killed.

Dominic Douglas

Dominic Douglas is the six-month-old son of Natividad and Travis.

Gloria Natividad Douglas

Gloria Natividad Douglas, known as Natividad, is a Hispanic woman, the wife of Travis Douglas and the mother of Dominic. This family joins Lauren's group quite early in the trek. With her husband, Natividad used to work as a maid for a rich couple, but she ran away when the man tried to seduce her.

Travis Charles Douglas

Travis Charles Douglas is a black man, the husband of Natividad. He used to work as a handyman and gardener for a rich couple. Travis is suspicious of Lauren's group at first but soon warms to them. He becomes interested in Lauren's idea of Earthseed.

Amy Dunn

Amy Dunn is a three-year-old girl in Lauren's neighborhood. She sets fire to the family garage. Later, she is accidentally shot dead.

Tracy Dunn

Tracy Dunn is Amy Dunn's sixteen-year-old mother. She was only twelve when her uncle made her pregnant with Amy. After Amy's death, Tracy disappears and is never found.

Jay Garfield

Jay Garfield is the head of the Garfield family, who are friends with the Olaminas. Jay, who is white, leads the search for Lauren's father after he disappears. Later he takes his family to the company town of Olivar.

Joanne Garfield

Joanne Garfield is the daughter of Jay Garfield, the girlfriend of Harry Balter, and Lauren's friend. Her friendship with Lauren cools when she divulges to her parents details of Lauren's plan for survival. After that, Lauren does not trust her anymore. Eventually, Joanne moves to Olivar with her parents.

Allison Gilchrist

Allison Gilchrist, known as Allie, is Jillian's twenty-five-year-old sister. After her father killed her baby because it would not stop crying, the two sisters burned the house down while the drunken father slept. Fleeing a life of prostitution and poverty, they took to the road. When Lauren's group pulls Allie and Jill out of the rubble of a house hit by an earthquake, they join the group. Allie takes charge of Justin Rohr.

Jillian Gilchrist

Jillian Gilchrist is Allison's twenty-four-year-old sister. She shares Allie's history of poverty and abuse. Neither she nor her sister can write, although they can read a little. Jill is shot dead when the group is attacked by a gang.

Bianca Montoya

Bianca Montoya is a pregnant seventeen-year-old Latino girl in Lauren's neighborhood. She plans to marry her boyfriend, Jorge Iturbe, and continue to live in the neighborhood.

Doe Mora

Doe Mora is the eight-year-old daughter of Grayson Mora.

Grayson Mora

Grayson Mora is the Latino father of Doe Mora. He joins Lauren's group toward the end of their trek. He is quiet, aloof from the group, but protective of his daughter. Like Lauren, he has hyperempathy syndrome.

Richard Moss

Richard Moss is the father of Aura and Peter Moss. He has three wives, including Zahra, whom he bought from her homeless mother when she was fifteen. Moss is an engineer for a big commercial water company. He has also put together his own form of religion, which emphasizes patriarchy and the subordination of women. Moss is killed when the neighborhood is overrun.

Zahra Moss

Zahra Moss is the youngest of Richard moss's three wives. Ross bought her from her homeless mother. Her new home is the first house she has lived in. When the neighborhood is destroyed, Zahra sees her baby daughter killed. But she escapes and heads north with Harry, who becomes her boyfriend. Zahra cannot read or write until Lauren starts to teach her.

Cory Olamina

Cory Olamina is Lauren's stepmother. An educated woman with a Ph.D., she teaches the neighborhood children. When the neighborhood deteriorates, she wants to move to Olivar but cannot persuade her husband to go. After her husband disappears, she takes over the teaching side of his job. Cory is killed when the neighborhood is attacked and burned.

Gregory Olamina

Gregory Olamina is Lauren's youngest brother. He is killed when the neighborhood is overrun.

Keith Olamina

Keith Olamina is the oldest of Lauren's three brothers and Cory's favorite, although he and Lauren do not get along well. He is twelve when the story begins. Keith is not very intelligent and dodges work and school whenever he can. His ambition is to leave the neighborhood and go to Los Angeles and make money. When he is thirteen, he frequently leaves the neighborhood for long periods. He acquires money and new clothes, but he will not say where he got them. After a few months of living dangerously, he is tortured and killed, possibly by the drug dealers he thought were his friends.

Lauren Olamina

Lauren Olamina is fifteen years old when the story begins. She lives in Robledo, California, with her father, stepmother, and three brothers. Her dead mother was taking the prescription drug Paracetco, and this was why Lauren contracted "hyperempathy syndrome," which means that she feels the physical pain of others in her own body. On the advice of her father, she tries to keep this condition secret, since she thinks she might be perceived as weak. She only confides in people she trusts.

Lauren is an academically gifted student. She finished her high school work early and has taken college-level courses. She also reads voraciously and is extremely well informed about history and current events. Although her father is a Baptist minister, Lauren has already lost her faith in the Christian God. She develops her own religion called Earthseed, based on the idea that God is Change. Change is her watchword. Even before disaster hits their community, she is certain that she does not want to live the life that is expected of her: to marry young, have children, and live in impoverished circumstances in Robledo. She also guesses that her neighborhood will be destroyed in the near future, and she makes plans to escape, reading everything she can about how to survive in emergency situations and how to live off the land.

When the disaster happens, Lauren shows that she is strong willed and determined and that she possesses great leadership qualities. She is the undisputed leader of the small group that heads north along the freeway, seeking a better life. She is ruthless, she kills when she has to, and she ensures that her group does what it has to do to survive. Gradually, she also instills in her companions a sense of ethics and community. Although she is tough, she also cares about others and shows compassion. She is rewarded when the group arrives at Bankole's land, where she can put her dream of founding an Earthseed community into practice.

Marcus Olamina

Marcus Olamina is Lauren's brother. At thirteen, he is already handsome, and he attracts girls. His friend is Robin Balter, Harry Balter's sister. Marcus is killed when the neighborhood is attacked.

Reverend Olamina

Reverend Olamina is Lauren's fifty-seven-year-old father and the husband of Cory. He is a college professor and dean and a Baptist minister. A very strict father, he severely beats Keith for misbehavior, which produces a permanent estrangement between father and son. He has also beaten Lauren, but she does not hold it against him. Reverend Olamina is a tough-minded man who does his best to protect his family in difficult circumstances. His own parents were murdered fifteen years earlier, and his first wife was a drug addict. Olamina goes missing from the neighborhood one day and is never found. He is presumed dead.

Wardell Parish

Wardell Parish is a strange and solitary man who lives in Lauren's neighborhood. His sister and all her children are killed in a house fire.

Justin Rohr

Justin Rohr is a three-year-old boy who is taken in by Lauren's group after his mother is killed just outside San Juan Bautista.

Emery Tanaka Solis

Emery Tanaka Solis is the twenty-three-year-old mother of Tori Solis. She married at thirteen and bore three children. After her husband died, she worked for an agribusiness conglomerate that made a virtual slave of her. She fell into debt, and the company took her two sons. She then fled with her daughter and headed north. They are taken in by Lauren's group toward the end of their trek.

Tori Solis

Tori is the nine-year-old daughter of Emery Tanaka Solis.

Curtis Talcott

Curtis Talcott is Lauren's boyfriend in Robledo. He wants to marry her and leave Robledo, but she says she must stay and help her family until she is eighteen. Although she says she will marry him if he waits for her, her heart is not in it. There is too much of herself that she is unable to share with him. She never sees him again after the neighborhood is attacked and burned, and she assumes he was killed, though she never knows for certain.

Kayla Talcott

Kayla Talcott is the mother of Curtis Talcott. After Reverend Olamina disappears, Kayla takes over some of his preaching and church work, even though she is not ordained.

Themes

Change

Lauren rejects traditional religion. Based on her experience, she sees no relevance in a belief system focused on the Christian God. Instead, she forms her own religion based on her observation that everything in the universe changes. Change is the one constant in life. People can either accept change and work with it for the betterment of themselves and their community, or they can resist it,

Topics For Further Study

- Research the history of illiteracy in the United States. What can be done to tackle illiteracy in the United States? How have educational methods developed over time to accommodate new finds or theories in literacy studies? Develop a political platform, a curriculum, or a tutorial that employs some of the methods for dealing with illiteracy that you encounter during your research. Try to propose some of your own resolutions and include them in your project.

- In the novel, water is scarce and expensive. Research the topic of water supply. Is water likely to become a scarce commodity in the twenty-first century? If so, what regions of the world already have this problem or will have this problem? Will the United States be affected and, if so, which areas?

- There are many sides in the current debate about global warming and climate change. Study the arguments about whether global warming is currently happening or not, about the effects of

global warming on the environment as well as industry, and about who is responsible for helping industries comply with environmental sanctions aimed at reducing harmful emissions. Document your findings and prepare to debate with other members of your class by picking the argument with which you agree most and developing a strong defense for your position.

- Research the history of company towns in the United States in the nineteenth century. Write an essay that explains how your research compares with the description of Olivar in the novel. Is Butler's representation of Olivar historically accurate? Does the author leave out important elements that you found in your research? If so, what are those elements?

- Is Butler's pessimistic vision of America in the 2020s convincing? Are such developments likely or unlikely? Can you see ways in which America might develop differently?

---

hoping in vain that things will carry on the way they always have done.

For Lauren, change is God. This God shapes humans and is in turn shaped by them. God is dynamic process, not a static, transcendental lawgiver and judge. Change is an irresistible force, and humans can harness it to promote the spiritual evolution of the race. According Lauren's Earthseed religion, each human life is a seed that can sprout into something valuable and productive if it can adapt to changing realities. By yielding to change, this human earthseed can also shape it constructively. The consequences of failing to do so are death and chaos. The ultimate expression of Earthseed, its destiny, is "to take root among the stars," to spread human life to other planets and galaxies.

Freedom

Lauren's trek north is a journey toward freedom. She is escaping the prison of a walled

community in which there is no hope for a full, productive, free life. Most of the people her group accumulates on the way are fleeing from some kind of slavery or exploitation. Zahra Moss is escaping an oppressive marriage that rests on a belief in male superiority. Harry has turned down a chance to go to the company town of Olivar, in which the residents give up their freedom and their rights in order to buy security. Jill and Allie flee from a life of prostitution in which their pimp was their father; Travis and Natividad escape from menial service to a rich man who thought he had the right to seduce Natividad; Emery Solis and her daughter are escaping virtual slavery to an agribusiness that keeps them in permanent debt and even takes Emery's sons away. Bankole, too, is escaping from conditions of life similar to those that Lauren was enduring. He seeks freedom on the land he owns in the coastal hills. The members of Lauren's Earthseed community who decide to settle there will at least be free to shape their own destiny, although there is no guarantee they will survive.

Loss and Restoration of Community

The novel is divided into two halves. The first half, set in Robledo, shows how the social order in California in 2024 has broken down. Society is split into several groups. The rich live in walled estates, with lavish security systems. The middle classes, much threatened and impoverished, live in walled communities and try to maintain a semblance of normal life. But jobs are scarce, and no one has any prospects. Inflation has eroded the value of money, and essentials such as water are expensive. In Lauren's neighborhood, people try to grow as much of their own food as they can. For meat, they rely on eating rabbits. Everyone in the community over the age of fifteen is trained in how to use guns, since they cannot rely on a corrupt police force for protection against the thieves who regularly break into their community. Outside, in unwalled areas, the rule of law and the sense of community have totally collapsed. Homeless, dirty, desperately poor people roam the streets, along with drunks and drug addicts. Many are addicted to a drug that makes them commit arson, because they love to watch things burn.

The second part of the novel presents a gradually emerging contrast between the lawlessness and brutality of life amongst the traveling bands of refugees and the sense of community and mutual responsibility that eventually characterizes Lauren's group. Lauren's quest is to recreate what an ideal community should be. At first, because of the dangerous situation she is in, she is ruthless, trusting no one and looking out only for herself and her two companions. But as she continues to travel north, she does not shut out the voice of compassion. A key moment is when she pulls Allie and Jill out of the rubble of a house. Bankole, who has never lost his sense of values, says to her, "I was surprised to see that anyone else cared what happened to a couple of strangers." Another key moment comes when Emery and her daughter are found in the group's camp. Lauren goes out of her way to feed them, offering them two of the five sweet pears that she had bought only two days earlier. Seeing her example, other members of the group share what food they have. When Lauren puts out the idea that Emery and the girl could join their group, Harry tells her she is going soft. "You would have raised hell if we'd tried to take in a beggar woman and her child a few weeks ago." But Lauren is not going soft. She is simply demonstrating that in spite of the degradation and danger all around her, humans can still show that they care about each other. Then, when Jill is killed, Lauren comforts the grief-stricken Allie with a hug. The message she conveys is "*In spite of your loss and pain, you aren't alone. You still have people who care about you and want you to be all right. You still have family.*" When Lauren's new "family," a heterogeneous, multiracial group that spans several generations, arrives at their destination, they have learned to take care of each other. They are ready to develop a community based not on fear or exploitation but on mutual respect and shared values.

Style

Dystopia

A dystopia is an unpleasant, sometimes frightening, imaginary future world. Dystopias usually take undesirable aspects of present-day society and depict a world in which those aspects have become dominant. In *Parable of the Sower*, Butler creates a dystopia by magnifying some disturbing social trends that occurred in the United States in the late 1980s and early 1990s. These trends included the widespread use of designer drugs (custom-made, mind-altering drugs such as Ecstasy). In the novel, use of the drug pyro reaches epidemic proportions. It makes people commit arson because doing so feels better than sex. Another trend in the 1990s was the increasing popularity, particularly in California, of gated communities protected by security fences. These become the walled communities in 2024 California. In both cases, the walls go up because of fear of crime. Homelessness, illiteracy, and global warming were other issues in the 1990s that appear in larger form in the novel.

Image and Metaphor

The novel takes its title from the parable of the sower in the gospel of Luke. The sower is like the spiritual teacher who spreads the word of truth. Some people listen; others do not—just as seeds take root in some places but not in others. In the *New Testament*, the sower is Jesus; in the novel, it is Lauren. The metaphor of the seed occurs again in the name Lauren gives to her new religion, Earthseed. It is also reflected in the name of the first Earthseed community: Acorn. The acorn image occurs earlier in the novel, too. Lauren loves to eat bread made with acorns rather than wheat or rye.

Her father tells her that he had a difficult time persuading his neighbors to eat acorns. They wanted to cut down the oak trees and plant something else they considered more useful. Lauren learns from a book how to make acorn bread, and this helps to sustain their group as they travel north. The acorn image conveys the idea that the seeds of new life are always available, not only in nature but in humans, too.

Historical Context

Illiteracy

Rising rates of illiteracy became a matter of public concern in America in the late 1980s and early 1990s. In 1989, it was estimated that 13 percent of seventeen-year-old Americans could not read or write and that twenty million Americans had problems with literacy. Some could not read or write at all, and this often resulted from poverty or being in culturally disadvantaged families. Others were partially literate and could read street signs and grocery lists but not much more. Often this was due to undiagnosed learning disorders such as dyslexia. According to a 1987 National Assessment of Educational Progress government survey, although 96 percent of those between twenty-one and twenty-five years old had basic reading skills, less than 48 percent were capable of reading a map well enough to use it properly. In the 1993 National Adult Literacy Survey by the Department of Education, over 40 percent of the adult population fell short of the literacy skills needed to succeed on a day-to-day basis.

Gated Communities

In the late 1980s, fear of rising crime in urban areas led to a growth in the number of gated residential communities in the United States, particularly in California and other western and southern metropolitan areas. These were communities where access was controlled through gates and security guards. Sometimes fences topped with barbed wire surrounded the community. An example of a gated community is Canyon Lake, located seventy miles east of Los Angeles. Created in 1968, it incorporated as a city of its own in 1990. Gated communities proved an effective deterrent against crime, and their numbers increased throughout the United States in the 1990s. In 1997, there were about twenty thousand gated communities, which increased to around fifty thousand by 2000.

Fear of Crime

Fear of crime was a prominent feature of life in the United States at the time *Parable of the Sower* was written. According to a 1994 Gallup Poll, 52 percent of the people in the United States named crime as the most important social problem, up from only 9 percent in a similar poll conducted eighteen months earlier. A 1993 poll showed that 87 percent of U.S. residents thought that crime was higher than a year earlier. This was not in fact true, since the crime rate fell from 1991 to 1994, but people thought it was true. There was a particularly strong fear in urban areas of street crime and random, gang-related violence. Fear of crime led legislators and the public at large to call for harsher punishments for criminals. In California, a "three strikes" law was passed in 1994. It mandated a sentence of twenty-five years to life for a third felony conviction if the previous felonies were serious or violent.

Homelessness

Homelessness in America increased drastically during the 1980s, to an estimated two million people in 1989. Some experts argue that the policies of the Reagan administration were to blame for cutting welfare programs and making massive cuts in the budget of the Department of Housing and Urban Development (HUD). HUD was the main government sponsor of subsidized housing for the poor. The situation was not helped by the fact that poverty also increased during the 1980s. In 1978, 24.5 million people lived below the federal poverty line; by 1988 this had risen to 32.5 million. The gap between rich and poor also increased. Another factor in the rise of homelessness in the 1980s arose from concerns about the rights of the mentally ill. It became harder to commit people to mental hospitals against their will. The result was that many mentally ill people ended up on the streets. It is estimated that one-third of the homeless during the 1980s were mentally ill and that a similar proportion had problems with substance abuse.

Climate Change

Concerns about global warming, an increase in Earth's average surface temperature, were first raised in the 1980s. The phenomenon was also known as the "greenhouse effect." Many scientists believed that global warning was caused by an increase in emissions of gases such as carbon dioxide resulting from the burning of fossil fuels for energy production. In 1988, James Hansen, director of the Goddard Institute for Space Studies at NASA, told a U.S. Senate committee there was strong evidence that global warming was being

Many of the futuristic urban communities in Parable of the Sower *are fortified in walled cities perhaps like this one from Italy's medieval era at Monteriggioni*

caused by human activity. He warned that if global warming were not reversed, it would cause catastrophic climatic changes. Throughout the 1990s, scientists warned of extreme weather including floods, heat waves, droughts, and hurricanes that would occur as a result of global warning.

Critical Overview

Although Four Walls Eight Windows, the original publishers of *Parable of the Sower*, tried to present the book as similar to the fiction of other African American writers such as Toni Morrison and Toni Cade Bambara, reviewers seemed still to regard it as science fiction. This did not prevent the novel from receiving high praise. For Faren Miller, in *Locus*, it "presents what is simply the most emotionally and intellectually appealing religion I've encountered in nearly four decades of reading sf." Miller commented on the grim nature of the world depicted and the religious issues Butler presents but added that the novel "functions beautifully as fiction, brimming with living characters and the crazy complexity of life."

Hoda Zaki, in *Women's Review of Books*, pointed out that Butler drew extensively on African American history:

> [I]mages of slavery remind us of the U.S. past: slaves hiding their attempts at self-education and literacy, and fleeing cruel overseers; Lauren's band of survivors, which recalls the Underground Railroad; the pervasive feeling that freedom, work and security lie to the north.

Zaki also pointed out that Butler shows characters from a variety of racial backgrounds in positive roles that are not usually found in science fiction novels about the future. Zaki concluded, "In a world increasingly polarized ethnically and racially, [Butler's] work contributes a needed critical element to the genre of science fiction."

In a glowing review in the *New York Times Book Review*, Gerald Jonas commented that although religious awakenings are common in science fiction of the future, they are often arbitrary and conventional, but Butler "dares to take Lauren's revelations seriously," and this enables her to show how Lauren's ideas capture the allegiance of her followers. Jonas concluded that the novel succeeded on many levels: "A gripping tale of survival and a poignant account of growing up sane in a disinte-grating world, it is at bottom a subtle and disturb-ing exposition of the gospel according to Lauren."

Criticism

Bryan Aubrey

Aubrey holds a Ph.D. in English and has pub-lished many articles on twentieth-century litera-ture. In this essay, Aubrey discusses Parable of the Sower *in terms of dystopias, utopias, archetypal patterns, coming-of-age novels, and the character of the narrator, Lauren.*

Butler is a writer of great originality whose work does not fit neatly into categories. Although she is usually referred to as a science fiction writer and *Parable of the Sower* was reviewed in the sci-ence fiction section of the *New York Times Book Review*, there is in fact little science fiction in it. Butler pays scant attention to the technological as-pects of her near-future society, merely mention-ing in passing "Window Wall" televisions and the newest "multisensory" entertainment systems that include such things as "reality vests" and "touch-rings." Much more important to Butler's purpose is the fact that almost no one in Lauren's Robledo community can afford these items.

Parable of the Sower properly belongs to the category of dystopia. Dystopias come in many forms. George Orwell's *1984* (1948), for example, depicts an oppressive, totalitarian society. A more recent form of dystopia is the "cyberpunk" novel, such as Neal Stephenson's *Snow Crash* (1992), in which highly sophisticated information technolo-gies exist alongside environmental degradation, rampant crime, and the domination of ruthless cor-porations. Yet another form is the feminist dystopia, in which women are systematically op-pressed, as in Margaret Atwood's *The Handmaid's Tale* (1986) and Suzy McKee Charnas's *Walk to the End of the World* (1974).

Parable of the Sower resists easy classifica-tion, though, since it has elements of a number of different kinds of dystopias. It offers some censure of the political system, although that is not the au-thor's main target. In Butler's 2020s, the federal government seems to have become irrelevant rather than oppressive. It wastes money on space pro-grams and makes futile attempts to tackle home-lessness and unemployment by passing legislation that restricts workers' rights.

> " As Lauren matures over a period of three years, she becomes a visionary, a prophet, and a charismatic leader, who also has formidable, practical organizing skills."

The all-powerful corporation, at the heart of many "cyberpunk" dystopias, makes an appearance in the novel as the company town of Olivar, where people get protection from crime and unemploy-ment but at the expense of individual rights and freedoms. The reader is left in no doubt that Lauren and Harry make the right choice when they elect not to go to Olivar. Feminist elements also appear in the novel, although it does not present a sys-tematic portrait of the institutionalized oppression of women. Women have the opportunity to become astronauts and go on the latest mission to Mars. In-deed, a female astronaut is killed on Mars. But in contrast to that, Butler presents many examples of men behaving badly to women. Richard Moss, for example, adopts a quasi-religious patriarchal fam-ily system that creates a system of virtual slavery for his many wives. Apparently, this is a common practice amongst middle- and upper-class men. Butler delivers a crushing verdict on Moss when she describes him, after the catastrophe over-whelms Lauren's neighborhood, lying stark naked in a pool of his own blood. So much for patriarchy.

To add to the complexity of this novel, it might be pointed out that within the dystopia is also a vi-sion of utopia. Utopian works, of which the proto-type is Sir Thomas More's *Utopia* (1515–1516), depict an ideal society. Lauren's vision of Acorn, a self-reliant community built from scratch on a few hundred acres of farmland, in which the new, enlightened religion of Earthseed is to take root, is a utopian vision. It is still in the future, and there is no guarantee that it will succeed, but the verses from Lauren's "Earthseed: The Books of the Liv-ing," which appear as epigraphs to each chapter, are constant reminders that within this miserable dystopia a utopia is ready to spring up. Lauren, of course, thinks her religion is new, and some ele-ments of it are, particularly the vision that it is the

What Do I Read Next?

- *Parable of the Talents* (1998) is Butler's sequel to *Parable of the Sower*. The Earthseed community that Lauren founded is collapsing. Her followers are enslaved, her daughter is kidnapped, and she is imprisoned by religious fanatics. But Lauren continues to believe in Earthseed and must find a way for the Acorn community to survive.

- Neal Stephenson's bestselling *Snow Crash* (1992) is a fast-paced, near-future dystopia, in which the United States is a collection of city-states controlled by corporations and the Mafia controls pizza delivery. The hero, named Hiro Protagonist, is a computer hacker (and samurai swordsman) who battles with a deadly designer drug called Snow Crash, that is also a sinister, world-endangering computer virus.

- *A Clockwork Orange* (1962), by Anthony Burgess, is a grim dystopia narrated by Alex, a member of an extremely violent teenage gang. When Alex is imprisoned, he is subjected to a new government-sponsored treatment program designed to cure his violent behavior. He comes out of it as a model citizen but has no free will nor the capacity to do good or experience pleasure.

- *The Handmaid's Tale: A Novel* (1986), by Margaret Atwood, is a near-future fable in which the United States has become the Republic of Gilead, controlled by religious fundamentalists. Women are strictly controlled and have no rights. Atwood's target is the Christian right's views about the proper role of women. She attempts to show what might happen if such views are taken to their logical conclusion.

destiny of Earthseed to colonize the stars. But its central idea, "the only lasting truth is Change," was expressed over two-and-a-half-thousand years ago by the Greek philosopher Heraclitus, whose famous phrase was "All is flux; nothing is stationary." Even in 2024, it appears that there is still nothing new under the sun.

Be that as it may, within the dystopian/utopian framework of her novel, Butler manages also to touch on the archetypal pattern that mythologist Joseph Campbell in his book *The Hero with a Thousand Faces* (1949) described as the "monomyth." In the monomyth, the hero hears a call to adventure, leaves his familiar environment, and journeys to an unknown or unfamiliar realm, where he undergoes many trials. He then returns to his society to bestow a boon on his fellow man. It is not difficult to see a similar pattern, with some variation, in *Parable of the Sower*, as well as some of the standard elements in a coming-of-age novel. Lauren—a female protagonist, of course, not a male one—is only fifteen when the novel begins. On the threshold of maturity, she must decide what she believes and what she wants to do with her life. When another neighborhood girl,

Bianca Montoya, gets pregnant at seventeen and decides to marry her boyfriend, Lauren knows that this is the life expected of her too—to marry young, have children, and remain in poverty. Lauren would sooner commit suicide than endure such a life. Like many a strong-willed fifteen- or sixteen-year-old, she clashes with her stern father, who, as the representative of the older generation, is more conservative and cautious than she. Lauren knows she must break with the old ways of doing things, just as she has already broken with the religion of her father, which does not speak to her personal experience. She boldly plans to encounter life beyond the walled neighborhood that is all she has ever known, and she does not falter when this "call to adventure" finally comes. When she shepherds her small group on their dangerous journey north, like the hero of the monomyth, she faces many dangers in an environment where the rule of law, and human kindness, no longer exists. The boon she brings is a vision of renewed hope for humanity—an agrarian, back-to-nature utopian community that will act as a counterpoint to corrupt cities and lawless countryside where all civilized values have been destroyed.

It is Lauren, then, who carries much of the interest in the novel. She is far more well developed by the author than any of the other characters, most of whom, except perhaps for Bankole, remain somewhat sketchy. (Bankole, incidentally, has something in common with the archetype of the wise old man. His ethical values are not impaired by the chaos around him, and it is he who guides the group to their safe haven.) Lauren is certainly an unusual, even strange, figure. She is something of a child prodigy, since even at fifteen she has a sophisticated understanding of the world and an emotional maturity well beyond her years.

As Lauren matures over a period of three years, she becomes a visionary, a prophet, and a charismatic leader, who also has formidable, practical organizing skills. No one in her group ever disputes that she is their leader, and she never lets them down, usually one step ahead of the others in anticipating danger and taking steps to avoid it.

In an interview with Rebecca O. Johnson, published in *Sojourner: The Women's Forum*, Butler commented on her character Lauren, but in a way that some readers might find surprising. She says she found it hard to write the book "because I knew I would have to write about a character who was power-seeking. I didn't realize how much I had absorbed the notion that power-seekers were evil." Butler thus found herself out of sympathy with her main character. She got around the problem by deciding that "power can be a tool. . . . [M]oney, knowledge, religion, whatever is common among human beings, can be beneficial or harmful to the individual and is judged by how it is being used."

An author's views of her own work must be respected, but it does not mean that other views are not possible. It might be interesting, for example, to discover how many readers reach the conclusion that Lauren is a power seeker. Certainly she has a missionary desire to promote certain ideas; she wants to persuade and lead, but those personal qualities do not of themselves make her a power seeker. Lauren's situation in life is as much forced on her by circumstances as created by her own will. Earthseed, the religion she creates, teaches humility before the irreducible fact of change. It does not sound like a religion that calls for a messiah figure or an autocratic leader.

If the creative and resourceful Lauren does seek power, it is not from any egotistical or selfish desire to dominate others. This would be doubly hard for Lauren since she is an empath. She has the capacity to feel the pain of the oppressed to an unusual degree. The origins of this "hyperempathy" lie in her mother's abuse of a drug named Paracetco when she was pregnant with Lauren. In creating this detail, Butler builds on a distressing fact that emerged in the early 1990s: Some babies born to cocaine-addicted mothers were addicted to cocaine from birth. Lauren emphasizes that her condition is a delusion (the doctors call it "organic delusional syndrome"), but delusions are real to those who suffer from them. She is also encouraged to keep her condition a secret, since it is perceived as a weakness. The pain of others has the power to disable her completely, but sometimes a person's greatest weakness is also the source of her greatest strength.

It is not hard to see in fifteen-year-old Lauren as she rides her bicycle in an unwalled area, absorbing the distressing scenes ("I tried not to look at them, but I couldn't help seeing—collecting—some of their general misery") an echo of the legend of the Buddha, who as a young man walking in the street was awakened to the reality of human life by the sight of old age, sickness, and death, from which he had previously been shielded. From this arose his desire to find the cause of suffering and the means by which it might be removed. Just as the compassion of one man gave rise to one of the world's great religions, so the vision of a young girl, in entirely different circumstances, in a different time and place, and in a different way, gives rise to Earthseed, a religion that embraces suffering as an inevitable part of the change that is the fundamental principle of life itself.

Source: Bryan Aubrey, Critical Essay on *Parable of the Sower*, in *Novels for Students*, Thomson Gale, 2005.

Madhu Dubey

In the following essay excerpt, Dubey identifies "current urban problems" in the changing communities of Parable of the Sower, *and argues that "investing literature with broadbased social value" to resolve such dilemmas is problematic.*

In "The Politics of Fiction, Anthropology, and the Folk: Zora Neale Hurston," first published in 1991, Hazel Carby seeks to account for the recent academic revival of Zora Neale Hurston's southern folk aesthetic. Carby argues that Hurston's writing, locating authentic black community in the rural south, displaced the difficulties of representing the complex and contested black culture that was taking shape in the cities and that the current academic reclamation of Hurston's work illustrates a parallel logic of displacement. Carby concludes with the suggestion that present-day critics of

> " ... the novel thoroughly discredits the enduring image (revived in recent times) of the city as a marketplace of abundant and diverse consumer options."

African-American literature and culture "begin to acknowledge the complexity of [their] own discursive displacement of contemporary conflict and cultural transformation in the search for black cultural authenticity. The privileging of Hurston ... at a moment of intense urban crisis and conflict is perhaps a sign of that displacement."

Carby's provocative argument can be extended beyond its specific reference to the academic recovery of Zora Neale Hurston, and applied to the turn toward southern folk culture taken in so much of the criticism surrounding novels by Toni Morrison, Alice Walker, Gloria Naylor, Ntozake Shange, and others. Although most of these writers have published city novels, criticism on these novelists has tended to privilege those selected texts and textual elements that help consolidate a black feminine literary tradition derived from southern folk culture. Following Carby's logic, we might argue that these critical texts are executing a "discursive displacement" of problems of urban literary representation, but this displacement is itself an oblique form of response to the widely prevalent rhetoric of contemporary urban crisis. This rhetoric, magnetized around the notorious term "underclass," tends to frame the issue of urban crisis essentially as a crisis in black culture and community. In popular media and academic discourses, the underclass is commonly represented as a recalcitrant urban mass polarized against an expanding black middle class and caught in illicit culture of poverty. Given the public sway of these discourses, it is not surprising that so much recent African-American literature is framing urban crisis as a problem of representation, and grappling with the questions of whether and how the writer can bridge class divides and speak for, as well as to, a wider black urban community. This problem of representation is exacerbated by the fact that contemporary literary readerships are highly specialized and restricted as well as racially and culturally diverse, and are certainly not coextensive with "the black community."

The southern folk aesthetic exemplifies a "discursive displacement" of this crisis in literary representation in the sense that, if black community is perceived to be irreparably fractured in the contemporary city, the folk domain of the rural south operates as a site where integral black communities can be imaginatively restored. These face-to-face models of community are typically bound together by ties of place, distinctive cultural modes of knowing (clustered around the term "conjuring") and styles of communication (oral tradition). The turn toward southern folk culture works essentially to guarantee the writer's ability to identify, address, and speak for a wider black community. For example, Alice Walker declares, in a much-quoted passage from her essay "The Black Writer and the Southern Experience," that "what the black Southern writer inherits as a natural right is a sense of *community*. Something simple but surprisingly hard, especially these days, to come by." If we accredit current discourses of urban crisis, black community *does* appear surprisingly hard to come by these days, requiring as it does difficult acts of mediation across intraracial class, regional, and cultural distinctions. The literary turn toward a rural southern past helps short-circuit this labor of mediation, furnishing community as the writer's "natural right." Alice Walker's, remembered image of wholesome southern community hinges on a "co-operative ethos" that mitigates intraracial class divisions, precisely the ethos that is often said to have dissolved in the contemporary city.

Houston Baker, in his study of black women novelists, specifies the type of community implicit in the southern folk aesthetic, as he opposes the "mulattoization"—or racial dilution—of black urban culture to "a field of 'particular' or vernacular imagery unique to the Afro-American imagination," a field Baker situates in the rural south. Even Addison Gayle, a prominent advocate of the city-based Black Aesthetic of the 1960s, has more recently argued that black southern folklore gives us "the genesis of a racial literature"; despite "the fact that modernization, urbanization, and all the concomitant evils have come to the South," the African-American writer who taps into southern folklore can be "one with his community, and his works ... validated and legitimized by the community itself." As these passages suggest, the southern folk aesthetic stakes a claim to crisis-free literary representation, and strives to recover, in Toni Morrison's words, "a time when an artist could be genuinely representative *of* the tribe and *in* it." Morrison's use of the word "tribe" (and, elsewhere, "village") invokes a metaphor of organic community that serves to secure the contemporary writer's claims to literary representation, and that bespeaks the difficulty of affirming the writer's social function within the more complex and conflicted conditions of contemporary urban community.

The critical currency of the southern folk aesthetic has obscured those African-American novelists who explicitly engage the difficulties of writing an urban fiction that cannot configure its reading audience as an organic racial community. In this essay, I shall focus on one such novelist, Octavia Butler, whose recent novel, *Parable of the Sower* (1993), addresses several concerns feeding into a contemporary crisis of urban literary representation. Octavia Butler is a prolific writer whose novels have usually been targeted at a restricted science-fiction readership and, with the exception of *Kindred*, have therefore remained outside the critical purview of the African-American women's fictional tradition. Butler's latest novel merits attention because its unusual approach to questions of community broadens and complicates influential current accounts of black women's literary tradition. If, as Hazel Carby contends, southern folk aesthetics exemplify a discursive displacement of urban crisis, *Parable of the Sower* attempts squarely to confront this crisis through its starkly dystopian urban setting. The novel self-reflexively deploys scientific modes of knowing and textual forms of communication (rather than the magical epistemology of "conjuring" or oral tradition) in order to assess the writer's role in mediating urban crisis. The novel forcefully rejects localist and organic notions of community, reaching instead for more complex ways of representing communities that are not coextensive with places or with discrete cultural traditions. In what follows, I treat *Parable of the Sower* as a lens that clarifies the dangers of advancing folk resolutions to current urban problems. I then go on to examine Butler's resolution to dilemmas of urban literary representation, which depends on the very same model of organic community that her novel struggles to discredit as an unrealistic and undesirable ideal. As I shall argue, the contradictory terms of this resolution reveal not only the difficulty of investing literature with broad-based social value within contemporary urban conditions, but also the constraints placed by current discourses of urban crisis on the African-American literary imagination.

If the urban migrations of the first half of the twentieth century constituted a mass movement of African-Americans from "medieval America to modern" as well as a collective effort to seize "the larger and more democratic chance," the reverse literary turn toward the rural south in the last decades of this century may be read as a form of "desperate pastoralism" born out of acute disenchantment with the failed promise of urban modernity for African-Americans. As so many urban historians have observed, the American city at the end of the twentieth century is typified by two contradictory but interdependent trends—hardening racial and economic divisions on the one hand, and on the other a promiscuous intercourse between cultural signs of racial difference that maintains the mirage of a "consumer democracy." Locating authentic black community in a segregated folk domain, the southern aesthetic enables writers to divest from the illusory pluralism promised by the contemporary city.

Parable of the Sower similarly exposes the hollowness and duplicity of recent American ideologies of urban development. The novel takes as its point of departure an uncannily credible future in which ideals of the American city as a "consumption artifact" have devolved into a precarious urban order founded on economic and racial inequality. Octavia Butler has said in an interview that in this novel she "made an effort to talk about what could actually happen or is in the process of happening." The dystopia presented in *Parable of the Sower* is so closely extrapolated from current trends, as Stephen Potts observes, that it produces a shock of familiarity rather than estrangement. Butler identifies the walling of communities as one process that is actually and already occurring in contemporary urban America. And, in fact, the novel's depiction of walled neighborhoods as spatial manifestations of a segregated urban order based on unequal distribution of economic resources uncannily resembles both John Edgar Wideman's journalistic description of contemporary Los Angeles as a city structured by "invisible walls" and Mike Davis's grim account of "Fortress L.A."

Set in Robledo, a "little city" near Los Angeles, during the years 2024–27, the first half of *Parable of the Sower* presents a walled neighborhood whose residents armed themselves to protect their property against threats of looting and arson. The streets outside this enclave are occupied by an urban underclass made up of "the street poor—squatters, winos, junkies, homeless people in general" who are "desperate or crazy or both."

Inhabitants of the walled neighborhood are too fearful of street violence to send their children to the few schools that still exist; few jobs are available even for the educated. Past patterns of production and consumption have so thoroughly stripped the earth of its natural resources that even water has become an expensive commodity. Vegetable gardens, fruit trees, and livestock provide the means of subsistence for the relatively well-to-do, such as the residents of Robledo, whose struggle to preserve their property, their families, and their community ends when their neighborhood is destroyed by pyromaniacs, users of a popular drug that stimulates arson.

Projecting widespread scarcity and heightened class and racial antagonisms as the probable results of current patterns of production and consumption, the novel thoroughly discredits the enduring image (revived in recent times) of the city as a marketplace of abundant and diverse consumer options. It is the gated community rather than the vibrant and heterogeneous marketplace that Butler presents as the epitome of contemporary urbanism. Lauren Olamina, the eighteen-year old protagonist and narrator of the novel, describes Robledo as "a tiny, walled, fish-bowl cul-de-sac community." The novel's only other extended image of urban order is equally, if not more, dystopian. Olivar, a city bought out and controlled by a multinational company, offers its citizens employment, a "guaranteed food-supply," and security from the "spreading chaos of the rest of Los Angeles County." But the safety of a company town like Olivar is based on a system of labor exploitation that seems "half antebellum revival and half science fiction." Corporations pay their workers wages that barely meet living expenses, forcing them into a cycle of debt slavery that perpetuates their dependence on the company. The order of this privatized city is maintained by the suspension of "'overly restrictive' minimum wage, environmental, and worker protection laws," so that corporations can do away with money wages altogether and hire labor in exchange for room and board.

The gated communities of Olivar and Robledo sketch a future scenario in which American cities can no longer continue to function as systems supporting an equitable organization of production and consumption. In response, the novel's protagonist urges other characters to seek more viable economic and ecological alternatives, such as living off the land. This turn to a simple agricultural economy is certainly a logical consequence of the novel's refusal to equate current directions of urban development with the promise of progress. Lauren's mother remembers a past when this urban promise seemed tangible, when cities were "a blaze of light." In the novel's present, however, "lights, progress, growth" are discredited as the thwarted goals of urban development. In its critique of an urban order rationalized by ideologies of conspicuous consumption and in its turn to a modest agricultural order, *Parable of the Sower* decidedly recalls novels such as Toni Morrison's *Song of Solomon* and Gloria Naylor's *Mama Day*, which affirm primitive social orders situated in an imaginary rural south as alternatives to contemporary capitalist cities organized as artifacts of consumption. As Susan Willis has argued, seemingly nostalgic images of the rural south in black women's fiction often serve as Archimedean levers for criticizing urban capitalism.

Parable of the Sower shares this critique but refuses the polarization of rural and urban spheres that bolsters the southern folk aesthetic. Raymond Williams warns, in *The Country and the City*, that "we need not, at any stage, accept the town and country contrast at face value," because literary constructions of this contrast so often repress the realities of agricultural labor and thereby blind us to the functional interdependence of country and city in advanced capitalist economies. Butler is careful not to disguise the harsh facts of agricultural labor or to represent the rural sphere as an elsewhere to the urban capitalist economy. Emery, the only farm worker in the novel, has worked for an agribusiness conglomerate that paid wages in company scrip and practiced a form of exploitation through debt as pernicious as the debt slavery common in privatized cities such as Olivar. By means of such exact parallels between conditions of labor in rural and urban areas, the novel resists constructing an idealized fiction of the countryside to ground its opposition to urban capitalism.

Butler even more emphatically refuses the retrospective stance that typically characterizes rural-based critiques of urban conditions. Commenting on the literary method of using a fabricated rural past as a "stick to beat the present," Raymond Williams remarks on its tendency to turn "protest into retrospect," a tendency that curtails the radical reach of rurally grounded critiques of urban capitalism. In *Parable of the Sower*, Butler clarifies the strongly conservative (and conservationist) ideologies that tend to accompany a retrospective critical stance toward the present. The adults in Robledo are "still anchored in the past, waiting for the good old days to come back"; as Lauren frequently points out, this backward vision prevents them from reckoning with the many changes that have already occurred and from imagining future social transformation.

In explicit opposition to the "dying, denying, backward-looking" posture of her community, Lauren searches for a belief system that can "pry them loose from the rotting past" and push them into building a different and better future. To this end, Lauren establishes her own religion, which she names Earthseed. This name comes to her as she is working in her garden and thinking of the way "plants seed themselves, away from their parent plants." Based on her observation that "A tree cannot grow in its parents' shadows," Lauren envisions members of the Earthseed community (which, at this point in the novel, exists only in her imagination) as "Earthlife . . . preparing to fall away from the parent world," "earthseed cast on new ground," far from the familiar spaces of home, family, and neighborhood.

Butler's seed metaphor carries both a critical and a constructive response to conditions of urban crisis that strikingly diverges from the southern folk resolution to urban problems, crystallized around the metaphors of roots and ancestry. Taking their cue from Toni Morrison's essays, "Rootedness: The Ancestor as Foundation" and "City Limits, Village Values," critics including Karla Holloway, Joanne Braxton, and Farah Jasmine Griffin configure the ancestor as a repository of southern folk tradition and a means of combating the presumed fracture of black urban community. The ancestor, as a bearer of collective folk memory, helps displaced city-dwellers to preserve their roots in the rural south; these roots support the foundation of "village" models of home, family, and community that alone can withstand urban alienation and dislocation. In this conception of the ancestor as the root or foundation of urban community, a remembered and imagined rural past grounds a critique of the capitalist city as well as an alternative vision of social order.

In contrast, Butler's critique of the capitalist city does not take its bearings from the past (whether real or imagined). If the metaphor of roots points toward consolidation of past values as a positive response to present urban problem, in *Parable of the Sower*, attachment to the "apparent stability" of home, family, and neighborhood obstructs action directed at change. Like the gated community, home, too, in this novel is figured as "a cul-de-sac with a wall around it." This is not to suggest that Lauren does not draw emotional solace from her home, family,

and neighborhood. Butler has said in an interview that family seems to her to make up "our most important set of relationships" and, in fact, other novels by Butler have been criticized for the heavy redemptive weight they place on family. *Parable of the Sower* fully grants the sustaining value of home and family, but the novel sketches an emergency scenario of such wholesale urban devastation that these constructs cannot offer refuge from or guide a viable critique of dystopian urban conditions. As exemplified by the reactions of the adults in Robledo, people often react to perceived crisis by conserving familiar structures and values in an attempt to fend off the inevitability of change. This defense of traditional values associated with an idealized past often serves dubious political ends, as is obvious from contemporary discussions of the urban "underclass" that promote familial stability (associated either with rural southern life or with a "golden age of the ghetto") as a resolution to structural economic and political problems. The seed metaphor in *Parable of the Sower* suggests a valuable corrective to such approaches, urging as it does the necessity of discarding ideas and ideologies rooted in the past that aim only to stabilize, not to transform, present social conditions. Home and family in Butler's novel cannot escape or counter the systemic logic of urban poverty and unemployment. The novel delineates the broad national and international economic processes that impinge on every home and every neighborhood, clarifying the futility (and impossibility) of constructing urban communities on "village" foundations. Lauren's aspiration to seed herself away from the shadow of home and family signals her readiness to relinquish available mirages of stability and to embrace drastic change and rupture if these are the only means to future survival and growth. This readiness is expressed in the central principle of Lauren's Earthseed religion: "When apparent stability disintegrates, as it must—God is Change."

Both the name of Lauren's religion, Earthseed, and its governing metaphor of seeding suggest notions of place and community other than those inhering in the roots metaphor, which consolidates cultural and ancestral traditions as bulwarks against modem urban forces of displacement. Lauren's religion assumes mobility across space as its necessary and enabling condition. Recognizing that all visionary schemes of social transformation require an imagined elsewhere to inspire and focus action, Lauren writes that the "heaven" or "destiny" of Earthseed is "to take root among the stars." By this Lauren literally means that the future of the human race lies in extrasolar space. The importance of this image of heaven is its orientation toward a future space that can only be reached by means of modern technology. The extraterrestrial direction of Earthseed, a common enough science fiction device, hyperbolically conveys the expansive globalism of the novel's vision, a vision far removed from the localism of folk models of place-bound community.

I do not mean to suggest here that mobility is in itself a forward-looking urban value or that localism is necessarily aligned with nostalgic folk models of community. In fact, urban community movements have often sought to conserve the use values attached to specific neighborhoods as the only available means of resisting the instability of an urban space that is repeatedly deformed and reformed by the dictates of capitalist exchange value. As Logan and Molotch have persuasively argued, contradictions between use and exchange values, between place as the site of lived community and place as commodity, are at the root of "truly urban conflict." Poor neighborhoods inhabited by racial minorities have been especially vulnerable to the rapid conversions of urban space over the last two or three decades; the forcible dislocation of these residents has been the invariable byproduct of urban renewal and gentrification projects intended to raise property values. In this kind of urban context, mobility can hardly be affirmed as a more progressive stance than efforts to defend the use values of places and communities against the disembedding forces of capitalist spatial turnover.

This conflict between urban use and exchange values is dramatized in a recent novel, *Tumbling*, by Diane McKinney-Whetstone, which depicts a low-income black residential neighborhood in Philadelphia that forms the site of a closely knit community modeled on the southern "village." Residents band together to protest and obstruct an urban renewal project undertaken by real-estate developers and subsidized by the city administration, which threatens to raze the neighborhood. Despite the residents' efforts, their neighborhood church is bulldozed to clear the space for highway construction. *Tumbling* ends with the lines, "They would not be moved. No way, no way." In the novel's closing scene, residents form a makeshift community on the debris of the church in a last-ditch and ultimately futile effort to defend the use value of their neighborhood—futile because the community lacks the political and economic power to overcome the urban "growth machine" jointly run by "place entrepreneurs," city officials, and political leaders.

It is because neighborhoods and communities are imbricated in wider and unequally structured grids of exchange value and political power that struggles to preserve local value and communal integrity are almost always unsuccessful. For this reason, *Parable of the Sower* insists that readiness to move—to outer space, if need be—is crucial to survival in modern capitalist cities. Like *Tumbling*, the first part of *Parable* laments the inevitable defeat of movements to maintain local and communal self-sufficiency. The Robledo neighborhood cannot be sustained because its relative financial and social stability is structurally interconnected to the extreme instability of the poor and the pyromaniacs who throng outside the walls of Robledo and who eventually raid and burn down the neighborhood.

Just before the destruction of Robledo, Lauren Olamina preaches a funeral sermon for her father (who has disappeared and is presumed dead) and for the ideal of self-contained, stable, place-bound community that Lauren associates with an older way of life. Lauren's sermon commemorates her father's attempts to preserve the integrity and durability of locale and community: "We have our island community, fragile, and yet a fortress. Sometimes it seems too small and too weak to survive. . . . But . . . it persists. . . . This is our place, no matter what." This is, however, a funeral sermon and Lauren is mourning the death of traditional conceptions of community rooted in a fixed and impermeable sense of place. At the end of her sermon, a member of the community begins to sing the spiritual, "We Shall Not Be Moved," to which Lauren mentally responds, "We'll be moved, all right. It's just a matter of when, by whom, and in how many pieces." Appropriately enough, then, the first half of the novel traces the literal destruction of Lauren's home, neighborhood, and community in Robledo, and the second half describes her journey north (with a band of fellow travelers she picks up on the way) toward a new home and community. The novel ends soon after the group reaches its destination. The entire action of the novel reveals the impossibility of maintaining "village" ideals of bounded community rooted in a stable locale. In this sense, even as it presents the complete collapse of actual cities, the novel insists on an urban understanding of place as the inescapable basis for constructing alternative images of social order.

In contrast to the Robledo community, based on the principle of self-contained localism, the journey section that constitutes the bulk of the novel presents community as process rather than settlement. This section traces the contingent formation of a community on the move—"born right here on Highway 101," as Lauren puts it—unified not by its attachment to past or place but by a common set of practical objectives that must be continually adjusted to meet changing circumstances. When Robledo burns down, halfway through the novel, Lauren runs into two survivors of the neighborhood, Harry and Zahra, who share her will to move toward a better life. The other fourteen people who join the group in the course of the journey north are distinguished primarily by the fact that most of them are racially mixed, and therefore "natural allies" in a society that frowns on miscegenation. Most members of the group have suffered some form of injustice, whether caused by poverty, forced prostitution, child abuse, or debt slavery. The sole purpose that unifies this group of diverse people is their shared resolve to move toward a better future.

Even though the itinerary of this "crew of a modern underground railroad" is explicitly calculated to bypass cities, which are sites of danger, their operation as a community is emphatically urban in most crucial respects. Despite the natural reference of its name, Earthseed is definitely not an organic community unified by collective memory, ethnicity, shared cultural heritage, or attachment to place. If, in order to resist the "mulattoization" of urban community, the southern folk aesthetic strives to recuperate cohesive racial communities consisting of cultural insiders, the Earthseed community, in contrast, is racially and culturally mixed and thus demands constant efforts of mediation and translation. The boundaries of this community, the porous lines between insiders and outsiders, friends and enemies, must be continually redrawn; they must "embrace diversity or be destroyed." The process of finding unity in diversity is necessarily risky and difficult, requiting the ability to interpret unfamiliar cultural codes and the alert balancing of suspicion and trust typical of urban social interactions. This group makes collective decisions by way of rational argument and persuasion rather than by appeals to past precedent or tradition.

Given the novel's insistence on this thoroughly urban conception of community, the settlement established by Lauren and her Earthseed community at the end of the novel surely appears puzzling. The journey that takes up most of the second half of the novel ends in Humboldt County in northern California, on a piece of property owned by Bankole, one of the group of travelers who journey north with Lauren. Bankole offers the group (which by the end of the novel consists of four men, five women, and four children) rent-free use of his land. Several

geographical features of Bankole's property make it a suitable (though not ideal) place for establishing an Earthseed community. Most importantly, arable land and a dependable water supply make the property amenable to gardening and farming. The economy projected at the end of the novel is small-scale, primitive, and self-sufficient in the sense that farming, breeding livestock, and building shelters are expected to take care of basic production and consumption needs. It is clear that jobs paying money are scarce in neighboring towns and, given that several members of the community are former debt slaves or throw-away laborers, working Bankole's land seems preferable to selling labor to "strangers" who "shouldn't be trusted." One of the more valuable characteristics of Bankole's land is its isolation; because it is "far removed from any city" and "miles from everywhere with no decent road," it is relatively immune to attack from outsiders. That the area's distance from cities constitutes a strongly emphasized advantage is not surprising considering that cities, as centers of asymmetrical accumulation, have been shown throughout the novel to be the most vulnerable to criminal violence targeting the scarce commodity. The Earthseed community plans to guard its settlement by assigning members to keep watch at night and later by training dogs to protect the property.

How is this settlement different from the walled and heavily guarded neighborhood of the beginning of the novel? We have seen that the Robledo community was destroyed because its goal of local self-sufficiency was unviable given its dependence on a wider, starkly inequitable economic order. The community at the end of the novel does acknowledge, though it does not adequately reckon with, the inevitability of such connections. Despite some affinities with arcadian rural communities such as the island of Willow Springs in Gloria Naylor's *Mama Day*, the Earthseed community cannot be regarded as arcadian, in that it does not assume the essential moderacy, simplicity, or stability of human needs. The potentially destabilizing desire to accumulate surplus, on the part of individuals and the group, is expressed in Harry's remark that he wants a job outside the community that will pay money as well as in the community's plan to sell surplus produce in nearby towns. The members of the Earthseed community insist on the provisional nature of their settlement; as Lauren points out, there are "no guarantees," and should their experimental community fail (as most member of the group expect it to do), they will have to be prepared to move on.

Yet the Earthseed community also aims impossibly to maintain local self-containment and stability. The novel's concluding image of community does not suggest a more workable balancing between use and exchange value, between localism and mobility, than does its opening image of the walled cul-de-sac neighborhood. As we have seen, Butler's representation of Robledo forcefully repudiates notions of place-bound community, and the journey section of the novel reaches for a more complex way of imagining community that is not coextensive with place, and place that is conceived as a "concrete abstraction" rather than as a self-enclosed site of social meaning. Butler wrestles with the difficulties of writing a fiction adequate to this understanding of place and community, yet the Earthseed settlement at the end of the novel ends up establishing an insulated, agrarian, face-to-face model of community that is not so different, after all, from the organic communities associated with southern folk aesthetics. In this respect, the Earthseed community is symptomatic of the difficulty that limits the contemporary literary imagination seeking utopian urban alternatives. Its small-scale, self-sufficient, agrarian ideal is rife with contradictions: even if we know that any truly alternative social vision requires wholesale transformation of global economic order, we end up thinking small because the abstraction of this order makes it difficult to grasp and imagine large-scale change. Or, in Manuel Castells' succinct expression, "When people find themselves unable to control the world, they simply shrink the world to the size of their community."

Source: Madhu Dubey, "Folk and Urban Communities in African-American Women's Fiction: Octavia Butler's *Parable of the Sower*," in *Studies in American Fiction*, Vol. 27, No. 1, Spring 1999, pp. 103–28.

Lisbeth Gant-Britton

In the following essay, Gant-Britton explores how Butler creates "new patterns for the future" for African Americans in Parable of the Sower.

Ideas [are weapons] and their creators run the world. Christianity is an idea. Islam is an idea. Buddhism and Hinduism are ideas . . . Capitalism and Socialism were ideas before they became reality . . . One's place in the world is partly due to the ideas that a culture has forced on one, and/or the ideas that a person 'freely' accepts and uses.

Haki R. Madhubuti, *Claiming Earth*

Thought is no longer theoretical. As soon as it functions it offends or reconciles, attracts or repels, breaks, dissociates, unites or reunites; it cannot help but liberate and enslave. Even before prescribing, suggesting a future, saying what must be done, even

before exhorting or merely sounding an alarm, thought, at the level of its existence, in its very dawning, is in itself an action—a perilous act.

Michel Foucault, *Language, Counter-Memory, Practice*

Many writers are speculating these days about what the United States may be like in the twenty-first century. However, few of them are African American, and fewer still are black women. Octavia Butler is one of them. Her novel *Parable of the Sower*, like its 1998 sequel *Parable of the Talents*, offers a vision of one potential American future, one which may take women of colour and other marginalized peoples beyond ourselves as we are constituted today. The only African American woman with a substantial body of science fiction writing to date (ten novels), Butler has a vision worth examining. She considers the central question of how a black woman writer may project a liberated and liberating future while at the same time figuratively endeavouring to suture the still-open wounds of an embattled past and problematic present.

Reviewing the literature by African American women writers, I noted that until recently, fiction by multiply-oppressed women has been more concerned with re-envisioning the past or finding voice in present oppositional discourses, than it has been with imagining a world of the future. Many black women writers have seen literature as the primary way they could re-envision an egregious history. This work is definitely vital and ongoing, and I believe it should go on. But at the same time, we stand at the border of a new millennium. And even though that millennium is itself an ideological construction, it does provide an 'in-between' space—as postcolonial and cultural critic Homi Bhabha puts it in *The Location of Culture*—a present-future juncture which becomes the terrain, if you will, for elaborating new 'strategies of selfhood' and 'new signs of identity.' These moments are 'innovative sites of collaboration and contestation,' as Bhabha says, 'in the act of defining the idea of society itself' (1994, pp. 1–2). Further, as Paul Ricoeur observes in *Time and Narrative,* each fictive temporal experience unfolds its own world, its own 'time.' This 'time' is meaningful to the extent that it portrays features of each text's unique temporal experience in relation to the cultural dilemma under consideration in the narrative.

In terms of an American context, at the present time, black Americans are situated at one of the most paradoxical junctures we have inhabited since the Reconstruction. Many African Americans in the middle and upper classes enjoy unprecedented material prosperity and societal influence. Indeed, in 1996, a black man was publicly considered as the Republican party's possible presidential, then vice-presidential candidate. At the same time, though, a post-civil rights backlash surged that has included some 200 black churches being burned. Against the backdrop of this paradox of progress, we hurtle through time. What kinds of futures are we, as a society, creating in the process?

Hortense Spillers notes that for many years black women writers have had no choice but to develop their own tradition of diegesis to narrativize the complexity of African American women's experiences in order to combat the mental oppression of already-circulating mis-characterizations. She aptly points out that new traditions of agency are not born. They are made in the face of social and cultural assaults—even if they must be fashioned as a patchwork of 'discontinuities':

> '[T]radition' for [the] black women's writing community is a matrix of literary *discontinuities* that partially articulate various periods of consciousness in the history of an African-American people. This point of paradox not only opens the future to the work to come, but also reminds us that *symbolic discontinuity* is the single rule of terministic behavior that our national literature has still to pursue. The day it does so, the reader and writer both will have laid sight on a territory of the literary landscape that we barely knew was possible. (Spillers' emphasis, 1985, p. 251).

That our literary 'landscape' might one day evolve into something 'we barely knew was possible,' as Spillers puts it, is an appropriate metaphor for the central questions in *Parable of the Sower*. How does one begin to make a new tradition out of a legacy of discontinuities?

Octavia Butler's novel, *Parable of the Sower* is an exploration of continuity amidst discontinuity. It is set in a decidedly dystopic future. In fact, in this novel, Los Angeles and its surrounding areas are the trope of a failed future. The entire West coast, and a good portion of the rest of the country, is barely livable in the year 2025. L.A. of course, was once an icon of utopian promise in America itself. But in this twenty-first century situation, all that is left are remnants of the reification of such an ideal. The city's infrastructure has crumbled, services are at a standstill, water costs twice as much as gasoline (which is largely unavailable anyway), and those few families who still have jobs are huddled together in makeshift walled communities to keep out the majority of the population, which is homeless, drug-crazed and violent. The wealthy lived in armoured walled enclaves, with privatized police and fire departments.

> **"** She considers the central question of how a black woman writer may project a liberated and liberating future while at the same time figuratively endeavouring to suture the still-open wounds of an embattled past and problematic present."

At first glance, all that we may perceive in Butler's novel is a legacy of compromise and practicality. Yet we also glimpse an immense potential hidden in this narrative. *Parable* contains innovative strategies of agency for women of colour, but they are embedded within the work. Such hidden futurity is vitally important because it signals dormant subjectivity within otherwise seemingly impenetrable circumstances of domination. By subjectivity one may include moving from victimization to agency or autonomy. Charles Scruggs develops a similar idea in *Sweet Home: Invisible Cities in the Afro-American Novel* when he argues:

> in the novels of Wright, Baldwin, Ellison, and Morrison, the visionary city is always present within the tangible, and often terrible, conditions of black urban life. The critique of a society or of social conditions—even the realistic depiction of the most wretched horrors—inevitably implies something different and better . . . Often the visionary city lies dormant, asleep; but it contains within its dormant state the potency of dream and the possibility of making the dream manifest, if only temporarily (1993, pp. 2–3).

Scruggs's definition of an invisible city is an example of the invisible agency we may uncover in *Parable*. Possible new paradigms are born when the central characters stare straight into the face of impossibility (in the case of overcoming a failed economy for example) and effect change anyway. One may argue that the changes Butler's characters make are barely enough for the protagonists to save themselves. But that is precisely the point. In these novels, this hidden theorizing, these deeply-embedded new goals, often manifest themselves as no more than the presence, rather than absence of alternatives. But for many exploited people, change is often a matter of starting with almost nothing and making incremental advancements. As D. Soyini Madison comments in *The Woman That I Am:*

> I remember my mother ... speaking quietly but forcefully in a tone that could scare a bull. She would wilfully declare: 'Being the woman that I am I will make a way out of no way.' These were *mother's* words, but they are also the words and the will of *all* women of color who assert who they are, who create sound out of silence, and who build worlds out of remnants (1994, p. 1).

As Madison's observation attests, potentially fruitful agency is hidden within her mother's simple declaration. The unarticulated aspects of the older woman's commentary are rich with the unspoken but potentially instructive theory of a women of colour. Such embedded theories may include continued efforts to heal still unresolved aspects of black women's various pasts, while many of these women continue striving, if only for limited agency, in the present and future.

These embedded theories relate to what Bhabha characterizes as 'in-between' spaces which are opened up at this present-future juncture and which provide the terrain for elaborating what he calls new 'strategies of selfhood,' 'new signs of identity; and innovative sites of collaboration and contestation, in the act of defining the idea of society itself' (1994, pp. 1–2). Indeed, this transformational potential against all odds which Butler builds upon, has been the mainstay of many black writers' indomitable challenge to a past and present that do not seem capable of being significantly changed.

In *Black Looks,* bell hooks describes the 'response to the traumatic pain and anguish that remains a consequence of white racist domination' (1992, p. 169). She suggests that the residue of this pain and anguish continues to inform and shape the psychic state of black people, influencing how we view the world, and I would add, the future. This residue is also continually 'stirred up' by contemporary sociopolitical problems which recur, and which unfortunately still include issues such as the enslavement of peoples of colour in America and other countries, even in this day and age. Julia Kristeva in *The Powers of Horror* describes this continuing residue in psychoanalytic terms as 'phobic,' specifically naming the dilemma 'abjection.'

> The phobic has no other object than the abject. But that word, 'fear'—a fluid haze, an elusive clamminess—no sooner has it cropped up than it shades off like a mirage and permeates all words of the language with nonexistence, with a hallucinatory, ghostly glimmer. Thus, fear having been bracketed, discourse will seem tenable only if it ceaselessly confronts that otherness, a burden both repellent and

repelled, a deep well of memory that is unapproachable and intimate: the abject (1982, p. 6).

Butler's project is consistent with both of these issues. It is concerned with the transfer of trauma from one generation to the next, as demonstrated by *Parable*'s main characters. The black father dies, having only managed to keep his family alive during society's rapid deterioration. His daughter Lauren, the protagonist, carries on in his name. But she boldly attempts to mould a new future instead of coping with the present. The daughter's decidedly forward-looking vision contrasts with Toni Morrison's concept of 'rememory' in *Beloved,* in which discursive healing is seen almost exclusively as a backward-looking project to allow African American men and women to engage and re-envision what Morrison calls 'unspeakable things unspoken.'

But in Butler's *Parable of the Sower,* we see a shift of that past-oriented temporality of 'rememory' forward. We then have a model which allows readers to conceptualize the future in a broader manner. Butler's model privileges proactive rather than reactive thinking. This different attitude is potentially more empowering for the novel's characters of colour, since it assumes a certain authority on the part of previously marginalized peoples to engage and shape critical sociopolitical issues, in an effort to be part of the transformational process rather than to be at the mercy of it. As Susan Willis states in *Specifying,* black women's writing in particular often imagines the future within the present. It sees the future born out of the context of oppression. It produces utopia out of the transformation of the most basic features of daily life—everything we tend to take for granted (1987, p. 159).

Butler's novel focuses primarily on the Olamina family, and in particular, on daughter Lauren. The Olamina parents are an African American professor and his second wife, a Latina. Both have doctorates and own their own home. Despite regular assaults by homeless people, the father refuses to leave what little security he knows to seek what might be a safer place farther north. In the twentieth century, the elder Olaminas—a multiracial, professional couple—would most likely be characterized as progressive. But in the twenty-first century, they represent the last generation of Americans to have been socialized into what Butler describes as a dying capitalism. In fact, their daughter regards them as clinging to a conservative world view that focuses narrowly on the past and present, rather than one which embraces change as necessary for the future.

Daughter Lauren has been born into this post-technological age. She is ready to embrace Bhabha's 'vision and construction . . . to take [her] beyond' herself. She is already conscious of the ways in which the decaying dominant socioeconomic system in the novel structures her subordination through its abandonment of poor and working people. For instance, Lauren observes how the country's cloistered twenty-first century elite configures the master narrative of 'progress' as a panacea for the future, so it privileges the European and Japanese transnational corporations who set about to privatize entire American cities and towns. From her subject position as a downwardly mobile (in a socio-cultural as well as economic sense) working poor person, Lauren is ready to create a new world with fresh possibilities.

Even before her entire family is killed by marauders, she works from her interstitial position—multi-racial, female, youthful—to refashion the received master narrative of an omnipotent Christian God upon which her family depends. She reconfigures it into a new imaginary conceptual space and calls her new written ontology 'Earthseed: The Books of the Living.' In it, she reverses her father's references to a supposedly all-powerful Christian God. She inverts the human/supernatural positionality. She argues instead that 'God exists to be shaped . . . There has to be . . . a better destiny that we can shape.'

What does it mean that her father's God now exists to be changed by people, rather than the other way around? Empowerment. Subjectivity in Lauren's eyes. New definitions and enactments of selfhood. In this way, Butler's young protagonist is an example of the kind of proactive oppositionality that black feminists Stanlie James and Abena Busia outline in *Theorizing Black Feminisms.* These critics argue that many black women are often characterized solely as 'victims' because of their experiences of multiple interrelated oppressions, including but not limited to, racism and ethnocentrism, sexism and classism. But James and Busia agree with feminist critic Catharine Stimpson that when people of colour theorize, it provides us with opportunities to 'think, imagine, speak, and act' that can transform an individual from victim to activist. Indeed, this kind of development can transform a whole community, perhaps even an entire society as well.

It is significant that in *Parable,* all of the elders in the Olamina community are killed off or move away, whereas Lauren, with her newly-minted master narrative, is one of the few to survive. Here Butler seems to be dramatizing the death of an old worldview, leaving Lauren alive to pursue the work of creating a new one. At first, Lauren's new goals exist solely in the realm of the imaginary. They're more fantasy than reality, initially, no more than an example of the presence, rather than absence of alternatives. Yet, as she struggles to have them accepted, we witness Lauren's continual, gradual empowerment. As she 'sows' the seeds of these ideas in the minds of others, so do they grow. With this belief as her basis, Lauren attempts to reposition herself both physically and mentally within twenty-first century struggles against subalternization and dominance.

After Lauren's family is murdered, she has to create a new family for herself. So, she gathers together a prototypical new community from a cross-section of people of different races, ages, genders and classes. Then in a kind of Harriet Tubman-like Underground Railroad, she leads the group to northern California. She even disguises herself as a man part of the time as Tubman sometimes did. Because of gangs of starving people on the road, Lauren and her group even have to walk and hide along the freeway like escaping slaves. This metaphor is by no means accidental. In Butler's post-technological future, many people of all races are forced to work virtually as slaves for transnational corporations who dole out just enough wages for them to subsist. But Lauren struggles not to be demoralized by this system. Instead, she tries to use it as a catalyst for change. She writes:

> All successful life is
> Adaptable.
> Opportunistic,
> Tenacious,
> Interconnected, and
> Fecund.
> Understand this,
> Use it.
> Shape God

We see Lauren attempting to escape as much from mental and emotional slavery as from physical slavery. As such, her efforts resonate with Audre Lorde's admonition that:

> Our future survival is predicated upon our ability to relate within equality . . . The future of our earth may depend upon the ability of all [people] to identify and develop new patterns of relating across difference.

Thus, Lauren, in nurturing her new dream, becomes one kind of model for African American and other oppressed women who want to move away from narratives that construct them as being less than capable of constituting change.

In this way, Lauren's ontology also relates to Molara Ogundipe-Leslie and Carole Boyce Davies' idea in *Recreating Ourselves* of a transformational discourse which seeks to change the epistemological bases on which the futures of people of colour may be formulated. But Davies warns in *Black Women, Writing and Identity,* that women of colour may also—consciously or unconsciously— participate in systems of oppression in the pursuit of their own goals of freedom. Davies cites a Caribbean-born woman as an example. The woman sends her children into the U.S. military, thinking it is their only hope for a better future. The mother does this—fully understanding that should another U.S. invasion of a Caribbean country such as the one in Grenada occur, her own children might well have to kill some of their Caribbean relatives (Davies, 1994, p. 27).

Indeed, in *Parable,* once Lauren herself is rendered parentless and homeless, she declares to her comrades, 'I mean to survive.' She explains that she has never stolen or killed, but that if it means staying alive, she will. And she does. This characterization indicates that we can't assume a benevolent direction for all efforts at change by women of colour—even though they may have good intentions. But Lauren's characterization as a survivalist is problematic in at least one other respect too. It reinforces representations of African American womanhood that configure women as robust, able to take care of themselves and others—closer to a male heroic mythological image. Also, these representations risk projecting the novel's Anglo American women by contrast into the mythical position of 'damsel in distress.'

Ricoeur critiques the 'remythicizing' effort in *Time and Narrative* in his reference to certain novelists' speculations (such as Virginia Woolf in *Mrs. Dalloway*) on time as it relates to their universe. He observes that the subject is interpellated by the fictional view of time as set forth in the text. In *Parable,* myths, despite their sometimes flawed appearance, recur throughout Butler's narrative project and do form an important subtext. For instance, the U.S. President is a mythical figure who periodically emerges in the novel. He is named President Donner. His authority in the crumbling country derives largely from his successful manipulation of the myth of a return to the 'good old days.' His continued relationship to, and reliance on, the narrative of 'progress and development' on which this country was originally founded, demands nothing less than a willing suspension of disbelief, a voluntary amnesia on the part of these poor citizens who now suffer in this text in the mid-twenty-first century. Donner asks these people to ignore their recognition that the very reason the land and atmosphere they have inherited are so ravaged, is because of that original quest for development in the first place. Yet he still asks them to participate in a romantic expectation of a future which Butler suggests is impossible to achieve in a post-technological twenty-first century, given the dearth of renewable resources to run anything. (For instance, computers exist in *Parable,* but there are hardly any sustainable resources such as water to generate electricity.)

Therefore, the president is effectively asking already oppressed peoples in this novel to participate in a kind of mental split to preserve a fiction which will further oppress them in the face of their devastating reality. He is actually asking them to look backward in the guise of looking forward. As such, President Donner is a symbol of a dislocated, schizoid future for the U.S. He continues to exist as a figurehead by pointing towards a future which can no longer be realized on the old, historical trajectory. Lauren describes Donner as a 'human banister.' She says 'he's like . . . like a symbol of the past for us to hold on to as we're being pushed into the future.' We may say then that subscribing to Donner's point of view amounts to a construction of the future based on absence. The poor and working people in the text share Donner's sense of time only to avoid coming to terms with the grim future that really lies in front of them.

Donner's very name suggests mythological time. He reminds us of Donner and Blitzen in the Santa Claus myth. In German, Donner and Blitzen means 'thunder and lightning.' And in French, 'donner' means to give, but President Donner is the bearer of a gift that is not really a gift at all. Finally and most ominously, Donner's name brings to mind legends of cannibalism, as it alludes to the account of the Donner travel party that got trapped in the Sierra Nevada Mountains in 1846, and some members had to eat one another. In *Parable,* President Donner metaphorically feeds off his near-starving people.

The President is actually one of three father figures with whom Lauren cannot agree; the others are God the father and her own father. Lauren's father doesn't believe in the Donner-endorsed abundance myth, but he is set in his reliance on an omnipotent God—so much so that he even declares pollution to be God's will. Lauren and her younger brother Keith both reject the idea of God the father, and rebuff their own father's views as well. But they demonstrate those rejections in different ways.

Keith runs away to the world outside of their walled neighbourhood when he is just fourteen. He relies on a kind of secularized mythical time based on virtual reality. This 'timeless' time is enabled by a device called the 'TV window' which one can enter and experience, instead of just looking at, as we do today. Keith joins a band of homeless who steal equipment so they can spend their time being mentally somewhere else or effectively nowhere else, in a kind technological heterotopia or utopia. As such, they are a reminder of William Gibson's cyberpunks in *Neuromancer* and the computer hackers who 'jack' into the Internet. The 'net' enables Keith and his cohort to leave their corporeal reality behind and participate in a widely expanded range of temporal and sensual experiences. Sadly, Keith doesn't realize that he has simply traded one ephemeral enclave for another.

Lauren opts to substitute her Earthseed philosophy for what she considers to be her father's parochial world-view. Armed with Earthseed, she remythicizes time by speculating that humanity has the potential to be on a plane with that of the Christian God. Earthseed's altered temporal perspective centres around change. Instead of continuously trying to back away from what Lauren perceives as the grim reality of their future, either through cosmological, religiously-oriented time or secularized mythical time, she advocates a push forward in which time is more actively manipulated, as signified by her aphorisms embracing change.

These tenets add a dimension of the heroic quest to her group's journey north, which begins essentially as a local struggle. In one sense, Lauren as the Emancipator reminds us of Odysseus. She also reflects both Jesus and Moses, sowing seeds for a democratization of God's spirit. But for Lauren it is not a question of stoically sacrificing herself for the next generation. Rather, it is more an issue of becoming the next generation within the present one, that is, demonstrating transformation and change at the intersection of the present and the future. Thus, a kind of doubling takes place in the text, in which the men and women in the novel continue to exist in their 'present,' but because they also attempt to reconstruct themselves as the Earthseed collective, they're already no longer the same.

Lauren's double role as teenage girl and symbolic male leader of the group illustrates this conjunction. Rather than thinking of her temporary masquerade as a man strictly in terms of gender performativity, we could also regard it as a kind of temporal performativity. Symbolically, Lauren is both her present-day self as well as being the leader of the new, utopic community. She even dreams of their leaving earth altogether and founding a community on Mars, as they trudge along the decrepit freeway from Los Angeles to northern California.

In this way, Lauren both prefigures new black heroes to come, as well as reminds us of black figures who remade themselves in the crucible of history. In the often-quoted passage in his *Narrative of the Life of Frederick Douglass,* Douglass delineates how, after finally standing up to his vicious overseer, Covey, he was already a different man, although he had not yet escaped from slavery. He says, 'My long-crushed spirit rose, cowardice departed, bold defiance took its place; and I now resolved that, however long I might remain a slave in form, the day had passed forever when I could be a slave in fact.' Later, this defiant self-deterministic attitude would be reflected in the Harlem Renaissance's credo of the 'New Negro.' And Langston Hughes talks about this emancipatory spirit in his essay, 'The Negro Artist and the Racial Mountain.' Similarly, Lauren, vulnerable, but feeling less than vulnerable observes:

> We are all Godseed, but no more or less
> so than any other aspect of the universe,
> Godseed is all there is—all that
> Changes.

On a metatexual level, Butler seems to be suggesting in *Parable* that for African Americans of any class to mediate authoritatively in the larger American society may remain a stiff task even in the future. But Lauren takes on the politics of self-authorization on both contemporary and historical levels, and in so doing, pushes the limits of the fictional formula. The space created by this forcing of the limits becomes 'the places of difference,' as theorist Valerie Smith puts it. Like Douglass and others, Lauren and her Earthseed comrades make a journey that is symbolic of the terms of cultural engagement that Bhabha suggests will be produced performatively in the future—not the result of preformed sociocultural beliefs, but developed fluidly out of changing circumstances (Bhabha 1994, p. 2).

Of course, whether Butler's characters eventually make it to Mars is secondary to the fact that they are willing to try. Thus, we could say that this dystopic 'cautionary tale' as Butler calls it, ends on a utopic note. This forging of possibility from the terrain of impossibility reminds me of what Chicana poet and theorist, Gloria Anzaldua says in *Making Face, Making Soul.* She says that the mere fact that many women of colour, who are normally enslaved by or have to service social and cultural systems in some way, escape long enough to create new patterns for the future, is an amazing feat in and of itself. As Anzaldua puts it, 'Our art is a sneak attack while the giant sleeps, a sleight of hands when the giant is awake, moving so quickly, they can do their deed before the giant swats them. Our survival depends on being creative.'

Source: Lisbeth Gant-Britton, "Octavia Butler's *Parable of the Sower*: One Alternative to a Futureless Future," in *Women of Other Worlds*, edited by Helen Merrick and Tess Williams, University of Western Australia Press, 1999, pp. 278–94.

Robert Butler

In the following essay excerpt, Butler places Lauren within "a direct line of descent" of African American heroines and examines her psychological, spiritual, and physical journeys toward freedom.

> I am not going to spend my life as some kind of twenty-first-century slave.
>
> So we became the crew of a modern underground railroad.
>
>   *—Parable of the Sower*

Octavia E. Butler's fiction takes the African American journey motif one step further by projecting it quite literally into the future. Eight of her ten published novels are set in futuristic societies in which her heroic figures cope with and transcend various kinds of entrapment by undertaking an interesting assortment of open journeys.

Patternmaster (1976) describes a society that is controlled by an all-powerful ruler who dominates the inward and outward lives of his subjects by ruthlessly imposing a "pattern" of thought and behavior on them. Teray and Amber, the novel's dual heroes, seek to break away from this form of "physical slavery" and "mental slavery" by setting themselves in open motion. Amber, who is presented as an "independent" woman who is a "houseless wanderer," helps Teray overcome the tyranny of his brother Coransee by entering a liberating world of free space and motion. After killing Coransee, he breaks free of the "patterns" that have crippled him and he is able to experience physical and psychological freedom that is described in terms of open motion:

> The canopy of awareness first seemed almost as broad as the sky itself.
>
> Feeling like some huge bird, he projected his awareness over the territory. He could see, could sense, the

lightly wooded land dotted with ruined buildings. He could see the distant ranges of hills, was aware of the even-more-distant mountains. The mountains were far beyond his striking range. In fact they were near Forsyth, still over a day's journey away, but he could see them. He swooped about, letting his extended awareness range free through the hills and valleys.

All of Butler's patternist novels are centered in this quest to transcend the mental structures and social institutions that imprison people in roles defined by hierarchical societies that are essentially feudal in character. Anyanwu, the heroine of *Wild Seed*, escapes various forms of slavery in Africa and America by becoming a fugitive in search of free space. A "shapeshifter" who can, like the Greek god Proteus, always change her outward forms to escape the entrapments that authority figures design for her, she becomes at several points in the novel a bird flying away from danger or a dolphin who can be "cleansed" by swimming in the sea. Like Ellison's invisible man, her identity is essentially fluid and indeterminate, always moving to new stages of development. Her antagonist Doro, however, has a rigidly fixed personality and is described as "a tortoise encased in a shell that gets thicker and thicker each year." Whereas Anyanwu's function in the novel is to free herself and others from oppressive ideas and social structures, Doro is intent on building slave communities in Africa and America that give him absolute power over his subjects.

Imago (1989), likewise, presents two worlds in conflict, a "hierarchical" society that freezes people into static roles and a free society of Onkali, "space-going people" who envision life as a dynamic process of discovery and growth. While human beings dominate each other and kill those who do not fit into the "patterns" that they have constructed, the Onkali are engaged in an ongoing quest, a "long, long search for new species to combine with to construct new life forms." Fully intending "to leave the solar system in perhaps three centuries," they envision life as a colossal open journey, an ongoing search for fresh space providing new life.

Butler's fiction, therefore, clears new space for African American literature by using a science fiction mode in which black writers have rarely shown interest and infusing this mode with social and political themes that are relevant to contemporary black people. But her work is also in the main tradition of black American literature dating back to the slave narratives. In a 1984 interview with Margaret O'Connor she pointed out that much of her fiction was inspired by "the narratives of Frederick

Douglass and others who endured slavery." Indeed, most of her work can be seen as signifying powerfully on the slave narratives, projecting them into the future and probing the residual effects of pre-Civil War slavery in present day and future America. Like the authors of nineteenth-century slave narratives, Butler envisions freedom as a radically open journey that must be experienced on physical, mental, and spiritual levels.

Parable of the Sower, published in 1993, is an appropriate book with which to conclude this study of the African American journey motif, because it not only imagines the open journey in fresh ways but it also signifies meaningfully on every major text examined in this study. The social world envisioned in the novel clearly echoes the nightmarish city depicted in *Native Son,* a deadening place of walled neighborhoods that trap the masses and walled estates that protect the rich from the misery they have created. Lauren Olamina, the novel's central character, describes her community of Robledo in terms that are strikingly similar to the way Bigger Thomas perceives the ghetto that threatens him. As she travels through her neighborhood she observes that

> A lot of our ride was along one neighborhood wall after another; some a block long, some two blocks, some five. . . . Up toward the hills there were walled estates—one big house and a lot of shaky little dependencies where the servants lived. . . . In fact we passed a couple of neighborhoods so poor that their walls were made up of unmortared rocks, chunks of concrete, and trash. Then there were the pitiful, unwalled residential areas. A lot of the houses were trashed—burned, vandalized, infested with drunks or druggies or squatted in by homeless families with their filthy, gaunt, half-naked children.

In such a "dangerous" and "crazy" place people are reduced to the same "fear and hate" that afflict everyone in *Native Son,* Physical movement is so dangerous that very few people dare to venture out of their walled communities and, when they do, they are either murdered like Lauren's father, tortured like her brother, or raped like the four-year-old girl to whom Lauren has become a surrogate sister. Social mobility has been destroyed by a devastated economy and intellectual growth has been stamped out by the complete elimination of any systems of education. Robledo becomes a frightening metaphor of America in gridlock, a world that closely resembles the nineteenth-century plantation that trapped Frederick Douglass and the twentieth-century ghetto that immobilized Bigger Thomas. But America in the twenty-first century is even worse than it was in the past, for slavery has

> **This outward movement triggers inward journeys that are psychological, spiritual, and moral in character. As their external surroundings become more spacious, their inward selves deepen and mature."**

been universalized to include all ethnic and racial groups in all regions of the country. All America has become a massive plantation, a gigantic ghetto.

Like Ralph Ellison and Charles Johnson, who sometimes portray the city as a Dantean underworld, Butler depicts an urban society that has "gone to hell" and is "teetering on the abyss." Butler's America has degenerated to such a point that it is seen in apocalyptic terms as a new version of "Jericho" and "Babylon," a culture that is paralyzed and on the verge of collapsing under the weight of its own corruption. Like Ishmael Reed, Butler envisions America in the first quarter of the twenty-first century as having returned to a condition of "slavery" in which "the country has slipped back 200 years."

But *Parable of the Sower,* like the vast majority of classic African American journey books, does not present a vision of apocalyptic despair or an enervating nihilism. The heroine of the novel can save herself and others by constructing "a modern underground railroad" taking them north to liberating new spaces. Such spaces not only take the form of an actual "sanctuary" in the external world but also become mental, spiritual, and moral frontiers within the self. For Butler envisions the self as most African American picaresque writers do, as a protean process of limitless becoming rather than a completed state of being rooted in a particular place. Her heroine therefore is in a direct line of descent from Hurston's Janie Crawford, Walker's Ruth Copeland, Morrison's Pilate, and Williams's Dessa Rose, since all of these heroines transcend social roles that "place" them in restrictive identities by experiencing open journeys toward social freedom and personal transformation.

Lauren Olamina's central task is to find a way of moving from such constricting places to liberating spaces. Early in the novel she fears that "there are no safe places to move." Her own small city of Robledo is "a dying and backward place" where nearly all social institutions and moral values have collapsed and, as a result, a sense of community has been destroyed, reducing people to a bleakly Darwinian struggle for existence in a jungle of selfishness and violence. Feral dogs roam freely in the streets, which are populated mainly by "the street poor." Drug-maddened "crazies" burn down the few vestiges of civilization such as churches and makeshift homes while police and firemen refuse to do their jobs without extra payment, which very few citizens can afford. Things get worse when one moves beyond Robledo to places such as Los Angeles, which is described as a "carcass which is filled with maggots," or southern Mississippi and Louisiana, which are experiencing cholera epidemics caused by a hopelessly polluted water supply. A new community in a suburb of Los Angeles called Olivar offers an equally dim prospect. A town that has been "bought and privatized" by a gigantic multinational corporation intent on reducing its citizens to the "debt slavery" found in early-twentieth-century company towns, Olivar is an even "bigger dead-end" than Robledo.

The novel's opening scene clearly dramatizes Lauren's desire to escape from such a trap. The book begins with her describing a "recurring dream" that she has whenever she feels confined, "twist[ing] on [her] own personal hook." She pictures her neighborhood as a "crouching animal" that is "more threatening than protective" and then imagines herself as in a room whose walls are "burning." In sharp contrast with these grim images of paralysis and death are hopeful images of open motion and space. She envisions herself as "learning to fly" or "levitate" and, as the fire spreads through the room that threatens to become her coffin, she flies through a "door" which brings her into open space illuminated by "cool pale, glinting light" that allows her to look up at "the broad sweep of the Milky Way." Her vision is further clarified and enriched when she comes to see the stars as not only "free" but "windows into heaven. Windows for God to look through and keep an eye on us."

The entire novel is telescoped in this remarkable opening scene because it clearly equates place with death and open movement in free space with a new life. Lauren's physical journey begins after her family and home have been destroyed by several acts of senseless violence. Her old life gone, she does what most American and African American picaros do in such situations—she instinctively

lights out for new frontiers, "heading North" into what she hopes will be a "better life." Like Frederick Douglass, she sees the North as an indeterminate space rather than a definite place. She knows that actual places such as Oregon are "closed" because its citizens are deeply afraid of the refugees who might settle there and thus cause additional economic and social problems. Armed with a backpack containing only her journals, poems, and seed, she sets herself in quintessentially American pure motion, desiring only to "just run and run." She knows exactly what she is leaving but has only the vaguest notion of where she is heading. As she joins the "river of people" who have become fugitives in their own land, she asks herself, "Where were the westward walkers going?" Her very American answer is "To something . . ."

Her physical travels bring her to progressively larger and freer forms of open space, which offer her relief from a social world that is literally "falling apart" from massive earthquakes and morally disintegrating from sociopathic behavior. She avoids cities that have been overrun by scavengers, cops, private security guards, druggies, and other "predators" intent on "destroying what's left." When she and her growing group of companions reach the Pacific Ocean, an enormous open space that is described as "half a world of water," they begin to sense a better life. Psychologically and physically refreshed by the water that cleanses them and the sheer space that fires their imaginations, they notice that the many people camping on the beach have also been "lulled" by the ocean into less violent, more humane behavior. They later reach an area outside of Sacramento that they marvel at, "rich country" that has not been affected either by earthquakes or human violence, a world that offers them "more water, more food, more room . . ." After Taylor Bankole joins them, they direct themselves toward the "safe haven" of his three hundred acres of farmland in northern California, a "godsend" that offers them a "better life" by giving them a sanctuary from the bondage of the past.

This outward movement triggers inward journeys that are psychological, spiritual, and moral in character. As their external surroundings become more spacious, their inward selves deepen and mature. Although Lauren has just turned eighteen when her voyage begins, she soon realizes that her experiences on the road have made her a "woman" and not just a "kid." No longer is she imprisoned by the "walls" of her own life; she now can break free of all restrictions that have held her back in the past and shape a radically new self. As she stresses in a poem she writes late in the novel:

> The self must create
> its own reasons for being.
> To shape God.
> Shape self.

Implicit in Lauren's dynamic view of the self as a process that is always developing is a religious vision that is clearly nonteleological, a theology that regards God and the universe as always changing, always evolving. Lauren emphatically rejects the static views of God that she has received from her Baptist upbringing. She moves away from her father's "fortress church," which is surrounded by walls and protected by armed guards and barbed wire, because such a church is grounded in rigid dogma and narrow morality that stifles her spirit. In a larger sense, she rejects traditional notions of God as a "big-daddy-God or a big-cop-God or a big-king-God," because such stale concepts reduce God to an unchanging place in "nature," making him an authority enforcing the mechanical rules of a hierarchical society that oppresses people.

She comes to see God as pure process, a dynamic life force that is always changing:

> . . . God is Pliable
> Trickster,
> Teacher,
> Chaos,
> Clay.
> God exists to be shaped.
> God is Change.

This sense of God leads her eventually to develop a new religion called Earthseed, a free and open religion that reflects the dynamic, protean nature of the soul and God. Rather than imagine her religion in conventional terms as a church with "walls" and a solid "foundation," she pictures it in terms of open motion, as seeds that are

> . . . windborne, animalborne, waterborne, far from their parent plants. They have no ability at all to travel great distances under their own power, and yet, they do travel. Even they don't have to sit in one place and wait to be wiped out. There are islands thousands of miles from anywhere—the Hawaiian Islands, for example and Easter Island—where plants seeded themselves and grew long before any humans arrived.
>
> Earthseed.
>
> I am Earthseed. Anyone can be. Someday I think there will be a lot of us. And I think we'll have to seed ourselves farther and farther from this dying place.

Her religion of Earthseed is centered in this symbol of open motion—traveling in a free but purposeful manner away from a "dying place" to a new

space offering new life. In this sense Earthseed is a creative center to her life (she *becomes* Earthseed) in which all of her journeys mix with and enrich each other. Her movements through nature, the self, and God become one in this free but "unifying, purposeful" vision of "life on earth."

The vehicle that empowers her as she takes these psychological and spiritual journeys is art, her writing of her poems and Earthseed journals. Like Charles Johnson and Ishmael Reed, who consider art as a means of constructing an authentic self, Butler sees her writing as a way of consciously shaping and purposefully directing her life. When Lauren is asked by a friend how people can survive in the disintegrating world of twenty-first-century America, she replies, "[U]se your imagination"— that is, refuse to accept the "patterns" imposed by a repressive society and create your own directions. Lauren's writings therefore are critically important in her attempts to fashion a journey for herself that will not only move her beyond "walls" but also enable her to avoid the "abyss" with which her society confronts her.

It is not surprising therefore when she reveals early in the novel, "I have to write to keep from going crazy." Later, when vandals destroy her family and bring her old life to a horrifying close, she senses that her writing is her only chance to avoid madness and move toward a new life:

> I have to write. I don't know what else to do. . . . I'm jittery and crazed. I can't cry. I want to get up and just run and run. . . . Run away from everything. But there isn't any away.
>
> I have to write. There's nothing familiar left to me but the writing. God is change. I hate God. I have to write.

In a physical world of traps and terror where there seems to be no "away" into which one can escape, writing creates a "way" leading to inward and outward movement that is salvific. First of all, writing becomes a "way" in the sense that it is a means to empower the self by inducing and enriching self-consciousness. Secondly, writing is a "way" in the sense that it can direct movement in a flexible but purposeful manner, thus creating pathways to outer experience that the self freely maps out. Lauren's writings finally achieve both functions, enabling her to imagine a redemptive space called Earthseed and then move consciously toward this space. While the social world that others have constructed has produced violence and anarchy that rob Lauren of anything "familiar," thus making her "crazed and jittery," her writing allows her to picture her life as a clean slate upon which she can write her own identity, freely journeying to spaces within herself to which society has tried to block admission.

Acorn, the Earthseed community that her writings help her to imagine and construct, finally provides her and her fellow travelers with a new life of limitless growth, what Ellison described at the end of *Invisible Man* as a world of "infinite possibilities." The community that they establish is a socially open space whose purpose is to "take root among the stars," to become a world of ongoing growth that is in harmony with the protean nature of the human self and nature. Such a fluid society encourages them "to grow ourselves into something new," thus overcoming the slavery that has characterized their previous lives. Jillian and Allison Gilchrist shed their former roles as prostitutes and become the parents of Justin Rohr, the orphaned boy whom they rename Adam. Bankole, whose marriage was destroyed when druggies killed his wife in order to steal her medicine, marries Lauren, who in turn recovers the kinship relationships she lost when her family was destroyed by a variety of predators. The Douglasses, a racially mixed couple who were persecuted by conventional society, are fully accepted in the new society. Harry and Zahra also marry, transforming their previously empty lives. All of these people, who come from a wide assortment of races and backgrounds, become a multicultural community, an "interesting unit" committed to renewing the human race.

But although this Earthseed community is built on Bankole's land, which is "free and clear" of debt and is also an "empty" and "wild" space offering a fresh start, it is not idealized by Butler as a final resting place, a fixed and stable end point for their travels. Even though the land has an excellent supply of uncontaminated water and has a substantial "garden" for growing fruits and vegetables, it is not perceived either by the characters or the author as a place that can solve their problems permanently. For such a world is not immune to the ravages of the socio-paths and psychopaths who have blighted the society from which they came. When Lauren's group reaches their much sought-for promised land, they discover to their horror that Bankole's house has been burned to the ground, his sister and her family have been butchered, and his farm has become "a huge ruined garden." At best, this place is only "a possible sanctuary," a temporary way station providing them with some degree of rest before they reembark on their journeys to safer spaces.

What these spaces might be is never made exactly clear, just as the end points of journeys taken by picaresque heroes such as Huck Finn, the invisible man, and Ruth Copeland are never precisely defined. Their "new home" cannot be found on any maps because it is a space to be quested after, not a place that can be inhabited. Like the "home" over the River Jordan celebrated by the spirituals, it is a state of mind and a spiritual ideal. The future for Butler's characters, therefore, is liberatingly indeterminate, something that must always be creatively shaped and reshaped as they move and develop.

Source: Robert Butler, "Twenty-First-Century Journeys in Octavia E. Butler's *Parable of the Sower*," in *Contemporary African American Fiction*, Associated University Presses, 1998, pp. 133–41.

Madelyn Jablon

In the following essay excerpt, Jablon explores how Butler transcends the science fiction and fantasy genre by incorporating elements of black history and serious social commentary into Parable of the Sower.

Octavia E. Butler's *Parable of the Sower* also relies on social and political ideas to extend the boundaries of fantasy. In *Fantasy and Mimesis,* Kathryn Hume outlines four types of fantasy: escapism, expressive literature, didactic literature, and perspectivist literature (xiv). Butler's novel fits Hume's classification of didactic literature or "the literature of revision." This classification of fantasy literature "calls attention to a new interpretation of reality" as it "tries to force the readers to accept the proffered interpretation of reality and to revise their worlds to fit this interpretation." The authors of didactic fantasy literature offer "at least a token program of reform," which may be religious or moral, as in Bunyan's *Pilgrim's Progress,* or social and political, as in John Steinbeck's *The Grapes of Wrath* (xiii). Butler addresses moral, religious, social, and political themes. One lesson she teaches is that there is a continuum from personal to political, from religious to social and communal. As Mosley revises categories of the personal and collective, so does Butler. The second revision of genre is evident in Butler's use of positive and negative examples for instruction. She presents both utopia and dystopia, encouraging readers to imitate the actions of some and refrain from imitating the actions of others. Butler's heroine, Lauren, also defies classification. Hume distinguishes between "stories which center on a hero" and "stories which use a superhuman saint or messiah" (104). Lauren combines characteristics of both. Like the folk hero, she has imperfections and personal idiosyncrasies that make her human. Like the messiah, she espouses "new interpretations of the cosmos" and "assigns new meanings to life" (105). Through the introduction of a new religion, Lauren fits Northrop Frye's definition of a hero in the "high mimetic mode" (she is superior to other people but not to her environment), but the plot in which she appears is that of a romance. It commences with her living with her family as a member of a walled community. The dissolution of that society at the hands of villains who live outside the walls begins her journey and entry into a nonrational world governed by violence. She undergoes tests and trials, survives, and emerges a triumphant new leader (Hume 152). The story also fits the pattern of a tale of initiation. The novel traces Lauren's development from a fifteen-year-old girl living under the watchful eye of an overprotective father to an independent eighteen-year-old woman who is beginning her life's work and a mature relationship. The novel employs a variety of archetypes for the purpose of demonstrating that romances tell the story of the ego gaining control over the id. In Butler's novel, the unconsciousness is the world beyond the wall, outside the community, and the people residing on either side of the road that Lauren travels. The Satan worshipers in Butler's tale are cannibals, scavengers, thieves, and drug users whose survival depends on the destruction of others. Arrival at Bankole's farm represents a return to order, a celebration of community values and hope for future generations, and, of course, a subsuming of the id to the control of ego and superego.

Freedom is the subject of this, Butler's tenth science fiction novel. Like her earlier novels, it integrates historic elements to introduce this subject. There are references to slavery and to the African Diaspora. The novel can be read as an allegory of the slave narrative. In this apocalyptic tale, Lauren Oya Olamina, the daughter of a Baptist minister, leads a diverse group north to establish Earthseed. The story Lauren records in her diary begins in 2024 and describes the destruction of the walled community in Robledo, California. It describes the three-year journey north on Route 101 toward the freedom represented by the land owned by Taylor Franklin Bankole on the coastal hills of Humbolt County. Lauren describes her group as the "crew of the modern underground railroad." She figures as a Sojourner Truth leading the way north, persevering because of her own stubborn refusal to live "as some kind of twenty-first century slave" (155).

Bankole's observation that the "country has slipped back 200 years" is validated by the histories of those who join the group. Emery's sons have

> **Butler addresses moral, religious, social, and political themes. One lesson she teaches is that there is a continuum from personal to political, from religious to social and communal."**

been taken from her and sold for payment of debts owed to the company store. Allison and Jillian Gilchrist run away from a father who is trying to sell his daughters. Grayson Mora and Doe Mora are runaway slaves, as are Travis, Gloria, and Dominic Douglas, whose flight to Canada is assisted by the wife of the slavemaster who knows of her husband's desire for Gloria.

In her discussion of *Wild Seed* and *Kindred*, Butler's previous novels, Sandra Y. Govan observes that the writer "links science fiction to the Black American slavery experiences via the slave narrative." In an interview, Butler explains how history affects her writing. She begins by recalling a visit to Mount Vernon, where she listened to the presentations of tour guides whose memorized speeches obscured the historical truth by referring to "slaves" as "servants." As preparation for writing science fiction, Butler read slave narratives but realized that she "was not going to come anywhere near presenting slavery as it was. [She] was going to have to do a somewhat cleaned-up version of slavery, or no one would be willing to read on." Although she may refrain from portraying the African American experience of slavery as history, her cleaned-up science fiction version provides a frightening degree of verisimilitude. Govan describes Butler's references as follows: "Butler treats the reoccurring themes of casual brutality, forcible separation of families, the quest for knowledge, the desire to escape, the tremendous work loads expected of slaves as effectively as any of the narratives or documentary histories discussing the slavery experience." Butler rescues the past from the obscurity that results from identifying "slaves" as "servants."

When Christopher Charles Morpeth Donner assumes the office of president in 2024, he dismantles the space program, suspends "overly restrictive worker protection laws," and encourages foreign investments in company towns such as Olivar. This former middle-class suburb of Los Angeles has been purchased by Kagimoto, Stamm, Frampton, and Company, a Japanese-German-Canadian enterprise, which has taken control of municipal utilities such as the desalination plant that provides the town's water and corporate-owned power and agriculture industries. Because most people are unemployed, the company is able to staff its operations with highly qualified workers who soon become in debt to the company. This is what happens to the Solis family. Emery's husband, Jorge Francisco Solis, becomes ill with appendicitis and dies as a result of inadequate medical care. Emery must work to pay off the debt that her husband, a company-town employee, has incurred. Because she is unable to do so, her two sons are taken from her and sold into slavery. Afraid that her daughter will also be taken, she flees.

When Cory, Lauren's stepmother, urges her father to consider applying to Olivar, her father echoes the words of the Bible and the ex-coloured man who said he had sold his birthright for a mess of pottage when he crossed the color line: "This business sounds half antebellum and half science fiction. I don't trust it. Freedom is dangerous, Cory, but it's precious, too. You can't just throw it away or let it slip away. You can't sell it for bread and pottage."

Unlike the ex-coloured man, Lauren's father, a dean, professor, and Baptist minister, knows the cost of freedom and is unwilling to relinquish it for the safety and security that company towns represent. This is Butler's special blend of fact and fiction, the historical past and the imagined future. Addressing this issue of fact and fiction in the creation of Olivar, Lauren says:

> Maybe Olivar is the future—one face of it. Cities controlled by big companies are old hat in science fiction. My grandmother left a whole bookcase of old science fiction novels. The company-city subgenre always seemed to star a hero who outsmarted, overthrew, or escaped "the company." I've never seen one where the hero fought like hell to get taken in and underpaid by the company. In real life, that's the way it will be. That's the way it is.

Lauren distinguishes between science fiction and reality. Reference to the "company-city subgenre" sets the fictional world apart from the real world. Her plot summary develops a set of oppositions between "real" and "fictive" worlds. Fiction features a hero who outsmarts or escapes the company town. "Real" heroes succeed in gaining

admittance to these towns. Cory, Lauren's stepmother, debuts for this role of hero when she urges her husband to apply to Olivar. Her daughter, Lauren, will fulfill the destiny of the fictional hero. *Parable of the Sower* sets up this dichotomy between real and fictive world, leading the reader to expect that once the definitions of "real" and "fiction" have been established, the novel will attempt to traverse the boundaries. Contrary to these expectations, the novel follows the plot outline of the subgenre. Lauren, the hero, establishes the first Earthseed community. This community, aptly named Acorn, is a cooperative rather than a corporate venture. The novel announces its "fictionality" and meets all the necessary criteria of the subgenre.

These definitions of fiction and reality are complicated by Lauren's own discussions of them. This hero-character, a writer and reader, defends the belief that imaginary and real worlds intersect. As an initial effort to convert others to Earthseed, Lauren asks her followers to read and think about how what they read can assist them in improving their lives. Lauren agrees that the good old days that their parents discuss will never return, but she feels that the future is not devoid of hopeful possibilities. The past cannot occur again, but the future can be good. Joanne asks what can be done to prepare for the future. As if eagerly awaiting an opportunity to address this question, Lauren answers by instructing her to read all the books she can. Joanne scoffs, "Books aren't going to save us," and Lauren responds:

> "Nothing is going to save us. If we don't save ourselves, we're dead. Now use your imagination. Is there anything on your family bookshelves that might help you if you were stuck outside?"
>
> "No."
>
> "You answer too fast. Go home and look again. And like I said, use your imagination. Any kind of survival information from encyclopedias, biographies, anything that helps you learn to live off the land and defend ourselves. Even some fiction might be useful."

Lauren reconciles fictive and real worlds by stressing the importance of imagination to survival: "Use your imagination," she tells Joanne. "*Even some fiction might be useful*" (italics for emphasis). Of course, fiction, as the previous passage suggests, is exactly what Lauren is engaged in, and it has already assisted her by providing her with important information about the character she is playing. Lauren defends her author and the genre of science fiction against the argument that it has no bearing on "reality." Even though we may know the story before we finish or even begin the book, because fiction engages our imaginations, it is useful to our individual and collective survival. Keith, Lauren's stepbrother, leaves the walled community to enter the real world outside. Before he is killed, he returns home several times with such valuable commodities as chocolate candy bars and currency. When Lauren inquires into his procuring of these items, he confides that he lives in an old, deserted building with thieves, prostitutes, and drug addicts and that he is valued by this group because he can read and write: "They stole all this great stuff and they couldn't even use it. Before I got there they even broke some of it because they couldn't read the instructions." So, as Lauren correctly surmises, Keith reads for a living, helping his friends learn to use their stolen equipment. This would seem to suggest that reading—in and of itself—will not help us to survive. To be an effective tool in our salvation, reading must be accompanied by imaginative thought. The evidence that suggests this is Keith's brutal murder. Lauren teaches her traveling companions to read by way of the exercise book she created to explain Earthseed. This book—which we shall look at shortly—requires imagination to assist with survival.

After disclosing the meaning of Earthseed, Lauren says, "I've never felt I was making any of this up. . . . I've never felt that it was anything other than real: discovery rather than invention, exploration rather than creation. All I do is observe and take notes, trying to put things down in ways that are as powerful, as simple, and as direct as I feel them." By referring to her discovery of something that already exists, Lauren advances the platonic descriptions of artistic invention. Earthseed is a component of Lauren's religion, and the title of a book she is writing on the subject. In this passage, she embellishes her ideas concerning the interplay of real and imaginary worlds:

"You believe in all this Earthseed stuff, don't you?"

"Every word," I answered.

"But . . . you made it up."

I reached down, picked up a small stone, and put it on the table between us. "If I could analyze this and tell you all that it was made of, would that mean I'd made up its contents?"

Elsewhere she explains that she is discovering or imagining something that already exists. She says: "I never felt that I was making any of this up—not the name, Earthseed, not any of it. I mean I've never felt it was anything other than real: discovery rather than invention, exploration rather than creation."

Imagination is a gateway to truth. And Lauren's book, *Earthseed: The Book of the Living,* exemplifies this idea. She contrasts it with the Tibetan and Egyptian Books of the Dead by saying that there may already be a book of the living, but she doesn't care. As a collection of verse, it explores the nature of God and the role of humankind. It is her own book of Psalms. Thirty-one excerpts are interspersed in the diary that serves as the frame.

According to Hume, literature is the product of two impulses: fantasy and mimesis. Although the mimetic has been celebrated and studied, while fantasy has been regarded with suspicion or trivialized (she reminds us that Plato banned it from the Republic)—Hume believes it is an equal component in the creation of literature and "an impulse native to literature and manifest in innumerable variations from monster to metaphor." Butler's novel investigates these ideas about literature by transforming them into fiction.

Lauren never told her father that she was not a Baptist. He was a minister, and she didn't want to hurt his feelings, especially since the family jeopardized their lives by practicing their religion. When the novel opens, a group is traveling to a church outside the city wall in order to be baptized in a church rather than at home with bath-water. Although Lauren finds comfort and consolation in her religion, especially the community it fosters, she also takes issue with its portraiture of God. Rather than believe in "a big-daddy-God or a big-cop-God or a big-king-God, . . . a kind of superperson," she sees God as change. "From the second law of thermodynamics to Darwin evolution, from Buddhism's insistence that nothing is permanent and all of Ecclesiastes, change is a part of life." Lauren believes that "God *is* change" and that humans can affect the changes that occur. She compares her beliefs to those of Benjamin Franklin, Thomas Jefferson, and the Deists. She says they believed God was something "that made us then left us on our own." Lauren disagrees with this image of God as "a big kid, playing with toys." Instead, she believes that people have control over their lives and that "God exists to be shaped." She calls this "godshaping," and when things don't go well she admonishes herself, "Poor Godshaping. Lack of Forethought." Lauren's religion celebrates the role of the individual in shaping his or her destiny. In this context, prayer becomes a way of imagining things into occurrence:

God can't be resisted or stopped, but can be shaped and focused. This means God is not to be prayed to. Prayers only help the person doing the praying, and then, only if they strengthen and focus that person's resolve. If they're used that way, they can help us in our only real relationship with God. They help us to shape God and to accept and work with the shapes that God imposes on us. God is power, and in the end, God prevails.

But we can rig the game in our own favor if we understand that God exists to be shaped, and will be shaped, with or without forethought, with or without our intent.

The supreme will of the individual is set against a backdrop of Agamemnon. As the reader travels with Lauren along Route 101, he or she sees the destruction of civilization: scavengers profit from the demise of others, children and women are victims of the lawless activities of men, three-year-olds and seventy-three-year-olds are raped to death by outlaws. The biggest threat are the paints, men and women who shave their heads and paint their faces blue, green, or yellow. Paints take a drug—pyro (also known as blaze, *fuego,* flash, and sunfire), which affects their neurochemistry and makes watching the "leaping changing patterns of fire a better, more intense longer-lasting high than sex." Lauren says, "It's like they [the paints] were f—g the fire, and like it was the best f—k they ever had." At the close of the novel, Lauren's tribe of converts cover their bodies with wet rags to protect themselves from the "orgy of burning" that is consuming "dry-as-straw Southern California."

Cory compares the discord to Babylon, while Joanne compares the devastation to Jericho, but Lauren consoles herself with the parable of the widow and the story of Noah, focusing on the "two-part nature of this situation": "God decides to destroy everything except Noah, his family, and some animals. *But* if Noah is going to be saved, he has plenty of hard work to do." This fictional world ends as the Bible predicts, and the salvation of humankind takes place with the birth of the Earthseed community and the resurrection of Bankole's farm.

Unlike the old world, where race was a barrier and interracial relationships were condemned, the world that Lauren creates welcomes people of all races and ethnicities. The children of Earthseed are part white, Mexican, Japanese, Black, and Black Latino. When Lauren looks at them she sees the future of humankind. Thelma Shinn discusses the role of race in Butler's utopian future. She says, "By combining Afro-American, female, and science fiction patterns, she can reveal the past, the present, and a probable future in which differences can be seen as challenging and enriching rather than

threatening and denigrating and in which power can be seen as an interdependence between leader and those accepting that leadership, each accepting those limits on freedom that still allow for survival of the self."

The title of the novel announces its fictionality: it is a parable, a story with a religious or moral slant, but unlike the original biblical tale, it suggests hope for the future. The sower's seed doesn't bear harvest, but Lauren's Earthseed "falls on good ground," bearing "fruit a hundredfold."

Source: Madelyn Jablon, "Metafiction as Genre," in *Black Metafiction: Self-Consciousness in African American Literature,* University of Iowa Press, 1997, pp. 156–65.

Sources

Johnson, Rebecca O., "African-American, Feminist Science Fiction," in *Sojourner: The Women's Forum,* Vol. 19, No. 6, February 1994, pp. 12–14.

Jonas, Gerald, Review of *Parable of the Sower,* in *New York Times Book Review,* January 2, 1994, p. 22.

Miller, Faren, Review of *Parable of the Sower,* in *Locus,* December 1993, pp. 17, 19.

See, Lisa, "An Interview with Octavia Butler," in *Publishers Weekly,* Vol. 240, No. 50, December 13, 1993, pp. 50–51.

Zaki, Hoda, Review of *Parable of the Sower,* in *Women's Review of Books,* Vol. 11, Nos. 10 and 11, July 1994, pp. 37–38.

Further Reading

Butler, Octavia, and Stephen W. Potts, "'We Keep Playing the Same Record': A Conversation with Octavia E. Butler," in *Science-Fiction Studies,* Vol. 23, No. 70, November 1996, pp. 331–38.
    Butler discusses the science-fiction genre, responses to her work, and themes her work addresses.

Fry, Joan, "An Interview with Octavia Butler," in *Poets & Writers Magazine,* Vol. 25, March/April 1997, pp. 58–69.
    Butler discusses a range of topics, including her favorite writers and where the philosophical ideas in *Parable of the Sower* come from.

Wiloch, Thomas, Review of *Parable of the Sower,* in *Bloomsbury Review,* May/June 1994, p. 24.
    Wiloch applauds Butler for not following the pattern of most science fiction. She is not content to tell a standard adventure story but instead turns it into a character study of a young woman.

Tambourines to Glory

Langston Hughes

1958

Tambourines to Glory, published in 1958, is the second of Langston Hughes's two novels. (His first, *Not without Laughter*, was published in 1930, almost thirty years earlier.) It tells the story of two women, the religious Essie Belle Johnson and her conniving friend Laura Reed, who open a storefront church in Harlem. Essie sincerely wants to use her beautiful singing voice to bring people to God, and hopes to make enough money through the church to bring her daughter up from the South to live with her. But Laura wants only the money, which she uses for gambling, drinking, and attracting young men. The novel is rich with the spoken and sung voices of the African American community of Harlem, and derives its humor from the lively and generally appealing scoundrels who twist religion and morals for their own earthly gain.

Hughes had written a musical play version of *Tambourines to Glory* in 1956, and he changed the story only slightly to create the novel. Several of the novel's thirty-six brief chapters read like a play script. The novel as a whole is noticeably without extended descriptive passages, characters' unspoken thoughts, and other qualities that often distinguish prose fiction from drama.

Author Biography

James Langston Hughes was born on February 1, 1902, in Joplin, Missouri. His unusual middle name

Langston Hughes

had been the birth name of his mother, a teacher. His father was a lawyer and businessman. Hughes grew up mainly in Lawrence, Kansas, a lonely child drawn to reading and writing. His first poem, "The Negro Speaks of Rivers," was published in the June 1921 issue of the magazine *Crisis*, edited by the sociologist and political leader W. E. B. DuBois. It became one of Hughes's best-known and most anthologized poems.

After a year at Columbia University in New York, Hughes took simple jobs, traveled around the world, and continued to publish poems. He returned to the United States in 1924, already recognized as one of the most talented young African American poets in the movement known as the Harlem Renaissance. Hughes thrived in the atmosphere of Harlem, soaking up jazz and blues music, leftist politics, and racial pride. Within the next six years he would graduate from Lincoln University in Pennsylvania and publish two highly regarded collections of poems, *The Weary Blues* (1926) and *Fine Clothes to the Jew* (1927), and a novel, *Not without Laughter* (1930). Through the next twenty-five years Hughes published more poetry, some of it rather radical politically, as well as plays, short stories, essays, and a weekly newspaper column. His writing explored and celebrated the African American experience, often incorporating musical elements and themes.

Throughout this period, Hughes won writing contests and received fellowships and grants to help support his work. Although he was an important and respected writer, Hughes never enjoyed financial security until the late 1940s, when he wrote the lyrics for a successful musical theater production. For the first time, he was able to own his own home. He hoped to repeat that success in 1956 with a new play, *Tambourines to Glory*, which he rewrote and published as a novel in 1958. However, the novel did not sell well and the play lost money.

By the 1960s, with a new Civil Rights movement led by a new generation of men, African Americans regarded Hughes more highly as a historic figure than as a writer of significant new work, although he continued to publish. Hughes died of congestive heart failure on May 22, 1967, in New York City. His last poetry, about civil rights, was published after his death.

Plot Summary

Chapter 1

Tambourines to Glory is divided into thirty-six chapters, each a separate scene with its own title. The first, "Palm Sunday," is the longest at six pages, and it introduces the main characters, the setting, and the idea that triggers the plot. On a Palm Sunday in Harlem, two friends are reminiscing over their younger days when they attended church occasionally. Essie Belle Johnson and her neighbor Laura Reed both grew up in the American South, and came to New York City as young adults, specifically to the African American section called Harlem. Both are about forty, living in one-room kitchenette apartments in a run-down building, and barely getting by on welfare. Essie dreams of having enough money to bring her daughter Marietta up from Virginia to live; Laura thinks only of the next drink, the next bet on the numbers, and the next man. Playfully, they discuss opening a church and getting rich off the collection plate. As they sing a hymn they are uplifted for a moment, and Essie is moved to strengthen her relationship with God.

Chapters 2–5

The next morning, Essie tells Laura that she really intends to start a church. She believes that God will answer their prayers, and that he has already touched her life. Laura is willing, though she sees the church only as a way to get money. They agree that when the weather is warm they will buy a Bible and a tambourine and start praising on the street corner. Laura will preach, Essie will sing, and they will use the tambourine to keep time and to gather collections.

Chapters 6–8

With a tambourine from the Good Will Store, the Reed Sisters, as they call themselves, offer their first worship service at the corner of 126th Street and Lenox. The two dozen people who stop to hear them are moved enough to join in the singing, shout "Amen," and throw some change in the tambourine. On their first night of preaching, the Reed Sisters take in $11.93. Although they had agreed that the first night's collection would go toward purchasing a Bible, Laura takes out almost four dollars for liquor and a bet. Over the next several nights, Laura's habit is to preach, divide the money, and go look for a man or a drink, but Essie stays to talk with the people in the crowd. They think she can help them, and she wonders whether it is true.

Chapter 9

The church is a success. Laura tells the crowds that "since God took my hand, I have not wanted for nothing." The Sisters have been able to pay the rent and eat regular meals. Laura urges the crowd to put money in the tambourine to help her stay on God's path, and they do. One old woman, Birdie Lee, accepts salvation and takes a turn shaking the tambourine to God's glory. She is so energetic and rhythmic that she draws in more people. Although Laura does not like sharing the spotlight, she sees that letting Birdie Lee stay with them is good for business. Like many chapters, this one is sprinkled with snatches of lyrics from the hymns sung by Essie, Laura, and Birdie Lee.

Chapters 10–13

As autumn begins, Essie, Laura, and Birdie Lee find a three-room apartment to house their church. The first convert in the new location is Chicken Crow-for-Day, a lifelong gambler, drinker and womanizer. His conversion draws others. Soon, Essie has two thousand dollars in the jar where she keeps God's money. She is still uneasy about the church. She can see that she and Laura are doing some real good in the lives of other people, and she herself feels more energetic and engaged than ever before. But she knows that for Laura it is all just a scam. Essie wonders whether they are truly serving God.

Media Adaptations

- The novel *Tambourines to Glory* was adapted by Hughes from his own musical play of the same title, with songs by Jobe Huntley. It was produced in New York in 1963, and is available in *Five Plays by Langston Hughes*, Indiana University Press, 1963.

- Music from the play was recorded in 1958 on *Tambourines to Glory: Gospel Songs by Langston Hughes and Jobe Huntley*, performed by the Porter Singers. The original recording was Folkways album FG 03538. Still in the Folkways archives, it can be ordered as a custom CD from Smithsonian Folkways Recordings.

Chapters 14–15

Chapters 14 and 15 are entitled "Enter Buddy" and "Enter Marty." Buddy is Big-Eyed Buddy Lomax, who takes Laura out for a drink after services. Buddy is handsome, sophisticated, flashy and young, and Laura is flattered and excited to be seen with him. Before long, Buddy spends most nights with Laura, and has gotten her to go along with a plan to sell tap water as blessed Holy Water from the Holy Land. Marty is a white man who pulls the strings and controls the money behind Buddy's schemes. Essie and Laura will never meet him, but he will do favors for them and look for ways they can help him as well.

Chapters 16–18

Marty gets Essie and Laura an apartment on the ninth floor of a new building overlooking the park, jumping them ahead of all the people on the waiting list. Essie is more uncomfortable than ever with Buddy and Marty in the picture. She refuses to accept any of the proceeds from the holy water, so Laura uses it to buy a Cadillac. Laura is so dazzled by Buddy's skills in bed, and his new ideas for bringing in more money from the church, that she buys him a convertible, caters to his every whim, and pretends not to notice when he spends time with other women.

Chapters 19–20

Almost a year after the church began, it is the largest independent church in Harlem, and has outgrown its quarters. Marty arranges for Laura and Essie to take possession of a condemned theater that could never pass a fire inspection, and the Tambourine Temple is born. The new church seats a thousand people, and has a marquee where Laura can enjoy seeing her name in lights. Essie has been studying the Bible and reading other religious books. She is a true believer, and she hopes that Laura will start to believe also.

Chapters 21–28

Marietta arrives to live with her mother and Laura. She is sixteen, innocent and lovely, and Buddy is attracted to her immediately. On Marietta's first day in Harlem, Laura catches Buddy kissing her. Marietta is also courted by C. J., a young guitar player from the church, who offers her less excitement but a more solid Christian relationship. Meanwhile, Marty has Laura begin a new practice of calling out "lucky texts" from the Bible, and slyly encouraging the congregation to bet on those numbers during the week. This increases the amount in the collection plate, and is good for Marty's gambling businesses. To keep suspicion off Laura and Buddy, Buddy pretends to be converted during a service, but Essie sees through him. As Laura adds a fur coat and a chauffeur to her lifestyle, she and Essie grow farther apart. Finally, Essie and Marietta move to a small house of their own in the suburbs, coming to town only for services.

Chapters 29–35

Just before a service one night, Laura notices a hundred dollars missing from her purse. She confronts Buddy, who admits without remorse that he has taken it and savagely tells her that she would be too old to hold his interest without her money. Suddenly, Buddy's infidelity and cruelty is too much, and Laura stabs him to death with Essie's pocket knife. When the body is found, Essie is suspected, and Laura joins in accusing her. In jail, Essie sings gospel songs and prays, accepting her situation as punishment for not ridding the church of Laura's corruption. Eventually Birdie Lee testifies to having witnessed the crime, and Laura confesses. Before the police take her away, she moves all her cash into the church bank account.

Chapter 36

With Laura gone, Essie, Marietta, and C. J. will lead the church in a new direction, starting a day care and other new programs to improve the lives of community members. Essie preaches and sings, praising God, and shakes the tambourine to the glory of God.

Characters

Sister Birdie Lee

Birdie Lee is a "little old lady" who is called to God during one of the Reed Sisters' street corner services. She had followed God in her younger days, but since then she "backslid, backslid, backslid." Now she has determined to stay on the path of righteousness. As is typical in this kind of service, Birdie Lee shouts out her story, or "testifies," right in the middle of Laura's preaching. She grabs the tambourine, sings a song of praise, and shakes the tambourine "so well that the whole corner started to rock and sway, feet to patting, hands to clapping." From that moment, she is a member of the church, and from that moment Laura resents her, because Laura perceives Birdie Lee as competition. Birdie Lee is a faithful member of the church, helping with the scrubbing when they move the church into the apartment, and joining in the rejoicing when Crow-for-Day is converted. In the end, her weak bladder proves Laura's undoing, when a need to rush to the toilet puts Birdie Lee in a position to witness Buddy's murder. Birdie Lee saves Essie from prison and makes up for all her past sins by promising to testify once more and tell what she saw.

C. J.

C. J. is a young Christian boy who plays guitar in the band at the Tambourine Temple. He is in his first year at City College, studying chemistry, and is sweet and polite if a little dull. When Marietta comes to Harlem, he is the natural one to court her. As the two fall in love, C. J. struggles, with Marietta's firm insistence, to keep his lust under control. By the end of the novel, the two are engaged to be married.

Chicken Crow-for-Day

Chicken Crow-for-Day—tall, thin, and aged sixty-five—is the first person converted after the Reed Sisters open their church indoors. By his own account, he has been a life-long sinner, who spent his time drinking, gambling and chasing women. Dramatically, as he announces his salvation before a crowd, he pulls a pistol and a knife out of his pockets and flings them through the window into the street. With the support of the congregation, he apparently does change his life. Crow-for-Day stays with the church as it grows, eventually earning the titles "Brother" and "Deacon."

Essie Belle Johnson

Essie Belle Johnson is an unemployed woman of about forty, living on welfare in Harlem. She came up North from Richmond, Virginia, years ago, and has been trying ever since to get together enough money to bring her daughter to live with her. Essie does not have much education or many skills, and she is passive, prone to sitting and staring at the wall in "long, long, very long pauses," but she has a beautiful singing voice. When she and her friend Laura start to joke about starting a church as a way to raise money, Essie thinks and prays about it and makes a sincere connection with God. She and Laura do form a church, with Laura preaching and Essie singing, and they make a success of it. Even before she decided to pray, Essie lived a quiet life. She did not drink or gamble or chase men. Her only close tie was with Laura, who lived quite a different life. For five years, Essie and Laura have been neighbors and friends, sharing scraps of food and looking after each other in spite of their differences. Now that they are the Reed Sisters, partners in the church, Essie is less comfortable with Laura's sins. She prays that Laura will find God, and she scolds Laura about her behavior, but she does not try to exert any control over Laura's actions. Essie refuses to take any of the money from the phony Holy Water, but neither does she speak against the scheme.

The church grows larger and more successful, and Essie sees this as a sign that her work is blessed by God. With every hymn she sings, her faith grows deeper. She turns her energy inward, into private study of the Bible and of religious writers, and withdraws emotionally from Laura. After Buddy starts sleeping at the new apartment with Laura, and Marietta arrives, the distance between the women increases until Essie and Marietta take a small house outside Harlem. It is not until Laura kills Buddy and frames Essie for the crime that Essie realizes her passiveness has worked against God's plans for her. "I should have riz in my wrath and cleaned house," she thinks, instead of "just setting doing nothing but accepting what comes, receiving the Lord's blessing whilst the eagle foulest His nest." When Essie is released from jail and returns to the church without Laura, she is a new woman, full of energy and plans for the future.

Marietta Johnson

Marietta is Essie's daughter. She has grown up in Richmond, Virginia, in the home of her grandmother, and has not lived with her mother for more than two of her sixteen years. Essie's greatest wish has been to get enough money together to bring Marietta to live with her, and after about a year of running the church she is able to send for her. In June of the second summer, after school gets out, Marietta comes North on the Greyhound Bus, as so many people have before her. She is polite, well-mannered, fresh and pretty; to Buddy she looks like "a tiny, a well-formed, a golden-skinned, a delicate-featured, a doll-handed, a pretty-as-a-picture, a blossoming peaches-and-cream of a girl." Buddy tries to move in on Marietta on her first day in Harlem, but Essie thinks the Christian boy C. J. is a better match for her. Although she found Buddy's passion exciting, Marietta agrees. Marietta and C. J. begin a swift but chaste courtship, and by the final chapter Marietta is already planning to begin nursing studies in the fall and to marry C. J.

Buddy Lomax

"Big-Eyed" Buddy Lomax is the latest in Laura's string of young men. One night after services, Buddy walks down the church aisle and asks Laura to go out for a drink. He takes her to the Roma Gardens, which seems very elegant to Laura, and he is handsome, "a six-foot, a tower-tall, a brownskin, a large-featured, a big-handed, handsome lighthouse-grinning chocolate boy of a man." Like Laura, he likes flashy cars and clothes, he likes to drink and gamble, and he is as charming as he is dishonest. Together the two scheme to get more money from the church through the sale of phony Holy Water and through announcing "lucky texts" from the Bible that are really coded messages for playing the numbers. Only Laura believes that Buddy really loves her and is faithful to her; others can see that he is casually sexy and sexist in his dealings with her, crudely praising her large breasts and using her for sex when there are no younger women available. To keep his favor, Laura buys Buddy new clothes and a car, and gives him cash that he spends on gambling and on entertaining other women. When Marietta comes to town, Buddy makes a play for her with Laura and Essie in the next room, and Laura sees him kissing Marietta. Soon afterwards, Buddy steals a hundred dollars from Laura's purse. She confronts him in the basement of the church, and he cruelly reminds her of the difference in their ages, and admits that he stays with her only because of her money. When he pulls her in for a kiss, Laura stabs him to death with Essie's knife.

Marty

Marty is the white man behind Buddy's schemes, the man who can pull strings and get things done. He is able to get an apartment for Essie and Laura, putting them ahead of people who have been waiting longer. He arranges for them to take possession of the fire-trap theater with no inspections or licenses. Later, when his illegal numbers operation is doing poorly in Harlem, he improves his business by having Laura announce "lucky texts" during church services, encouraging the congregation to bet on the numbers in Bible verses. Marty is never seen or heard from directly in the novel—all of his communications come through Buddy.

Laura Reed

Laura Reed is Essie Belle Johnson's best friend, another woman from the South now living on welfare in Harlem. She is a little younger than Essie, with a good figure and a taste for life. She likes to drink and to gamble, and she has a string of men who pass through her life but do not stay. Laura does not really seem happy with her fast life, sharing her money and her body with men so that she will not be alone, but she does not dare slow down. When the women come up with the idea of starting a church, it is just a money-making idea for Laura. Her mother and her bootlegging stepfather did not raise her to be religious, and she does not believe in God now. But she sees no harm in taking money from those who do believe, if they are willing to give it, and she soon finds that the faithful are indeed willing to put their coins in the tambourine for a chance to be closer to God. After the first street corner service, when the women collect $11.93, Laura goes back on her promise to put all of the money toward a Bible; she takes out $3.93 for her "earthly needs"—some liquor and a bet.

The two women run the church as partners, although their motivations and their methods are as different as they could be. Laura is an effective preacher, but she does not mean anything she says from the pulpit. She uses her share of the money from the collections for gambling, clothes, high-priced liquor, a fur coat, a Cadillac, a chauffeur, and presents for Buddy, while Essie sets hers aside for the Lord's work. Laura is eager to help Buddy by selling fake Holy Water and calling out the numbers of "lucky texts" to support the gamblers. She enjoys seeing her name in lights on the new church marquee, and has a wardrobe of shiny robes to wear while she is preaching. She loves having Buddy in

her bed, and tries to believe she can trust him. Greedy for more money, she sees only Essie and Buddy standing in her way: "One's *too* honest, and the other one ain't honest enough." Laura murders Buddy and tries to frame Essie for the crime. In the end, she is in jail, alone again, out of money, and still wanting a drink.

Themes

Faith and Religion

The central tension in *Tambourines to Glory* is between Essie, who sincerely believes in God and wants to help people find peace through faith, and Laura, who sees the church simply as a way to get money. The difference originates in their childhood: Essie's mother insisted Essie attend church every week when she was a girl, but Laura "seldom went . . . and never regular." Although neither woman has been to church in years, Essie has happy memories, especially of the music. And when the two are joking about starting a church and Laura sings, "Precious Lord, take my hand, lead me on," she starts to mean it. From the first, Essie and Laura expect different things from the church, and each finds what she is looking for. As the narrator explains, "Playing and singing and talking were the only things about their corner that interested Laura, but these were the least that interested Essie." Essie wants to help the people who stop to hear them; Laura wants to help only herself. Essie finds a new engagement with her own life—a community, and a way to bring her daughter to live with her. Laura gets money, a fur coat, a Cadillac, and a handsome young man.

The question that repeatedly troubles Essie is one of the central questions of the novel: "Is we doing right?" Is the Tambourine Temple a force for good, although it originated as a scam? Does it matter that Laura's motives, at least, are impure? The fact is, the church really is helping people change their lives. Chicken Crow-for-Day does stop his "Sniffing after women, tailing after sin, gambling on green tables," and Birdie Lee gives up drinking. Essie finds the energy to get off her chair and shake off her lethargy. Marietta and C. J. will have a safe and comfortable—if a little dull—life together. And the Tambourine Temple, with Laura out of the picture, is going to open a day care center, a clubhouse, and a playground. Amused as he was by charlatan preachers who made themselves wealthy, Hughes could not ignore the contributions the

Topics For Further Study

- Research the career of the gospel singer Mahalia Jackson. In what ways is she a role model for Essie? What does Laura admire about her?

- How important is race to *Tambourines to Glory*? How would the story be different if all of the characters were white, or Latino, or if people of different ethnic groups lived in the neighborhood?

- Why does the trick with the Holy Water from the Jordan River work? People living in Harlem must know that these two women would have no way of actually obtaining water from Jordan. What makes them believe the words on the bottles?

- In what ways are the challenges faced by Essie and Laura, living in New York City after growing up in the South, like those faced by any other immigrants (for example, like people who came to New York from Puerto Rico or from China)? In what ways are they different?

- Research the economic opportunities for under-educated poor people today. What kinds of jobs are available for people with a high school or less level of education? What kinds of financial aid are available for higher education? What kinds of housing are available for someone working a minimum-wage job? What industries and businesses are located in big cities? Are poor people better off today than they were in 1958?

- Would *Tambourines to Glory* make a good movie? What changes in the story would have to be made in order to make the story appealing to today's audiences? Who would you cast in the leading roles?

---

churches made to their communities, and the changes a faith in God made in people's lives. Ultimately, perhaps it does not matter whether the preacher is sincere or even whether God really exists, especially for people with so little else to believe in. As the narrator explains about one of the Reed Sisters' songs, "For many there living in the tenements of Harlem, to believe in such wonder was worth every penny the tambourines collected."

But in the end, Good triumphs over Evil. Laura and Buddy are punished for their faithlessness. Buddy loses his life. Laura loses her self-respect, her freedom, her Cadillac, and her partnership and friendship with Essie. Although Laura also gives up all of her cash, putting it into the bank in the church's name before her arrest, by the end of the novel Laura has still not turned from her wicked ways. Her final two lines are "I have nothing now, Essie, but Jesus—since He comes free" and "Maybe somebody'll buy me a drink." Essie accepts her hours in jail and her suffering as penalty for her gravest error: failing to drive Laura and Buddy from the church. As she says, "Religion has got no business being made into a gyp game."

Ghetto Life

Just as *Tambourines to Glory* is a humorous but largely accurate portrayal of the storefront churches of Harlem in the middle of the twentieth century, it also illuminates other aspects of lower-class Harlem life. One of the great contributions of Hughes and other writers of the Harlem Renaissance was that their work portrayed the daily lives of African Americans, realistically and respectfully, in ways that American literature had not done previously. The lives of the lower class were especially invisible to the reading public. While many knew about the Harlem Renaissance, about the intellectual life of Harlem, and about the exciting night life available to wealthier whites and blacks, the underclass was nearly invisible. Hughes knew that Laura and Essie and Buddy and Birdie Lee were not the people who would buy his novel; his intention was to tell their stories to people who knew only one side of Harlem.

The building where Essie and Laura live is a large apartment building with "a courtyard full of beer cans and sacks of garbage." The building has been carved up into a surprising number of tiny "kitchenette" units, each with a gas burner and a sink. Essie and Laura, who dream of one day having a two- or three-room apartment, have welfare as their only source of income, but everyone else who lives on their floor has a job. Laura has held several jobs in the past, but has not been able to hold one very long. The available work does not pay well, since it has not enabled even the working residents to find better housing. The women are often hungry. Even Essie, who does not waste money on gambling or alcohol, often has no more than rice to eat if Laura cannot contribute a bit of meat or vegetables to the pot.

Almost all of the characters in the novel and in the neighborhood are African American, but there are white men behind the scenes making profits. (It has been estimated that in 1929, eighty percent of Harlem's businesses were owned by whites.) Laura urges passers-by to put some of their money in the tambourine rather than giving it to "the paddys [Irishmen] that owns these Harlem guzzle joints," or, in other words, "instead of it all going right to the white man." White police officers, apartment managers, and fire inspectors will take bribes to overlook violations or grant favors. The mysterious Marty, another white man, is in charge of the numbers racket in the neighborhood. Men like Buddy can earn a decent living working for the gambling or sex trades, but all assume and accept that white men are in charge.

This Harlem is populated with "pimps and gamblers and whores," and although she has never had any trouble, Essie carries a knife for protection. But there is also the young artist who paints beautiful murals on the church walls, and C. J., who attends college and plays the guitar. Hughes is not presenting Harlem as bad or dangerous, but as a place pulsing with life of all sorts, with "Auto horns . . . honking, taxis flying by, arc lights blinking, people passing up and down the street, restaurants and bars full." Even for the poor it is an exciting, teeming city—"Mighty magnet of the colored race . . . Harlem, a chocolate ice cream cone in New York's white napkin."

Style

Scenic Method

Tambourines to Glory is a short novel—barely one hundred pages in the *Collected Works of Langston Hughes* edition—yet it is divided into thirty-six chapters, several just over a page long.

Most of the chapters are self-contained, small glimpses into brief moments in the lives of the characters. Chapter 1, for example, is six pages long and takes about fifteen minutes to read (if one sings along with the characters); it describes a conversation that would last about fifteen minutes in "real life." The only background information, after a two-sentence exposition that identifies the day as Palm Sunday, is provided by the characters as they speak to each other. Throughout the novel, there is little explanation or reflection from the narrator, only the briefest description of settings, and no extended internal monologues. Sixteen chapters begin abruptly with one of the characters speaking or singing; twenty-two end this way. A few chapters begin with brief tag lines that identify the passing of time ("The next morning," "The winter prospered them," "When June came"), but changes in Essie's and Laura's fortunes and behavior are communicated directly by their speaking or their actions.

The novelist Henry James (1843–1916) frequently structured his novels this way, and Hughes may have been inspired by his work. More likely, the structure of *Tambourines to Glory* arises from the fact that it was a play before it was a novel. Although the play version comprises only thirteen scenes, the novel echoes the play's reliance on foregrounded speech and action, rather than on reflection or exposition, to carry the plot and theme forward.

Foreshadowing

Foreshadowing is a device used by authors to suggest or prepare for something that is going to happen later. *Tambourines to Glory* uses foreshadowing to set up Laura's killing of Buddy, so that when it happens it feels like a natural outcome of what has come before, instead of a sudden unconnected idea that has sprung into the author's mind. In Chapter 3, Hughes makes the first mention of Essie's knife, "a long pearl-handled knife" with "a little button on its side" that releases a "thin sharp blade." Essie uses the knife to clean her fingernails, and returns it to her coat pocket, where she keeps it for protection. As the narrator confirms, there is really no other reason for Essie to carry this knife, and the scene of Essie cleaning her fingernails has no particular purpose in the action of the novel, other than to introduce the idea of the knife.

Throughout the rest of the novel, there are occasional references to the knife in the pocket, or to the fact that, although Laura buys a new fur coat, Essie is content with her heavy old black one. In Chapter 29, just before Laura kills Buddy, Laura and Essie quarrel over Laura's fur coat. Laura says, "You keep on wearing your old rags if you want to, with that same old Lenox Avenue knife of yours in that ragged pocket. What are you protecting?" With the knife in Essie's pocket fresh in the reader's mind, Hughes is able to make the murder scene move swiftly, without interrupting it to explain what Laura is taking out of Essie's coat. Although some of the early references to the knife are worked in somewhat awkwardly, the excitement and drama Hughes achieves in the climactic scene through foreshadowing make up for that awkwardness.

Dialect and Diction

An important element that adds to the liveliness of *Tambourines to Glory* is Hughes's use of various African American urban dialects of the 1950s. Contemporary reviewers of the work almost universally praised Hughes's success at capturing the sounds of real speech. The novel, having originated as a play, contains a great deal of dialogue (Chapters 1 and 15, for example, are almost entirely conversations between two characters, with little exposition or description), and each character's way of speaking reflects something of her background or personality. Essie and Laura retain a trace of the South in their informal speech, as when Essie says, "Somehow I kinder like to keep my head clear," and Laura replies, "Woman, you sound right simple." Their speech is full of colorful metaphors, such as the many ways Laura describes her various lovers ("Old racoon," "chocolate boy with the coconut eyes," "my king-size Hershey bar"). And it is by their grammar and by their pronunciation of "likker" and "lemme" and "gonna," as much as by their clothing and their living situations, that Hughes flags them as members of the socioeconomic underclass.

As Essie begins to study the Bible, she begins to drop phrases from it into her speech. When Laura is preaching, she speaks with a distinct rhythm and repetition: "Turn! I say turn! Turn your steps toward God this evening, join up with us, and stand up for Jesus on this corner. . . . Talk, speak, shout, declare your determination. Who will stand up and testify for Him?" Buddy's speech marks him as a young man who knows the latest style, when he calls Laura "baby" or "sugar" or "kiddo," when he talks about money as "a few Abe Lincolns and some tens" or "fifty simoleons" and when he describes that "sharp little chick" Marietta as "stacked, solid, neat-all-reet, copasetic, baby!" Marietta, newly arrived from the South, speaks in a way that is slightly more formal, more quiet, more shy than the others' speech patterns.

Hughes was primarily a poet, and he had spent decades developing his instinct for the sound of language. Additionally, he had written the play form of the story first, so many of the lines spoken by the characters were crafted to be said aloud. None of the differences in speech are pointed out by the narrator or commented upon by the characters. Just as he trusts the reader to somehow hear the lyrics of the hymns sung throughout the novel, Hughes trusts the reader to hear and interpret the different ways of speaking.

Historical Context

The Great Migration

Between about 1890 and 1930, some two-and-a-half million African Americans moved from the American South to cities in the North, in what came to be called the Great Migration. Although the slaves had been freed, there were still few opportunities in the South for good jobs and property ownership, because the economy in the South was faltering, and because Jim Crow laws in the South increasingly made life difficult for African Americans. Legally and culturally, African Americans could be and were denied the vote, employment, housing, and other basic needs. In the large cities of the North, especially along the East Coast, factories needed workers. The largest migration occurred during World War I and afterward, when factories needed workers to replace those who had gone to fight, European immigration was low, and there was an increased need for the manufacture of certain wartime goods. More than a half million African Americans, like the *Tambourines to Glory* characters Essie Belle Johnson and Laura Reed, left their homes in the South and came North. Though they typically received only the lowest, unskilled jobs, and although they earned less than white employees doing the same work, many of these African American migrants still found greater opportunity than they had left behind in the South. But families like Essie's were common. Adults frequently left children behind with relatives, hoping that in a few months or years they would earn enough to bring their children North with them. For single women, especially, this dream was in many cases never realized, as hoped-for jobs did not materialize.

In New York City, as in other cities and as with other immigrant groups, African Americans congregated in one section. Harlem, on the northern end of the island of Manhattan, became a

Compare & Contrast

- **1950s:** African Americans are still moving from the rural South to big cities in the North, hoping for good jobs and equal opportunity. Segregation, racism and a weak economy hinder many of their efforts.

  2000s: The Great Migration is over, and is reversing. Since the 1960s, many African Americans, especially from the middle class, have left the North and moved to large cities in the South.

- **1950s:** Harlem is in economic decline as middle-class African Americans move out, leaving only the poor behind. Half of all housing units are unsound.

  2000s: Harlem is gradually being gentrified as middle- and upper-class African Americans return. They are buying and fixing up formerly run-down homes, causing housing prices to rise dramatically. Former President Bill Clinton opens an office in Harlem, and wealthy black business owners are opening businesses there.

- **1950s:** Public schools in the South are segregated, by law and by custom. Many black students attend all-black schools, even after a 1954 Supreme Court decision rules that separate schools are inherently unequal.

  2000s: Public schools across the United States are by law open to all students regardless of race or creed, but schools in many large cities are segregated by socioeconomic class because middle-class families have left the cities or can afford to send their children to private schools.

- **1950s:** Public transportation in the Northern United States is more integrated than in the Southern states. After 1955, interstate trains and buses are forbidden by law to segregate their passengers. Boycotts in Montgomery, Alabama, and Tallahassee, Florida, force the integration of local public transportation in 1956.

  2000s: Interstate bus travel tends to be segregated by socioeconomic class, with only poorer people and young people choosing bus travel. Within New York City, public buses, subways, and commuter trains are used by a wide variety of people from different races, religions, and social classes.

---

magnet for migrating African Americans. It then grew into a center for African American thought and culture in the 1920s and 1930s. The mingling of rural Southern people and Northern people used to big cities, and the interplay of their various artistic, social, and religious traditions, produced a rich and lively new culture. The movement known as the Harlem Renaissance fed Langston Hughes and other important writers, musicians and artists, who for the first time portrayed urban black life realistically and sympathetically.

The Storefront Church

A direct result of the Great Migration was the creation in Harlem and other Northern cities of a large number of "storefront" churches. Most of the African Americans who came to Harlem were from small rural towns where they were well-known, and where their church membership gave them a standing in the community that their working lives did not. Coming to large cities, they found large impersonal churches with hundreds of members, preachers who led a different kind of service than they were used to, and different kinds of music. Additionally, these churches tended not to be located in the very poorest neighborhoods, where new immigrants settled. Some immigrants delighted in the size and the prestige of the modern urban churches, but many felt lost and unwelcome.

To meet their spiritual needs, African Americans began to form loosely organized churches in local neighborhoods, often led by semi-literate preachers (with or without any ministerial training), holding meetings on street corners or in abandoned or condemned stores or houses. These churches were Christian, but typically not affiliated with any major denomination. Preachers spoke in stark terms about heaven and hell, about sin and redemption, and led the singing of spirituals and old folk songs that the rural congregation knew. Members of the congregation felt free to shout out or start a song, as they had done at home. During the 1920s, nearly two-thirds of the churches in Harlem were of the storefront variety. Only a few eventually outgrew their storefront locations and moved to larger venues, or built permanent structures. Because new churches were forming all the time, whenever a new mass of uneducated poor people moved into a neighborhood, it was relatively easy for charlatans to establish churches for the sole purpose of making money. Like Essie and Laura, they may have had no experience and questionable motives; also like Essie and Laura, they may have done some real good in peoples' lives.

Gospel Music

The music called "gospel music" was a particular form created and perfected by African Americans during the 1920s, a fusion of the blues and old-style Christian hymns. This music was frequently sung in urban churches, giving a new city edge to the traditional hymns that people had been singing down South. The song that Essie and Laura sing in Chapter 1, for example, "Precious Lord, Take My Hand," was a popular song in this tradition, written by Thomas A. Dorsey. Hughes loved this kind of music, wrote reviews and columns about it, and incorporated it into several plays and into this novel. Over the years, gospel music remained an important part of worship, but also became a style of music for commercial entertainment. Flashily dressed singers performed gospel music in theaters and clubs. Hughes noticed with amusement that many gospel singers were more interested in money than in the Lord. And many of them did make good money.

In Chapter 10, Laura comments that, "These gospel songs is about the only thing the white folks ain't latched onto yet. But they will, as soon as they find out there's dough in 'em." She mentions Mahalia Jackson (c. 1911–1972), a famous gospel singer with a remarkable voice. Jackson herself had become a commercial success, equally well-known among black and white people through radio and television appearances, but her faith would not allow her to sing hymns in nightclubs. (Laura quotes her in Chapter 21: "You know what Mahalia Jackson says: 'The church will be here when the night clubs are gone.'") Instead, Jackson sang a concert in New York's

Carnegie Hall and other respectable venues, and released record albums, thus helping make gospel music available to a larger and more diverse audience without compromising her convictions.

Critical Overview

Compared with the poetry, little critical attention has been paid to Hughes's prose, and the novel *Tambourines to Glory* has yet to receive serious critical analysis. In fact, several reference works completely overlook *Tambourines to Glory*, listing *Not without Laughter* (1930) as Hughes's only novel. But, because of Hughes's importance, the novel was widely, if not always favorably, reviewed upon publication in the most important periodicals of the day.

Most critics admired the novel's humor and liveliness, and were captivated by the author's obvious affection for his characters. In the *Saturday Review*, Richard Gehman wrote that the novel "develops with a natural, effortless simplicity and an unassuming authority," and that it "is full of vitality, earthiness, joy, unashamed religious feeling, and humorous perspective." Arna Bontemps, in a review for the *New York Herald Tribune*, called the writing "as ribald, as effortless, and on the surface as artless as a folk ballad," and commented on the "fondness and humor" with which Hughes created his characters. Reviewers were nearly universal in feeling that even though Essie and Laura and Buddy made mistakes and caused some mischief, it was impossible in the end not to like them.

Even the most favorable reviews considered the novel only a slight work. Critics who found weaknesses in the novel generally faulted the plot itself, especially the violent ending. In the *New York Times Book Review*, Gilbert Millstein acknowledged "the consistently high quality of Hughes's production over the years," but described *Tambourines to Glory* as a "minor effort . . . with an industriously contrived climax." LeRoi Jones (now Amiri Baraka), himself a well-regarded African American writer, was much harsher in his *Jazz Review* article, describing the novel's "horribly inept plot."

For readers of all colors in the 1950s, novels by African American writers or featuring African American characters were something of a novelty. A few of the reviews by white writers are interesting now, more than fifty years after they were written, because of the dated language and ideas they express, even as they praise *Tambourines to Glory*. Marion Turner

Traffic on a busy street in Harlem, New York, the setting for Tambourines to Glory

Clarke, for example, writing in the *Baltimore Evening Sun*, admired the novel as "rough and unvarnished but pulsing with the life of a vigorous race." Marty Sullivan, in the *Fort Wayne News Sentinel*, called the novel a "blessed exception" to a trend toward didacticism in novels with African American characters, and also finds it "a fine look into the colorful, earthy and endlessly inventive Negro speech."

When *Tambourines to Glory* was reissued in 2001 in Volume 4 of *The Collected Works of Langston Hughes*, critics again had an opportunity to consider the long-neglected novel, which had gone out of print. Reviewing the volume for the *Journal of Modern Literature*, Roland L. Williams Jr. finds more to praise in Hughes's intentions "to honor and hearten blacks" than he does in the actual writing. Still, he admires the novel's presentation of an important period in history, and assures readers that "they will come to dig the roots and branches of black music."

Criticism

Cynthia Bily

Bily teaches English at Adrian College in Adrian, Michigan. In this essay, Bily examines

Hughes's novel and an earlier poem through a Marxist lens.

Essie Belle Johnson, one of the main characters of Langston Hughes's novel *Tambourines to Glory*, is numb. Her only goal since she arrived in the North has been to get enough money for a two- or three-room apartment so she can bring her daughter to live with her. After more than a dozen years, however, she has only a one-room kitchenette in the Rabbit Warren, a building of tiny one-room units housing as many as three or four people each. The view out her window is of "a courtyard full of beer cans and sacks of garbage." There is no child care for these crowded families; children coming home from school entertain themselves until their parents come home from work. But paying rent on this awful place takes most of Essie's monthly check, so that she has a hard time getting food. She and Laura pool their resources when they can, but in Chapter 4 they have nothing but a pot of rice for dinner, as neither of them can come up with a bit of meat or even some gravy for flavoring. Essie spends a lot of her time sitting, her mind "kind of empty" in one of her "long, long, very long pauses." Essie has given up on trying to find a good job, and lives off welfare, but it was not always this way. She tells her friend Laura Reed, "It ain't easy to get ahold of money. I've tried. Lord knows I've tried to get ahead." As a poor, African American, overweight, under-educated woman in the 1950s, Essie does not have much chance of improving her situation. She is resigned to her fate.

Laura has more energy, but she does not see herself as a contributor, or even a potential contributor, to society. Her relief investigator wonders why she cannot hold a job, but Laura thinks of the welfare check as "white folks' money" and sees no reason why she should work for it if she can get the same amount without working. She has dreams of accumulating cars and furs, but she has no vision of herself doing satisfying or important work. Like Essie, Laura does not have many options. Her most marketable asset is her body—the curvy figure and large breasts with which she can attract a man. Once her beauty is gone, she will have no way to escape her situation. Essie and Laura are the only two people on their floor who do not have jobs to go to, but their lack of industriousness is obviously not the only reason they do not have decent housing—apparently, even many hard-working people cannot find anything better than the "Rabbit Warren." As Laura reminds Essie, no one can get an apartment in Harlem "unless you got enough money to pay under the table."

> "Why do many poor people accept their poverty instead of challenging the system that keeps them poor? Because they have accepted another ideology—religion—that teaches them that God is in control, and that their reward will come later, when they reach Heaven."

Essie and Laura, ground down by their poverty, are sad at times, and they dream of better days, but they are never angry. Why not? In a wealthy industrialized nation that produces millionaires and mansions, why should there be people who cannot earn a fair wage and live in a decent home? Essie believes she simply "was borned to bad luck." Where did she get the idea that she cannot change her life?

In the nineteenth century, the philosopher and economist Karl Marx asked similar questions. He wondered why poor people around the world—who outnumber wealthy people by far—did not join together in revolution to make their lives better. Why would thousands of factory workers settle for low wages when a few corporate heads were earning millions from the labor of the many? Capitalist societies, Marx argued, drove people to compete with each other instead of helping each other, and to seek out material goods that are not useful except as signs of status, instead of using surplus money to support others who need it. In the *Communist Manifesto* (1848), he and economist Friedrich Engels predicted that eventually the working classes would seize control, abolish private property, and distribute wealth evenly and fairly.

According to Marxist theory, lower-class people are trained to accept belief systems, called ideologies, that keep them apart from each other and kept them in the lower class. Why do relatively low-income Americans fight against relatively low-income Iraqis, instead of joining together to seize wealth from the people who control it? Because they have accepted an ideology called nationalism that

What Do I Read Next?

- The first volume of Hughes's autobiography, *The Big Sea* (1940), covers approximately the first thirty years of his life, including his early encounters with salvation and African American churches.

- Hughes is best known as a poet, and *The Collected Poems of Langston Hughes* (1994), running more than seven hundred pages, shows the depth and range of his poetic talents. The poem "Tambourines" is similar to the song Essie sings at the end of the novel.

- *Tambourines to Glory* has sometimes been compared to *Elmer Gantry* (1927), a novel by Sinclair Lewis about a phony preacher who comes to lead a large church in the Midwest. The tone of Lewis's novel is somber and judgmental, without Hughes's humor and musicality.

- *One Way to Heaven* (1931), by Countee Cullen, another novel about life in Harlem, examines the tensions between lower-class and middle-class African American society.

- *All God's Chillun Got Wings* (1924) is a play about racial prejudice in Harlem. Written by Eugene O'Neill, a white playwright, the play shows the struggles facing a white woman who marries a black man.

- *Canaan Land: A Religious History of African Americans* (2001), by Albert J. Raboteau, describes urban storefront churches and how they grew out of the "Great Migration," while providing a context within the larger story of religious tradition.

---

teaches them that their primary loyalty is to their country, not to others in their social class. Why do many poor people accept their poverty instead of challenging the system that keeps them poor? Because they have accepted another ideology—religion—that teaches them that God is in control, and that their reward will come later, when they reach Heaven. In a work called *Critique of the Hegelian Philosophy of Right* (1844), Marx famously called religion the "opiate of the masses." He meant that religion worked like the drug opium, keeping all who used it calm and unquestioning.

Marx's ideas were argued about and expanded on over the next century, and formed the basis for the socialist government of the former Soviet Union. Hughes considered and reconsidered these ideas throughout his long writing career, and often explored the connections between racism and class conflict in his work. In the 1930s, much of Hughes's writing took a strident political tone, as in his 1932 poem "Goodbye Christ," published in the labor journal *The Negro Worker*. In this poem, perhaps his most controversial, the speaker tells Jesus Christ that although "You did all right in your

day, I reckon," he has outlasted his usefulness and should exit the stage. They have "sold [Jesus] to too many," and "ain't no good no more." In this period, Hughes was more outraged than amused by those he saw as phony preachers using religion to become wealthy or famous. He believed they were complicit in keeping poor believers poor and quiet. The poem's speaker lists several specific offenders:

> And please take Saint Ghandi [sic] with you when you go
> And Saint Pope Pius
> And Saint Aimee McPherson
> And big black Saint Becton
> Of the Consecrated Dime.

The poem suggests a replacement for Jesus, "a new guy with no religion at all": "Marx Communist Lenin Peasant Stalin Worker ME."

These first four historical figures were examples for Hughes of how ideology can be misused. Mohandas Gandhi, the leader in the 1930s and 1940s of the independence movement in India, organized nonviolent acts of civil disobedience by Indian peasants. Pope Pius XI, head of the Roman Catholic Church from 1922 to 1939, opposed labor movements and communism. Aimee Semple McPherson, an evangelical preacher in the 1920s, founded the Church of the Four Square Gospel and became a millionaire before financial and sexual scandals eroded her following. And George Wilson Becton was the founder of a church in Harlem, the World's Gospel Feast, which asked members for donations of "consecrated dimes." By linking these four, the angry speaker of *Goodbye Christ* presents them as equally harmful.

Some twenty-five years later, Hughes's ideas about religion and Marxism had undergone change. He came to admire Gandhi and supported his efforts in the early 1940s, and he became less admiring of Stalin and the Soviet Union. But even though Hughes's answers were becoming more moderate, he could still be seen wrestling with some of the old questions. In *Tambourines to Glory*, Laura refers to two of the names on Hughes's list when she and Essie first think about starting a church: "Remember Elder Becton? Remember that white woman back in depression days, Aimee Semple McPherson, what put herself on some wings and opened up a temple and made a million dollars?" By 1958, when both Becton and Semple were long dead, Hughes's opinion of their sanctity had not changed, but he was able now to treat their deceptions with humor instead of pure anger. For Laura, of course, Becton and McPherson are good examples—of how to fleece poor believers.

Marxist theory would say that *Tambourines to Glory* presents a society that has unevenly distributed its material goods and the means to acquire them. In the beginning, Laura and Essie have so accepted their lower-class status that they do not try very hard to move up. Later, Essie and Laura and Buddy improve their status through varying degrees of underhandedness, but there simply are not many other options open to them. For example, no matter how successful they become, they could never get an apartment without the support of Marty, "The fixer, the man behind the men *behind* the men." The economic system is not set up to fairly distribute housing.

Laura demonstrates Marx's idea that a capitalist economy teaches people to value the wrong things. Laura does not care about helping the members of her church. Capitalism teaches competitiveness, a "me first" way of dealing with other people. As Laura says to Essie, who wants to stay after services and talk to the people, "You've done helped yourself. You might *can* help them. . . . but why bother?" Laura has no qualms about taking

nickels and dimes from people who can scarcely afford to give them. She does not want a more just world, or a better life for everyone—she wants a fur coat, a Cadillac, and a chauffeur. None of these things has what Marxists call a "use value"; that is, they do not have any real purpose. A worn black coat is just as warm as a fur, and a smaller car (or the bus) would get Laura where she needed to go. Essie's plain black robes serve her just as well as Essie's colorful satin robes with contrasting trim. The things Laura has been trained to want have only "sign value," or the power to impress other people. Laura's wasteful spending is an example of conspicuous consumption.

Essie demonstrates some qualities that Marxists would admire. She is not greedy or competitive. She thinks that "maybe that is the way to help ourselves—by helping others." She never takes ownership of the money she takes in from the church, but thinks of it as God's, and she lends it freely to Birdie Lee when Birdie Lee needs to get a tooth pulled. Essie will not take any of the profit from the fake Holy Water. But Essie does not challenge the way things are. She does not wonder why God would set up a system that dooms millions of people to starvation while others feast. She does not encourage her followers to take political action to try to change the structure of society. What would happen if the thousand members of the Tambourine Temple spent an hour a week converging on City Hall, or the White House, instead of gathering to sing and pray? Essie accepts basic inequalities, and uses her resources to make small improvements within the existing structures.

Hughes never gave up on his idea that some form of a socialist economy would be more just than capitalism. Ultimately, *Tambourines to Glory* condemns the unequal distribution of power, material goods and hope that capitalism fosters. But what Hughes acknowledges in *Tambourines to Glory* is that, while religion may in fact be an "opiate for the masses," the churches often do work that no other institution will do. With Laura out of the picture, Essie will use the Tambourine Temple's money to provide day care for working mothers, a clubhouse, and a playground. Marietta will help care for the sick. True, in a just society, day care and health care would already exist for everyone who needed it. But in the meantime, in an unjust capitalist society, a church whose leader has a social conscience can stand as an oasis of equality and compassion.

Source: Cynthia Bily, Critical Essay on *Tambourines to Glory*, in *Novels for Students*, Thomson Gale, 2005.

People congregate inside a storefront Baptist church in Chicago, Illinois, in 1941

Joyce Hart

Hart is a freelance writer and author of several books. In this essay, Hart examines the significance of the metaphor of the tambourine in Hughes's Tambourines to Glory.

In Langston Hughes's *Tambourines to Glory*, the tambourine is used as a major metaphor in the story. The metaphor starts with the realization of the double use of the tambourine. First, the musical instrument is used as an inexpensive and simple accompaniment to street-corner singing, a way to help attract a crowd and keep that crowd involved. But once the crowd is roused, the tambourine then takes on a different meaning as it is turned upside down and passed around much like a beggar's bowl, into which donations are dropped and then carried away. This is the beginning of the metaphor, but it goes a lot deeper when one realizes the similarities between the tambourine's two different sides and the two main female characters of this story.

Essie and Laura are women on the edge. They live in tight quarters on a tight budget. And when a brilliant idea about an easy way of making money crosses Laura's mind, she quickly convinces Essie that it could be their ticket out of poverty. "Say,

Essie, why don't you and me start a church." Essie can sing and Laura knows how to preach. What more could they need? And with this, the two women, whom Hughes patiently describes as two different sides of a similar coin, set off to convert their neighborhood. Their motives may have been somewhat related to each other at the beginning of their venture but as the story develops, it is their expanding differences that stretch them far apart, inevitably forcing their connection to snap.

Essie is a pious woman, innocent and full of love. And when she sings, people stop to listen and eventually join in. Essie is the musical side of the tambourine. Her rhythm is smooth and steady. And the songs she sings are soothing and uplifting. She makes the people around her want to forget their troubles, turn their hearts to God, and believe. Sinners repent, and the psychologically wounded begin to heal. As musical as Essie is, she is like the tambourine in another way too. She needs to be played. She sits all day, alone in her apartment, doing nothing to better herself. She is lonesome but does nothing to ease that pain. She misses her daughter, but does not work toward bringing her child to her. She just sits in a corner and collects dust. Without Laura prompting her, like someone gently beating a hand against the skin of the tambourine, no one would hear Essie's music. Nothing new would happen in Essie's life. Someone needs to pick her up, turn her around, and pump the music out of her.

Laura is the motivator. "You God's handmaiden," Essie tells Laura, "even if you do not always act like a holy maiden do." But Laura is also the open, cupped hand. No matter what she does, she is always asking someone to help her. It is not that she is incapable of taking care of herself, but she is better at prompting others to nourish her. She eats at Essie's house. She sleeps with men who buy her presents. And when she begins to preach, it is not redemption of lost souls that she is seeking. She preaches to make people believe that in giving her money they will be saved. Laura is manipulative and uncaring and hollow. Whereas Essie is open and honest, Laura always has a scheme. Laura is the tambourine turned on its head. People look at the tambourine, and they see an instrument of music, so they do not question the emptiness of the "bowl" formed by the underside of the tambourine. They listen to Laura and think they are hearing the music of God talking to them. In gratitude for inspiring them, they dig into their pockets when Laura passes through the crowd with her concave tambourine, and they do their best to fill it up. At first,

> " Essie touches the essence of humanity, and it makes her real. So when she sings with that tambourine in her hand, the people not only hear the music, they also feel it."

only nickels and dimes drop into the tambourine. But as time goes by, that tambourine's appetite increases. The more Laura gets, the more she wants. There is one big difference, however, between a real tambourine and Laura. Whereas the real tambourine has a finite capacity, Laura's greed is endless.

The title of Hughes's novel uses the plural form of the word *tambourine* despite the fact that the main characters of this story own only one tambourine. They start out with one tambourine and one bible. So why does Hughes use the plural form? What other tambourine is he referring to? Maybe he uses the concept of more than one tambourine to exemplify the differences in the two main characters, anticipating the eventual split between Essie and Laura at the end of the novel. And if this is so, then his meaning of *glory* more than likely reflects two different definitions.

Essie is one type of tambourine, and because her tambourine differs from Laura's, the version of glory that she represents is most likely defined in different terms. Glory for Essie implies beauty and grandeur. And Essie does exemplify both. Her beauty reigns best when one looks inside of her. She gets caught up with Laura's ideas of starting a church not for the money but rather for the peace of mind, the inspiration, and the passion of doing good works. She does not deny herself the rewards of her trade, but she puts aside most of it with an eye to sharing the benefits with those who need it the most. "This is the Lord's money," Essie tells Laura. And as the narrator relates: "Essie did not think it [the money] belonged to her. Essie thought it ought to go in some way to the works of God." She uses the money to enhance the church, enlarging it so more people can come. She wants to add a nursery or pre-school and a medical clinic. Essie's glory is the beneficial side of pride—a confidence that she can do good.

Several young people stand in the doorway of a storefront church in Chicago, Illinois, like the one founded by the main characters in Tambourines to Glory

Laura's glory is something else. It is more along the lines of credit and fame. She could care less about anyone else's pain or conversion, unless, of course, it means more profit. She buys sparkling things that make her stand out in a crowd, boasting that she has done well for herself. She takes on a young, flashy lover for the same reason. Laura's glory is all wrapped up in her pride. Hers is a superficial glory. It does not feed her soul, but rather threatens to destroy her.

Laura's jealousy and greed have taken control of her. "I wish Essie would get holy enough or lazy enough or something to quit my Temple," Laura thinks to herself near the end of the story. "All they [the congregation] have to do is see her up there, and they feel happy." Essie is getting in the way of Laura's money-making scheme: "But look at the money I would make without her." These sentiments that come out of Laura sum up Hughes's intent for writing this novel. The empty tambourine, the one turned upside down, will always be empty, no matter how many times it is filled up with coins. The instrument was made to create music not to collect funds. Just as, in Hughes's vision, the instrument of the mind, body, and soul was made to create goodness and compassion. Essie's dreams were answered, and the answers fulfilled her. She wanted to do something worthwhile with her life. She also wanted the means of bringing her daughter back to her. She took advantage of Laura's ideas and impetus to manifest her dreams. And she was duly rewarded. But she never stopped making music. She enjoyed singing, but the singing was not an end in itself. The singing was an expression of her love and compassion for the people around her. In helping others, she helped herself.

Laura, on the other hand, represents for Hughes all the things that are wrong in a community. Laura is a charlatan and a leech. She has an insatiable hunger for material things. Her goals are ambiguous, and therefore she can never reach them. She wants money, but how much money will ever be enough? Even Laura refers to money as the "apple of evil," at one point, as if she recognizes to some degree that money will eventually be the cause of her being kicked out of paradise. But she does not pay any attention to her own thoughts. Instead, she tells Essie to don the fancy white robe Laura has bought for her. "Just being robed in goodness," she tells Essie, "is not enough for the type of folks we attract. They like color, glitter, something to look at." But of course, Laura is dead wrong. Her values are all mixed up. The riches that the congregation is looking for has very little to do with money and glitter. But Laura lives too close to the surface to understand that. She flits from thought to thought without taking the time to meditate on any one of them. She complains that all that Essie does is sit, exhibiting a passiveness for which Laura is incapable. While Essie sits, Laura schemes. And it is during this quiet time that Essie reaches something so deep inside of her that it connects her to all the people who come to the church. Essie touches the essence of humanity, and it makes her real. So when she sings with that tambourine in her hand, the people not only hear the music, they also feel it.

At the climax, Laura puts on her scarlet robe. And as she stabs her boyfriend in the back, Hughes writes: "Her scarlet robe swept upward like velvet wings." Then he adds: "Laura's fists went up into the air and their fingers opened like two frightening claws." Through these two descriptive phrases, should any reader be left that does not quite grasp what Laura has become, Hughes creates the image of a fallen angel. After her hideous crime, Laura ascends to the altar, and the Tambourine Choir (yes, the tambourines are now multiplied) joins her in a song that contains the lines: "I'm going to lay down

my soul / At the foot of the cross, / Yes, and tell my Jesus / Just what sin has cost . . ." This is Laura's last assault on the church she has helped to create. For she sings words that have, for her, no meaning. She has just killed a man and is about to send her best friend to jail for the crime. She is an empty tambourine, indeed.

Then, in the final chapters, one of the congregation saves Essie's life, just as Essie had saved hers. "Oh, if I had just brought my tambourine," Birdie Lee says at the prison, "I would shake it here in jail to God's glory, to you, Sister Essie, who by your goodness lifted me up out of the muck and mire of Harlem and put my feet on the rock of grace." And that, by Hughes's account, is what the tambourine is really meant for. It is to be played for God's glory, a glory that he uses Essie to elucidate. The final song that Hughes ends this novel with begins: "If you've got a tambourine, / Shake it to the glory of God!" And that is just what Essie did.

Source: Joyce Hart, Critical Essay on *Tambourines to Glory*, in *Novels for Students*, Thomson Gale, 2005.

John W. Parker

In the following review, Parker follows Hughes's representation of the black gospel tradition in Tambourines to Glory, *noting the way the characters succeed by commercializing religion.*

Since the publication of *The Weary Blues*, poetic account of the enchantment, romance, and tragedy that was Harlem's back in the Twenties, Langston Hughes has maintained a healthy nostalgia for the Harlem scene, not only because it marks the point of his departure as a man of letters, but likewise because it remains a city within a city, a widely-discussed experiment in large-scale living in the urban ghetto. The impact of the Black Metropolis both as a place and a symbol is illuminated by such Hughes publications as *Shakespeare in Harlem* (1942), *Montage of a Dream Deferred* (1951), *Simple Takes a Wife* (1953), *The Sweet Flypaper of Life* (1955), and now *Tambourines to Glory*. A casual glance at the dates of these volumes attests to the fact that by and large each follows the other in rapid succession.

Tambourines to Glory is an urban folk tale which results from the skillful fusion of some thirty-six smaller segments into a whole more meaningful by far than any of the parts. Such organization as the book displays stems from its consistency in mood and atmosphere and from the unity of action exhibited by the characters. Artistically handled, too, is the selection and arrangement of the details in such a way as to assure suspense and movement. Starting as it does *in medias res*, *Tambourines to Glory* has a middle, but scarcely a beginning or an end.

The volume turns mostly upon the sham and pretense of two attractive Harlem tenement women who, with their names on the relief rolls and time on their hands, set about to establish an independent, unorthodox church, the predominance of their own worldly interests notwithstanding. Only Essie's half-hidden seriousness of purpose and the power that sometimes stems from the singing of powerful hymns lighted up an otherwise drab, second-floor kitchenette in which the idea of a new church was crystallized.

These gospel racketeers, wisely enough, gauged their public utterances to the gullibility of unsuspecting people, and suppressed in their own hearts the knowledge that whiskey, loose women, the numbers game, and the Gospel of Christ make strange bedfellows. Just the same, the church prospered and before long the Reed Sisters (as they elected to designate themselves) moved the church from the corner block to a converted theater building with a thousand seats and their names in lights on the marquee.

The total situation, however, leaves much to be desired. The two-dollar downpayment on the Bible for the new church resulted from Laura's having hit the numbers. In the absence of proper credentials, Laura and Company found it necessary to produce cash periodically to keep back the law-enforcement officers. And with too many men on her hands and whiskey to buy, Laura frequently put in late appearances at the church services. Before long, however, tragedy settled down upon the enterprise. Laura finally stabbed her boy friend, Big-Eyed Buddy, landed in prison, and left it to Essie and Birdie Lee to purify the church for the first time in its brief history.

Tambourines to Glory is in no sense a satire upon organized religion, or even upon cults as such, but rather a close-up exposé of the manner in which what sometimes passes as religion turns out to be nothing more than a commercial venture in the hands of unscrupulous racketeers.

Touched upon in this new novel are several themes treated elsewhere in Hughes' published writings. One observes, for instance, that the characters fall for the most part in the category of the nothings, not the dicties; that the author shuns sweetness and light and digs into the difficulties that aggravate men here and now; that an underlying Darwinian emphasis takes its toll upon

conventional morality; and that fallen women, wandering irregularly from bar to bar, abound. Mr. Hughes cites facts, but does not draw conclusions; himself a Harlemite, he continues to laugh with the people, not at them.

All in all, *Tambourines to Glory* underscores a wide knowledge of the New York ghetto (and by implication others around the world) in a period of increasing racial awareness.

Source: John W. Parker, "Another Revealing Facet of the Harlem Scene," in *Langston Hughes: The Contemporary Reviews*, edited by Tish Dace, Cambridge University Press, 1997, pp. 589–90.

Le Roi Jones

In the following review, Jones discusses the position of Tambourines to Glory *between the more subjective folk tradition of "Negro literature" and the more universal idea of the "Negro in literature."*

I suppose, by now, Langston Hughes's name is synonymous with "Negro Literature." For many, he is the only Negro in the world of books. This, of course, is unfortunate. But in quite another sense this is as it should be. Hughes is probably the last "major" Negro writer who will be allowed to write what could be called a "Negro Literature" (as differentiated from literature in general): to impose upon himself such staggering limitations.

Now, don't for a moment take this to be a plea for "assimilationist" literature (i.e., novels, etc. written by Negroes that assiduously avoid any portrayal of Negro life in much the same way that the "Black Bourgeoisie" avoid any attempt to connect them, even vicariously, with blues, jazz, "greens" or anything else even remotely "Negroid"). I am merely saying, that the Negro artist, and especially the Negro writer, A. E. (After Ellison), has come too far and has experienced so much that cannot be, even vaguely, attributed to the "folk tradition." And that to confine all of his thinking, hence all his writing to that tradition (with no thought as to where that tradition has got to; what significance that tradition has, say, in relation to the macrocosm of American life in general, or for that matter, man's life on earth) is to deny that there is any body of experience outside of that tradition. A kind of ethnic solipsism. Poet Robert Creeley says (in quite another context . . . but with the same general implications . . .) "A tradition becomes inept when it blocks the necessary conclusion: it says *we* have felt nothing, it implies others have felt more." This does not mean that the Negro writer, for instance, ought to stop using Negro Life In America as a theme; but certainly that theme ought only to be a *means*. For the Negro writer to confuse that means with the end (let us arbitrarily say that end is "art") is stultifying and dangerous. For these reasons, Hughes, to my mind, is a folklorist. He abdicated from the world of literature just after his second book of verse (*Fine Clothes to the Jew:* 1927); since then, he has sort of crept backwards and away from significant literature, until finally (with this book) he has gotten to a kind of meaningless ethnic name-dropping.

I am pretty well acquainted with the Negro in literature. I know of Hughes's early writing: his first novel (*Not without Laughter,* 1930), his early poetry (some of it very beautiful, a rough mixture of spoken blues, Masters, and Imagists). I know of his affiliation with the "Harlem School" (Claude McKay, Jean Toomer, Countee Cullen, and a few others) and the importance and merit of the "School" (Toomer's novel *Cane* is among the three greatest novels ever written by a Negro in America. The others: Richard Wright's *Native Son*, Ralph Ellison's *Invisible Man*). I also know of the "School's" (or at least Hughes's) wonderful credo . . . "To express our individual dark-skinned selves without fear or shame. If the white people are pleased we are glad. If they are not, it doesn't matter . . . If colored people are pleased, we are glad. If they are not, their displeasure doesn't matter either." This credo almost singularly served to notify the world that the Negro artist had got to the point where he was ready to challenge that world solely on the basis of his art. Hughes's attitude, along with the even fiercer attitude of Claude McKay, and the more intellectually sound attitudes of Jean Toomer and Countee Cullen, was a far cry from the "head patting" parochial "literature" of Chesnutt, Dixon, Dunbar and the so-called "Talented Tenth" of the 1890's. Hughes and the rest were interested in dispelling once and for all the Negro novel of apology. . . . (For example, from an early novel by a Negro, Charles Chesnutt; he relates an incident where "A refined Afro-American is forced to share a Jim Crow car with dirty, boisterous, and drunken Negroes.") . . . of fawning appeals for "an alliance between the better class of colored people and the quality white folks." The "School" was also reacting against the need for a Negro artist to be a pamphleteer, a social organizer, or, for that matter, anything else except an artist. This, of course, was the beginning of the Negro in literature; and the beginning of the end for a "Negro literature."

"Negro literature" is simply *folk literature*, in the sense I choose to take it. It has the same

> **"** Of course, when a folk art does have enough breadth of intellectual, emotional, and psychological concern to make its presence important to those outside of its individual folk tradition, then it has succeeded in thrusting itself up into the area of serious art."

relationship to literature *per se* (that is, to that writing which can be fully significant to all the world's peoples) that any folk art has to art in general. It is usually too limited in its appeal, emotional nuances, intellectual intentions, etc. to be able to fit into the mainstream of world art. Of course, when a folk art does have enough breadth of intellectual, emotional, and psychological concern to make its presence important to those outside of its individual folk tradition, then it has succeeded in thrusting itself up into the area of serious art. And here, by "serious," I mean *anything* containing what Tillich calls an "Ultimate Concern" (God, Death; Life after—the concerns of art) and not as some people would have it, merely anything taught in a university. "Negro Literature" is only that; a literature of a particular folk. It is of value only to that particular folk and perhaps to a few scholars, and certain kinds of literary *voyeurs*. It should not make pretensions of being anything else.

Of course, utilizing the materials of a certain folk tradition to fashion a work of art (the artist, certainly, must work with what he has, and what is closest to him) can lead to wonderful results: Lorca, Villon, Joyce and Dublin, Faulkner, Ellison. But merely relying on the strength and vitality of that tradition, without attempting (either because one lacks talent or is insincere) to extend the beauty or meaning of that tradition into a "universal" statement cannot result in art. Bessie Smith is certainly in the folk tradition, but what she finally got to, through that tradition, is, as they say, "something else." *Nobody Knows You When You're Down and Out*, could almost be sung by Oedipus leaving Thebes. As Pound said of great literature, "language charged with meaning to the utmost possible degree." That is art. A work that never leaves or points to some human reference outside a peculiar folk tradition is at best only folklore.

Ralph Ellison is a Negro writer. His novel *Invisible Man* won the National Book Award as the best American novel of 1952. It is among the best books written by an American in the last twenty years. The novel clearly deals with what is superficially a "Negro theme." Its characters are primarily Negroes, and its protagonist is a Negro. And although it is this "Negro theme" that gives the book its special twist, the theme is no more than a point of departure for Ellison. It is no more a "folk tale" than Faulkner's *The Sound And The Fury*. Ellison's horrifying portrait of a man faced with the loss of his identity through the weird swinishness of American society is probably made more incisive by its concentration on one segment of that society. Ellison uses the folk materials; jazz, blues, church songs, the southern heritage, the whole phenomena of Harlem. But he "charges them with meaning," extending the provincial into the universal. He makes art. Ellison, by utilizing the raw materials of his environment and the peculiar cultural heritage of the Negro, has not written a "Negro novel" but a novel. Ellison is a Negro writing literature and great literature at that.

To get back to Langston Hughes. Hughes and the "Harlem School" proposed (the credo was written around 1926 in *The Nation*) essentially to resist writing mere folklore. They were to become "full-fledged" artists; though bringing in the whole of the Negro's life. Jean Toomer's novel *Cane* succeeded; some of Cullen's poetry, and Langston Hughes's early verse. Toomer's is perhaps the greatest achievement. His *Cane* was the most significant work by a Negro up until Richard Wright's *Native Son*. Cullen's failure to produce great art is not reproachable. He just wasn't talented enough perhaps. Perhaps Langston Hughes is not talented enough, either. But there are the poems of his early books. "The Negro Speaks of Rivers" is a superb poem, and certainly there must be something else where that came from. And though he is never as good as a prose writer, *Not without Laughter*, his first novel, with all its faults, did have a certain poise and concern nowhere after so seriously approached. Some of the famous "Simple" pieces (started as a series of sketches for *The Chicago Defender*), at their best, contain a genuine humor; but most of them are crushed into mere half-cynical yelping (through a simulated laughter) at the almost mystical white oppressors. At any rate, Hughes has not lived up to his credo. Or perhaps the fault is that he has only lived up to a part of it. "To express our individual dark-skinned selves." Certainly, that is not the final stance of an artist. A writer must be concerned with more than just the color of his skin. Jesse B. Simple, colored man, has to live up to both sides of that title, the noun as well as the adjective.

Since this is a review of a particular book rather than a tract on the responsibilities of the Negro artist, as it must seem I have made it, I must mention the book, *Tambourines to Glory*. There's not much I can say about the book itself. Probably, if a book of similar literary worth were to be written by another author it would not be reviewed (probably, it would have never gotten published). But the Negro writer (especially Hughes, since he is so well known as such) raises certain peculiar questions that are not in the least "literary." I have tried to answer some of them. But the book is meaningless, awkward, and never gets past its horribly inept plot. In fact, were it not for, say, the frequent introduction of new characters within the book, it would be almost impossible to distinguish the novel, itself from the blurb summary on the jacket. "Laura Reed and Essie Belle Johnson, two attractive Harlem tenement women with time on their hands and no jobs, decide to start their own gospel church on a street corner. Laura wishes to make money. Essie honestly desires to help people." The characterizations don't get much past that.

Even as a folklorist Hughes leaves much to be desired. His use of Harlem slang is strained and rarely precise. When a Harlem con man "Big-Eye Buddy" is trying to make little Marietta (from the South), he says hiply . . . "Men don't start asking a sharp little chick like you what school you're in." "Sharp?" Marietta replies incredulously. Buddy says, "Stacked, solid, neat-all-reet, copasetic, baby!" It reeks of the Cab Calloway—Cotton Club—zoot suit era. No self-respecting young Harlemite hipster would be caught dead using such passé, "uncool" language today. As they say, "Man, that stuff went out with pegs." At least a folk artist ought to get the tradition of the folk straight.

But there are so many other faults in the very structure and technical aspect of the novel, as to make faults in the writer's own peculiar stylistic device superflous. None of the basic "novelistic devices" are used correctly. Any advance in the plot is merely stated, never worked into the general texture of the novel. By mentioning the landmarks of Harlem and its prominent persons, occasionally, and by having his characters use a "Negro" dialect to mouth continually old stock phrases of Negro dissatisfaction with white America, Hughes apparently hoped to at least create a little atmosphere and make a good folk yarn out of it. But he doesn't even succeed in doing that this time.

It's like a jazz musician who knows that if you play certain minor chords it sounds kind of bluesy, so he plays them over and over again; year in, year out. A kind of tired "instant funk." Certainly this kind of thing doesn't have anything much to do with jazz; just as Hughes's present novel doesn't really have anything to do with either literature *per se*, or, in its imperfect and shallow rendering, the folk tradition he has gotten so famous for interpreting.

Source: Le Roi Jones, "*Tambourines to Glory*," in *The Jazz Review*, Vol. 2, June 1959, pp. 33–34.

Sources

Bontemps, Arna, "How the Money Rolled In!" in *New York Herald Tribune Books*, December 7, 1958, p. 4.

Clarke, Marion Turner, "Selected New Books in Review: Fiction of Harlem, Ireland, Maine," in *Baltimore Evening Sun*, November 21, 1958, p. 28.

Gehman, Richard, "Free, Free Enterprise," in *Saturday Review*, Vol. 41, No. 47, November 22, 1958, p. 19.

Hughes, Langston, "Goodbye Christ," in *The Collected Poems of Langston Hughes*, edited by Arnold Rampersad, Knopf, pp. 166–67; originally published in *Negro Worker*, November–December 1932, p. 32.

———, *Tambourines to Glory*, in *The Collected Works of Langston Hughes: The Novels*, Vol. 4, edited by Dolan Hubbard, University of Missouri Press, 2001, pp. 211-325.

Jones, LeRoi, Review of *Tambourines to Glory*, in *Jazz Review*, Vol. 2, June 1959, p. 34.

Millstein, Gilbert, Review of *Tambourines to Glory*, in *Langston Hughes: Critical Perspectives Past and Present*, edited by Henry Louis Gates Jr. and K. A. Appiah, Amistad Press, 1993, p. 39; originally published in the *New York Times Book Review*, November 23, 1958, p. 51.

Sullivan, Marty, "'Folk Tale' of Harlem is Praised," in *Fort Wayne News Sentinel*, November 22, 1958, p. 4.

Williams, Roland L., Jr., "Respecting the Folk," in *Journal of Modern Literature*, Vol. 24, Nos. 3–4. Summer 2001, p. 534.

Further Reading

Emanuel, James, *Langston Hughes*, Twayne, 1967.
   The first book-length study of Hughes and his work, this volume offers a solid introduction to the writer's major themes, although it focuses on the poetry more than on the prose and mentions *Tambourines to Glory* only in passing. It includes a chronology of important dates and an annotated bibliography.

Hughes, Langston, and Milton Meltzer, *A Pictorial History of the Negro in America*, Crown, 1956.
   Hughes wrote the text to accompany an extensive collection of photographs, cartoons, graphic art, and other illustrations accumulated by Meltzer. The book is arranged chronologically, beginning with the slave trade, and includes several illustrations from Harlem and the Harlem Renaissance.

Miller, R. Baxter, *Langston Hughes and Gwendolyn Brooks: A Reference Guide*, G. K. Hall, 1978.
   The half of this book concerning Hughes includes a critical overview that covers responses to all of Hughes's writings, as well as a comprehensive annotated listing of major reviews and criticism published between 1924 and 1977.

Ostrom, Hans, *A Langston Hughes Encyclopedia*, Greenwood Press, 2002.
   Ostrom explains that each entry in this alphabetically arranged work is intended for a general reader with no particular knowledge about Hughes or the times in which he lived. Included are entries for individual works, as well as for broader topics such as "Harlem" and "religion."

Rampersad, Arnold, *The Life of Langston Hughes*, 2 vols., Oxford University Press, 1986–1988.
   This sweeping and thorough two-volume work is the definitive biography of Langston Hughes. It is also an insightful look at the first three-quarters of the twentieth century. Hughes's fascination with music is a thread that carries through the biography. Hughes's working and re-working the material that became *Tambourines to Glory* in both novel and play forms is detailed in the second volume.

The Violent Bear It Away

Flannery O'Connor

1960

The Violent Bear It Away, published in New York in 1960, is Flannery O'Connor's darkly humorous Gothic novel about a Southern boy's spiritual awakening. It charts the spiritual and physical journey of fourteen-year-old Francis Marion Tarwater, raised by his great-uncle in the backwoods of Alabama to be a prophet. Tarwater travels to the city, where he struggles against the need to deny his spiritual inheritance and the call of God. O'Connor paints a macabre picture of Southern life and religious fundamentalism and parodies the blind self-assurances of modern secular thinking. The novel is unsettling because it offers no easy truths; its hero is an unlikable boy who learns that doing God's work entails violence, unreason, even madness. It is not, as might be expected, a parody of religious fanaticism, but a psychological study of the mysterious, frightening, and sometimes offensive nature of the religious calling. Stark religious symbolism and Biblical allusions unite to explore themes of spiritual hunger, faith versus reason, and the battle for the soul. O'Connor wrote the novel over eight years while suffering from lupus, publishing the first chapter as a story, "You Can't Be Poorer Than Dead," in 1955. Her last major work to be published in her lifetime, *The Violent Bear It Away* contains elements found in much of O'Connor's fiction. Her only other novel, *Wise Blood* (1952), fuses humor and horror to examine questions of faith, suffering, family relationships, and intellectual versus religious understanding. The novel was not particularly well received when it

first appeared; many critics found it strange and impenetrable. But, to some extent because of O'Connor's reputation as a master of the short story, the novel is now considered an important work in the Gothic tradition and acknowledged to be O'Connor's best work of longer fiction.

Author Biography

Mary Flannery O'Connor was born in 1925 in Savannah, Georgia, the only child of a middle-class Catholic family. Her father was a realtor who had once had literary ambitions, and her mother came from a prominent Georgia political family. From an early age O'Connor, a shy and quiet girl, had literary aspirations, which were encouraged by her father; at the age of six she began writing and illustrating her own stories. In 1938, the O'Connor family moved to Milledgeville, her mother's hometown, after her father showed symptoms of lupus. O'Connor attended Peabody High School, where she contributed drawings and articles to the school newspaper and submitted short stories to literary journals.

In 1940 O'Connor's father died, and she and her mother moved to her mother's family farm, Andalusia. After graduating in 1945 from the Georgia State College for Women (now Georgia College), where she edited the college newspaper and literary magazine, O'Connor enrolled in the Writer's Workshop at the University of Iowa. At Iowa, she was mentored by Paul Engle, the director of the program, and made other important literary contacts.

Her first short story, "The Geranium," was published in 1946. In 1947, O'Connor received her master of fine arts degree and won the Rinehart-Iowa Fiction Award, which consisted of a cash prize and an option on her first novel by the publisher Rinehart. For one semester she worked as a teaching assistant while she worked on that novel, *Wise Blood*. The following year, she lived for seven months at an artists' colony in Saratoga Springs, New York, where she met the poet Robert Lowell, the critic Alfred Kazin, and others from New York literary circles.

In March of 1949 she moved to New York City. Six months later she moved to Connecticut, where she stayed at the farmhouse of Robert and Sally Fitzgerald, a couple she met in New York. At the end of 1950, after exhibiting symptoms of lupus, O'Connor moved back to Andalusia. *Wise Blood* was published two years later to largely negative re-

views, but O'Connor immediately set to work on her second novel, *The Violent Bear It Away*. She continued to write short stories, for which she won three O. Henry Awards. Her health continued to decline, and after 1955 O'Connor began to use crutches. Still, she continued to travel, lecture, and write, supporting herself with literary grants.

A committed Catholic her whole life, O'Connor even traveled to Rome for an audience with the Pope in 1958. By the end of the 1950s, largely on the strength of her short stories, O'Connor was viewed as a major American writer. In 1960, *The Violent Bear It Away* was published, but it, too, was poorly received. For the last few years of her life, as her lupus progressed, O'Connor concentrated on writing nonfiction. She died on August 3, 1964 at her mother's home in Milledgeville. In 1972, she was posthumously awarded the National Book Award for *The Complete Short Stories*.

Plot Summary

Overview

The main action of *The Violent Bear It Away* is simple and occurs over seven days, but much of the novel consists of flashbacks that recall incidents in the lives of the main characters. As events are brought to mind through the memories of various individuals, the author provides insight into their psychological and spiritual natures, reveals the motivations behind their actions, and offers an intimate family history clouded by personal feelings, religious and intellectual beliefs, and emotional confusion. The novel is divided into three sections, each covering a period in Francis Marion Tarwater's journey of spiritual self-discovery.

Chapters 1–3

The novel opens with the burial of Mason Tarwater, young Francis Marion Tarwater's great-uncle, at his farm in rural Powderhead, Alabama. Although Tarwater will not learn this until the end of the novel, it is explained that Buford Munson, who has come to get his jug filled from old Tarwater's still, has buried the old man in the proper Christian way because the nephew is passed out drunk. A history of this family is woven into the events that are taking place, but incidents are not described in order of their occurrence. What emerges is that old Tarwater considered himself a prophet. His religious teaching was that of a Christian fundamentalist who despised the trappings of

Media Adaptations

- *Comforts of Home*, a Web site dedicated to Flannery O'Connor, can be found at http://www.mediaspecialist.org/index.html (accessed November 24, 2004). This site has links to biographical information about the author and critical analyses of her work.

- *A Student's Guide to Flannery O'Connor*, http://www.geocities.com/Athens/Troy/2188 (accessed November 24, 2004), reviews O'Connor's short stories, presents theme paper topics, and has available for order every book written by or about the author.

- The Flannery O'Connor–Andalusia Foundation, Inc. maintains a Web site http://www.andalusia farm.org/ (accessed November 24, 2004) with information about the activities taking place at the Andalusia property where O'Connor lived and worked.

secular modernity; he followed an ancient religious and moral code, and, like an Old Testament prophet, saw himself as a voice crying out in the wilderness. He was committed to a psychiatric hospital for four years, after which he stole his nephew, Rayber, from his parents. Rayber eventually rejected his uncle's teachings, became a schoolteacher, and married Bernice Bishop, a social worker. Rayber's pregnant cousin died in a car accident before she gave birth to Francis Marion, who Rayber took to raise.

After being released from the asylum, Mason lived with Rayber for a few months. Rayber studied him and wrote an article about him in a "schoolteacher magazine," describing him as an all-but-extinct specimen—a religious fanatic. Outraged, Mason kidnapped Francis Marion from Rayber and raised him in the woods to be a prophet as well. Rayber and his wife attempted to retrieve young Tarwater from Powderhead, but gave up after the old man shot Rayber twice, rendering him almost completely deaf (he uses a mechanical hearing device). After this incident, old Tarwater promised Rayber: "THE PROPHET I RAISE UP

OUT OF THIS BOY WILL BURN YOUR EYES CLEAN." Rayber and his wife had a mentally disabled child, Bishop, whom Rayber has taken care of on his own after his wife left him. Mason tried and failed to kidnap Bishop, and Rayber refused to let the old man baptize Bishop, so the old man ordered Francis Marion to finish the job. He also instructed young Tarwater to bury him in the proper Christian way in anticipation of the Second Coming.

Tarwater is skeptical of his great-uncle's teaching, rejecting the idea that he too is a prophet. As Tarwater had set about burying his great-uncle's body, he was visited by an inner voice, that of a "stranger" who later becomes a "friend"—and who represents the devil—who counseled him that he need not do the old man's bidding, that perhaps the old man had not taught him the truth. Young Tarwater passes out drunk, but that night he returns to Powderhead and sets fire to the house, believing he is also burning his great-uncle's body and thus denying him his chance for Resurrection. Tarwater leaves for the city in search of Rayber, believing he has rebelled against his great-uncle's wishes. He gets a ride into the city with an opportunistic copper-flue salesman named Meeks, who suggests to Tarwater that his great-uncle may have misled him. Meeks is another incarnation of the devil as he tempts Tarwater. When he arrives at his uncle's house, Tarwater is repulsed by the sight of the young disabled boy Bishop; Tarwater realizes that he has come to baptize Bishop after all. Rayber sees Tarwater's arrival as an opportunity to undo his uncle's false indoctrination and educate the boy in the proper way, to develop him into a "useful man."

Chapters 4–9

Rayber's enthusiasm to "save" the boy soon dissipates, as he finds Tarwater sullen, angry, and difficult. Tarwater does not hide his skepticism of the schoolteacher, whose rationalist arguments echo very much those of Tarwater's own inner voice—the voice of his friend, the devil. Rayber buys the boy new clothes, which Tarwater rejects, and gives him food that he does not eat, despite a deep hunger. Rayber asks his nephew to take some standardized tests, his ultimate goal being to ferret out the center of the boy's "emotional infection," but Tarwater refuses. Rayber continually tries to psychoanalyze the boy, attributing his behavior to his upbringing and thinking of ways to fix his problems. Rayber also wants to give Tarwater what he is unable to give his own son because of his disability. Throughout the section, it is shown how Rayber struggles with his love for Bishop.

One night, Tarwater steals out of the house to attend a religious gathering he has seen advertised. Rayber follows him through the city to the revival meeting, where a young girl named Lucette preaches about Christ's coming and asks the audience for money so her parents can continue their missionary work. As he hides outside in the bushes and listens to Lucette, Rayber recalls his own dysfunctional childhood. At the end of the meeting Lucette stares at Rayber and speaks about the man whose ear is "deaf to the Holy Word." Rayber tries to switch off his mechanical hearing device but cannot, and he flees and waits outside for Tarwater. The boy claims that he attended the service only "to spit on it."

Rayber decides to take Tarwater to a natural history museum to teach him about evolution and science. As they walk through a park to the museum, Rayber stops to tie Bishop's laces and is suddenly gripped with an uncontrollable love for the boy. He remembers an incident in which he tried to drown his son but could not, changing his mind at the last moment because he could not imagine life without the boy. The three of them continue walking, and they come to a fountain, which Bishop tries to jumps in. Tarwater moves to baptize him, but Rayber snatches the boy away at the last moment, realizing what his nephew is trying to do.

Frustrated by his inability to cure Tarwater, Rayber decides to take him back to Powderhead so he can shock him into facing his past and thus get through to him. He tells Tarwater they are going on a fishing trip, and they check in at the Cherokee Lodge, which is near a lake. Tarwater, who had eaten little in the city, has a huge meal at the lodge. He also shows some unexpected kindness to Bishop by tying his shoe. During the stay at the lodge, Tarwater's "friend" visits him repeatedly, and Tarwater recognizes that this voice's demand for a sign from God is what has kept Tarwater from baptizing Bishop. Tarwater tells his friend that he would have drowned Bishop in the fountain rather than baptize him, and his friend approves of such an action, saying he should do it to prove that he was not going to baptize the boy. Later Rayber takes Tarwater fishing and tells him how he tried to drown Bishop and also tells Tarwater that he wants to save him. Tarwater, after his heavy meal, vomits into the lake, leaves the boat, and swims to shore.

Rayber takes a trip to Powderhead with Bishop, and when he returns he offers to let Tarwater baptize Bishop so he can overcome his internal conflict. Tarwater is horrified by the offer, but that afternoon he takes Bishop out in a rowboat. From his room, Rayber hears Bishop's wail. He knows that Tarwater is drowning his son, but he does nothing to stop him.

Chapters 10–12

Tarwater hitchhikes back to Powderhead with a trucker, whom he tells he has drowned Bishop and thus proven he is not a prophet. He admits, though, that he also baptized him by accident. The truck driver gives Tarwater a sandwich that he is unable to eat and drops Tarwater a few miles from Powderhead. There, Tarwater tries unsuccessfully to get a drink from one of his neighbors, who chides him for what he has done to his great-uncle's house. He is then picked up by a stranger, a man in a lavender shirt and Panama hat who drives a lavender and cream-colored car. Tarwater accepts alcohol and marijuana from the man and passes out. He awakens naked, his hands tied with a lavender handkerchief. He sets fire to the forest, then takes the road to Powderhead. At the farm, Buford Munson tells him that he buried the old man with a cross over him. Tarwater has a vision of a multitude being fed from a single basket of loaves and fishes, and he has a great hunger. He stays there until night, his hunger growing as flames from the forest fire encircle him. He throws himself on his great-uncle's grave and smears a handful of dirt from it on his forehead. Then, Tarwater returns to the highway, the burning woods behind him, and travels back to the city to preach the Word to the children of God.

Characters

Bernice Bishop

Referred to by Mason Tarwater and his great-nephew Francis Marion Tarwater as "the welfare woman," Bernice Bishop is mother to the mentally disabled boy, Bishop, and she is ex-wife to George Rayber. Bernice Bishop appears only in the past, in the novel's many flashbacks. It is learned in one of these flashbacks that Rayber attempted to "rescue" the young Tarwater from his uncle, that his wife accompanied him, and that she was repulsed by the boy's expressionless response to his great-uncle's violence; she declared that she could not live with him. Although Bernice is trained as a social worker, Bernice Bishop left Rayber after the birth of their "dim-witted" son in part because the son reminded her of her husband's uncle, Mason Tarwater. Rayber also recalls that Bernice has returned only once in the past two years, and only to ask that her son be institutionalized.

Lucette Carmody

Lucette is the young girl of eleven or twelve at the Christian revival meeting who preaches the love of Jesus and the Second Coming. She sees George Rayber hiding outside the window and calls him a "damned soul" and echoes old Tarwater's words when she says to him, "The Word of God is a burning Word to burn you clean." Rayber believes she is exploited by adults, and her exploitation makes him recall his own childhood.

Meeks

Meeks is the copper flue salesman with whom young Tarwater catches a ride into the city after he has set fire to his great-uncle Tarwater's house. Meeks is described as a "stranger" and "friend"— one indication that he is among the several incarnations of the devil that the boy encounters (and one of the three that drive him). The salesman is driven by his love of money, but he claims he loves the people to whom he sells. His discussions about love and technology suggest that his views parody those of George Rayber. Meeks hopes to take advantage of Tarwater's backwoods innocence for his own profit.

Buford Munson

The first sentence of the novel introduces "a Negro named Buford Munson," who buries the elder Tarwater because the old man's great nephew Francis Marion is too drunk to finish the job. On his return to Powderhead at the end of the novel, the young Tarwater finds out from Munson that the old man has indeed been buried with a cross over him in anticipation of the Resurrection.

Luella Munson

Buford Munson's daughter, who, Francis Marion Tarwater learns, took care of George Rayber while Rayber's mother, Mason Tarwater's sister, "sat in her nightgown all day drinking whiskey out of a medicine bottle."

Bishop Rayber

Bishop, the mentally disabled and dumb son of the schoolteacher, George Rayber, and of Bernice Bishop, is innocent, uninhibited, and largely unaware of what goes on around him. It is not his actions, but rather others' reactions to him, throughout the novel that are of most interest. His great-uncle Mason Tarwater had tried to kidnap and baptize Bishop as an infant, but his father rescued him and will not, on principle, allow his son to go through what he thinks as the meaningless ritual of baptism. Bishop's mother leaves him in the care of his father. Bishop's father struggles with his love for the boy, and at one point had tried to drown him but found he could not do it. Francis Marion Tarwater, the protagonist of the novel and the boy's cousin, takes it as his mission to baptize Bishop. Bishop is attracted to water throughout the novel; at the end of the novel he is baptized, then drowned, by the younger Tarwater.

George Rayber

Referred to as "the schoolteacher" by his uncle, Mason Tarwater, and his great-nephew, Francis Marion Tarwater, George Rayber is the symbol in the novel of earthly knowledge, of rationalist belief that conflicts directly and violently with the Tarwaters' spiritual understanding. According to Mason Tarwater, Rayber's mother (Tarwater's sister) was a whore who spent her time reading and drinking whiskey, neglecting her son entirely. His insurance salesman father was absent much of the time. When he was seven, Rayber was kidnapped by Tarwater and baptized. When his parents came to reclaim him four days later, Rayber did not want to leave. But Rayber later rejects his uncle's teaching, returning when he is fourteen to tell the old man he no longer believes. Some ten years later, Rayber's cousin dies in a car crash just before giving birth to a son, Francis Marion Tarwater, and Rayber takes the boy to raise him. Rayber's uncle, newly released from a mental asylum, comes to live with him shortly thereafter, and Rayber studies him and writes a story about him in a "schoolteacher magazine." Mason Tarwater, infuriated, kidnaps the baby and leaves Rayber with the warning: "THE PROPHET I RAISE OUT OF THIS BOY WILL BURN YOUR EYES CLEAN." Rayber and his wife attempt to rescue young Tarwater, but give up after Mason shoots Rayber twice, leaving him deaf in one ear and suffering a permanent limp. Rayber has a young son, the "idiot child" Bishop.

Rayber is in charge of his school's testing program, and he subscribes to modern rationalist and psychological theories that he believes can measure and evaluate human desires and motivations; he rejects the spiritual but is continually drawn by it. Logic tells him his dim-witted son is of no use to him or anyone else, but he feels an uncontrollable love for the boy. This is one of the reasons Rayber failed in his attempt to drown his son. Rayber wears thick glasses and uses an electric hearing aid that he can turn on and off—physical signs that he is the modern rationalist who has eyes but sees not and who has ears but hears not. Rayber represents not only the typical modern man but also the Pharisee and the devil, as he makes it his mission to convince Francis Marion Tarwater that he has been indoctrinated into false religious beliefs and tries to give him a proper, non-religious education.

The Stranger/The Friend

Throughout the novel, Francis Marion Tarwater is counseled by an "inner voice" of a stranger or friend who aims to steer him off the path of righteousness. This is the voice of the devil, who is also transformed physically into the man who rapes him at the end of the novel—the man in the lavender shirt and Panama hat who drives a lavender and cream-colored car.

Francis Marion Tarwater

Francis Marion Tarwater, usually referred to simply as "Tarwater," is the protagonist of the novel whose journey to the city to baptize his cousin constitutes the novel's central action. He is a dour, often silent teenager, but a sense of violence lurks beneath his expressionless surface. Tarwater was born in a car wreck in which both his parents died. He was taken to be raised by his uncle, the schoolteacher George Rayber, but his great-uncle Mason Tarwater, a self-proclaimed prophet, stole him. Mason raised his great-nephew in the isolation of Powderhead, a clearing deep inside the woods in Alabama, with the idea of his great-nephew being a prophet as well. Before Mason Tarwater dies, he instructs his great-nephew to give him a proper Christian burial and tells him that his mission is to baptize his cousin, the mentally defective boy Bishop. But an inner voice of a "stranger"—later a "friend"—counsels Tarwater to reject this duty. Instead, Tarwater burns down his great-uncle's house and leaves for the city.

In the city, Tarwater struggles against the impulse to perform the baptism his great-uncle has ordered. He also resists the psychological-rationalist teachings of his uncle, Rayber, and finds himself repulsed by and drawn to Bishop. Tarwater slowly recognizes that he has come to baptize the boy after all. But he continues to listen to the counsel of his "friend," who tries to talk him out of his mission. This is the voice of the devil, and throughout the novel Tarwater wrestles against his temptations. In the end, Tarwater drowns Bishop but, just before he does so, he baptizes the boy. Tarwater flees to Powderhead, where he has a vision, then returns to the city to fulfill his mission as a prophet of God.

Tarwater is complex and hard to define, mirroring the complexity of the novel's theme and handling. The name "Tarwater" links two disparate elements, one black and impenetrable, one cleansing. The boy is at once a prophet from the wilderness and a confused backwoods boy who is spiritually hungry (the constant references in the book to his physical hunger underscore this). He appears naive, but his rejection of the modern world and its trappings is clear and articulate. He attempts to reject his uncle's spiritual legacy, but he cannot. He struggles between doing the devil's work and God's, finding that the latter's teaching is fraught with violence and unreason. He is violent, and a great deal of violence is done to him—he sets fire to a house, he murders a boy, he is raped. He is the prophet Elisha who succeeds his great-uncle, a latter-day Elijah; he is St. Christopher as he baptizes, then drowns, his cousin; he is John the Baptist come to show the way. At the end of the novel he unwittingly performs the action that confirms his status as a prophet, and he finally accepts his role as a messenger of God.

Mason Tarwater

Mason Tarwater, the "old man" who reckons himself a prophet, is the great-uncle of, and spiritual guide to, Francis Marion Tarwater, the novel's protagonist. Mason charges his great-nephew Tarwater with the task of baptizing his cousin, the idiot boy Bishop. The novel opens with Mason Tarwater's death. It is soon learned in a series of flashbacks how the old man kidnapped his great-nephew Tarwater from his nephew, the schoolteacher George Rayber, and raised Tarwater to be a prophet and continue his work. The young Tarwater also recalls how the old man had been committed to an insane asylum for four years by his sister. After returning from the asylum, Mason stayed with his nephew, Rayber. But it turned out that Rayber was studying Mason to write an article about him in a "schoolteacher's magazine," characterizing him as a fanatic, a specimen of a breed "now all but extinct." Infuriated, old Tarwater, who had also kidnapped Rayber when he was young and baptized him, stole Francis Marion to raise him as a prophet to "burn [Rayber's] eyes clean." When Rayber attempted to rescue the boy, the old man shot him, impairing Rayber's hearing and leaving him with a limp.

Mason Tarwater, for all his crazy ways, is God's representative in the novel and one of the two forces that wrestle for Francis Marion Tarwater's soul. Francis Marion struggles against his great-uncle's teachings but cannot reject them. Old Tarwater is repeatedly contrasted to Rayber, who represents the devil, as Mason rejects modernity and rationalism, embraces fundamentalist religious principles, and believes in actions over words. Old Tarwater, it is recounted, viewed himself as the prophet Elijah and his great-nephew as his successor, Elisha. He shielded the boy from what he viewed as the evil influences of the city—modern life, and secular, rationalist thinking. He has little time for those who do not heed the word, labeling most people "asses or whores." Young Tarwater remembers the old man disappearing into the woods for days on end and on his return looked "as if he had been wrestling a wild cat, as if his head were still full of the visions he had seen in his eyes. . . ." Mason is an authentic prophet of the wilderness who recognizes the violence and unreason inherent in any truly spiritual understanding and undertaking.

The Truck Driver

One of the three drivers in the novel that represent the devil, the truck driver gives Francis Marion a ride back to Powderhead after he has murdered the boy Bishop. The truck driver is indifferent and needs someone to talk to so he does not fall asleep at the wheel. His indifference echoes that of George Rayber, the novel's main representative of the devil.

Themes

Religion and Violence

The title of the novel is taken from Matthew 11:12. At the beginning of Matthew 11, Jesus preaches to the multitudes about the prophet John the Baptist, who he says will not wear "soft robes" or preach a gentle message. Christ then says, in the verse that provides the novel's epigraph: "From the days of John the Baptist until now, the kingdom of heaven suffereth violence, and the violent bear it away." There have been two interpretations of the verse. The first says that, since the time of John the Baptist and Christ's ministry, the kingdom of heaven has been advancing forcefully, and the "violent," meaning the eager, ardent multitudes of godly men, will take it by force—displaying their strength through action. The implication is that the faithful will one day attain the kingdom of heaven. Another interpretation is that unbelievers, such as Pharisees (the "violent" in this case) try to undermine the work done by Christ and John the Baptist, doing violence to the kingdom of God in

this way. In the novel, both of these interpretations are explored, and the conflict surrounds the attitudes of the believer and the skeptic, the faithful and the godless, as they battle for young Francis Marion Tarwater's soul.

There are numerous instances of violence throughout the novel: kidnappings, a shooting, a drowning, arson, and a rape. Violence is never glorified, but it is used to shock readers into understanding the seriousness of the religious subjects being explored. The drowning of Bishop, for example, draws into relief the intense nature of baptism that for many has become something of a trivial rite. The rape of Tarwater by the stranger underscores in a brutal way the violation of his soul by the devil. O'Connor uses violence repeatedly in her novel to emphasize that religion is not soft or pretty, that God's will is sometimes frightening, and that ordinary human moral standards cannot be applied when it comes to understanding God and his ways.

The Battle for the Soul

The Violent Bear It Away is a novel about psychomachia, or the struggle between good and evil, spirit and flesh, God and the devil within the human soul. Young Tarwater has been reared by his great-uncle (who represents God) to be a prophet, but he listens to an inner voice (that of the devil), and chooses to deny his spiritual inheritance. He is thence tortured by doubt, indecision, and the continuous and confounding pull of his religious calling. This internal battle is played out especially vividly in his perplexing, uncontrollable desire to baptize his cousin Bishop. The devil in the form of his inner voice, as well as three drivers—the salesman Meeks, the truck driver, and the stranger who gives him a ride in his lavender car—and his uncle George Rayber, also repeatedly tempt Tarwater away from his faith. Tarwater is shown struggling against their worldly views. In the end, Tarwater succumbs to his religious calling, and it is less a victory than a capitulation when he embraces his role as a prophet of God. Another battle for the soul is waged between the Tarwaters and Rayber; the Tarwaters want to baptize Rayber's retarded son Bishop and Rayber tries to prevent them from doing so.

Spiritual Hunger

Central to the novel is the question of spiritual hunger and the idea that, ultimately, only God can satisfy the longing that torments the human soul. Throughout the novel, young Tarwater has a profound, gnawing hunger that cannot be appeased. His great-uncle has taught him that Christ is the

Topics For Further Study

- Do you think that Francis Tarwater is a true prophet, a madman, or something else? How do you think people can recognize when someone is a true prophet, if there is such a thing? Research the life of one of the biblical prophets mentioned in the novel (Moses, Elijah, Elisha, John the Baptist) and write a short essay about him. Do you see any parallels in the life of your chosen prophet and the life of Tarwater?

- Research the Christian rite of baptism. What is the symbol of the rite, according to the Catholic Church? Is there any variation among the other sects of Christianity, such as Methodism or Lutheranism? What do you think O'Connor does when she uses drowning as a symbol for baptism in her novel? Write a short essay in which you discuss O'Connor's understanding and treatment of baptism in the novel.

- Who do you find to be a more sympathetic character: Francis Tarwater or George Rayber? Why? Who do you think would be more sympathetic to most modern-day readers? Create a dramatic debate between the two characters in which each presents his point of view. Whose do you think is more compelling? Does your audience agree?

- Look for stories in the newspaper about religious believers who commit violent acts in the name of their faith. How are these people portrayed by the media? Is there an assumption of their insanity? Do you think there is any justification for what they have done?

Bread of Life, but he continually resists this truth and his spiritual calling, yet does not understand the emptiness he feels. Tarwater cannot eat the foreign food his uncle offers him, and craves for the food his great-uncle used to prepare. On his way to the revival meeting, Tarwater stops by a bakery and stares longingly at a single loaf of bread, which emphasizes the spiritual nature of his hunger. At the Cherokee Lodge, Tarwater overeats and vomits into the lake. After he kills Bishop and travels back to Powderhead, he cannot eat the sandwich given to him by the trucker, complaining that his stomach does not allow anything inside it. The idea of Christ as the Bread of Life and recurring images of loaves and fishes serve to deepen this theme. At the end of the novel, Tarwater has a vision of a multitude—his great-uncle among its number—being fed loaves and fishes by Christ from a single basket. It is only then that he becomes aware of the object of his hunger and realizes that "nothing on earth would fill him."

The Spiritual Journey

The obvious subject of *The Violent Bear It Away* is Francis Tarwater's passage to self-realization and his spiritual awakening. Images of roads, paths, cars, boats, and travel figure prominently in the novel to underscore this important theme. In each of the three parts of the book, Tarwater travels, first from Powderhead to the city, then within the city (to a revival meeting, to a museum) and to the Cherokee Lodge, and finally back to Powderhead. He has various guides along his journey: his great-uncle, who tries to lead him down the difficult path to redemption; Rayber, who wants life's journey to be predictable and devoid of feeling; and other incarnations of the devil who try to steer him away from his goal and off the path of righteousness. It is significant that Tarwater is born in a car wreck, that three of the incarnations of the devil that tempt him are drivers, and that in the end it is his own shadow in the moonlight that "clears a rough path toward his goal." The journey to God, it is seen, is no easy one. O'Connor's exploration of this theme presents her unique, grotesque vision of the beauty and terror of the divine.

Faith versus Reason

As Francis Tarwater struggles to come to terms with his faith, he is tempted by the devil in the guise of his uncle, the schoolteacher George Rayber. Rayber is a secular humanist who scoffs at the fa-

natical faith of his uncle Mason Tarwater and believes that reason is the only true guide as humans
learn how to live. In his published study of his uncle in the "schoolteacher magazine," Rayber argued
that the old man had imagined the need to be
"called" out of a feeling of insecurity, so he "called
himself." Rayber believes too that a person's intelligence and emotional states can be measured
and the results can be used to better his or her life,
to "fix" or "save" it. Thus, he tries to convince his
nephew to take standardized tests, which the latter
refuses. Rayber also tries to convince Tarwater that
religion is superstition, while reason and science
have brought impressive human advancements,
such as flying. To this Tarwater replies, "I wouldn't
give you nothing for no airplane. A buzzard can
fly." Although Rayber thinks he can read his
nephew "like a book," he does not understand him
because he does not have the requisite tools or understanding to really see or hear what is going on
around him; cold logic and reason are inadequate
to make sense of the mystery of life. Because of
this, Rayber struggles against the love he has for
his disabled son; he cannot make sense of it using
logic, and it overwhelms him and renders him helpless. Rayber had, at Tarwater's present age of fourteen, rejected the spiritual life and chosen the way
of reason. The novel shows how Tarwater makes
his own choice about what path he is to follow.

Style

Southern Gothic

The Violent Bear It Away is an example of
Southern Gothic, a style of writing that is characterized by its setting in the American South and its
grotesque, macabre, or fantastic incidents. Southern Gothic literature explores and critiques Southern culture by focusing on the supernatural, and
describing people who are spiritually or physically
deformed but still portrayed with empathy, their humanity as well their limitations spelled out in
often violent terms. O'Connor's characters in *The
Violent Bear It Away* are near-caricatures, and dam-
aged in some way, but their essential humanity
makes the reader care about their plight. The protagonist Tarwater is a sullen, angry boy, emotionally wounded and a "backwoods imbecile" as his
uncle, Rayber, calls him. But O'Connor makes the
reader care about his journey to self-realization.
Other characters' deformities are more obvious:
Bishop is mentally defective, Rayber is lame and

uses a hearing aid, and old Mason Tarwater is
"crazy." They are grotesque, but their defects are
described with a blend of humor and horror so they
are more than mere types. It is through the lens of
their distorted visions that the author presents her
own darkly ironic understanding of God, faith, and
freedom. Within the genre of Southern Gothic,
O'Connor uses her unique satirical voice in *The Violent Bear It Away* to create a disquieting and
morally complex story about the funny and tragic
nature of religious fanaticism and the place of spirituality in the modern world.

Religious Imagery and Symbolism

The Violent Bear It Away is a deeply religious
novel, one that offers up a dark and disturbing portrait of spiritual states, faith, and Christian fanaticism. Religious symbolism permeates the work, and
everywhere there are Biblical allusions and references. The dominant images in the novel—water,
fire, loaves and fishes, and eyes—are all religious in
nature. They emerge organically from the story but
are also interconnected and woven together, taking
on multiple forms to enrich the religious questions
and concerns. Throughout the novel, fire and water
are purifying forces that serve also to destroy. The
book, of course, is about baptism; both Tarwater and
Bishop are drawn to water; and the turning point of
the action is Bishop's drowning. Tarwater also believes that if he is sent on a mission from God it
would be to do more than to baptize an idiot boy,
thinking about how Moses struck water from a rock.
The two events that signify Tarwater's spiritual denial, and then rebirth, involve fire—at the beginning
he sets his great-uncle's house ablaze, and at the end
he sets fire to the forest before assuming the mantle
of a prophet. Early on in the novel, Tarwater mistakes the lights of the city for fire. The fire of pu-
rification is also used to describe old Tarwater, who
"learned by fire," and who tells Rayber that his great-
nephew will "burn" the schoolteacher's eyes clean.
Tarwater also imagines that God will talk to him as
he did to Moses, from a burning bush, which does
happen in his final vision. It is significant, too, that
even the name Tarwater unites these central elements of fire and water.

The images of the loaves and fishes are related
to fire and water; loaves are baked over fire and
fish come from water. The fish might be viewed as
symbolic of the human soul (Christ is the "fisher
of men"), and only Christ, as the Bread of Life, can
satisfy the human soul. Old Tarwater is also described as having eyes that "looked like two fish
straining to get out of a net of red threads." Ray-

ber takes Tarwater to a natural history museum to show him how humans are descended from fish. And the drowning incident takes place on the fishing trip. Images of loaves include the bread in the bakery that Tarwater stares at longingly, and the sandwich given to him by the truck driver that he cannot eat, because his hunger is not physical but spiritual. At the end of the novel, Tarwater sees his great-uncle gathered with the multitude being fed loaves and fishes by Christ from a single basket.

There are descriptions and references throughout the novel to eyes, which reveal a great deal about people's characters and beliefs. Rayber wears glasses, mirroring his spiritual blindness; Tarwater's eyes at the end are "scorched," "singed"— purified; the stranger who rapes Tarwater has lavender eyes, signaling the fact that he is the devil (in ancient times snakes were said to hide under lavender bushes); and old Tarwater's eyes are referred to as "fish-colored," and Tarwater is deeply attracted by them. Again, images have religious overtones, are interconnected, and constantly reinforce ideas through repetition and as they are transformed. Other important images in the novel that are used are: roads or paths, which emphasize Tarwater's spiritual journey; hats and clothes, markers of holiness and identity; and earth, which symbolizes redemption and rebirth.

Historical Context

Two Americas: United States Culture in the 1950s

The 1950s were characterized by affluence in much of American society, as Americans put the hardships of the Second World War behind them and enjoyed unprecedented economic growth. As a whole, the nation did indeed flourish. Between 1945 and 1960, the U.S. Gross National Product grew by 250 percent, unemployment hovered around 5 percent or less, and inflation was low. Government spending stimulated growth through public funding of schools, veterans' benefits, welfare, interstate highways, and armaments for the Korean War. Families moved to suburbs, where they needed cars, which sparked a boom in the automobile industry and stimulated the construction of more roads. The increase in mobility contributed also to the rise of motels, fast-food restaurants, and gas stations.

Scientific and technological innovations such as the jet plane, the development of mass communications through radio and television, and the creation of consumer goods such as dishwashers and garbage disposals created a culture in which modernity, progress, consumption, and conformity were prized. Television programs fed Americans a diet of cookie-cutter idealizations of suburban life filled with racial and gender stereotypes. Popular culture depicted marriage and feminine domesticity as a primary goal for American women, and the education system reinforced this portrayal. This revival of domesticity as a social value was accompanied too by a revival of religion. Religious messages began to infiltrate popular culture, and religious leaders such as Billy Graham became celebrities. For many Americans—largely white, urban or suburban, educated, and middle-class— the decade was a golden age, as the economy boomed. Americans enjoyed social stability and new, exciting opportunities for success.

There were, however, a great many other Americans who struggled on the fringes of the economic boom during the 1950s, dispossessed by the very industrialization and expansion that was the backbone of the nation's success. As automation increased efficiency in production, big business flourished, until less than half a percent of American corporations controlled more than half of the nation's corporate wealth. Technology drastically cut the amount of work needed to successfully grow crops, and many small-scale farmers were forced to give up their land to rich companies who used chemicals and harvested crops with new machinery. Large numbers of black farmers, in particular, moved from the countryside to cities, and the number of inner-city ghettoes expanded rapidly. Some of the most destitute regions in the country were found in the rural South, where blacks continued to live in shantytowns and the decline of the coal industry eroded the only significant economic support many poor white communities had known. Rural areas often lacked adequate schools, health care, and services, and many people who lived there were almost entirely shut off from the mainstream of American economic life. The needs of these disadvantaged groups went largely unanswered, and their living conditions deteriorated rapidly.

This contradictory nature of American culture was explored in many works of literature of the decade. Saul Bellow produced a number of novels examining the difficulties of urban Jews finding fulfillment in modern urban America. J. D. Salinger's *The Catcher in the Rye* (1951) tells the story of a young boy who, despite his family's outward material success, feels completely alienated

Compare & Contrast

- **1950s:** Americans are enduring the cold war years, a military stalemate between two international superpowers, the U.S.S.R. and the United States. Both countries are secretly developing nuclear weapons programs, and many Americans fear a nuclear attack from communist adversaries.

  Today: The September 11, 2001 terrorist attacks on the World Trade Center and the Pentagon prompted America's global war on terror, preceding a U.S. war with Iraq. Americans live under the fear of terrorist attacks by those who oppose its policies, particularly terrorist cells in the Middle East.

- **1950s:** North Korea attempts to invade South Korea in June 1950. The United States responds by sending munitions and supplies to South Korea. Before the end of the month, the United States is engaged in a war with North Korea.

  Today: After defeating Saddam Hussein in a full-scale military attack, the United States continues to occupy Iraq. Battles ensue between Iraqi insurgents and U.S.-led forces over strategic cities. The state of the U.S.-led occupation, along with morality and faith, become major campaign issues in the November 2004 presidential election.

- **1950s:** Twenty-two percent of Americans live in poverty, most of them in newly created inner-city communities and in rural areas, as wealthier Americans move to the suburbs.

  Today: Eleven percent of Americans live in poverty, most of them in rural areas. The rate of poverty for minorities living in rural areas is especially high, and one of out four rural Hispanics, African Americans, and Native Americans lives below the poverty line.

- **1950s:** Television presents idealized portraits of suburban American life in such shows as *Father Knows Best* and *The Adventures of Ozzie and Harriet*. Rural life and inner-city life are rarely portrayed.

  Today: Television presents far more hard-edged depictions of American suburban life in *The Sopranos* and *The Osbournes*. Most television programs focus on urban and suburban people and situations, and there are few portrayals of rural life in major television programs.

- **1950s:** Radio and television popularize the new Protestant evangelical movement in Christianity, with preachers such as Billy Graham and Oral Roberts presenting their message to audiences using mass media in an outgrowth of revival-tent preaching. The vast majority of these religious leaders are from the South.

  Today: Television evangelists remain popular, particularly in the Midwest and the South. Two well-known and controversial evangelists, Pat Robertson and Jerry Falwell, have achieved particular notoriety for their assertion that the September 11, 2001 terrorist attacks in New York City constituted divine retribution for what they regard as rampant sexual immorality in American society.

- **1950s:** Fourteen percent of Americans live in rural areas. There is mass migration away from the rural South, as African Americans move to the North to escape racial oppression and find higher-paying jobs.

  Today: Seven percent of Americans live in rural areas. Over forty percent of this population lives in the rural South, where poverty, illiteracy, and poor health conditions continue to be widespread.

Illustration of the visions of the Old Testament prophet Ezekiel

from society. The African American writers Richard Wright, Ralph Ellison, and James Baldwin published works condemning racism and called into question the myth of the American Dream. The Beats, a group of nonconformists led by Allen Ginsberg, author of the poem *Howl* (1956), and Jack Kerouac, the author of *On the Road* (1957), rejected uniform middle-class culture, stressed the importance of intuition and feeling over reason, and sought to overturn the sexual and social conservatism of the period. They also fuelled protests against the death penalty, nuclear weaponry, and racial segregation. Although O'Connor's fiction is not concerned with the cultural trends of the 1950s, her work is firmly rooted in the American South of that time. She depicts a society that is at the margins of American society—that is shut off from the mainstream. Her works are populated not by successful, beautiful people with comfortable suburban lives, but by grotesques and misfits who are struggling against the horrors of modern life and clinging to the values and traditions of the past. Her protagonists rebel against modernism and the changes it brings. Like other writers of the decade, she exposes in her writings the fact that the economic success, technological advances, and cultural trends of the 1950s have had unsettling and alienating effects on American life.

Critical Overview

O'Connor's first novel, *Wise Blood*, received hostile reviews when it first appeared in 1952; most readers missed the dark humor and religious intent of the highly unconventional novel. By 1960, O'Connor had earned something of a reputation for her short stories. Critics were more forgiving in their remarks about *The Violent Bear It Away*. However, few reviews were outright favorable, and most readers expressed confusion at the author's intent and took exception to the seeming anti-Catholic determinism in the novel, although most commended O'Connor's finely crafted prose. Sumner J. Ferris, for example, writing in *Critique*, praised the excellent construction of the novel, but maintained that because of its theme and locale the author's spiritual vision would not be taken seriously and, further, that O'Connor "will never be considered anything but a Southern woman novelist."

After O'Connor won the posthumous National Book Award in 1972 for her *Collected Stories*, critical opinion of her second novel softened further. Although commentators now still acknowledge that it is a difficult book to comprehend, it is emphasized that a close and careful reading reaps considerable rewards—indeed, this is essential to fully appreciate the power and deep complexity of the work. Numerous scholarly works have since been written on the novel, touching on a vast array of subjects—including the depiction of family, the difficult heroism of the protagonist, the significance of hats in the work, the importance of silence, the novel's multi-layered system of religious symbolism, and the spirituality and psychology of the main characters. Scholars have been aided in their discussions by O'Connor's letters about her novel, which point out, for example, that the main concern she had when writing it was to explore "the conflict between an attraction for the Holy and the disbelief in it that we breathe in with the air of the times," as she says in *The Habit of Being*. Critics continue to explore O'Connor's handling of this conflict, discussing issues such as her use of irony, humor, and religious symbolism grounded in the particular to emphasize her theme. The novel's complexity and unusual treatment of difficult spiritual questions, initially seen as its shortcomings, are now regarded as the work's strengths and evidence of O'Connor's original and uncompromising vision as a Christian and as a writer.

Criticism

Uma Kukathas

Kukathas is a freelance editor and writer. In this essay, Kukathas considers the relevance of O'Connor's religious vision for modern readers.

The Violent Bear It Away is about the fearsome nature of the Christian faith and calling, and about its strange, mysterious, and sometimes awful aspects. The novel tells the story of a young boy, Tarwater, who attempts to renounce his faith and his mission as a prophet, but is pulled back to God and redeemed finally through grace after he receives a holy vision. But the protagonist Tarwater's spiritual journey is bizarre, and the manner in which he comes to acknowledge the divine and assumes his role as a prophet of God is nothing less than horrifying. He kills his mentally retarded cousin by drowning him, but just before he does, he unwittingly baptizes the boy. Soon after, Tarwater is raped by a man who is the incarnation of the devil; Tarwater sees for the first time what evil is, and turns back to God. After seeing a vision, he accepts the mantle of prophet and goes forth to preach this message to the modern world.

To many contemporary readers, Tarwater is certainly a most unlikely prophet, and his spiritual

odyssey might appear to be one that leads to madness rather than salvation. But O'Connor, writing in a letter in 1962, insisted that "Tarwater's call is real. . . . [H]is true vocation is to answer it. Tarwater is not sick or crazy but really called to be a prophet—a vocation I take seriously, though the modern reader is not likely to." For O'Connor, Tarwater is not a parody of a religious fanatic. He is not a psychological study of a disturbed boy who plays out in his psychoses the indoctrination of his insane, controlling evangelical great-uncle. He is not a satirical portrait of an ill-educated boy from the backwater. He is, for O'Connor, a boy who first rejects, then hears and answers the call of God; he is a spokesperson for the Christian faith. Tarwater is someone who is aware of the truth of the divine. But how is a modern reader supposed to take this—and Tarwater—seriously? Why does O'Connor think that using an unlikable redneck hero, exploring his tortured psyche, and describing his insane-seeming actions will point readers to the truths of the Christian faith?

In her essays and letters, O'Connor frequently noted that her fiction was written with a Christian purpose—that she wrote as a Catholic. She thought of herself as a prophet of sorts, as an artist who could speak forth truth to her society. In fact, while she was writing *The Violent Bear It Away*, O'Connor often signed her letters with variations of the name "Tarwater." One of her main concerns as a Christian, which she writes about in her non-fiction and which is a major theme of *The Violent Bear It Away*, is that modern life and secular thinking stifle true understanding of the divine. O'Connor felt that most people viewed religion with apathy, that they thought lazily about morality and spiritual questions. She took it as her role to jolt them out of their complacency to face the harsh realities of God's message. In her essay "The Fiction Writer and His Country," she declares:

> The novelist with Christian concerns will find in modern life distortions which are repugnant to him, and his problem will be to make them appear as distortions to an audience which is used to seeing them as natural; and he may be forced to take ever more violent means to get his vision across to this hostile audience. When you can assume that your audience holds the same beliefs you do, you can relax a little and use more normal ways of talking to it; when you have to assume that it does not, then you have to make your vision apparent by shock—to the hard of hearing you shout, and for the blind you draw large and startling figures.

By using large, grotesque characters like Tarwater, and depicting his detestable actions and other horrific events, O'Connor presents a repugnant picture of modern society and the problems it faces. She does this to show to her readers that the faith she speaks of is no easy, comfortable path but one that sometimes entails suffering, violence and destruction. The truths in her vision of Christianity fly in the face of all that modern readers find reasonable, and she means to show that it cannot be ignored, nor sugar-coated. O'Connor uses Tarwater as her protagonist to illuminate two major concerns: that modern secular beliefs hinder understanding of God and that God's message is mysterious, unfathomable, but not to be ignored simply because it is difficult to stomach.

By making the hero of her story an unsophisticated boy from the backwater, O'Connor underscores the idea that the beliefs of educated, rational intellectuals are seriously misguided. On a superficial level, Tarwater seems like a "backwards imbecile," as his uncle, George Rayber, calls him. But Tarwater surveys the world that Rayber introduces to him and quickly finds it spiritually hollow. Tarwater's spiritual guide and teacher is his uncle, Mason Tarwater, who "taught him Figures, Reading, Writing, and History beginning with Adam expelled from the Garden and going on down through the presidents to Herbert Hoover and on in speculation toward the Second Coming." Although the details of his education sound comical, Tarwater is no idiot; he has a sound understanding of religious teachings and a keen mind. His inner voice (of the "stranger") articulates reasoned arguments about the limitations of religion—showing that Tarwater understands and anticipates rationalist objections to faith. Throughout the novel, Tarwater is drawn to Mason's fervent evangelical beliefs even though he struggles to deny their truth. Tarwater goes to the city to seek out Rayber, the representative of reason, of modern humanistic rationalism, but soon Tarwater rejects Rayber's views. It is old Tarwater's vision, the vision of faith, that he embraces and which triumphs against secular ways of seeing. Tarwater's rejection of Rayber's belief—that reason and science can save the world and humanity—are spelled out in a humorous episode in which Rayber tries to impress upon the boy the achievements, such as flying, that humans have accomplished. To this Tarwater replies, "I wouldn't give you nothing for no airplane. A buzzard can fly." Tarwater articulates, in his unsophisticated speech and ultimate choices, that the trappings of modernity, secularism, and rationalism cannot show humans the light, but are a hindrance to ultimate salvation.

Tarwater is a sullen, unlikable boy who is not easy to sympathize with or identify with. The

> O'Connor felt that most people viewed religion with apathy, that they thought lazily about morality and spiritual questions. She took it as her role to jolt them out of their complacency to face the harsh realities of God's message."

reaction to him by readers is likely to be similar to that of the woman at the Cherokee Lodge: that he is mean and that there is something evil about him. He exhibits no endearing traits that might attract readers to him. If anything, he seems like a troubled boy from a dysfunctional home whose behavior is the result of brainwashing and isolation, and we feel sorry for him. But O'Connor uses this complex, frightening figure to make a bold statement that, like other prophets before him, Francis Marion Tarwater has been chosen by God for reasons that are incomprehensible to people. Tarwater himself does not understand why or if he is chosen. O'Connor explores his confusion, anger, and defiance of his calling. She also examines the suffering he undergoes before he is finally redeemed. He is tortured by the need to be his own person, as Rayber would want him to be, and to be an instrument of God. He is tormented and tempted by voices inside his head. On the one hand, then, what O'Connor seems to be offering is a portrait of someone struggling with mental illness. But part of O'Connor's genius is that she is able to paint Tarwater in such a way that this interpretation of him is perfectly reasonable, even probable. Thus the reader can easily believe, like Rayber does, that Tarwater's problem can be quantified and fixed by human intervention. But the author insists that what reason would have us think is true is simply not true. Tarwater is not mad, although all reasonable indications point to that. He is a prophet, and what appears to us as a descent into madness is a journey away from the temptations of reason to an acceptance of God's frightening and awesome power working through him. By choosing this unlikely hero as God's instrument, O'Connor intensifies the

What Do I Read Next?

- *Wise Blood* (1952) is O'Connor's first novel. It tells the story of young Hazel Motes who, like Francis Tarwater, is caught in a struggle against his innate faith.

- O'Connor's most celebrated collection of short stories, *A Good Man Is Hard to Find and Other Stories* (1955), is a classic of Southern Gothic literature that tells of the underside of life in the rural South.

- The posthumously-published *The Habit of Being: Letters of Flannery O'Connor* (1988) offers a self-portrait of an author who otherwise revealed very little of herself.

- The subjects of O'Connor's essays in her prose collection *Mystery and Manners* (1969) include writing, religion, teaching literature, and the grotesque in Southern fiction.

- In *Under the Banner of Heaven: A Story of Violent Faith* (2003), Jon Krakauer recounts the chilling story of Dan and Ron Lafferty, Mormon brothers who in 1984 murdered their sister-in-law and infant niece in the name of a divine revelation, and it explores one type of modern-day religious fundamentalism in the United States.

- In *Lost Revolutions: The South in the 1950s* (2000), Peter Daniel chronicles the changes that transformed the South in the period following World War II and describes the culture that developed from poverty, religious fundamentalism, and racial obsessions.

- *A Curtain of Green and Other Stories* (1941) is the first collection of stories by Eudora Welty, another Southern woman whose work contains elements of horror and humor.

- *Terror in the Mind of God: The Global Rise of Religious Violence* (2003), by Mark Juergensmeyer, explores the mindset of those who perpetrate and support violence in the name of religion.

---

mystery of the divine and satirizes modern humans' hostility toward it.

The violent acts committed by Tarwater in the novel intensify readers' dislike of him, but O'Connor uses those acts to emphasize to readers the seriousness of her subject. As she noted in many of her essays, modern people misunderstand the nature of God and religion. People view God as a Santa Claus figure, and expect religion to make them happy and comforted. But this, O'Connor insisted, is not what religion is all about. As she wrote in a letter in *The Habit of Being*, "What people don't realize is how much religion costs. They think it is a big electric blanket, when of course it is the cross." By making her protagonist perform horrible, violent acts in his journey to spiritual awakening, O'Connor stresses the point that Christianity requires that people reexamine their morality, that they acknowledge the limitations of their knowledge, that they submit to the incomprehensibility of the divine. The behavior of Tarwater and his old uncle might strike readers as immoral and ungodly. Old Tarwater makes liquor for a living, kidnaps his nephews, and shoots Rayber. Young Tarwater sets his property ablaze and drowns his cousin. But God does not judge them for doing these things, and in fact, those acts are either done in God's name or used to bring them closer to him. Again, by insisting actions that appear insane are necessary for the will of God, O'Connor startles readers into paying attention to the message of Christianity in a way that has not been made palatable and is thus meaningless. With the drowning of Bishop, O'Connor shocks her readers into to looking anew at the meaning of baptism. She uses violence and horror to insist to readers that they need to really look without rose-colored glasses at the awesome nature of religion and faith.

In *The Violent Bear It Away*, O'Connor draws large and startling figures, and she shouts her message so modern, apathetic readers will take note. She uses Tarwater—a strange, violent, grotesque figure—to present her vision to a hostile audience and show them in extreme terms the importance, difficulty, and urgency of God's message. O'Connor insist that her readers take Tarwater seriously because what he has to say and show is of dire importance, difficult though it may be to fathom and to stomach. In some ways, Tarwater is larger than life because he is used to emphasize O'Connor's beliefs about the intense, bizarre, and incomprehensible nature of God. But any attempt to rationalize that he or his vocation are not to be taken entirely seriously, is to then assume the rationalist position that O'Connor rejects. By presenting an extreme character and extreme situations, O'Connor forces modern readers to look at the most terrible aspects of Christianity. Like a prophet, she presents an uncompromising vision, which she views as necessary to point readers to the mysterious and unpalatable truths of the Christian faith.

Source: Uma Kukathas, Critical Essay on *The Violent Bear It Away*, in *Novels for Students*, Thomson Gale, 2005.

Catherine Dybiec Holm

Holm is a freelance writer, as well as a genre novel and short story author. In this essay, Holm looks at how O'Connor develops complex human characters who drive this intense and dark story.

In Flannery O'Connor's *The Violent Bear It Away*, the reader gets an in-depth look at religious fundamentalism. O'Connor skillfully lets the reader see the effects of such fundamentalism through the eyes of an old man who thinks he is a prophet, a boy who is cynical and questioning beyond his years, and a schoolteacher who believes that salvation comes within oneself rather than from Jesus. O'Connor develops this disturbing story through these complex characters. Using her own understanding and portrayal of human nature, the author allows the reader to draw his or her own conclusions about the effects of fundamentalism and extremist thinking. It is this treatment of such disturbing issues that makes this story infinitely powerful. The author does not shy from violent outcomes. Because the story skillfully builds to horrific events, through the motives and actions of O'Connor's well-developed characters, the outcomes of the story are powerful, disturbing, and ultimately not surprising.

Religion shows up in the first sentence of the story in the form of a burial, which must be done properly in the Christian way. Point of view shifts often in this story, but the common thread of faith runs throughout the book. From the point of view of the old man, the reader can imagine how enraged

> " O'Connor's characters, even those who are not as extreme as the old man, often long for greatness to appear, religious or otherwise. Who has not wished for life to be better, fuller, richer?"

this character had been when he realized his nephew had been "creeping into his soul through the back door" and had completed a written study about the old man. To the old man, a call from God prompted him to rescue young Tarwater and raise the boy in the backwoods. "The Lord himself had rescued the old man. He had sent him a rage of vision." The old man's visions are often full of rage, and accompanied by extreme action. Other characters in *The Violent Bear It Away* think the old man is crazy, but the reader does not feel authorial judgment. O'Connor does this by letting the reader into the head of the old man. The reader knows his thoughts, feels his emotion, and even feels sympathy for the old man at times. This use of craft by the author is important—it allows the reader to experience the old man's thoughts and motives, especially in terms of his extreme behavior.

Thanks to O'Connor's treatment and description of the old man, a reader of any faith (or no faith) can feel the disappointment of this character, who awaits a powerful vision and instruction from his God. The old man wants excitement; he wants the sun to burn the world and God to speak to him through fire. Instead, he receives the ordinary. The old man lies to the schoolteacher about impending death, and takes a perverse delight in the concern that is suddenly revealed on the schoolteacher's face. The schoolteacher, for an instant, reveals a "stricken look, plain and awful," when he learns of the old man's death. The phenomenon of longing for passion and direction in life, or of longing for excitement and drive and importance and love, is an urge that any reader can relate to, religious or not. It is through telling detail such as this that O'Connor makes her characters remarkably human and real, winning at least some degree of empathy from the reader.

O'Connor's characters, even those who are not as extreme as the old man, often long for greatness to appear, religious or otherwise. Who has not wished for life to be better, fuller, richer? Often, the characters are not rewarded with visions or experiences of greatness. While this may be interpreted by some as authorial cynicism, it gets at the heart of the human condition and adds to the complexity of these characters. Even the boy wishes for, or at least waits for, the greatness and thundering presence of God. It makes sense that he would expect this, having been raised with the extremism of his great-uncle. In one case, O'Connor uses such a situation to show the stark contrast between what is wished for, and what is:

> There was a complete stillness over everything and the boy felt his heart begin to swell. He held his breath as if he were about to hear a voice from on high. After a few moments he heard a hen scratching beneath him under the porch.

With a few short sentences, O'Connor has given the reader dark humor, the dichotomy between wished-for greatness and ordinary reality, and a reminder of the boy's poor, backwoods setting.

The boy is again disappointed on his first trip to the city. In a place full of 75,000 people, none will look at him; none will meet his eyes or shake his hand. O'Connor captures the impersonality of the city with her efficient and effective prose when she describes "the mass of moving metal and concrete speckled with the very small eyes of people." Even though the boy resists the pull of his so-called destiny, he also longs for purpose, to be called by God as his great-uncle was called. He says of the city, "When I come here for good I'll do something to make every eye stick on me." It is a dark foreshadow of the book's ending. Even when his great-uncle recounts the story of the boy's baptism as a baby, the boy is sure that he was fully and cognitively aware of the events around him. The boy desperately wants to believe he is different, special, and beyond ordinary. At the same time, he is so burdened by his so-called destiny to baptize Bishop, that he drowns the child, in order to be free of that destiny.

Young Tarwater provides a foil to contrast the extremism of the old man. Interestingly, for the reader, the contrast between the two is not as simple as the old man being a believer and the boy being an adamant disbeliever. The layers within the boy's logic make the contrast between the two more interesting, and more realistically human. It also makes the boy another surprising character. Again, O'Connor has avoided creating stereotypical, flat characters and given the reader some nuances of

personality to think about. When the old man is sure that young Tarwater's first task (when the old man dies) will be to baptize the dim witted child of the schoolteacher, young Tarwater has other things in mind:

> "Oh no it won't be," he said. "He don't mean for me to finish up your leavings. He has other things in mind for me." "It's no part of your job to think for the Lord," his great-uncle said. "Judgment may rack your bones."

Ironically, the old man has assumed a God-like position over the boy, by telling the boy that there is no question about young Tarwater's future duties to God. But the more interesting thing about this exchange is young Tarwater's presence of mind to not automatically accept direction from an authority figure, and to have some thoughts about his own direction. Still, visions of greatness constantly clash with the mundane ordinariness of everyday life. The boy continues to believe that greatness will be part of his life. After all, he was born in a car wreck. Young Tarwater is sure that being born in such a way "set his existence apart from the ordinary one . . . the plans of God for him were special." Again, the author effectively captures the human longing for meaning. And yet, the rational Rayber gives the boy pause:

> Rayber smiled, then he laughed. "All such people have in life," he said, "is the conviction they'll rise again." The boy steadied himself, his eyes still on the banner but as if he had reduced it to a small spot a great distance away. "They won't rise again?" he said.

O'Connor shows the reader that the boy has a mind of his own. The boy feels a "charge of excitement," almost a "sensual satisfaction," when the great-uncle tells him of the schoolteacher's fortitude. The schoolteacher will raise his child Bishop as he pleases. Similarly, Young Tarwater will shape his destiny the way in the way he wants. It is ironic that Bishop who will be raised as if he is "free" probably does not have the mental capacity to understand and implement these advantages.

When young Tarwater comes to the city, despite years of influence from the old man, the boy intends to find out how much of what his uncle told him was true. Somehow, the boy realizes that there may be other versions of reality and belief in the world beyond the old man and his backwoods home. It is the boy's consistent edginess, doubt, and argumentativeness that make him a well-rounded and interesting character; it is also these flaws that send him over the edge.

The schoolteacher is also a foil to the great-uncle's beliefs, providing the possibility for change

Biblical issues and events, like the one depicted here in Gustave Dore's engraving of Jesus walking on water, influence the characters in The Violent Bear It Away

in the direction of young Tarwater's life. The schoolteacher somehow managed to shed what he considers old Tarwater's brainwashing and is free of old Tarwater's "idiot hopes" and "foolish violence." When the old man realizes he is reading about himself in the magazine, the schoolteacher offers his own, contrasting understanding of being born again. "You've got to be born again, Uncle, by your own efforts, back to the real world where there's no saviour but yourself." But the schoolteacher recognizes the common link between himself, the boy, and the old man—the potential for great internal emotion and violence. The schoolteacher is able to stop himself in the act of violence, but the boy is too far gone to know better.

Bishop, perhaps, presents the greatest enigma in the story. This child links the schoolteacher, the old man, and young Tarwater. To the schoolteacher, Bishop is formed in the "image and likeness of God." To young Tarwater, Bishop looks like a young and innocent old man. To the old man, and to young Tarwater, Bishop represents young Tarwater's calling—he must be baptized. The schoolteacher experiences surges of terrifying and unexplainable love around Bishop. And it is ironic, perhaps intentionally so, that the schoolteacher, who spends less time seeking greatness than the

boy or the fundamentalist old man, encounters the greatness and expansiveness of true love—quite beyond the ordinary. Also ironically, the schoolteacher spends his life trying to squelch the greatness within himself. But for all his effort, he still has moments when "his hated love gripped him and held him in a vise." Rayber knows that he has a divided self—both rational and violent. He warns young Tarwater not to go to extremes; that extremes are only for violent people: "He had kept it from gaining control over him by what amounted to a rigid ascetic discipline. He did not look at anything too long, he denied his senses unnecessary satisfaction."

In the end, violence is what young Tarwater resorts to in order to escape his destiny. "I proved it by drowning him. Now all I have to do is mind my own bidnis until I die," young Tarwater tells us, "I don't have to baptize or prophecy." But Tarwater's destiny is planted too deeply within him, like the seed that he shares with the schoolteacher and the old man. And in the end, the act of violence and rape committed against Tarwater sends him over the edge and plants him firmly into the destiny that he resisted, the destiny of becoming a prophet. Tarwater has achieved his greatness, and has surpassed the mundane everyday life, but at great cost to himself and to others. And the reader has experienced a disturbing and powerful story through the experiences and motives of these effectively drawn characters.

Source: Catherine Dybiec Holm, Critical Essay on *The Violent Bear It Away*, in *Novels for Students*, Thomson Gale, 2005.

Joyce Hart

Hart is a freelance writer and author of several books. In this essay, Hart examines the various combatants in the battle between good and evil in O'Connor's novel The Violent Bear It Away.

There has long been a discussion about the characters in Flannery O'Connor's *The Violent Bear It Away*. This dialogue revolves around not just how the characters act and what their motives are but also includes an exchange of ideas concerning what each character represents. This is obviously a novel about the battle between good and evil, but on which side of this battle do the characters stand? And, maybe more importantly, which of the characters wins the battle? Is old man Tarwater a representative of good or evil? And where does that put Rayber, the character who stands diametrically opposed to the old man? And then there is the third main character, the young boy Francis Marion Tarwater who teeters somewhere in the middle of the two extremes of old Tarwater and Rayber. Does the young boy capitulate toward evil by the end of the novel? Or does he see his way clear to the bright light of goodness? And last but not least, just what is goodness? Or at least, how does this novel define this abstract quality?

The reviews were mixed when *The Violent Bear It Away* was first published. O'Connor believed that this was to be expected. She concluded that most readers would not be able to understand the concepts that she portrayed in this short novel. Not only were her ideas abstract, the beliefs that inspired her story were formed by an in-depth study of obscure Catholic dogma. But there are other reasons why readers might have had (and probably still have) trouble comprehending O'Connor's attempt to define good and evil as well as the interior discourse that her characters face in trying to claim goodness in their fictional lives. One major reason for the confusion could be caused by the fact that her characters appear to be muddled in their own thinking. Or it might be that the author herself is unsure about what defines goodness and evil.

Take Old Man Tarwater, for example. In letters to her friends, as published in *Flannery O'Connor, Collected Works*, O'Connor refers to old Tarwater as a natural man. In her way of thinking this is so because the old man does what he wants, when he wants, to whomever he chooses. Cultural or societal rules mean nothing to him. He is a man of very strong convictions, most of which come directly from his interpretations of the Bible. His analysis of this ancient text is unfettered by other historic accounts or by the outcome of intellectual study. Old Tarwater lives his life based on his instincts. And it is these personal intuitions that help elucidate the Biblical phrases that he reads. The Bible, for instance, says what it says because old Tarwater believes that is what it says. He believes himself to be a prophet—a man to whom God speaks directly. Therefore, accordingly, what Tarwater believes is what God wants him to believe. Old Tarwater's actions, he believes, are directed by God, regardless of society's judgment. In his mind, Tarwater 's motives, thoughts, and actions are all good.

In today's world, however, old Tarwater would be hounded by the FBI until he was shackled and taken to prison. He kidnaps not just one child but two children. And he would have kidnapped a third child, Bishop, but he never gets the chance. He does, however, manage to steal his nephew, Rayber, when Rayber was just a child. Later, the old man takes the young Tarwater boy back to his isolated shack in the woods. When Rayber tries to reclaim the young boy, Tarwater shoots Rayber. Then, after Rayber abandons the idea of rescuing young Tarwater, the old man teaches the boy to lie to state authorities who come to register him for school. This is all done in the name of God, in the name of a religion that has only one member: Old Man Tarwater. He believes he is saving the young boy as he tried to save Rayber before him. And he instructs the young boy to continue his work upon his death.

Then at the other end of the social spectrum, there is Rayber. O'Connor has created this character as the antithesis of the old man. Rayber is all about society and the modern emphasis on science versus superstition. Rayber's world is comprised of so-called facts. He is an intellectual, whose beliefs rely heavily on the results of very precise empirical tests. Whereas old man Tarwater gives free rein to his emotions, which in turn feed his intuitions and inspire him, Rayber confines his feelings, keeping them under control so they will not interfere with his reasoning processes. "To feel nothing," O'Connor writes of Rayber, "was peace." Rayber fears his emotions will drive him insane. "The longing [emotion] was like an undertow in his blood dragging him backwards to what he knew to be madness." If he allows his emotions freedom, he is concerned he will turn out to be just like the old man. If he is to experience any emotion, he concludes, it will be under the rigid controls of his intellect.

On the positive side, Rayber raises his mentally impaired son, providing him with as much stimulating experiences as possible. He sees to the child's needs and at moments admits to himself that he loves the child. Although this love is frightening, Rayber cannot escape it. And when young Tarwater wanders into town, Rayber takes him in without hesitation. Rayber's hope and goal is to rehabilitate the young Tarwater. Rayber believes that the old man has brainwashed the young boy. He knows this to be true, because the old man had tried to do the same thing to Rayber. The old man had wanted Rayber to see the world as he saw it. And Rayber knows that young Tarwater is struggling in trying to decipher the world. He recalls his own challenges in trying to measure the meaning of life, on one hand, according to old Tarwater's beliefs and on the other hand, on the personal experiences he was living through on his own. Rayber senses that young Tarwater is doing the same; and he wants to support him in his efforts, secretly hoping to convince him that the old man was wrong and Rayber's vision of the world is right.

But Rayber, like old man Tarwater, has a very dark side. He admits to having tried to drown his son, Bishop, an act he had performed in order to rid himself of his emotions for the child. He could not pull it off, however, because in the midst of his attempt, he realized that the ache of not having his son in his life would have been as great as the ache of having him alive. But this insight does not prevent Rayber from secretly and passively allowing young Tarwater to drown Bishop.

Rayber lies on a cot in the hotel room, waiting "for a cataclysm. He waited for all the world to be turned into a burnt spot between two chimneys." With these words, the reader understands that Rayber subconsciously wants not only young Tarwater but also Bishop to be somehow removed from his life. He wants there to be nothing but their ashes remaining, much as he believes that there was nothing but ashes left of old Tarwater once the house at Powderhead was burned down. He wants all memories of his kin, the people who rouse the most emotions in him, to be gone. This will give him peace, he concludes. So when he hears his son yell out in the night as Rayber stares out of the window that overlooks the lake on which young Tarwater is drowning Bishop, Rayber does nothing. He merely remains "standing woodenly" at the

> **If this is how O'Connor delineates the difference between good and evil, it is no wonder that is it difficult for readers to determine who has won the battle in this muddled novel."**

window. And in the end, when silence returns to the dark night, when the full impact of Bishop's drowning hits him, Rayber feels no pain.

Finally there is young Tarwater. Who is this character? If old man Tarwater represents the emotional prophet of God, and Rayber represents the rational man of modern society, then young Tarwater might be the bridge between the two. Or at least that is what the reader is led to believe as the young boy begins his journey into town after the old man dies. Whereas the old man and Rayber are more definitely sure of where they stand, young Tarwater wavers. For instance, young Tarwater insists to Rayber that he is fully aware of how the old man has tried to brainwash him and has therefore risen above it all. "With me," he tells Rayber, the old man's teachings "fell on rock and the wind carried it away." He believes he is unaffected, although Rayber points out that young Tarwater, if he were truly untouched by the old man, would not be so obsessed with baptizing Bishop. Young Tarwater ponders Rayber's accusations about his obsession with baptizing Bishop and then denies it. Even when he relates the details of the drowning to a stranger, young Tarwater says, "It was an accident. I didn't mean to." But it is not the drowning that he is referring to. It is the baptism. "The words just come out of themselves but it don't mean nothing." Young Tarwater has more remorse, at this point, for the so-called accidental baptism than he does for the premeditated murder. And it is the baptism and death of Bishop that creates the fork in the road that young Tarwater is traveling on.

Whereas previously, Tarwater had been exploring the secular world, bringing his strange concepts of the world to the city, he now begins his return to Powderhead and social obscurity. But O'Connor is not finished with him yet. She conjures up yet one more trial for the young boy. In a letter to Louise Abbot, O'Connor writes that as she interprets it, "hell is what God's love becomes to those who reject it." And since immediately after Bishop's drowning, young Tarwater states that there is no sense in baptizing because one cannot be reborn, O'Connor drops the boy into another scene that resembles hell. She has him drugged and raped. Then to emphasize her symbolic language, she has young Tarwater set the scene ablaze.

So where does the battle between good and evil take place in this novel? And who represents which side? The old man is a self-professed prophet directed by God. This should put him on the side of good. But he commits crimes against society, which would deem him bad. Rayber, as seen through the eyes of modern culture, may appear confused but not evil. And young Tarwater, who commits the most serious crime would be, at the least, classified as corrupt. According to law, the old man, young Tarwater, and Rayber might all have spent time in jail. But is this a true accounting of good and evil? And more specifically, is this what O'Connor had intended?

In a letter to John Hawkes on September 13, 1959, O'Connor writes, "The modern reader will identify himself with the school teacher, but it is the old man who speaks for me." With this statement, readers have the first clue as to where the author has placed her characters on the goodness spectrum. For O'Connor, old man Tarwater was the most natural of the characters and therefore the most "good." In contrast, Rayber was a secular man, a man of the world. And not only was Rayber involved with social customs, he was at the leading edge. Rayber was a man of modern science, trusting the tenets of the new world of psychology as much as the old man trusted the laws of the Bible. But in O'Connor's mind, as she states in a letter to William Sessions on September 13, 1960, Old Man Tarwater was true to "his own character." In contrast, as O'Connor writes to Alfred Corn on July 25, 1962, Rayber fought "his inherited tendency to mystical love"; and when Rayber watches the drowning of his son, Bishop, by his not stopping the murder, he "makes the Satanic choice."

"Sin is sin," O'Connor writes to Dr. T. R. Spivey on August 19, 1959, "whether it is committed by Pope, bishops, priests, or lay people." And yet she quickly dismisses the murder of Bishop and young Tarwater's involvement in it. She writes to "A" on July 25, 1959: "Someday if I get up enough courage I may write a story or a novella about Tarwater in the city. There would be no reformatory I assure you.

That murder is forgotten by God and of no interest to society." So, according to O'Connor, young Tarwater follows in old Tarwater's footsteps—along the path of goodness. If this is how O'Connor delineates the difference between good and evil, it is no wonder that is it difficult for readers to determine who has won the battle in this muddled novel.

Source: Joyce Hart, Critical Essay on *The Violent Bear It Away*, in *Novels for Students*, Thomson Gale, 2005.

Clinton W. Trowbridge

In the following essay excerpt, Trowbridge examines how O'Connor used symbolism and allusions in The Violent Bear It Away *to convey the idea that man's desire for the spiritual is answered only through faith in Jesus Christ.*

The difficulty, yet at the same time the beauty and power, of *The Violent Bear It Away* derives from the fact that so much of its meaning is communicated through its imagery as contained in its figurative language. For Flannery O'Connor, symbols, figures of speech in general, were not simply ways of saying things. Rather, they were tools of language to penetrate into the heart of mystery. She took them so seriously that she would have us take them literally. They were used to make a work not more suggestive but more explicit. As Robert Fitzgerald wrote in his introduction to *Everything That Rises Must Converge*:

> She could make things fiercely plain, as in her comment, now legendary, on an interesting discussion of the Eucharistic Symbol: 'If it were only a symbol, I'd say to hell with it.'

Basic to the novel is the idea that only Christ can really satisfy man's spiritual hunger. Yet no one was more afraid of being too explicit about her themes, and so she wove this idea into an intricate web of figures of speech and Biblical allusions, all of which rise naturally out of the concrete world of her fiction, so that, for the unsuspecting, they can be overlooked as merely decorative. First of all, she takes the idea of man's spiritual hunger literally and makes the parable of the loaves and the fishes serve as the major, and thus controlling, image of the novel. What seem to be more obviously important images—fire and water—really derive from the loaves and fishes as she uses them; for loaves are baked, after all, and fish swim. It is in fact just this sort of literal connection between things, this making things "fiercely plain," that is essential to recognize if we are to read her work as she would have it read. The parallel that old Tarwater makes between himself and Elijah and between the young

Tarwater and Elisha, a parallel which runs through the novel, is but another instance of the fire and water images, for Elijah used his cloak to part the waters and was taken to heaven in a chariot of fire; and Elisha was to receive a double portion of his spirit if he saw him ascend. Moses and the burning bush and Jonah and the whale are likewise logical figures through which to view the young Tarwater. Even the name "Tarwater," though it has other important suggestions, seems to be a literal yoking of these two elements. Nor are these connections between images ones that I am making. They are made by Miss O'Connor herself, though in a manner that one is likely to overlook.

The fishes are introduced early in the novel in what at first seems to be merely a comic, though certainly vivid, way of describing old Tarwater's death. The image is slipped to us, characteristically, in a simile. One of the things O'Connor teaches us is to take her similes literally. Old Tarwater has just died, at the breakfast table, and the young Tarwater is being impressed with his spirit. As we discover by the end of the novel it is a kind of laying on of eyes.

> He was a bull-like old man with a short head set directly into his shoulders and silver protruding eyes that looked like two fish straining to get out of a net of red threads. . . . Tarwater, sitting across the table from him, saw red ropes appear in his face and a tremor pass over him. It was like the tremor of a quake that had began at his heart and run outward and was just reaching the surface. . . . His eyes, dead silver, were focussed on the boy across from him.

> Tarwater felt the tremor transfer itself and run lightly over him.

The idea of the loaves is presented, even more deceptively, in one of Miss O'Connor's funniest scenes. Tarwater is sitting on his great-uncle's coffin wondering how to go about burying him, and a former conversation between himself and the old man occurs to him and is dramatized for us. Old Tarwater had climbed into the coffin after finishing it and had instructed the boy in what to do with him when the time came.

> [He] had . . . climbed into it . . . and had lain there some time, nothing showing but his stomach which rose over the top like over-leavened bread. . . .

> 'It's too much of you for the box,' Tarwater said. 'I'll have to sit on the lid to press you down or wait until you rot a little.'

The conversation continues and the boy begins to anger the old man with the threat that he will not carry out his instructions, that he will allow the despised Rayber to cremate him. It is this that the old man most fears, and still in his over-leavened con-

> "That it literally comes full circle, that the novel ends in Powderhead where it began, dramatizes Tarwater's inability to escape; that it ends with his acceptance of his rôle as prophet shows that he has been travelling the path toward salvation, that the stages of his journey were also stations of the cross."

dition he shouts: "He don't believe in the Resurrection. He don't believe in the Last Day. He don't believe in the bread of life . . ." Highly comic, this connection between the literal and the figurative, between the old man lying in his coffin and the crowd eating the multiplied loaves and fishes, brings into the novel the silent country of the dead, the dead who will receive the multiplied loaves and fishes if they are faithful, as well as all the hosts of the holy to whom man ought to owe his allegiance. It is actually this promise of salvation and fulfillment that lies behind the threatening words of the old man:

> The old man grabbed the front of his overalls and pulled him up against the side of the box and glared into his pale face. 'The world was made for the dead. Think of all the dead there are,' he said, and then as if he had conceived the answer for all the insolence in the world, he said, 'There's a million times more dead than living and the dead are dead a million times longer than the living are alive,' and he released him with a laugh.

It is the silent world of the dead, among whom his great-uncle eats the multiplied loaves and fishes eternally, that haunts Tarwater until, at the end of the novel, unable to resist its pressure any longer, he accepts his rôle as prophet. There, in a vision, he sees his great-uncle surrounded by a vast multitude, impatiently awaiting the single basket that is being passed among them:

> The boy too leaned forward, aware at last of the object of his hunger, aware that it was the same as the old man's and that nothing on earth would fill him. His hunger was so great that he could have eaten all the loaves and fishes after they were multiplied.

"Jesus is the bread of life," the old man had told Tarwater, but the whole action of the novel consists in Tarwater's trying to escape this truth. Even as he resists it, however, he senses that eventually he must succumb. What he most fears and seeks to run away from is what even he knows is the true object of his quest. He is, like the narrator in Thompson's "The Hound of Heaven" (whose first name he shares), being pursued; though, at the end of the novel, because he has been caught, he starts in pursuit of others, compelled by the command that he "GO WARN THE CHILDREN OF GOD OF THE TERRIBLE SPEED OF MERCY."

Fish, bread, silence; along with these, and images that derive from them, there is the image of the road. Because this image is central to the structure of the novel, I will begin with it, returning later to a discussion of the others.

Tarwater, born in a wreck, walks, runs, or rides almost continually during the come of the novel, so much so that the work itself could rightly be termed picaresque. The road symbolizes his spiritual journey in several ways. That it literally comes full circle, that the novel ends in Powderhead where it began, dramatizes Tarwater's inability to escape; that it ends with his acceptance of his rôle as prophet shows that he has been travelling the path toward salvation, that the stages of his journey were also stations of the cross.

Old Tarwater and Rayber are the opposed moral forces of the novel, and Tarwater has to choose which to follow. Once again taking literally what is usually passed over as a figure of speech, Miss O'Connor envisions each as a guide. Tarwater imagines following his great-uncle's commands in these terms:

> His black pupils, glassy and still, reflected depth on depth his own stricken image of himself, trudging into the distance in the bleeding stinking mad shadow of Jesus, until at last he received his reward, a broken fish, a multiplied loaf.

Much later in the novel, Rayber explains to Tarwater: "The old man told you to baptize Bishop. You have that order lodged in your head like a boulder blocking your path." Rayber would also lead the boy down a path, but it is unobstructed only because it is empty, because it lacks any kind of feeling. He even knows that this is so himself. Miss O'Connor has Rayber express this awareness in the following image, in which the tight-rope metaphor succinctly expresses the narrowness as well as precariousness of his way of life:

> He kept himself upright on a very narrow line between madness and emptiness, and when the time

came for him to lose his balance, he intended to lurch toward emptiness and fall on the side of his choice.

Characteristically, the road image is introduced in a wonderfully funny, and indeed epic, simile early in the novel. The old man is boring Tarwater with the constantly repeated story of Rayber's four days with him:

> The story always had to be taken to completion. It was like a road that the boy had travelled on so often that half the time he didn't look where they were going, and when at certain points he would become aware where they were, he would be surprised to see that the old man had not got farther on with it. Sometimes his uncle would lag at one point as if he didn't want to face what was coming and then when he finally came to it, he would try to get past it in a rush.

Witty as this extended comparison is, its real significance lies in the fact that what is really being made vivid is not how old Tarwater tells stories and how young Tarwater listens to them, but the image of the boy and his guide trudging painfully along toward the goal of the boy's redemption. One of the delights of reading Miss O'Connor's fiction lies in appreciating the wit involved in such passages. The opening paragraph of "Good Country People" is one of the most amusing of these. Here, however, there is more than the pleasure in her wit. She is building the structure of imagery through which she would have us see deeper into her novel.

There are other guides, variously demonic, who accompany Tarwater on his flight: three are drivers; the other, Satan himself, takes up his place in Tarwater's mind as the voice of the "stranger" right after his great-uncle's death. He becomes so powerful that he gradually seems to take on physical being. As Robert Fitzgerald says of him: "There are few better representations of the devil in fiction than Tarwater's friend, as overheard and finally embodied in *The Violent . . .*"

These four characters, all tempters, serve to dramatize in an extreme form different aspects of Rayber's philosophy, a philosophy that Miss O'Connor equates with the Satanic *non serviam* and which she sees as the basic evil of modern man. To the Existentialist, Rayber's words may sound heroic; for Miss O'Connor they are the words of the devil:

> 'The great dignity of man,' his uncle said, 'is his ability to say: I am born once and no more. What I can see and do for myself and my fellowman in this life is all of my portion and I'm content with it. It's enough to be a man.'

The copper flue salesman, Meeks, is the most amusing, most broadly satirical, of these portraits. He might be said to represent the hypocrisy and fundamental irrationality of Rayber's attempt to harmonize self-interest and selflessness. His advice to Tarwater, in fact his whole philosophy of life, is a parody of Rayber's, and as such serves to reveal what lies behind Rayber's gospel of love. To Tarwater he says that "love was the only policy that worked 95% of the time." Both Meeks and Rayber are in awe of man's triumphs over nature. Meeks tells Tarwater that "the greatest invention of man . . . was the wheel," and advises him "to learn to work every machine he saw." Tarwater's indifference here matches the reply he gives to Rayber's eulogy on man's conquest of the air: "A buzzard can fly." The Meeks shall indeed inherit the earth, Flannery O'Connor seems to be saying, but that's all it will be: dirt.

The truck driver from Detroit dramatizes the moral indifference, blind determination and real contempt for his fellows that we see in Rayber when his philosophy is too severely tested. When Tarwater tells the truck driver that he has just drowned a boy, the man says, "Just one?" His desire for sleep matches Rayber's longing for nothingness. The one is kept awake, the other kept alive, through grim determination. As Rayber lies on his bed waiting for what he somehow knows will happen—the drowning of Bishop—Miss O'Connor writes: "He told himself that he was indifferent even to his own dissolution. It seemed to him that this indifference was the most that human dignity could achieve, and for the moment . . . he felt he had achieved it. To feel nothing was peace."

The pervert who picks up Tarwater in his car is related to Rayber in a more symbolic but even more sinister sense. He is Tarwater's "friend" reappearing in another guise to take his revenge on his betrayer, for Tarwater had momentarily banished him when he uttered the words of baptism over Bishop even as he drowned him. Yet his "kindness" to Tarwater suggests the darker motives that possibly underlie Rayber's concern for Tarwater, and the two are symbolically identified through the combination corkscrew-bottleopener that Rayber gives Tarwater as a peace offering and that the pervert takes with him as a talisman after ravishing the unconscious body of his victim.

At the end of the novel, when Tarwater accepts his rôle as prophet and starts toward the city, it is something within himself—the result of his acceptance of God's grace—that guides him, not any human figure; and Miss O'Connor emphasizes this fact in a simile which, once again, we must take literally in order to understand its real significance.

The moon, riding low above the field beside him, appeared and disappeared, diamond-bright, between patches of darkness. Intermittently the boy's jagged shadow slanted across the road ahead of him as if it cleared a rough path toward his goal.

So much for road imagery and the various guides that almost succeed in destroying Tarwater. His great-uncle is ultimately the more powerful figure and much of that power can be seen in the way Miss O'Connor uses images more directly connected with the reward that comes at the end of the road: the loaves and the fishes.

Old Tarwater's eyes are several times in the novel referred to as "fish-colored." To Rayber they stand for the fierce pull, the insane attraction, of the old man's absurd vision of a world transfigured. He manages to resist them; though his breakdown at the end suggests that he has not entirely escaped them. To Tarwater they stand for the vitality and ever-watchful presence of his great-uncle's character, and they haunt him throughout the action until he finally gives in to their demands. As the secret sign used by the early Christians to proclaim their identity to each other, the fish that are contained in old Tarwater's eyes serve to dramatize the fact of his own redemption and thus constantly remind us that he is the real hero of the novel. To Rayber, the old man is a "type that's almost extinct." Yet Miss O'Connor, with characteristic wit, both symbolically dramatizes Rayber's own deep attraction for the old man's views and satirizes man's pride in his past, which oddly coexists with his pride in his progress from the past, when she has Rayber take Tarwater to the natural history museum to introduce him to "his ancestor, the fish, and to all the great wastes of unexplored time" in order to stretch the boy's mind.

When Tarwater first leaves Powderhead, he does so thinking that he has burnt up his great-uncle and in so doing rid himself of his influence. What he has actually done, Miss O'Connor tells us, not directly but through her imagery, is to release upon himself the full power of his great-uncle's spirit and to receive, without knowing it, a double portion of that spirit.

> . . . he began to run, forced on through the woods by two bulging silver eyes that grew in immense astonishment in the center of the fire behind him. He could hear it moving up through the black night like a whirling chariot.

Elisha prayed that he would receive a double portion of Elijah's spirit and was told he would if he saw him ascend to heaven. Later his prayer is granted when he sees him ascend in a chariot of fire. Tarwater has prayed, in effect, to be "shut" of the whole business, but the effect is the same. What Miss O'Connor would seem to be emphasizing is the irresistible nature of God's grace, which, ironically, here operates through the very act that was meant to deny it.

The old man had instructed Tarwater that his first mission as a prophet would be to baptize Bishop, and it is largely through Bishop that he works after his death. It is Rayber, ironically, who sees the real significance that Bishop has for Tarwater—ironically, because he is unaware at the time that Tarwater has been told to baptize him.

> Nothing gave him pause—except Bishop, and Rayber knew that the reason Bishop gave him pause was because the child reminded him of the old man. Bishop looked like the old man grown backwards to the lowest form of innocence, and Rayber observed that the boy strictly avoided looking him in the eye.

The similarity between the two, yet Bishop's greater holiness, is emphasized, and again in a simile, early in the novel when Tarwater recalls his first meeting with Bishop:

> The little boy somewhat resembled old Tarwater except for his eyes which were grey like the old man's but clear, as if the other side of them went down and down into two pools of light.

Just before Tarwater drowns Bishop, the old man himself seems to be forcing him on, though to the baptism, not the drowning, through the eyes of the child:

> He [Tarwater] looked through the blackness and saw perfectly the light silent eyes of the child across from him. They had lost their diffuseness and were trained on him, fish-colored and fixed.

Then, too, the child is a sort of fish. There is his general attraction to water, dramatized in the scene in the park where he lurches into the fountain. And when Rayber recalls his own unsuccessful attempt to drown the boy, he describes Bishop's struggles as if they were those of a fish:

> A fierce surging pressure had begun upward beneath his hands and grimly he had exerted more and more force downward. In a second, he felt he was trying to hold a giant under. Astonished, he let himself look. The face under the water was wrathfully contorted, twisted by some primeval rage to save itself.

It is comically ironic that Rayber has taken Tarwater on a fishing trip, fishing for his soul, as it were, while Tarwater, unaware of what he is doing, acts the part that has been prepared for him and sets in motion all that is to come when he carries out his great-uncle's instructions and baptizes Bishop as he drowns him.

As Tarwater recollects the drowning and accidental baptism of Bishop, it becomes clear that it is the silent land of the dead, symbolized in the

great whale that swallowed Jonah, that has taken possession of him. A great fish has swallowed him and for a moment he is seen as a fish himself. Yet it is only by taking literally what most would pass over as a figure of speech that we understand this and see that this is for Tarwater the moment of his soul's redemption, unaware of it as he is. Recalling the scene, "he grappled with the air as if he had been flung like a fish on the shores of the dead without lungs to breathe there." And it is really Bishop who acts upon him, who, the imagery and figures of speech suggest, drowns him into the spiritual life, the life that all along he has been fleeing:

> The boy . . . saw suddenly that the bank loomed behind him, not twenty yards away, silent, like the brow of some leviathan lifted just above the surface of the water. He felt bodiless as if he were nothing but a head full of air, about to tackle all the dead. . . . The water slid out from the bank like a broad black tongue. . . . While he stood there gazing, for the moment lost, the child in the boat stood up, caught him around the neck and climbed onto his back. He clung there like a large crab to a twig and the startled boy felt himself sinking backwards into the water as if the whole bank were pulling him down. . . . He might have been Jonah clinging wildly to the whale's tongue.

At the end of the novel, just after Tarwater has accepted his great-uncle's hunger as his own, Miss O'Connor describes his change in an extended water image which, if we take the figures of speech literally, makes it clear that Tarwater's soul, just redeemed, is now buoyed up by the waters of the spirit, that he will now swim, fish-like, in the procession of prophets that have preceded him.

> He felt his hunger no longer as a pain but as a tide. He felt it rising in himself through time and darkness, rising through the centuries, and he knew that it rose in a line of men whose lives were chosen to sustain it. . . . He felt it building from the blood of Abel to his own, rising and engulfing him. It seemed in one instant to lift and turn him.

It is characteristic of Miss O'Connor that she should develop her controlling images with wit as well as infuse them with Biblical overtones and allusions. Overcome with a thirst that cannot be quenched by the waters of a well, that is made worse later on by the doped liquor that the pervert presses upon him, Tarwater trudges toward Powderhead after the drowning of Bishop. He passes a country store where he and his great-uncle had sometimes traded. The Sybil-like, angel-like proprietress, as Miss O'Connor describes her, aware of how he has treated old Tarwater, fixes her eyes on him with a "black penetration":

> She spotted him across the highway and although she did not move or raise her hand, he could feel her eyes

reeling him in. He crossed the highway and was drawn forward. . . .

We would pass over the "reeling him in" and "drawn forward" as merely amusing, though vivid, figures of speech if it were not for our recognition of what was being said when we take the words literally. Ever since the moment of his great-uncle's death, when the tremor that passed through the old man seemed also to pass through the boy, Tarwater has been caught, on the line of the great fisher of souls, so to speak. His acts of rebellion, his acts of violence, all are but the thrashings of a fish that imbeds the hook ever deeper into its jaws with each exertion. Now he is being reeled in for judgment, and though he is not caught yet, we recognize that he has really been caught all along. For his redemption to be secured, for him to be finally brought in, all that remains is for the pervert (Satan) to drug him into insensibility and ravish what is left of his unredeemed life. Dead to his old life, he accepts capture and his new soul floats on the waters of spirit.

As the fish is the central image for the soul, and so symbolizes it, so the bread is symbolic of what nourishes the soul—the spiritual life. The images that cluster around this central image are literally related to it, just as water, thirst, struggle are literally related to the image of the fish. These images are: the seed from which the grain grows that is used to make the bread; and fire, the fire in which it is baked.

The idea that old Tarwater has left his mark both on Rayber and on young Tarwater is presented early in the novel in an image which calls up the parable of the sowers. Tarwater is recalling an argument with his great-uncle about old Tarwater's effect on Rayber. The old man boasts:

'The truth was even if they told him not to believe what I had taught him, he couldn't forget it. . . . I planted the seed in him and it was there for good. Whether anybody liked it or not.'

'It fell amongst cockles,' Tat-water said . . .

'It fell in deep,' the old man said. . . .

Later, Tarwater taunts Rayber with the old man's words:

'It's you the seed fell in,' he said. 'It ain't a thing you can do about it. It fell on bad ground but it fell in deep. With me,' he said proudly, 'it fell on rock and the wind carried it away.'

Rayber, furious, curses at the boy and says:

'It fell in us both alike. The difference is that I know it's in me and I keep it under control. I weed it out but you're too blind to know it's in you.'

At the end of the novel, just after Tarwater has heard the command that he go to the city to prophesy to the children of God, Miss O'Connor writes: "The words were as silent as seeds opening one at a time in his blood." Again in the guise of a figure of speech, she tells us something central to our understanding of her work. The seeds of the spiritual life have been in Tarwater all the time, but they had to enter his blood—his new life—in order to open.

In the course of the novel, Tarwater grows increasingly hungry. Though the unappetizing food Rayber serves him might be reason enough for the boy's hunger, clearly it comes to more than that; and, once again, it is by taking a figure of speech literally that we see Miss O'Connor's intention:

'Jesus is the bread of life,' the old man said. . . . The boy sensed that this was the heart of his great-uncle's madness, this hunger, and what he was secretly afraid of was that it might be passed down, might be hidden in the blood and might strike some day in him and then he would be torn by hunger like the old man, the bottom split out of his stomach so that nothing would heal or fill it but the bread of life.

Tarwater's hunger, like his thirst, is a spiritual one, but it is Miss O'Connor's great gift to see far things up close and, through ordinary physical images, to give reality to states of the soul. Often she does this comically, as in the scene between Tarwater and the truck driver toward the end of the novel in which only the reader sees the wit as well as deeper significance, the *double entendre* of their dialogue.

'I'm hungry,' he said.

'You just said you weren't hungry,' the driver said.

'I ain't hungry for the bread of life,' the boy said. 'I'm hungry for something to eat here and now. I threw up my dinner and I didn't eat no supper. . . . When I come to eat, I ain't hungry,' Tarwater said. 'It's like being empty is a thing in my stomach and it don't allow nothing else to come down in there.'

Sometimes she drops the symbolic detail so casually that, unless we are looking for it, we are apt to pass over its significance. During the evening chase that eventually ends up at the "Carmodys for Christ," Rayber sees Tarwater staring into a shop window, his face "strangely lit" and looking "like the face of someone starving who sees a meal he can't reach laid out before him." He determines to return the next morning and buy whatever it is that has brought such a response from the boy. "Everything a false alarm," he thought with disgust, when he sees that the boy had been merely looking in the window of a bakery, empty except for "a loaf of bread pushed to the side that must have been overlooked when the shelf was cleaned for the night."

"If he had eaten his dinner, he wouldn't be hungry," thinks Rayber, failing, of course, to recognize the symbolic loaf, just as Tarwater himself is undoubtedly unaware of the reasons behind its attraction for him.

At the end of the novel, what Tarwater most fears comes to him. Not only do the dreaded seeds open in his blood, but, as he walks across the field of corn at Powderhead, toward the grave of his great-uncle, his stomach seems to split open:

> . . . his hunger constricted him anew. It appeared to be outside him, surrounding him, almost as if it were visible before him, something he could reach out for and not quite touch. . . . Instantly at the thought of food, he stopped and his muscles contracted with nausea. He blanched with the shock of a terrible premonition. He stood there and felt a crater opening inside him, and stretching out before him, surrounding him, he saw the clear gray spaces of that country where he had vowed never to set foot.

His eyes have been "scorched" and appear "seedlike" as he uses a firebrand to protect himself from the "stranger," now referred to as his "adversary."

> His scorched eyes no longer looked hollow or as if they were meant only to guide him forward. They looked as if, touched with a coal like the lips of the prophet, they would never be used for ordinary sights again.

Tarwater is now prepared for his final vision. He has passed from the ordeal by water through the trial by fire, and he is ready to be "healed" and at the same time "filled" by the bread of life. The country that now stretches before him is the silent country of the glorified dead, and this is his entry into it. He has become one with his great-uncle; and, accepting his call as a prophet, he now sees himself as one in a line of prophets, "who would wander in the world, strangers from that violent country where the silence is never broken except to shout the truth."

The silent country is the country of the redeemed dead, and Miss O'Connor weaves images of silence and noise through her novel to make correct, and therefore real, the spiritual atmosphere of redemption and damnation.

It is the memory of the voice as well as the eyes of old Tarwater that Tarwater tries to escape during the course of the novel. The memory might fade, however, were it not for the fact that through various images his great-uncle exerts a silent, continual, and finally unbearable pressure on him. This pressure, Miss O'Connor seems to suggest, is actually the inexorable force of God's will. Since it is presented most often in the image of the sun, it is also the force that burns Tarwater's eyes clean.

Source: Clinton W. Trowbridge, "The Symbolic Vision of Flannery O'Connor: Patterns of Imagery in *The Violent Bear It Away*," in The *Sewanee Review*, Vol. 76, No. 2, April–June 1968, pp. 298–318.

Sources

Benoit, Raymond, "The Existential Intuition of Flannery O'Connor in *The Violent Bear It Away*," in *Notes on Contemporary Literature*, Vol. 23, No. 4, September 1993, pp. 2–3.

Bieber, Christina, "Called to the Beautiful: The Incarnational Art of Flannery O'Connor's *The Violent Bear It Away*," in *Xavier Review*, Vol. 18, No. 1, 1998, pp. 44–62.

Burns, Stuart L., "*The Violent Bear It Away*: Apotheosis in Failure," in *Sewanee Review*, Vol. 76, 1968, pp. 319–36.

Buzan, Mary, "The Difficult Heroism of Francis Marion Tarwater," in the *Flannery O'Connor Bulletin*, Vol. 14, 1985, pp. 33–43.

Cash, Jean W., "O'Connor on *The Violent Bear It Away*: An Unpublished Letter," in *English Language Notes*, Vol. 26, No. 4, June 1989, pp. 67–71.

Donahoo, Robert, "Tarwater's March toward the Feminine: The Role of Gender in O'Connor's *The Violent Bear It Away*," in *CEA Critic*, Vol. 56, No. 1, Fall 1993, pp. 96–106.

Ferris, Sumner J., "The Outside and the Inside: Flannery O'Connor's *The Violent Bear It Away*," in *Critique*, Vol. 3, No. 2, 1960, pp. 11–19.

Giannone, Richard, "The Lion of Judah in the Thought and Design of *The Violent Bear It Away*," in the *Flannery O'Connor Bulletin*, Vol. 14, 1985, pp. 25–32.

Grimes, Ronald L., "Anagogy and Ritualization: Baptism in Flannery O'Connor's *The Violent Bear It Away*," in *Religion and Literature*, Vol. 21, No. 1, Spring 1989, pp. 9–26.

O'Connor, Flannery, "The Fiction Writer and His Country," in *Mystery and Manners*, Noonday Press, 1969.

———, *Flannery O'Connor: Collected Works*, Library of America, 1988.

———, *The Habit of Being: Letters of Flannery O'Connor*, Farrar, Straus, Giroux, 1979.

———, Letter to Grace Terry on August 27, 1962, quoted in Cash, Jean W., "O'Connor on the *The Violent Bear It Away*: An Unpublished Letter," in *English Language Notes*, Vol. 26, No. 4, June 1989, p. 69.

———, *The Violent Bear It Away*, 13th reprint, Noonday Press/Farrar, Straus and Giroux, 1960.

Olson, Steven, "Tarwater's Hats," in *Studies in the Literary Imagination*, Vol. 20, No. 2, Fall 1987, pp. 37–49.

Paulson, Suzanne Morrow, "Apocalypse of Self, Resurrection of the Double: Flannery O'Connor's *The Violent Bear It Away*," in *Literature and Psychology*, Vol. 30, No. 3–4, 1980, pp. 100–11.

Scouten, Kenneth, "The Schoolteacher as a Devil in *The Violent Bear It Away*," in the *Flannery O'Connor Bulletin*, Vol. 12, 1983, pp. 35–46.

Shaw, Patrick W., "*The Violent Bear It Away* and the Irony of False Seeing," in *Texas Review*, Vol. 3, No. 2, Fall 1982, pp. 49–59.

Swan, Jesse G., "Flannery O'Connor's Silence-Centered World," in the *Flannery O'Connor Bulletin*, Vol. 17, 1988, pp. 82–89.

Wilson, Carol Y., "Family as Affliction, Family as Promise in *The Violent Bear It Away*," in *Studies in the Literary Imagination*, Vol. 20, No. 2, Fall 1987, pp. 77–86.

Zornado, Joseph, "A Becoming Habit: Flannery O'Connor's Fiction of Unknowing," in *Religion and Literature*, Vol. 29, No. 2, Summer 1997, pp. 27–59.

Further Reading

Bloom, Harold, ed., *Flannery O'Connor*, Chelsea House Publications, 1999.
This volume gathers together some of the best criticism on O'Connor's work, including *The Violent Bear It Away*, and also features a short biography on the author, a chronology of her life, and an introductory essay by Bloom.

Magee, Rosemary, *Conversations with Flannery O'Connor*, University Press of Mississippi, 1987.
The interviews with O'Connor in this collection were conducted over the span of her writing career.

Martin, Carter, *The True Country: Themes in the Fiction of Flannery O'Connor*, Vanderbilt University Press, 1969.
This is a study aimed at students that concentrates on the religious themes in O'Connor's fiction.

McMullen, Joanne, *Writing against God: Language as Message in the Literature of Flannery O'Connor*, Mercer University Press, 1996.
Religious symbols and images in O'Connor's fiction are analyzed in depth in this book.

Spivey, Ted R., *Flannery O'Connor: The Woman, the Thinker, the Visionary*, Mercer University Press, 1995.
Spivey's bio-critical study analyzes O'Connor's work and discusses her life, family, and influences.

Glossary of Literary Terms

A

Abstract: As an adjective applied to writing or literary works, abstract refers to words or phrases that name things not knowable through the five senses.

Aestheticism: A literary and artistic movement of the nineteenth century. Followers of the movement believed that art should not be mixed with social, political, or moral teaching. The statement "art for art's sake" is a good summary of aestheticism. The movement had its roots in France, but it gained widespread importance in England in the last half of the nineteenth century, where it helped change the Victorian practice of including moral lessons in literature.

Allegory: A narrative technique in which characters representing things or abstract ideas are used to convey a message or teach a lesson. Allegory is typically used to teach moral, ethical, or religious lessons but is sometimes used for satiric or political purposes.

Allusion: A reference to a familiar literary or historical person or event, used to make an idea more easily understood.

Analogy: A comparison of two things made to explain something unfamiliar through its similarities to something familiar, or to prove one point based on the acceptedness of another. Similes and metaphors are types of analogies.

Antagonist: The major character in a narrative or drama who works against the hero or protagonist.

Anthropomorphism: The presentation of animals or objects in human shape or with human characteristics. The term is derived from the Greek word for "human form."

Antihero: A central character in a work of literature who lacks traditional heroic qualities such as courage, physical prowess, and fortitude. Antiheroes typically distrust conventional values and are unable to commit themselves to any ideals. They generally feel helpless in a world over which they have no control. Antiheroes usually accept, and often celebrate, their positions as social outcasts.

Apprenticeship Novel: See *Bildungsroman*

Archetype: The word archetype is commonly used to describe an original pattern or model from which all other things of the same kind are made. This term was introduced to literary criticism from the psychology of Carl Jung. It expresses Jung's theory that behind every person's "unconscious," or repressed memories of the past, lies the "collective unconscious" of the human race: memories of the countless typical experiences of our ancestors. These memories are said to prompt illogical associations that trigger powerful emotions in the reader. Often, the emotional process is primitive, even primordial. Archetypes are the literary images that grow out of the "collective unconscious." They appear in literature as incidents and plots that repeat basic patterns of life. They may also appear as stereotyped characters.

Avant-garde: French term meaning "vanguard." It is used in literary criticism to describe new writing that rejects traditional approaches to literature in favor of innovations in style or content.

B

Beat Movement: A period featuring a group of American poets and novelists of the 1950s and 1960s—including Jack Kerouac, Allen Ginsberg, Gregory Corso, William S. Burroughs, and Lawrence Ferlinghetti—who rejected established social and literary values. Using such techniques as stream of consciousness writing and jazz-influenced free verse and focusing on unusual or abnormal states of mind—generated by religious ecstasy or the use of drugs—the Beat writers aimed to create works that were unconventional in both form and subject matter.

Bildungsroman: A German word meaning "novel of development." The *bildungsroman* is a study of the maturation of a youthful character, typically brought about through a series of social or sexual encounters that lead to self-awareness. *Bildungsroman* is used interchangeably with *erziehungsroman,* a novel of initiation and education. When a *bildungsroman* is concerned with the development of an artist (as in James Joyce's *A Portrait of the Artist as a Young Man*), it is often termed a *kunstlerroman.* Also known as Apprenticeship Novel, Coming of Age Novel, *Erziehungsroman,* or *Kunstlerroman.*

Black Aesthetic Movement: A period of artistic and literary development among African Americans in the 1960s and early 1970s. This was the first major African-American artistic movement since the Harlem Renaissance and was closely paralleled by the civil rights and black power movements. The black aesthetic writers attempted to produce works of art that would be meaningful to the black masses. Key figures in black aesthetics included one of its founders, poet and playwright Amiri Baraka, formerly known as LeRoi Jones; poet and essayist Haki R. Madhubuti, formerly Don L. Lee; poet and playwright Sonia Sanchez; and dramatist Ed Bullins. Also known as Black Arts Movement.

Black Humor: Writing that places grotesque elements side by side with humorous ones in an attempt to shock the reader, forcing him or her to laugh at the horrifying reality of a disordered world. Also known as Black Comedy.

Burlesque: Any literary work that uses exaggeration to make its subject appear ridiculous, either by treating a trivial subject with profound seriousness or by treating a dignified subject frivolously. The word "burlesque" may also be used as an adjective, as in "burlesque show," to mean "striptease act."

C

Character: Broadly speaking, a person in a literary work. The actions of characters are what constitute the plot of a story, novel, or poem. There are numerous types of characters, ranging from simple, stereotypical figures to intricate, multifaceted ones. In the techniques of anthropomorphism and personification, animals—and even places or things—can assume aspects of character. "Characterization" is the process by which an author creates vivid, believable characters in a work of art. This may be done in a variety of ways, including (1) direct description of the character by the narrator; (2) the direct presentation of the speech, thoughts, or actions of the character; and (3) the responses of other characters to the character. The term "character" also refers to a form originated by the ancient Greek writer Theophrastus that later became popular in the seventeenth and eighteenth centuries. It is a short essay or sketch of a person who prominently displays a specific attribute or quality, such as miserliness or ambition.

Climax: The turning point in a narrative, the moment when the conflict is at its most intense. Typically, the structure of stories, novels, and plays is one of rising action, in which tension builds to the climax, followed by falling action, in which tension lessens as the story moves to its conclusion.

Colloquialism: A word, phrase, or form of pronunciation that is acceptable in casual conversation but not in formal, written communication. It is considered more acceptable than slang.

Coming of Age Novel: See *Bildungsroman*

Concrete: Concrete is the opposite of abstract, and refers to a thing that actually exists or a description that allows the reader to experience an object or concept with the senses.

Connotation: The impression that a word gives beyond its defined meaning. Connotations may be universally understood or may be significant only to a certain group.

Convention: Any widely accepted literary device, style, or form.

D

Denotation: The definition of a word, apart from the impressions or feelings it creates (connotations) in the reader.

Denouement: A French word meaning "the unknotting." In literary criticism, it denotes the resolution of conflict in fiction or drama. The *denouement* follows the climax and provides an outcome to the primary plot situation as well as an explanation of secondary plot complications. The *denouement* often involves a character's recognition of his or her state of mind or moral condition. Also known as Falling Action.

Description: Descriptive writing is intended to allow a reader to picture the scene or setting in which the action of a story takes place. The form this description takes often evokes an intended emotional response—a dark, spooky graveyard will evoke fear, and a peaceful, sunny meadow will evoke calmness.

Dialogue: In its widest sense, dialogue is simply conversation between people in a literary work; in its most restricted sense, it refers specifically to the speech of characters in a drama. As a specific literary genre, a "dialogue" is a composition in which characters debate an issue or idea.

Diction: The selection and arrangement of words in a literary work. Either or both may vary depending on the desired effect. There are four general types of diction: "formal," used in scholarly or lofty writing; "informal," used in relaxed but educated conversation; "colloquial," used in everyday speech; and "slang," containing newly coined words and other terms not accepted in formal usage.

Didactic: A term used to describe works of literature that aim to teach some moral, religious, political, or practical lesson. Although didactic elements are often found in artistically pleasing works, the term "didactic" usually refers to literature in which the message is more important than the form. The term may also be used to criticize a work that the critic finds "overly didactic," that is, heavy-handed in its delivery of a lesson.

Doppelganger: A literary technique by which a character is duplicated (usually in the form of an alter ego, though sometimes as a ghostly counterpart) or divided into two distinct, usually opposite personalities. The use of this character device is widespread in nineteenth- and twentieth-century literature, and indicates a growing awareness among authors that the "self" is really a composite of many "selves." Also known as The Double.

Double Entendre: A corruption of a French phrase meaning "double meaning." The term is used to indicate a word or phrase that is deliberately ambiguous, especially when one of the meanings is risqué or improper.

Dramatic Irony: Occurs when the audience of a play or the reader of a work of literature knows something that a character in the work itself does not know. The irony is in the contrast between the intended meaning of the statements or actions of a character and the additional information understood by the audience.

Dystopia: An imaginary place in a work of fiction where the characters lead dehumanized, fearful lives.

E

Edwardian: Describes cultural conventions identified with the period of the reign of Edward VII of England (1901-1910). Writers of the Edwardian Age typically displayed a strong reaction against the propriety and conservatism of the Victorian Age. Their work often exhibits distrust of authority in religion, politics, and art and expresses strong doubts about the soundness of conventional values.

Empathy: A sense of shared experience, including emotional and physical feelings, with someone or something other than oneself. Empathy is often used to describe the response of a reader to a literary character.

Enlightenment, The: An eighteenth-century philosophical movement. It began in France but had a wide impact throughout Europe and America. Thinkers of the Enlightenment valued reason and believed that both the individual and society could achieve a state of perfection. Corresponding to this essentially humanist vision was a resistance to religious authority.

Epigram: A saying that makes the speaker's point quickly and concisely. Often used to preface a novel.

Epilogue: A concluding statement or section of a literary work. In dramas, particularly those of the seventeenth and eighteenth centuries, the epilogue is a closing speech, often in verse, delivered by an actor at the end of a play and spoken directly to the audience.

Epiphany: A sudden revelation of truth inspired by a seemingly trivial incident.

Episode: An incident that forms part of a story and is significantly related to it. Episodes may be either self-contained narratives or events that depend on a larger context for their sense and importance.

Epistolary Novel: A novel in the form of letters. The form was particularly popular in the eighteenth century.

Epithet: A word or phrase, often disparaging or abusive, that expresses a character trait of someone or something.

Existentialism: A predominantly twentieth-century philosophy concerned with the nature and perception of human existence. There are two major strains of existentialist thought: atheistic and Christian. Followers of atheistic existentialism believe that the individual is alone in a godless universe and that the basic human condition is one of suffering and loneliness. Nevertheless, because there are no fixed values, individuals can create their own characters—indeed, they can shape themselves—through the exercise of free will. The atheistic strain culminates in and is popularly associated with the works of Jean-Paul Sartre. The Christian existentialists, on the other hand, believe that only in God may people find freedom from life's anguish. The two strains hold certain beliefs in common: that existence cannot be fully understood or described through empirical effort; that anguish is a universal element of life; that individuals must bear responsibility for their actions; and that there is no common standard of behavior or perception for religious and ethical matters.

Expatriates: See *Expatriatism*

Expatriatism: The practice of leaving one's country to live for an extended period in another country.

Exposition: Writing intended to explain the nature of an idea, thing, or theme. Expository writing is often combined with description, narration, or argument. In dramatic writing, the exposition is the introductory material which presents the characters, setting, and tone of the play.

Expressionism: An indistinct literary term, originally used to describe an early twentieth-century school of German painting. The term applies to almost any mode of unconventional, highly subjective writing that distorts reality in some way.

F

Fable: A prose or verse narrative intended to convey a moral. Animals or inanimate objects with human characteristics often serve as characters in fables.

Falling Action: See *Denouement*

Fantasy: A literary form related to mythology and folklore. Fantasy literature is typically set in non-existent realms and features supernatural beings.

Farce: A type of comedy characterized by broad humor, outlandish incidents, and often vulgar subject matter.

***Femme fatale*:** A French phrase with the literal translation "fatal woman." A *femme fatale* is a sensuous, alluring woman who often leads men into danger or trouble.

Fiction: Any story that is the product of imagination rather than a documentation of fact. Characters and events in such narratives may be based in real life but their ultimate form and configuration is a creation of the author.

Figurative Language: A technique in writing in which the author temporarily interrupts the order, construction, or meaning of the writing for a particular effect. This interruption takes the form of one or more figures of speech such as hyperbole, irony, or simile. Figurative language is the opposite of literal language, in which every word is truthful, accurate, and free of exaggeration or embellishment.

Figures of Speech: Writing that differs from customary conventions for construction, meaning, order, or significance for the purpose of a special meaning or effect. There are two major types of figures of speech: rhetorical figures, which do not make changes in the meaning of the words, and tropes, which do.

***Fin de siecle*:** A French term meaning "end of the century." The term is used to denote the last decade of the nineteenth century, a transition period when writers and other artists abandoned old conventions and looked for new techniques and objectives.

First Person: See *Point of View*

Flashback: A device used in literature to present action that occurred before the beginning of the story. Flashbacks are often introduced as the dreams or recollections of one or more characters.

Foil: A character in a work of literature whose physical or psychological qualities contrast strongly with, and therefore highlight, the corresponding qualities of another character.

Folklore: Traditions and myths preserved in a culture or group of people. Typically, these are passed on by word of mouth in various forms—such as legends, songs, and proverbs—or preserved in customs and ceremonies. This term was first used by W. J. Thoms in 1846.

Folktale: A story originating in oral tradition. Folktales fall into a variety of categories, including legends, ghost stories, fairy tales, fables, and anecdotes based on historical figures and events.

Foreshadowing: A device used in literature to create expectation or to set up an explanation of later developments.

Form: The pattern or construction of a work which identifies its genre and distinguishes it from other genres.

G

Genre: A category of literary work. In critical theory, genre may refer to both the content of a given work—tragedy, comedy, pastoral—and to its form, such as poetry, novel, or drama.

Gilded Age: A period in American history during the 1870s characterized by political corruption and materialism. A number of important novels of social and political criticism were written during this time.

Gothicism: In literary criticism, works characterized by a taste for the medieval or morbidly attractive. A gothic novel prominently features elements of horror, the supernatural, gloom, and violence: clanking chains, terror, charnel houses, ghosts, medieval castles, and mysteriously slamming doors. The term "gothic novel" is also applied to novels that lack elements of the traditional Gothic setting but that create a similar atmosphere of terror or dread.

Grotesque: In literary criticism, the subject matter of a work or a style of expression characterized by exaggeration, deformity, freakishness, and disorder. The grotesque often includes an element of comic absurdity.

H

Harlem Renaissance: The Harlem Renaissance of the 1920s is generally considered the first significant movement of black writers and artists in the United States. During this period, new and established black writers published more fiction and poetry than ever before, the first influential black literary journals were established, and black authors and artists received their first widespread recognition and serious critical appraisal. Among the major writers associated with this period are Claude McKay, Jean Toomer, Countee Cullen, Langston Hughes, Arna Bontemps, Nella Larsen, and Zora Neale Hurston. Also known as Negro Renaissance and New Negro Movement.

Hero/Heroine: The principal sympathetic character (male or female) in a literary work. Heroes and heroines typically exhibit admirable traits: idealism, courage, and integrity, for example.

Holocaust Literature: Literature influenced by or written about the Holocaust of World War II. Such literature includes true stories of survival in concentration camps, escape, and life after the war, as well as fictional works and poetry.

Humanism: A philosophy that places faith in the dignity of humankind and rejects the medieval perception of the individual as a weak, fallen creature. "Humanists" typically believe in the perfectibility of human nature and view reason and education as the means to that end.

Hyperbole: In literary criticism, deliberate exaggeration used to achieve an effect.

I

Idiom: A word construction or verbal expression closely associated with a given language.

Image: A concrete representation of an object or sensory experience. Typically, such a representation helps evoke the feelings associated with the object or experience itself. Images are either "literal" or "figurative." Literal images are especially concrete and involve little or no extension of the obvious meaning of the words used to express them. Figurative images do not follow the literal meaning of the words exactly. Images in literature are usually visual, but the term "image" can also refer to the representation of any sensory experience.

Imagery: The array of images in a literary work. Also, figurative language.

In medias res: A Latin term meaning "in the middle of things." It refers to the technique of beginning a story at its midpoint and then using various flashback devices to reveal previous action.

Interior Monologue: A narrative technique in which characters' thoughts are revealed in a way that appears to be uncontrolled by the author. The interior monologue typically aims to reveal the inner self of a character. It portrays emotional experiences as they occur at both a conscious and unconscious level. Images are often used to represent sensations or emotions.

Irony: In literary criticism, the effect of language in which the intended meaning is the opposite of what is stated.

J

Jargon: Language that is used or understood only by a select group of people. Jargon may refer to terminology used in a certain profession, such as computer jargon, or it may refer to any nonsensical language that is not understood by most people.

L

Leitmotiv: See *Motif*

Literal Language: An author uses literal language when he or she writes without exaggerating or embellishing the subject matter and without any tools of figurative language.

Lost Generation: A term first used by Gertrude Stein to describe the post-World War I generation of American writers: men and women haunted by a sense of betrayal and emptiness brought about by the destructiveness of the war.

M

Mannerism: Exaggerated, artificial adherence to a literary manner or style. Also, a popular style of the visual arts of late sixteenth-century Europe that was marked by elongation of the human form and by intentional spatial distortion. Literary works that are self-consciously high-toned and artistic are often said to be "mannered."

Metaphor: A figure of speech that expresses an idea through the image of another object. Metaphors suggest the essence of the first object by identifying it with certain qualities of the second object.

Modernism: Modern literary practices. Also, the principles of a literary school that lasted from roughly the beginning of the twentieth century until the end of World War II. Modernism is defined by its rejection of the literary conventions of the nineteenth century and by its opposition to conventional morality, taste, traditions, and economic values.

Mood: The prevailing emotions of a work or of the author in his or her creation of the work. The mood of a work is not always what might be expected based on its subject matter.

Motif: A theme, character type, image, metaphor, or other verbal element that recurs throughout a single work of literature or occurs in a number of different works over a period of time. Also known as *Motiv* or *Leitmotiv.*

Myth: An anonymous tale emerging from the traditional beliefs of a culture or social unit. Myths use supernatural explanations for natural phenomena. They may also explain cosmic issues like creation and death. Collections of myths, known as mythologies, are common to all cultures and nations, but the best-known myths belong to the Norse, Roman, and Greek mythologies.

N

Narration: The telling of a series of events, real or invented. A narration may be either a simple narrative, in which the events are recounted chronologically, or a narrative with a plot, in which the account is given in a style reflecting the author's artistic concept of the story. Narration is sometimes used as a synonym for "storyline."

Narrative: A verse or prose accounting of an event or sequence of events, real or invented. The term is also used as an adjective in the sense "method of narration." For example, in literary criticism, the expression "narrative technique" usually refers to the way the author structures and presents his or her story.

Narrator: The teller of a story. The narrator may be the author or a character in the story through whom the author speaks.

Naturalism: A literary movement of the late nineteenth and early twentieth centuries. The movement's major theorist, French novelist Emile Zola, envisioned a type of fiction that would examine human life with the objectivity of scientific inquiry. The Naturalists typically viewed human beings as either the products of "biological determinism," ruled by hereditary instincts and engaged in an endless struggle for survival, or as the products of "socioeconomic determinism," ruled by social and economic forces beyond their control. In their works, the Naturalists generally ignored the highest levels of society and focused on degradation: poverty, alcoholism, prostitution, insanity, and disease.

Noble Savage: The idea that primitive man is noble and good but becomes evil and corrupted as he becomes civilized. The concept of the noble savage originated in the Renaissance period but is more closely identified with such later writers as

Jean-Jacques Rousseau and Aphra Behn. See also Primitivism.

Novel of Ideas: A novel in which the examination of intellectual issues and concepts takes precedence over characterization or a traditional storyline.

Novel of Manners: A novel that examines the customs and mores of a cultural group.

Novel: A long fictional narrative written in prose, which developed from the novella and other early forms of narrative. A novel is usually organized under a plot or theme with a focus on character development and action.

Novella: An Italian term meaning "story." This term has been especially used to describe fourteenth-century Italian tales, but it also refers to modern short novels.

O

Objective Correlative: An outward set of objects, a situation, or a chain of events corresponding to an inward experience and evoking this experience in the reader. The term frequently appears in modern criticism in discussions of authors' intended effects on the emotional responses of readers.

Objectivity: A quality in writing characterized by the absence of the author's opinion or feeling about the subject matter. Objectivity is an important factor in criticism.

Oedipus Complex: A son's amorous obsession with his mother. The phrase is derived from the story of the ancient Theban hero Oedipus, who unknowingly killed his father and married his mother.

Omniscience: See *Point of View*

Onomatopoeia: The use of words whose sounds express or suggest their meaning. In its simplest sense, onomatopoeia may be represented by words that mimic the sounds they denote such as "hiss" or "meow." At a more subtle level, the pattern and rhythm of sounds and rhymes of a line or poem may be onomatopoeic.

Oxymoron: A phrase combining two contradictory terms. Oxymorons may be intentional or unintentional.

P

Parable: A story intended to teach a moral lesson or answer an ethical question.

Paradox: A statement that appears illogical or contradictory at first, but may actually point to an underlying truth.

Parallelism: A method of comparison of two ideas in which each is developed in the same grammatical structure.

Parody: In literary criticism, this term refers to an imitation of a serious literary work or the signature style of a particular author in a ridiculous manner. A typical parody adopts the style of the original and applies it to an inappropriate subject for humorous effect. Parody is a form of satire and could be considered the literary equivalent of a caricature or cartoon.

Pastoral: A term derived from the Latin word "pastor," meaning shepherd. A pastoral is a literary composition on a rural theme. The conventions of the pastoral were originated by the third-century Greek poet Theocritus, who wrote about the experiences, love affairs, and pastimes of Sicilian shepherds. In a pastoral, characters and language of a courtly nature are often placed in a simple setting. The term pastoral is also used to classify dramas, elegies, and lyrics that exhibit the use of country settings and shepherd characters.

Pen Name: See *Pseudonym*

Persona: A Latin term meaning "mask." *Personae* are the characters in a fictional work of literature. The *persona* generally functions as a mask through which the author tells a story in a voice other than his or her own. A *persona* is usually either a character in a story who acts as a narrator or an "implied author," a voice created by the author to act as the narrator for himself or herself.

Personification: A figure of speech that gives human qualities to abstract ideas, animals, and inanimate objects. Also known as *Prosopopoeia*.

Picaresque Novel: Episodic fiction depicting the adventures of a roguish central character ("picaro" is Spanish for "rogue"). The picaresque hero is commonly a low-born but clever individual who wanders into and out of various affairs of love, danger, and farcical intrigue. These involvements may take place at all social levels and typically present a humorous and wide-ranging satire of a given society.

Plagiarism: Claiming another person's written material as one's own. Plagiarism can take the form of direct, word-for-word copying or the theft of the substance or idea of the work.

Plot: In literary criticism, this term refers to the pattern of events in a narrative or drama. In its simplest sense, the plot guides the author in composing the work and helps the reader follow the work. Typically, plots exhibit causality and unity and have a beginning, a middle, and an end. Sometimes, however, a plot may consist of a series of disconnected events, in which case it is known as an "episodic plot."

Poetic Justice: An outcome in a literary work, not necessarily a poem, in which the good are rewarded and the evil are punished, especially in ways that particularly fit their virtues or crimes.

Poetic License: Distortions of fact and literary convention made by a writer—not always a poet—for the sake of the effect gained. Poetic license is closely related to the concept of "artistic freedom."

Poetics: This term has two closely related meanings. It denotes (1) an aesthetic theory in literary criticism about the essence of poetry or (2) rules prescribing the proper methods, content, style, or diction of poetry. The term poetics may also refer to theories about literature in general, not just poetry.

Point of View: The narrative perspective from which a literary work is presented to the reader. There are four traditional points of view. The "third person omniscient" gives the reader a "godlike" perspective, unrestricted by time or place, from which to see actions and look into the minds of characters. This allows the author to comment openly on characters and events in the work. The "third person" point of view presents the events of the story from outside of any single character's perception, much like the omniscient point of view, but the reader must understand the action as it takes place and without any special insight into characters' minds or motivations. The "first person" or "personal" point of view relates events as they are perceived by a single character. The main character "tells" the story and may offer opinions about the action and characters which differ from those of the author. Much less common than omniscient, third person, and first person is the "second person" point of view, wherein the author tells the story as if it is happening to the reader.

Polemic: A work in which the author takes a stand on a controversial subject, such as abortion or religion. Such works are often extremely argumentative or provocative.

Pornography: Writing intended to provoke feelings of lust in the reader. Such works are often condemned by critics and teachers, but those which can be shown to have literary value are viewed less harshly.

Post-Aesthetic Movement: An artistic response made by African Americans to the black aesthetic movement of the 1960s and early '70s. Writers since that time have adopted a somewhat different tone in their work, with less emphasis placed on the disparity between black and white in the United States. In the words of post-aesthetic authors such as Toni Morrison, John Edgar Wideman, and Kristin Hunter, African Americans are portrayed as looking inward for answers to their own questions, rather than always looking to the outside world.

Postmodernism: Writing from the 1960s forward characterized by experimentation and continuing to apply some of the fundamentals of modernism, which included existentialism and alienation. Postmodernists have gone a step further in the rejection of tradition begun with the modernists by also rejecting traditional forms, preferring the anti-novel over the novel and the antihero over the hero.

Primitivism: The belief that primitive peoples were nobler and less flawed than civilized peoples because they had not been subjected to the tainting influence of society. See also Noble Savage.

Prologue: An introductory section of a literary work. It often contains information establishing the situation of the characters or presents information about the setting, time period, or action. In drama, the prologue is spoken by a chorus or by one of the principal characters.

Prose: A literary medium that attempts to mirror the language of everyday speech. It is distinguished from poetry by its use of unmetered, unrhymed language consisting of logically related sentences. Prose is usually grouped into paragraphs that form a cohesive whole such as an essay or a novel.

Prosopopoeia: See *Personification*

Protagonist: The central character of a story who serves as a focus for its themes and incidents and as the principal rationale for its development. The protagonist is sometimes referred to in discussions of modern literature as the hero or antihero.

Protest Fiction: Protest fiction has as its primary purpose the protesting of some social injustice, such as racism or discrimination.

Proverb: A brief, sage saying that expresses a truth about life in a striking manner.

Pseudonym: A name assumed by a writer, most often intended to prevent his or her identification as the author of a work. Two or more authors may work together under one pseudonym, or an author may use a different name for each genre he or she publishes in. Some publishing companies maintain "house pseudonyms," under which any number of authors may write installations in a series. Some authors also choose a pseudonym over their real names the way an actor may use a stage name.

Pun: A play on words that have similar sounds but different meanings.

R

Realism: A nineteenth-century European literary movement that sought to portray familiar characters, situations, and settings in a realistic manner. This was done primarily by using an objective narrative point of view and through the buildup of accurate detail. The standard for success of any realistic work depends on how faithfully it transfers common experience into fictional forms. The realistic method may be altered or extended, as in stream of consciousness writing, to record highly subjective experience.

Repartee: Conversation featuring snappy retorts and witticisms.

Resolution: The portion of a story following the climax, in which the conflict is resolved. See also *Denouement.*

Rhetoric: In literary criticism, this term denotes the art of ethical persuasion. In its strictest sense, rhetoric adheres to various principles developed since classical times for arranging facts and ideas in a clear, persuasive, appealing manner. The term is also used to refer to effective prose in general and theories of or methods for composing effective prose.

Rhetorical Question: A question intended to provoke thought, but not an expressed answer, in the reader. It is most commonly used in oratory and other persuasive genres.

Rising Action: The part of a drama where the plot becomes increasingly complicated. Rising action leads up to the climax, or turning point, of a drama.

Roman a clef: A French phrase meaning "novel with a key." It refers to a narrative in which real persons are portrayed under fictitious names.

Romance: A broad term, usually denoting a narrative with exotic, exaggerated, often idealized characters, scenes, and themes.

Romanticism: This term has two widely accepted meanings. In historical criticism, it refers to a European intellectual and artistic movement of the late eighteenth and early nineteenth centuries that sought greater freedom of personal expression than that allowed by the strict rules of literary form and logic of the eighteenth-century neoclassicists. The Romantics preferred emotional and imaginative expression to rational analysis. They considered the individual to be at the center of all experience and so placed him or her at the center of their art. The Romantics believed that the creative imagination reveals nobler truths—unique feelings and attitudes—than those that could be discovered by logic or by scientific examination. Both the natural world and the state of childhood were important sources for revelations of "eternal truths." "Romanticism" is also used as a general term to refer to a type of sensibility found in all periods of literary history and usually considered to be in opposition to the principles of classicism. In this sense, Romanticism signifies any work or philosophy in which the exotic or dreamlike figure strongly, or that is devoted to individualistic expression, self-analysis, or a pursuit of a higher realm of knowledge than can be discovered by human reason.

Romantics: See *Romanticism*

S

Satire: A work that uses ridicule, humor, and wit to criticize and provoke change in human nature and institutions. There are two major types of satire: "formal" or "direct" satire speaks directly to the reader or to a character in the work; "indirect" satire relies upon the ridiculous behavior of its characters to make its point. Formal satire is further divided into two manners: the "Horatian," which ridicules gently, and the "Juvenalian," which derides its subjects harshly and bitterly.

Science Fiction: A type of narrative about or based upon real or imagined scientific theories and technology. Science fiction is often peopled with alien creatures and set on other planets or in different dimensions.

Second Person: See *Point of View*

Setting: The time, place, and culture in which the action of a narrative takes place. The elements of setting may include geographic location, characters' physical and mental environments, prevailing cultural attitudes, or the historical time in which the action takes place.

Simile: A comparison, usually using "like" or "as", of two essentially dissimilar things, as in "coffee as cold as ice" or "He sounded like a broken record."

Slang: A type of informal verbal communication that is generally unacceptable for formal writing. Slang words and phrases are often colorful exaggerations used to emphasize the speaker's point; they may also be shortened versions of an often-used word or phrase.

Slave Narrative: Autobiographical accounts of American slave life as told by escaped slaves. These works first appeared during the abolition movement of the 1830s through the 1850s.

Socialist Realism: The Socialist Realism school of literary theory was proposed by Maxim Gorky and established as a dogma by the first Soviet Congress of Writers. It demanded adherence to a communist worldview in works of literature. Its doctrines required an objective viewpoint comprehensible to the working classes and themes of social struggle featuring strong proletarian heroes. Also known as Social Realism.

Stereotype: A stereotype was originally the name for a duplication made during the printing process; this led to its modern definition as a person or thing that is (or is assumed to be) the same as all others of its type.

Stream of Consciousness: A narrative technique for rendering the inward experience of a character. This technique is designed to give the impression of an ever-changing series of thoughts, emotions, images, and memories in the spontaneous and seemingly illogical order that they occur in life.

Structure: The form taken by a piece of literature. The structure may be made obvious for ease of understanding, as in nonfiction works, or may be obscured for artistic purposes, as in some poetry or seemingly "unstructured" prose.

Sturm und Drang: A German term meaning "storm and stress." It refers to a German literary movement of the 1770s and 1780s that reacted against the order and rationalism of the enlightenment, focusing instead on the intense experience of extraordinary individuals.

Style: A writer's distinctive manner of arranging words to suit his or her ideas and purpose in writing. The unique imprint of the author's personality upon his or her writing, style is the product of an author's way of arranging ideas and his or her use of diction, different sentence structures, rhythm, figures of speech, rhetorical principles, and other elements of composition.

Subjectivity: Writing that expresses the author's personal feelings about his subject, and which may or may not include factual information about the subject.

Subplot: A secondary story in a narrative. A subplot may serve as a motivating or complicating force for the main plot of the work, or it may provide emphasis for, or relief from, the main plot.

Surrealism: A term introduced to criticism by Guillaume Apollinaire and later adopted by Andre Breton. It refers to a French literary and artistic movement founded in the 1920s. The Surrealists sought to express unconscious thoughts and feelings in their works. The best-known technique used for achieving this aim was automatic writing—transcriptions of spontaneous outpourings from the unconscious. The Surrealists proposed to unify the contrary levels of conscious and unconscious, dream and reality, objectivity and subjectivity into a new level of "super-realism."

Suspense: A literary device in which the author maintains the audience's attention through the buildup of events, the outcome of which will soon be revealed.

Symbol: Something that suggests or stands for something else without losing its original identity. In literature, symbols combine their literal meaning with the suggestion of an abstract concept. Literary symbols are of two types: those that carry complex associations of meaning no matter what their contexts, and those that derive their suggestive meaning from their functions in specific literary works.

Symbolism: This term has two widely accepted meanings. In historical criticism, it denotes an early modernist literary movement initiated in France during the nineteenth century that reacted against the prevailing standards of realism. Writers in this movement aimed to evoke, indirectly and symbolically, an order of being beyond the material world of the five senses. Poetic expression of personal emotion figured strongly in the movement, typically by means of a private set of symbols uniquely identifiable with the individual poet. The principal aim of the Symbolists was to express in words the highly complex feelings that grew out of everyday contact with the world. In a broader sense, the term "symbolism" refers to the use of one object to represent another.

T

Tall Tale: A humorous tale told in a straightforward, credible tone but relating absolutely impossible events or feats of the characters. Such tales were commonly told of frontier adventures during the settlement of the west in the United States.

Theme: The main point of a work of literature. The term is used interchangeably with thesis.

Thesis: A thesis is both an essay and the point argued in the essay. Thesis novels and thesis plays share the quality of containing a thesis which is supported through the action of the story.

Third Person: See *Point of View*

Tone: The author's attitude toward his or her audience may be deduced from the tone of the work. A formal tone may create distance or convey politeness, while an informal tone may encourage a friendly, intimate, or intrusive feeling in the reader. The author's attitude toward his or her subject matter may also be deduced from the tone of the words he or she uses in discussing it.

Transcendentalism: An American philosophical and religious movement, based in New England from around 1835 until the Civil War. Transcendentalism was a form of American romanticism that had its roots abroad in the works of Thomas Carlyle, Samuel Coleridge, and Johann Wolfgang von Goethe. The Transcendentalists stressed the importance of intuition and subjective experience in communication with God. They rejected religious dogma and texts in favor of mysticism and scientific naturalism. They pursued truths that lie beyond the "colorless" realms perceived by reason and the senses and were active social reformers in public education, women's rights, and the abolition of slavery.

U

Urban Realism: A branch of realist writing that attempts to accurately reflect the often harsh facts of modern urban existence.

Utopia: A fictional perfect place, such as "paradise" or "heaven."

V

Verisimilitude: Literally, the appearance of truth. In literary criticism, the term refers to aspects of a work of literature that seem true to the reader.

Victorian: Refers broadly to the reign of Queen Victoria of England (1837-1901) and to anything with qualities typical of that era. For example, the qualities of smug narrowmindedness, bourgeois materialism, faith in social progress, and priggish morality are often considered Victorian. This stereotype is contradicted by such dramatic intellectual developments as the theories of Charles Darwin, Karl Marx, and Sigmund Freud (which stirred strong debates in England) and the critical attitudes of serious Victorian writers like Charles Dickens and George Eliot. In literature, the Victorian Period was the great age of the English novel, and the latter part of the era saw the rise of movements such as decadence and symbolism. Also known as Victorian Age and Victorian Period.

W

Weltanschauung: A German term referring to a person's worldview or philosophy.

Weltschmerz: A German term meaning "world pain." It describes a sense of anguish about the nature of existence, usually associated with a melancholy, pessimistic attitude.

Z

Zeitgeist: A German term meaning "spirit of the time." It refers to the moral and intellectual trends of a given era.

Cumulative
Author/Title Index

I

I Am the Cheese (Cormier): V18
I, Claudius (Graves): V21
I Know Why the Caged Bird Sings
    (Angelou): V2
The Immoralist (Gide): V21
In Country (Mason): V4
In the Castle of My Skin (Lamming):
    V15
In the Time of the Butterflies
    (Alvarez): V9
Invisible Man (Ellison): V2
Irving, John
    A Prayer for Owen Meany: V14
    The World According to Garp:
        V12
Ishiguro, Kazuo
    The Remains of the Day: V13

J

James, Henry
    The Ambassadors: V12
    The Portrait of a Lady: V19
    The Turn of the Screw: V16
Jane Eyre (Brontë): V4
Japrisot, Sébastien
    A Very Long Engagement: V18
Jewett, Sarah Orne
    The Country of the Pointed Firs:
        V15
The Joy Luck Club (Tan): V1
Joyce, James
    *A Portrait of the Artist as a
        Young Man:* V7
July's People (Gordimer): V4
Juneteenth (Ellison): V21
The Jungle (Sinclair): V6

K

Kafka, Franz
    The Trial: V7
Keneally, Thomas
    Schindler's List: V17
Kerouac, Jack
    On the Road: V8
Kesey, Ken
    *One Flew Over the Cuckoo's
        Nest:* V2
Keyes, Daniel
    Flowers for Algernon: V2
Kim (Kipling): V21
Kincaid, Jamaica
    Annie John: V3
Kindred (Butler): V8
Kingsolver, Barbara
    Animal Dreams: V12
    The Bean Trees: V5
    Pigs in Heaven: V10
Kingston, Maxine Hong
    The Woman Warrior: V6

Kinsella, W. P.
    Shoeless Joe: V15
Kipling, Rudyard
    Kim: V21
Kitchen (Yoshimoto): V7
The Kitchen God's Wife (Tan): V13
Knowles, John
    A Separate Peace: V2
Koestler, Arthur
    Darkness at Noon: V19
Kogawa, Joy
    Obasan: V3
Kosinski, Jerzy
    The Painted Bird: V12
Kundera, Milan
    *The Unbearable Lightness of
        Being:* V18

L

Lamming, George
    In the Castle of My Skin: V15
The Last King of Scotland (Foden):
    V15
The Last of the Mohicans (Cooper):
    V9
Laurence, Margaret
    The Stone Angel: V11
Lawrence, D. H.
    Sons and Lovers: V18
Lee, Harper
    To Kill a Mockingbird: V2
Lee, Lilian
    Farewell My Concubine: V19
The Left Hand of Darkness (Le
    Guin): V6
Le Guin, Ursula K.
    Always Coming Home: V9
    The Left Hand of Darkness: V6
Leroux, Gaston
    The Phantom of the Opera: V20
Les Misérables (Hugo): V5
Less Than Zero (Ellis): V11
A Lesson Before Dying (Gaines): V7
Lewis, Sinclair
    Babbitt: V19
    Main Street: V15
Like Water for Chocolate (Esquivel):
    V5
Little Women (Alcott): V12
Lolita (Nabokov): V9
London, Jack
    The Call of the Wild: V8
    White Fang: V19
*The Lone Ranger and Tonto Fistfight
    in Heaven* (Alexie): V17
A Long and Happy Life (Price): V18
Look Homeward, Angel (Wolfe): V18
Looking Backward: 2000–1887
    (Bellamy): V15
Lord Jim (Conrad): V16
Lord of the Flies (Golding): V2
Losing Battles (Welty): V15

Love in the Time of Cholera (García
    Márquez): V1
Love Medicine (Erdrich): V5
Lowry, Lois
    The Giver: V3

M

Machiavelli, Niccolo
    The Prince: V9
Madame Bovary (Flaubert): V14
Maggie: A Girl of the Streets
    (Crane): V20
Mailer, Norman
    The Naked and the Dead: V10
Main Street (Lewis): V15
Malamud, Bernard
    The Fixer: V9
    The Natural: V4
The Maltese Falcon (Hammett): V21
Mama Day (Naylor): V7
*The Mambo Kings Play Songs of
    Love* (Hijuelos): V17
Mann, Thomas
    Death in Venice: V17
Margret Howth: A Story of To-Day
    (Davis): V14
Markandaya, Kamala
    Nectar in a Sieve: V13
Marmon Silko, Leslie
    Ceremony: V4
Mason, Bobbie Ann
    In Country: V4
The Master and Margarita
    (Bulgakov): V8
The Mayor of Casterbridge (Hardy):
    V15
McCullers, Carson
    The Heart Is a Lonely Hunter: V6
    The Member of the Wedding: V13
Melville, Herman
    *Billy Budd, Sailor: An Inside
        Narrative:* V9
    Moby-Dick: V7
The Member of the Wedding
    (McCullers): V13
Memoirs of a Geisha (Golden): V19
Méndez, Miguel
    Pilgrims in Aztlán: V12
The Mill on the Floss (Eliot): V17
Mitchell, Margaret
    Gone with the Wind: V9
Moby-Dick (Melville): V7
Moll Flanders (Defoe): V13
Momaday, N. Scott
    House Made of Dawn: V10
Mori, Kyoko
    Shizuko's Daughter: V15
Morrison, Toni
    Beloved: V6
    The Bluest Eye: V1
    Sula: V14
    Song of Solomon: V8

Cumulative Author/Title Index

Cumulative
Nationality/Ethnicity Index

Subject/Theme Index

Boldface denotes discussion in *Themes* section.

A

Abandonment
The Immoralist: 129–131
Adultery
The Maltese Falcon: 211–212, 214
Adventure and Exploration
Dusklands: 16–19
Kim: 161–162, 171
Nausea: 230–232
Africa
Dusklands: 1, 4, 10–11
The Immoralist: 114–117, 119,
121–123, 132–133
The Maltese Falcon: 189–191,
194–196, 203–205, 212–213,
215–217, 219
Age of Reason
Emma: 31, 34
**Age of Reason Or Age of
Enlightenment**
Emma: 31
**Alcoholism, Drugs, and Drug
Addiction**
Parable of the Sower: 233–235,
240
Alienation
The French Lieutenant's Woman:
75–76, 78–81
Allegory
Juneteenth: 146–147
The Maltese Falcon: 207–209,
212–213, 215
Parable of the Sower: 263, 266

American Northeast
Tambourines to Glory: 268,
274–277
American Northwest
Juneteenth: 150, 153–154
American South
Juneteenth: 136, 138–139, 145
Tambourines to Glory: 268,
275–276
American West
Parable of the Sower: 233–234,
240–241
Anger
Kim: 175
Apartheid
Dusklands: 8, 10–11
Appearance vs. Reality
The Maltese Falcon: 211–215
Arthurian Legend
The Maltese Falcon: 207, 215
Asia
Dusklands: 2, 3, 8–11, 16–18
Kim: 169, 172
The Maltese Falcon: 189–191, 197
Atonement
Emma: 21, 24–25
Juneteenth: 151–152, 154,
156–158
The Violent Bear It Away:
312–316
Authoritarianism
I, Claudius: 104–106, 109

B

The Battle for the Soul
The Violent Bear It Away: 296

Beauty
Emma: 56, 58–59, 61
Betrayal
Juneteenth: 151, 154
The Maltese Falcon: 211,
213–215
Bildungsroman
The French Lieutenant's Woman:
77–78
Black Arts Movement
Parable of the Sower: 246–249
Buddhism
Kim: 163–165, 169–171

C

Capitalism
Parable of the Sower: 248–250
Tambourines to Glory: 279, 281
Change
Parable of the Sower: 238
**Change, Transformation,
Metamorphosis, Rebirth**
Nausea: 225
Christianity
Dusklands: 4, 9
Juneteenth: 151–152, 154
Kim: 171–172
The Violent Bear It Away:
291–292, 298, 300, 302–305
City Life
Parable of the Sower: 241,
246–252
The Violent Bear It Away:
299–300
Civil Rights
Juneteenth: 144–146

Freedom

The French Lieutenant's Woman:
67, 71–75, 77–79, 88–91
The Immoralist: 127
Nausea: 227
Parable of the Sower: 239

G

Ghetto Life

Tambourines to Glory: 273

God

The French Lieutenant's Woman:
72–73, 88–89, 91–93
Juneteenth: 151–152, 154
Parable of the Sower: 234–235,
238–239, 255–258, 260–261,
265–266
Tambourines to Glory: 267–270,
272–273, 275, 283, 285
The Violent Bear It Away: 290,
293, 296–298, 302–310,
312–316

Gothicism

The Violent Bear It Away:
290–291, 298

Gratitude

Emma: 52–53, 57, 59–61

Greed

The Maltese Falcon: 214–215

Grotesque

The Violent Bear It Away:
297–298

H

Happiness and Gaiety

Emma: 54, 56, 61–62
Juneteenth: 138–139, 143–144,
147–149, 152–159

Harlem Renaissance

Tambourines to Glory: 273, 276

Hatred

Emma: 45, 49, 58–62
Kim: 164–165, 171, 173
The Violent Bear It Away: 302–305

Heaven

Tambourines to Glory: 279–280
The Violent Bear It Away:
311–313

Heritage and Ancestry

Parable of the Sower: 249, 251

Heroism

Emma: 21–22, 32–33, 37–38,
48–52
The French Lieutenant's Woman:
74, 78, 92
The Immoralist: 133–134
The Maltese Falcon: 202, 207,
211–212, 214
Nausea: 230–232
Parable of the Sower: 258–259,
262–264

The Violent Bear It Away:
302–303

History

Dusklands: 5, 8–9, 16
I, Claudius: 95–96, 101–113
Juneteenth: 136, 138–139,
144–146, 150–152
Kim: 164, 174
The Maltese Falcon: 190–191,
196
Nausea: 223
Parable of the Sower: 242
The Violent Bear It Away: 291,
293, 299

Homelessness

Parable of the Sower: 234–235,
240–241

Homosexuality

Emma: 51–52
The Immoralist: 114, 119,
122–123, 132–134
The Maltese Falcon: 195

Honor

The Maltese Falcon: 208

Hope

Tambourines to Glory: 267, 270,
275–276

Humility

Emma: 50, 52–55, 57–59

Humor

Emma: 31, 33, 37, 40
The French Lieutenant's Woman:
77–78, 90
Tambourines to Glory: 267,
272–273, 277
The Violent Bear It Away: 290,
298, 301–302

I

Identity

Kim: 170

Imagery and Symbolism

Dusklands: 16–18
The French Lieutenant's Woman:
74–75, 77, 89–90
The Immoralist: 129–134
Juneteenth: 144–146
Kim: 169–171, 173
Parable of the Sower: 246–247,
249, 253, 255, 257
Tambourines to Glory: 282
The Violent Bear It Away: 310,
312–316

Imagination

Parable of the Sower: 262,
264–265

Imperialism

Kim: 161, 169, 172, 174–175

Insanity

Juneteenth: 138–139, 144
The Violent Bear It Away:
302–304

Irony

Emma: 21, 24, 31–33, 37–40
The French Lieutenant's Woman:
78, 88–91
The Immoralist: 134
Juneteenth: 150–151
The Maltese Falcon: 203,
208–209

K

Killers and Killing

Dusklands: 4–5, 7–10
I, Claudius: 97–98, 101, 103
Juneteenth: 138–139, 154
The Maltese Falcon: 187,
189–191, 194, 199–201,
203–204, 206, 208, 213,
215–216, 218
Parable of the Sower: 235–236,
240

Kindness

Emma: 44–48
The French Lieutenant's Woman:
76–78

Knowledge

Emma: 31–32, 34–35
Kim: 163–164, 169, 172–174
The Violent Bear It Away: 290,
298

L

Landscape

Dusklands: 4, 8–11, 16–18
The Immoralist: 119, 121, 124,
130–131
Kim: 161, 163–166, 171, 173
Parable of the Sower: 235–236,
239, 241, 252–254, 256–260,
262
The Violent Bear It Away:
292–293, 297–298

Law and Order

Dusklands: 3, 8, 10
I, Claudius: 96, 98
Juneteenth: 138–139, 145–146
The Maltese Falcon: 187–191,
194–198, 203, 204–206,
209–210, 212–219
Parable of the Sower: 235,
239–241
Tambourines to Glory: 270,
273–276
The Violent Bear It Away: 308,
310

Life Versus Death

The Immoralist: 119

Limitations and Opportunities

Emma: 51–52, 54–55, 59
The French Lieutenant's Woman:
74–76, 78